READ ALL
ABOUT IT!

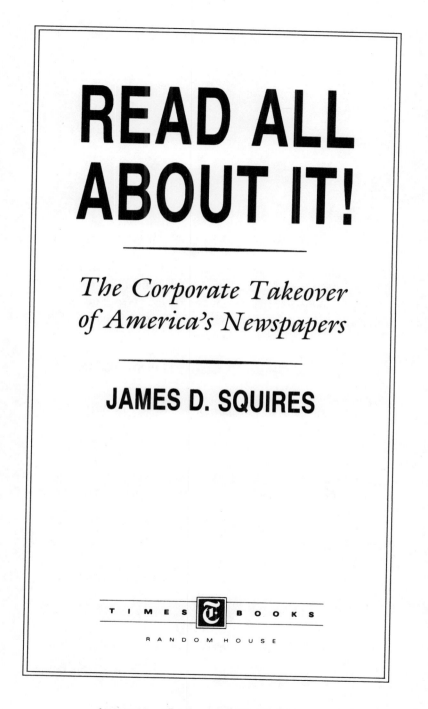

READ ALL ABOUT IT!

The Corporate Takeover
of America's Newspapers

JAMES D. SQUIRES

T I M E S 𝕿 B O O K S

R A N D O M   H O U S E

Library of Congress Cataloging-in-Publication Data

Squires, James D.
    Read all about it! : the corporate takeover of America's
newspapers / James D. Squires
        p.   cm.
    ISBN 0-8129-2101-1
    1. Chicago tribune.   2. American newspapers — History.
3. Consolidation and merger of corporations — United States.
I. Title.
PN4899.C4S68   1993
071'.3 — dc20   92-50498

Manufactured in the United States of America

9   8   7   6   5   4   3   2

First Edition

In memory of Nat Caldwell, Gene Graham, and Bill Jones, whose journalism defined the noblest traditions of the free press, and in appreciation of journalists everywhere still struggling to uphold them, especially my former colleagues at The Tennessean, The Orlando Sentinel, *and the* Chicago Tribune.

A free press should always fight for progress and reform, never tolerate injustice or corruption, always fight demagogues of all parties, never belong to any party, always oppose privileged classes and public plunderers, never lack sympathy with the poor, always remain devoted to the public welfare.

— JOSEPH PULITZER

Acknowledgments

I would like to thank the Joan Shorenstein Barone Center on Press, Politics and Public Policy, Harvard University, and the Seigenthaler Chair of Excellence in First Amendment Studies, Middle Tennessee State University, without whose support this book would have been impossible; David Halberstam and Amanda Urban, without whose encouragement it would never have been written; Paul Golob and Steve Wasserman, without whose help it would never have been completed, or readable; and John Seigenthaler and Clayton Kirkpatrick, without whose confidence there would have been no rich and rewarding newspaper career from which to draw these lessons in the first place.

Contents

READ ALL
ABOUT IT!

1

Stop the Press, I Want to Get On

For me, Walter Lippmann said it all. The famous columnist's words best defined the mission of a free press. There was something solid and sacred in the idea of being "the beam of a searchlight that moved restlessly about bringing one episode and then another out of the darkness into vision."

Like generations of reporters before me, I had signed on to the legacy of old Joseph Pulitzer. Though wrestling in the gutter of yellow journalism with one hand, he had simultaneously raised the other in oath that newspapers existed solely to oppose the plunderers and predators of a free society.

Gathered around a corroded coffee urn in the city room of the Nashville *Tennessean* a quarter of a century ago, my fellow reporters and I danced to the music of Lippmann's words, finding in them the anchor for our judgment that journalism was an oasis in the desert of capitalism, a business with a conscience and a higher purpose. As if proof was somehow to be seen as words on a page, my colleagues passed around a tattered magazine clipping in which the late Peter Lisagor, then one of America's most renowned reporters, defined his job as "walking down the center of the street, opening the shutters and raising the shades on windows on either side."

God, that sounded wonderful. And in the hands of Amon Carter Evans, *The Tennessean*'s thirty-two-year-old publisher, the beam of Lippmann's searchlight was restless indeed. He had sworn to shine it through any window anywhere on anyone. And who was to doubt him? After all, he was born to the cloth, or, in his case, to the newsprint. He was the son of Silliman Evans, the first editor of the *Chicago Sun*, a newspaper founded for no reason other than to oppose the isolationist policies of conservative *Chicago Tribune* publisher Robert R. McCormick and to make sure that Chicagoans knew every story had at least two sides. Silliman Evans went on to become a crusading publisher himself and named his second son after yet another of the breed, Amon Carter of Fort Worth, who had given him a start in the business. The journalistic mission of *The Tennessean* mattered to the Evans family in Nashville the same way the mission of *The Courier-Journal* mattered to the Binghams in Louisville and that of *The New York Times* mattered to the Ochses and the Sulzbergers. Such commitment flowed from heart to mind like ink to a press — the lifeblood of a true institution of democracy.

Amon Carter Evans could not have been over five and a half feet tall, but in my twenty-year-old eyes he stood a full foot taller the day when he came out of his office, sleeves rolled up, tie askew, and strode across the city room in John Wayne–size steps. At the desk next to mine, he stopped — and declared war. In somber tones I had heard only at funerals or in church, he ordered Nathan G. (Nat) Caldwell, *The Tennessean*'s best reporter and a man who had won the Pulitzer Prize for exposing John L. Lewis's corrupt behavior as head of the United Mine Workers, to drop everything else and launch an investigation of the phosphate mining industry. "Go to Florida, New York, anywhere you have to," Evans said, "and take a photographer. They [the phosphate miners] are raping the land."

His words were music to my ears. That's why I had gotten into the business. Yes, *The Tennessean* was a business — sort of. All American newspapers were, always had been, and always would be. Successful survival in the marketplace was the key to their financial independence. It was what made them distinct from the rest of the world's press. But newspapers were a different kind of business. My colleagues and I all knew, for instance, that if hard times ever hit *The Tennessean*, young Evans had promised to sell his family stock in American Airlines and use the proceeds to subsidize the newspaper's relentless quest for open shutters, lifted shades and episodes in darkness that needed illuminating. None of us had actually heard him say that, of course. No one really knew if he even owned any airline stock. But we told one another the story anyway, in the same breath that we told the one about our idol, Pulitzer, and the famous judge Morgan Stanley. In 1904, Pulitzer had asked Stanley to be on his board of directors. Stanley agreed, but characteristically offered an unsolicited opinion that Pulitzer's newspapers had one defect: they didn't stand by their friends.

"A newspaper should have no friends," said Pulitzer.

"I think it should," Stanley replied.

"If that's your opinion," Pulitzer responded, "then I wouldn't make you one of my trustees if you gave me a million dollars."

Both stories were testaments to the indomitable spirit of American journalism. And it was such romantic notions that had drawn my generation to the craft in the first place. We called it a "profession" and believed it to be, every bit as much as medicine or law. And even the few among us with the brains to pass college algebra and the money to go on to become doctors or lawyers were convinced they had chosen the higher calling. What could be more honorable, more vital and more precious to this free society than being part of a business expressly guaranteed by the U.S. Constitution?

The newspapers were making money in the 1960s, but none of us knew how much, or cared. To the bliss-blinded ignoramus of the typewriter, the salient fact of newspaper economics was that the good ones profited less than the bad ones because good journalism costs more. Even the old journalist-proprietors agreed that the definition of "quality" journalism was journalism practiced selflessly in the public interest. Their elite huddled together in the front seats at the newspaper publisher meetings and looked down their noses at the merely profit-minded. When the profiteer Frank Munsey, who had specialized in low-value, high-profit newspapers around New York, died in 1925, he was eulogized by William Allen White, the legendary Kansas newspaper editor who was then journalism's conscience: "Frank Munsey, the great publisher, is dead. Frank Munsey contributed to the journalism of his day the talent of a meat packer, the morals of a money changer and the manners of an undertaker. He and his kind have about succeeded in transforming a once-noble profession into an eight percent security. May he rest in trust." Maybe it was just another business to Munsey, but not to journalism's royalty. Their models — and ours — were the Ochs and Sulzberger families, owners of *The New York Times*. When faced with newsprint rationing during the Second World War, *The Times* had chosen to print news over advertising, thereby establishing moral superiority over virtually everyone else. And because it was *The Times* that emerged to be the most important paper in the nation, the decision had been good business, too. In the backs of city rooms all over the country, reporters revered *The Times*' owners for that leadership — for setting the standard that high-mindedness returned better profits in the long term.

The Times' power and influence had little if any relationship to its value as a business. In fact, in the early 1960s, *The Times* was only marginally profitable, often just above the break-even point, sometimes below. Yet it had the most important voice in the land. And along with the *New York Herald Tribune*, which had an even greater propensity for red ink, *The Times* employed the country's best and most famous journalists, people like Tom Wicker, David Halberstam and James Reston. Both Wicker and Halberstam had passed through *The Tennes-*

sean's city room in their youth, along with a dozen or so other big-name reporters on other larger, famous newspapers. To my colleagues and me they represented the gods of journalism. When you read a Wicker clipping in *The Tennessean*'s library, or were awarded the desk where Halberstam was sitting when he got the call to join *The Times*, you knew that you had made the right career choice, that you were in the right place. You hadn't taken a job, you had answered a calling. We knew that those who had answered it before us were measured not by the way they dressed, the size of their houses or the cars they drove, but by the courage they had shown, the good they had done and the respect they had gained among their peers in the process.

My role models were the editors and publishers who had stood up to the government, who had told the truth when it was not popular or profitable to do so, the people who had seen journalism as the tool with which to abolish slavery, to oppose war, to stand up to Fascism and racism. The greater the risks they took, the more consistent and persistent their stands, the taller they stood in my eyes.

As a young reporter I was dispatched on temporary assignment to Washington in the early 1960s, to cover a congressional committee investigation of the Ku Klux Klan, which had been flexing its muscles anew around the South. *The Tennessean* did things like that then, sending kid reporters out on big stories, traveling first class on their maiden airplane rides to New York and Washington in quest of bylines and, more important, confidence-building experience. That's what Silliman Evans had taught *Tennessean* editors to do. That's how great reporters were made — and the reputations of great newspapers, too. *The Tennessean* couldn't really afford this, of course; it made up for it by not paying you anything. So there I was, barely old enough to vote, in the capital of the United States of America, living in a cheap hotel and trying to figure out if everyone who passed was somebody important I ought to know. One morning, after a session of heavy coffee drinking in *The Tennessean*'s one-person bureau office at the National Press Building, I discovered that the key needed for entry to the men's room had been misplaced. Since I was to meet a friend at the Washington bureau of *The New York Times* for lunch, I waited. Upon arrival there, hours later and in agony, I fumbled frantically in front of the urinal trying not to wet my pants. But before relief came, I heard the voice of a man standing at the next urinal. "Good morning, young man," he said. "You must be new to *The Times*. I've never seen you around here before. I'm Scotty Reston." Not only did the sight and sound of the distinguished *Times* man strike me dumb and make me forget my own name, but it locked my bladder. I could only stand there in pain, unable to speak — or pee.

In those days, the sight of a *Times* reporter in a southern city to cover the region's struggle over civil rights could inflict the same kind of bladder paralysis — or worse — on mayors, sheriffs and local police chiefs. And a single *Times* dispatch could bring the national newsmagazines and newly feared network television crews streaming to the scene of whatever social or political injustice had been reported on the paper's pages. It was an era when newspapers, especially big, important ones, could focus the na-

tional attention. Not everything that was true then was
true before or has been since. *The New York Times* was
not always so revered. Not many of the great publishers
were as altruistic as the Sulzbergers about profits, and not
many agreed with Pulitzer about newspapers not having
friends. On the contrary, many newspaper barons culti-
vated the most powerful of friends and rewarded them
on the same pages where they were punishing their adversaries.

The owners of the American press have historically
been men of wealth, power, politics and eccentricity, who
only out of a sense of modesty assumed titles such as
Captain and Colonel. In their minds King and Your Majesty were better suited. They built what they owned,
mastered what they built and wielded vast political power
until they became too old and infirm to do so. Some
didn't even stop then. Still, they were independent and
rambunctious forces in society, ever ready to exercise
power and strong enough to do what they wanted. What
they usually wanted most was to publish, which they did
at any cost, for this was the source of both their power
and their fulfillment.

Because these men were so different and their causes
so diverse, the press was by nature rife with contradictions
and conflict at every level. Their enemies and adversaries
ranged from foreign governments and U.S. presidents to
the publisher across the street. Few of their battles were
undertaken without risk of both credibility and profits.
The signatures of newspaper barons like Hearst, Pulitzer
and Scripps were scrawled across the political landscape
in their corporate editorial policies. Often these men —

ultimately to their detriment—personally paid more attention to what their newspapers stood for than to the quality of their reporting or the size of their profit margins. But these policies were usually the constructs of conscience and often elaborate declarations of the political and social philosophy of a single individual.

If a publisher changed his friends or his politics, the shift was generally evident in the tone of his newspaper's editorial voice. The Hearst newspapers, for example, underwent a dramatic evolution in editorial philosophy as their founder matured from antiestablishment, populist rabble-rouser to a member of the country's conservative elite. Pulitzer remained a populist to the day he died. Readers may have disagreed with the public stance taken by these publishers, but they never had to wonder where they stood.

The press lords of the past understood that the core business that kept newspapers financially independent—the sale of advertising—is by nature problematical. They knew that a newspaper might well print bad news about some business that regularly bought advertising space. John S. (Jack) Knight, who built the nation's most highly regarded group of newspapers in the 1950s and '60s, was extolled by *Newsweek* for his business prowess. "Few major newspaper combines have grown so healthy so fast," the magazine said. But it was not Knight's bottom line that was his source of pride and political power. It was his personal opinion column, which set the tone for his newspapers. He became known for a willingness to take unpopular editorial positions that cost his newspapers revenue and profits, at least in the short term. In the early 1960s, for example, Knight's flagship *Miami Herald* championed the defense of a fragile coastal environment by opposing a huge oil refinery proposed for Biscayne Bay—at a time when the city was hungry for jobs and economic growth. To the chagrin of friends who shared his personal fondness for wagering, Knight also fought a legalized gambling initiative that would have made Miami an international Las Vegas and sent his newspaper's advertising revenues soaring.

Claiming and reflecting a different reason for being set the press apart from the rest of society. Its drum skipped a beat every now and then, giving the press a sort of ragtime quality—unpredictable and even explosive, but never bland, dependent or monolithic. Its leaders could disagree to the point of dueling in the street, then come together on a matter of press rights or First Amendment principle. Yet this fraternalism almost never bridged the normal divergence of editorial opinion or business interests. Even when the trade groups such as the National Advertising Council or the American Newspaper Publishers Association lined up behind some matter of financial significance, there was always among newspapers a contrary wave of dissent and maverick opinion. The press almost never found itself presenting a single editorial voice in its own financial interests. For instance, many publishers openly opposed the newspaper industry's exemption from antitrust laws that was lobbied through Congress in 1969 by the seven largest newspaper groups, which then together owned only seventy-four papers. Dow Jones and *The New York Times* editorialized against it and the Bingham family's *Courier-Journal* called the legislation a "governmental favor" that threatened "the independence of the press."

As an institution the press compelled its members only to respect the public confidence that had given and sustained its life. In this sense, the press as an institution was embracing Pulitzer's notion that newspapers should have no friends. And nowhere was it more united in this regard and different from the rest of private enterprise than in its relationship with the government. For most of its 200-year life, the press asked nothing from the government but to be left alone. Time after time that independence was underscored, explained and upheld in law. And within the press itself, it was nurtured and enforced by the most powerful of human influences — peer pressure.

The history of the American press, ancient and modern, is replete with instances where peer pressure by the press elite was critical in preserving the best traditions of a free press. None is more illustrative than the case of the Pentagon Papers. In 1971, against the advice of his lawyers, *New York Times* publisher Arthur Sulzberger allowed *The Times* to publish the first installment of what had previously been a secret government history of the debacle in Vietnam. Immediately, Nixon's White House, citing endangered national security interests, got a court to temporarily restrain *The Times* from further publication.

Then *The Washington Post* obtained its own copy of the papers and prepared to publish, leaving the final decision in the lap of Katharine Graham, the new and untested publisher of the newspaper that previously had been run by her father and her husband. Had Mrs. Graham chosen not to publish, her decision would surely have been cited as evidence by the government that *The New York Times* had been wrong to do so. Mrs. Graham earned her place in press history alongside John Peter Zenger and Horace Greeley by fearlessly risking her social position and family fortune for no other reason than that it was the right thing to do.

The most remarkable aspect of her decision was that she made it while standing on such shaky ground, not only legal but financial. It came early in her stewardship of the company and only two days after another monumental decision — to sell stock in the previously family owned enterprise on Wall Street. Indeed, the fear that the badly needed infusion of public cash would be retarded, if not utterly nullified, by a fight with the federal government had been cited by her lawyers and business advisers as a reason to hold up publication.

Although she was among the first to risk Wall Street's money for journalistic principle, courting financial ruin in the pursuit of the press function had long been part of American newspapering. The influence of peer pressure was at Mrs. Graham's side throughout the decision-making process in the presence of Eugene Patterson, then *The Post*'s managing editor and agent of the paper's editor Ben Bradlee, who was pleading the case for publication from his home by telephone. Patterson has recalled that the biggest stumbling block was Fritz Beebe, the paper's longtime business manager, who was arguing that publication could damage the stock sale and that nothing would be harmed by waiting. But Patterson argued persuasively that if *The Post* did not publish, Mrs. Graham would be abandoning her industry obligation to Sulzberger and *The Times*. How could she ever sit down at the dinner table with him again if *The Post* chose not to publish? Such a decision certainly would be cited by Nixon's lawyers as evidence that Sulzberger had been wrong and irresponsible, and *The Post* would be thereafter regarded as the paper that had let *The Times* down. Even worse, Mrs. Graham would not be welcome in her own newsroom, which Patterson assured her, would be empty of himself, Bradlee and others who felt as strongly. Patterson believes to this day that these considerations enabled Mrs. Graham to make a decision she basically did not like, or fully understand.

The peer influence felt by Mrs. Graham was in essence the heart of the old press culture, a comfort with risk in both business and politics. It was an ethic preserved by the elite and enforced on the rest whenever necessary to preserve the special role of the press in society. Mrs. Graham, like Amon Evans and his counterparts, shared and cherished an appreciation of her business as one with a unique constitutionally protected role in the democracy and one whose durability lay in that definition. In no sense, however, was this a guard against imperfection. Because those who owned journalism practiced it as their personal preserve, the press was as prone to excess and hypocrisy as any other line of human endeavor.

Hearst and Pulitzer, two of the most important influences in newspaper history, have been unable to escape consensus opinion that in 1898 they instigated the Spanish-American War just to serve their New York circulation war. Hearst's reputation for megalomania finally got him memorialized by Orson Welles in *Citizen Kane*, a movie caricature of the American press which is actually quite villainous and not entirely undeserved. Hearst once got so angry at Stanford University that he banned its name from his San Francisco newspaper, referring to the university's football team as "the boys from Palo Alto."

A. J. Liebling, the great press critic of his time, always likened the press to the black stallion of children's literature, alternately owned by good masters, who fed and brushed him and put him up at night, and bad ones, who left him out in the cold to starve. That is the way a young journalist of thirty years ago saw all press proprietors, as good and evil struggling for control of the oars that would propel the American ship of state toward the ideal democracy which was always out there on the horizon. Well-intentioned or not, it was the struggle between good publishers and bad that kept the country from stalling in stagnant water.

In time, the edge of my own idealism, which had been honed in Amon Evans's city room, would be dulled by the reality of the young publisher himself. At twenty-five years old, with six years' experience as a reporter, including a stint as a Washington correspondent, I took my first step into newspaper management by becoming night city editor of *The Tennessean*. But it was two more years before I began to understand what a paradoxical world I had entered. By 1970, Evans's *Tennessean* had given me just about every possible opportunity a newspaper of 100,000 daily circulation could afford — and far more than a backward, poorly educated young son of a mill worker could expect. It had gotten me a college degree, the first in the history of my family, and sent me off to national political conventions, to travel with presidents and to cover firsthand historic national events such as the assassinations of John F. Kennedy and Martin Luther King, Jr., and the election of Richard M. Nixon. Journalism had given me a seat at the table, a spot from which to watch and participate in the progress of democracy. And it was on the strength of such employer largesse and *The Tennessean*'s journalistic reputation that I was awarded a Nieman Fellowship at Harvard University at age twenty-seven. Yet when I returned to Nashville, after studying urban government up north for a year, I learned that my homecoming assignment would be to tutor the publisher's closest friend, a local politician, on urban affairs in preparation for his campaign for mayor. After providing me the Nieman feast, *The Tennessean* had fed me a fish bone, which stuck in my craw, a sharp and painful ruination of the meal.

Nonetheless, the juxtaposition of Liebling's good and bad masters was fixed in my mind that day in 1971 when Amon Carter Evans assembled *The Tennessean* staff to tell us that our hated afternoon rival, the *Banner*, had been sold by the Stahlmans, the Nashville family who had owned it for years. Then he welcomed into the newsroom and introduced to us Allen H. Neuharth, a former *Miami Herald* news executive, whom Evans identified as a representative of the *Banner*'s new owners, the Gannett Company of Rochester, New York. Neuharth's appearance left no one with the impression we were looking at the future of newspaper journalism.

Neuharth favored sharkskin suits in those days, and

those looking down our noses at him around the city desk thought the one he was wearing fit him as perfectly as the smug impression on his face. Somebody near me wondered out loud "where the shark ends and Al begins." I had seen Neuharth only a few months before, working the hallways of a meeting of the Southern Newspaper Publishers Association, wearing a glistening houndstooth sport coat, a black open-collar shirt and a nondescript necklace. After he had gotten off an elevator, I had heard a Florida publisher comment to a companion that Neuharth reminded him of a "banty [bantam] rooster." Indeed, Neuharth struck me as a man with the ability to strut even while sitting down.

Except for their political views, the Stahlman and Evans families were a lot alike. The senior Stahlman, James G., who liked to be called Major, was the *Banner*'s publisher. He kept a sword in his office, which we all knew was there for protection against the Communists his editorial page said were constantly stalking everything American. One morning when he saw the fuse of an unexploded firecracker protruding from a drain sewer outside the building where *The Tennessean* and *Banner* shared offices, he called the FBI and reported a bomb scare. Neuharth later would call Major Stahlman "the biggest S.O.B." he'd ever met, a remark the old publisher would have taken as an insult and returned twofold, maybe at sword point, had he not died before Neuharth said it. So detested was Stahlman's *Banner* in *The Tennessean* city room that the news of its "sale into chains" was greeted with glee. Gannett, the owner of only small newspapers at the time, was not known or respected for its journalism. The consensus opinion among the rag-gedy-ass reporters laughing up their sleeves was that the *Banner* had gotten what it deserved. No one realized that the smartest man in the room by far was Neuharth and that his purchase of the failing *Nashville Banner* was but the first step in his quest of the more prestigious and profitable *Tennessean.*

Because the *Banner* and *The Tennessean* were part of a joint operating agreement, under which the business operations of the competing papers had been merged, Gannett's purchase of the afternoon newspaper made Neuharth and Evans business partners. On the day Neu-harth came to *The Tennessean*, Evans was still angry be-cause the Stahlmans had not told him about the deal. The two men stood side by side in the newspaper's city room that day, matching swaggers and stretching to their tall-est, two cock pheasants marking territory. We saw it as a face-off between the good master and the bad, not the old and the new. We believed that the health of journal-ism was only as good as the young reporters, and as one of our number, David Halberstam, would tell a meeting of newspaper editors twenty years later: "They cannot be better than their publishers and editors." In turn, the publishers and editors couldn't be better than their own-ers and the values ingrained in the institution.

But however good or bad Evans was as a publisher, he represented the independent and diverse nature of the press — a nature that had always kept it from becoming a monolith like the oil, steel and auto industries, and thus less vulnerable to pressure from either profitmongers or the government. And however fearful we were of Neuharth, none of us lounging around *The Tennessean* that day could see clearly what his coming really meant. Our skepticism of the new owners he represented was then nothing more than a new sprout in our contempt for the old. It was the nature of reporters of every era to believe that the levers of the press gates were so disparate that even if they fell into the hands of barbarians, they would somehow always remain open. For all our supposed skill as observers and analysts, we placed our faith in the character of individuals to determine and protect the values of the institution. Had we believed Neuharth to be a Pulitzer or a Sulzberger, we would have welcomed his owning the *Banner*, or, for that matter, us. Never for an instant did we see that the real threat represented by Neuharth had little if anything to do with individual character or personal commitment to journalism. What none of us then understood was that Neuharth symbolized the coming of an era of press ownership of an entirely different nature, a system beyond his control or that of anyone else.

What was happening to *The Tennessean* was a classic example of the dilemma facing families who sought to pass their newspapers to a new generation. Amon Evans was precisely the kind of owner constantly being stalked in the early 1970s by Neuharth's Gannett Company, which because of its voracious appetite for acquisition was rapidly becoming known as "the predator." From a company with 27 small dailies and revenues of $250 million in 1963, Neuharth built a $3.4 billion media giant whose holdings today run the gamut from billboards to satellites and include 93 newspapers, the most of any

American company. When Neuharth took Gannett's stock to sell on Wall Street in 1967, only two newspaper companies had preceded him—Dow Jones, publisher of *The Wall Street Journal* and Times Mirror, publisher of the *Los Angeles Times*. Both had offered the public a non-voting class of stock to raise investment capital and had structured their offerings so as to keep control in the hands of the owning families. The big New York and Chicago papers with which Wall Street was most familiar were earning little then, due to labor-intensive production systems and rising newsprint costs. Neuharth knew he was peddling a vastly different kind of business, one based on newspaper monopolies in small towns poised on the brink of industrial growth. So he presented the newspaper business in general and Gannett in particular on Wall Street in a way it had never been presented anywhere to anyone before; he billed it as "a dependable profit machine in good times or bad."

This was a most important departure, for it was something that neither the old independent owners nor their succeeding generations were in a position to do. Newspapers had always been among the most cyclical of businesses. The press titans took their profits and built their fortunes when times were good. When recessions came along, they were able to adjust by accepting little or no profit, if necessary. Because they relied on equipment that was decades old, the 1960s and '70s found many of these publishers debt free. With no interest to pay and no stockholders but family to worry about, a year of low or no profit would not bring the wolf to the door.

On Wall Street, Neuharth's promise of a recession-proof earning machine was startling news. Unlike the big newspapers in competitive environments, Neuharth pointed out, the Gannett papers would show big profits by consistent natural growth in good times and — when times were hard — by cutting newsprint and raising advertising and circulation prices to the limit of market resistance. It was a truth about monopoly newspapers that none of the old publishers would dare to admit. But it was also one few if any had dared to exploit. With a few notable exceptions, like Hearst and McCormick, who tended to do business in competitive markets, press proprietors seldom flaunted their wealth. Politically active publishers like Silliman Evans in Nashville, Barry Bingham in Louisville and the Cowles family in Des Moines had built incredibly valuable newspaper franchises, while hiding that fact from local advertisers. At the same time, high-profit-margin operators like Samuel I. Newhouse seldom called attention to themselves, or their riches, so as not to raise the ire of either the public or the government. As a result they were not perceived as any more wealthy than the local hardware distributor or the town's leading bank or automobile dealer — which is how the public thought it should be. The job of the press had been to finger the robber barons, not join hands with them.

While Neuharth was convincing Wall Street investors to underwrite his ambition, people like Amon Evans couldn't get around the problems of rising newsprint and labor costs and inheritance taxes. Not many newspapers were turning the kinds of profits Neuharth knew were possible, and second- and third-generation publishers like

Evans were having trouble making ends meet, especially where there were multiple heirs. The problems of inheritance were even more onerous. Because of federal and state tax consequences, a family often lost 70 percent or more of its equity if it tried to pass the newspaper on. This left little choice but to sell the properties or to take them to public ownership in a way in which the family equity was diluted but its value was not, as both Dow Jones and Times Mirror had done.

Some of the newspaper families would hang on until the middle of the 1980s, trying to preserve independence and individuality. Most of them, especially the tradition-drenched Evanses, viewed Neuharth the same way sanctimonious churchmen might welcome a whore in the sanctuary. They avoided his eyes and the seats beside him. But they could not avoid looking, and many of them found both his appearance and his style seductive. He had the look of money, and it would not be long until, like the hypocritical churchmen, they were inviting him to slip into their back doors under the cover of darkness. And like Evans, the overwhelming majority would eventually take the money and run, thus delivering their family jewels into the soft, manicured hands of cool, conservative corporate America.

In his book *Confessions of an S.O.B.*, Neuharth referred to his conquest of the Nashville family newspapers, first the *Banner* and then *The Tennessean*, as a "little deal" and wrote disparagingly of Evans as an easy mark. Evans finally sold, Neuharth said, because he needed "big bucks" to pay off wife number five and marry wife number six.

When the numbers-oriented, professional profit makers began entering the temple of journalism in the early 1970s, they saw what people-oriented publishers like Evans had been blind to: four people doing the work of one machine. It took no genius to realize that a business being threatened by the first great technological invention — television — might be saved by the second — the computer. The good business described by Neuharth might just be an extraordinary one. They were right. What television did to the nature and culture of press ownership, the computer did to the nature and culture of press function. Together they would transform a business whose profitability had always depended on the quality of people into one whose survival depended on the efficiency of equipment.

Between 1975 and 1990, newspaper production work forces would be cut by 50 percent or more. Presses that once required 12 to 14 workers would now run with 6 or 7. Typesetting that used to demand huge departments, employing from 50 to 300 skilled, unionized craftsmen, would disappear completely. Paper handling and loading, once requiring waves of manual laborers, would be done by computerized conveyor systems, robotic cranes and remote-controlled flatcars. Human photoengravers would be replaced by laser beams, and film processors by computer processes.

Almost overnight, a loud linear world of words etched in hot lead by hot, sweaty and ink-stained people would become a place of digitized images and antiseptically clean, quietly humming, air-conditioned machines. The transition would be both a boon to the profit seekers and a trauma for the protectors of tradition. Waste and redundancies that clogged newsrooms and production departments and threatened the economic health of the printed press would be eliminated. But so would a lot of other things, among them the free spirit that had been the soul of the American press since its inception.

Looking back on it now, I can see that I should not have been surprised. Still, I can't help but mourn the passing of publishers like Amon Carter Evans. He was every inch the typical offspring of the typical independent newspaper publisher who dominated the industry during the first half of this century. He and his kind ran the nation's press as if it belonged to them — which it did. Evans's interest in phosphate miners and the environment was most likely rooted in his love for duck hunting. His zeal for investigative journalism had been ignited only when the land "rapists" had begun dredging operations on a west Tennessee lake, destroying his most prized duck blind.

As far as anyone knows, Evans never had to sell his stock in American Airlines, if indeed he had any. Instead, in 1978, with his number of marriages climbing higher than his newspaper's profit margin and unable to get around the inheritance taxes that threatened his family fortune, he sold *The Tennessean*, not to another of his kind, but to Neuharth's Gannett Company, an owner as representative of the future of the free press in America as the Evans family had been of its past — and for a paltry $50 million.

I was not there to see it. In 1972, a year after I'd returned from Harvard, the employment opportunities that often follow Nieman Fellowships lured me north to a far bigger and more famous newspaper, the *Chicago Tribune*. There I would quickly learn that my education as a journalist had hardly begun.

2

The Ghost in the Machine

IT IS A QUITE A WAYS from the backroads of Tennessee to the marble-lined hallways of the *Chicago Tribune.* No American newspaper but *The New York Times* can match the *Tribune* in richness of tradition or worldwide fame. Its reporters were among the first ever accredited to cover the Congress of the United States. And there was a time when only the *Tribune* and *The Times* had permanent reporters assigned to cover the White House. The *Tribune's* founder, Joseph Medill, called the meeting that resulted in the formation of the Republican Party. He personally recruited, schooled and promoted Abraham Lincoln as a candidate for president, and then along with Horace Greeley convinced the nation that the abolition of slavery was worth going to war over. But it was Medill's grandson, Colonel Robert Rutherford McCormick, who ensured the *Tribune's* survival and amassed its power. He had been dead for seventeen years by the time I was offered a job as the *Tribune*'s national political writer, but stories about the McCormick era still shaped the *Tribune* in the eyes of journalists. In newspaper lore, the publisher still loomed as large as the great Gothic tower he had built at the highest point on Michigan Avenue as a monument to himself and a home for his newspaper. And to a prospective employee from the hills of Tennessee, his legacy was as intimidating as the Tribune Tower's lobby, where the Colonel's words are inscribed on great chunks of marble along with those of the great men of law and letters. It was like walking through a giant marble copy of Bartlett's *Familiar Quotations*.

My eyes went directly to the huge American flag displayed in the corner to count its stars. For it was there in the lobby, according to the story, that McCormick once personally ordered a mutilation of the flag — the removal of the star representing the state of Rhode Island. Like many of his decisions, it was a crime of passion, an angry gesture at the Rhode Island legislature for passing some horse-racing legislation he didn't like. He also banned the name of the state from the newspaper for a time, and ordered maps altered accordingly. A half century later, an unsuspecting artist would remove one of these ancient and fraudulent maps from the newspaper's archives and use it — minus Rhode Island — as an illustration for a travel story.

For four decades, the adrenaline and lifeblood of the *Tribune* pumped from the heart of the man running it. Its news, editorial columns and employee relations reflected the personal agenda of the Colonel. A lot of the paper's policies, for example, stemmed from a running feud between McCormick and President Franklin D. Roosevelt, which went all the way back to their prep school days at Groton. Roosevelt told a *Tribune* reporter once that the animosity arose out of a rivalry for the attention of a young lady, an allegation McCormick dismissed as "another of Frank's shallow lies."

Their feud was roaring full blast in 1937 when, with war brewing in Europe, Roosevelt came to Chicago for a bridge dedication speech, which he was to deliver from a spot directly across the Chicago River from Tribune Tower. On the side of a warehouse bearing the name of his newspaper, McCormick sent FDR a message in orange letters several feet tall: "THE CHICAGO TRIBUNE — UNDOMINATED" — which indeed it was, except by McCormick himself.

The Colonel went to his grave in 1955 convinced that Roosevelt had used the power of the White House in an effort to destroy the *Chicago Tribune*. A decade earlier Roosevelt had died knowing full well that McCormick and his newspaper had tried everything possible to do the same thing to his presidency.

By the time I arrived at the *Tribune* in the fall of 1972, my glasses tear-frozen to my face by an early winter wind, the long dead Colonel was still plainly in charge. His empire — including his personal fortune, the *Tribune*, the New York *Daily News*, radio and television stations in New York and Chicago and a massive newsprint business in Canada — was all safely in the hands of the management trust he had counted on to keep things just as they were. And they had not disappointed him.

If a business can be run from the grave, the *Tribune*

was. Don Maxwell, who had succeeded the Colonel as editor, once confessed that he would awaken in the middle of the night certain that he had just talked on the telephone to McCormick—and that the Colonel's instructions had been very specific.

Although the paper began life as a progressive social force dedicated to the abolition of slavery, the *Tribune*'s long association with the Republican Party and McCormick's hatred of Roosevelt had established it as perhaps the country's most important conservative voice. But with Maxwell apparently taking directions over very long distance telephone lines, that voice became shrill and ugly. The *Tribune*'s political writers, mostly polemicists and ideologues, wrote vengefully, as if their jobs still depended upon their willingness to spread the Colonel's political views. In 1964, the newspaper editorially opposed the Civil Rights Bill which was being pushed through Congress by Illinois's great moderate Republican senator, Everett Dirksen. Well into the 1970s, the *Tribune*'s editorial page clung to the '40s and '50s, and its political reporters continued to punish McCormick's targets as if he were still reading their copy. Shortly after my arrival in the Washington bureau, one of my senior colleagues, a *Tribune* man from his gray, cropped hair to his heavy wing tip shoes, reported an "exclusive" story, the lead of which read:

> Liberal Republican Sen. Chuck Percy of Illinois disclosed yesterday that he will seek his party's presidential nomination in 1976.

"Jesus Christ, not again," said a Republican source on Capitol Hill. "Not again."

This was the *Tribune* style, with which the industry was familiar and of which it was contemptuous. But in my job interview, Maxwell's successor, Clayton Kirkpatrick, had assured me that the days of that kind of reporting were numbered. I had asked him why the *Tribune* would want to hire a political reporter from a newspaper like *The Tennessean*, which had been as liberal and progressive as the *Tribune* had been conservative. "This is not the old *Tribune*. We've changed," he said. "We like the way David Broder of *The Washington Post* writes politics. That's how we want you to do it."

That was good enough for me. A willingness to change was obviously part of my own makeup. Although I didn't appreciate it at the time, the change of going from *The Tennessean* to the *Tribune* was like passing between acts of the same Greek tragedy.

In Chicago, the newspaper executives got married less often, but just as in Nashville family money problems were on their minds. And they were running the Colonel's business the same way Amon Evans had run his father's *Tennessean* — into the ground. In those days there were about 200 private stockholders of Tribune Company, only one of which mattered — the family trust, which held 54 percent of the stock. As long as the family trust was in effect, the *Tribune* and the New York *Daily News* were run as if Colonel McCormick and his cousin Joseph Patterson were still alive. Both grandsons of the famed Medill, they were alike in many ways — patriotic, entrepreneurial and strong-willed — but they differed widely in style and political philosophy. As young men, they actually alternated running the powerful *Tribune* for nearly ten years, swapping the jobs of editor and business manager. This caused the paper to career wildly between McCormick's reactionary conservatism and Patterson's progressive socialist populism. Realizing that the *Tribune* was not big enough for the two of them and that the schism would kill it, McCormick helped his cousin found the *Daily News* in 1919. (And in what only could have been an act of blind and ironic benevolence, he later helped Patterson's daughter Alicia found *Newsday*, the paper that would eventually help to wreck the *News*.)

In their separate spheres, the cousins prospered. Their papers became the franchise newspapers in the nation's two largest cities, unique and identifiable voices with vast and important constituencies. From Chicago, McCormick's *Tribune* rose as the strident voice of midwestern Republicanism and commerce; in New York, Patterson's *News* spoke for the rambunctious, ethnic, urban working class. Although they earned less money than people thought, each paper was an immensely profitable enterprise by the standards of that era. For a while, McCormick's *Tribune* was the largest circulation full-size newspaper in the country, selling more than a million copies a day worldwide. Although it had shrunk to less than 800,000 by 1972, the *Tribune* (and its sister afternoon paper, *Chicago Today*) dominated the nation's second most important urban market. And in the Big Apple, the tabloid *News* had grown to be the nation's circulation leader, reaching 2.5 million copies sold per day in 1949. By the 1970s, it was still the leader, but with a million less circulation. In both cities, the company also owned the most important independent television station, WPIX in New York and WGN in Chicago.

Tribune Company owned television stations in New Orleans, Denver and Atlanta as well, along with extensive cable franchise holdings. In the 1960s, two important Florida newspapers, *The Orlando Sentinel* and the Fort Lauderdale *News and Sun-Sentinel*, had been added to the empire. Both cash cows, they had been left virtually untouched by the Colonel's successors and were operating much as they had been when purchased. Under the terms of the family trust, the Chicago management trustees were in charge, but the New York minority representatives could veto almost everything involving large expenditures of money. So, except for the purchase of the two Florida papers, there were none. In the world of business, the company's reputation was for no debt, no energy and no imagination. And in the world of journalism, it had little respect. The journalism elite considered the *Tribune* and the *Daily News* mediocre at best, and the Florida papers were considered miserable.

But what *Tribune* editor Kirkpatrick told me in my hiring interview was accurate. The *Tribune* was indeed in the throes of a change, necessitated in part by the imminent expiration of the family trust in 1975, and in part by a larger revolution in the way all American newspapers would be owned and managed. In the space of a few years, the McCormick-Patterson empire would be reconstituted as a modern media conglomerate and would seek to ele-

33

vate management control and standardization over journalism's traditional strengths, freedom and individuality.

Compared with the spartan existence at *The Tennessean*, where as city editor I had neither assistant city editors nor even a warm body to answer the telephone, the *Chicago Tribune* was fat with people. Counting the staffs of the *Tribune* and *Chicago Today* — which were merged in 1974 — and a large suburban newspaper group known as the Trib, there were close to 1,000 reporters, editors, photographers and clerical people involved in print journalism. Editorial costs represented up to 20 percent of the company's revenues, or more. The advertising, production and circulation departments were just as labor intensive — and everybody was treated like family. Not only were *Tribune* employees among the best paid in journalism, but the fringe benefits were unequaled. Each year the company's profits were shared with employees, with every nonunion worker eligible to receive between 5 and 10 percent of his or her annual pay — the exact percentage determined by the company's operating profit. In those days, 10 percent was a very good year.

Such generous labor policies reflected Colonel McCormick's larger vision of the role of the press as an institution. He and his contemporaries understood that both the quality of journalism they practiced and the size of their profits depended on the number and quality of the people they employed.

Although McCormick and Patterson had opposed America's entry into the First World War, both cousins nonetheless volunteered for combat duty, to underscore that their opposition ought not to be construed as concern for their personal safety. And once war was under way, they were fiercely patriotic and supportive. For the rest of their lives, they would use their military titles: Colonel McCormick and Captain Patterson. In the Second World War, the Colonel rewarded *Tribune* employees who went to war by continuing to pay them up to 70 percent of their salaries even though he hired replacements. When the war was over, the returning veterans were given their jobs back, but the replacements were kept, too. Naturally, this meant that by the 1960s and '70s the *Tribune* had not only one of the biggest staffs in journalism, but also the oldest. I didn't realize how old until August 1974, when President Nixon, facing certain impeachment, decided to resign. As the news editor of the Washington bureau, I wrote, edited and transmitted to Chicago a story reported by the newspaper's White House correspondent, the late Aldo Beckman, which disclosed Nixon's still-secret decision. During a telephone conference call, the acting managing editor in Chicago asked me for a headline recommendation, and I suggested, "Nixon to Quit." The editor, new on the job, asked what "the count" was on the headline, meaning how long would it be in the *Tribune*'s standard 120-point banner headline type. Before I could respond, another voice on the conference hookup said, "Same as 'Great War Ends' — I wrote that one, too." And indeed he had. The employment of many of the *Tribune* copy editors spanned the eras of both Hitler and Nixon.

Besides superannuated desk men, McCormick bequeathed a more important legacy to the journalists who

followed him. The legal doctrine prohibiting "prior restraint" on publishing — the basis on which the Pentagon
Papers case was decided — owes its existence to the single-
minded efforts of Robert McCormick. In 1929, on the
eve of the Great Depression, McCormick put his money
and the power of the *Tribune* behind a lawsuit that resulted in a landmark Supreme Court decision known as
Near v. Minnesota. In this case, the Court ruled that the
government may not suppress in advance the First
Amendment rights of any newspaper — not even the race-
baiting, anti-Semitic, seditious rag published by Jay Near
in St. Paul.

At the time, McCormick was both feared and hated by
much of the journalistic establishment, most of whose
members disagreed with his strident and vindictive editorial policies. Yet the peer pressures of press ownership
finally brought the establishment — and its money — behind him in support of an absurd and hateful newspaper
they all abhorred. To do otherwise, McCormick had convinced them, would undermine the foundation of their
business.

Unlike those who would follow them, McCormick and
his contemporaries also understood perfectly the social
and economic nature of their business. Reflecting what
was surely the family perspective, Captain Patterson once
wrote:

> Newspapers start when their owners are poor, and
> take the part of the people, and so they build up a
> large circulation, and, as a result, advertising. That
> makes them rich, and they begin, most naturally, to

associate with other rich men — they play golf with one, and drink whiskey with another, and their son marries the daughter of a third. They forget all about the people, and then their circulation dries up, then their advertising, and then their paper becomes decadent.

Walter Trohan, who was McCormick's friend, his Washington bureau chief and a *Tribune* journalist for thirty-eight years, wrote in his memoirs that the two qualities that characterized the *Tribune* under McCormick — courage and consistency — apparently died with him. Certainly, neither had been resurrected by the time I went to work there seventeen years later. As is often the case, the successors of great men are often men easily led. And those who succeeded McCormick atop Tribune Company fit the mold. They were reactive by nature, a succession of salesmen, accountants and engineers more concerned about the financial implications of operating Lippmann's searchlight than about what it illuminated. When Liebling was setting up his "kindly master" and "cruel master" categories, he knew nothing of this kind of press proprietor, who is not really an owner at all but a manager or presider. When put into the Black Beauty analogy, these people can be most accurately characterized as not knowing which end of the stallion to feed and which to clean up after. But they do know that if Black Beauty can't win the race, it's off to the dog food factory. Survival, more than advancement, would become their goal.

In ways unimaginable to me when I arrived in 1972,

the Colonel's ghost still haunted his magnificent twenty-fourth floor office, with its fabulous hand-carved ceiling moldings and the infamous door which mysteriously vanished into the wall, confounding visitors about how they had entered. As a new member of the Washington bureau, I was dispatched to meet the publisher on my first day of work, and I guess I must have been expecting to see McCormick himself, because I was disappointed to find in his stead a mousy, nondescript man in a brown suit named Harold Grumhaus. The meeting lasted only a few seconds, thankfully, since Grumhaus (hardly an imposing giant of journalism) acted as if he wished I had not come. On the way out, I was introduced to J. Howard Wood, Grumhaus's predecessor as publisher and the Colonel's immediate successor in that post. Though allegedly retired, Wood was still prowling the executive suite.

Fresh from this ghoulish initiation, I set about my work covering the 1972 presidential election. My first story for the famous *Chicago Tribune*, for more than a century the voice of Republican conservatism, was a dispatch from George McGovern's presidential campaign. I filed it from Baltimore on a Sunday afternoon, dictating it to a tape-recording machine at the *Tribune*'s national desk, my first time ever. At *The Tennessean* people took dictation, even though there were very few of them. Then I flew with the McGovern campaign to Cleveland, where I checked in again with the newspaper.

"Did you get the story?" I asked the national deskman, a veteran named Larry Fein.

"Yes, we did," he said.

"How is it?" I wanted to know.

"We don't know yet," he said, politely. "We don't have the grits off of it yet."

"The grits?"

"Oh, I mean we are having some difficulty understanding your accent."

Before long, they were calling me Jim Bob behind my back. I wasn't at *The Tennessean* anymore.

None of us who came to the *Tribune* in the early 1970s was hired because the newspaper needed another journalist. It just needed younger ones, a different kind of employee to deal with the different kind of challenges posed by the rise of television and suburbanization — a struggle for relevancy that twenty years later is yet to be won.

The realization within Tribune Company that the world of newspapers was changing did not even begin to dawn until after the three men McCormick had knighted from his deathbed had been removed from Tribune Tower by either death or retirement. One of the first things the designated trustees did upon the Colonel's death in 1955 was to enact a mandatory retirement age of sixty-five. One, Chessor Campbell, an advertising executive, died within five years, but when the other two — publisher Wood and editor Maxwell — turned sixty-five, they didn't want to go. And who could blame them? They had all the power and perks of ownership, including the Colonel's imperial life-style, his Wheaton estate, his Canadian fishing lodge and the most powerful social and political positions in Chicago. So they created for themselves hang-around jobs that were exempted from the rule, including chairman of the Tribune Company board, chairman of the finance committee and editorial consultant. Maxwell died on the sidewalk outside Tribune Tower. Wood, who became the first chairman of the company after turning sixty-five, stayed around to look over the shoulder of his successor, Grumhaus, until it was nearly time for Grumhaus himself to retire.

The second generation of trustees, or directors as they were now called, was not unlike the first, except that, having had less personal contact with McCormick while he was alive, they were less sure of what he wanted done. Whatever else McCormick had been, he'd been an activist and a leader. And so anxious were McCormick's employees to follow him that many of their mistakes, such as the famous "Dewey Defeats Truman" headline, were made in their haste to get where they thought he wanted to go.

Soon after my arrival, the power at Tribune Company was passed to a new publisher, Stanton Rufus Cook, who would hold it — formally anyway — for almost twenty years. An engineer by education and by nature, Cook had joined the *Tribune* while the Colonel was still alive. John Malone, a Chicago inventor and newspaper buff, claims he was in McCormick's office on the first day Cook was brought in by the paper's production director to greet the publisher. After Cook had departed, Malone said he asked the Colonel, "Where'd he come from?"

"An oil company. He's a production engineer," McCormick replied.

"Well, what does he know about newspapers?" Malone wanted to know.

"Not a thing," said McCormick.

"Then, why did you hire him?" Malone said he asked.
"Because he is a tall upstanding man."

Cook may have been anointed by the Colonel himself,
but the *Tribune*'s power was most often wielded by the
paper's longtime company general counsel, Donald Reuben. No power vacuum anywhere near Don Reuben goes
unfilled. He had filled one first inside the law firm of
Kirkland & Ellis, which McCormick, himself a lawyer,
had founded in 1908. It was Kirkland & Ellis that McCormick sent before the Supreme Court to argue against
prior restraint and it was to Kirkland & Ellis that the
Colonel's men deferred — not only in matters of law and
politics but also where law and politics affected business.
To whatever degree the powers of a publisher can be
usurped by the newspaper's attorney, Reuben had
usurped them. The Chicago trustees may have controlled
the management, but Reuben was the man behind the
trustees.

He could have had the top *Tribune* job himself, he
contends, but instead engineered the elevation of Cook.
Reuben also arranged for lifetime employment contracts
(in six figures) for four other top managers as part of the
deal. His arrogance and candor, however, could get him
in trouble. In 1977, he was asked by a friend in the Carter
administration for an assessment of the new *Tribune*
chairman he had installed. Reuben unflatteringly characterized Cook as a lightweight, and after a memo quoting
him found its way back to *Tribune* editors, the relationship
between Reuben and Cook was never quite the same.

That Reuben actually might have turned down the
top spot at Tribune Company — had it been offered — is

understandable. He had a better job. Once described by
Fortune as the single most powerful attorney in the country, Reuben had among his clients in the 1970s and '80s
not only Tribune Company but also the Archdiocese of
Chicago, the Chicago Bears, the city's taxi industry and
its wealthiest family — the Pritzkers, who owned the Hy-
att hotel chain. And inside Tribune Company, there was
no doubt that he was the single most powerful influence.

Reuben's interests ran mainly to the exercise of the
newspaper's political clout, locally and in Washington. In
the 1970s, he was the man to see if you wanted to get
along with the *Tribune* in Chicago. The politicians and
labor bosses knew him as the most effective way to communicate with the newspaper. Editorial reaction to some
government or civic initiative could often be predeter-
mined simply by calling Reuben, who would then call
Tribune executives with his opinion on what was about to
surface. They would in turn give him theirs, which he
would relate back to the caller. What Reuben thought on
the matter and how *Tribune* editorial opinion eventually
fell were seldom at odds — particularly on matters of politics and elections, including judicial appointments, where
Reuben's judgment was considered supreme. Tribune
Company was particularly paranoid about the possibility
of strikes by union employees (a legacy of Colonel
McCormick's "publish at any cost" philosophy), and the
directors looked to Reuben for their protection in court.
This paranoia was not without foundation. The *Tribune*'s
great embarrassment, the infamous "Dewey Defeats Truman" headline, came in the middle of a 1948 printers'
strike, the only one the Colonel ever had to endure. As

it would do again in 1985, the *Tribune* published anyway, using inexperienced editorial people to do composing room work. Not only was the "Dewey Defeats Truman" headline wrong, it was printed badly garbled and upside down through most of the edition. Next to Reuben himself, it was the unions he was supposed to keep under control that exerted the most influence on the *Tribune*, on its executives and on the future of its business.

When Cook became a director in 1972, the editorial side of the paper was in the hands of Maxwell's successor, Clayton Kirkpatrick, a man of extraordinary patience and pragmatism who had spent most of his career caught between the surge of inevitable change and massive institutional resistance to it. After the excesses of the Colonel and, more damaging, those of his feeble mimic Maxwell, Kirkpatrick was good for the *Tribune* in that he was a wonderful repository for power that best goes unexercised. But the characteristics for which he was most admired also prevented him from being a strong and inspiring leader. The caution and indecision which marked his stewardship were also qualities he shared with Cook. Together the two men would define the personality of the newspaper and the company during the '70s.

In 1974, the year Cook became publisher, I almost quit because I could not distinguish between the reticence that came from walking in the Colonel's shadow and outright cowardice. As might be expected, the *Tribune* had come late to the Watergate story. For months, its coverage had consisted mainly of White House denials of *Washington Post* stories. But after the election, I was made the paper's sole reporter on the story, which by this time was populated by old friends of mine from Tennessee politics. These included the Watergate prosecutor, James F. Neal, and the staff of the ranking member of the Senate Watergate Committee, Howard Baker. It was not long before *The Washington Post* ran out of exclusives, and the *Tribune* suddenly became very competitive. For the first time in anyone's memory, the newspaper was being cited on the nightly network news broadcasts and quoted in *The New York Times* as the source of news on important Watergate developments.

My run-in with Kirkpatrick began when Dan Thomasson of Scripps Howard and I, working together, uncovered an extraordinary story—a secret which President Nixon had twice cited obliquely as "the grave national security matter" that had caused him to create the band of "White House plumbers" who ultimately committed the Watergate burglary. The "leak" Nixon had ordered the "plumbers" to plug, it turned out, concerned an internal fiasco in which Admiral Thomas Moorer, chairman of the Joint Chiefs of Staff, had ordered navy officers and enlisted men to spy on and pilfer documents from Henry Kissinger while Kissinger was making secret trips to China as Nixon's national security adviser.

When the White House found out we had the story, Alexander Haig, the president's chief of staff, telephoned Kirkpatrick and told him publication would be a serious breach of national security. I told Kirkpatrick that was bunk. For days the issue went unsettled and the story unpublished. Because of our friendship, Thomasson withheld his dispatch while I tried to convince the *Tribune*. In desperation one day, I told Kirkpatrick that *The*

Washington Post had the story and was about to publish it. Somewhere in that Tower, I surmised, the ghost of the Colonel still lurked, and with luck it might be a competitive spirit. But this was not the case.

My strategy only spurred Kirkpatrick to telephone Ben Bradlee to find out if *The Post* had the story, and if so, why he had not published it. "Kirk, I don't think we have that story," Bradlee told him. "But if I did I would sure as hell run it." Only then did the *Tribune* wiggle loose from the hold that had been put on by the telephone call from San Clemente. The White House, of course, denied the report, leaving my career delicately suspended from the limb until *The Post* and *The New York Times* confirmed the story a few days later.

The next time I called Chicago with an exclusive — a twenty-four-hour head start on the text of the Watergate tapes — the response was quite different. The *Tribune* scooped the rest of the press by a full day on publication, and, a few days later, ended its long love affair with Richard Nixon and the Republican Party. Based on the unsavory nature of the president's comments in the transcripts, Kirkpatrick wrote an editorial calling on Nixon to resign, ultimately a major factor in the collapse of his support among Republicans in Congress. The *Tribune* had indeed begun to change — slowly.

3

Steam Buckets and Bottom Lines

COLONEL McCORMICK had never thought himself capable of making mistakes. More important, no one could fire him for making them. His successors never experienced that comfort, even when the company's stock was tightly held and controlled by management. Over much of the two decades following McCormick's death, they guarded the legacy as if they were sitting on the edge of a razor blade. What they feared most was the sight and smell of their own blood, which was beginning to ooze. My own hiring and the spate of others that followed were not the manifestation of restlessness for change but in fact the direct result of a *Tribune* reader measurement survey that drew blood. The paper's mastery at building circulation had been buried with McCormick, and readership had been declining steadily since his death. In response, Tribune management had called in pollster Ruth Clark, a pioneer researcher who taught the newspaper business to live by the reader survey. Her assessment of those reading the gray lady of Chicago was that *Tribune* readers were a lot like the newspaper's staff — old, boring and not long for this world. Your readers are dying, Clark told the Colonel's stunned men, and if you don't do something, your newspaper will die, too. All over the country, newspaper owners were hearing the same message.

By 1972, television had really begun to divert America's attention, and the household penetration of newspapers began only its second period of decline in history. (The first had followed the development of radio.) Afternoon newspapers, especially those in competitive markets, were already on the road to extinction.

In the nation's second largest market, the only newspapers left to threaten the *Tribune* were the *Sun-Times* and the *Daily News*, both of which were owned by the Marshall Field family. This fact was in itself a disturbing prospect for the *Tribune* and a telling commentary on the overall industry, for survival — not profit — had always been the goal of the Field newspaper empire. As long as it remained a viable competitor with the *Tribune*, big newspaper profits would be only a dream — or the contents of the mail the company received from its monopoly markets in Florida. This kind of competition between Tribune and Field was what had always held down press profits — and also what had held up the institution's dedication to vigorous journalism.

As had become the custom since McCormick's death, the *Tribune* was letting the Field papers choose both the weapons of war and the battleground. So each day a bitter front-page struggle was waged for supremacy of single-copy sales inside the city limits of Chicago, where the tabloid *Sun-Times* and the jazzy, well-written *Daily News* had a natural advantage. Tribune Company had let Field convince retail advertisers that city readership, not total market circulation, was the key to market supremacy. According to Ruth Clark, the *Sun-Times* had the momentum as well. Chicago readers considered it the leader in sports, the best paper on local news, the paper of the future and the paper most relevant to their lives.

Such a bleak outlook, Tribune managers knew, would be enough to stir McCormick in his grave. Over the years, his newspaper had taken on and defeated all comers in Chicago. Both William Randolph Hearst and Jack Knight had come to the nation's second city with the idea that it was big enough for two press barons. Both had left convinced that it was not.

Although the modern newspaper war between Tribune and Field lacked the energy and imagination of those fought by the old press lords, it retained one of their important characteristics — each company was privately held and answerable for its performance to no one but family stockholders. In this regard Chicago was fast becoming an anachronism. But this apparent absence of stockholder pressure for profits in Chicago newspapering was deceiving. Both the Field heirs, brothers Marshall III and Ted, were far less dedicated to their grandfather's public service mission of keeping the Colonel's paper honest. Increasingly, they had become preoccupied with their own pursuits in real estate and moviemaking. This meant that, despite its vigor and market position, the *Sun-*

Times might have less staying power than the *Tribune*, which would be there for the long haul.

Though it would be a full decade before Wall Street would get a look inside Tribune Company, the pressures to increase profitability and stock value were intensifying. When the McCormick family trust expired in 1975, the stock would be automatically distributed to the individual heirs, instantly creating a number of unhappy New Yorkers who would want to cash in. In this sense, the company's twenty-year insulation against reality provided by McCormick's will had worn thin. Finally, Tribune Company would begin to feel the kind of financial squeeze that elsewhere on the newspaper landscape was creating a media gold rush. The Washington Post Company had gone public. So had *The New York Times* and Jack Knight's newspapers. And Gannett's acquisition rampage was getting into high gear.

During the 1970s, Tribune Company's version of professional management took its flagship newspaper on a series of hundred-mile-an-hour U-turns. Budget cuts, for example, were often imposed only a few weeks after the launch of new and costly reader-building projects. New sections, such as a recreation section called "Venture," would be abruptly abandoned when they failed to produce instant circulation or advertising gains. Editorially, the newspaper was just as schizophrenic, still the old McCormick *Tribune* at heart but with a face-lift and a new wardrobe to suit advertising and circulation goals that seemed to change by the minute. This caused the newspaper to veer and tilt like an overloaded ocean liner in a storm, and it was not uncommon for people to fall off, some of them pushed while others jumped.

In the fall of 1976, I jumped at the opportunity to edit *The Sentinel*, the *Tribune*'s financially lucrative but editorially bankrupt monopoly-market newspaper in Orlando. I didn't know I was signing on for front-line duty in a newspaper revolution already well under way in smaller and medium-sized cities where the local printed press no longer faced competition.

Through most of the next decade and a half, my companion in the trenches was Charles T. Brumback, a product of Culver Military Academy, Princeton University and thirty years of relatively union-free newspapering in Florida. Fifteen years my senior, he was my school of newspaper economics in the same way *The Tennessean* had been my education in journalism.

I remember my first lesson: "If there is anything in this world I am an expert on," Brumback told me during an argument over newsprint usage in 1977, "it is columns of numbers. I've been looking at them all my life." The discussion, over how much newsprint should be devoted to columns of election vote results, was a harbinger of things to come. Basically, newspapering is a simple business. About three fourths of all costs can be broadly characterized as either newsprint or labor. Any pursuit of cost reduction leads very quickly to reduction of the size of the newspaper or the size of the staff. Over the next thirteen years, Brumback's dogged pursuit of cost reduction became legendary among Tribune Company employees, typifying a new style of newspaper management that would by 1990 be running the entire industry.

Brumback came to Tribune Company along with the Orlando newspaper from Martin Andersen, a Florida version of Colonel McCormick who was as much a merchandise retailer as anything else. Andersen used his circulation department to deliver goods bought through the ads of his newspaper, had an escalator installed in his newspaper building just in case he ever wanted to convert to a department store and equipped his pressroom as a bomb shelter in the event Fidel Castro attacked Florida. Under Andersen and the early Tribune Company management, the paper was right-wing and shrill. It seemed to be angry at its readers, publishing along with each letter to the editor an editor's retort, such as, "How stupid can you get?"

Serving mainly as the paper's chief financial officer, Brumback, a wealthy native of Toledo, was known at *The Sentinel* for blunt talk, baggy suits and a habit of turning off the lights. He must have been a man of extraordinary patience as well, because Andersen and his successor, Bill Conomos, were both strong-willed and dictatorial. Conomos was particularly erratic, sometimes abusive and quick to fire. Brumback survived him for a decade, before being put in charge when Conomos was himself fired for terrorizing the place in late-night temper tantrums.

Tribune management quickly found Brumback to be uniquely suited for the new way of doing things. His expertise was not newspapers; it was money. Brumback came to appreciate earlier than most newspaper managers that while union strength remains in numbers, the engine of American industry runs most profitably now with the fewest people possible. He also took note that machines are quiet, dependable capital assets that depreciate according to the tax schedule, while people are loud, are less reliable and come trailing pensions and medical benefits that accumulate above the bottom line for years and years to come.

With the engineer Cook at the top of the company, taking advice only from Reuben, the lawyer, and the company's financial officer, John W. Madigan, a stocks-and-bonds man, the accountant Brumback was a natural fit in the company hierarchy. He spoke the new company language. And he understood far better than I that this language included a new definition of "quality." To the new management team, quality newspapers were not necessarily those that served up the best journalism to their communities, or that won prestige and respect within the journalism fraternity, but rather those whose profits would earn them distinction on Wall Street as a "quality" business. Tribune Company was headed for public ownership as soon as its profitability reached the levels necessary to be termed a "quality" stock investment.

Although I would report to Cook, Brumback and Madigan for my entire executive career in newspapering, the man who ultimately would have the most influence on the way I had to do business was forty miles away on the Florida coast, at Cocoa Beach. Al Neuharth had nothing to do with Tribune Company directly, but he was writing this new definition of a "quality" newspaper and drawing the blueprint by which Brumback and I would have to work for the next thirteen years. Universally feared and disdained by his peers, Neuharth would become the most controversial influence on today's newspapers.

Tribune publisher Stan Cook, a man much more typical of American business chief executives than Neuharth, always smirked at the mention of his name. Neuharth's antithesis in both style and substance, Cook set the tone for the other Tribune executives, including Brumback, who had seen Neuharth brazenly start from scratch a successful daily newspaper, *Today*, right in Martin Andersen's backyard. Their reaction — smiling and shaking their heads in either wonderment or dismay — was typical of the entire industry.

Once in the early 1980s at an editors' luncheon in Washington where President Reagan was to make an address, Neuharth arrived early, alone, and seated himself conspicuously at a center table at the front of the huge room. As the bearers of the great names of journalism, including the Chandlers, Sulzbergers and Binghams, arrived and headed for front-row seats, Neuharth waved and beckoned and offered repeatedly both his companionship and his prime table. Once he rose and walked halfway across the room to greet Katharine Graham of *The Washington Post*. But, one by one, those he sought out declined to join him. Some waved and smiled and stretched handshakes across tables, and some altered their courses so as to avoid him altogether. All, it seemed, had made prior seating commitments.

Finally, with virtually everyone else seated, Al was left standing alone beside an empty table. But even then he wore the look of a man who had been turning away supplicants, saving the table for more important but tardy companions, maybe the president himself. Finally, an old friend from Florida who had been watching the drama and listening to the exchanges deliberately moved to join him, bringing along a late-arriving group of reporters who had come to cover the president. Otherwise Al Neuharth, head of the nation's largest newspaper chain, in plaid coat, open-collared black shirt and gold chains, would have lunched alone at a white-covered table for 10 in the middle of a room of 1,600 people being addressed by Ronald Reagan.

A tough kid from tough country in South Dakota, Neuharth began by learning everything the Knight newspaper chain had to teach. But he found himself in line behind the titan of journalistic ethics, Lee Hills, who had become Jack Knight's alter ego, and rival Alvah Chapman, who had learned his newspapering at the knee of the respected Nelson Poynter of the *St. Petersburg Times*. Smart enough to know that, once set, the pecking order is hard to change, Neuharth left for a less obstructed pathway. He joined the thin management ranks of a small-town newspaper group headquartered in Rochester, New York, built by and named for its founder, Frank Gannett, a onetime candidate for the Republican presidential nomination. Soon, with all the swiftness and subtlety of a palace coup, he took management control by outthinking, outworking and outmaneuvering Gannett's chairman, an unsuspecting and beloved small-town publisher named Paul Miller. Then Neuharth began a revolution that, despite his retirement as Gannett chairman in 1989, is still under way. All his accomplishments, including the bold launching of the country's most widely circulated paper, *USA Today*, could never attain stature within the traditional press establishment, whose importance he helped diminish. Among the Walter Cronkites and the Ben Bradlees, Neuharth's name still draws the same sneers his appearance evoked when he walked into Amon Evans's city room.

But this disdain is both naive and hollow. For Neuharth long ago became the king and journalists his minions. Their culture might never be his, but his would surely become theirs. In his book *Confessions of an S.O.B.*, Neuharth adroitly drew the line between the old press world and the new one he hoped to create in the most illuminating terms. It was the line between Paul Miller and himself and their views of how to deal with the stock analysts they first encountered.

The affable, folksy Miller was still nominally chairman of the company, but Neuharth, second in command, had him pegged for what he was — a useless icon from another era. Not only would Miller never gain admittance for Gannett to the inner circle of press titans, but he was equally out of place on Wall Street. True to the style of his contemporaries, Miller had trouble focusing on the kind of business specifics the brokers wanted, Neuharth remembered. Instead, Miller tended to regale them with his personal travelogue for the week, which included a trip to Ohio to pick up his mother-in-law and a trip to Oklahoma to play golf with his newspaper buddies. "From that point on, we reduced Miller's role to handshaking," Neuharth confessed. Later, he would leave Miller out of the meetings with analysts entirely.

The results of Neuharth's candid and powerful sales

pitch still filled him with euphoria when he recalled it twenty years later. "Soon Wall Street media analysts and publications began to hype our Gannett stock," he boasted in *S.O.B.* One example he included was this tout by Wall Street analyst John Kornreich: "Gannett's basic media business is awesome. It is virtually an unregulated monopoly." Another publication, *The Wall Street Transcript*, offered a testament strikingly prophetic of the kind of management that would ultimately rule virtually all the nation's press institutions: "Gannett's management lives, breathes and sleeps profits and would trade profits over Pulitzer Prizes any day."

Gannett soon began hosting dinners for analysts, a practice later copied by many of the large media companies. Today, most of the media company chairmen, CEOs and financial officers make annual treks to Wall Street to pump their companies. In the beginning some even dragged along editors and star reporters, until they discovered how little interest they attracted.

Neuharth said there were only two reasons for newspaper company managers to go to Wall Street for financing: to make themselves wealthy or to amass power through bigness. Personal wealth, he wrote, was clearly the motive of many who followed him in the issuance of public stock, but his own motive was to gain for Gannett and himself financial resources to be used in quest of the professional power and prestige he had seen come to Jack Knight, the Grahams and the Sulzbergers. It was peer respect, far more than money, that Neuharth lived for, a prize that could never come to the head of a little group of small-town dailies whose common stock Frank Gannett had willed to a foundation bearing his name. And, in time, the sheer power of the company's size would influence the contest juries and the infrastructure of the industry to the point where he could no longer be ignored.

What Al Neuharth and the Wall Street culture brought most consistently and permanently to the management of the press was an overwhelming compulsion for high earnings. They became a requirement, a peer pressure, a never-quenched thirst for cash with which to acquire properties, service new debt and reward stockholders. For some they became as well the building blocks of executive careers and the kind of wealth that once went only to our most courageous and successful proprietor-entrepreneurs.

Charlie Brumback admired entrepreneurs, but he was not one. Like most of his counterparts in other media companies and at Tribune, he focused his ideas on cutting costs, not generating revenues. Similarly, his approach was that of a manager, not a leader. The first thing he did after being named president of the Orlando newspaper in 1976 was to enroll himself in the American Management Association's school for chief executive officers. Among the lessons he learned was that when confronted with a task about which you have not a clue, assign it to a trusted expert. Upon my arrival in Orlando later that year, Brumback made it clear that he considered me the expert on editorial matters, and I made with him what in retrospect turned out to be a Faustian bargain: let me decide what goes in the newspaper, what its editorial opinions will be, what time it goes to press and how it presents itself in the community, and I promise to run the tightest ship in the business. It was a deal designed to deliver both prizes and profits.

The papers we took over together — *The Sentinel* and, later, the *Tribune* itself — were both bloated with excess personnel, rife with waste and technologically retarded. Promising Brumback big profits in Orlando was a no-brainer. Later in Chicago, where we made the same deal, it was harder. But we both got lucky — I in getting my arms around the octopus newspaper and Brumback in his fight with the production unions. For thirteen years, our papers won journalistic and financial acclaim, including the approval of readers and stock analysts alike. The *Tribune* was consistently listed by our peers as one of the top ten newspapers in the country, an opinion buttressed by seven Pulitzer Prizes during my eight and a half years as editor.

My goal was to put out a better newspaper each day than the day before, one with more and better information reported by more and better journalists for more — and better — readers. Brumback's goal was to make more profit than last year, not just a little more but the most possible. When these goals collided, our respective rank within the company decided the outcome. His always took precedent over mine — no matter what.

The only battle I ever won with Brumback, the first, was a gift. My initial observation when I got to *The Sentinel* was that it was like the *Tribune* in one important respect: its face in the community was that of its lawyer, William Mateer. In addition to representing the newspaper, Mateer represented the county government, an obvious and troublesome conflict of interest. How could he be a party to the county commission's secrets and at the same time represent the reporters who were supposed to ferret them out? To make matters worse, his government client had complained so heatedly about the reporter assigned to the county beat, a young woman named Jane Healy, that she was about to be reassigned. I insisted that Healy stay on the beat, and she later won a Pulitzer Prize and became the newspaper's number two editorial executive. Brumback backed me on Healy, but he refused to fire Mateer, who had played a key role in getting rid of Brumback's predecessor. Charlie knew where the real corporate power resided.

The dispute got us both summoned to Chicago, not to Tribune Tower but to the office of the real boss, corporate counsel Don Reuben. There, with the lawyer's hourglass charge-a-meter running, Reuben and I had a full-scale debate over the legal and ethical definition of conflict of interest. It was a rout. Reuben, whose client list had always included Chicago's biggest newsmakers, ruled that Mateer had no conflict of interest. Case closed. I resigned on the plane ride home.

The next day, as I was about to clean out my new office, Brumback called to say that Mateer had agreed to quit representing the county. I stayed.

During the next four years Brumback and I increased the operating margins of the Orlando *Sentinel* from the mid teens — then average for the industry — to the low twenties. That was then among the industry's best. Soon *The Sentinel* was contributing nearly as much money to the corporate bottom line as the *Tribune*, which was three and half times its size. Furthermore, the newspaper's journalistic reputation had done an about-face in less than three years. One national newsweekly called us the most improved newspaper in the country, "most certainly in the top 15." Attracting the most interest was the newspaper's pioneering of zoned local news and advertising, which targeted four suburban counties around Orlando. Our tabloid "Little Sentinels" were among the first and most successful in the country. Then again, being successful with a monopoly newspaper in the mistake-proof, union-free environment of Orlando, Florida, did not require genius.

From my first day as editor in Orlando, I assumed the responsibility for marketing the newspaper, without resistance or fanfare, and for two reasons. First, Brumback didn't want to do it. Second, he had brought in another refugee from the internal wars of the *Tribune*, a marketing professional named Robert Holzkamp, to head up *The Sentinel*'s advertising sales. Holzkamp had one goal in life — to be such a success that he could return to the *Tribune* as advertising director. I made a deal with him, too, that we would work together to plan and execute every new product or marketing idea either of us could come up with. Unless we were together on a project, it was never launched. But if we were together, no one even tried to stop it. Some of them worked, some of them didn't. We quickly abandoned our bad decisions and buried them. The good ones we exploited. The revenue rolled in.

Holzkamp was a typical advertising executive in that he thought the newspaper ought never to offend any advertiser. He courted them judiciously and delivered their interests, needs and complaints to my office regularly. The serious problems, such as boycotts by car dealers or real estate brokers, we smoothed over together. Soon, the advertisers were as comfortable in my office as they were in his. Whoever caught them first would telephone the other. My deal with Brumback called for us to make money, and so long as Holzkamp and Brumback didn't try to influence the content of the news, I gladly made myself an advertising salesman. I spoke to their breakfast meetings, hosted their advertisers at lunch and, yes, even made sales calls. I never promised advertisers anything but a newspaper so compelling that their customers would have to read it every day. So what? The *Tribune*'s newspaper in Orlando, while never breaching its ethics, turned into one of the industry's most profitable businesses — and Brumback and I became the rising stars in the nation's fourth largest media company.

When we set our budget in Orlando, we worked from the assumption that we would have to surpass the previous year's profit by at least 15 percent, and by 20 or 25 percent if possible. This meant that no editorial improvement could be paid for without new advertising revenue above and beyond that needed to make the profit goals. The editorial departments thus became totally dependent on Holzkamp's willingness or ability to sell advertising. In short order, I resorted to the tactic of lumping a financially lucrative advertising project with a costly editorial one, letting the profits of one underwrite the other. If Holzkamp needed a special advertising promotion section extolling the virtues of Florida tourism, I produced it — as long as some of the revenue got siphoned off to pay for a new reporter or a larger news hole.

As long as I had what amounted to the publisher's power on editorial matters, this coziness did not seem to matter. I involved other senior editorial executives in the process. This kind of committee decision making, I assured them, was the only way to go. The papers got fatter and fatter, in both advertising and news. Gradually the operating committee got fatter and more powerful as well, and it began to exert subtle influence over the direction of the newspaper's content. Though I retained direct control over day-to-day news judgments, the marketing strategy often determined how editorial resources were allocated — not only how the newspaper was edited, but for whom it was edited.

This experience started me down a primrose path. I ended up with the same arrangement in Chicago, with an executive committee of vice presidents from circulation, advertising, editorial and production — myself the highest ranking — deciding how the *Tribune* filled its news and advertising columns every day. Advertisers were never able to influence news judgments, story tone or assignments, but the concept of marketing-driven editorial content — in the form of regular sections containing complementary news and advertising information — became a way of life.

From his perch in Cocoa Beach, Al Neuharth was also watching our progress closely. He telephoned one day and invited me to his house for dinner. He told me he had never seen a newspaper turn around as quickly as *The Sentinel* had. I must have hired a lot of new people, he said, and spent a lot of Tribune Company's money. He seemed startled to learn that there had been no new editorial hires, and no meaningful increase in budget. "They ought to let you run the *Tribune*, then," he said.

Later that year, in the fall of 1980, someone from Orlando was picked to run the *Tribune* — but it wasn't me. It was Brumback, whose record at *The Sentinel* so impressed the *Tribune*'s top executives that he was named president and chief executive officer of the flagship paper. Three months into 1981, with *The Sentinel* outearning the *Tribune*, Brumback showed up one Saturday carrying his Chicago staff's marketing plan. With a sheepish grin, he handed it to me to read.

"It's terrible," I said.

"I know," he replied. "The place is a mess. Why don't you come up and help me fix it?"

A few weeks later I was summoned to Chicago and offered the job of editor and executive vice president, which I did not want. What I wanted was to add Brumback's duties to mine in Orlando. Brumback had told me that I had been next in line on the "succession chart" — another feature of the new professional management system. The previous year he had even delegated to me the planning and budgeting process. Without prodding from Brumback, Holzkamp and I had promised a record year for 1981, with operating margins in the low twenties. But when Stan Cook came down to announce officially that the publisher's job was going to the *Tribune*'s general manager, a smiling, friendly fellow named Harold Lifvendahl, I asked him why I had not been given a shot at it. Cook looked me right in the eye and said, "You know, I think I left my hat either in Chicago or on the plane. I need to call and see if anyone found it." He walked off.

Later Brumback told me that Lifvendahl had been one of Reuben's golden parachute designates. "He's got a lifetime contract. They had to put him somewhere."

That I understood. But I was still fishing for some employer recognition of the journalistic rejuvenation of *The Sentinel*. Nobody at Tribune had ever said a kind word about *The Sentinel*, though other people were calling it the best newspaper in the state. (Actually, the *St. Petersburg Times* was better.)

Cook used to come in twice a year, accompanied by a squad of junior accountants — none of whom could hold Brumback's pencil. They would smile, kick the tires, pat a back or two and then say the financial goals we had set were inadequate. Never had they exhibited any knowledge of the quality of the newspaper. But they had given me some stock options, which Brumback assured me would be valuable someday and should be considered evidence of corporate approval. Still, at the time I wanted to hear that I had done a good job, that I was a great newspaper editor — at least from him. No dice.

So, I bargained on Chicago. Yet I wondered why they would want me there, where both the newspaper and the town were full of good editors. Brumback's reply — the closest he ever came to a compliment — was "You won't believe how much deadwood there is, how many people the *Tribune* has. There is fat everywhere. After what you have done at *The Sentinel*, I think you are the best person in the country to come in there and clean it out."

That was a disappointment. Up to this point, I had earned my pay, my recognition and my promotions on journalistic achievement — reporting, writing, outworking other reporters and other newspapers in the conduct of journalism. Now I was being offered one of the top jobs in my profession — editor of the famous *Chicago Tribune* — for no other reason than my ability to produce increasingly respectable newspapers on the cheap, more profitable each year than the last, without requiring additional resources. My first year in Orlando, *The Sentinel*'s editorial budget amounted to nearly 15 percent of the company's revenue. That figure dropped one percent each of the next four years.

"What you're saying," I told Brumback that day, "is that you want me in Chicago to get rid of the steam buckets."

His blank look said he had not been in Tribune Company long enough to hear the story. Once during the Colonel's reign, a worker failed to trim the trees properly at Catigny, McCormick's Wheaton estate. As punishment, he was assigned to Tribune Tower carrying steam in a bucket from the basement boiler room to the twenty-fourth floor. Arriving each time with his bucket empty, he was sent back to refill it — again and again. The remodeling of both the Orlando *Sentinel* and the *Chicago Tribune* into modern, high-profit newspapers required no more important skill than spotting and eliminating the "steam buckets," then transferring their salaries to product improvement — mainly newsprint — or to the bottom line.

At the time Brumback and I were plucked out of Orlando to run Tribune Company's most important business, the corporate view from the Tower was that our mission was urgent. Dying to go public, Cook was being told by Madigan, the company's chief financial officer, and others that the *Tribune*'s flagship business needed to be at least an "average" earner among newspapers, which was then 15 percent pretax on total revenues. It was doing only slightly more than half that in 1981. Meanwhile, the response of the newspaper's management to Ruth Clark's doomsday warnings had been to fall in love with the newest marketing tool of television and professional management — the reader research survey. *Tribune* researchers — who spent as much time in the office of my predecessor, Max McCrohon, as his subeditors did — had all Chicagoland divided laterally into five strata, the top being "Quintile One" with the highest demographic profile and "Quintile Five" being the lowest. Since Quintiles Four and Five don't read or have money to spend in response to advertisers, they were pretty much disregarded as helpful *Tribune* targets. The Colonel's paper always had been the paper of the blue bloods on the North Shore and the upscale suburbanites of the Northwest Corridor. The complication was that the *Tribune* advertising department had deferred to the *Sun-Times'* argument that city circulation numbers were more important in the battle for retail advertising. So while the *Tribune* was designing tailored feature news sections for suburban Ones and Twos, its front page was dominated by a tabloid kind of city news coverage designed to battle the *Sun-Times* for street sales.

Dependence on research came easily and quickly to newspapers, especially those in trouble. Not only do these surveys tell editors what readers say they want, but they also provide ammunition to support budget increases for more staff and more newsprint. When I got to the *Tribune* in July 1981, the editorial budget had been going up as fast as the national debt would under Reagan and Bush. Surveys are quite helpful in telling editors about the lifestyles of their readers and where to find them. But it helps to remember that newspaper readers always start out by saying the paper is too fat and end up by saying that they want more of everything; and nonreaders always say that the newspapers they are not reading are dull, are boring and contain nothing relevant to their lives. A readership survey of the *Chicago Tribune* in Iraq would produce the same results we always got in Du Page County. That's because the demographic profiles of Quintiles One and Two would be similar.

The other notable characteristic of Tribune management at the time — panic — had been a staple all through the post-McCormick era. When combined with research, panic becomes a blueprint for disaster, which is what Brumback and I had been brought in to avert. At the time, disaster was believed imminent. And it had come to light on a new frontier — for the press and for the *Tribune* — a weekly company "planning group" assembly of advertising, circulation, editorial, marketing and production executives. In 1981, this group, a pioneer in corporate-style committee management of newspaper content, had heard that the most recent reader survey showed that for the very first time in its battle with the *Sun-Times*, the *Tribune* was losing ground in Quintile Two. Suddenly, the *Sun-Times* was gaining and the *Tribune* declining in suburban areas that had been heavily *Tribune* for twenty years.

That survey result had gotten Brumback's attention as well. First of all, it was presented to him in a column of numbers, which he understood. And in his mind he combined it with another set of numbers he found equally disturbing — McCrohon's soaring editorial budget. McCrohon had been unable to show Brumback any plan for improving the *Tribune* without corresponding increases in staff and newsprint. Because Brumback knew someone who could do so — me — the combination cost McCrohon his job. After only two years as editor of the *Tribune*, McCrohon was ousted for no reason other than that he was caught between a new corporate management in need of higher profits and a new boss who knew very little about research and newspaper readers.

Not long after I assumed McCrohon's seat at the planning group table, it became apparent to me that my predecessor had been fired for nothing. The survey showing the *Sun-Times* gaining in the second most important demographic group had been meaningless. If the *Sun-Times* was indeed gaining on *Tribune* ground in the suburbs, I couldn't understand why there had been no impact on the overall circulation picture. The *Tribune*, still well ahead, should have been showing circulation losses in the suburbs, where *Sun-Times* penetration numbers were going up. The answer lay in the route-by-route circulation history: Chicago area newspaper readers at the time were simply upwardly and westwardly mobile. Wherever there was a circulation gain by the *Sun-Times* in a suburb, there was a corresponding *Tribune* gain in an adjacent suburb farther out. The *Sun-Times* penetration in Quintile Two had increased only because *Sun-Times* readers in Quintile Three city neighborhoods were moving westward and taking their newspaper habit with them. As a group these *Sun-Times* readers had attained a higher economic profile. The corresponding movement among *Tribune* readers was being reflected in higher incomes among Quintile Ones who were even farther west and were adding circulation numbers in areas where the *Sun-Times* had no home delivery distribution. The *Sun-Times'* "invasion of the suburbs" died that day on the planning group table, too late to save McCrohon's job.

But in properly analyzing the reader profile data for the two Chicago newspapers in the early 1980s, an interesting phenomenon popped up. The reader profiles of the two newspapers shifted dramatically on Sundays, when the *Tribune* nearly doubled the *Sun-Times* in circulation. On Sunday, nearly a half million people bought the *Tribune* who didn't read it daily. These included many daily *Sun-Times* readers, who either switched or bought both papers. The *Sun-Times*, in turn, sold fewer papers on Sunday than it did Thursday (its best day during the week), primarily to lower-income, inner-city readers, many of whom didn't buy it during the week. Thus, the demographic profile of the average reader of each newspaper was lowered on Sundays, but the disparity between the attractiveness of the *Sun-Times'* reader and that of the *Tribune*'s Sunday customer actually increased.

This Sunday *Tribune* advantage, I discovered, had been ignored for years. Because its Sunday circulation lead was so great and the *Tribune*'s ancient Tower printing plant was already producing at capacity, Tribune management had concentrated its marketing resources on the struggle for supremacy in daily street sales, where the tabloid *Sun-Times* had the advantage of mass-transit single-copy sales, in which many copies are discarded and read a second and third time. This aided the *Sun-Times*' readership figures immensely in the battle for retail advertising.

Considered in light of the increased pressure from corporate management for cost savings and profit, a change of strategy was in order. Winning the battle for Quintile Three inner-city readers should not be nearly as important to advertisers as the incredible advantage in reader quality the *Tribune* had on Sunday. When the *Tribune* increased Sunday printing capacity by opening a new $400 million offset-printing plant two years after Brumback and I arrived, we changed the marketing strategy, shifting news space, advertising and marketing support into the one day when we had the greatest natural advantage. The *Sun-Times* responded competitively, as it always did, shifting its own resources away from its best circulation days and its best audience to its worst.

This was the beginning of the end of the battle for supremacy in the Chicago market. Within a year, with the *Tribune* dramatically widening its lead in advertising share, the Field family gave up and sold its newspaper to Rupert Murdoch. The paper then lost its publisher, James Hoge, and its two best journalists, columnist Mike Royko and editorial page editor Lois Wille, both of whom joined the *Tribune*. The rest is history.

It was the last of the great newspaper circulation wars

in one of the greatest battlefields of them all. Colonel McCormick had won the previous one against Hearst by including more news and printing more newspapers than his opponent, by using every gimmick possible to sell or give them away and by having the local mob muscle necessary to push the other guy's circulating trucks into the Chicago River. Brumback and I won ours by not fighting a circulation war at all. Instead, it was an advertising-driven contest in quest of the highest-quality readers. We didn't hire more reporters, or include more news or print any more newspapers. We just shifted available resources to a day when circulation and advertising rates were the highest to generate more revenue. And the higher demographic profile of our readers combined with better reproduction of the advertisers' images by high-quality offset printing, led to a better and more desirable response to advertising — tipping the advertising balance to our side of Michigan Avenue once and for all.

This strategy was not something forced on me. It was in fact my idea, the very best way I could see to live within the framework of my deal with Brumback. If I could defeat Jim Hoge and the *Sun-Times*, which the editors and publishers before me had been unable to do, then I would make the profits necessary to keep my end of the bargain and make Brumback a success. In turn, Brumback would keep his word, which was to let me decide what one of the most important newspapers in the country said in its news and opinion columns. I may have been preoccupied with marketing strategy more often than I might have liked, but, as in Orlando, the deal worked to both our advantage.

4

The Dirty Little Secret

THE TWENTY-FOUR-STORY GOTHIC MONOLITH Colonel McCormick constructed to house his beloved *Tribune* on Michigan Avenue was built from the winning plans in a worldwide architecture competition in 1925. The most modern and most unusual newspaper plant of the era, it had many extraordinary features, including "cornerstones" from the world's most famous shrines and structures, many of them gathered by *Tribune* reporters dispatched to the sites solely for that purpose. Until about twenty years ago, it also featured one of the world's most unusual elevator arrangements. In the Tower itself and an adjoining annex, there was a virtual caste system of elevators: one set, accessible only with a special security pass, that sped directly to the Colonel's old office on the top floor; a second set serving all the floors below except one — the fourth floor; and a third set exclusively for the fourth floor, where the editorial department is located.

It's the "fourth floor only" elevators that were extraordinary because they represented the newspaper's devotion to a phenomenon peculiar to the American press — an internal separation between business and editorial functions known in the industry as "the division between church and state."

When I joined the *Tribune* as a reporter, the Colonel's rule that business side employees, especially those from advertising, stay off the fourth floor was still very much in force. Empty elevators skipping by the fourth floor while lines formed in the lobby waiting for a "fourth floor only" car attested to the tradition's formidable nature. By the time I left the *Tribune* seventeen years later, after nearly a decade as its editor, all the annex elevators stopped on every floor. Business side employees came and went at will. The hallowed separation between church and state was hardly more than a pretense. For this, no one was more responsible than I. And for the ease with which I let it happen, I can only offer the lamest of excuses, "I really didn't know at the time what I was doing."

Shortly before his death in 1989, C. K. McClatchy, scion of the California newspaper family that owned the respected *Sacramento Bee*, went against his "better judgment" and issued some public stock in his company, while retaining family control in the fashion of *The New York Times* and *The Washington Post*. But at the time he told me he was afraid that, like other newspaper publishers, he was letting the "camel's nose under my tent." I told him that many editors of my generation were beginning to feel the same way concerning our willingness to accom-

modate the wishes of advertising and marketing departments. "No, you let in the hump," he said. "The nose
got in a long time ago."

One thing about McClatchy, he was right a lot. We
had allowed in the hump. The camel's nose had gotten
into our tent when newspapers decided that in order to
compete with television they had to sell the quality of
their audience, just as television was doing.

Leo Bogart, retired executive vice president of the
Newspaper Advertising Bureau, a role in which he exerted
enormous influence on newspaper advertising policies,
remembers the early sightings of the camel because at the
time he was helping to lead it. In 1959 he was working
for Revlon, the cosmetics firm which was then riding high
from having sponsored *The $64,000 Question*, one of the
most popular shows on television, as that miracle infant
medium neared puberty. The scandal that the show was
rigged, with the winners picked in advance and given the
right answers by the sponsors, had just broken, and Revlon was concerned about how upcoming congressional
hearings on the matter would affect its business. And
rightly so; the hearings and investigations years later
would reveal that in rigging *The $64,000 Question* and
another Revlon-sponsored game show, *The $64,000 Chal-
lenge*, the producers were following the orders of Revlon
to make the shows more exciting in an effort to attract a
specific kind of viewer.

As Revlon's new marketing director, Bogart was asked
to research the matter. Working with a retired university
professor, he organized a survey using in-person inter-
views of a cross section of the public each night after the

televised hearings to gauge their impact on Revlon. (The survey disclosed no negative feelings.) What Bogart didn't realize at the time was that he was pioneering the technique of profiling for an advertiser the audience watching a precise moment of television. A decade later, the use of audience measurement as a sales technique had started to undercut the traditional economic underpinning of the nation's newspapers, which was the sale of advertising at rates based on total circulation. This development coincided with the passing of newspaper ownership into the hands of corporate managers less concerned with press tradition than with business profitability. The decline of the free press had begun.

Through much of their history, newspapers had been edited for and marketed to specific classes or socioeconomic groups. There were ethnic papers, labor papers, papers for the masses like Patterson's *Daily News* and papers like McCormick's *Chicago Tribune* for the ruling classes. By cutting into advertising revenue and changing people's information-consuming habits, television not only reduced the number of newspapers but forced the survivors initially to try to appeal across a wide spectrum of readers. By the late 1960s and '70s, newspapers were in enough financial trouble that they started to survey their own markets, using the tools of television marketing. They began to discover what distinguished readers from nonreaders and their readers from those of their competitors. And, for the first time, newspaper executives, following in the footsteps of their television and radio counterparts, began to construct audience profiles and share them with advertisers.

Nobody thought much about this at the time because the traditional walls separating the church and state of the press — editorial from advertising — were still firmly in place. But it was a critical development. Except for a few financial ads on business pages around the country, newspaper advertising had been placed without much consideration to surrounding editorial content or what segment of the population was reading the page. Readers were still believed to read all of the newspaper and content remained the private preserve of editors, or entrepreneur publisher-owners who thought and acted like editors. It was these executives — virtually all male, all white and all middle-aged — whose judgment constituted the prism of journalism through which the world saw itself. "News" might be more local than national, more crime than business, more sports than feature, more interesting to a white man than to a black woman. But it was a synthesized version of what had happened in the twelve hours preceding publication as seen from a particular perspective — regardless of who was reading the newspaper.

By the early 1970s, research experts like Ruth Clark were telling uncertain managers of then not-so-profitable urban newspapers like the *Chicago Tribune* and *The New York Times* that perhaps their way of doing things had become obsolete. *The Times,* as expected, resisted. In those days nothing so inconsequential as the need for more advertising revenue could possibly affect a news synthesis and distillation process so ingrained and smug that its editors boasted, "See, it goes in lively, but it comes out dull." At *The Times*, news had always been and would always be the serious business of serious men. But most everywhere else, especially in the profit-conscious corporations whose stock was publicly traded, the policy of business hands off the editorial department began to change.

At the *Tribune*, when Max McCrohon was named managing editor, soon-to-be publisher Stan Cook sent in a business and personnel manager with him — to help keep McCrohon organized and to serve as a communication link to the reticent Clayton Kirkpatrick. McCrohon's journalistic credentials, gentle nature and serendipitous style eased his entry into a newsroom that remained a bastion of McCormick-style journalism. But the personnel man, William Van Vlissingen, who represented the first appearance of the newspaper's business management on that side of the wall, eventually became such an anathema that news he had just wrecked his car on a snowy bridge elicited a cheer from the staff party he had left only minutes earlier. At the *Tribune*, Van Vlissingen was the nose of the camel, and the new generation of *Tribune* hires and the executives it spawned would not hold the line against the business intrusion with the rigidity and resolve of the men at *The Times*.

Neither would those elsewhere in industry. Eventually this business imperative to match up the editor's content with the advertiser's desired audience profile would be the battering ram that broke through the most revered and important press tradition — the wall between the editorial, which constituted the soul of the press, and the revenue-generating side that was always its heart. Between the time I went to Orlando as editor in December 1976, and the day I left the *Tribune* in December 1989, this separation — although still given lip service throughout the industry — had all but disappeared. Today, with few exceptions, the final responsibility for newspaper content rests with the business executive in charge of the company, not the editor. Editors such as myself who are willing to bridge the gap between editorial and business are now the standard in the nation's newsrooms. Those reluctant to do so don't last long. Although we justified the shift as necessary for our papers' survival, we were in effect surrendering the traditional editorial integrity of the press to the marketing interests of corporate owners. For the first time, American journalism has become truly a "news business" built on a successful three-way relationship between news content, advertising sales and target audience.

In their passionate pursuit of control over labor and other costs, the new managers of the press such as Brumback were only out to deliver what was demanded of them. All CEOs of publicly traded corporations eventually learn what Neuharth had when he first took Gannett's stock to the public market: investors are only interested in good news. And it must be delivered year after year.

In my last year in Orlando, *The Sentinel* outearned the giant *Tribune*. Subsequently, its cash-flow margins would surpass 30 percent and join the best Gannett or anybody else could produce. Over the next eight years, the *Tribune* profit margin tripled — from the high single digits to the midtwenties. During my last two years as editor — in 1988 and 1989 — the *Tribune* was among the best earners in the industry. It did not even feel the bite of the Bush recession until January 1992.

But long before that, my end of the bargain had become too heavy to hold up. Each year the operating departments were called on to do more with less, while the demands for increasing profits never ceased. I had become a smoke-and-mirrors magician, juggling from the right hand to the left, robbing Peter to pay Paul and lying to myself and my staff about how successful we were. Enough would never be enough. The kind of reinvestment needed to stop the decline in market penetration and advertising share would not be made. No bold new economic model would be adopted to provide the newsprint and staff to cover news. A marketing plan written in 1982 to take advantage of the *Tribune*'s massive new printing plant to improve substantially the quality of coverage of its key reader base — the Chicago suburbs — remained unimplemented when I resigned at the end of 1989.

Stalled by poor production planning when the plant opened in 1983, the plan never got off the ground. Then, a strike by three unions in 1985 resulted in a drastic reduction of production employees and a hiring freeze at the reduced level. This artificially inflated the newspaper's profits in 1986 and 1987 to levels which automatically became the base that had to be improved upon in succeeding years. From that point on, there would never be enough projected revenue for the editorial and advertising expansion called for in the plan.

Each year I would build into the initial budget proposal the hiring of enough entry-level reporters and advertising salespeople to expand local news coverage and advertiser service — about $1.5 million in payroll costs. Each year, they would fall by the wayside because corresponding increases in production costs — paper, ink and new press runs — meant that another $1 to $2 million was never available. In essence, the newspaper management was deciding that this proposed investment in people was not worth what it would return in increased circulation, improved household penetration and a higher level of involvement by small advertisers in the *Tribune*'s second most important market segment — the high-income residents of the city's northwest suburbs. True, the newspaper was at the time paying off its plant and investing $50 million to buy back a large share of its circulation system from independent distributors. But it was also setting profit records during those years, dumping more than a half billion dollars to the corporate bottom line during the 1980s.

My experience was hardly unique. During that decade, in newspapers all across the country, there were editors and publishers feeling the same pinch. Each day they tried to serve up both good journalism and whatever cash flow was being demanded by the corporate management. Basic and much-needed improvement that would have greatly enhanced the quality of journalism provided for readers was talked about, planned for and then either watered down or postponed altogether while newspapers and their corporate owners became the earnings stars of Wall Street investors. This decade of corporate development changed the nature of the *Tribune* and other newspapers across the country as dramatically as if they had been converted to fried chicken franchises. The pressure to profit became a straitjacket for the free press. And for the most part the people lacing it up did not understand or give much thought to what they were doing.

Newspaper publishers and editors had always tried to sell newspapers, Brumback would say, adding that "this has never been a philanthropic endeavor." Of course he was right. But in the past when market and reader pressures forced newspapers to change the style of their mission, as was the case many times, the owners did so always mindful not to alter the basic relationships. Some characteristics of the press were not to be tampered with. For example, newspapers were always deliberately "underpriced" — sold for less than the value of the paper they were printed on. *The New York Times* and many others during the Second World War were published on days when there was no advertising to support the news. The price, the frequency and some aspects of the content, such as the expression of unpopular editorial opinion and public service announcements, were viewed as inviolate essentials of the franchise. Newspapers that were bland, cowardly, incomplete or uninterested in the public's business were considered the weak sisters of the marketplace.

The proprietors knew from press history that it was prudent business to put long-term reader trust ahead of advertiser relationships and long-term advertiser relationships ahead of short-term profits. Some years they bit the bullet and made nothing because to do otherwise would have meant gouging their advertisers or short-changing their readers. Historically, papers have been able to expand in their markets, improve their products, pay their debts and still make their owners rich by averaging 10 percent annual profit. A 10 percent cash-flow margin used to be the goal for both *The New York Times* and the *Chicago Tribune*. In monopoly markets, averaging this kind of profit is a no-brainer, especially if the owners confidently ride the margins up to 12 and 13 in good times and down to 7 and 8 in bad.

C. K. McClatchy, a good businessman but an even better journalist-proprietor, once looked at his business manager and ultimate successor, Erwin Potts, and said, "Do we really need to make this much?" McClatchy was a firm believer in the old hierarchy of priorities: the readers first, employees second and owners third. It was what kept both communities and employees convinced that the press was a special business.

Now, there no longer is even the illusion that public service is the first goal of the institution. Despite all the lip service by news executives to the needs and interests of the consumers, the true priorities of the new press ownership were never more clearly stated than by Philip J. Meek, who heads the publishing group of Capital Cities/ABC, which numbers among its press holdings ABC News, *The Kansas City Star* and the *Fort Worth Star-Telegram*. Writing on newspaper profits in the *Washington Journalism Review* in 1990, Meek said, "Management's obligation is to balance profit optimization, franchise strengthening, community service and employee development within the context of whatever external conditions exist. Excessive multiples [the relationship between earnings and purchase prices] . . . require a shorter-term view and more emphasis on profits near term."

The first part of this statement, translated from the turgid prose of Wall Street, is pretty tame stuff: "We're going to provide as high a quality journalism as we can and still make our budget number." The colonels, generals, and kings of journalism all uttered similar pledges at one time or another. But simply working within a realistic budget and returning a reasonable profit is not what Meek was talking about when he referred to "multiples" and "external conditions."

In a memorable speech delivered as part of a journalism lecture series at the University of California, Riverside, in 1988, McClatchy explained in the language of the press what Meek would later say in the language of Wall Street. "There are many [newspaper] chains . . . that face great pressure to bolster the bottom line," McClatchy said. "Cap Cities [and others], for example, are burdened with very large debts. These pressures fight against quality."

McClatchy was using Cap Cities as an example of those who buy pieces of the press already earning respectable profits — as almost all the monopoly newspapers bought by Gannett and others were — and finance them on the expectation that those profits can be doubled and tripled. This shackles the papers as businesses for decades.

Monopoly newspapers in big metropolitan markets — such as those in Kansas City, Fort Worth, San Jose, Orlando and Fort Lauderdale — can easily hold market positions and still return pretax profits in the 20 to 35 percent range. When they are owned by companies with big debt obligations or ambitious acquisition goals, these monopoly newspapers are asked to maintain or improve contributions to corporate earnings without fail. Businesses whose revenue base rests on retail, help wanted and real estate advertising — all cyclical economies — are hard-pressed to produce consistent numbers without sacrificing improved news coverage, staff development and — most important — market penetration.

During the 1980s, the *Chicago Tribune*, *The Orlando Sentinel* and the Fort Lauderdale *Sun-Sentinel* were the workhorse profit makers of Tribune Company. Sometimes the *Tribune* alone contributed 30 to 50 percent of the company's total profits as the broadcast and newsprint holdings faltered. During the last half of the decade, these newspapers were consistently in the 25 to 35 percent range in operating income. Yet year after year plans for significant editorial investment and circulation promotion that would expand their markets and enhance survival were restricted or postponed so the big earnings could fall to the bottom line.

The corporate responsibility of the new managers of the press demands that they weigh the payback from using the newspaper's profits to improve the quality of journalism against the return on investment in an acquisition or another line of business. And because most newspapers are owned by companies diversified in the media, the result is that the highly profitable local newspapers in monopoly markets have been financing the international competition among media conglomerates. Cap Cities/ ABC, Gannett, Times Mirror and Tribune Company, among others, have all been scrambling to position themselves for global competition with the likes of Time Warner, Rupert Murdoch and the media giants of Europe.

A rather typical newspaper purchase of the last two decades occurred in 1986, when the New York venture capital firm of Adler & Shaykin paid $145 million for the struggling *Chicago Sun-Times*, which was still managing a double-digit cash flow despite having a lousy plant and having lost the market leadership position to the *Tribune*. Despite the paper's adequate earnings, no publicly held corporation was interested in acquiring it for the simple reason that the *Tribune*'s dominance meant that the *Sun-Times* would never make the kind of excessive profits Wall Street had come to expect from newspaper-owning corporations.

This meant that if the newspaper was to survive, it had to be picked up by an eccentric owner and run as a charity case the way Murdoch did with the *New York Post* for a decade, or run on the cheap by a bone-picker publisher like William Dean Singleton. A former reporter and throwback to the old journalism-proprietors, Singleton is a rare bird indeed. Because he has to finance his acquisitions with junk bonds and by any other means possible, he has to run a tight ship, too. And he can wring blood from a turnip. Unlike his corporate counterparts, however, Singleton is not in the entertainment business. He hires old-style journalists, who do their best to cover the news with whatever money Singleton can make available. When Singleton has it, he spends it on news coverage. In two cities where there is still real competition, Houston and Denver, his *Post*s are fighting an uphill battle against better-financed corporate giants.

Even Singleton rejected the chance to own the *Sun-Times*, leaving it to be "saved" by a leveraged buyout in which the newspaper's assets were pledged to secure a high-interest loan that would soak up its cash flow. The *Sun-Times'* only real asset is its riverfront building, estimated to be worth between $70 and $100 million at the time. In effect, the buyers simply put up only $7 million equity on a $145 million deal and pledged the future earnings of the newspaper to support the purchase of a piece of real estate they believed would appreciate significantly. This left the *Sun-Times* alive, but without resources to modernize its printing process or significantly improve its competitive position. As the real estate market declined and appreciation did not materialize, the newspaper was left to limp along, with no more committed purpose than to service a real estate debt.

True, Chicago is better off with two daily newspapers than with one. But the real significance of the demise of the *Sun-Times*, is this: with its only competitor gasping on life support, the *Tribune*'s decision to take its record profits to the bottom line year after year is infinitely easier. The number one paper in the market will gradually increase its market share without having to invest. There was no pressure for the *Tribune* to hire more reporters, improve advertising service and use more newsprint. Instead, we just opened up a storefront in a neighborhood, shifted a few reporters and advertising representatives from one place to another and congratulated ourselves.

While the plight of the *Sun-Times* was tied to the interest payments of real estate speculators, its shackling by debt is no different from that of many other dailies whose earnings must be shifted to finance other corporate obligations or speculative adventures by wheeler-dealer CEOs in search of a Wall Street reputation. The press is rife with heavily indebted corporate ownership.

Time magazine, the one newsweekly that has indisputedly earned a spot among the elite of American journalism, is a classic case. Its founder, Henry Luce, was a typical press baron whose main interest was influencing American public opinion on social and political issues, even if it meant publishing only his version of the truth in *Time*. Nonetheless, for over sixty years after its founding in 1923, *Time* was the major profit center of the publishing giant it spawned, regularly returning a pretax profit of between 15 and 20 percent of revenues — often half the total profit of Time Inc. For years *Time* was considered among the richest of news organizations, boasting resources that even the big newspapers envied. No more. The merger of Time Inc. and Warner Communications in 1990, the largest in media history, created a behemoth of a company, but one saddled with $11 billion in debt. Two years after the deal was closed, Time Warner stock had dropped from the $200 per share merger offer price to $99, and its management was struggling with debt, unhappy stockholders and one another. Once an important and influential voice in the conduct of public policy, *Time* magazine, like its sister subsidiaries, has no more compelling purpose today than to carry its share of the corporate parent's debt burden.

Paying corporate debt service or financing international adventures does not sell well as the reason for tight budgets and skimpy newspapers, either within the newspapers or in the communities they serve. So corporate demand for ever-increasing financial performance is often explained in a less than candid fashion. "Declining market penetration, not profit levels, is forcing an analysis of priorities," Cap Cities' Meek maintained in 1990. "What information readers want to cope with — with the increasing demands on their daily lives — must be the constant objective of any newspaper, not what the newsroom professionals think the readers need and the newsroom wants."

Meek's explanation is a perfectly accurate, respectable and expected explication of the competitive strategy of any business that must survive in the marketplace. But it encompasses both outright deception and the kind of ill-conceived, shortsighted management philosophy that has already wrecked much of America's once vaunted manufacturing capability.

A permanent frown seems to have formed on the faces of media company executives over the twenty-year decline in market penetration levels of daily newspapers. But if penetration levels are their real concern, why do today's newspapers not just employ the tactic proven so successful to Japanese manufacturers in quest of market share? Offer higher quality at a lower price. Any newspaper circulation director in the industry knows that except in rare instances newspaper circulation is a direct function of copies distributed, pricing and promotion expenses. Give any of them more copies, a lower price and some money to spend and they will give you the circulation numbers. And if the newspaper is good, the readers can be retained. Presto: improved penetration. That's really how they go about staying even.

But improved quality, better service, and lower pricing all negatively affect a newspaper's bottom line in the short term. Why they are not employed is the dirty little secret of newspapering, an essentially flawed and outmoded economic model that bases advertising rates on total circulation numbers, and that by its very nature, discourages both too much quality and too many readers. Because advertisers want only high-income, well-educated readers, publishers don't really want higher penetration in their market. They want what magazine publishers have always wanted — higher penetration in the top 35 percent of the market. But unlike magazine publishers, newspaper owners can't just admit that and begin basing rates on audience profiles.

Why? There are two good reasons.

One, doing so would mean abandoning the practice of charging advertisers for all circulation, which would destroy the single unifying economic principle of the industry, without anything to replace it; and this would be interpreted as a public confession to what all smart advertisers already suspect — that only a fraction of the newspaper readers they pay to reach even see their newspaper advertisement and an even smaller fraction is demographically inclined to respond to it.

Two, it would mean abandoning the legal basis on which the printed press has always stood before legislatures and courts wrapped in the flag of the First Amendment. It is on this second point that the dirty little secret of newspapering gets really dirty. The newspaper industry claims the right to put vending machines on public streets and in airports, the right to sit in courtrooms, the right to see public records, to question the president, the right to have a front-row seat at the war — all on the basis that it is an institution exercising the people's right to know. Never does it claim the right to such access on the basis that it is in the business of delivering advertising information for profit.

Nowhere does the Constitution define "the people" as the predominantly white upper 35 percent of the population between twenty-five and fifty years of age who make $50,000 a year. Yet newspapers routinely control costs and enhance profits by cutting off circulation that is unprofitable because it lacks value as a quality audience. When the customer is difficult to service, is hard to collect from or does not make enough money, the market penetration of which Meek and his counterparts speak so often and so covetously is deliberately given up.

For example, in the early 1970s, when gasoline prices soared during the oil embargo, newspapers with state and regional circulation arbitrarily pulled the plug on readers they could cut off without having to reduce advertising rates. According to former editor Bill Kovach, the Cox-owned newspapers in Atlanta — the *Journal* and *Constitution* — kissed off 50,000 people in south Georgia in an effort to recover rising fuel costs. One of Charlie Brumback's first cost-saving moves at the *Chicago Tribune* when he took it over in 1980 was to cut off between 25,000 and 40,000 readers outside Chicago whose numbers had never been counted in the rate base for Chicago retailers. These readers had not been counted because it was more profitable for the *Tribune* to strip the ads and save the newsprint than to deliver the ads and charge the retailer for the added circulation.

By reducing circulation efforts among low-income, minority readers, newspapers actually improve the overall demographic profile of their audiences, which they then use to justify raising advertising rates. Thus, with few exceptions, the profitability of newspapers in monopoly markets has come to depend on an economic formula that is ethically bankrupt and embarrassing for a business that has always claimed to rest on a public trust: the highest profitability comes from delivering advertising sold at the highest rates in a paper containing the fewest pages and sold for the highest possible retail price to the fewest high-income customers necessary to justify the highest rate to advertisers. Of course, such a strategy can't possibly produce anything but declining market penetration, for which television and illiteracy are getting the blame.

Businesses truly worried about penetration and market share would not have newspapers' uninterrupted record for consistent price increases in both advertising and circulation. Except for four or five cities where there has been head-on newspaper competition, both advertising and circulation prices have risen consistently for twenty years even as newspapers' share of advertising and their household penetration have declined. In Lexington, Kentucky, for example, where Knight-Ridder has a monopoly and publishes what is perhaps the best newspaper in the state, the *Herald-Leader* costs 50 cents at retail outlets. Until the last few years, you could buy a fat national edition of *The New York Times*, with twice as much news content as the *Herald-Leader* and much higher attendant distribution costs, on a Boston street for the same price.

The explanation lies in the difference between the attractiveness to advertisers of a Kentucky tobacco cutter and a Harvard professor. In Boston, *The New York Times* has to compete for the professor — an attractive consumer — with *The Boston Globe* and other publications. You could get *The Globe* for 35 cents. In Lexington, it's the *Herald-Leader* or nothing. And the *Herald-Leader* is one of those wonderful press monopolies that already has all the good demographic profile customers in its market. Al Neuharth's parting words on his retirement in 1989 were that newspapers were still selling themselves too cheaply. They should be a dollar a copy, he advised, advocating the precise strategy he sold to Wall Street: Price maximizes revenue and holds down printing and distribution costs while culling from the circulation base the unwanted low-income reader.

This approach, when applied to advertising policy, has a similar effect. Small advertisers are driven out of the newspaper to other, cheaper media, such as free weeklies and shoppers. This creates an underclass strata of advertisers and their customers, who are excluded from newspapers and ultimately alienated from them. But this is undeniably the most productive use of newsprint. The cost of paper, printing and circulation makes it more profitable to publish fewer pages of high-rate advertising than more pages of low-rate advertising.

Profit optimization, then, is compelled less by declining penetration than by the corporate owner's many and varied cash needs — not the least of which in many instances is huge debt incurred by companies caught up in the acquisition mania of the 1980s. Newspapers purchased by expanding groups were immediately pressed into service to finance the next deal. Today there are monopoly markets all over the country with circulation histories like that in San Bernardino, California, where Gannett bought *The Sun* in 1969, and Nashville, where it bought *The Tennessean* a decade later. When Gannett bought *The Sun*, it had about 77,000 daily circulation. In the twenty years since, population in the market has increased 63 percent. The newspaper's circulation is still around 77,000 daily, barely even. San Bernardino is next door to Riverside, where *The Press-Enterprise* is still controlled by a local publisher, Howard Hays, even though Dow Jones owns half the stock. During the same twenty-year period, *The Press-Enterprise* circulation nearly doubled, 82,230 to 156,508.

In 1979, the year Gannett took over *The Tennessean* from Amon Evans, the Nashville market had 800,000 people and *The Tennessean*'s circulation was 139,000 daily. Ten years later, the market had grown to more than a million — a 25 percent increase — and *The Tennessean*'s circulation was still 139,000. The reason was simple. *The Tennessean* needed new presses in order to build its circulation. But because it was the dominant newspaper in a joint-operating agreement, the Nashville profits were substantial and, more important, not threatened by competitors. So *The Tennessean* had to wait until 1991 to begin its quest for circulation. The money was needed elsewhere. Once it got the presses, circulation began to climb.

In all fairness, television and other social trends affecting how Americans live have hurt newspaper readership. Many white, high-income readers have moved to the suburbs where the newspapers were not and their places in urban areas have been taken by minorities with higher incidences of illiteracy and nonreading habits. These facts are often cited by media company investment analysts and the corporate media management as reasons for their incessant gloom-and-doom predictions about newspapers.

But there might be an even better explanation. Ben Bagdikian, a former reporter, journalism professor and one of the few people who know enough about the evolution of the news media to legitimately call himself a critic, points out in his book *The Media Monopoly* that there have been only two periods of documented decline in newspaper readership during the twentieth century. The first, between 1930 and 1940, was clearly the result of the Great Depression and the growth of radio. The second — and by far the biggest — came between 1965 and 1980. In 1965, long after radio and television had become entrenched, readership was still 105 newspapers per day for each 100 households. Today, after twenty-five years of the new ownership, it is 64 per 100 households, down 39 percent.

There is no corresponding profit index available because industry profits have been a well-kept secret, kept first by wily old publishers who did not have to tell anyone but the Internal Revenue Service, and now by corporate reports that hide the profits of individual newspapers in group numbers. But the old profit margins were known by industry insiders, and today's margins can be easily extrapolated by experts willing to count advertising lines and interpret rate cards. Using those sources and methods, a comparable earnings index for the industry between 1969 and 1989 shows that under the new ownership, newspaper profits have increased as fast as penetration has declined.

The monopoly papers that groups like Knight-Ridder, Gannett and Thomson began collecting in the 1970s had cash flows in the 7 to 12 percent range, depending on how many family members were feeding at the trough and how good a newspaper the owner felt obligated to provide. Some margins were higher — in the twenties. But assuming average margins were somewhere between 8 and 12 percent in 1969, the profitability of newspapers had about doubled by 1990. The average cash-flow margins of papers owned by the public companies — which are usually higher than those of individual papers still family owned but lower than those of groups of papers owned privately — were 20.5 percent in 1985, 19.5 per cent in 1986, 19.2 percent in 1987, 16.5 percent in 1988, 19.5 percent in 1989 and 16.5 percent in 1990.

One fact the industry has not tried to hide is that profit records are poorer in towns without monopoly papers. During the 1980s, in cities where there was still real newspaper competition — Dallas, Denver, Houston, Las Vegas, Little Rock and San Antonio — usually only one paper was truly profitable, and Gannett-size operating margins were unheard of. But in those cities, the circulation and market penetration track records for the last twenty years were much better than the rest of the industry's. In Dallas, 1990 circulation was up 147,743 daily over 1970. In Houston, it was up 169,000; Denver, 110,055; Las Vegas, 65,091; Little Rock, 57,770; San Antonio, 89,572. In these cities, they still marketed the newspapers the way they always did — in the interest of penetration and market share.

At the end of the decade, both newspapers in Houston changed hands. The *Chronicle*, owned by a family charitable trust, was sold to the Hearst Corporation. *The Post*, owned by the Hobby family, went to Singleton, who had actually outbid Hearst for the *Chronicle* but lost. At the time the papers each sold on the street for 25 cents a copy. Late in 1991, Singleton, in need of profit to show his debt holders, raised the price of *The Post* to 35 cents. When circulation refused to decline, the Hearst-owned *Chronicle* went to 50 cents a copy. *The Post* followed. Since then the two papers have lost 70,000 single-copy buyers between them — but both papers are more profitable.

Absurdly, the economic decline in 1990 sent newspaper industry stock into a deep depression, as if the collapse of the whole business was imminent. Newspapers responded not by improving quality and increasing sales efforts, as they would have if attacked by a new competitor, but by cutting back content and laying off employees. Expansion plans were canceled, editorial bureaus closed and special editions scuttled. By 1992, the economy had claimed as victims several more papers, all in competitive markets. Gone were the *Arkansas Gazette*, the *Dallas Times Herald* and *The Knoxville Journal,* all closed by owners who could not make their debt payments. In addition, the New York *Daily News* slid into bankruptcy and a little closer to extinction.

John Morton, an analyst for the brokerage firm of Lynch, Jones and Ryan in Washington, explained the hubbub. "All that is really happening is that instead of being two or three times more profitable than most businesses, newspapers this year [1990] are reduced to being only one or two times more profitable," he told the industry's magazine, *Presstime.* "For newspapers, a recession means only that earnings may not grow and may decline, but it does not mean earnings disappear. There is nothing shabby about an average operating profit margin of 14.9 percent, even if it is down from 17.7 percent for the same period in 1989. There are lots of industries that do not see 15 percent margins in the midst of their biggest booms in history."

It took two straight years of recession and the near collapse of the retail department-store industry before average newspaper profits fell back into line with what other industries made in their very best years. In 1991, Knight-Ridder, which publishes the highest-quality papers of any group owning more than ten, reported that its newspaper division had operating profits of $259 million on $1.9 billion in revenues, or 13.5 percent. If most newspaper companies did break out profit numbers for individual newspapers, these numbers would show many of them making 35 percent in good years, and 20 percent in years when they have slashed staff and reduced news pages. Moreover, the numbers would show monopoly newspapers gouging advertisers and readers with rate increases to subsidize competition or diversification elsewhere.

To appreciate the certain consequences of excess profit making and failure to reinvest in quality improvement, one has only to look at the great earnings eagles of the past. One by one, railroads, textiles, steel, automobiles and network television failed to reinvest enough of their earnings in long-term product improvement. The combination of shortsightedness and the onslaught of new technology eventually turned them into buggy whip makers.

In *The Reckoning*, David Halberstam's study of how the Detroit auto industry's shameful neglect of research and development brought about its near destruction by the Japanese, the author quoted Ford designer Gene Bordinat's recollections of a conversation he had with Chrysler executive Lynn Townsend. Bordinat had gone directly to Townsend with his concern over the declining level of quality he was witnessing in the entire industry. "Hell, Gene, all the public wants is its splits [stock splits]," Townsend replied. "That's all you have to give them."

Why then do the press managers keep plunging down the same path? The answer is the same you might get from a crack smoker in a Washington, D.C., tenement, or the big spenders in the deficit-ridden Congress. They can't stop. And the core of this addiction is the kind of careerism, quest for personal wealth and peer pressure so common to the Wall Street culture. Exorbitant compensation from fees and bonuses based entirely on profits has been widely blamed for the many headline-making scandals involving insider trading, junk-bond financing and illegal trading in government bonds. American business spends 70 percent of payroll costs on its executives. The American press does the same.

While many of the old press barons became fabulously wealthy in the news business, most did so by reinvesting their profits and building long-term equity in their companies. Many were cautious about displays of personal wealth and paid their top executives modestly. In 1965, when Jack Knight's family was the sole owner of his newspaper empire, the old publisher paid himself a relatively modest salary of $202,000. More important, he paid his editors and reporters on the basis of their journalistic skills.

But the new corporate ownership has brought to the press a system of executive compensation based primarily on profits. The more cash a newspaper or broadcast operation returns, the more those managing it receive in their pay envelopes. In many instances, this compensation is tied directly to company stock, either in the form of lucrative stock options or in "phantom shares," in which the executives receive the benefit of improvements in stock prices resulting from their management. Under this system, executives in place at the time of initial stock offerings, stock splits or mergers can become extremely wealthy. Because they are frequently among the company's biggest individual stockholders, their personal wealth climbs with the stock price, or in salary and bonuses tied to it.

In 1989, Tribune Company paid its top fourteen executives $17 million in salary and bonuses. In the preceding three years, Charlie Brumback alone had earned more than $9 million and the company's top executive, Stan Cook, about $11 million — mostly in stock options. This level of compensation is typical of the industry and extremely important in a world where executives are judged primarily on their ability to produce profits. Once a profit standard is set by an executive, he must exceed it the following year to be judged a success on Wall Street. An executive who does not equal or surpass the earnings record of a predecessor is frequently labeled inferior by stock analysts.

At every meeting of newspaper industry executives I attended in my thirteen years as an editor, charts and graphs were displayed showing the rate of annual decline in readership and advertising market share. Never did I see a chart on newspaper industry profits or executive salaries. No such records are kept. But if they were kept and graphed, the profit and executive pay lines would be the inverse of those for readership and market share.

From 1976 to 1989, my compensation (salary and bonus) rose nearly 400 percent, from $75,000 to $350,000, not counting stock options, which over the same period equaled the total of other compensation. Because executive bonuses are tied to profits, they are ratcheted up along with profits.

As stockholders, executives who effect acquisitions and mergers are among those who benefit most from them. Warner Communications chairman Steven Ross is said to have made $196.6 million on the deal that created the new giant Time Warner Co., with its $11 billion debt. Two years later, in 1991, all the company's subsidiaries were caught in budget crunches that resulted in the reduction of 605 jobs in journalism. *Time* lost 44 people. Assuming each employee cost the company $100,000, this saved Time Warner $4.4 million. The previous year, the company had paid Ross $4 million in salary and bonus, in addition to paying him $74 million on the Time Warner stock swap.

One of the papers that folded in 1991, *The Knoxville Journal*, had been brokered to Gannett a decade earlier by a group of businessmen that included then U.S. Senator Howard Baker and Lamar Alexander, who would go on to become governor of the state and secretary of education in the Bush administration. It was all legal, ethical and above board. But the group collected several million dollars in fees, all of which ultimately had to be recovered from the newspaper's share of a profitable joint operating agreement with Scripps Howard. A decade later, after being discarded by Gannett, the paper died, leaving Knoxville with a single newspaper. The sale of the *Baltimore Sun* papers to Times Mirror in the mid-1980s is a similar case. The sale was brokered by the *Sun*'s publisher, Reg Murphy, who was reported to have received between $13 and $16 million for his efforts. In 1991, after Murphy retired, the new management said that as part of cost reduction requirements it needed to rid the papers of at least 260 employees through buyouts or attrition.

All this adds up to a new system of ownership in which management drains traditional press institutions of the wealth derived from decades of service within a particular community — often for short-term personal gain — and then refuses to sustain them through cash-flow problems five or ten years later. It is not that these businesses could not be returned to profitability but that they might never be profitable enough to satisfy debt loads or stockholder demands. Many of these papers had been in business for one hundred years or more — under all kinds of owners. But with this new system of ownership, the wealth the press accumulates in good years is never there to see it through the bad ones.

In the process, the basic relationships between the institution and its readers and advertisers are radically altered. And as has happened in the rest of American industry, so too has the crucial partnership between employer and employee been severed. To meet financial goals, ownership has had to view employees the same way it does newsprint, as a "cost center" that can be shrunk at will to maintain profit levels. This has resulted in a new era of employee distrust and disaffection, the same kind of fractured owner-worker relationship that is often blamed for the decline and perhaps the ruin of the American automobile industry. The significance of the analogy cannot be overstated. However important the automobile industry was to the economic health of the United States during the twentieth century, the free press has been to the country's social and political welfare for twice as long.

5

Profits over Principle

O N THE DAY I WAS HIRED as editor of the *Chicago Tribune*, Stan Cook announced a far more exciting acquisition — the Chicago Cubs.

"What do you think of that?" he asked me, obviously elated that Tribune Company now owned the city's favorite baseball team.

"You know, it creates some problems for the newspaper," I responded, trying to be gentle.

"Not at all," he said. "It'll be great."

At that very minute, twenty floors below us in the Tower, the staff of the *Tribune* had their noses out of joint in a big way. When they perceive a betrayal by their owners — rightly or wrongly — reporters are quick to frenzy, spinning like an angry dog biting its own tail.

The story of the purchase of the Cubs by the city's largest press owner had been broken first by WBBM radio, and then by the *Chicago Sun-Times*. Both the *Trib-*

une and WGN had been scooped on the news being made by their owners. This same phenomenon occurred at *Time* magazine eight years later when the story of its parent company's merger with Warner Communications was broken by rival *Newsweek*, even though *Time* editors knew what was going on. Such dysfunction, which appears to be a natural by-product whenever a modern institution of the press is put in the position of reporting on itself, is the symptom of a more basic conflict between the culture of the press and that of corporate America, which has engulfed it. Both the Tribune-Cubs and Time-Warner deals illustrate how this conflict weakens the press internally, by alienating the owners from the journalists, and externally, by changing the way it is perceived and treated by the public and the government. By carefully orchestrating information flow — normally a smart business decision — the corporations hurt their press subsidiaries and damaged the most important asset of any press organization — its credibility.

In announcing the merger, Time Warner officials had been careful to point out that being part of an international entertainment conglomerate would in no way tarnish its journalistic jewel, *Time* magazine. But the way the corporation handled the story had already embarrassed the magazine in front of its peers and its constituency. The corporate culture's secrecy and control of information had eclipsed *Time*'s journalistic competitiveness, in effect censoring it on one of the biggest financial merger stories in history. Time Warner's $11 billion debt later censored the magazine even more by putting it under such severe financial pressure to perform financially.

Henry Luce might have bought himself a movie company, but he would have made sure that his magazine broke the story. His journalistic pride was every bit equal to, if not stronger than, his lust for money.

When it comes to information, the nature of the press is to disclose it in the public interest. The nature of American business, by contrast, has always been more like that of government — not to disclose at all, or to disclose as little as possible in the manner most beneficial to image or financial interest. *Time* magazine getting scooped on the Time-Warner merger was only the beginning of the problems for Time Inc. journalists. Two years later, Graef Crystal, a respected writer for *Fortune* who compiled the magazine's yearly report on executive compensation, quit his job in protest of what he called the "overinvolvement" by Time Warner officials in his evaluation of Time Warner Chairman Steven Ross's $39.1 million pay. Crystal put his finger right on the important point: "After all, none of the other 199 companies in my study were accorded the privilege of challenging my valuation methodology." Early in 1992, when N. J. Nicholas, Jr., the ranking Time executive left in the merged company, was forced out, the magazine did not make the mistake of not covering the story. This time it savaged Nicholas, the loser of the power struggle and the man primarily responsible for the stringent budget requirements under which the magazine had been laboring — and to whom *Time*'s editors and reporters would no longer have to report. The winners fared better.

No one enjoys the publication or broadcast of embarrassing, unflattering or personal information about him-

or herself, and this is particularly true of big-shot chief executives accustomed to having things their own way. Following a *Tribune* series on defense contractors, Stan Cook told me that Lester Crown, whose family controls General Dynamics, had said he was willing to spend $1 million to buy the *Tribune* a new editor. Crown was angry that the series had mentioned the suspension of his security clearance after accusations that he had been trying to buy political favors with campaign contributions.

This kind of sensitivity prevails at the top of a half dozen major news media owners. Even the potential of information about the corporation moving uncontrolled is anathema to most corporate managers. Imagine NBC News, with General Electric as its owner, doing tough investigative reporting on the company's role as a defense contractor, or its problems with environmentalists; *Time* magazine taking on the entertainment business; or the *Chicago Tribune* writing critically about other baseball team owners, or lumber interest practices in Canada. And these news organizations are still run by people with journalistic backgrounds. They will contend publicly that they would never be deterred from the pursuit of a good story involving their parent companies. Perhaps not — if it fell into their laps and could not be avoided. But they would avoid such stories if at all possible. The news director who spends NBC's resources investigating GE won't be news director very long. The reporter or editor at *Time* whose reporting is considered "negative" by corporate management will soon end up like the compensation expert at *Fortune*, in another line of work.

As the major news-gathering organizations have been

taken over by media conglomerates — or transformed into corporate behemoths of their own — the price of economic success has been measured in sagging employee morale and the diversion of profits away from reinvestment in product research, market expansion and employee development. The less obvious but more important loss, however, has been a change in the posture of the press in the eyes of its public constituency. An entertainment company is viewed differently by the public than a newspaper. The company that owns the city's baseball team has a different set of problems with its constituency than an institution of the press would normally have. When Cubs tickets were impossible to buy, Tribune Company's television station WGN would often show to its home audience pictures of celebrities in the crowd who had managed to get them. The next day I would get letters at the *Tribune* blaming the newspaper for not making tickets available to the average Chicagoan.

But to the executives at Tribune Company, buying the Cubs was a good business move — a "must" buy, made to keep the team out of the hands of a new owner who might sell the right to televise Cubs games to a Chicago station other than Tribune's. Loss of that important programming to one of its competitors would have had a double impact on WGN — reductions in both revenue and audience. But for the newspaper, being a corporate sibling of the famous baseball franchise became a nightmare — a constant source of tension within the sports staff, a political liability in the newspaper's relationship with the public and a regular cause of corporate bickering. Time after time in the next nine years, being owned and managed by the same people who managed the Cubs created management and credibility problems for the *Tribune*.

My editorship of the Colonel's newspaper began and ended in squabbles over the Cubs, and with the man who ran them, John W. Madigan, a former Salomon Brothers investment broker who also served as Tribune Company's chief financial officer, and who today is the *Tribune*'s publisher and head of all the company's newspapers. Again and again we butted heads over what I considered conflicts between the interests of the *Tribune* and those of the corporate executive suite. Differences in style and background caused part of the gulf between Madigan and myself, but as much as anything else we personified the clash between the corporate mentality that now runs the press of this country and the resistance to it from journalists who are rapidly changing their colors or disappearing from positions of authority and influence.

Trying to run the flagship newspaper in the corporate headquarters town of a modern media conglomerate is like trying to thread a needle with a finger in your eye. William Allen White once wrote that there are three things no man can do to the satisfaction of everyone else — make love, poke the fire and edit the newspaper. Although I had the title of editor and executive vice president, everyone who outranked me in the corporate power structure — and often their wives and secretaries — had been editing the *Tribune* for years. It was no wonder the paper had been reeling and lurching through a losing battle with the *Sun-Times*. Before I could edit the *Tribune*,

I had to get it back. This, it turned out, was a process costly to future corporate relations.

News-gathering organizations are a lot like high-stakes poker games. The ranking decision maker starts out with a finite number of "chits," equal stacks of yeses and noes. The yeses are used up early in your tenure, leaving you with only noes. Over the years, the noes steadily dwindle, as your skin gets thicker and thicker, your list of enemies longer and longer and the ground you're standing on smaller and smaller. Then you run out of noes and ground, and the only friends you have are people too far down in the organization to help you. Just getting a place at the table — in poker parlance, the ante — can deplete your capital before you get started. I never had more chits than when I returned to the *Tribune* in 1981. But I had to spend them quickly just to get my arms around the newspaper.

My watch began with a deluge of criticism from Cook and Madigan about the newspaper's coverage of the Tribune Company purchase of the Cubs. I doled out some yeses. The paper's coverage had indeed been dismal, reflecting the way the reporters felt about the story. In instances like this, reporters don't want to look like tail waggers for the corporation, so they snarl and sulk off in the corner, which is what the *Tribune* sports department did. But the Tribune hierarchy loved the *Sun-Times'* coverage, which was the work of the city's most respected baseball writer, Jerome Holtzman. Since Holtzman's skill and integrity were both above question, I promptly seduced him away from the *Sun-Times* and put him in charge of *Tribune* baseball coverage. With the announcement of his hiring went a memo to the two men to whom I reported directly — Cook and Brumback. It explained again the difficulties the *Tribune* would have covering the baseball team to the satisfaction of the twenty-fourth floor and asked that they please leave editorial judgments to Holtzman and others in the department.

Complaints about corporate interference were not limited to the sports department. Madigan had a propensity for telephoning subeditors and reporters with personal requests, only some of which would be characterized as editorial. These included coverage of high school athletic events at New Trier High School, where his son attended; efforts to get the *Tribune* automotive writer to speed up delivery of parts for his Saab; personal escort service on his vacations abroad; calls from his wife to the features department for coverage of her club activities and regular postings from his secretary on the important dead among the business elite. In my memo to Cook and Brumback, I pointed out that since Madigan had been named to oversee the team operations, it would be particularly helpful if he quit calling the newspaper with requests for coverage on other matters as well.

Having his hands removed from those levers was no doubt painful for Madigan at the time, and costly for me in the long run. His wife, her feelings hurt, visited me to make a case for more coverage of her hospital auxiliary on the North Shore. Madigan himself agreed only to quit calling others in editorial. He continued to call me, which quickly reduced my stack of noes. One morning Madigan's secretary phoned to tell me that someone her boss thought important had died. Indeed, the dead man had been important. So was Madigan. So I assigned an obituary for the following morning edition. It was not scheduled for the afternoon paper, which in those days was a limited replate in which makeovers were held to a minimum to cut costs for Brumback.

When the afternoon paper landed in Madigan's office, he called me in the newsroom and angrily demanded to know why the obit had not made the afternoon edition when he had promised the family that it would. Because the afternoon edition news editor had determined the ones he had already put in were more important, I replied. This was insufficient. One word led to another and finally to a regrettable explosion in which I suggested that he come down to the fourth floor and edit the newspaper. In turn, I offered to go up to his office, count money and invest pension funds. The relationship never got much better.

There were a number of less personal collisions that were far more illustrative of the difference of opinion between corporate manager and journalist about how the press ought to conduct its business. Of these, the most important is the brokering of the newspaper's editorial power by executives outside the editorial decision-making process. Corporate executives generally feel that newspapers under their control should reflect their opinions. If they don't, how can they explain that to the other executives who read the paper and with whom they associate? In the old days, this was never a problem. At the *Tribune*, for example, all opinion expressed clearly belonged to Colonel McCormick. He ordered the editorial policy, and wrote many of the editorials himself. After his death,

Don Maxwell and the editorial board could not keep that power concentrated. It spread all over the building, including corporate headquarters, because the publisher doubled as chief executive officer of the parent company. When I became editor, editorial policy was being decided in several ways. Unimportant decisions — at least those deemed uninteresting and unimportant by Cook and Madigan — were being left to an editorial board formally presided over by the editor but often dominated by the editor of the editorial pages. Lobbying on the really important stuff, however, such as political endorsements and editorial opinion for or against important local issues, often began in the offices of Tribune executives or their attorney, Don Reuben. Prominent Chicagoans knew that the way to sell the *Tribune* something was to sell it first to Reuben, Cook or Madigan in a private conversation. Then either one of them would call the editorial page editor to set up an appointment or (as was more often the case) Cook would end up personally escorting the caller to the editorial board offices. Sometimes other Tribune executives, including advertising and financial people, would be among the delegation. Even worse, these visitors were frequently not only lobbyists for a particular civic or financial cause but also members of the Tribune Company board of directors. They would all sit around in what amounted to a joint editorial board/corporate executive committee. Often the board, or its leader, was summoned off the fourth floor to meet with a delegation of visitors in some other executive's office, where the appearance of the publisher patting the visitor on the back, or discussing a civic meeting they had just attended, was taken as a signal of which way editorial board opinion should fall.

This procedure was particularly troublesome in the case of Reuben, who was frequently at the center of political and business activity. Not only did he represent the most powerful private interests in the city, but he also was considered a powerful insider in the administrations of Mayors Richard J. Daley and Jane Byrne. On a matter such as a new publicly financed stadium for the Bears, for instance, Reuben often could influence or at least ascertain what the *Tribune*'s editorial opinion would be before the issue was ever raised publicly. After Tribune Company purchased the Cubs, there were few local stories left in which the reporters could find out the news before the executives did. Many times the special interests would have the same conversations with Tribune executives and with the *Sun-Times* publisher, James Hoge. A former journalist, Hoge would go back, leak to his reporters and scoop the *Tribune*, whose executives would still be moping around respecting pledges of secrecy.

Stopping these corporate strong-arm tactics became my most difficult problem — and ultimately my most rewarding accomplishment. That I was able to do it was solely the result of my handshake deal with Brumback, which we had carried over from our days in Orlando. The way we saw it, my job was to appoint a good board and manage it to a consensus opinion that was in the best interest of the *Tribune* and its readers — and in a manner that kept Cook satisfied and off Brumback's telephone.

The showdown had come early in my editorship when the editorial page editor — an amiable, loyal *Tribune* man

named John McCutcheon, whose father had been Colonel McCormick's front-page political cartoonist — told
me that an editorial board meeting had been scheduled
for the corporate suite. Canadian lumber interests, among
them Tribune's extensive timberlands and massive paper
mills in Quebec, were trying to generate editorial opposition to a pending protectionist tariff being considered
by Congress. Cook's office had telephoned and in effect
ordered the board to a joint meeting with Canadian officials and Tribune corporate and paper mill executives. I
told Cook the Canadians ought to send representatives
to a board session on the fourth floor like everybody
else and meet with Tribune corporate visitors separately.
Everyone in the corporate suite took offense. A test of
wills ensued, resulting in the editorial board staying
home. Instead, I went to the meeting to represent the
Tribune. No policy was breached because none was at
stake. The *Tribune* traditionally opposes all forms of pro-
tectionism. But the gauntlet had been thrown down over
how and where newspaper editorial policy would be decided.

Taking Reuben out of the *Tribune* editorial policy
turned out to be far easier than removing Madigan. That's
because Madigan wanted to get rid of Reuben, too. At
our best, however, neither of us was a match for him.
Only as a result of a fluke accident was Reuben's influence
extinguished. In another of those world-class ironies of
which Chicago seems so capable, Reuben, the master
expert on conflicts of interest, got caught in one of his
own making.

One of the most successful market-driven twists in the

definition of "news," at which I had become quite adept, was a gossip column called "INC." It was nothing more than a mass-produced political and celebrity rumor mill, written in a bitchy, glitzy style by two very good female reporters. When done well, such a column is an editor's hemorrhoid because half the information in it makes somebody mad or uncomfortable enough at least to threaten suit, for either libel or invasion of privacy. As a result, the libel expert in Reuben's office, Larry Gunnels, was a frequent caller to "INC." 's headquarters, but always at my request.

One day he called and asked the "INC." writers about a column item in which they alleged that an organized crime figure had been allowed to use a private airstrip in Wisconsin owned by the prominent and wealthy Pritzker family. The reporters, believing that I had prompted Gunnels's inquiries, revealed to him the source of the information. But I had not put the call in to Gunnels. Reuben had ordered the telephone call on behalf of another client — the Pritzkers — a clear conflict of interest. I complained to Cook, and the resulting flap ended Reuben as the *Tribune*'s First Amendment lawyer. Gunnels, who said he had been ordered to make the call, was hired to work directly for the *Tribune*.

With the corporate executives removed from the newsroom, I set about reexamining the tone and thrust of the *Tribune*'s news coverage, its editorial voice, its employment policies and its image in the community. My deal with Brumback meant, among other things, that for the first time in history women named something other than McCormick and Patterson would appear on the mastheads of Tribune newspapers, first in Orlando and later in Chicago. Two of the six editorial names on the *Tribune*'s masthead during my tenure were those of women, and they made as much money as the men. The deal also meant that, for the first time ever, minorities would be represented on the newspaper's editorial staff in other than token numbers. Two minority *Tribune* reporters would win the Pulitzer Prize during the 1980s. Today the editorial page editor of the newspaper is black, and the predecessor who hired him was a white woman hired and promoted while I was editor. More important, the *Tribune*'s prizewinning journalism focused on local issues — minority housing, gang warfare, corruption in the city council, the plight of the underclass and the quality of Chicago schools. Other prizewinners covered genetic engineering and child abuse.

By devising and controlling a marketing strategy that produced profits, I ensured also that the *Tribune* put the resources it had to the best possible use — high-quality journalism in the public interest. I extolled the virtues of this strategy in my annual lecture at the American Press Institute, the industry's think tank in Reston, Virginia. Get in bed with the advertising department, I told the young editors assembled, but get paid for it in freedom and newsprint. The hope was that financial success and market domination would eventually quench the corporate appetite for more profits, and that security from takeover and peer ridicule in the world of the CEO would translate into a less pressurized business climate in which the *Tribune* and other newspapers could put more reporters, better editors and more newsprint to better use.

I was wrong about that, or at least I didn't last long enough to see it. It looked like a good compromise at the time, a proper course considering the alternative. It was not unlike the bargains I saw being struck all around me by journalists of my generation who have had to deal with the corporatization of the press. But what we failed to take into account was that the increasing dominance of the corporate culture was changing the way the press views itself as a business. Inevitably, it will change the way the press is viewed by others — the public and, more important, the government. Witnessing the corporatization of Tribune Company convinced me that corporate ownership of the press assures that newspapers will soon become indistinguishable from any other business.

Traditionally, the strength of the press has been rooted in its diversity and independence. Together these qualities kept it from becoming monolithic and therefore kept it less vulnerable to subjugation by any force, particularly government. It is harder to capture or control things that do not have a common set of goals — or weaknesses. From time to time, newspapers joined in loose coalitions to exempt newsboys from child labor laws or to keep down postal rates, but even these activities fit neatly into the press's classic position of freedom from government control.

One tenet of the old press was that strong, forcibly stated opinions were not only good journalism but good business as well. The newspapers of spirit and conviction, not the bland and tame, were the ones that grew into the grand and gloriously valuable franchises that constituted the bulk of media company wealth. Jack Knight's opinion column was a source of both personal pride and corporate editorial power. Colonel McCormick's greatest passion was his editorial rumblings. He acquired a voice in Washington and published a Paris edition of the *Tribune* in quest of greater resonance. The Hearst, Pulitzer and Scripps Howard newspapers all had corporate editorial policies unrelated to profits. They were in most cases the articulation of their owners' gut beliefs on what was right or wrong about the country. Having a podium was their reason for being in the newspaper business in the first place. The New Deal was no threat to Colonel McCormick's financial interests; he opposed it because he hated Franklin Roosevelt. Newspaper profits had nothing to do with the dramatic evolution in editorial philosophy the Hearst papers endured as their founder matured from antiestablishment populist to conservative Republican. Joseph Pulitzer's social conscience did not waver with good times or bad.

Today's owners have other considerations on their minds. In the last decade, each of the two largest American newspaper companies launched a new paper — Gannett's *USA Today* and Knight-Ridder's *El Nuevo Herald*, a Spanish-language newspaper for Miami's Cuban community. As different as these papers are in nature and mission, they had one thing in common — an editorial voice shaped by marketing considerations rather than convictions. Neither company really wanted to have an opinion. Both *The New York Times* and *The Wall Street Journal* are marketed nationally. Their voices, liberal and conservative respectively, are strong and distinct. But the country's newest national newspaper, *USA Today*, initially adopted an editorial policy designed to avoid all contro-versy. Although its editorial page has begun to take stronger stances as its market position has stabilized, at the outset *USA Today*'s editorial opinions could never be characterized as positions strongly held and forcibly stated. Whatever moderate stance *USA Today* assumes, it makes sure the editorial page is soaked with opposing views.

It is ironic that this delicately balanced, marketing-driven editorial approach was perfected by John Seigen-thaler, a man who is regarded in the industry as a throw-back to another era. He accepted the job as *USA Today*'s first editorial director, while remaining the publisher of the Nashville *Tennessean*, where the editorial page he had overseen for thirty years had been one of the nation's strongest and most consistent voices for social democratic progress. His appointment and mission at *USA Today*, however, reflected Al Neuharth's marketing genius. Who was going to criticize Seigenthaler for having no opinion?

In Miami, the Knight-Ridder marketing decision was considerably more complicated and painful. There, the need for the Spanish-language edition was rooted in the Cuban-American community's unhappiness with the moderate foreign policy stance and tone of *The Miami Herald*. The Cubans are considerably more hawkish and hot-blooded than the cool and evenhanded *Herald* edi-tors, putting Knight-Ridder in the unenviable position of either expressing the *Herald*'s liberal views in Spanish (which would undoubtedly dampen the Cubans' enthusi-asm for the new newspaper) or having to explain why it chose to speak opposing views out of the same corporate mouth. In the end, Knight-Ridder decided that, when speaking Spanish, it would just keep its opinions to itself. Instead of having an editorial opinion of its own, *El Nuevo Herald* simply makes space available for the opinions of others.

Such conflicts between traditional press obligations and new financial considerations are impossible to hide from the public or the government. The old journalist-proprietors nourished and cherished journalism as society's most valuable forum for the expression of opinion — and did not have to answer to Wall Street analysts demanding 35 percent profit margins. Since the advent of corporate ownership, however, economic necessity has become an increasingly unifying and homogenizing force. To protect their profits, the new media conglomerates now seek government favoritism, just like any other special interest. In the late 1960s, many newspaper owners prevailed upon the Nixon administration to support an exemption from antitrust laws for failing newspapers in the same city. Many of the strongest voices in journalism rose in protest, sounding an important alarm. For the first time, they said, the press had flung itself begging at the feet of the very politicians it was supposed to monitor. And by arguing that such government intrusion was necessary to preserve editorial competition, the industry as a whole was publicly prostituting the principle of the free press to protect its profits. It was the sprouting of clay feet. And in the two decades since, those feet have grown like Pinocchio's nose.

In 1982, the American Newspaper Publishers Association sent its chairwoman, Katharine Graham, to lobby for restrictions to prevent the American Telephone & Telegraph Company from using its telephone monopoly to compete with newspapers for advertising. The ANPA sent out letters urging all newspaper publishers to lobby for passage of legislation so clearly in its economic interest. But still there was diversity. A number of publishers refused to follow the ANPA's lead because they believed that urging government regulation of information flow is contrary to the tenets of press freedom. Among those declining to write such editorials was the *Chicago Tribune* editorial board, which found the position in conflict with its long conservative tradition against government regulation of business. In that instance, Tribune Company's management clearly saw preservation of the independent editorial stance of its flagship newspaper as being more important than industry solidarity. Jack Fuller, then a board member and eventually my successor as editor, remembers the decision as a point of pride that the *Tribune* refused to compromise a matter of principle and take up the positions of the liberal *New York Times* and *Washington Post*, to which it considered itself a conservative alternative.

Seven years later, during my last year as editor of the *Tribune*, the newspaper's editorial board reaffirmed its position against government regulation of information flow with an editorial opposing efforts to renew federal regulation of the cable industry. Again this conflicted with an active ANPA lobbying campaign, but this time Stan Cook, outraged at what was simply an orderly restatement of *Tribune* policy, personally ordered the position reversed. Cook gave me two good reasons why corporate financial interests were suddenly prevailing over the editorial policy of individual papers: profits and peer pressure. First, he said that because the company had gone public in 1983, it now had obligations to stockholders it had never had before; and second, the original editorial had embarrassed Charlie Brumback (since promoted to chief operating officer), who had promised other industry CEOs that he would lead the lobbying campaign in favor of government regulation. A few days later I wrote and published the contradictory editorial, reversing years of policy. "Things change," Cook said.

But there was another dynamic at work as well. During the 1980s Tribune Company had divested itself of its cable interests. When the *Tribune* refused to support government regulation of the cable industry in 1982, that decision had been in the corporate financial interest as well. Anyone watching the flip-flop closely — as readers, politicians and judges do — could reasonably conclude that whatever the *Chicago Tribune* editorial page recommends to be in the public interest on the cable business might be more accurately viewed as what is in the newspaper's financial interests. Such a crabbed view of journalism's mission is hardly what Walter Lippmann had in mind.

According to the *Tribune*'s logic, it was better to embarrass me and the editorial board and silence one of the oldest and loudest voices in the press against government regulation of business than to adhere to principles that might reduce corporate profits. And as the 1980s came to an end, I was not the only editor suffering embarrassment because of the new pressures of corporate journalism. If my good friend David Lawrence was not embarrassed, he should have been. Lawrence, as a result of his superior talent and energy, had been given the toughest jobs in the Knight-Ridder organization, first as editor and then as publisher of the sagging *Detroit Free Press*. In one of the few remaining competitive markets where Knight-Ridder was a major player, the *Free Press* was locked up with *The Detroit News*, only recently purchased by Gannett, in mortal combat that had produced more than $100 million in operating losses over a decade.

In an effort to rid their companies of the kind of sorry financial performers Wall Street would not tolerate and at the same time preserve competing editorial voices, Knight-Ridder and Gannett sought to solve the problem with a joint operating agreement, which because it is an exemption from antitrust laws, had to be approved by the Justice Department. At the time, Attorney General Edwin Meese III was under fire from most of the press for a ridiculously shady and sleazy performance in office. But once he took the Detroit JOA case under advisement, the fire from the *Free Press* and from Knight-Ridder's *Miami Herald* cooled significantly. At one point editorial cartoonists at both newspapers were told by their editors that Meese cartoons were prohibited until after he ruled on the JOA. No doubt those censorship decisions were made — as the managements at both papers insisted — with no input from corporate headquarters. But the point is that they were prudent decisions being made by some of the best and most respected newspaper editors in the press today, including Lawrence in Detroit and Jim Hampton in Miami. The corporate journalism ethic has become so strong and pervasive that it works automatically. The new monolithic press now wears its financial interests on its face for everyone to see.

6

Follow the Money

S OME MIGHT ARGUE that corporate ownership came to
the press just in time to save a decadent enterprise
from dying of squalid and decrepit management. Al
Neuharth may well be right in saying that the changes he
wrought in the industry would have occurred with him
or without him and that the way he changed newspapers
actually helped them to survive longer than they might
have otherwise. Like the rest of us, he was part of two
generations of press leadership caught between opposing
forces: loyalty to journalism's traditional obligation to
gather and publish serious information important to democracy, and the stark financial realities of continuing to
use newspapers for that purpose. The balance we used to
strike does not appear to be the way to keep a word-based
business alive in the new information order, which is
basically a world of visual images.

Whenever Gannett bought a newspaper, which it did

sixty-nine times during Neuharth's tenure, the old management, when retained, was given a guide for operations. Inevitably, it included a list of the best-earning comparable properties within Gannett, a number of which earned between 30 and 40 percent or higher. These profit standards became the goals not just for the new "Gannettoids" but for every company whose stock was evaluated by Wall Street. In similar fashion, when the nation's press owners followed Neuharth to Wall Street and offered their stock for sale as he had, the new buyers handed them an operations model as well. And the model was Gannett itself: over twenty-two years of consecutive quarterly earnings growth; revenue increases from $186 million in 1967 to $3.1 billion in 1989; net earnings increases from $14 million to $219 million; stock dividends up from 4.8 cents to a $1 a share.

Christopher Shaw, a media acquisition specialist on Wall Street, was among those whose advice to media investors always included what became known as the Gannett formula — the acquisition of 15 percent margin newspapers that could be turned into 40 percent earners two years later by minimizing costs and raising advertising and circulation prices to the limit. "No one will buy a 15 percent margin paper without a plan to create a 25 to 45 percent margin," Shaw said.

More important, perhaps, the Gannett financial statements became the basis for establishing the market value of newspapers, which were to be among the hottest properties in the coming era of acquisition. Instantly, companies that did not insulate family or management through the issuance of separate classes of stock became vulnerable to both greenmail and breakup. Until junk bond money began drying up at the beginning of 1990, fear of takeover was the number one concern in the media's executive suites. Operating strategies clearly began to reflect the advice of the takeover defense specialists, who said that the best deterrent to takeover was to keep the market value of the company at the highest possible level. And the only way to do that was by continually increasing earnings to support the stock.

Even the *St. Petersburg Times*, one of print journalism's shiniest faces, found itself mud wrestling for its independence in 1989 with corporate raider Robert Bass. The *Times*' legendary editor-publisher, Nelson Poynter, had bequeathed the newspaper and his other properties to a nonprofit institute dedicated to the preservation and improvement of print journalism. Though the *Times* had always been in the forefront of the "publish first, truth always, and be damned later" school of journalism, it suffered an attack of journalistic paralysis when confronted with the pressure of surprise takeover by a notorious corporate raider. While *Times* executives pondered what to do, the news of the Bass greenmail was broken by its competitor, the *Tampa Tribune*. Bass, who had captured a 40 percent block of the *Times*' voting stock from a dissident Poynter heir, finally pushed the guardians of the *Times*' legacy into a corner and forced them to buy the stock back at the cost of significant company indebtedness. Although no one will put a price tag on the battle, it may have cost more than $100 million, money that otherwise would have gone toward better journalism.

At one point in the 1980s, the combination of Neuharth's unquenchable thirst for ownership and his free-spending ways drove newspaper prices up so high that no one but Gannett could afford them. In the middle of the decade, when he went after three respected dailies — *The Detroit News, The Des Moines Register* and the Louisville *Courier-Journal and Times* — Neuharth had begun to flaunt his power and was obviously out to embarrass the press establishment that had shunned him. Although all three papers were considered plums, his avowed determination to buy them was enough to drive away most other suitors.

In Des Moines, for example, everyone expected to be outbid. Their only hope was that the descendants of the Cowles family, one of the old-time proprietors with a reputation for quality over profits, would refuse to sell to Gannett. Fat chance. The premium Neuharth had established for a monopoly newspaper had long eclipsed their ancestor's principle.

For the *Register*, a medium-sized daily in a depressed farm economy market, he put $165 million on the table, nearly $30 million over the bid of his nearest competitor and $50 million more than Katharine Graham would offer. The size of the sale price staggered young Charles Edwards, the Cowles heir who ran the paper. "If my grandfather had known these newspapers could make this kind of money," said Edwards, now the paper's publisher under Gannett, "he never would have died."

Although they were among the last newspapers purchased by Gannett, Louisville and Des Moines were among the most important deals for Neuharth personally and to the industry. Because of their reputations for journalistic excellence and integrity, their sales signaled the end of an era. Both were prompted by family members squabbling over how to claim their inheritance — the phenomenon that Neuharth had begun to exploit twenty years earlier. In two decades the old family proprietors had been virtually wiped out. Even more significant, the two papers were viewed as perhaps the final bastions of the independent, public service–oriented journalism around which has grown up so much myth and legend. *The New York Times, The Washington Post,* the *Los Angeles Times* and *The Wall Street Journal* were believed to be held safely in the hands of management beholden to families that had long controlled them, and the *St. Petersburg Times* had been willed to a nonprofit foundation. But except for those five, most of the big independent daily newspapers in the country already had been gathered up in the acquisition mania. With the sales of the *Des Moines Register* and the Louisville *Courier-Journal and Times,* the final maidens had lost their virtue.

Tribune Company was invited to bid on both newspapers. Des Moines was a natural fit, better for Tribune than for Gannett. I urged the company to pursue the purchase seriously. By building a satellite plant on the Iowa-Illinois border that would print both newspapers, we could have had early morning home delivery across two states, an advertising sweep from the shores of Lake Michigan all the way to Kansas and Nebraska. We never had a chance. Tribune Company always based its purchases on a formula that relied on projected revenues, which are invariably underestimated to avoid risk. Tribune never took editorial people along when inspecting properties, relying instead on advertising, production and financial people, mainly, Brumback once told me, to ensure confidentiality. Editors played the same nonexistent role in acquisitions as they did in other important company decisions. Neuharth, by contrast, seldom went anywhere without his editorial people. Indeed, they often headed up the actual acquisition and transition teams, particularly when Gannett was courting the old journalism elite who owned the papers in Louisville and Des Moines. In addition to courting the sellers, Neuharth was willing to manipulate the numbers to support what he wanted to do. Wall Street was never his boss. It was just another obstacle to be overcome.

The style in which Neuharth built Gannett and handled Wall Street was clearly the most important force in the concentration of press ownership in relatively few hands. Responsibility for this development is often laid at Neuharth's feet as proof of his villainy. But concentration of ownership in itself is not the problem. Considering the financial condition of the industry and the management of many of the newspapers at the time, adding them to corporate portfolios may well have saved their lives. In the same way, blaming Neuharth personally for the shift in emphasis of newspaper content across the board is also misdirected and unfair.

All Neuharth did was what the other press barons before him had done — buy newspapers he wanted to own and run them the way he thought best. The scope of his influence is no more attributable to his willingness to lead than it is to the willingness of the rest of the industry to follow. Whether the managers of the press like Neuharth or not, he became the model of success for a whole generation of less innovative and less courageous bureaucrats who found themselves atop a business that should be led, not managed.

This was particularly true inside some of the most important media companies, where the successors to McCormick, Hearst, Pulitzer and Knight, while denigrating Neuharth's style and tactics, could not formulate their own. For all the independence they showed once he had captured Wall Street, they might as well have just sold out to him.

In recent years, companies rich in journalistic tradition (and still sensitive to its demands) have hired corporate chief executives who are well equipped to balance the company's financial interests against the survival of the free press. James K. Batten, a former reporter, was groomed for the chairmanship of Knight-Ridder, which owns more metropolitan dailies than any American company other than Gannett. Batten, who assumed this post in 1989, sounds like most of his peers when he contends publicly that his job is really little different from that of his predecessors. "Through my more than thirty years in this business, conscientious editors, publishers and corporate people have struggled to strike a wise and proper balance between the obligations to readers and communities, and to their newspapers' owners," he wrote in 1990 in the *Washington Journalism Review*. "It's not a perfect or painless process, but in Knight-Ridder at least, it works. Over the years we have become ever more convinced of this article of faith: ultimately, journalistic quality and financial success go hand in hand."

As good as that sounds to the public and to the anxious journalists down in the ranks, it just does not work that way. Journalistic quality and financial success went hand in hand only when the ownership of the press was willing to temper its financial success in the interest of journalistic quality. In today's world, it works the other way around. There are still exceptions, of course, famous ones such as *The New York Times* and *The Washington Post*, where family interests still supersede those of other stockholders from time to time. The reality today, however, is that most newspapers in the United States are owned by corporations whose management makes no distinction between their business and any other. And even in the more sensitive and sophisticated companies, the old definitions of journalistic quality are no longer valid. The "quality" that once satisfied readers, attracted advertising support and returned 10 percent operating margins is now appreciated only by an elite group of journalists and news junkies. Just getting people to buy and read a newspaper today is as difficult as getting an agreement on what quality newspaper content should be.

Wherever the managers of media companies and the high priests of journalism gathered during the 1980s — at Stanford, Northwestern, Harvard or on Wall Street, they were told the same story: 70 percent of the Fortune 500 companies in 1955 are no longer in existence today. Most of them dropped off for the same reason the Swiss no longer dominate watchmaking, a tale told over and over to the newspaper managers by consultants and financial advisers. The Swiss invented the quartz watch, but they refused to change the way they made watches and sold the invention to the Japanese. Now the Swiss are but a part of the Japanese watch industry. They can still make the finest watches but not the finest watches that sell in the greatest numbers and return the most profit to their makers. The Japanese watchmakers do that.

This analogy has great resonance within the newspaper industry, among both preservationists like Batten who feel the need to address the issue of quality journalism and those like Brumback who believe that "quality" is what sells.

But in any context, discussion of newspaper quality invariably turns to *The New York Times* and *The Wall Street Journal*. Because of its extraordinarily large editorial staff and the generous space it allots to news reporting each day, *The Times* has been cited by David Halberstam as an example of a paper still more committed to quality journalism than most. Likewise, David Laventhol of the *Los Angeles Times* (an editor turned publisher who understands the intricacies of the industry's problem as well as anyone) has cited *The Times* and *The Journal* as examples of the durability of traditional journalism when practiced by companies still committed to traditional standards of excellence. But *The Times* and *The Journal* are "quality" to Halberstam and Laventhol for entirely different reasons. Halberstam defines quality as a big news space filled with serious news of government and important events written by superior journalists. Laventhol views *The Times* and *The Journal* as "quality" because they long ago matched up a superior journalism product with a desirable target audience and created the kind of "quality brand" image with readers that ensures long-term survival and profitability.

Yet perhaps the most important perspective on "quality" journalism is that of A. Roy Megarry, publisher of *The Toronto Star*, one of 122 newspapers owned by the Canada-based Thomson group, and one who typifies the new breed of newspaper executive. Megarry evaluates the future effectiveness of *The Times* and *The Journal* in more critical terms — as carriers of advertising. And while he concedes that these two papers are "quality," he likens them to the best horse and buggy at the Indianapolis 500.

Megarry likes to point out that in a typical year (1988), *The New York Times* and *The Wall Street Journal* had to sell 660,000 new subscriptions at reduced prices just to increase their combined total circulation by 23,000. This is akin to Rolex and Mercedes giving rebates. Even worse, had they not offered reduced subscriptions, they would have lost more subscriptions than they gained. This means that the very best quality newspapers must discount to stay in business.

The significance of this commercial weakness comes in the startling realization that these two newspapers are already precisely what most of the others are still struggling to become. Their "highest quality" journalism has already been precision-tuned to fit the perfect advertising target: the nation's highest-income, best-educated, most influential, discriminating and free-spending buyers. These newspapers long ago found their niche — a large homogeneous slice off the top of the market who have similar interests, life-styles and buying habits. They no longer have to trade bad readers for good. They no longer have to balance the needs and interests of one segment of the market against those of a dramatically different one. They don't have to struggle to develop an editorial content that reaches from bank president to cabdriver, or sell themselves to the readers of *Vanity Fair* and the viewers of *Wrestlemania* on cable television. It is a sobering sight for the management of the mainstream press, which has been struggling mightily to get the perfect combination, to look at the two high-flyers and see that their circulation numbers and advertising revenue labor under the same intense pressures as their own.

So, declared Megarry in a now infamous speech to a Canadian press group, "maybe we are fast approaching the time when the publishers of mass circulation newspapers will finally stop kidding themselves that they are in the newspaper business and admit they are primarily in the business of carrying advertising messages."

Whether their loyalties are in the newsroom or in the boardroom, the managers of newspapers get the same message: traditional newspaper content, no matter what the quality, is becoming progressively less relevant to people's lives, while advertisers are seeking ever more efficient ways to market their goods and services. Newspaper publishers are word merchants in a world where technology now routinely lures their customers live and in color to the base of the Berlin Wall to hear the crash of it collapsing and to watch the emancipated dancing through the gaps. It takes them outside the door of international summit meetings, beneath falling bombs along the streets of Baghdad and the sands of the Arabian des-

ert — simultaneously, if they like — or high in the skies
to watch opposing armies light the night like shooting
stars.

With each generation more visually oriented than the
last, with such new, enthralling access to the world as
close as the remote control button, an ever smaller number of people have need for the prism of written journalism. What can the reporter and editor contribute twelve
hours later to events people have already seen and heard?
To some readers, a great deal. But they are a dying breed,
and surveys suggest that they do not seem to be remaining
attentive to the printed word in numbers sufficient to
constitute a critical mass, even for *The New York Times* or
The Wall Street Journal.

Meanwhile, still another technology — this one driving
the cash register at the corner grocery — identifies and
catalogs not only who is shopping for groceries at the
moment, but what their habits suggest they might buy on
the next visit. Eventually this information will find its way
to smart product manufacturers like Procter & Gamble
and Quaker Oats, who long ago discovered that newspaper advertising is hardly the most efficient way to deliver
discount coupons and trial offerings. They are all tired of
paying for readers who dump the food section and their
coupon inserts into the garbage can before they take their
papers apart to look for the entertainment section. Soon
such vital ingredients in the marketing message as discount coupons and introductory samples will be delivered
by electronic means or direct mail, making the traditional
newspaper grocery ad nothing more than a memory. Now
that the computer cash register can record who is buying

what and send them electronic mail, who needs to pay for all that unnecessary newspaper circulation?

It is against such a backdrop that for the last half dozen years newspaper preservationists and Wall Street interlopers alike have been huddling in think tanks in Florida and California and in publisher meetings in Reston, Virginia, and New Orleans, quietly searching for the unspeakable — an alternative to both the traditional content and the traditional form of newspapers. Armed with circulation records, advertiser wish lists, surveys of reading habits, studies of television-watching behavior and demographic profiles, they seek simply to find out what will sell. If and when that is determined, quality journalism will be newly defined accordingly.

"Editorial quality" once meant how well a news organization covered and reported the news according to standards set by editors and reporters. The definition of "news," and, correspondingly, "quality," has broadened considerably in recent years as a result of the rise of women into senior editing positions and the diversification of staff to reflect minorities to a greater degree. There is now more coverage of issues of particular interest to women, more coverage of personal health, the family, religion and social behavior. This is the way news content always changed in the past. Succeeding generations of professional journalists trained and experienced in gathering and judging news shaped the news the same way a baker trained in the kneading and baking of bread produced bread. As the tastes and talents of the bakers varied, so did the final loaves.

For over two years now, at the *Boca Raton News,*

Knight-Ridder has been experimenting the same way Procter & Gamble comes up with new products for households, by trying to find out exactly what people want to read and to design a definition of news that will encompass these values. Preliminary results suggest that when and if a Knight-Ridder newspaper for the baby-boom generation emerges, it will look a lot like Gannett's *USA Today*. Likewise, Gannett has decided that its best hope is to make all its papers more like its national flagship by the year 2000.

If this trend holds, the newspapers that survive corporatization will be quite different from what they have been for the last 200 years. It is certain that they will be consumer driven and relatively free from information that is unpleasant, complex, unattractive or dull. According to the maxims of the new journalism, if it does not attract readers or advertisers, it cannot possibly be "quality editorial" and therefore a proper use of company resources.

I stayed on as editor of the *Chicago Tribune* a year too long, just to make sure that a massive piece of journalism — two years of investigation into how the U.S. government and the scientific community had reacted to the AIDS crisis — would get published. It was a story as long as this book, but not unlike dozens of other series the *Tribune* and other good newspapers run routinely. The story, researched and written by one of journalism's best reporters, Pulitzer Prize winner John Crewdson, prompted investigations by the National Academy of Sciences and the United States Congress. It created an international furor in the scientific community, and it won the *Tribune* accolades from laymen and scientists alike for reporting with extraordinary accuracy a complex medical story of the utmost public interest. But among Tribune Company executives, only one — an eminent scientist on the board of directors — offered a word of positive acknowledgment. Because of its length and subject matter, the story was glumly received by Tribune top management and frequently cited later as evidence that my tenure and status as a newspaper editor had surpassed my judgment on how to use newsprint. Over the years I had often allocated the same amount of space to a wide variety of inane subjects, such as the annual festival of homes, a real estate industry promotion, and regular tributes to the Florida tourism industry, which could be sold to advertisers. For those I was written notes of congratulation and extolled in Tribune Tower as a great editor.

Nowhere in the press has the adoption of the television culture been harder to swallow or claimed more casualties than among the dwindling but still influential core of journalism purists in the nation's newsrooms. These people subscribe to Lord Northcliffe's definition of news as "something somebody wants to suppress." Peel back the slick, pin-striped cover of a news executive at *The New York Times, The Wall Street Journal*, Knight-Ridder or Times Mirror, and you are likely to find a hardheaded ignoramus of the typewriter generation who is still traditional enough to consider journalism a sacred trust to be guarded in the public interest.

Among them are a number of intelligent and strong-willed people. And now and then, the sound of one of them self-destructing in the path or the wake of the corporate steamroller will echo across the landscape. In the last few years, these have included some big-name editors of famous newspapers, such as Bill Kovach of the *Atlanta Constitution*, Katherine Fanning of *The Christian Science Monitor* and, most recently, Eugene L. Roberts of *The Philadelphia Inquirer*. My own departure from the *Chicago Tribune*, considered premature by everyone but myself and a few Tribune corporate executives, has often been included on the list — erroneously. Like some other "purists" who loved their work and considered it important, I tried to adjust to the new business paradigm and to excel at cost cutting and profit making in exchange for total control of editorial policy and news content. I stayed too long and accepted too many bonuses to make a martyrs' list.

More illustrative of the newsroom revolution now under way is Gene Roberts's retirement in 1990 (five years ahead of schedule) from atop Knight-Ridder's most widely acclaimed and highly regarded newspaper. Known to a legion of admirers as "the frog" because of a crouched appearance and an ability to conduct complex conversations with a series of one-syllable grunts, Roberts was far and away the most widely respected newspaper editor in the business. His newspaper collected Pulitzer Prizes two and three at a time — seventeen in eighteen years — and his brand of journalism came to symbolize the mission of several generations of journalism's best. Roberts believes the most important news is news of government, particularly the arcane and complex underbelly that remains hidden from public view, and any news organization with a higher priority is a news organization in need of reform.

With the establishment of *The Inquirer* as a temple of this kind of journalism, Roberts himself became a powerful political force inside the Knight-Ridder organization and a role model for editors at its twenty-seven other papers. But this position also placed him and *The Inquirer* in direct conflict with Knight-Ridder's market-driven, customer-service brand of corporate journalism.

Whatever *The Inquirer*'s reputation nationally, it had the reputation inside Knight-Ridder as an underachiever in circulation and profits and top-heavy with expensive editorial staff. Roberts's reputation and his ability to lead people cut two ways. If his paper were exempted from the corporate marketing strategy or earnings formulas, how could Batten and his deputy, Anthony Ridder, nominally Roberts's boss, impose them on anyone else?

Several publishers in the chain, including some of the most respected and most successful, had complained to Ridder and Batten frequently about corporate leniency toward Roberts and *The Inquirer*'s "editorial excesses." One of *The Inquirer*'s reporting projects, an opus on the disappearance of the white rhinoceros in South Africa, was widely ridiculed in executive circles and effectively exploited to undercut Roberts's status. "I think it is fair and accurate to say that however great Gene Roberts is as a journalist, as an editor he was a negative factor to the profitability and the circulation of *The Inquirer*," said Rolfe Neill, a former editor and publisher of *The Charlotte Observer*, one of the chain's best and most successful newspapers. "In today's world, a great editor cannot be an obstacle to profitability and circulation growth."

Knight-Ridder ultimately had to decide whether Roberts and *The Inquirer* would follow the company line or become the core of companywide resistance to cost control and profit enhancement policies. Welcome, Jack Knight and Gene Roberts, to the world of A. Roy Megarry.

Although oversimplification is a pitfall when writing about personality conflicts and intrigue in corporate boardrooms, the oversimplification often constitutes the nugget of truth that is most important and best remembered. Whatever its complications, the Roberts departure will never be viewed among the purists as anything but Knight-Ridder's willingness to sacrifice quality in the name of corporate profit making. But the greater and more important truth was that Roberts's definition of quality was no longer in step with that of his company or the industry in general.

Perhaps more important, Gene Roberts represented something no longer valued by corporate journalism. He was a leader. Newspapers don't win seventeen Pulitzer Prizes in eighteen years without leaders. Leadership is what built the franchises the managers are now managing. But, as I found in my own case, only the reporters and editors miss leaders. For the most part, Knight-Ridder's top executives and some of Roberts's management peers actually cheered his departure. And as difficult as it might have been for Batten to watch the company's most celebrated journalist walk out the door, he had no choice. A choice between Roberts and Ridder, Batten's likely successor, was no choice at all, particularly if it were ever to be voted on by the company's board of directors or the analysts of Wall Street.

In the end Batten's performance as company chairman would be evaluated on the financial performance of *The Inquirer* over the next five years, not by how many Pulitzers it won or how many journalism medals got cast in Roberts's image. No matter that Batten and the rest of the preservationists still have one foot firmly planted in the old world, the other is resting precariously on the thin ice of the new. Long term, the overall quality of Knight-Ridder newspapers might be damaged more by Batten losing his job than by Roberts losing his. "We all know that Batten is just another guy in a gray suit who has to answer to stockholders," said one of his top editors. "The first time he gives the wrong answers, there will be another guy in a gray suit in there to replace him. And it is likely to be somebody less understanding about what we do than Jim."

Yet the concern that former reporter Batten would feel over the loss of a news executive such as Gene Roberts makes him a bit of an iconoclast himself. Few chief executives running companies that own news-gathering businesses can actually appreciate the skills and qualities that distinguish good journalists from mediocre ones. The lawyers, accountants and salesmen now rapidly becoming the top press management would never have held Roberts in such high esteem in the first place because of his insistence on costly journalism to fill in around the advertising.

Qualities such as news judgment, community knowledge, skill at attracting, managing and leading a news staff — even the skill of publishing profitable newspapers — are secondary to belief in and commitment to the corporate ethic of stockholders first, foremost and always. Corporate press owners would rather have a news executive with no conflicts about where his or her heart is. The culture gap here is simply too great to bridge. When Al Neuharth, in his quest for press titandom, made an unsuccessful move to acquire the CBS television network in 1985, he got close enough that he and the network's CEO, Thomas Wyman, were discussing the membership of a merged board. "Just don't expect me to keep that fucking Cronkite on the big board," Neuharth remembers Wyman telling him. "Putting him on the CBS board when he retired as anchorman was the dumbest thing I ever did."

Why would the head of CBS feel that way about someone who had built so much of the company's image and made the stockholders so much money? Because Cronkite was constantly carping for more money and television time to be devoted to "quality news programming." In the fall of 1990, presenting the first annual Theodore H. White Lecture at Harvard University, Cronkite complained about the amount of space devoted to soft news features in *The New York Times* these days and said he cannot understand why "newspapers don't just turn their reporters and editors loose and let them cover the news."

Today's news executives would respond to Cronkite that they are doing just that. They have more reporters and more editors — all better educated and with an improved sense of ethics. Journalism salaries are higher, and reporters have more sophisticated equipment at their disposal than ever. Editorial budgets are bigger, too, though the proportion of newspaper revenue devoted to editorial has dropped by 30 percent or better in the last fifteen years.

But these changes mask a larger point. The issue is that the owners and managers of the new media are no longer content to let quality journalism be defined by a new, better-educated, more diverse class of journalism professionals. They want news content defined in advance by target audience responses to surveyors' questions and then designed to fit inside the elite and narrow parameters of the most desired advertiser targets with a single goal — attainment of the corporation's financial objectives. They now define leaders in journalism as those best able to design newspaper content to reach the most desirable advertiser audience in numbers sufficient to achieve the company's financial objectives.

This is precisely the fear that haunted John S. Knight when in 1969, as he struggled with the problems of age and inheritance taxes, he decided to follow Al Neuharth to Wall Street and sell public stock in what was to become Knight-Ridder. "I do not intend to become your prisoner," he told stock analysts in his initial meeting. "As long as I have anything to do with it, we are going to run the newspapers."

Jack Knight's successors have in fact become prisoners. They still run the newspapers, but they are now compelled to find the most profitable way to deliver information, even if it means abandoning their traditional form, their traditional function and their traditional definition of excellence.

Two years before Knight took his company public, his newspapers made $8 million net profit on revenues of $123 million, or less than 7 percent. And they were regarded as the best newspapers in the land. The same kind of performance got "the frog" run out of the temple in Philadelphia.

7

Good-bye to All That

M Y FRIEND BILL KOVACH had no idea what he was up against. Kovach, a marvelous journalist, had spent his entire career at the Nashville *Tennessean*, when it was owned by the Evans family, and in the warm bosom of *The New York Times* editorial department, where "the corporation" is still the Sulzberger family. However, in 1986 he became editor of the Atlanta *Journal* and *Constitution*, which were owned by Cox Communications, a privately held corporation run like a publicly owned one. In less than two years at Atlanta he assembled one of the best staffs in the country and created the most journalistic excitement the industry had seen in a decade. Kovach's papers would ultimately win two Pulitzer Prizes for his first year's work, but before he could collect them, he was pressured out of his job by Cox corporate executives, mainly because he and they lived in separate worlds. On the surface, the dispute centered on Kovach's resistance to the corporation's efforts to model the newspapers after *USA Today* in appearance and content. But that was only the pressure point designed to explode the deeper, more important conflict between the corporate fish and the journalist fowl.

Kovach's destruction was rooted in Cox's discovery that he was not and would never be a corporate manager. Not only was he not malleable, but he also possessed both the tendency and the ability to lead — and the potential to overshadow his bosses among journalists. Those responsible for the financial performance of the Atlanta newspapers could not tolerate at their helm a high-profile leader who still believed that journalists, and not a corporation's financial interests, should direct the press. It's the rare corporate mogul (Charlie Brumback, for one) who does not feel the need periodically to let his peer group know who really decides what the newspaper says and does. In this sense the corporate managers have the same appetite for power that the old proprietors had, but with none of the qualifications for executing it. But editors such as Kovach, Gene Roberts and Ben Bradlee are forever blocking the way, making tinkering, cost cutting and power playing long, tedious and unpleasant exercises.

Having figured out that Kovach's "hot button" was his disdain for *USA Today*–type editorial content, Cox newspaper president David Easterly pushed it until he got the explosion he wanted. It was no secret in the industry that when Kovach was hired — on the advice of former *Boston Globe* editor Tom Winship — Easterly had preferred Ron Martin, who had been *USA Today*'s managing editor from its inception. Once Kovach was out, Easterly simply hired the editor he had wanted all along. Not only does Martin share Easterly's concept of modern newspaper content, but he is a skilled corporate operator and unlikely to make anyone forget that Easterly is the real boss of the South's most important newspapers.

In the long run, it made more sense for Easterly to get rid of Kovach while he was still a "high priest" of journalism. Very soon he would have a become a "pope." "Pope" is how former *Los Angeles Times* publisher Tom Johnson, now president of CNN, refers to a particular status in the journalism hierarchy, attached to certain jobs and accomplishments. Among the "pope" jobs are the editorships of *The New York Times*, *The Washington Post*, the *Los Angeles Times* and the *Chicago Tribune*. Some journalists, like Gene Roberts, become "popes" no matter what job they have. Kovach was already a "pope" among reporters. In another year or two atop the Atlanta newspapers, he would have been one among editors as well. But as both Roberts and I can attest, in the world of corporate journalism, even the "popes" are no longer invincible.

The marriage of corporations and journalism is an unnatural, unhappy union. The best journalists are naturally skeptical individuals with a healthy disrespect for authority, pomposity and ruling classes. They understand and appreciate the ideal of democracy that one man's vote and voice are as important as another's. And they have a well-honed apparatus for detecting two staples of the corporate culture — bullshit and insincerity.

As a matter of routine, newspaper publishers have always had to both defend and endure invasions of their own privacy and the goring of their own oxen because their publications claim those practices as both constitutional rights and civic obligations. When as publisher of the *St. Petersburg Times*, Eugene Patterson was arrested for driving while under the influence, he ordered his newspaper to publish the story on the front page.

But when it came to negative publicity — or any publicity at all — concerning Tribune Company, the corporate skin was thin as tissue. One day in the mid-1980s, Larry Gunnels, by this time general counsel of Tribune Company, showed up in my office in a tizzy. He had just been ordered by John Madigan to stop Kristie Miller, the only descendant of the Colonel on the company board of directors and representative of the largest individual stockholder, from taking notes during the board meetings. "Tell her she can't do that," Madigan had ordered. "She's writing a book." God forbid — a McCormick exercising freedom of speech.

To Tribune executives, reporters from other publications who wrote about the company were all potential assassins, either out to grind a personal ax or in pursuit of some destructive plot hatched by a competitor. But the reporters who most terrified the executive suite were those on their own payroll. Tribune Company journalists, particularly on the sports and entertainment beats, who found themselves having to write about their employer were constantly subjected to microscopic scrutiny for signs of hostility or disloyalty. Only the independent, irascible Mike Royko, the *Tribune*'s best and Chicago's favorite columnist, could flail the ownership or management of his beloved Cubs without evoking a corporate complaint. Tribune bosses were smart enough to know that Royko was doing them a favor by continuing to love and exhort the Cubs in his column, and, more important, they knew complaining about what he wrote was risky. Should their complaints be passed on, Royko was likely to write a second column excoriating them for trying to censor him.

For at least a decade, my predecessors had tried repeatedly to hire Royko away from the *Sun-Times*. When we finally pulled it off (by luring the *Sun-Times'* best and most respected editor, Lois Wille, across Michigan Avenue first), I promised Royko absolute freedom from editorial interference, fear of which had deterred him from entertaining the *Tribune*'s offers in the past. The deal was this: if managing editor Dick Ciccone or I detected in the column anything libelous or anything we thought Mike might regret writing, we would mention it to him. But he wrote what he pleased, which every now and then meant a blast at the Cubs' ownership. This lack of complaining about Royko did not, however, reflect corporate affection for him. On the contrary, the corporate mentality toward journalists who cannot be controlled was often reflected in petulant behavior.

In my early days as editor of the *Tribune*, the Cubs were covered by a typically sharp-tongued, sartorially inelegant doubting Thomas of a reporter who found little to like in the swaggering style of the team's general manager, Dallas Green. Hardly a week passed without some complaint from the twenty-fourth floor about the "tone" of

Cubs coverage. Anything other than totally complimentary stories which portrayed the company as a paragon of both success and virtue had problems of "tone." These usually brought me a call or visit from one of the three executives who outranked me. Ironically, considering their fear of reporters not in their employ, they were most often accompanied by a clipping or a transcript of a more flattering account from competing media. Cook and Madigan, who moved about as if they were joined at the hip, even wrote the same kinds of notes. Typical was one from Cook after the *Sun-Times* published a much longer story on Tribune Company's annual stockholder meeting than the *Tribune* did. "Looks like they gave us a lot better coverage than we gave ourselves." Another from Madigan on the appointment of his successor as president of the Cubs, "Their coverage was much better than ours."

Tribune executive suite sensitivity to the Cubs was matched only by sensitivity to the federal government. Cook enjoyed a particularly cozy relationship with the Department of Defense, which had long ago singled him out as a news executive after its own heart. As *Tribune* publisher, he repeatedly accepted their invitations to inspect their bases, ride in their planes and race over the terrain in their tanks in simulated combat. Hardware of any kind fascinated him. After all, as the successor to a man who had called himself Colonel, had named his estate after the battle of Catigny and had built a museum to his old army division, Cook developed an interest in things military that could fairly be characterized as obsessive. To make matters worse, he was constantly being harangued by two peers from corporate America whose wealth and social status stemmed from their control of huge military contractors — Lester Crown of General Dynamics and Robert Malott of FMC Corporation. Half the complaints from the publisher's office during my years as editor stemmed from objections by these two, or by the Pentagon itself. I never knew which. I responded by beefing up the *Tribune*'s defense coverage, which became much admired, including prizewinning journalism on the procurement scandal involving General Dynamics, and the travails of FMC's controversial contribution to modern warfare, the Bradley Fighting Vehicle.

Finally, I hired a bright marine retiree from the office of the secretary of defense to cover military affairs. If Cook wanted military expertise, he could have it. The problem was, the marine colonel turned out to be one tough reporter, who often knew and reported what the Pentagon was not telling as well as what it wanted everybody to know. Almost from his first column, he became the source of a two-year running dispute between myself and the publisher over his credentials as a journalist. Cook seemed to think he "just isn't catching on," while I thought he was magnificent. I never had orders to fire him, but the suggestion was planted in my office at least once a month, for no other reason than the constant battering Cook was taking from Pentagon public affairs officers and their friends in the defense contracting business. I had the same kinds of problems with economic coverage while Cook served as president of the Chicago Federal Reserve Board, an absurd appointment for a newspaper publisher to accept.

Editorial arm-twisting took many forms at the *Tribune*.

During most of my tenure as editor, the editorial board kept up a constant drumbeat against the special-interest lawmaking that characterized the Chicago City Council and the Illinois State Assembly. Both groups retaliated by passing laws specifically aimed at damaging Tribune Company's financial interest — prohibiting the Cubs from playing night baseball. When the Cubs sent their lawyers to lobby the politicians, they were told in effect that their cause would be helped if the *Tribune* editorial page was brought under control. Conversely, every time the editorial page shouted at the lawmakers, their response was to accuse the newspaper of being angry over the night baseball prohibitions. When the political boss of the legislature, House Speaker Michael Madigan (no relation to John), finally allowed a bill through authorizing the Cubs to play a limited number of night games, he insisted on personally conveying the news not to the head of the Cubs but to the publisher of the *Tribune*.

This kind of conflict between corporate interest and journalistic independence was not peculiar to the *Tribune*. It goes on every day at virtually every news-gathering organization. In a sense the situation at the *Tribune* was better than at most newspapers. My unique thirteen-year arrangement with Brumback, who had no interest in setting news or editorial policy, in effect granted me the publisher's power on policy — unless Cook, who actually held the title, expressed some special interest. Except for the order to reverse the editorial on telephone company regulation, I was able to fend off all direct corporate efforts to influence the *Tribune*'s news and editorial policies. During all my years of reporting to Brumback and

Cook, I was never called on the carpet or reprimanded for the way I did my job. Bonuses, salary raises and stock options beyond all reason and expectation were routinely lavish, and I came to recognize them as rewards for what they considered a job well done.

Even though I could prevail in arguments with the publisher and resist pressure to corporatize the company's flagship newspaper, the frequency of my resistance was not without cost. Differences of opinion about employee relations and the effect of the constant ratcheting of earnings from the *Tribune* and other newspaper properties set me apart from others at the top of Tribune Company — and set me up for a fall.

In 1989 there was unrest in the executive suite. Stan Cook would turn sixty-five in 1990, at which time he would have to retire from all his offices, save that of chairman. A power struggle soon developed between the two strongest contenders for his job, John Madigan and Charlie Brumback, preoccupying the top management of the company for over a year.

Madigan, who was fifty-four at the time and the second-ranking corporate executive, had expected to succeed Cook. He spread his anticipation around Chicago business circles, prompting speculation to that effect in the newspapers and business journals. But Tribune Company had never been run by anyone who had not previously been in charge of the *Tribune* itself. It also wasn't likely that the Tribune board of business executives would go for Madigan, an unproven manager, over Brumback, who had been the company's best cost cutter and profit maker in the 1980s. Yet Madigan had dismissed Brumback as a competitor because Charlie was only four years younger than Cook.

For me a choice between the two was no choice at all. I urged Brumback to make a run for it. He was reluctant to do so overtly, but it was clear he thought he had a chance — and he didn't discourage my offer to be his campaign manager. An informal poll of chief executive officers from the other Tribune properties produced none who favored Madigan. Many cheered me on, quietly, because they did not want to be on the losing side should Madigan win. The newspaper industry landscape is well populated with former Tribune Company executives who once considered themselves rivals with Madigan. And after they were gone, no matter how successful they had been, Tribune never had anything good to say about them.

Fully aware of the risks and the consequences, I campaigned for Brumback with the few contacts I had on the board, including Cook. This included a speech to the board, which Cook had conveniently arranged for me, in which I extolled Brumback's business acumen, his value as my mentor in that regard and his wisdom in leaving the editorial decisions to the journalists. In campaigning for Brumback, I made a point of citing his meticulous efforts to avoid any conflicts of interest. He once even ordered all Tribune executives to refrain from making political contributions. When I told him this was unconstitutional, he said he didn't care, that they were all making too much money to sue. He was also unlike most corporate press moguls in that he kept a low profile and never flexed the newspaper's muscles for his personal gain. When he showed up in a city where the *Tribune* had people, cars and equipment, he made his own arrangements and went his own way. If Brumback called a bureau or a reporter, it was just to show courtesy.

Naturally, the journalist in me could not help but contrast this style with that of Madigan, who was notorious for using *Tribune* reporters as travel guides, translators and facilitators in meeting heads of state or foreign dignitaries. In this sense, anyway, the imperious Colonel still lived. When Madigan traveled, it was VIP all the way. The reporters didn't seem to mind. One even took the opportunity to ask him for a raise. But the editors in the Tower considered his actions a flagrant abuse of power. Madigan had never had an official connection to the newspaper, and there was no justification for his forays other than his personal comfort and enjoyment. Often he contacted reporters without discussing his plans with the editors. On one occasion he invited one of his former travel guides, the *Tribune*'s Israel correspondent, to address a meeting of company directors and chief executive officers. Had Madigan bothered to check with the newspaper, he would have learned that the reporter had been called back to Chicago to discuss a number of problems with his performance, including an allegation of plagiarism that would ultimately result in his resignation.

Among my complaints to Cook about Madigan was one I believed to be most revealing. It concerned the purchase of a fur coat for his wife by one of the *Tribune*'s advertisers. As advertising salesman had told me that Madigan wanted to avoid paying Illinois sales tax and had asked that the coat be delivered to another company executive who maintained a residence in a neighboring state. He also told me that Larry Gunnels had firsthand knowledge of the matter, so one day in my office I asked Gunnels about it. He turned white and began to stammer. Finally, he said that he couldn't talk about the affairs of one client with another client. "Just don't ask me anything about Madigan," he pleaded.

But I knew that the executive had been asked to bring the coat to Madigan at the office. I also knew that Gunnels knew all about it. If the *Tribune* had had this kind of information on a Chicago politician or some other public figure, we'd have printed it. I wanted an explanation. Instead, Madigan fired my lawyer. In all fairness, though Gunnels was terrific on First Amendment law, he was not trained or suited to be a corporation general counsel. He was among eight or ten executives I saw during my time at the *Tribune* who were promoted regularly — sometimes beyond their abilities — handsomely rewarded all along the way and eventually dumped as scapegoats for some corporate failing. Another was George Van Wagner, a super advertising salesman who in my memory never failed to deliver the revenue he promised. But as director of advertising for the *Tribune*, he was an uncommunicative manager not easily sold on Brumback's new ideas for cost cutting. Though Van Wagner had earned his stripes, I shared Brumback's preference for Robert Holzkamp (our old friend from Orlando) as advertising director because he was easier to work with. My approach would have been to find Van Wagner a job in the company where he could be both happy and productive. After all, he had spent his entire professional life there. But this view ran counter to the corporate culture, which holds that if fired executives leave with pockets full of severance pay, the company conscience is salved. That Van Wagner would end up in a small town in Louisiana with an unhappy family that finally fell apart was of no concern. Being dumped by Tribune Company does not make re-employment an easy proposition.

Meanwhile, as usual, Brumback was traveling a lower-profile, less treacherous and more direct road to beating out Madigan — by delivering record-breaking profits to the bottom line. They were beautifully charted in color for presentation to the board in his year-end 1988 summary and his 1989–1991 forecast. But this time, the crown on Brumback's prodigious profit-making reputation would come at the expense of the editorial department and what remained of our personal relationship.

In his plan for 1989, Holzkamp, ever the magician, had surprised me by predicting for the first time in our history together that he could produce all the revenue I wanted to spend — and still beat our record 1988 profits. I had long ago quit anticipating a year in which I would not have to better the previous one. The only question was by how much. By this time, the *Tribune* was producing a 22 percent operating margin, and Holzkamp was confident that we could improve on that performance. I thought I had the budget process whipped. But at the final presentation, Brumback — also for the first time ever — said that he did not believe Holzkamp's optimistic forecast. A recession was certain, he said, and he sent us back to trim another few million from costs just in case. As the day neared for Brumback to take our budget plan to the corporate executives, we were still a million dollars short in cost reductions. Absolutely convinced that we would never need to do it, I told Brumback I would freeze editorial employment replacements for six months, thereby saving the equivalent of ten to fifteen full-time jobs — roughly $1 million. He accepted the offer and promised me that the jobs could be filled if revenue held up the way Holzkamp and I thought it would.

On the way out of town to make a speech, I heard that an anticipated industrywide increase in the cost of newsprint, which we had figured on for 1989, had been rescinded. This meant a windfall for our budgeting process. Four or five million dollars would fall right to the bottom line. I never gave my ten jobs another thought. But when I returned, I learned that Brumback had put both the newsprint cost reduction and my jobs into his charts. These figures enabled him to promise to ratchet up profits even more — about two points on the operating margin — in a year when the rest of the newspaper business was in recession. This addition made all of Brumback's chart lines the same in every category from 1982 to 1989 — a perfect set of corporate guidelines on revenue, cost reduction and productivity improvement. There was no chart on the editorial budget as a percentage of total revenue, but it would have shown the same consistent pattern — an inexorable decline.

Charlie won the succession battle that day, but he lost a good friend — and I lost the support I needed to keep running the *Tribune*. Clearly, once the battle with the *Sun-Times* had been won, there was no need for improving editorial quality. After all, that costs money.

What I didn't realize until after Brumback's promotion was that the Gunnels dispute had undermined the other half of my support base — with departing publisher Cook. After Madigan had decided that Gunnels was inadequate as corporation counsel, I had made an effort to salvage him as a First Amendment lawyer. Great at preventive medicine, Gunnels had saved the company from dozens of lawsuits simply by teaching editors how to avoid attracting them in the first place. After his firing as general counsel, Cook and Brumback had agreed to let Gunnels remain as in-house legal adviser to the *Tribune* and other journalism properties.

But all this changed when Cook gave Madigan a consolation prize — Brumback's old job as president of the *Tribune*. Rather than tell Madigan the truth — that Brumback had beaten him out because nobody thought him qualified for the top job — Cook told Madigan it was because he lacked newspaper operating experience. As part of the deal, Cook also reneged on his promise to let Gunnels stay. Suddenly and without explanation, he was given notice to vacate his office and pick up his severance. After five years in the job, he was harshly and unceremoniously fired in a manner quite typical of corporate employee relations at the highest levels, where golden parachutes and stock option bonanzas at least cushion the fall. At these heights the employer-employee relationship that has become so impersonal at the lower echelons remains highly personal, even whimsical. Only the callous disregard for people remains the same.

Yet Gunnels had done nothing to get fired other than be in the path of a domino effect caused by the change at the top of Tribune Company. Because corporate bosses face such pressure for short-term financial performance of the companies they head, they want their own teams in place as quickly as possible. A new corporate CEO can mean a complete housecleaning of top executives and an invalidation of their job performances for no other reason than the comfort of the big boss. Newspapers that changed publishers within Tribune Company, with rare exception, also changed editors, and usually advertising directors, too. Within a year after Brumback succeeded Cook and Madigan succeeded Brumback, every department head Charlie had been responsible for hiring at the *Chicago Tribune* had been replaced.

In fact, both Cook and Brumback said up front that it was Madigan's decision to fire Gunnels. "John didn't feel comfortable with Larry anymore. He had been running his mouth about John's personal business," Cook told me. Brumback's explanation was that Madigan was concerned about the relationship between Gunnels and myself: "He didn't want you two sitting down there talking about him."

The job of publisher and CEO of the *Tribune* carries with it automatic membership on the company board of directors, and a seat on the management trust, which votes the largest single bloc of company stock. A job like that must be filled with a corporation man who can always be counted on to put stockholder interest above that of reader, journalist, tradition, free press or God Almighty himself, should it come down to it. Plainly, I did not qualify. My old nemesis Madigan plainly did.

That my seventeen years with the company — and my

twenty-seven-year newspaper career—had to be sacrificed as part of the decision is a little harder for me to
explain, or accept. In all my years at the *Tribune*, I had
received nothing but positive performance evaluations,
raises, bonuses and good peer reviews. Since my resignation, the most difficult question for me to answer is the
one asked most often: "Why on earth would you leave
one of the most important, best-paying and more powerful jobs in journalism when you were at the height of your
career?" The simple but painful explanation is because
the people running the corporation that owned the *Tribune* wanted me to leave. And even though it was the
hardest thing I ever had to do, I wanted to leave, too.

Madigan's first acts as my new boss were to send me
the signals he wanted me to leave. Just as Easterly had
done to Kovach in Atlanta, Madigan pushed all my hot
buttons in short order. Among the first things he asked
me for was help in planning his family vacation to China
and for contacts in New York and Washington for a
family trip. He wanted an escort to the United Nations
in New York and a tour of important buildings in Washington, D.C. On his very first trip as head of the *Tribune*,
he accepted a free airplane ride back to Chicago from
Secretary of Transportation Sam Skinner, at taxpayer expense, for which I had to insist that the newspaper reim-
burse the government. Also it quickly became clear that
the *Tribune* would be returning to the old way of making
editorial policy, with politicians first pleading their cases
in private to the ranking executive at social events or in
one-on-one meetings, then coming to the editorial board
as an afterthought. One day I came in to learn that an

editorial board meeting with an elected official had been moved off the editorial floor to a conference room near Madigan's office, where the official had gone first.

Almost immediately I began to get memos on content, as if moving into Brumback's office had suddenly imbued Madigan with journalistic expertise. Among the first memos was one suggesting that "we be tougher" on a Chicago investment group. A copy of a negative story about the company that day in *The Wall Street Journal* was included. A few days later, *The Journal* retracted its story and apologized for the criticism, which it said had been a mistake.

In case any of these messages had been misunderstood, Madigan replicated the firing of Gunnels, this time dismissing a sixty-year-old former suburban policeman who had the misfortune of getting lost while on an errand to deliver Madigan's wife someplace. The employee, Earl Jessup, had originally been hired as a driver for my predecessor, Max McCrohon. He'd performed the same function for me for a few years. When Brumback had wiped out all company-owned vehicles for executives as a cost-saving measure, Jessup had been reassigned to oversee the editorial motor pool. When Madigan became company CEO, he wanted a driver. I offered him the one already on the payroll. But what Jessup had done satisfactorily for two editors over ten years he could not do for one corporate manager for three months. A few weeks later, I learned that on Madigan's orders Jessup was about to be dismissed by the company's new personnel director, someone he didn't even know. I intervened and handled the firing myself.

All the hot buttons pushed and all the signals sent, my handshake deal with Cook and Brumback clearly had been breached. The final stages of corporatization had come to the Colonel's newspaper in short order. The new corporate culture revealed itself most pointedly that October, when the Cubs reached the National League playoffs, causing the regular corporate free-for-all over who gets how many tickets and how good they are, including use of the company's private skybox. Even though it is not nearly the best place from which to watch a baseball game in Wrigley Field, Madigan considered a seat in the box a kind of corporate Krugerrand with which to reward loyalty and good behavior. He told me the editorial department had been allotted two of the precious box seats for the first playoff game and asked for nominations. Mine were Mike Royko and cartoonist Jeff Mac-Nelly, two of the team's most avid fans and the newspaper's most valuable assets. MacNelly was fine, Madigan said, but he shook his head and turned up his nose at the suggestion of Royko, a journalist for whom he had nothing but disdain. "Not him," he said. "He doesn't like us. He doesn't even speak to me in the elevator."

Royko would not have accepted the invitation anyway, preferring to watch the game with friends in the reserved seats, with tickets we had already made available to him. He would have been offended at the idea that he was being given a single ticket for no other reason than to "hobnob with bigwigs" — to him more of a burden than a privilege. This is the difference between the corporate and journalistic mind-sets. Madigan, the ultimate organization man and corporate ladder climber, couldn't possibly understand why anyone would not be thrilled at the prospect of an exclusive, comfortable, catered seat at Wrigley Field in a box of important people. Royko (and most of the other good journalists I know) could never understand why anyone would want to ruin a wonderful experience like a Cubs game at Wrigley Field by turning it into a corporate cocktail party in which he is expected to make conversation with strangers.

Madigan's reward is not only Royko's punishment but also an expression of a corporate classism that most journalists find repugnant. To Madigan, famous journalists like Royko, MacNelly and Ann Landers are celebrity assets no different from Geraldo Rivera and Joan Rivers, or the Cubs' multimillion-dollar ball players, whose fame and personal image are to be exploited for corporate gain. They are rolled out and exhibited like art treasures for the viewing pleasure of those to whom Tribune Company would like to sell something. While some of these employees come to enjoy being exhibited, others want to be regarded as no different from the average reporter or pressman — except in their pay envelopes, of course. Madigan's petulant attitude toward Royko is illustrative of corporate mentality. What the corporate brain trust cannot control, it does not trust and cannot be comfortable with — until it's gone. Like Royko, I fell into that category.

There was no way for someone who had fought Madigan's ascent to power as vigorously and openly as I had to remain a power at the newspaper. But having had a long and successful stint at running it, I was content to let somebody else try. So when Madigan's promotion was announced in December 1988, I offered my resignation effective immediately or whenever Madigan thought it would most benefit the newspaper. My goal, however, was not to leave Tribune Company altogether. I hoped to stay around long enough to make sure that the newspaper honored its commitment to reporter John Crewdson to publish his remarkable investigation of the AIDS virus discovery and to serve as program chairman for the 1989 convention of the American Society of Newspaper Editors, of which I was scheduled to be president in 1993. Then I hoped I might do for myself what I had tried to do for other fallen Tribune Company executives — salvage at least something from seventeen years with the same company. Whenever Madigan was ready to change editors, I told him, I would gladly move to Washington and write a regular political column, for either the *Tribune*'s editorial page or the paper's syndicate. The Tribune had not had a successful Washington columnist of its own in years, although the syndicate distributed several. I left the choice to him.

Although we met daily and never had a cross word in the ten months of my reporting to him, I was summoned to Madigan's office just before Thanksgiving in 1989 and told that he had decided to accept my offer of resignation. The columnist deal was no longer an option. All he wanted to do was negotiate severance. That was a big matter with me, too, considering the devastation Brumback had wreaked on Tribune pension and health insurance plans in his zeal to cut costs wherever possible. Nearly twenty years' service, thirteen among the highest paid executives, meant about $35,000 a year pension and no health benefits. So we had a lawyer fight over what I was due and how long I would agree not to compete against the *Tribune*. My lawyer won, mainly because Madigan wanted me out of Chicago quickly and there was enough money set aside in my long-term executive perk portfolio to pay for it. This amounted to about $1 million. It was a typical corporate divorce in that when a corporation is through with an executive, it is quite willing to part with the stockholders' money to get rid of him, even if his skills are still valuable to the company. The papers I designed and ran during my thirteen years had made Tribune nearly three quarters of a billion dollars — more money than any other newspapers they owned or operated during any comparable time in the company's history.

For the $1 million in good-bye money, Madigan also asked for a vow of silence about the terms of my leaving and anything else that had happened at Tribune Company during my employment. In other words, if you want the money accumulated in your executive compensation package, you can't take notes or write a book. Considering the corporate mentality, that demand was not surprising — even from a newspaper publisher. Of course, Tribune Company should have known me well enough to anticipate my answer, which was that they could not buy my freedom of speech with their money, much less with mine. The "gag order" clause was stricken from the severance agreement.

Out of curiosity, though, I did ask Madigan why — after nearly a year of picking my brain about newspaper operations and marketing strategy — my resignation suddenly became in order without the column option. He stammered more than Gunnels had when I'd asked him about the fur coat. I took these notes on his answer: "I ... uh ... you ... uh ... I guess ... it is because ... well ... you ... you have never shown me the proper reverence."

"Reverence"? I assumed he met *deference*. Surely he didn't mean *reverence*, which I had always reserved for the Omnipotent or, since I am Catholic, for the real Pope if ever I meet either of them. Maybe he did mean *reverence*. In any case — deference or reverence — he was certainly right about my not showing it. And I don't blame Madigan for wanting the satisfaction of choosing the day of my unemployment. Had I been he, I would have refused to enter the building until I had cleaned out my desk. Maybe that's the difference between an old journalist-proprietor type and a modern corporate manager.

In one sense, the *Tribune*'s letting me go reflected nothing more complicated than a practical decision made in the interest of harmony in the executive suite. The place simply wasn't big enough for both Madigan and myself. But in another, far less personal way, that decision reflected an important transformation in the free press — the willful destruction of the journalistic soul that had always made the press a business different from the rest. In that regard, my resignation was no different from that of Bill Kovach in Atlanta, the premature retirements of Eugene Roberts at Knight-Ridder and Kay Fanning at

The Christian Science Monitor — or even the on-time departure of Ben Bradlee from *The Washington Post*.

The one thing we all had in common was that corporate newspapering was glad to see us go. Of the five editors, I was probably the most corporatized, the least rigid, the most likely to compromise in the interest of getting all the masters served. It pains me now to have to say that. *The Sentinel* and the *Tribune* were modern and market-friendly, colorful and more likely to experiment with and stretch the definition of news. In that regard they pioneered roads that all newspapers, including the most serious and respected, are now traveling. The *Tribune*'s commitment to serious journalism remained such that it could hire the best reporters from *The Philadelphia Inquirer* and *The New York Times*. Yet the paper was market-oriented enough to earn the praise of the industry's best marketer — Al Neuharth. He wrote that the balance struck by the *Tribune* between old and new produced "the nation's best newspaper." The accolade was appreciated. But my senior colleagues Bradlee and Roberts, both of whom are my friends and mentors, would have cringed. Kovach, alongside whom I grew up in *The Tennessean* newsroom, who is so close to me that I would want him to be a pallbearer at my funeral, would have been insulted to the point of publicly renouncing the praise.

But whatever the shadings of our journalistic principles, we are vastly different from what corporate ownership wants to see in the editor's office. Even in companies where preservationists such as Jim Batten of Knight-Ridder or Peter Kann of Dow Jones are still influential, the nature of the ownership and its attendant pressures have created a new breed of publisher and news executive that is a significant mutation. The leaden creatures of journalism, once dipped in the gold of business, become a new alloy with the awareness and conscience of their old peer group but the instincts and reactions of the new. With each new acquisition and merger and the coming of each new generation of management, fewer and fewer decisions about the future of the press are being made by people who appreciate the importance of the need for an arms-length relationship with the government in the conduct of democracy.

The newspaper empires of Scripps Howard, Hearst, Tribune Company; the magazines of Henry Luce and all three network news operations answer to corporations headed by accountants, lawyers, investment bankers and deal makers. Hundreds of other small newspapers are owned by foreign interests or similar companies who view and manage them as if they were dry cleaners.

I spent a few minutes of my final day as editor of the *Chicago Tribune* with my longtime partner Charlie Brumback, defining the modern newspaper publisher. Among our conclusions were that it is no disqualification for the job never to have worked on a newspaper, set editorial policy, hired a reporter, written or executed a marketing strategy, explained the newspaper's news coverage to an angry group of readers or managed a paper to profitability. However, not "acting and talking" like a corporate executive *are* disqualifications — at least they were in my case.

"You don't talk like us," Brumback said.

Thank God. As ridiculous as that sounds, a line has

been drawn in all but the most sensitive and tradition-bound media companies that separates journalist from corporate executive, leader from professional manager and journalism from the information business. Straddling it, which was once possible, gets increasingly difficult the higher you rise in the executive ranks. If you are a journalist, rather than an accountant or an M.B.A. (which are preferred), you either cross over — to everyone's satisfaction — or you don't. Straddling won't do. In retrospect, I guess it was a line that during my years as a *Tribune* executive I could never get across in my own mind. Likewise, I clearly had not crossed it in the eyes of the Colonel's successors.

My eventual disqualification should have dawned on us all — myself included — that beautiful September Saturday in 1986 when the top executives of Tribune Company traveled to the Virginia coast to attend the commissioning of a nuclear submarine, the USS *Chicago*. Accompanied by our wives, Cook, Brumback, Madigan and I took the corporate jet to Newport News, where the submarine had been built and where Tribune Company had just bought the only newspaper in town, the *Daily Press*. It was a typical corporate command-performance social event, in which the goal was to introduce the company in a new market. To make the event more compelling, the company that had manufactured the submarine was Newport News's most important employer, and its CEO was an old school chum of Cook's. Along with the late Harold Washington, then mayor of Chicago, and actor Charlton Heston, who delivered the dedication speech, the Tribune contingent was treated by the navy as VIPs.

After the ceremony, the entire crowd of more than a thousand was invited to tour the submarine, which could be boarded by only six or eight people at a time crossing a narrow walkway suspended above a canal. Naturally, Cook, the military hardware aficionado, wanted to tour the ship. But the schedule for the Tribune VIPs, prepared by our marketing department, called for us to visit our newly acquired newspaper property. The size of the crowd made it likely that the tour would go on for hours, so the navy suggested we visit the newspaper and return, which we did in three long, black limousines.

Upon our return a couple of hours later, hundreds of Newport News residents were still gathered, patiently waiting to be escorted across the catwalk. It was plain to me that the new owners of the town's only newspaper were about to create an unfortunate image — that of exiting chauffeur-driven limousines and being escorted to the front of a line of people who had been waiting their turn all afternoon. Quietly I suggested to Brumback and our marketing people that under the circumstances we might want to go to the end of the line. No one in the party would hear of it. My reasoning had no standing in the world of the corporate executive. They looked at me as if I were a kook.

Thus it was that my wife and I stood at the rear of the crowd and watched the three highest-ranking Tribune Company executives — and then a second contingent of lower rank — get in front of their newspaper's readers. Insignificant over the long haul, that incident was nonetheless indicative of the kind of display of power and privilege that an institution sensitive to the public interest ought best avoid. With corporatization has come an addiction to position and special privilege as entitlements. This is alien to the nature of newspapers. The press is not supposed to break in the front of the line; it is supposed to tell everyone who does.

8

Chicago to New York: Drop Dead

To the bloated, labor-intensive world of old-time newspapering, like that which still existed at the *Chicago Tribune* and the New York *Daily News* in the 1980s, the mandate of the new obligation to Wall Street meant having to radically restructure the traditional owner-employee partnership. Today, conflict between the financial goals of modern newspaper management and the employee legacies of the paternalistic past is routine.

In 1985, three of the *Chicago Tribune*'s thirteen unions surprised us with a strike. Ironically, it turned out to be a gift to the *Tribune* and Charlie Brumback's career from the self-centered leaders of the typographical union, whose members were in the midst of a referendum on whether to join the Teamsters. The drivers' union, a Teamsters local, had a no-strike clause with the *Tribune*, so the printers' leadership knew that the drivers would cross the picket line. They did, and the printers' strike was broken (although, eight years later, the printers are technically still on strike.) For rank-and-file workers, Brumback would become, as one of their leaders termed him, the Saddam Hussein of American journalism.

During the strike, a faulty air-conditioning connection forced the company to dig a crater forty feet deep near where pickets were marching on lower Michigan Avenue. Invariably, some pedestrian around the imposing and historic Tribune Tower would ask the reason for such a huge hole. "Charlie Brumback dropped a quarter," a picket would reply. Depiction of management as a skinflint is common in labor disputes, but, in Brumback's case, it was an uncommonly good fit.

For the *Tribune*, the savings resulting from the 250 jobs lost by the union in the process helped Brumback achieve in five years the double-digit profitability he had only hoped would come in ten. But the outcome was also a victory of sorts for the union leaders, who saw the Teamsters' referendum defeated and their own leadership preserved. It was a simple case of self-preservation on the part of elected union leaders, an attitude that has been as responsible as mechanization for the decline of organized labor. Perhaps even more important, it gave Brumback a false sense of confidence in dealing with unions and the reputation of an ogre in the eyes of the old-world New York employees at the *Daily News*, who had already seen enough of Chicago management.

Brumback is a man of few words, some of which are decidedly harsh. Before the 1985 strike at the *Tribune*, he told employees doing page pasteup that they were engaged in "idiot work." Early in the New York *Daily News* strike in 1990, he would call the *News* a "newspaper for immigrants." When his words failed — as they sometimes obviously did — he was not opposed to taking action. Once when a teenage son repeatedly ignored his entreaties to lower his stereo, Brumback walked into the room, lifted the stereo up and nonchalantly dropped it to the floor, smashing it. "There," he said, "now it is turned down." It was that volatile combination of words and action that eventually earned Brumback extraordinary notoriety within labor circles as a ruthless union buster who wouldn't balk at sending armed guards and snarling security dogs into newspaper halls and back shops, or recruit the homeless as scab circulation workers.

Brumback has been accused of deliberately provoking the Chicago strike. The charge is false. The international union provoked it. When it happened, no one was more surprised than Brumback. "Goddamn," he said, when I telephoned him at home. "I didn't think they'd do it." He was surprised that night because the labor relations expert he had hired to deal with the unions, a tough cookie from Lee Newspapers named George Veon, was not expecting a strike either.

Veon had whipped the unions at Lee's newspaper in Madison, Wisconsin, and had endeared himself to Brumback with personnel policies such as an order asking employees to identify and label all personal telephone calls and to discuss with him "any call over five minutes' duration." It was only after some of Veon's tactics earned the *Tribune* unfair labor practice citations that Brumback discovered and employed the architect of the eventual disaster at the *Daily News*, Nashville attorney Robert Ballow, an affable but hard-nosed former circulation director.

Unfair labor practices or not, both Brumback and Veon were feted as heroes within Tribune Company. No single event was more important in Brumback's subsequent elevation from CEO to chairman. Careers aren't made in media companies today on tactfulness in employee relations. They rise on the heat of blazing balance sheets and scorched-earth cost cutting.

Brumback had won the CEO's job with a string of thirteen straight record profit years at his properties, many of them built by stripping the costly remnants of the old paternalistic culture from every crack and crevice of a workplace replete with liberal employee benefits programs, including profit sharing, heavily subsidized medical insurance and redundant, wasteful employment policies. Part of my job was to sell the changes to the most skeptical of employees, the journalists. It has always been the mission of editors to rally happy troops to the publisher's cause. But it was far easier to rally them behind a call for the rise of the proletariat or throwing the bums out of City Hall. That's what reporters used to sign on for — that and the fun of having the leader himself show up in the pressroom calling you by your first name and throwing around white envelopes containing ten-spots. It is something else again when the Holy Grail is the constant improvement of return to shareholders and the leader tromps around in hobnail boots, brandishing disdain like a truncheon and dropping it on the toes of employees to whom he is trying to sell fewer jobs and less pay.

For five years after Tribune Company went public in 1983, the value of its shares appreciated 23 percent a year, triple the average of the rest of the industry. During the same period, profits rose at a 23 percent clip as well, while revenues increased only 9 percent. The company consistently showed a return on equity in the range of 17 to 18 percent, equal to that of the New York Times Company and Times Mirror Company.

But as profits and executive salaries soared, the unavoidable corollary was the perception among employees that the company had betrayed them. Indeed, general disregard for the pride and morale of employees became the hallmark of our worker relations. Our company and others in the press signed on to one of the most self-destructive misconceptions ever adopted by American business — that employees can somehow be motivated to do good work by threats of unemployment, and that they can be misled about why their salaries and benefits are shrinking.

Brumback's kick-'em-in-the-groin policies soon became a model for emulation and part of a new Tribune Company culture. For example, John Madigan sought to out-Brumback Brumback at almost every turn. In early 1989, Madigan railed at a staff meeting about the high quality and high cost of meals laid on for *Tribune* veterans at their annual dinners during Brumback's tenure, costs which were sometimes as much as fifteen to twenty dollars per person. He drew pained expressions all around the table, but no rebukes, when he declared, "These kinds of people aren't used to this kind of quality. They've never been to country clubs or first-class restaurants. Why should we have to provide something like that?"

Nowhere was this attitude more evident or costly than at the New York *Daily News*. Overshadowing all of our success in Orlando and Chicago, both in the Colonel's old office on the twenty-fourth floor of Tribune Tower and in the trading pits of Wall Street, was the company's one great albatross — *Daily News* labor costs. Because of its visibility to stock analysts in the capital of world business, the *News* became for Tribune Company as compelling a force as Time Warner's $11 billion debt or Al Neuharth's burning ambition. Nobody could claim success until the *Daily News* was fixed. And to those high in Tribune Tower, it seemed the *News* had been broken forever.

One February morning in 1979, the then CEO of Tribune Company, Stan Cook, square jawed and silver haired, bounced onto a TWA jet at New York's La Guardia Airport, bound for San Francisco and a visit with his daughter, who was attending Stanford University. A one-time air force navigator, the effervescent Cook loved to fly, and he was effervescing — even more than usual. But when he saw who else was traveling that day, he instantly lost his fizz.

There in the seat beside him sat Joseph Barletta, a young labor lawyer Cook had dispatched from Chicago two years earlier on the intrepid mission of improving the profitability of the *Daily News*. Though Barletta was then the paper's general manager, he might as well have been a hijacker. And in a sense he was.

Barletta was not the sort of Tribune Company executive Cook preferred — not tall, striking in appearance or likely to engage in frothy small talk. He was a tough guy, short, thick, swarthy and bold enough to bring up bad news, which he planned to do. In fact, he had plotted to intercept Cook, going to the length of arranging for the seat next to him. He knew from experience that the only way to get Cook's attention to trouble was to ambush him with it. For the next two and a half hours, Barletta pummeled Cook with a carefully planned presentation, including cost analyses, revenue projections and workplace efficiency studies. They all added up to a simple conclusion: the *Daily News*, then the nation's largest-circulation newspaper, with a $300 million revenue base, was actually insolvent and living on borrowed time. Costs were rising faster than revenue, and by 1981, Barletta told Cook, the *Daily News* would begin to drown in red ink.

Barletta's presentation, a summary of what had happened all over the newspaper industry in the 1960s and 1970s, suggested that the *News*'s lower-middle-class readers had not only become less desirable to advertisers but were moving to the suburbs, where they were harder to reach. But the biggest problem was that the newspaper itself, like those elsewhere, was technologically retarded, bloated with labor costs and dependent on perpetual advertising and circulation price increases for new revenue.

Cook, now five years into his leadership of Tribune Company, didn't like what he heard. Barletta's analysis did not bode well for plans to take the company public, a step most of Tribune's competitors had already taken. But Barletta persisted.

"Well, what do you want me to do about it?" he remembers Cook snapping at him somewhere over the Rockies. The CEO then turned his attention to the inflight cowboy movie. Later he would tell the tale of Barletta's airborne entrapment with great indignation to friends in Chicago and from that point on grimace at the mere mention of his name.

Cook did not heed Barletta's warning. Indeed, over the next decade, although everyone seemed to agree that the venerable *Daily News* was dying a slow death, no one knew how to save it. Ten years later, when Cook reluctantly relinquished the chief executive's job of the giant media conglomerate, he was no closer to finding a satisfactory answer to the problem.

At Tribune Company, the first commandment of Chicago politics — "Don't make no waves, don't back no losers" — was as much an axiom of the corporate boardroom as of the ward headquarters back room. The *Daily News* had been a "loser" by newspaper earnings standards, smearing the parent company's bottom line with red ink for the last ten years.

The *Daily News* was a truly great and unique newspaper, which at midcentury had boasted 2.4 million circulation and 4.0 million readers daily. As late as the middle of the 1980s, it was still capable of producing $500 million in annual revenue, and it was selling a million copies a day when its nine unions went on strike in the fall of 1990. But the combination of its huge circulation and its flabby labor force made the *News* a most dirty spot on an otherwise gleaming ship and a natural target for anybody concerned about the value of Tribune stock. Labor costs at the *News*, for example, constituted 47 percent of revenues, compared with about 25 percent at the company's more profitable newspapers in Chicago, Orlando and Fort Lauderdale, making acceptable profit levels impossible. Any other of the big media companies would have been just as sorry as Tribune was to own the *News*. Tribune Company ridding itself of the New York millstone was in principle no different than Times Mirror Company dumping the Dallas *Times Herald* and *The Denver Post*, Gannett bailing out of Little Rock, or *The New York Times* selling its little daily in Harlan County, Kentucky.

The true significance of this to Tribune Company — and an important clue to understanding the company's management tactics — was signaled at the beginning of 1990, when an analyst for a New York investment firm, Furman Selz Mager Dietz and Birney, concluded that Tribune Company would be better off without the *Daily News*. If Tribune could lower the cost of programming its television stations — which was a certainty sometime within the next few years — and either turn the *News* into an average newspaper earner or shed it, the report said, the company's stock would have a private market value of perhaps $100, two and half times what it was selling for at the time. The potential of more than doubling the company's $3.3 billion value made the millions ultimately risked by taking a strike at the *News* strike a paltry wager.

That the company under Brumback's leadership appeared willing to face up to this "critical challenge" was billed as a bold and encouraging enough sign to make it a good long-term investment. Indeed, despite the recession and its negative impact on media company stocks, Tribune stock rose 8 percent on January 15, 1991, the day it was announced that the strike might result in the newspaper closing. Between the day the strike began and the day the paper was eventually sold, price per share increased by more than 20 percent, which dwarfs the estimated $130 to $150 million the company suffered in strike losses.

Publicly, in what is both the best and the worst of tabloid traditions, Tribune Company claimed that the *News* was strangled by a serial killer — the same crime-infested New York unionism which had murdered a half dozen other papers in the city in the last quarter of a century. Specifically, it blamed organized crime influence in the Newspaper and Mail Deliverers Union of New York for destroying first the newspaper's distribution system and eventually its advertising support.

"I came here prepared to fight organized labor," declared the company's combative labor negotiator, Robert Ballow. "And I ended up fighting organized crime." For their part, the unions claimed that for years Tribune Company had tried to starve the newspaper to death, finally sending in its own assassin in the slow-drawling, quick-witted Ballow with a contract to carry out a "hit" on the *Daily News* unions.

"Tribune Company sent him here to kill the unions," said Theodore Kheel, a union adviser and veteran New York labor mediator. "And if they killed the *News* instead, that was all right, too. The Tribune Company has wanted to get out of the newspaper business in New York since 1982, and if they could not break the unions, they would close the *News* or sell it. It was a no-lose proposition for the company from the beginning."

Tribune Company relished its image as a particularly austere and feudal proprietor. Late in the summer of 1990, with a strike certain, the company finally sent Robert Holzkamp to New York, ostensibly to work the same revenue miracles he had pulled off in Orlando, Fort Lauderdale and Chicago. By January, with no advertisers left to cultivate, Holzkamp, an ever-loyal and supremely decent man, was still demonstrating the company's extraordinary piety by trying to impose the Tribune work culture on an unhappy and demoralized sales staff, many of whom were guilt-stricken for having crossed picket lines. He did not hesitate to implement his mocked and detested "tidy office" policy of no paper left on desktops and no unauthorized decorations beyond a single family photograph. It was, the New Yorkers noted, pathetically akin to Custer disciplining an unkempt soldier as the Indians charged.

Against such a backdrop, throughout more than a year of negotiations with *News* unions whose contracts had expired, Tribune refused to budge an inch. Until the final days, when federal mediator William J. Usery finally forced it to specify job and wage levels it considered acceptable, the company's bargaining position was simply that it had the right to set those levels. The point was not lost on labor expert Kheel, who interpreted the company's insistence on this "management rights clause" as an effort "to get the unions to ratify their own irrelevancy."

When pressed for specific union concessions acceptable in return for not closing or selling the *News*, Tribune talked in terms of a 50 percent reduction in the union work force of 2,300 and 40 percent pay cuts for those who remained — demands considered outrageous by union leaders.

Widely condemned by journalists, politicians and newspaper lovers everywhere, Tribune Company's tactics seemed to mystify smart and influential people all over New York, including the mayor of the city, the governor of the state and the spiritual leader of the newspaper's many Catholic readers, John Cardinal O'Connor. To them, the company fit snugly into the second category of Liebling's definition of newspaper owners — the cruel and starving masters.

Yet on Wall Street, Tribune Company was not only clearly understood but publicly applauded. "More than many other media companies, they really have the shareholder in mind," an analyst for Goldman, Sachs told *The New York Times* a month into the strike. "They are simply more efficient than other media companies." Such praise from such a source would have insulted the press-lord journalist-proprietors of yesterday, who would have grumbled, "What the hell do they know about the newspaper business?" But to the new owner-managers of the modern American press establishment, an accolade from Wall Street is a tribute of the highest order. In fact, it is virtually the only one that matters.

Blaming the company, the unions or both equally in this case is easy because the *Daily News* was clearly victimized. But no one person, company or union killed the newspaper. It was a victim in the same sense that its mother institution — the free press itself — has become a victim. They are casualties of change in the nature of press ownership and the role newspapers play in the lives of Americans. Swirling in the throes of the lightning-fast technological revolution and scrambling madly for the profits demanded by Wall Street, the newspapers' subtle strength and the secrets of their durability were first ignored and finally lost.

To understand how the *Daily News* came to flounder in such confused and clumsy hands is to understand the ending of a long and complicated chapter in the life of one of the country's most important but least understood businesses. The story of the *News* is in one sense the familiar saga of incompetence, ambition and greed so often ascribed to each other by labor and management during a strike in any business, ailing or healthy. But in a broader, more important sense, what happened to the *News* may well have been the final frame in an epic, a snapshot capturing the slow death of a great American institution — a sort of obituary for *Citizen Kane* and the traditional free press of which he was such a villainous caricature.

Being owned by Tribune Company all its life was for the *Daily News* like being born into a family with a history of mental illness. For forty years, under Patterson and then the family trust, the *News* lived as a distant cousin who had changed the spelling of his name and boycotted family reunions. But in 1975, when the trust expired, the Captain's *News* fell into the hands of the Colonel's men, largely thanks to the efforts of longtime company attorney Don Reuben, who engineered a revamp of the company board which left Patterson's heirs unhappy minority stockholders.

Over the next five years, Tribune Company would slowly try to take control of the *News*, which would never be the same again. By the end of the 1970s, the changes attendant to the prospect of Tribune Company selling its stock to the public, with effective control remaining in the hands of a new management-run trust, had ignited a bitter Chicago–New York conflict. This struggle took the simple form of a concerned management trying to save a business from dying by ridding it of waste and redundancies — in the case of the *News*, the clogged production and circulation departments. But the real significance lay elsewhere and is emblematic of the experience all over the industry during the last twenty years. Whether the newspaper business survived or not, modern management seems to have been unable to take over the press without eliminating that long-standing spiritual dependency between an institution important to democracy and the human beings who had made it so.

At many newspapers, employees came to realize that their only choice was between change and extinction. In newsroom after newsroom, journalists have had to accept the reality that the management's commitment to quality, community and tradition stops wherever the buck does. So have the union craftsmen, whose jobs had been passed down within families for generations and who had come to believe that the blood in their veins was as blue with the ink of the free press as that of any reporter, editor or publisher.

Like the old newspaper owners, newspaper workers

viewed themselves as something special. Today they have come slowly and painfully to the realization that they are not. But none came later or more reluctantly than the employees at the New York *Daily News*. As a group they will go down as a sort of Thelma and Louise of journalism, more willing to plunge off the cliff to certain death than to accept the inevitability of an imprisoned existence.

For a dozen years the *News* employees had taken every bomb and missile Chicago lobbed at them. When Barletta was sent out in 1977, his was as much a reconnaissance and intelligence mission as anything else. And like a lot of forward observers sent into enemy territory, he would become a casualty, the first of a long list of Tribune Company executives whose careers would disappear into what would become known back in Chicago as "the black hole on Forty-second Street." For over a decade, the company dropped into it publishers, editors, production managers and financial officers as if it were chumming sharks.

After the avalanche of bad news from Barletta, Cook had fired the *News*'s publisher, Tex James. Firing James was exactly what Barletta wanted him to do. But the firing came only because Robert M. Hunt, then Cook's best friend and most influential adviser, had decided after hearing Barletta's analysis that he wanted James's job. Hunt, who was president of the *Tribune* at the time, had grown impatient in Chicago because Cook had no plans of giving up the title or power of publisher until forced to by age and company bylaws.

Hunt, raised in the *Tribune*, where upscale advertising lineage poured in over the transom and home delivery subscriptions in the richest suburbs kept it coming, never had a chance. His approach to marketing the *News* was to create a disaster called "Tonight," an upscale afternoon edition which peaked in circulation the first day and then went steadily downhill. It was hardly any wonder. At one point, "Tonight" was running house ads urging its readers to read *The New York Times*, rather than the *Daily News*, in the morning.

The millions of dollars "Tonight" lost before folding not only nearly wrecked the franchise but all but wrecked the Cook-Hunt friendship. With the *News* expected to lose $50 million in 1982, Cook asked Hunt to try to wring concessions from the paper's unions to reduce the deficit. While Hunt was hard at the task, the pressure from investment bankers over how red ink would affect the company going public overwhelmed Cook. The effort to sell the *News* out from under his best friend turned into a second debacle for Cook when he learned that between $80 and $160 million in underfunded employee benefits and other liabilities made the *News* impossible to give away and too expensive to close. Finally, in an embarrassing reversal, Cook came to New York, declared the *Daily News* a great newspaper and vowed the company would turn it around.

At a meeting with the embattled Hunt and other executives on the eighth floor of the *News* in the spring of 1982, Cook, who specialized in awkward pep-rally exhortations, actually took off his suit jacket and rolled up his shirtsleeves to demonstrate what would have to be done to save the *News*. Then he asked for questions.

An irritated Jim Wieghart, then the *Daily News* executive editor, had one. "When Bob Hunt made a mistake with 'Tonight' he admitted his mistake and publicly apologized for it. Are you willing to admit your mistake and apologize for trying to sell the *Daily News?*" With the room quiet as a stone, Cook looked down at the conference table and turned away from Wieghart the way he had from Barletta. "Are there any other questions?" he asked solemnly.

The discomfort of the moment would characterize the relationship between the *News* and Tribune Company for the rest of the decade. Two years later, after Hunt had gotten $40 million in union givebacks to enable the *News* to show a $30 million profit for 1984, Cook sent Hunt back to the unions for more. But he had already used up his chits and did not want to face them again. Instead, Hunt came to accept what his friend Barletta had told him when he tried to talk him out of coming to the *News* — that the situation there might well be hopeless. Hunt telephoned Cook and quit as *News* publisher in a conversation so agonizing that, following it, Cook told confidants he thought Hunt needed psychiatric counseling. Virtually the entire team of *News* executives assembled by Hunt ultimately went down with him, a frequent occurrence when a Tribune property endured an embarrassment or changed CEOs. They included Wieghart, who had continued to be undiplomatically public in his criticism of Cook's attempts to sell the *News.* In Hunt and Wieghart, Tribune had what is a necessary accompaniment for every management failure in a publicly held company: a scapegoat carcass to hand the stock analysts on Wall Street.

When Jim Hoge succeeded Robert Hunt in 1984, he took over a newspaper that was holding its breath. The only man in Chicago with a jaw as square as Cook's, and still something of a wunderkind at forty-eight, Hoge had quit as publisher of the *Chicago Sun-Times* when it was purchased by Rupert Murdoch. Skepticism about Hoge's management skills (he had lost the *Sun-Times–Tribune* battle and had presided over the closing of the Chicago *Daily News*) was overcome by Cook's long-standing admiration of his range of social acquaintances and his ability to keep significant advertising in the *Sun-Times* even in its decline.

Despite his extensive social network, Hoge has never been a bundle of warm fuzzies. Most of his friends agree with his first editor at the *News*, Gil Spencer, who said it was possible only to "know Hoge vaguely." But those who admired him believed the opportunity at the *News* was more a marriage of convenience than a natural attraction. "He is basically an upscale, top-of-the-market editor who would be more comfortable doing *The Times* or the *Tribune*," said Spencer, adding that "it is hard for Hoge to really give himself to the *News* because he doesn't really give himself to anybody."

At the same time, there was a saying in former Chicago Mayor Richard Daley's patronage machine that "we don't want nobody that nobody sent." In this case, it applied to the *News* employees. They didn't want nobody that Chicago sent. To many of them, patrician Hoge, who enjoyed prominence among the city's richest, most famous and most beautiful people, was an unusual choice to save the newspaper of the poor and ordinary.

"Whether Hoge was right for the *News* is not as important as whether the unions perceived him to be right," said Joe Kovach, the newspaper's news editor (now retired) and a much respected bastion of knowledge and stability in its newsroom for a quarter of a century. "And to the unions, Hoge was, well, a pussy. They thought he was more interested in his image among the important people. And they didn't believe he was tough enough to earn their respect."

Hoge's image was of some concern back in Chicago as well. Conversation in the executive suite sometimes reflected the worry that if Hoge were smart and lucky enough to save the *News*, he might be smart and lucky enough to ingratiate himself with the Tribune Company board of directors and succeed Cook as CEO. Madigan's assistants delighted in telling the story that one of them had been dispatched to New York to talk with Hoge, but that Hoge had insisted on holding the conversation while on a walk to lunch through the city. The conversation had been hampered, the assistant complained to Madigan, because Hoge had walked on the inside with his head turned so he could see his reflection in the store windows.

Hoge's youthful appearance and mannequin profile were often the subject of twenty-fourth-floor chatter, usually by ladder climbers trying to draw out Cook's feelings toward him. All of them knew that Cook, who put a lot of stock in personal appearance, had once profusely thanked a business magazine interviewer who had remarked that he thought Cook and Hoge shared a physical resemblance. The reporter had wondered to the amusement of others present whether the resemblance had been a consideration in Hoge's hiring. But Hoge's detractors usually turned the conversation to his habit of heavy cigarette smoking, which Cook abhorred, and the future of "things in New York," which invariably brought a frown to his face. That Hoge could ever nestle snugly into such an uncomfortable bosom was always ruled out by company insiders.

The trivial nature of Tower concern about New York, internal company rivalries and a lot of other Tribune Company problems ended abruptly when Cook finally got around to giving up some of his power to Brumback at the end of 1988, naming him chief operating officer. By then the New York frown had frozen solid on the face of the company, for reasons ranging from the chilly reception of Wall Street to continuing labor problems and cloudy profit prospects. Brumback acknowledged that "fixing New York one way or another" was both his mandate and his challenge.

Ultimately, even Hoge's critics had to compliment his efforts. Under Hoge and Spencer, the *Daily News* did better than it had in years. For a while it even made a little money. In 1987, Hoge won another $30 million in union concessions, allowing the paper to break even and computerize the business reporting operations. Searching for a middle ground between the *News*'s unions and the Chicago management became for Hoge a consuming passion, and, toward the end, the cause of a bitter and painful disappointment.

Hoge's relationship with Tribune Company, the subject of much conjecture, was hardly mysterious to anyone who had spent much time around both parties. However aloof and introverted Hoge might appear, he was an open book of warm fuzzies compared with the somber, disciplined and inscrutable nature of Tribune Tower. As long as Cook was CEO, Hoge's plans to improve production facilities and editorial quality at the *News* were met mainly with slow corporate handwringing over union intransigence. Only when Brumback took over at the beginning of 1989 did Hoge get the mandate to join the battle seriously. Brumback's first act was to dispatch Roy Eugene Bell, his best manager, operations expert and alter ego, to help Hoge. His second was to make sure Hoge knew and appreciated Nashville attorney Ballow, who had been fighting Brumback's court battles stemming from the 1985 *Tribune* strike. The new CEO's orders to all three men were the same: "Fix it, sell it or shut it down." The directive was never altered or revised.

Working for Brumback instead of Cook was "the difference between daylight and dark," Hoge told a friend early in 1989. "This guy makes a decision."

The strike strategy, however, was clearly the preserve of the bare-knuckled Ballow. For years, Ballow had been the scourge of the minor leagues. With the persistence of a used car salesman and the patience of a nun, he had beat up on newspaper unions in places such as Seattle and Kansas City, impressing corporate honchos like Cap Cities/ABC's Thomas Murphy in the process. At seminars all over the company, he had offered to bet his reputation and any publisher's money that his hard-nosed tactics would work in the big arenas, too. In New York, his tactic was to block the door to agreement, albeit good-naturedly, until everybody got very tired and frustrated.

Not until his opponents had reached the point of exhaustion and were quarreling among themselves would he open a small hole, through which only a select number could return — at a crawl.

From the fall of 1989, when he stepped forward as the *News* negotiator, until the fruitless final stage of mediation in late February 1990, Ballow made no attempt to negotiate contract specifics. Only when Usery, the mediator, succeeded in pushing Hoge and Brumback into the negotiations did the company back off its bargaining strategy of insisting first and foremost on a tough management rights clause that gave it the right to decide such things as job manning and work rules up front.

Union leaders regarded the clause as a concession of their own irrelevance, a message to workers that the unions had surrendered the collective bargaining process and the framework of the traditional work contract. It was a message of foreboding they knew would reverberate beyond the *News* to the pressrooms and mail rooms of *The New York Times* and the *New York Post* and into unions halls and boardrooms all over a city in which union influence still exceeds all other. "A deal like that would have made Mr. Brumback an industry hero all over the country, which is apparently what he wanted," says the union adviser Theodore Kheel. "And it would have finished the unions in New York."

If that was Brumback's intention — as Kheel believed — to insist on a deal so onerous that the unions could not possibly accept it, he picked in Ballow the right man for the job. Insisting on the management rights clause was routine business for a good company labor relations lawyer, Ballow said, and it would have worked, too, if he and the rest of the *News* management had not miscalculated both the ability of the unions to physically intimidate the newsstand vendors and their political clout to get away with it. Ballow said he didn't understand that until a few days into the New York strike, when it became apparent that there was more to the *Daily News* distribution system than met the eye.

His first hint came from a nineteen-year-old black man from Harlem who came into the *News* and complained that he had not been delivered his 20,000 newspapers. A check turned up no record of his being a distribution agent, but hungry for distributors, the *News* offered to sell him 20,000 papers for the standard rate of twenty-eight cents apiece. "But I only pay twenty cents," he insisted. The picture emerging was of an underhanded scheme in which *News* employees were selling the man the papers from the so-called odds room, one of hundreds of scams and side businesses being conducted as part of the paper's distribution system.

Many newsstand dealers ultimately came to understand the meaning of sympathy for the rights and needs of organized labor. And those slow to understand often went home at night with their noses in a different spot on their faces from where they had been in the morning. A month into the strike, when the rest of the city had begun to ignore the intimidation tactics as a factor, Ballow knew the options had been reduced to two — sell or close. "There was something else at work here that was a lot stronger than unionism," acknowledged Ballow. "And everybody knew what it was."

What everybody knows now is that a lot of drivers at the *News* were into more than the newspaper-selling business; that daily access to the street carries with it the opportunity for all kinds of other activity, from engaging in petty thievery to collecting street taxes for the crime syndicate. And what everybody knows — too late — is that when this battle got into the trenches, the streets of New York, the unions employed unadulterated, white-knuckle street tactics.

Not only did the unions take out the newsstands and thereby whip the *News* management economically, but they won the public relations battle as well. Union political power pushed Mayor David Dinkins, Governor Mario Cuomo and John Cardinal O'Connor out into the streets behind the union boycott, easily overriding allegations of mob influence. In the end, the Colonel's men were no match for the Captain's crew, unable even to win a popularity contest against Mafia godfathers — much less the mayor and the cardinal.

While Ballow can be forgiven his naïveté, the Chicagoans should have known better. In Chicago, one man's "mob" is simply another man's organization. The Colonel's *Tribune* did not win the newspaper wars of Chicago by waging them on the street with Sunday-school teachers. More than one opposition circulation truck — and driver — have been dumped into the Chicago River over the years. A fertile field for any McCormick biographer would be to explore the relationship between the old publisher and Al Capone, the city's street power of his time.

Moreover, the Tribune men should have known what

Chicago's professional football and baseball teams learned long ago, that winning in New York is never easy or final. Someone once wrote about the Yankee fans in the Bronx — after they finally lost a World Series to the Dodgers in Brooklyn — "They still have a shot at blowing up the buses." And that perverse sense of victory at any cost seemed to be what *News* crime reporter and guild strike leader Jerry Capeci was expressing when Hoge emerged from a Tribune board meeting on January 15, 1991, and announced that the paper would close if it were not sold. "We've won the strike against the *Daily News*," Capeci crowed. "We've already destroyed the *Daily News*. The announcement by Hoge is proof of it."

Like Capeci, the *News*'s cramped, decrepit and filthy production plant in Brooklyn stands as monument to the time warp which marked New York newspapering (except for *Newsday* of Long Island, a Times Mirror Company property) during the last half century. In the *News* labor-management wars, the Brooklyn plant took on the significance of a killing field. At one point during the union negotiations, Ballow actually offered to give it to the drivers' union as part of a deal. Later, when Usery convened top management and union leaders in a single meeting, Hoge declared the plant "worthless" — which driver boss Michael Alvino said explained "why Ballow was willing to give it to me."

While the rest of American newspapering had proceeded relatively quickly and calmly to clean, offset, vivid color printing, relics like the Brooklyn plant and their union-mandated working conditions kept New York's newspaper world black and white on good days, and a dirty, fuzzy gray on others. They also kept employer-employee relations in another era.

Early in his tenure at the *News*, when Hoge visited the Brooklyn plant, he was told by workers there that he was the first publisher they had seen since Patterson himself, who died in 1946. "Where are the white envelopes?" they asked. Hoge did not know what they were talking about. When Patterson had visited in the old days — which he did frequently — he'd brought envelopes full of cash, in denominations from one to a hundred dollars and passed them out at random.

Such paternalism fostered the employee loyalty that once made newspapers both great businesses and great places to work. But it also produced a lot of employees like the *Daily News*'s Joe Hopper. The major obstacle between the *News* and the drivers' union of which Hopper was a member was the wage and working arrangements granted over the years, which allowed the core of senior drivers, including some important to the union leadership, to earn $20,000 to $30,000 above their $60,000 salaries, in either unworked overtime or special payoffs.

Each morning after the papers were printed and loaded for delivery, Hopper appeared in the circulation offices with a list of *News* circulation trucks. Each day the list was the same, nothing but a photocopy of a list of circulation equipment the *News* already knew it had. For this task alone Hopper was paid $85,000 a year. According to Ballow, the deal was traced back to a bargaining trade-off years earlier with one of Alvino's predecessors. The discovery of the Joe Hopper case sent the jovial, chipmunk-cheeked Ballow into negotiator's ecstasy. He promptly rolled it into his standard diatribe and dumped it on the bargaining table like a bundle of dirty laundry.

"We will no longer pay anyone for work that is not done," he declared during a mediating session. "We can't have people who make $85,000 a year for doing nothing." It caught the equally good-natured Alvino by surprise. "Name me one member of my union that gets paid $85,000 for doing nothing," he retorted.

"Joe Hopper," said Ballow.

"Name another one," said Alvino, reducing both sides of the table to howling laughter.

It was not funny in Chicago. Hopper was promptly dropped from the regular payroll to the satisfaction of an indignant Tribune Company management, only to surface a day or so later on another one. Instead of being off the rolls, Hopper had managed to find a place on "The Medill Plan," a liberal salary benefit payroll for sick and disabled workers named after the newspaper's founder. Such unbridled union influence, and the nakedness of the exploitation, was viewed at once as an outrage by management and as an entitlement by the core union membership. But it was so ingrained that Ballow, a Southern Baptist, likened his efforts to get the union to give up such "outrages" to his church's missionary efforts in Spain: "Every year we send people to Spain, where everybody is Catholic, to try to talk them out of being Catholic. They look at us like we are crazy. That's the way I felt in New York talking to the unions, like I was trying to talk Catholics out of being Catholic."

In bargaining sessions and in their public pronouncements, the union bosses contended they were only asking for what their members were entitled to. But privately, in conversations with Ballow and others, they were more candid in the assessment of their problems. "I may be president of this union," Alvino told Ballow more than once, "but when I tell people they are going to get less pay next year than this year, I ain't got nobody behind me."

In the end, the essence of the strike boiled down to an agreement with the drivers, and the drivers' intransigence boiled down to the sentiment expressed in a widely rumored but understandably unverifiable off-the-record conversation between Ballow and Alvino. During a recess in the bargaining, the union leader was reported to have put his arm around Ballow's shoulder and said, "Bobby, our problem is that we can't get a legitimate deal for my guys as good as the illegitimate deal my guys already got."

Illegitimate or not, the deals made in the interest of publishing and of a loyal, enthusiastic work force were the key to the success of the old press barons and at the same time a curse to those who followed them because they bound the newspapers to timeworn, labor-intensive methods of production. And they imbued the owner-worker relationship with all the love-hate qualities of a family, which is why newspaper strikes are like divorce, with all the attendant resentment, bitterness, and sense of betrayal.

What Tribune Company unsuccessfully tried to overcome in New York was the last sturdy remnant of what had once been the fabric of the business — a willingness by the owners of the press to share an inordinate amount of their wealth and control with employees in exchange for uncommon loyalty and missionary zeal in the pursuit of uninterrupted publishing.

The extent to which the *Daily News* situation has been misunderstood and erroneously reported can be measured by the extent to which the company has been accused of miscalculating the depth of union sentiment in New York and of how far it extended into the soul of the *News*. There could have been no mistaking it. Patterson had been among the first publishers to adopt the five-day workweek and the first to recognize the New York Newspaper Guild, actually having invited it to organize the *News*. Such goodwill toward unionism was not a family trait, but pragmatism was.

Although Colonel McCormick's *Tribune* was dependent on blue blood, not blue collars, he nonetheless valued the owner-employee relationship to the point that the *Tribune*'s labor contracts set the standard for Chicago, before and after McCormick's death. Traditionally, Tribune Company's labor relations ranged from cave-in to rollover, with the cost of labor settlements hinging on how well Reuben, its political powerhouse lawyer, got along with an individual union leader. To the leading papers in a competitive market, the cost of a settlement was never as important as the swiftness and decorum with which it was reached. To the old press barons, it was always better to keep the presses running and keep mining the gold, even if you took home a lesser share of it.

New York newspapering, for all its strikes and bluster, was no exception. Through the years union appeasement proved an efficient if not intentional way to choke the life out of competitors. The *News* and *The New York Times*, both rich in readers and advertisers and not true competitors with each other, could flout economics and prosper anyway. (*The Times* still does, hiding labor excesses similar to those of the *News* under a billion dollars in annual advertising and circulation revenue.) Time and again over the years, while the rest of the industry reduced production work forces as they installed machines, *The Times* and the *News* installed their machines while agreeing to union contracts on wage, benefit and work rules that only strong, immensely profitable newspapers could afford. That's how the *News* came to have fourteen men on a press when five would do, 36,000 hours of unworked overtime per year and five-figure salaries for guys who work fifteen minutes a day — in short, between $50 and $70 million in excess labor costs.

In the mid-1970s, when the *News*'s Barletta was still trying to call Tribune boss Cook's attention to the need to streamline operations and accept new technology, newspaper owners elsewhere already had begun doing something about it. In 1975, *Washington Post* publisher Katharine Graham, new at the game and not a member of the old-boy publisher network, locked out her striking pressmen and printed her newspaper in nonunion shops while she repaired the damage done to the *Post* pressroom by union arsonists. Her success had the same effect on newspaper management attitudes as President Reagan's devastation of the air traffic controllers' union had on the national climate six years later.

Having never allowed a woman anywhere near a senior management position, the Colonel's successors in Tribune Tower watched as much in amazement as in approval.

Out of a combination of curiosity and friendship, they sent the *Tribune*'s top press expert to help Graham rebuild. And no Tribune man watched the whipping of the unions by the woman at the *Post* with more relish than Charlie Brumback, who then was just beginning to set earnings records at Tribune Company's solid gold newspaper franchise, *The Orlando Sentinel*. His profit margins and productivity measurements for employees would eventually become the standard for all Tribune newspapers, including the *Daily News*.

In the case of the *Daily News*, a compromise settlement in which both the *News* and its employees pitched something in the pot in the interest of preserving an important newspaper voice was certainly possible. It would have been gleefully greeted by publisher Hoge, who wanted nothing more than a deal that would keep the paper alive and himself in charge of it; and, though the unions would find it hard to believe, the personal preference of the vilified Tribune boss Brumback was unquestionably that the *News* emerge as the biggest, healthiest newspaper in New York, and one still Tribune-owned.

But the hard truth is that the old system of press ownership was gone and the new system was beyond the control of employed managers like Hoge and Brumback. There was no way they could have made a deal that would have satisfied Tribune Company earnings requirements as seen by the stock analysts. To make the New York *Daily News* a viable newspaper property over the next twenty years and consistently profitable in the face of competition would have required a minimum investment of a half billion dollars, which would have had to be repaid out of the newspaper's earnings. This was impossible without a kind of high-tech, minimum-staff plant. Tribune Company had no hope of getting the nonunion work environment it wanted. So after over seventy years of existence, the once-proud and still-famous *Daily News* of New York had to become Tribune Company's sacrifice to Wall Street, the new lord and master of the American press. And the Colonel's company could no longer live up to the defiant title he had once bestowed on it — "Undominated."

Beaten, embarrassed, and having lost $250 million over eleven years, Tribune Company finally gave British media mogul Robert Maxwell $60 million just to take the bruised old lady of the New York streets off its hands. Maxwell's willingness to do so was generally viewed by the American media industry as nothing more than an eccentric rich man opening his door to the homeless — a charitable act for which he was applauded but for which there was absolutely no economic justification, although Wall Street raised Tribune's stock one percent upon the news. Little did they know at the time how much the heavily indebted Maxwell needed the $60 million in cash. Today, with Maxwell dead and the paper limping out of bankruptcy, it will take a publishing miracle to return it to a social and political force in the nation's largest city.

9

The Death of Journalism

LIKE A LOT OF IMPORTANT STORIES, the corporate take-over of America's newspapers was long in the development and did not occur without warning. Nearly a half century ago, a group of do-gooders funded by *Time* founder Henry Luce and headed by the great educator Robert Maynard Hutchins suggested that trends in the communications industry were threatening the freedom of the press in this country. Terming this a "problem of peculiar importance to this generation," the Commission on Freedom of the Press wrote:

> The modern press is a new phenomenon. Its typical unit is the great agency of mass communication. The agencies can facilitate thought and discussion. They can stifle it. They can advance the progress of civilization or they can thwart it. They can debase and vulgarize mankind. They can endanger the

peace of the world; they can do so accidentally, in a fit of absence of mind. They can play up or down the news and its significance, foster and feed emotions, create complacent fictions and blind spots, misuse the great words, and uphold empty slogans. Their scope and power are increasing every day as new instruments become available to them. These instruments can spread lies faster and farther than our forefathers dreamed when they enshrined the freedom of the press in the First Amendment to our Constitution.

All of that was probably true then, and it is even truer today. These words could have been written just as easily by 1988 presidential contender Gary Hart, jailed evangelist Jim Bakker or any American president since Franklin Roosevelt who's had a quarrel with his treatment by the press.

But like a lot of outfits formed to study things, the Hutchins Commission had the right concerns for the wrong reasons. It feared — in 1946 — that the concentration of media ownership in fewer, more powerful hands would result in a monopoly of ideas and the inability of the varied elements of democracy to communicate freely with one another. At the time there were still competing newspapers in 117 cities, a dozen newspaper chains owning seven or more papers, three separate worldwide press services, four national radio networks, 200 separate book-publishing houses individually owned and a dozen or so big magazine empires. But the trend foreseen by the commission has continued beyond its wildest fears. In 1990, all major media, from newspapers to movies, are dominated by twenty-three companies. Fourteen companies control half the 1,600 or so daily newspapers — down from twenty just seven years earlier. More than half the revenue from all media is collected by seventeen firms. But so far, the commission's concern that like-minded, power-hungry owners would somehow stifle the spread of ideas and restrict access to channels through which the country expresses itself has been unfounded. Concentrated ownership of the media has so far proven to be a problem only in the sense that it would have to be broken by government, which in itself is more threatening and repugnant to a democratic society than is monopoly.

But in the forty-six years since the Hutchins group held its meetings, something just as insidious and threatening to democracy has occurred. What Dr. Hutchins and his colleagues could not possibly foresee was that the 9,000 or so television sets in the United States in those days would by 1960 multiply to 45 million, and by 1990 to three times that number; and that the incredible growth of the most important communication tool ever would result in the institution of the press being surpassed as the nation's main source of information and being swallowed up by "the media," a constantly expanding, earthly equivalent of a black hole.

News, which the Hutchins Commission defined as "a truthful, comprehensive, and intelligent account of the day's events in a context which gives them meaning," was still what the press pursued when I became a reporter on the Nashville *Tennessean* in 1962. And the practice of journalism was still its overriding mission over a decade later when as Washington bureau chief of the *Chicago Tribune* I reported the Watergate scandal and the resignation of Richard Nixon.

But during the next fifteen years, the wonderfully romantic and satisfying world of public service newspapering I had climbed into from a newsboy's cradle had become a heady, high-pressure world of business, preoccupied with cost control, return on assets and the courting of consumers. And by the time I left the press in 1989, the definition of "news" had changed dramatically. No longer is "news" only information that has passed through the prism of journalism, where it has been distilled by the collective judgment of professional journalists. "News" is whatever information anyone can get placed somewhere in the vast information collection and distribution system known as "the media." That this information is important, relevant, accurate or delivered in a context which gives it meaning is far less significant than whether it is titillating, controversial or entertaining. What people want to read, watch and listen to is now more important in the evaluation of "news" than any of the more traditional considerations. This has convinced me that what the news media do for a living today is no longer journalism at all.

News organizations still employ journalists who still spend their days gathering and assembling information for presentation, much of it related to natural events. And out of pride, most of them will insist publicly that they still constitute a prism of journalism, in that their collective judgments — based on training and experience — are exercised daily in deciding what reaches their readers, listeners and viewers. And in fact, they go through the motions of all this.

But during the last decade, the culture of the press has changed from that of an institution dedicated to the education of the public to that of its rival, television, which is dedicated to entertaining consumers for a profit. At the same time, the new corporate owners of the press have taken the responsibility for "news" content out of the hands of trained, experienced professional journalists whose goal was peer recognition for quality journalism, and put it into the hands of trained, experienced professional business managers whose goal is peer recognition for successful business management. And because of dramatic advances in technology, the exercise of this "news" judgment process occurs in a world in which organizations gathering and distributing information have a greatly enhanced ability to focus national and world attention instantly on a single issue or event.

Ironically, the decline of journalistic values has occurred just as the very nature of modern communications technology — the instant transmission of digitized photographs via satellite and cable directly onto the screens of television sets — has made the news media capable of the best journalism ever. What can beat a live telecast of what is happening? In America, the ability of the media to touch people's lives directly is unprecedented today and far exceeds the capabilities of the old printed press. With the growth of cable television, the use of the television screen for receiving information continues to soar. The average American third-grader now spends more hours in a week watching television than going to school. The amount of information delivered by television into the average American home increases by 8 percent annually. More than 60 percent of all American homes are now wired for cable television, which means that they have access to between thirty and fifty channels of digitized electronic images. Cable installations, too, are going up 8 percent each month, and very soon, with the substitution of fiberoptics for existing cable technology, the number of information channels will rise to 150. The rapid proliferation of VCRs and the increasing capacity for data storage on compact discs assures that within a few years Americans will be capable of receiving, cataloging and storing more information than any people in history.

By all rights then, each generation of Americans should be better informed and better equipped to participate in democracy than the preceding one. But this is not the case. If the surveys are accurate, the most information ever gathered is now being distributed to the least informed, least interested and most unfocused population in the country's history. Even though most people now get their news from television rather than newspapers, news is not what they watch television for. In most American cities, all three nightly network newscasts plus Cable News Network (CNN) and the *MacNeil/Lehrer News Hour* on public television still reach only about half the total television audience. According to a 1990 survey by Times Mirror Company, only 43 percent of the public now watch television news on an average day. When the Gallup Organization did the same poll in 1965, 52 percent watched the news. During the same period, regular reading of newspapers dropped from 71 percent to 43 percent.

If a tuned out, turned off, passive audience is an indication, television as a builder of citizens has so far proceeded as Edward R. Murrow predicted it might, "merely to distract, delude, amuse and insulate us."

To the extent that the average American has any image of the press today, that image is overwhelmingly of the celebrity television journalist. During the Gulf War, network anchors Peter Jennings, Tom Brokaw, Dan Rather and Bernard Shaw all experienced significant increases in their public recognition and approval ratings. Shaw, who was in Baghdad the night the bombing started, and his CNN colleague Peter Arnett, the only Western reporter who remained in Iraq throughout the war with the technological capability to transmit pictures, were both feted as war heroes upon their return. The nation's most prestigious universities competed to host Arnett's speeches, and the American Society of Newspaper Editors chose him rather than a print journalist to address the war at its annual convention. Despite a quarter century of brilliant work as a war correspondent for the Associated Press, Arnett was virtually unknown outside journalism. Now he is known to and approved of by 30 percent of the country, and his name has been added to the list of television celebrities Americans have come to associate with the best journalism. From the moment back in 1976 when Roone Arledge began ABC News's push toward respectability by hiring Barbara Walters away from NBC for the then unheard of salary of $1 million, television news has been a popularity contest of personalities and electronic gadgetry — not unlike that waged in the 1920s and '30s by the major movie studios. Not that Walters, Arnett and the other stars of television news aren't good journalists; most of them, in fact, are superb. But the nature of their craft has changed the shape of journalistic competition, as practiced and as seen by the public — and as a result has changed the public's expectations of the press.

As celebrity identification has increased, the "brand-name" quality associated with tradition-rich news organizations such as the Associated Press, United Press International, NBC, CBS and Time Inc. has begun to give way to conglomerates in which "news" is just another subsidiary cost center or to companies that see information gathering as a purely technical function.

Because the basic motivation of press owners has changed, the behavior of the press is changing as well. Newspapers no longer compete with one another to produce the best journalism, which is the most accurate portrayal of reality possible. Instead, they compete with one another — and with other forms of entertainment — for the attention of consumers. Again the goal is not enhancing professional distinction among journalists or bringing the society face to face with what it needs to know but rather conquering an audience for advertisers.

Because most of the world can now see "news" as it happens, the traditional skills of the journalist to recognize, get to, judge and accurately report events in a proper context have been diminished in value and replaced by a kind of electronic competition in which money, equipment and marketing appeal decide the outcome. Once a piece of entertaining information enters the system, it becomes "news" whether it deserves to be or not, and remains "news" until it is overrun by a fresher or more entertaining piece of information.

Once this new "information-gathering" apparatus has focused the nation's attention on an event, such as a sensational rape trial, the acts of a cannibalistic serial killer or sexual misconduct by a famous person, the traditional values involved in judging and editing news go out the window. Each story is played and replayed over and over again until it finally plays out as an attention getter. Today, "news" is no longer the written word. It is a visual image. Even inside the nation's newspaper newsrooms, first reports of events most often are delivered by television pictures. Once a hostage taking, a raging fire or a search for disaster victims begins to unfold before the nation's electronic eye, the traditional "editing" process of journalism is eclipsed.

Some famous brand-name news organizations may still retain and apply news judgments and values, but even the fewer rules are being applied less rigorously. As recently as the early 1980s, if *The New York Times* and *The Washington Post* ignored a story, they could keep it from becoming one. If both papers deemed a piece of information doubtful or unimportant, then the wire services, newsmagazines and networks would be skeptical of it, too. While it might make a paper here and there, or even a radio talk show, the story would soon fade from the public consciousness. Today this power is meaningless. The allegations of promiscuity and marital infidelity against presidential candidate Bill Clinton in 1992 were checked and dismissed by most major news organizations. But once they surfaced in a supermarket tabloid, they became television "info-tainment" — and, suddenly, front-page "news" and an important election factor.

The journalism establishment has in effect lost control over the content of its newspapers. The instantaneous delivery of information by an entertainment medium, to increasingly passive recipients, now dictates "news" to the press. The competitive pressures to report that something has captured the public's attention become irresistible. Then, the fact of the capture itself becomes legitimate "news" as well.

Less obvious but equally destructive to the prism of journalism has been the internal pressure from the owners of the press to use news organization resources in the most profitable way. A large share of news coverage re-sources — journalists, equipment, newsprint or airtime — are preplanned, programmed and targeted much the way prime-time entertainment television is. Almost no editor or news director today has the authority to alter or add content to newspaper or broadcast formats unless it fits into a preconceived and approved marketing plan.

Corporate ownership's preferred tools for determining the best use of newsprint and airtime are the reader-viewer survey and the industry think tank. When sug-gested product improvements don't fit into the company's marketing strategy, they seldom see the light of day, no matter what their journalistic value. Furthermore, audi-ence research often shows that what would attract the most readers or viewers is expanded news coverage, par-ticularly of local areas. But this is also the most costly and labor intensive of content improvements, and is seldom if ever the most profitable use of resources. As a result, it almost never occurs. For all their attention to "news" content, the managers of the new corporate media engage in a self-delusion common to the rest of American business in the last few years: that quality is not a function of money. They are more than satisfied that their editorial costs have risen steadily at about the level of inflation over the last twenty years, which is a misleading statistic. It is far more instructive (and revealing) to look at the relative allocation of the newspaper's revenue within particular departments. Except in extraordinary circumstances — such as the major expansion of *Newsday*'s staff for its incursion into New York and the expansion of once tiny newspapers in exploding Sun Belt markets — I have found no major newspapers or groups of newspapers serving monopoly markets whose editorial expenditure as a percentage of revenue has increased in the last fifteen years. While my sample was random and unscientific, it showed that, as a percentage of total revenue, editorial budgets have steadily declined since the mid-1970s. When I became a newspaper editor in 1976, the average editorial department's share of revenue was between 13 and 15 percent. Today, it is 10 percent at a good newspaper and a lot less at the bad ones. During the same period, editorial departments assumed a large part of what had previously been production department functions — mainly typesetting, page composition and proofreading.

A few companies, such as Dow Jones and Times Mirror, appear dedicated to seeking new ways of packaging and marketing the more traditional news content. But most have concluded that "quality" is related more to the nature of the "news," and in the last decade they have set out in quest of the news content of the future. Usually, after all the surveys and marketing exercises, the so-called product improvement translates into a shift of emphasis — and existing resources — toward news about celebrities and sports figures, titillating details of the personal lives of the rich and famous and a preoccupation with reporting the latest, the most trendy and most provocatively wretched of human travails. This double-barreled, marketing-driven remake of the press is a more serious and pervasive result of the influence that infected local television news with a "happy talk" format during the 1970s. And the new definitions of "news" actually mirror the subjects developed as television entertainment programming and selected for the so-called investigative reporting undertaken by television news shows to pump up their audience share during "sweeps" or ratings periods.

In the final analysis, these companies are not preparing themselves to better cover, judge and report what is going on, but rather to better gather and report information that will be most watched or read. They are primarily concerned then not with the preservation of the free press or the conduct of democracy but with development of the information business in its most profitable form, whatever that may be. Anything else, under the rules of their ownership, is a betrayal of their stockholders.

In its struggle for relevance and financial security in the modern information age, the press as an institution appears ready to trade its tradition and its public responsibility for whatever will make a buck. In the starkest terms, the news media of the 1990s are a celebrity-oriented,

Wall Street–dominated, profit-driven entertainment enterprise dedicated foremost to delivering advertising images to targeted groups of consumers. The pressure to appeal is so great at one southern metropolitan daily that an assistant managing editor now regularly monitors the the morning disc jockey chatter for guidance as to the makeup of the afternoon edition front page.

Across the media spectrum — from the front pages of the most respected newspapers to the sleaziest television dramatizations or exposés — the story of a public official's sex life or a celebrity's excessive behavior is more likely to qualify as "quality" editorial than a disturbing war photo or a wordy explanation of the savings and loan crisis or the AIDS epidemic. News, whether print or broadcast, must be "info-tainment" in order to reach and be accepted by a generation of visually oriented Americans with the attention span of a flashbulb, and it must produce enough profit to satisfy a generation of ownership that can appreciate no other purpose of journalism.

Even *The New York Times*, which has always prided itself on publishing only the news that is "fit to print," is not immune. Within the space of a single week in the spring of 1991, the once staid paragon of journalistic virtue ran front-page stories on the late-night antics of the Kennedy clan bachelors in connection with an alleged rape in West Palm Beach and on Kitty Kelley's unauthorized biography of Nancy Reagan — the so-called "news" of which was a suggestion that the former First Lady had had secret, intimate lunches with old, blue-eyed, paunchy, gray-toupeed Frank Sinatra.

In the world of media, it is becoming increasingly difficult to distinguish the news from the entertainment, the journalist from the entertainer, or the true light from the false. Even the great names in broadcast news are losing their luster. Since the late William Paley gave up control of CBS in the mid-1980s, its once robust and dominant news organization has become a pale ghost of its former self. At NBC, the defense contractor culture of new owner General Electric appears to have overwhelmed both that of television entertainment programming and that of network news excellence. Rumors persist that GE would like to sell NBC and its costly news operation. The most often mentioned buyer is the kind of company most likely to own big American news organizations in the future, another entertainment giant — Walt Disney. Some experts believe that one or more of the networks will abandon news altogether before the end of the decade in the pursuit of more profitable programming.

Among newspaper companies, the trend is clearly toward diversification and away from what many executives consider the threatened if not already obsolete business of pure journalism. Knight-Ridder has said it will gradually reduce its newspaper holdings and invest more heavily in electronic information services. Among the many reasons I was so easily expendable at Tribune Company is that journalism, particularly newspaper journalism, has no real place in the company's future. No one ever uses the word. The company bills itself as an "information and entertainment" conglomerate and hopes that newspapers will become a smaller factor in its total business. The growth expectations are in programming for its independent television stations, development of regional cable outlets and use of newspaper resources to produce advertiser-driven special products such as free weeklies tailored for niche markets. Once newspaper labor forces are reduced to the bone, made technologically cost efficient and laced up in the straitjacket economic model, they can be presided over by an accountant. The last thing a company like Tribune needs anymore is a creative, high-energy journalist trying to report more news. Neither print nor television journalism is profitable enough these days to be the core business in a publicly traded corporation.

In 1992, this company—which for almost ten years could not afford to take advantage of its magnificent printing plant to improve the franchise of its flagship newspaper—agreed to pay a thirty-two-year-old second baseman who hits below .300 nearly $7 million a year to play for the Chicago Cubs. Under the arrangement Ryne Sandberg, a perennial All-Star, will collect nearly $50 million from Tribune Company before the decade is over. The explanation lies in this shift in the corporate culture. Sandberg is essentially an entertainer, someone whose name makes the Cubs more attractive as programming for the company's television stations. Entertainment is where the fun, the excitement and the future lie in the view of the owners of the American press. This is the only possible reason that a company built by the work of journalists in Chicago, New York and Florida would believe that one second baseman is worth more to its future than 117 additional reporters and advertising salespeople for its newspapers—all of which have been restricting staff growth and newsprint for the last ten years.

Many media experts believe that news will eventually become the preserve of a handful of global conglomerates offering integrated information services. Japanese and European consortiums already have a head start in the global news business. In 1991, Meta International, the company that put millions of tiny computer terminals in French homes and revolutionized the information business, announced it will try the same thing in San Francisco. Using the telephone lines of Pacific Bell, the company offers a free terminal and dozens of information services including sports and entertainment news for less than ten dollars per month. Rival American services such as Prodigy — a joint venture by Sears and IBM — are available only to personal computer owners. Regional telephone companies are anxious to enter the news delivery business but must overcome opposition from the newspaper industry, which insists that the government prohibit them from doing so on monopoly telephone lines. Only a few American media giants — none of them famous news brand names — are considered big and strong enough to compete in this international news and information arena with the Bertelsmann group from Germany, Hachette of France and such globe-trotting entrepreneurs as Rupert Murdoch.

In fact, the two American firms given the best chance — Capital Cities/ABC with its satellite capacity and billion-dollar cash flow, and the Time Warner amalgam — are no longer rooted in the culture of the press. Instead, each presents the face of an entertainment company, whose services happen to include news. Time Warner, struggling to reduce its debt load, spends a disproportionate amount of time courting foreign partners, none of whom would have a natural appreciation for the traditions of the American free press.

For all its imperfections, the "press" traditionally has been a people-oriented, privately owned, public-spirited, politically involved enterprise concerned primarily with the preservation of democracy. That in itself was a major reason it survived in basically the same form for 200 years. But the loss of that distinctive character means among other things that this news medium now has no better chance of survival than any other business, nor should it have. Under the new order, it is no longer an institution dedicated to the public interest, but rather a business run solely in the interest of the highest possible level of profitability.

So what?

So, for two centuries the press has served as the trusted channel between the government and the governed. In keeping that moral commitment as an integral part of the system, the press has made both itself and the democracy it serves models for the rest of the world. At every cross-roads in our history, nothing has been more valuable in the American experience than the incessant catalyzing of the press. It fell to the press to stir the colonies to revolution in the first place. A hundred years later, it was the newspaper voices of abolition that ultimately propelled the nation to the twin brinks of destruction and greatness over the slavery question — the Civil War. Another century later, it was dramatic press accounts of oppression in the South that produced desegregation across the land, as well as a public rebuke of the war in Vietnam. Between

1960 and 1974, the press played a vital role in an unprecedented empowerment of the citizenry — the extension of participatory rights to minorities in new civil rights legislation and a similar enhancement of the roles of women and youth by the feminist and peace movements.

In such a system, it is the reporting of unfettered truth about how things are and ideas of how they might be made better that motivates a citizenry to act and educates it to courses of action. People cannot govern what they cannot see. And whatever its imperfections, the unquestioned purpose of the old business of journalism was to provide America with an accurate reflection of itself and the understanding necessary to preserve freedom.

But since 1972, when newspaper penetration began to decline in America, the levels of public interest in and understanding of complex social and political issues have steadily declined according to every available measurement. An authoritative study of public opinion polling by the Times Mirror Company shows that through the 1960s, adult Americans regardless of age were equally informed about and interested in the great issues and news events of their time. But since the mid-1970s, interest and knowledge among young adults has declined until it is now only half that of older Americans. As understanding has waned, so has participation in the most important of democratic expressions — voting.

Despite technical superiority and an unprecedented ability to disseminate information, the media of today are serving what survey after survey has shown to be the least informed, most uninvolved citizenry in the history of the republic. Rather than educating and challenging citizens, the press's purpose has become attracting and entertaining consumers, increasingly with distorted and unreal images that are the antithesis of those produced by good journalism.

Case in point: in the 1960s, brilliant foreign correspondents, including David Halberstam of *The New York Times* and Peter Arnett of the Associated Press, reported the disturbing nature of the Vietnam War in the printed press for years without much reaction from the public. Then, the networks — still owned by old-time entrepreneurs like David Sarnoff and Bill Paley — sent their cameras out to record what these journalists were writing about. Sarnoff and Paley were intent on establishing television news as a legitimate part of the free press, and it was the nightly news film dispatches of reporters like CBS's Morley Safer that set fire to the nation's conscience and burned up Lyndon Johnson's presidency.

By contrast, twenty-five years later, the most compelling piece of Gulf War journalism — an old-fashioned press photo — could find no place in the new American news media. New York–based photojournalist Ken Jarecke, who was working the Gulf for *Time*, submitted to his editors a single grisly picture that captured the essence of the entire conflict — an Iraqi soldier burned to a crisp while trying to escape a truck that had been bombarded from the sky. Not only did the photo not make *Time* magazine but the Associated Press picture editors also refused to transmit it, blaming their decision on the culture of today's press. "Newspapers will tell us, 'We can't present pictures like that for people to look at over break-fast,' " said an AP official. So much for an accurate reflection of the reality of war.

At a time when the rest of the world is realizing the importance of a free press, this most vital American institution — as intended and guaranteed by the U.S. Constitution, as preserved many times by the Supreme Court and as articulated and practiced by the important journalists of our history — is in danger of disappearing altogether from the American experience. Journalism, the mirror through which the society has seen itself, has been drastically distorted, its practice commercialized and appropriated for a decidedly different purpose. Without much notice, its role as the information provider for the democracy is being diminished and eclipsed by a successor far more efficient at delivering information but one without brand-name credibility, proven conscience or character references.

If the American public is ever again to see a clear and consistent distinction between serious journalism and what passes today for "quality news" programming, it will probably be the result of the resurrection and reestablishment of brand-name credibility among the electronic information sources that now constitute the only mass media. Most likely this must be done by people like Ted Turner, himself a throwback to the old journalist-proprietors, or by the great journalism families whose tradition-drenched offspring are still the major forces at such institutions as *The New York Times* and *The Washington Post*. As long as there is a Sulzberger or a Graham in charge, those companies will be among the last to place profiteering above the commitment of good journalism.

So far, there are only faint rays of hope here and there that simple news gathering can still be a business. The success of Turner's CNN has at least raised the possibility that more and better news coverage can attract both an audience and advertisers — at least for television. It was incredible to see how quickly CNN was able to take the news franchise away from the more established networks, especially during the Gulf War. But there is no evidence that news is a good business even on television except in times of crisis or huge national disasters. Of all the major media company executives surveyed at the end of the 1980s, only those from CNN talked both of establishing brand-name journalism credibility and of significant increases in the number of journalists to be employed during the 1990s.

It may well be that the values and traditions of the free press will have to find refuge and nourishment in that other "public sector" of our economy — the world of non-profit foundations and educational institutions. The law as a public-interest institution has remained rooted in the nation's law schools, long after commercialization in a world where the only legal positions regularly taken are those bought and paid for. In the same way, perhaps public service journalism can survive — at least in some ivory tower — so it can eventually take root in the new world of electronic information delivery.

Once again, it may be the indefatigable Al Neuharth who is pioneering the way. When he retired as Gannett chairman in 1989, he took with him the Gannett Foundation, which owned company stock worth $700 million (up from $4.5 million when he took over the company twenty years earlier). The saga and its possible implications are a joint memorial to irony. When Frank Gannett died, his will created the Gannett Foundation, on the principle that a charitable trust dedicated to the independence of the free press in America would own and control his newspapers. This would ensure, the will said emphatically, that while the papers remained profitable enough to be vital, "profits should be secondary to basic ideals."

But as Neuharth built the small company into a giant, setting Wall Street earnings records in the process, the profits were anything but secondary. Gannett's 1990 annual report to stockholders was virtually an apology for what would have been considered a boom year by most businesses — $377 million net earnings on $3.4 billion revenue, or an 11.5 percent margin during the worst newspaper industry recession in twenty years. At least one stockholder, however, was not sympathetic. The foundation, now run by the departed Neuharth, declared that in order to remain a financially viable charity and give away the required 5 percent annually, it needed to sell its 15.9 million shares of company stock, then valued at $670 million. With takeover always a threat, Gannett did not want a bloc of stock that large floating around. So it had little choice but to agree to buy it back — a move which led Standard & Poor's to lower the company's credit rating from AA to AA−. Now even greater financial performance must be squeezed out of Gannett's newspapers (already locked into constant need for 30 percent

plus cash flows) to service new debt from the buyback of
its own stock from a foundation the company had always
controlled.

In what is probably the best deal he ever made, Neuharth in effect stole the foundation from Gannett. The
maneuver smacked of the same creative genius and bold
spirit that had sustained the industry all those years. In a
final flourish of entrepreneurship, Neuharth had in effect
spun himself off into a separate, tax-exempt, nonprofit
enterprise whose sole business is the preservation of free
speech. At the same time, the new debt incurred by Gannett made it a less likely takeover target by outsiders.
Neuharth was Houdini, freeing himself after twenty-five
years from the straitjacket of his own making.

Like those of the titans of old, the fortune he had
amassed can be spent to protect and preserve the press —
and the legacy of "the founder" — precisely as Frank Gannett had intended. Except that Neuharth promptly
changed the name of the Gannett Foundation to Freedom
Forum (quite appropriately in view of the circumstances)
and set about making his customary waves through the
industry. In less than two years, he has in characteristic
fashion created a storm of controversy over the lavish
style in which the foundation lives, saved the Oakland
Tribune (the nation's largest minority-owned newspaper)
from financial demise and created a significant new center
on First Amendment law at Vanderbilt University. The
forum already sustains the nation's best media research
center, at Columbia University, and is certain to enhance
Neuharth's long-established role as the standard setter
for minority employment in the newspaper business.

Meanwhile, the Gannett newspapers run on extremely frugal budgets, just like those demanded by Wall Street elsewhere in the industry.

Neuharth's new foundation activism can be important because he forces emulation. His affirmative action efforts at Gannett, aimed at improving the percentage of women and minorities in both journalism and upper management, have set the industry standards for years. Not only was his reputation as the leader of minority development widely envied, but his policies were widely copied. Gannett is not the only media company whose growth into a multibillion-dollar corporation greatly enriched a charitable trust. Tribune Company's Robert R. McCormick Charitable Trust is now one of the two or three largest foundations in Chicago. An equally rich trust set up by John S. Knight has long been among the most active forces for First Amendment freedom and journalism. Virtually all the big media companies, public and private, sustain large, active foundations.

Surely, the newspaper foundations and the communications scholars of academe can see and appreciate what the big media companies continue to ignore or deny — that as a species journalism is on the endangered list. Journalism, as the Hutchins Commission report explained a half century ago, is a diary of what happened, an hourly or daily account of what has transpired since the last chronicle. Once it is compelled to entertain or to be planned in order to achieve a marketing goal, it ceases to exist. Who is there now to insist that journalism needs to exist in the interest of education — the government?

How much all of this ultimately matters to the enlight-

enment of the people, to the nurturing of ideas, to progress toward the horizon of an ideal democracy is a matter
for conjecture. It can be argued effectively that ignorance
cannot survive the flood of information, or, alternatively,
the size, speed and nature of the information flood assures
that it will all pass too fast to soak through and nurture
anything. There is ample evidence to support either hy-
pothesis.

Isn't a citizenry exposed to ten times as much information as the old press used to deliver better informed than
its predecessors, even if the sources are less credible and
the information unfiltered? Perhaps. But is a citizenry
that receives only those stories deemed "entertaining"
and "interesting" actually better educated? Obviously
not. Is a public that spends twice as much time on unsup-
ported allegations of sexual impropriety as the charges
deserve wasting time that might be spent on other, more
important issues? The debate is only beginning.

Of far more certainty is that, unlike the old newspaper-
dominated press, the new television-dominated media
business has no clearly defined, widely agreed-upon and
politically secure role in the political system. In recent
years, journalists have lost the right to protect the identity
of their sources and — ironically at the same time — the
right to betray and reveal them when they turn out to be
scoundrels.

If the public opinion surveys of the last few years are
accurate, what has not been lost in the courts has been
surrendered in a decline of public confidence in the press
as a public service institution. Polls show that fewer
Americans believe the news media have the right to pry

into the private affairs of public officials; that in pursuit
of the news journalists most often behave excessively and
in their own interest and, most recently, that the government was correct in its unprecedented censorship of the
press in the Gulf War.

On the horizon are even more legal conflicts between
the traditional rights of the press and those rights constitutionally guaranteed to others. For example, newspapers
and environmentalists have now squared off on the question of whether governments can require that newsprint
be made from recycled paper. With the evolution of media still incomplete and new technology emerging daily,
laws governing telecommunications and other forms of
transmitting digitized data are only in their infancy. All
of this ensures that the parameters of free speech and
the relationship between government and media will be
redefined in the months and years ahead, both in the
courts and in Congress.

But if recent history is an indication, when the redefi-
nition comes, the once vaunted power of the press to
influence its own destiny will be concentrated on preserving its profitability, not its constitutional mandate. In
Maryland in 1990, the newspaper industry exercised its
clout to defeat legislation that would mandate a more
environmentally sound policy of recycled newsprint. A
year earlier in Florida, media companies relied on a combination of editorial page advocacy and paid lobbyists to
mount a successful movement to repeal legislation which
extended the sales tax to advertising. In Congress, the
industry continues to concentrate its resources in a single-
minded effort to make sure that the telephone companies

can never use their wiring monopoly to compete with newspapers. That such an inclination is so pervasive and embraces such newspapers as the *Chicago Tribune*, which once raised its voice against every attempt by government to regulate business, is proof positive that the press has finally been homogenized in its economic interest, whether its goals serve the public or not.

The camel is in the tent for good. Corporate news media are here to stay. It is unrealistic to think that the new professional managers will ever accept smaller profits in the interest of better and more traditional journalism. Nor will the trend suddenly reverse itself and restore the purpose and priorities of the old press. The pressure to do so is ever so gradually being eased.

During 1989, my last year as editor of the *Tribune*, I met with John Curley, Neuharth's successor as Gannett chairman, at his stunningly elaborate corporate head-quarters in Rosslyn, Virginia, just across the river from Washington, D.C. I was there as an emissary from the American Society of Newspaper Editors to invite him, as a onetime editor now heading a large media company, to discuss the concerns expressed in these pages before a group of editors. "You mean, talk to a bunch of people like you?" He laughed. "Squires, you're over."

He was as right as Roy Megarry. I am over, just like the Colonel and the Captain and Walter Lippmann and union featherbedding in the pressroom; like the tougher-than-nails Bill Kovach, who is up at Harvard running the Nieman Foundation, and Gene Roberts, who has gone to teach journalism at the University of Maryland; like the journalism popes, Ben ("There ain't no quit in me")

Bradlee, who has gone off to spend his seventies raising a young son, and my old idol Scotty Reston, who now spends his eighties writing the country love letters, which the irresistible force Gene Patterson reviews for trade publications.

Me over, and not yet fifty? Well, maybe not quite. In the three years since my resignation, one — and only one — of my many acquaintances among media executives has called to suggest that I still have the journalistic skills and experience for which there is a need. Not surprisingly, it was Al Neuharth. What he wanted me for, quite appropriately, was to help him develop the idea to set up a museum for the press.

INDEX

Index

Index

Index

environmentalism, 232
Evans, Amon Carter, 15–17, 22–25,
    31, 55, 93
  Neuharth and, 19–20, 23–24
  newspaper finances and, 22–24
  passing of, 25
  physical appearance of, 4–5
  in selling *Tennessean*, 23–25
Evans, Silliman, 4, 8, 22

Fanning, Katherine (Kay), 140,
    169–70
Fein, Larry, 38
feminist movement, 224
Field, Marshall, family of, 47–48
FMC Corporation, 153
Fort Lauderdale *News and Sun-
    Sentinel*, 33, 84
Fortune, 42, 105–6
Freedom Forum, 229
Fuller, Jack, 121
Furman Selz Mager Dietz and
    Birney, 183

Gallup Organization, 212
Gannett, Frank, 54, 56–57
  foundation created by, 228–29
Gannett Company, 17–22, 54–57,
    83, 85, 101, 118, 125–31, 183,
    227–30, 233
  acquisitions of, 17–21, 25–26, 93,
    123, 125–26, 128–30
  affirmative action efforts at 230
  credit rating of, 228
  finances of, 20–22, 55–57, 78–79,
    95–96, 228–30
  Knight-Ridder's joint operating
    agreement with, 123
  operations model of, 126
  public ownership of, 21–22
  in redesigning definition of news,
    138
  reputation of, 18–19
Gannett Foundation, 228–30
General Dynamics, 106, 153
General Electric (GE), 106, 220
Goldman, Sachs, 186
Graham, Katharine, 53, 120–21,
    128

Pentagon Papers and, 13–15
  Washington Post strike and 204–5
Greeley, Horace, 14, 27
Green, Dallas, 151
Grumhaus, Harold, 38–40
Gulf War:
  government censorship during,
    232
  press coverage of, 213, 225–27,
    232
Gunnels, Larry, 115, 150, 169
  firing of, 158, 161–62, 164
  and Madigan's sales tax avoidance
    scheme, 158

Hachette, 222
Haig, Alexander, 44
Halberstam, David, 7–8, 19, 98
  on journalistic quality, 133
  Vietnam War covered by, 225
Hampton, Jim, 124
Hart, Gary, 208
Harvard University, 144, 233
Hays, Howard, 93
Healy, Jane, 59
Hearst, William Randolph, 22, 48,
    71
  editorial policy and, 118
  reputation of, 15–16
Hearst Corporation, 11, 96, 171
Heston, Charlton, 172
Hills, Lee, 54
Hobby family, 96
Hoge, James (Jim), 70–71, 113,
    192–96, 199–200
  Brooklyn plant visited by, 200
  Daily News strike and, 199, 205
  demeanor of, 192–93
  physical appearance of, 193
  unions' opinion of, 193
Holtzman, Jerome, 109–10
Holzkamp, Robert, 60–61, 63,
    158–60, 185
Hopper, Joe, 200–201
Houston *Chronicle*, 96
Houston *Post*, 96
Hunt, Robert M., 189–92
Hutchins, Robert Maynard, 207–9,
    230

Index

Index

Madigan, John W., 52, 66, 108–12,
150, 152, 155–59, 161–69, 193
author's resignation and, 163–69
and commissioning of USS
Chicago, 172
in competition for CEO position,
155–57, 159, 161
Cubs acquisition and, 109–10
Cubs ticket issue and, 165–66
editorial policy and, 110–12, 114
and firing of Gunnels, 158,
161–62, 164
sales tax avoidance scheme of
157–58
Tribune finances and, 179–80
Madigan, Michael, 154
magazine publishers, comparisons
between newspaper owners
and, 89
Malone, John, 40
Malott, Robert, 153
Martin, Ron, 148–49
Maryland, University of, 233
Mateer, William, 58–59
Maxwell, Don, 30–31, 39–40, 43,
112
Media Monopoly, The (Bagdikian), 94
Medill, Joseph, 27, 32
Meek, Philip J., 82–83, 88, 90
Meese, Edwin, III, 123
Megarry, A. Roy, 134–35, 142, 233
Meta International, 222
Miami Herald, 12, 17, 119, 123
Miller, Kristie, 150
Miller, Paul, 54–55
Moorer, Thomas, 44
Morgan Stanley, 5–6
Morton, John, 97
Munsey, Frank, 6–7
Murdoch, Rupert, 70, 85, 192, 222
Murphy, Reg, 101
Murphy, Thomas, 195
Murrow, Edward R., 213

Nashville Banner, 17–20
Nashville *Tennessean*, 3–5, 7–9,
16–20, 50, 147, 170, 209
Banner's rivalry with, 17–18
big-name reporters of, 8
circulation of, 16, 93–94

editorial policy of, 31, 119
finances of, 5, 25, 31, 93
journalistic mission of, 4
journalistic reputation of, 17
sale of, 23–26
Tribune compared with, 31, 34,
38–39
National Academy of Sciences
138
National Advertising Council, 12
NBC, 106, 213–14, 220
Neal, James F., 44
Near, Jay, 36
Near v. Minnesota, 36
Neill, Rolfe, 141–42
Neuharth, Allen H., 17–25, 52–57,
78, 125–31, 144–45, 180,
227–30, 233–34
accomplishments of, 54–55
acquisitions of, 23–25, 127–31
ambitions of, 56–57
in attempting to acquire CBS,
144
background of, 54
controversial influence of, 53
on cost of newspapers, 92
editorial policy and, 119
Gannett finances and, 55–57, 228
Gannett Foundation and, 228–30
newspaper finances and, 21–24
physical appearance of, 17–18,
23, 54
Sentinel's success and, 62–63
style and tactics of, 130–31
Tribune praised by, 170
New Deal, McCormick's opposition
to, 118
Newhouse, Samuel I., 22
Newport News *Daily Press*, 172–73
news:
Americans' declining interest in,
212–13, 224–25
definitions of, 137–39, 210,
214–16, 218–20, 231
as info-tainment, 216, 219–20
as preserve of global
conglomerates, 222–23
resources for coverage of 216–18
as visual images, 215
Newsday, 32, 199, 217
Newspaper Advertising Bureau, 74

Index

newspapers and newspaper industry:
advertising prices of, 91–92
antitrust exemption of, 12–13,
120, 123
circulation of, 91–92, 96
closing of, 96–97, 101
competition in, 208–9, 214
corporatization of, 138, 170–71,
174, 233
cost of, 81, 92, 98
and cost of newsprint, 160
decline of public confidence in,
231–32
declines in readership of, 94, 100,
212
diversification trend in, 220–21
editorial policy of, 11–12, 73,
76–78, 137–38, 217
establishing market value of, 126
in failing to reinvest in quality
improvements, 98
finances of, 5–7, 9, 11, 14–15,
21–25, 36–37, 50–51, 57, 75,
80–85, 88–102, 120–26,
131–33, 141–46, 175, 210,
216–19, 223, 228, 232–33
information publishing
obligations of, 125
inviolate characteristics of, 81–82
journalistic quality of, 6, 132–35,
137, 141–43, 188, 211, 214,
217–19
legal basis of, 12, 36, 89–90, 158,
161, 208, 229–30
marketing of, 75–76, 88–89,
91–96, 100, 136–38, 216–18
mission of, 3–5, 8, 14, 37, 81,
122
new priorities of, 82–83
news judgment process of,
210–11, 214–15, 217–18
owners of, 10–16, 22–23, 36–37,
89, 93, 95, 99, 101–2, 117–18,
120–21, 125, 130–32, 170–18,
186–89, 202–3, 205, 208–9,
211, 214, 216, 218, 221, 223
pope jobs in, 149
prohibiting prior restraint on, 36,
41
public's expectations for, 13,
214

qualifications of publishers of,
171–72
relationship between government
and, 13, 121–22, 232–33
in reporting on self, 104–6
social nature of, 12–13, 36
spirit of, 6
strength of, 117, 207–8
in struggle for relevance, 218
system of executive compensation
in, 99–101
takeover defenses of, 126–27
technological transformation of,
24–25, 39, 47
traditional image of, 223
in U.S. history, 223–24
workers in, 188–89
in world of nonprofit foundations
and educational institutions,
227–30
Newsweek, 11, 104
New York *Daily News*, 29, 31–32,
75, 175–78, 180–206
bankruptcy of, 97
Brooklyn plant of, 199–200
Chicago Tribune compared with,
32
circulation of, 32–33, 181–82
distribution system of, 197, 200
finances of, 180–84, 189–91, 194,
203–6
Hoge's management of, 192–95,
199–200
Hunt's management of, 189–91
labor costs of, 180–83, 186,
190–91, 194–95, 204, 206
marketing of, 190
"The Medill Plan" of, 201
sale of, 206
strength of unionism at, 197–98,
202–3
strike against, 177–78, 182,
184–86, 197–203, 205
Tonight" edition of, 190–91
Tribune Company's relationship
with, 187–92, 195
union-management negotiations
at, 184–86, 191, 195–203,
205
New York Herald Tribune, 7
New York Post, 85, 196

Index

Index

Index

Ender

BCNRRAX

Rxpt NCB

XXXCX PX

anyone Learned you

NHL

448

you anyone
learned

RAFI'S SONG

STONES OF EREBUS

AND THE

BY F. M. PERRIN

ILLUSTRATED BY MARK HEBER

Ankh Books,
P.O. Box 37010,
Winnipeg, Manitoba,
Canada R2M 5M3

Library and Archives Canada Cataloguing in Publication

Perrin, Frederic M. (Frederic Martial), 1955-
Rafi's Song: and the Stones of Erebus / Frederic M. Perrin

ISBN 0-9738036-0-6 (Hard Cover)

I.   Title.

PS8631.E775R33 2005   jC813'.6   C2005-905709-2

Printed in Canada by Friesens Corporation

The writing of <u>Rafi's Song and the Stones of Erebus</u> began as an unexpected quest of love and determination.

No true quest is ever journeyed alone and I would like to extend my sincerest gratitude to the following 'Companions' who, through miracles of their own, proved that dreams do come true: to editor Dr. Helga Schier, for understanding the book so well and for much thoughtful advice; to artist Mark Heber for the superb cover illustration and text layout; to artist Steve Penner for turning the book cover into a work of art; to publisher/author Dr. Judith Briles for her gracious mentoring and book testimonial; to publisher/author Kerry MacLean and school principals Vic Kuzyk and Tom Chan for their book testimonials.

And may the words written in the following pages and upon my heart forever proclaim my love for the greatest miracle of all – my wife Rachelle.

More Praise for

RAFI'S SONG

AND THE STONES OF EREBUS

"In weaving this beautiful tapestry of an eternal struggle between good and evil, Frederic Perrin uses every color of the literary rainbow in anointing this modern-day parable . . . destined to join the opus of Canadiana for our reading pleasure."

Thomas V. Chan, Educator, Author

"Frederic Perrin has woven a fantastic tale that will capture the imagination of even our most reluctant readers. I'm ordering multiple copies (of Rafi's Song) for our school's library."

Victor Kuzyk, Elementary School Principal

For Rafi and all the children: in your hearts
I hear the music of today; in your eyes
I see the miracles of tomorrow.

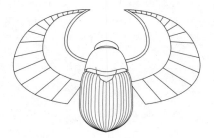

Proficy of Zodiacs

Scorpio, Toraus and
And A cancer one
will die Two shall
live all three sent
from the sky.
These last two gods
will stay on
earth. While the
other
parshis...

— leo

CHAPTER ONE

NEWTON'S APPLE

Rafiatu Malawi was the talk of Drumheller, Alberta. Some folks said it was because she lived in an apple (not a real apple as as you shall see), but as most folks said behind open newspapers and closed doors, it was Rafiatu's strange clothing and wild ways that put the drum back in Drumheller.

If Rafi (as her family and friends called her) dressed and behaved like normal children, Drumheller might have been any other small town in an otherwise large world, and this story could not begin. But Rafi was not like other children. She was ... How shall I describe her? First, try to imagine an eleven-year-old girl with the grace of a gazelle, the speed of a cheetah and the strength of a charging lion. Now, if you can imagine all of that dressed in clothes that make young children jealous, teenagers and fashion designers angry (because they did not think of it first) and adults gasp, then you have the right idea. Rafi was as different from you and I as a cactus is from a Hippopotamus.

As for Rafi's clothing – hats, shirts, pants, belts and even shoes – she made all of them herself in her bedroom under the stars when most people had the good sense to sleep. And if this was not enough to wonder about, every piece of clothing she stitched and sewed with nothing more than a needle in her hand and a song in her heart was unique in every way imaginable.

Words like 'bold,' 'daring' and 'unspeakable' followed her wherever she went. Her hats, if they could be called hats for they were made of grass and leaves instead of wool or cotton, were so unusual that, each year, birds competed to build their nests in them at the first sign of spring. Her belts, which hung about her waist in a dazzling display of freshly cut flowers and dandelions were looped and knotted so cleverly that visiting sailors often asked her for lessons. And her pants, in which no two legs were of the same cloth or pattern, changed color with the light so the townsfolk could argue at any time during the day or night about what color pants she was wearing and still be wrong. But that did not matter much since there were still Rafi's shoes to argue about, which never matched, and were at least as odd as her pants.

But it was Rafi's shirts that set the trend for the 'nouveau stitch' from Orkney to East Coulee. Decorated with odd things that other people might walk by or throw away, each shirt hung outside her pants in long tails that almost touched the ground, ending in brightly colored ribbons that caused folks on windy days to say: "There goes Rafi's kite." It was only when you passed by close to Rafi (which most folks avoided) that you realized her shirts were buttoned to her chin with smooth, colored stones, splashing rainbow cheeks and a cinnamon smile beneath autumn eyes that took your breath away if you looked too deep.

As for Rafi's wild ways, her favorite activity was jumping in the river. This was not unusual in a town blessed with hot summers, but Rafi never wore a bathing suit and jumped in the river, fully clothed, as often as she wished. Sometimes she would jump from the highest tree branches overhanging the river, and she would sing underwater for so long that tourists would dive in after her, thinking she had drowned. As you can imagine, this caused quite a stir at Town Hall, where tourists arrived daily by the bus load, dripping from head to toe, to complain to the Mayor about a strange girl singing in the river. Town Hall had the cleanest floors in North America.

Yet for all of Rafi's peculiarities, nothing she wore, said or did attracted as much attention or excitement as her hair. It was not that the townsfolk frowned upon the latest hair do's and don'ts so often blamed for raising eyebrows and wide grins on public streets, but Rafi's hair, streaked in alternating shades of chestnut and ebony, bore a large, white mark just above her bangs that looked exactly like the letter 'B.' How this could have happened no one knew, but when her mother revealed that, when Rafi was born, the doctor reported, "a letter is coming out," many people interpreted this as an omen of things to come.

This was not at all to the liking of the Mayor who was short, bald, and fat with a large, drooping mustache that flew like an arrow at the mere thought or mention of Rafi. Most of the time, it was hard to tell the difference between his face and a hairy, red tomato, which perfectly matched the red sash he wore on his black suit. He always looked grand and imposing. No one knew his name; even his wife had forgotten it. So, they simply called him 'The Mayor' or 'Your Excellency' and other names we cannot print here.

The Mayor was always in a bad mood unless, of course, he was in a worse mood, but screaming generally made him feel better. He wrote a list of all the people he screamed at in a small, black pocketbook that he kept in his suit pocket along with a sleek, black pen. Other than screaming, only tourists made him happy – lots of tourists – preferably rich, quiet and well behaved tourists who were not inclined to notice Rafi's odd behavior.

It was for this reason that signs were posted along the riverbank and throughout the town that read, 'No Singing in River!' There was also a twenty dollar fine for 'river singing,' but as none of The Mayor's minions could catch Rafi once she had left the river, the fine was never collected.

In fact, three years ago, the first day after Rafi and her family had arrived from Africa, unusual signs of every kind started popping up all over Drumheller. Each sign was a testimony to Rafi's challenging behavior and The Mayor's growing anger: 'No Dancing In Trees!,' 'No Talking to Animals! (Birds!!) (Or Bugs!!!),' 'Rainbow Hugging Prohibited!,' '$25 Fine For Walking Upside Down!,' 'Real Clothing Must Be Worn At All Times!' Before long, there were so many signs that the town ran out of space. However, a local entrepreneur who rented out hot air balloons to Town Hall – complete with The

Mayor's latest rules – eventually solved this problem.

But although Rafi could read very well, she did not understand why she should be prevented from doing things that seemed so natural to her. She could not imagine that anybody would get hurt hugging a rainbow. "Imagine," she would say to herself each morning before she opened the bright, green door of Newton's Apple where she lived with her parents and older brother, "just imagine the possibilities …"

And imagine she did. Sometimes, when people tried to speak to her as she lazed next to a flower bed or against a tree, she would say in the most serious voice: "Hush, it's not polite to interrupt – can't you hear them speaking?" In school, she would often quote trees, flowers, animals and even bugs in her assignments which, as you can imagine, stumped her teachers who had no way of verifying her sources. And since she often scored perfect marks without any appearance of studying, The Mayor banned all plants and animals from school premises, including earthworms and frogs (much to the objections of the biology teacher), to ensure that Rafi was not cheating on her tests. When she scored one hundred and thirty three percent on her next biology quiz, Town Hall created a new by-law stipulating that, before any school test or exam, classes were to be swept for spiders, fogged for mosquitoes, and all students were to be searched for lice.

The Mayor soon learned, however, that Rafi was not to be intimidated, and if anything, his schemes only inspired new levels of creativity. No one in Town Hall will ever forget the day she tied his shoelaces together during his speech on public safety. He went flying over the dais headfirst into Mrs. Grogblossom's lap who, unfortunately, was armed with a rolling pin. And while it has never been adequately explained how bubble bath came to be substituted for The Mayor's wine during a wine tasting festival, it had him talking in bubbles for a week. Naturally, bubble bath was banned from Drumheller the next day.

Yet The Mayor's stratagems were not without their effect on

Rafi. A gifted man, especially when it came to taking advantage of others, he knew Rafi's one weakness: rules. Not rules like making your bed or doing dishes (because there's no denying that beds must be made and dishes done), but rules simply made for the sake of denying others the freedom to express themselves in a not-so-free world. And so, shielded by his pocketbook and wielding his mighty pen like a sword, he set out to frighten Rafi as if he was a knight of old about to slay a dragon. Not surprisingly, he penned and posted so many rules in his pocketbook and about town that Rafi found it almost impossible to breathe.

Fortunately, Rafi's most guarded secret had escaped The Mayor's prying pocketbook – she was terrified of snakes. This was owing to the fact that she had been badly bitten by one after inviting it to tea along with a baby crocodile and a Hyrax when she was only three years old. Otherwise, she was sure that, once word got out and The Mayor had his way, Drumheller would be the snake capital of the world.

Yes, it was safe to say that Rafi captivated the valley. She never looked at anyone or anything the way ordinary people do. She preferred walking in the rain rather than complain about it, and she always knew how you felt before you knew yourself. When asked if she was magical, she would look at the grass beneath her feet or the clouds in the sky and say that it was magic just being alive, and that everyone was magical if they only took the time to capture the magic that was in the air or beating in their own heart. When asked whether she would like to be a famous dinosaur hunter like her father, Amos Malawi, the renowned paleontologist who worked at the local museum, or a sculptor like her mother, Myra, she would reply: "That would be wonderful, but I'm going to be an ambassador to the United Nations."

Most people shook their heads at such a notion. Ambassadors and nations required rules, regulations, and other impressive things like protocol, and it was hard for the townsfolk to imagine Rafi representing others when she was so different herself. The general opinion (shared by The Mayor) was that Rafi was a dreamer who could not follow rules, and one day would push The Mayor too far.

And some people said she was dangerous.

"Nuttin' no good never came out o' wearin' sticks and stones," warned Mrs. Thumbottom, the local gossip who lived across the street from Newton's Apple. Her face was pinched and hollow, and she pulled her lips so tight that local carpenters said they could use her mouth as a level. Her ears were unusually large for her small, square head but perfect for listening around tight corners when she did not want to be seen. Her nose, which was hooked like the end of a coat hanger and honked like a goose, could smell trouble before anyone knew they had any.

"And dem pants," she went on in slippers covered with so much cat hair they could have meowed, "yestiddy, one leg was green and the other blue, held together with twigs and a prayer if you get my meanin'." When she was not spying on the neighbors you could find Orly, as folks called her, scouring through the neighborhood garbage bins.

"I don't know, One Eighty Seven," said Mopsus, the local garbage collector who often checked his truck on his rounds to make sure he did not deposit Orly in with the rest of the trash. He smiled at the scowl the number put on Orly's face. It was recorded at Town Hall and well known throughout the valley that Orly was Drumheller's one hundred and eighty seventh resident (mainly because she told everyone one hundred and eighty seven times a day). But while she prided herself on such a low number, she did not like being called it to her face.

Mopsus was an Egyptian, or so he said, and since no one in Drumheller had ever been to Egypt, there was no reason to doubt him. He was also the town's resident philosopher, dispensing great wisdom at the sidewalk by the bin and by the bag to those who asked his advice. He was uncommonly beautiful for a garbage man, with keen dark eyes and a mop of braided hair, but this was just another oddity in an odd town – Drumheller had the finest looking garbage men in the whole world.

"And that hair," she persisted. The distaste on her face wrinkled like a navel trapped in a corkscrew. As if she did not want the garbage cans to hear what she was about to say, she leaned forward, which had the added benefit of revealing a chicken bone with some meat on it lying in the tall grass. On a jet of bad breath, a look of terror sprang from her eyes into Mopsus's face.

"It's the devil's workshop!"

"You mark my words, Orly," said Mopsus evenly, disliking her more than usual that morning. "There's something special about that child. I don't know what it is but I'll wager it's something good." He threw the last bag from the sidewalk into the back of his truck. "Too bad more people around here aren't like Rafiatu Malawi." Deliberately, he scooped up the chicken bone in one of his great hands, throwing it into the truck to join the rest of the garbage. Before Orly could say another word, he shot her an ugly look that scuttled her down to the Buzz and Blow, the local hair salon where Mrs. Wheeze cut and styled hair, and you could say whatever you wanted because everyone nodded no matter what blew under the dryers.

Other than Orly and The Mayor, everyone liked Rafi (although nobody liked to admit this in public). Since gambling had been banned, local residents placed bets with one another as to what Rafi would wear or do any given day that was guaranteed to send The Mayor into one of his positively 'raffing' conniptions and the hospital (where he kept a room). Predictably, each time after he was rushed to the hospital, Town Council would buy up all the pens and paper in town to write new by-laws so that new signs and balloons could be posted. "Laws," The Mayor would repeat from his hospital bed, "make Drumheller a respectable town."

His mood did not improve when someone handed him the results of a recent tourist survey that listed 'Rafi Spotting' as exciting as a visit to the town's world famous dinosaur museum. And his mustache almost popped from his head when one of his aides gave him a copy of <u>The Official Rafi Field Guide</u>, illustrated by a retired ornithologist. Sold in stores and included with bus tours, 'Rafi Spotters' could now match her previously seen couture or activities with the guide or draw her latest creations in the blank pages provided.

As usual, an emergency Town Hall meeting was called complete with three police cars, two fire trucks and an ambulance.

"We are talking about an eleven year old girl!" he screamed at anyone who was not already nodding or asleep. When The Mayor screamed, some people (including those awakened by the screaming) would start writing in thick books. Others (including some who were still asleep) would cross-reference the screaming of the day to see if it was covered by existing by-laws. This was not an easy task as there were no less than seven books of town by-laws with the eighth expected by the end of the month.

A warm wind hustled down the valley, which was home to six thousand residents, or Drumhellions according to Orly. School was out for the summer; so most children glued themselves to the Telemission (if you have ever watched it you know what I mean), worked summer jobs, or decorated the local mall while parents prayed for the coming of school. It has often been said that there were more dinosaurs than people in Drumheller, and to this day, it remains a fact that more dinosaur bones have been discovered in and around town than anywhere else on earth.

There was always a wind blowing in the valley, which kept kite makers happy, and naughty children (including some tourists) were told it was a dinosaur's breath. Everyone laughed at this, of course, (unless you were alone). But, at the slightest breeze or chill, everyone checked over their shoulders, making chiropractors the wealthiest citizens in town.

Riding the wind like a magic carpet, the red sun dipped early into the western canyons. As the night slowly darkened, the moon climbed up the stars to the heavens where it yawned and smiled over the sleepy valley. The night was as quiet as any the town had ever known except for the brushing of many teeth, many a good night (along with some slamming of doors) as, one by one, the lights clicked out of Drumheller.

At three and one half Newton's Apple, bright yellow lights stayed on. The house looked just like an apple you might buy at the store except that it was much larger, and where there might have been wormholes there were seven windows and a door. The walls, of which there weren't any because the house was perfectly round, were painted ripe red, bulging under a green roof that matched the door. From the roof grew a tall, brown chimney that looked more like a stem. In front of the Apple was a beautiful garden.

The garden at Newton's Apple was the envy of the neighborhood and the first stop of every bus tour. It seemed to grow from a storybook rather than from the soil. The trees were of every shape and color: Banana Birch, Laughing Coyote, Gorilla Mist, Dragon Spice, Elephant Ash, Redwood Roller, and Wistful Willow just to name a few. It was no wonder that songbirds throughout the valley chose the garden as their home. The flowers, which were a mystery even to the town's botanists bloomed brush strokes of every color, scenting the air with sweet perfume.

But by far the most striking feature in the garden was the marble fountain of a beautiful, young girl dancing in a bed of daffodils and holding a songbird in each of her uplifted hands. Rafi's mother, the sculptor Myra Malawi, had made the fountain. Myra's sculptures were displayed in art galleries throughout the world, and more than one jealous dinosaur hunter wondered if Myra secretly sculpted Mr. Malawi's growing collection of rare dinosaur bones.

Around the fountain was a short hedge of brambleberries, sharp with pointed leaves and thorns, and ripe with juicy blue and purple berries that stared out from the brambles like so many eyes. It was the only brambleberry bush in North America, which Rafi had grown from seeds she had brought from Africa. But that night, under the careless watch of the drowsy moon, four bloodshot eyes peered out from the hedge. Together, they watched the bright, green door of

Newton's Apple.

"Wake up, Dlop," said a scratchy voice. "You're on guard duty. Brat-a-rat-tat. A fat log of good you'll be if things get rough."

"I wasna asleep, you rat-faced salami," said another voice that squeaked like an injured hinge as two green eyes, looking more rested than the other four, joined the brambleberries. "Asleep indeed. Bree, if you must know, I was thinking."

"Yeh, you was thinkin' all right, Dlop," said a third voice, lower than the others and barbed with sarcasm. "Mebbee you always think with yer eyes closed, yer mouth open and droolin' on yer fat belly!"

Squeaks of laughter shook the brambleberries.

"Shut yer gob, Pud!" said Dlop, now fully awake and angry. "I was thinking how do we know that this is the right place? Tell me that, will ya? You tell me smarty-pants. Lots o' these holes have birdbaths and flowers 'neath the winders."

Pud licked his paw. "Well, bird brain," he said. "Mebbee if you could read like Bree you would know that this here place is three and one half Newton's Fig just like we was told." A short, hairy arm ending with razor sharp claws pointed to silver numbers on the bright, green door.

"And just like we were told," said Bree, watching the front walk with gray eyes that missed nothing, "we're on guard duty. So stay alert!"

"I'm not fat, am I?" asked Dlop.

"Quiet," snapped Bree. He scowled at a milk carton blowing across the garden. "Guards are supposed to guard when they're guarding. You'll wake the whole neighborhood with your squeaking. Worse, he'll hear us."

Dlop and Pud fell silent as a sharp breeze whistled through the hedge, dropping a load of brambleberries on their heads. Suddenly, the hedge seemed to close in on them, leaves and thorns scratching their arms and legs as the remaining brambleberries silently watched from the shadows.

"I don't wanna be a guard!" Dlop's screech reached beyond his small lungs. His big green eyes flooded with tears.

"Quiet, I tell you!" said Bree sternly as Pud stuffed Dlop's mouth with his tail. "This assignment is dangerous enough without you telling the world that we're here."

"Dangerous?" Dlop tried to squeak but Pud was sitting on his face.

Bree's voice softened as he looked at Dlop. "Look, Dlop," he said kindly, nodding at Pud. "It's not as bad as that. Besides, we're not guarding, are we Pud? We're on surveillance duty."

"Yeh, Dlop," said Pud, catching on. "We's on surveillance duty. Much more important than guardin', isn't it Bree?"

"You bet," said Bree, watching the empty street. "The boss told me not to tell you in case it swelled your heads, but there it is. We're surveillancing."

"Surveillancing," said Dlop importantly. He was now able to breathe again having bitten Pud's tail. "Well, why didn't you say so in the first place? Surveillancing. That's differen…"

"Why I …" snarled Pud. He licked his injured tail. His intensely blue eyes glared at Dlop who had fallen asleep. "Pssst, Bree," he whispered over Dlop's squeaks and snores, "what's surveillancing?"

"I heard that," said Dlop triumphantly. "See, I was thinking again."

Bree rolled his eyes. "Shut up!" he said. "Both of you!" He lifted his intelligent face and bear-like forepaws to the sympathetic moon. "How I got stuck with you two rat bags is beyond me."

"That's easy," said Dlop. "We're brothers!"

"Yeh." Pud punched Dlop on the arm. "Brudders to the end!"

Bree watched the front windows of Newton's Apple. "What end, I wonder?" he asked quietly.

The hedge rattled a little at the question, showering their heads with more brambleberries. Dlop's eyes grew to the size of plates and even Pud looked uneasy as a shadow passed over the moon.

"OK, Bree," said Pud. "Fess up. What are we surfing, I mean

guardin' here?"

Bree sniffed the air. His keen senses told him that rain was approaching from the north. But there was something else in the air that he could not put his whiskers on. Where it came from he could not say but his back stiffened and his whiskers bristled like bolts of iron.

"The boss says that we've got to surveill... watch this house. Something that happened today has even the boss on edge. I've never seen him look so worried. He says it could mean the end for the lot of us – especially Rafi."

Dlop found it hard to sleep. "The end?" he squeaked.

"What do you mean, Bree?" asked Pud. He took a thick bite out of a brambleberry. The juice stained his chin blue, matching his eyes. Finding the berry too bitter a meal, he spit it at Dlop.

"I don't know exactly," said Bree evasively, "but something was found today that should have been left unfound. Somehow Rafi is involved and so is ..."

"Not ..." Pud shivered. Dlop's eyes grew so big they almost joined at the middle.

"Triodon," said Bree softly.

Dlop pulled his ears over his eyes. "Triodon?" he asked. "There's only one thing that scares me more than ..."

Bree and Pud managed toothy, yellow grins. Dlop's fear of bats was well known.

As if the name had some unknown power, the air grew cooler and colder as the night closed in on the Apple. Whispering to one another, trees swayed back and forth as a storm gathered beneath the shivering moon. From across the garden, bright window light pierced the darkness yellow.

Then it started to rain.

"Triodon," said Pud in an uneasy voice. "You would think after millions of years he'd be dead."

Bree glared at the rain, which flew fast and furious, obscuring his view. "I wish it was that simple," he said.

Pud sniffed another brambleberry. "Rafi's finished," he said decidedly.

"Worse than that," Dlop squeaked under his breath. "We're finished!"

Bree listened carefully to the rain as bolts of lightning danced across the night sky. Predictably, thunder rolled, churning the heavens into a vast drum. He closed his eyes, cocking his ears above his head until they soared like satellite dishes. It was in this way he listened to the voices of the night: the fall of twig and petal, the wiggling of worms beneath his feet, the tuning of a wet crickets' band, and somewhere between the rhythm of rain and whoosh of wind … Was it his imagination or did he hear the sound of beating wings?

He gave Dlop's shoulder a brotherly squeeze. "Not yet, we aren't," he said. "According to the boss there's more to this Rafi than meets the eye." He squashed a brambleberry on Dlop's head where it sat like a purple crown. "Even when both eyes are open. We may yet have a chance."

"Against Triodon?" asked Pud doubtfully. He poked Dlop with a sharp claw to see whether he had fainted again or had simply fallen asleep. "He killed the …"

Bree scanned the sky, which was as wet and black as any night he had ever known. "Yes, Pud," he said grimly. "He killed them. All of them. And he's been killing ever since. But it's up to us now to do what we can. Every little bit helps." His gaze strayed to the roof and chimney of Newton's Apple.

"So shut up and keep your eyes on that house!"

An hour passed. Cold rain sliced through the garden, filling the fountain until it overflowed, running a moat around the hedge. The night was cold and long and damp, and soon the three brothers had huddled together for warmth until, one by one, their tired eyes flickered and then closed, leaving only the brambleberries to watch and whisper amongst themselves.

They were not alone. Unknown to Bree, Pud and Dlop, two

dark, winged creatures crouched in the shadows of a half dead tree in Orly's front yard. Blacker than the blackest night, and as silent as the deepest grave, they gazed across the empty street with piercing yellow eyes that flickered like gruesome candles in an ill wind. Shot with hatred, they burned with cruelty and malice, yet seemed as cold as ice. Above each pair of yellow eyes, two more eyes, blood red, and no less cold or cruel, cut like lasers through the night.

"Where's Megaera?" snarled a dreadful voice.

"She's with Lilith," snapped a second voice more dreadful than the first. "I thought you knew. She has a date with a man, Tis."

"You know I don't like being called Tis," the first voice hissed angrily. "Even to you, dear sister, it's Tisiphone, if you know what's good for you."

A cold silence gripped the shadows.

Tisiphone's chuckles broke the silence. "Oh, I get it," she said finally. "Date with a mantis. Alecto, you're so clever. Oh, won't he be surprised."

"More like dead, if I know Megaera," said Alecto. She bared a set of long, pointed teeth at Tisiphone.

"What about the others?" As if she already knew the answer, Tisiphone sneered at the hedge across the street.

Alecto gave a horrible laugh. Lodged somewhere between her pointed teeth was a smile.

She winked at her sister. "Ratatouille," she said hungrily.

"Beef Ratatouille," corrected Tisiphone. "Without the onions."

"How right you are, dear sister," said Alecto, although there was not a trace of fondness in her voice. "Without him, they're nothing. Once we're done here we can finish them off for sport."

Pinpoints of red glinted inches above Alecto's cruel eyes. "We've got work to do," a third voice interrupted. "Let's get to it without so much talk." Such loathing and wickedness was in this voice that Alecto and Tisiphone sounded kind in comparison.

"Yes," added a fourth voice impatiently. "Do let's get on with it!"

"Time to kill," said Alecto grimly.

"Time to die," spat Tisiphone.

"Remember," added a voice from the shadows above, "it's the girl we're after."

Alecto nodded. She raised her wing, which was barbed with deadly looking claws. Caught by the wind, it unfurled like a black flag. Taut over muscle and bone, the deeply scarred skin rippled with anticipation. As if by command the rain stopped, and an unwholesome darkness descended from the skies, wrapping itself around the Apple. From the east, a cold wind blew, bitter and hard as nails, driving confused rain clouds to the west. Then, under the watchful gaze of the worried moon, the eyes began to move.

Rising like disembodied ghosts, the eyes floated across the street, over a small fence and entered the garden at Newton's Apple. Deliberately, they hovered over the fountain, and then headed toward an open window. From inside the Apple, voices could be heard whispering excitedly.

East of the valley, the wind carried the sound of triumphant laughter.

CHAPTER TWO

ARMS AND DINOSAURS, STARS AND STONES

Folks lucky enough to be invited inside the Apple all agreed that this was a special treat. Nothing could compare to it, not even a visit to Madame Mool's Wax Works where awed spectators could see the world's most famous people made entirely of wax. Among other things, Madame Mool's featured a wax reenactment of the Spanish Inquisition with prisoners in varying degrees of torture that bore a remarkable resemblance to The Mayor. This was completely understandable since Madame Mool was The Mayor's first cousin, twice removed.

But Madame Mool's wax and wigs were no match for what awaited visitors once inside the Apple. The hallway looked more like a museum than a place in which to hang your coat or umbrella for it was filled with many of Mrs. Malawi's sculptures and an impressive array of Mr. Malawi's dinosaur bones. Some of the sculptures were so lifelike that unsuspecting guests would start conversations with them, conversations which developed into several promising relationships and at least one engagement on account of the stone and marble figures being such good listeners. Unfortunately, however, not everyone appreciated the ten-foot saber-toothed tiger, which served as both a coat rack and bottle opener and explained the fact that there were always more coats, umbrellas and unopened bottles in the Apple than there were people.

Beyond the hallway was an immense round room where the Malawis spent most of their time together and entertained their guests. Affectionately called the 'core,' this room was, in fact, many rooms and included a kitchen, living and dining area, and a small bedroom cleverly hidden behind a curtain of stringed seashells. This was Rafi's bedroom. Beside her bedroom, a round staircase of solid ebony, beautifully carved and covered with real ivy, wound its way up to the second floor and two more bedrooms, one for Rafi's parents Amos and Myra, and one for Rafi's brother Motu.

The core was as round as a billiard ball and stuffed with many unique and strange things that the Malawis had purchased abroad. There were lamps shaped like gorillas and giraffes, tables with claws, a crocodile tea set that snapped at dirty hands, chairs that squawked when you sat down, and a grandfather clock that looked like an old baboon and grunted the time.

But the true mystery of the Apple were the walls and ceiling of the core. Made entirely of precious hardwood – mostly mahogany, ironwood and bamboo – the walls and ceiling were carved by Myra into such breathtaking scenes of wildlife and people from Africa that Orly (looking through the windows from her house across the street) regularly reported unregistered 'squatters' to the Department of Immigration. It was only after the Malawis received a sharp letter from the Minister of Internal Affairs citing 'the harboring of illegal immigrants' that Myra regretfully covered the windows with red and yellow curtains, which spoiled her view of the beautiful garden.

Dead center in the core was a large, red sofa shaped like a donut with a bite taken out of it and sprinkled with soft, colorful cushions. Through the bite, the Malawis watched the Telemission.

"What's the world coming to?" Mr. Malawi asked disgustedly as he turned off the late edition Snews. He had hardly touched his dinner having spent the better part of the evening reading his newspaper upside down, which was a sure sign that he had something on his mind. He drained the glass of warm milk that Mrs. Malawi had given him to settle his stomach.

"Buildings blowing up, terrorists, war, more money spent on bombs than education ..." He looked up at Mrs. Malawi as she handed him a second glass of milk. "And now there's something worse than bills in the mail. Why if I had just one meteorite ..."

"Amos," said Mrs. Malawi, yawning. She knew from bitter experience not to encourage her husband in his views about how to improve humanity. "Tell the children about your discovery." After a long day of sculpting a life size statue of The Mayor for the police department firing range, she stretched out on the donut next to Mr. Malawi. Ignoring the cushions, she used his lap as a pillow.

"Yes, Pupa!" cried Rafi. She was thoroughly exhausted from a long day in which she had twice jumped in the river, taught a bus load of tourists how to swim, and then outrun the local authorities all the way to Town Hall where she delivered a lecture on the rights of bees. But every trace of sleep evaporated from her eyes at the news of her father's discovery. "What is it?"

"Yes, father," said Motu, Rafi's older brother by six long years. Although he was still in high school, Motu was studying to become a lawyer. According to everyone in town (including himself), he already knew more about the law than most people either sitting on the bench or in jail, a fact he never neglected to mention to Rafi when she flouted the laws of Drumheller.

"What did you find?"

Mr. Malawi slopped a little warm milk into his lap.

"Well," he said slowly, as if trying to remember his discovery. Mr. Malawi always spoke slowly where his work was concerned so as not to appear rushed or unscientific. Deliberately, he stroked his chin with the rim of the glass to give himself more time to think. Above the glass, he studied his family with penetrating deep brown eyes.

Unable to help himself, his gaze first fell upon Myra. She fell asleep on his lap even as he looked at her. Her peaceful smile, surrounded by locks of ebony hair, filled the room with the smell of lilies after a summer rain. Mr. Malawi remembered that smile from the first day they had met under his umbrella in a market in Mogadishu. Twenty-three years later, they still shared the same umbrella.

Next, he looked at Motu who sat brooding on the far side of the donut, his firm chin resting in his hand as if he was thinking about what he might say to a judge and jury. If Motu gave up his dream of becoming a lawyer he could just as easily become a model. He was as tall as he was handsome and one flash of his smile could light ice on fire.

Finally, his eyes turned to Rafi who sat on the carpet in the center of the donut like a little Buddha except that her toes were tucked impossibly behind her ears. A warm smile flooded his face. Three years ago, she had walked about town on her hands, toes tucked behind her ears, to protest the Drumheller Post Office's refusal to mail one of her letters to a passing cloud. By-Laws RM03-08-47 and RM03-08-48 remain posted throughout town to this day.

"Do you remember that T-Rex we've been excavating near Bowgett's Rock?"

"Of course," said Rafi. She had visited the site many times and even picked away at the jawbone the summer before.

"Well," said Mr. Malawi hesitatingly, "I removed a rib today and you'll never guess what I found."

"What did you find, Pupa?" cried Rafi, knowing that when her father spoke of his discoveries, even the world's greatest scientists stopped to listen.

As if he had already said too much, Mr. Malawi hid his face behind the glass. "Well," he said. "An arm."

"An arm?" said Motu, not fooled by the glass. "For once, this is interesting." Unlike Rafi, Motu did not share his father's passion for bones unless they were five feet six inches tall, female and named Joanna Clop.

"What kind of arm?"

Mr. Malawi looked over the glass with an important face. "Well," he said. "That's the most exciting part. I don't know."

The baboon clock grunted eleven times and swished its tail. That was enough for Motu.

"Thank you, father," he said dryly, "for that riveting discourse on your important discovery. If you don't mind, I'll catch it tomorrow night on VNN." His large hand waved good night. He did not know it, but more than a dozen girls in the valley included him in their prayers that night. With a deep sigh, he clopped up the stairs.

Rafi waited as another door slammed in Drumheller. She knew that her father would get to his point if allowed to do so in his own time.

"What about the arm, Pupa?"

"Well," said Mr. Malawi, looking suspiciously at the carved wooden faces on the walls and ceiling as if they had ears made of flesh and blood. Always cautious when it came to his work, he lowered his voice.

"I've never seen anything like it, Rafi," he said, a look of real bewilderment clouding his handsome face. "Birdlike, and yet not birdlike …" Mr. Malawi hesitated. For a moment or two, he pulled thoughtfully on his lip as if he was trying to extract the right words. Unable to find any, his voice sank to a whisper. "Five fingers. Human fingers. Separated by claws no less." His eyes widened at the implication. "Think of it, Rafi," he said almost dreamily. "A hand. Part bird. Part dinosaur. Part human. Curled into a fist. In the belly of a T-Rex. And …"

Rafi hung onto her father's words by the tails of her shirt. "And?" she cried.

"There was something inside the fist that made me think of you, Rafi."

Rafi was spellbound. She had always found her father's discoveries fascinating, no matter how small or seemingly insignificant they appeared to be. According to Rafi, little things were great things just waiting to be discovered.

"What was it, Pupa?"

Mr. Malawi gently guided Mrs. Malawi's head onto a cushion. He got up, crossed the room, and closed an open window. Outside, a heavy rain had begun to fall.

After locking the window, he returned to the donut and sat down next to Mrs. Malawi who still lay asleep. Tired and troubled, his face drooped as if it had been punctured into a flat tire. Gone was the sparkle in his eyes that belied the excitement he always felt but tried to hide when standing on the precipice of discovery. Clearly, whatever he had found at Bowgett's Rock was unexpected. But what had he found?

"Rafi, not a word, mind you, to anyone," he said quietly. "This could ruin my reputation."

Ignoring his request, the baboon clock grunted midnight to the swish of its tail.

Scratch, scritch.

Something brushed against the window. It was a high-pitched sound not unlike the sound a tree branch makes when scraped across glass. How the wind howled. If it were not for the rain, Rafi would have guessed that one of Orly's cats had gone for a midnight stroll in her mother's garden. She often wondered if Orly's cats spied on the Apple, having once before glimpsed a pair of yellow eyes staring at her through her bedroom window. But knowing that cats and rain make poor companions she thought nothing more of it and nodded encouragingly at her father.

"Dark night," he said, glancing at the window. "It's getting late. Perhaps we should talk about this in the morning."

Rafi would have none of that. "The arm, Pupa!" she pleaded. "Tell me about the arm!"

"What's that?" said Mr. Malawi, still watching the window. "Ah, yes," he said. "The arm." He drew a sharp breath.

"Inside the fist were three stones."

"Three stones?"

Mr. Malawi put his hand in his pocket. "Wait," he said, "there's more."

"More?" Rafi fell over backwards in her excitement, narrowly missing a coffee table shaped like an elephant with tusks for hanging mugs. What more could there be than an arm, part bird, part dinosaur, part human, in the belly of a T-Rex, its fisted hand holding three stones?

Mr. Malawi pulled his hand from his pocket. In his outstretched palm, rough from almost thirty years of digging, lay three black stones. They rolled ominously like black dice. Outside, peals of thunder shook the Apple as buckets of rain, driven to madness by the howling wind, slashed against the window.

He steadied his hand to keep the stones from falling.

"You see, Rafi?" he asked.

Rafi gazed intently at the stones. She gasped. Incredible as it seemed, white lines had been cut into each stone, cut so deep and with such precision that they could only have been made with a chisel.

"If these lines were made by some random geological event," observed Mr. Malawi, a definite air of finality in his voice, "then I'm an Albertosaurus." His free hand swept through waves of disheveled black hair. "If I didn't know better I'd say that these marks represent a language of some kind." He winced at his own words as if it pained him to say something so unscientific. "At first I thought they were letters, but the more I look at them I think they're runes."

"What are runes?" Rafi asked curiously. One by one, she turned the stones over in her father's hand, expecting to find more runes. There were none.

"The lines are only on one side," Mr. Malawi explained. "The other side is as smooth as a baby Velociraptor's bottom."

"What are runes?" repeated Rafi. With her fingertip, she traced the lines on each stone, which looked like the letters H, I, and X. The lines reminded her of something she had seen before, but she could not remember what exactly that was.

"I'm not a rune expert, Rafi," said Mr. Malawi, pleased at the interest glowing in his daughter's eyes. "But I seem to recall that they were a form of writing used by ancient tribes to communicate to one another. Some say that the Vikings invented them while others have said they emerged from the Latin alphabet. I don't think anyone really knows for sure. Certainly dinosaurs never used them, much less ate them. But, whatever their origin, I think experts generally agree that they had spiritual significance. You see the problem, don't you Rafi?"

"What do you mean, Pupa?"

"If this is some form of writing, it has no business in the belly of a T-Rex. By my reckoning, this T-Rex is over fifty five million years old. But writing wasn't invented until only a few thousand years ago. This discovery is like finding a Telemission in a Pyramid."

"Then how could runes ..."

Mr. Malawi shrugged his shoulders. "It's like I said, Rafi," he said wearily. He looked over his shoulder to see what grunt it was. "I'm no expert. You should ask Mopsus. He seems to know about these things. But that's not all ..."

Scritch, scratch.

Rafi turned toward the window. It was so dark she wondered if someone had sprayed over it with black paint. Above and around the Apple she could hear the wind howling in cold fury as it threw itself at the Apple, rattling the windows and whistling down the chimney as a river of rain pounded on the door. More eerily, she heard the sharp sound of cutting glass.

Mr. Malawi hung his head. As if he could no longer bear to look at the stones, his fingers cracked into a tight fist.

"I should have notified the museum immediately when I found the stones but instead ... something came over me ... I can't explain it," he said. He glanced at Mrs. Malawi as if he did not want her to hear what he was about to say.

"Maybe I was just imagining things ... After all, I'd had a long day, and I was dog tired but ..." he added sheepishly.

"But?"

Mr. Malawi poked Mrs. Malawi with his finger. It was only after he had poured a little of his milk in her hair without waking her that he was satisfied she was asleep and continued.

"You won't believe this, Rafi," he said, looking very uncomfortable, "but as sure as there's a T-Rex at Bowgett's Rock, I heard a voice whisper in my ear."

"A voice?" asked Rafi, delighted. Hearing voices did not surprise her. Just last week she'd had an argument with a caterpillar that had decided, on three separate occasions, to take up residence and start a family in one of her pockets. "What did it say?"

Mr. Malawi sighed. "It said that I should take the stones and give them to you, Rafi." He sighed again, more deeply. "Then it said I needed a shave and a haircut. That was when I remembered you saying just yesterday that you were looking for three special stones for your new shirt." His keen eyes looked searchingly at Rafi. "But, voice or no voice, it is clear to me that these stones were meant for you, Rafi."

"For me, Pupa?" Rafi could not believe her ears.

Mr. Malawi opened his hand. For the longest time he said nothing and merely stared at the stones as if struggling with an important decision. "Too late," he muttered more to himself than to Rafi as he continued to gaze upon the stones. "There's no going back now." He looked at Rafi.

"I took the stones, Rafi," he said, clearly ashamed at what he had done. "Like a thief in the night I took them, never thinking that I should have turned them over to the museum." Worry lines, almost as deep and white as those etched in the stones, crisscrossed his forehead. "I don't think I'll ever look at bones again without them reminding me of the bars in a jail," he said guiltily. He swept the air with his arms as if to erase the memory of his own words. "Anyway, I put them in my pocket and prepared the arm for the museum. I was so troubled about what I had done I completely forgot about the stones until your mother mentioned the arm." He glanced at Mrs. Malawi as she rolled on her side, still asleep. "She doesn't know about the stones, Rafi. They'll be our secret, at least for now."

Rafi looked at her mother's sleeping face. Certainly, she did not seem troubled about the stones. Questions tumbled through her mind, over and over, almost making her dizzy. Where did the stones come from? How did they get into the belly of a T-Rex? Were the lines on each stone a language of some kind and, if so, what did the lines mean? And whose voice had told her father to give her the stones?

Mr. Malawi leaned forward and planted a kiss on Rafi's forehead. The only man who could ever do so, he took her hands into his own and looked deep into his daughter's eyes. A wave of warmth flowed between them. For a moment, they sat as still as stone, father and daughter, deep in each other's thoughts as if they were one of Mrs. Malawi's sculptures. Then, with a wink and a smile, Mr. Malawi sat back on the donut and, low and behold, Rafi felt something smooth and hard in her hands. It was the strangest feeling too, for it felt light and heavy, hot and cold, and wet and dry all at the same time.

Barely able to contain her excitement, she opened her hands. Inside lay three black stones.

"Oh, Pupa," she cried, "they're beautiful!"

As if the stones had ears, the white lines suddenly pulsed with bright light. Mr. Malawi did not seem to notice; he was too busy staring at the window. As for Rafi, she weighed the stones carefully in her hand trying not to let them roll onto the floor, which they could easily have done for they were as smooth and slippery as wet granite.

Crack!

Something crashed against the window, shattering the glass. Spears of glass flew across the room in every direction, narrowly missing Rafi and Mr. Malawi who, grabbing his daughter, threw her to the ground. Instinctively, she closed her hand around the stones. With a start, Mrs. Malawi sprang from the donut.

"What was that?" she cried, rubbing the sleep from her eyes.

Together, they stared at the window. It was badly cracked with a big hole in the center as if someone had punched right through the glass. On the other side of the window, a grim darkness yawned. At the same time, they heard a horrible hissing and spitting as a volley of high-pitched screams launched into the night, first outside the window and then over the Apple. Then it stopped.

"Cat fight," declared Mr. Malawi, wondering aloud what a single Pterodactyl might do to the world's cat population. With a deep sigh, he went to get his hammer and a piece of wood to board up the window.

After cleaning up the glass, Mrs. Malawi announced that she was going to bed. Tomorrow, she noted, she would speak to Orly about cats running rampant in her garden. After kissing Mr. Malawi and Rafi good night, she headed upstairs.

Rafi was not so sure. She had often heard cats fighting beneath her bedroom window, but, never before, had she heard a cat scream like that. She looked at the window, which loomed in a picture of innocent darkness. She shuddered involuntarily. For a moment, one horrid moment that had made her spine tingle and her blood freeze, she was sure that she had seen a pair of yellow eyes glaring at her through the hole in the window. And such eyes, she thought. For the first time in her life, she felt as if she had just looked upon real hatred, a hatred so raw with evil and fevered with malice it made her skin crawl.

Mr. Malawi returned with a hammer, a plank of wood and some nails. After hitting his thumb several times with the hammer, he finally succeeded in covering up the window. He closed the curtains and turned around, revealing a furrowed brow at least twice as heavy as the hammer. Not wanting to add to her father's worries, Rafi decided not to mention the eyes in the window or the light she had seen in the stones.

"Well," he said wearily, sucking his thumb, "I'm off to bed. What a day! An arm, three stones, a voice and a broken window. I've never been so tired. If only I could curl up for a few million years …"

Rafi flung her arms around her father. "Thank you, Pupa," she said. "They are exactly what I was looking for. Don't worry. No one will ever know. The stones and your secret are safe with me."

Mr. Malawi returned her embrace. "That's my girl," he said. However tired he might have been, his arms were as strong as ever. "And you are well past your bedtime, young lady," he added, glancing

at the baboon, who, with a swish of its tail grunted that, if people
didn't start going to bed, it would soon be morning.

"Sing a tired old man a song and I'm off to bed," he said sleepily.
"You know your singing always helps me sleep better than warm
milk."

Rafi lay her head upon her father's heart. Then, in a low voice
so not to wake her mother or brother, she began to sing.

"Never has a daughter
Loved a father as do I,
Your heartbeats set to music
Living notes I long to try.

Hands as strong as Mountains,
In a touch of gentle rain,
You gave my life its magic,
Never said a word of blame.

In words as deep as Oceans,
On your shoulders tall and proud,
I stand upon a future,
Not a choice that makes a crowd.

Hugs of everlasting Fire
Light my path when I am down,
Warms my saddest frown to smile
Above dawn's darkest crown.

Bathed in truth, the sweetest Wind,
In the color of your eyes,
I see an Earth of Miracles,
Not a world of fashioned lies.

Could there be a dewdrop
Or a light up in the sky,
As precious as a father
Who taught me how to fly?

I love you, dearest father
As the ocean loves the sun,
And so I sing your Heartsong
That our hearts may live as one.

Thank you for your kindness,
You taught me right from wrong,
Gave me more than life to lay
Your heart upon my song."

"Where's Bree?" squeaked Dlop.

Pud spun hard on his tail, frantically checking the hedge. Bree was nowhere to be seen.

Above and around the hedge rose a terrific cacophony of cries and screams as if someone or something unnatural was torturing the night. There was a whoosh of wind followed by a soft thud and, suddenly, Bree was sitting where Pud had sat only seconds before. He was scratched from head to tail and his shoulder was bleeding.

"That was a close call," he said, gasping as if he found it difficult to breathe. With a bloodied paw, he painfully massaged his ribs. "Nothing broken," he announced, looking around the hedge. "Where's Pud?"

"Now Pud is gone?" cried Dlop. "Whiskers and tails! Oh, my …"

"Oh, my," said Pud, groaning from underneath Bree.

"Ghosts!" Dlop shrieked at the top of his lungs. "Ghosts and Gobbers!" Unsure as to which way he should run, he started digging a hole into which he plunged his face after he had only dug one inch. Dlop never had been any good at hide and seek.

Bree looked down at Pud. "There you are," he said.

Pud tried to look up at Bree. This was rather difficult as Bree was still sitting on his head.

"Where did you come from?"

"Oh," Bree pointed up at the sky as if he dropped through hedges all the time, "up there." He waved a paw toward the Apple. "And over there."

"P'haps you'd be kind enough to get off me and explain," Pud said graciously.

Bree licked his wounds as he watched the Apple through the brambleberries. "Yes," he said, "I think they have gone for now. Why there were only two, I can't explain."

"Only two?" Dlop gasped.

Bree examined his shoulder. The wound was ugly but not deep. He sliced a brambleberry neatly in two with his claw. He pressed one-half against his shoulder.

"It was late. You were both asleep and I think I was beginning to nod off myself when I heard a noise that sounded like wings ..."

"Wings?" Dlop's head swayed back and forth as if he was preparing to faint.

"Whatever it was," Bree continued, "it sounded like it was circling the Apple. At first, I thought it was the wind but then it stopped. I looked out but couldn't see anything so I went to investigate. There was no time to wake you. It was a foolish decision. As soon as I left the hedge I noticed that one of the windows had taken on the appearance of black wings ..."

"Black wings?" Dlop really did faint that time, his head landing in Pud's lap.

Bree looked gravely at Pud. "Then I knew there was no mistake. The enemy was upon us."

Bree massaged his shoulder. The wound was black with dried blood and brambleberry juice. "Something was cutting the glass. I figured that I had the element of surprise so I attacked. I climbed a tree and jumped onto the windowsill. I got in a few good bites only …"

Dlop fanned himself with Pud's tail. "Only …" he said.

"Only, it was I who was surprised. I hung on the best I could until I dropped in on Pud."

Pud's face flooded with a mixture of annoyance and admiration. "You're very brave, Bree," he said. "And very mysterious. We should have been there with you. We won't let you down again. Will we, Dlop?"

"Black wings?"

It was long into the night when the last light flickered out of Drumheller. The wind and rain had stopped and the moon had returned to its loft in the sky, frowning at the twinkle-toed stars as they danced the night away.

Through her bedroom window, Rafi watched the stars dance around the moon. An arm, three stones, a voice and a broken window; she wondered what it all meant. Whose hand held the stones that now lay buried in a sock under her pillow? It must be an awful thing to lose an arm, she reasoned. And why would someone in the process of losing an arm not release the stones? The stones were rare and beautiful indeed, but surely, not even the most precious stone on earth could replace the touch of a loving hand. She wondered whose hand had written upon the stones and why there were three. Tomorrow, she would tie them to her new shirt that hung by the window.

Far away, bright lights twinkled good night. From her small bed beneath the stars, Rafi made a wish. Then she lay her head upon her pillow, closed her eyes and hoped that the T-Rex had left the owner of the stones with its other arm intact.

Arms and dinosaurs, stars and stones, the day's miracles danced in her head as the stars grinned and the moon yawned. And then she fell fast asleep.

CHAPTER THREE

IN THE BEGINNING

Rafi lay dreaming on her bed next to the window. It was a horrid dream in which a one-armed dinosaur chased her up and down the valley and into Town Hall where it suddenly became The Mayor. Even with one arm, it was far more terrifying than any dinosaur she could have possibly imagined. It was the most unusual creature too, for it had the body of a man, two large and powerful legs, a long, scaly tail and great golden wings that spread like an eagle and screeched in the wind.

She opened her eyes. Her eyes were wet (along with everything else), and in the distance thunder rolled. Her first thought was that she had jumped in the river while sleeping, but a closer examination of her bedroom revealed this was not so. Everything looked normal. At the foot of her bed she could see her desk and dresser, and her night table sat in its familiar place next to the window. In large red numbers, a clock on the night table read 3:33:33. This, she concluded, blinking stupidly at the clock, would be a most unusual sight in a river. However, she reminded herself that last week she had seen a Telemission on the river bottom. But, as far as she could tell, it was not working even though it had been plugged into the mud.

Still unconvinced that she had not fallen in the river, she looked up at the ceiling. Illuminated by the moon's reflection off the windowsill, three sunken, carved faces stared back at her. Perhaps it was her imagination or a trick of the light, but, for a moment, she could have sworn one of the faces moved.

As she became more aware of her surroundings, she recognized the crack in the ceiling above her bed. This did much to convince her that she was in her bedroom and not in the river. She had never seen a river with a crack in it before. This was no ordinary crack. This was the crack that had appeared above her bed the very morning after Rafi and her family had moved into the Apple. Both Mr. and Mrs. Malawi had tried to conceal it, but however hard they tried, the crack had always returned by the next morning, looking like an odd letter U or a pot with the sides pushed in. She stared at the crack as if seeing it for the first time. Now, more than anything, it reminded her of the strange runes on the stones.

Fully awake and getting wetter by the minute, it suddenly occurred to her that, if she was not in the river, it should not be raining in her bedroom. In fact, she remembered closing her window that very night. Aside from the fact that it had been raining before she went to bed, it was always wise to close all windows after the local weatherman said it would not rain because he was a relative of The Mayor. Known far and wide as the 'whether man,' Pitch Pilgarlick was so bad at predicting the weather that competing stations from as far away as Lethbridge waited until he had made his forecast before making their own. By predicting rain when Pitch would call for sunshine, any weather station and its viewers were guaranteed one hundred percent accuracy.

Not at all displeased with lying on a wet bed, Rafi tried to remember the strange creature that had been chasing her in her dream. She could still feel its hot, black breath upon her neck. Several times in her dream she remembered turning around to shout at it, and was confronted with an awful face that changed every time she looked. At first, it seemed to have the face of a man, but it changed so much and so often she could not tell whether it was a man's face or that of a fish, lizard, insect, animal or bird. But the eyes were always the same. Wild and cruel, they glinted like hot lumps of coal.

Looking past the clock (which still blinked 3:33:33), she was surprised to see that her window was open, and what is more, it was held open by a large, green clothes peg. This struck Rafi as very odd because The Mayor had banned clothes pegs ever since the valley's school system shut down after she had arrived at school one day with different colored clothes pegs on her clothes, ears and in her hair. Orly had called the police, of course, but things got worse the next day when the students and staff of Drumheller staged school demonstrations clothes pegged from head to toe in every color of the rainbow. Courtesy of Orly, the army and VNN occupied the valley for three days thinking that aliens had contacted earth.

As Rafi pondered the only clothes peg in Drumheller, a strange noise called her attention to the desk. Thinking it wise not to move too suddenly, she looked down her nose toward the desk and was startled to see someone (or something) sitting at the desk (on it to be precise) and reading her school history book. Under different circumstances, she might have sat up to make its acquaintance, but before she could decide what to do she heard a sniffing sound coming from the dresser as something warm, wet and furry pressed against her cheek. And if this was not enough cause for alarm, an unpleasant odor filled the room.

Judging wisely that strange odors and wet fur go together, she slowly turned her head toward the smell. Imagine her surprise when she came face to face with a rather plump rat lying asleep on her pillow. Wondering what a UN ambassador would do under the circumstances, her first inclination was to scream, but the whiskered face seemed so content as it yawned and snuggled (and snored) that she thought better of it.

After hearing more sniffing (and a sneeze), she looked back at her dresser. She was startled to see yet another rat, slimmer than the first, wearing one of her green socks on its head and sniffing her perfumes. She had made them herself with flowers from her mother's garden. Seemingly pleased with the smell of the last perfume, the rat rubbed some under its armpits and onto its chin. Then, to Rafi's complete astonishment, it drank the remainder of the bottle, gargled, and spit what was left into her open sock drawer. Convinced that this was unusual behavior even for a rat, she wondered if this might be a perfect time to scream.

But before she could scream, new sounds directed her gaze back to the desk. Sitting on her computer mouse as if it was a stool sat the biggest rat of all, wearing half moon spectacles and (apparently) still reading her history book. It was the loudest reading, too, for the rat puffed and sighed, blowing its whiskers at the turn of each page as if what it read was immensely displeasing. With a snort of disgust, the rat slammed the book shut.

"We're not praying you know," said a tiny but rather severe voice from somewhere above the bed.

Surprised by the voice, Rafi looked up at the ceiling. This was easy to do because she was still lying on her back. But no one was there except the carved faces and the crack on the ceiling. As if it knew the answer to this riddle, the crack on the ceiling smiled. For a moment, she half expected the crack to open and drop some strange creature onto her bed. To her intense relief, however, it did not. Instead, it merely yawned as if having rats and voices in one's bedroom was as normal as a bolster or a pillow.

She had not forgotten about the rats. Slowly (so as to not attract their attention), and carefully (the rat next to her on the bed was still sleeping), she raised her head. As it turned out, she need not have had any fear of disturbing the rats. The rat on the dresser was busily brushing itself against her hairbrush, and the rat on the desk now wore a pencil behind its ear as it rapped on a calculator. The rat on the bed lay on its back, its paws and tail up in the air as if its stomach wanted rubbing.

The voice spoke again.

"We're not praying," it said as if to test her powers of observation, "we're 'preying'."

Sure that the voice was not part of a dream, Rafi looked everywhere above the bed. But, other than the cracked ceiling, nothing was there. Perhaps The Mayor was right. She was losing her mind. She closed her eyes and chuckled. What would Orly and The Mayor have to say about reading rats and voices in the dark?

"You should speak louder," said the rat on the desk.

"I can't speak louder," the voice complained. "Perhaps if I 'preyed' on her nose ..."

That was enough for Rafi. Not wishing to waste any time in ambassadorial protocol, she addressed the entire room as if it was an assembly. That way, all unknown visitors in her bedroom would have to reveal themselves at the same time.

"Who are you?" she asked nervously.

"Tut, tut, child," said the small voice, gentler than before. "Do not be afraid. I am not 'preying' right now. And I prefer ladybugs to children. There is nothing to fear. See?"

Something tickled Rafi's nose.

She crossed her eyes. A large praying mantis (exactly the same height and color as the clothes peg) was standing on her nose, its head bent down, one of its bulbous eyes almost touching her own. This was alarming to say the least (she forgot about the rats for a moment), but this mantis wore what appeared to be a red jacket and red harem pants, both of which billowed like miniature hot air balloons each time she breathed. She could only think that it was a relief the mantis was not wearing a skirt.

"Good mantis," she said, remembering her manners. "What is your name?"

Even if this was a 'preying' mantis, she reasoned that a courteous exchange was her best option until she had a fair chance of chucking it through the window. That the mantis was a male she was sure because the pants were far too short for its long legs. On its tiny chest, between the open folds of its jacket, grew a single curly hair above (what appeared to be) a small, red tattoo.

"I'm Krik," said the mantis, extending four handshakes at once, "from down under."

"You're from Australia?" Rafi asked in disbelief, although this discovery was hardly remarkable in light of the tattoo.

"Not that down under," said Krik, smiling. "You know, down, down under." One of his arms (or legs – one can never be sure with a mantis) squeezed her nose reassuringly. "But we'll come to that in due time. For now, it is enough for you to know that I won't hurt you."

Suddenly Krik puffed out his chest. His tiny chest grew and grew until the tattoo looked like a red heart with a black arrow running through it that read 'Mrok'. "But I could you know," he continued in the same voice that Rafi had heard when there was talk of biting noses. "I could have 'preyed' on your nose just now as you were sleeping, hopped out the window, and been long gone before you knew what bit you. But," said Krik, dwindling an inch and looking friendly again, "dear Rafi, I am not here to hurt you. In fact, my associates and I are here to protect you."

From where they stood on the desk and the dresser, the two rats bowed low. The rat on the dresser bowed so low it fell into the sock drawer.

"Protect me?" said Rafi. Fearfully, she gazed around the room.

"Yeh, dat's right, Rafi," said the rat in the sock drawer. Still wearing a sock on its head, the rat rested its chin on the edge of the drawer. "We's here to protect ya." The rat smelled its armpits, making an awful face. "We's brudders, ya know. Not Krik though," added the rat as if this needed an explanation. "My name's Pud, and, and over there," Pud continued, nodding toward the desk, "that's Bree. He knows everything. Reading, surfing, flying ... And we sees that you awreddy met Dlop." With pinpoint accuracy, Pud hit Dlop on the head with a rolled up pair of socks.

Not quite ready for introductions Dlop continued snoring, wrapping his tail around Rafi's ear.

"Yes," said Krik tersely. Filled with the purest amber, his clear eyes glared at Pud. "I was going to properly introduce you, but that will have to do. I can't do everything in a minute."

Encouraged by the friendly faces on and around her, Rafi sat up carefully on her bed. As for Krik, he rode her nose like a championship rider, and Dlop (still asleep) hung from her ear like a furry earring. If her mother had entered the room just then things might have taken a turn for the worse, but no one came, and Newton's Apple was as quiet as the soft moonlight illuminating Krik's small, green face.

"Hello, Krik," she said bowing, a difficult feat when you are bowing to someone standing on your nose. It was then that she noticed the mantis wore a brown satchel over its shoulder, which did not improve the outfit.

"I'm honored to meet you," she said truthfully. "Never have I met such a fierce and fashionable mantis before," she added, less truthfully. "I can only guess that you must be the leader of the League of Mantis."

Krik actually blushed. Other than a reddening of his skin and a confused gurgling in his throat, he made no further reply.

Rafi bowed her head to Bree.

"Hello, Bree," she said wonderingly, having never met a surfing rat before. Nonplussed, Bree cleaned his teeth with a paper clip as he sat cross-legged on the mouse.

"You are a miracle among rats indeed," she added, trying to imagine what a surfing rat might look like. "I didn't know rats could read – especially history – although I wonder if you enjoyed the book. And I'm sure that I've never heard of a surfing rat. Quite remarkable."

Bree snorted at the book. "Bubonic Plague, yeah, right," he said disgustedly. "Rafi, your history book is all wrong. Of course, what can one expect from a book written by Drogs? Blame the rats. Back in those times, it was the Drogs who needed a bath – not the rats. In fact, it was a rat doctor who eventually sorted the whole thing out. It's a bad rat – I mean rap. I'm surprised we haven't been blamed for rat music."

"Well," said Rafi wondering what a Drog was, but thinking this was not the time for such questions. "Perhaps when I am older we can plead your case before the United Nations. I'm sure they will listen to such a noble and worldly rat."

Bree bowed low.

Next, Rafi turned to Pud. Having converted his tail into a lasso he was climbing, knob by knob, back up the dresser. After making it successfully to the top, he blew a wet, perfumed raspberry at Bree.

Still wearing Dlop, Rafi bowed and smiled at Pud.

"Greetings, Pud," she said. "You are also a miracle. With an introduction like that you could be the Secretary General of the United Nations."

Pud blushed, burying his head in his armpit.

Finally, Rafi bowed to Dlop. This gesture was entirely lost on the rat as he swung from her ear like a snoring pendulum. "Dlop," she said soothingly, "dear little Dlop. I suspect that you are the greatest miracle of all."

Dlop made no reply.

"Didja hear that everyone?" blurted Pud. "I'm a sexy general!"

"Well spoken, Rafi," said Krik. He gazed into her eyes with wonder. "May I say on behalf of the League of Mantis and those gathered here, it is a great honor to meet you."

It was Rafi's turn to blush. She could not imagine, even for one second, why three rats and a mantis had taken up residence in her bedroom, and even more mysteriously, why they considered it an honor to meet her. Unaware of any town by-laws that should end the discussion, she leaned forward and smiled at Krik.

"Thank you, Krik," she said graciously. She unwound Dlop's tail from her ear, and placed him gently on the bed, stroking his soft fur. He purred like a kitten.

Rafi gazed sweetly at Krik with crossed eyes. "Perhaps you would be more comfortable on the bed," she said. The constant strain of looking up at the mantis was giving her a headache, not to mention a questionable future as a U.N. ambassador.

Krik hopped onto the bed. "Why, thank you," he said. In a flurry of green arms and legs, he removed his satchel, placing it on the bed as other arms and legs removed his jacket and pants. Having joined Krik, Bree took the clothing, jumped on the windowsill, dressed the clothes peg, and then returned to the bed. Only when this was completed to Krik's satisfaction did the mantis sit down in a modest chair of his own making using four of his long legs.

"Krik," said Rafi wonderingly and remembering the heart-shaped tattoo on his chest, "why do you wear clothes? And, if it is not too bold to ask, who is Mrok?"

Bree and Pud laughed. Even Dlop seemed to giggle in his sleep.

"Hrmmph," said Krik. A nasty, 'preying' look shot from his eyes. Apparently, this was enough to silence the rats.

"Well, if you must know, Rafi," he said testily, "Mrok is my wife."

"Your wife!" exclaimed Rafi. She was delighted in discovering a new miracle – a married mantis. "How wonderful!"

"Some would think so," snapped Krik in an irritated tone that did not quite agree.

"Not!" quipped Pud. As if he was a diver, he performed a magnificent half gainer onto the bed.

"Do you have children?"

Bree and Pud choked with laughter. Unable to contain themselves they fell into each other's arms, rolling over and over until Pud fell off the bed.

"Enough," Krik snapped from his chair. No longer green, his face had attained a lovely shade of puce. The look in his eyes as he glared at Bree and Pud could have cracked a carton of hard-boiled eggs. He stared the rats into complete silence, that is, except Dlop who snored and squeaked and purred as if nothing in the entire world, not even a 'preying' mantis, could disturb his sleep.

"No, Rafi," said Krik, glaring at Dlop. "I do not have children. But," he said, pawing his throat, "unlike many of my child rearing brethren, I still have my head."

"Your head?" said Rafi, wondering if she had missed something in Mr. Mockingstock's biology class. "I don't understand. What does having children have to do with your head?"

"Here it comes," said Bree.

"Ahem." Krik cleared his throat, ignoring the remark. "Perhaps you are unacquainted with the mating habits of the mantis. In order for Mrok to have children, I must first lose my head."

"How dreadful," said Rafi. She tried to remember all she could about the strange mating habits of the mantis. No wonder it is all so confusing, she thought. Depending on which side of the marriage you stood on, a praying or 'preying' mantis made perfect sense.

"Why do you wear clothes?"

Krik's face fired to an intense red that would have made a hot tamale proud. Glinting like daggers, his eyes transfixed the two rats before they could say another word.

"Mrok gave them to me to make me look ... er ... more attractive."

"I see," said Rafi, "so that is why ..."

"... I use the green clothes peg," said Krik. "You see, Mrok is strong and fast, but her eyesight is failing. More than once, she has bitten the clothes peg, thinking it was me, only to discover her mistake afterwards which certainly does little to improve her temper. But today she is far away." He lowered his voice, nodding at the clothes peg. For the first time Rafi noticed the top of the clothes peg was covered with bite marks. "Although I never take chances."

"Speaking of taking chances," said Bree seriously as he watched the window. "We've no time to lose."

"Precisely," said Krik. He stood up, reached into his satchel, and produced a gold pocket watch. Rafi peered over his tiny but muscular shoulder, which sported a fleur-de-lis tattoo. The face of the watch was most peculiar for it had the same number of arms and legs as Krik, several of them moving clockwise in erratic jumps while others swept forward and backward at dizzying speeds, all at the same time. After studying the watch for several seconds, during which time he frequently consulted the moon, the mantis returned the watch to the satchel and resumed his chair. He looked up at Rafi.

"Perhaps, Rafi," he said solemnly, "you are wondering why we are here."

"True," said Rafi, staring at the window along with Bree, "and wondering why I need your protection."

"Two questions," said Krik methodically as if he was a teacher in school. "Two questions to which I shall respond with one answer. Only where to begin? The beginning? The end? Before the beginning?" He gave Bree a deliberate nod.

Bree rubbed his right shoulder. With a single leap he landed on the windowsill and removed the clothes peg. Then he closed and locked the window.

"First," said Krik with a sudden air of formality, "do you have the stones, Rafi?"

"Yes," Bree added quickly. "The stones your father gave you last night. Do you have them?"

"The stones?" asked Rafi. She eyed Krik and Bree suspiciously. "What do the stones have to do with you?"

Equally suspicious, a moonbeam projected through the window into Krik's anxious face. For a 'preying' mantis, he suddenly looked pale and frightened.

"Everything," he said stiffly. There was something in his amber eyes that made Rafi think that she had nothing to fear from the mantis or even the rats who watched and waited (and slept) on her bed. Any fear she may have had concerning these strange visitors was swept away by her overwhelming desire to know more about the stones.

She reached under her pillow. The sock still lay where she had left it. She turned the sock upside down, half expecting it to be empty. To her intense relief, however, three black stones tumbled out of the sock into her open hand. As if from worlds away, the runes on each stone shone with a cold, blue light.

"Careful," said Krik anxiously. "Don't drop them or we'll all be stone. Place them gently on the bed so that I may see them."

One by one, Rafi placed the stones on the bed in front of Krik. Any thoughts she may have had that Krik would gather them up in his many arms and legs evaporated as soon as he reached into his satchel and pulled out a magnifying glass. For the longest time, and with many a sidelong glance at Bree, he inspected the runes on each stone. Apparently not satisfied with this inspection he reached into his satchel, pulling out a claw full of dust, which he threw upon the stones.

Rafi gasped. As if by some magic she did not understand the light in the stones changed color before her eyes. At first, the blue light seemed to die within each stone, but then it returned, growing rapidly in intensity and color. From blue, it changed to purple, from purple to green, from green to orange and then … Suddenly, three jets of red flame shot out from the stones, striking the carved faces that watched from the ceiling in silent repose, setting both the ceiling and the walls on fire.

"What is happening?" she cried helplessly. Before she could scream 'fire,' Krik silenced her with a wave of his claw.

"Shhh," he said grimly as if being burned alive was all in a day's work for a mantis. "No need to wake the others." He pointed a dusty claw at the walls and ceiling. "See? There is nothing to fear."

For reasons Rafi could never explain, or perhaps because of her growing trust in Krik, she waited. She did not have to wait for long. As if possessed with lungs that could rival the greatest wind, the runes on the stones inhaled the fire, flames and all, in less time than the blink of an eye.

Beyond words, she gazed around the burned and blackened room. Her heart sank. A gas explosion could not have been more complete in its destruction of the core. The donut had been fried to a crisp, three lamps were missing heads, the Telemission had melted, and half of the baboon clock's tail was missing. It was a miracle that her bed had not caught fire.

Dumbfounded, she gaped at the devastation wrought by the fire.

Krik turned excitedly to Bree. "There's no question about it," he said. "These are the Stones of Erebus."

"The Stones of Erebus?" Rafi asked weakly.

"Three of them to be precise," said Krik. "There are seven in all."

Rafi counted the stones on her bed. "Seven stones?" she asked. "Where are the others? And what are the Stones of Erebus?"

"Perhaps she should hear the song," suggested Bree.

Krik nodded. "It is time, Rafi, for you to understand." He turned to Bree and Pud. "Wake up Dlop and let's begin." He stood up from his chair, folding his arms behind his back just like a schoolboy about to sing a song. Behind him, Bree and Pud balanced Dlop on his tail. Standing on either side of Dlop, they formed a ratty chorus line. Then, under a spotlight provided by the brooding moon, Krik began to sing.

"Once upon a distant dream
In an age that Time forgot,
Before the children of the stars,
Before a moment thought,
Before the day, before the night,
Before the waning moon,
The Miracle of Miracles,
Watched a promise bloom."

After the word 'bloom,' Bree and Pud sang the chorus. "Bloom," sang Bree. "Bloom," sang Pud. After an awkward silence, Pud pulled Dlop's tail. "Doom," sang Dlop as Pud continued to pull his tail. Only after Dlop finally said something that sounded like 'bloom,' did Krik continue.

"On sunlit wings she learned to walk
Upheld in love and pride,
Round the Milky Way she danced,
Great Heavens, how she cried!
Tears of green, tears of blue,
As trees and oceans once forlorn,
Sang a wishful melody
And so the Earth was born."

"Born," sang Bree.

"Born," sang Pud.

"Mourn," sang Dlop after a pull on his tail.

"Heaven's hand drew seven stones
Cast by day upon the night,
Three stones for Wisdom, Beauty, and Grace,
One stone for Fire bright,
One stone for Ocean, one for Wind
One stone for Mountain tall,
Seven stones for seven daughters
Shall rule the fate of all."

"All," sang Bree.

"All," sang Pud.

"Fall," squeaked Dlop, whose tail was beginning to hurt.

"That was wonderful," said Rafi, clapping her hands. It was hard to know whether the song was finished because Dlop kept squeaking and did not stop until Pud released his tail.

"Only, what does it mean?"

Krik assumed a stance that was neither praying nor 'preying.' Tiny as he was, he straddled the bed like a green giant.

"In the beginning," he said in an important voice, "before you were born, before ..."

"... anyone was born ..." Pud shouted excitedly, having heard the story before.

"... when rats had the good sense to be silent," Krik retorted angrily, "there were seven stones. Seven stones, given to Earth after she was born to rule the world. And in return, she gave one stone to each of her daughters: Mountain, Ocean, Fire and Wind ..."

"That's three!" yelled Pud.

"Four," corrected Krik, who was looking more like a 'preying' mantis by the second. "And one stone was given to each of her youngest daughters – the three Fates – Wisdom, Beauty, and Grace. Together, Earth's daughters ruled the world. There was peace and happiness in the water, on the land and in the air. First, came the sweet grasses. Then the whispering trees. The sky became full of wings and song. Life grew as it had never grown before. Animals walked the earth ..."

"That's when the rats came, Rafi," said Pud, excitement pouring from his eyes, "I'll bet we was here even before bugs like Krik."

"That," said Krik, desperately trying to maintain his composure, "is a matter of debate. If I may continue ..."

"I ate a bug once," said Pud, sticking out his tongue. "Tasted like chicken."

Unable to go on, Krik collapsed in his chair. If it had been a real chair Rafi was sure that he would have thrown it at Pud. However, sitting seemed to help the mantis, and after a few moments of glaring at Pud, he rose from his chair and continued his story.

"Then came the dinosaurs ..." he said.

"Dinosaur rats, Rafi," said Pud. He stretched out his paws until they could go no further. "Big rats. Rats so big ..."

"... that the others hated them," snarled Krik, who was turning even redder than before. "All creatures, great and small, lived in harmony together for many years. But one day a new creature was born who was not like any of the others. His name was Triodon." Krik turned to Pud, but Pud, along with Dlop, had suddenly decided that it was best to hear the rest of the story from under Bree's knees.

"Triodon," repeated Krik, louder than before. He obviously enjoyed the silence. "He could not call any of the others father, mother, sister or brother. He was different from them all. Yet their faces were upon him and there was something of him in all of them. At first, he was friendly to the others but they shunned him because he was different. No one would walk or talk or sleep with him nor let him play in any of their games. And so he grew lonely in a world teeming with life."

"How terrible," said Rafi, "how can people, I mean, creatures, be so cruel?"

Krik nodded grimly. "Cruel indeed. Yet Triodon walked alone. With every step his heart grew heavier and heavier until even the sound of his own breath became wearisome, and his sadness turned to anger, his anger to hatred and his hatred to stone. And as each passing day brought him nothing but misery, he resolved to have his revenge. Not only with those who mocked or shunned him, but with all living things. And as he sat alone in the salted bitterness of his own tears, he remembered the legend of the seven stones. In that fateful moment he decided that, if his fate upon Earth was to be ruled by the thoughtlessness of others, he alone should rule Earth."

"This story is so sad," said Rafi. She wiped her tears on the bed sheet. "My heart goes out to Triodon. If only they had embraced difference instead of rejecting it."

"Wisely said, Rafi," said Krik. "But it was too late. Triodon's heart was black with hatred, and even as the others laughed at him, he plotted their destruction. With his great wings he flew to Wind and said: 'Mother Wind, your sister Ocean begs that you send your stone to her that she may stop Fire from destroying all life upon Earth. She sends me as her humble messenger that I may take the stone to her and return it safely to your keeping when all is done.' Not wishing to see the skies without wings, Wind gave Triodon the stone and said: 'When Earth is safe from my sister Fire, bring me this stone so that none alone may rule Earth.' And Triodon lied. 'I will.' And so Wind was deceived."

Krik paused.

"Next, aided by his powerful tail, Triodon swam to the bottom of Ocean and said: 'Mother Ocean, your sister Fire begs that you send your stone to her that she may stop Mountain from destroying all life upon Earth. She sends me as her humble messenger that I may take the stone to her and return it safely to your keeping when all is done.' Not wishing to see her waters bitter and empty of life, Ocean gave Triodon the stone and said: 'When Earth is safe from my sister Mountain, bring me this stone so that none alone may rule Earth.' And Triodon lied. 'I will.' And so Ocean was deceived."

Krik paused again.

"Protected by his thick scales, Triodon then made his way into Fire and said: 'Mother Fire, your sister Mountain begs that you send your stone to her that she may stop Wind from destroying all life upon Earth. She sends me as her humble messenger that I may take the stone to her and return it safely to your keeping when all is done.' Not wishing to see her flames unable to bring new life upon the soil, Fire gave Triodon the stone and said: 'When Earth is safe from my sister Wind, bring me this stone so that none alone may rule Earth.' And Triodon lied. 'I will.' And so Fire was deceived."

Rafi leaned forward on her bed. She was so fascinated by Krik's story she failed to notice that Dlop was sleeping on her head. His tail dangled between her eyes. As for Bree and Pud, they stood next to the window as rigid as stone soldiers, but there was not a trace of sleep in their eyes.

Krik went on with his story.

"Finally, on his great legs, Triodon descended deep into Mountain and said: 'Mother Mountain, your sister Wind begs that you send your stone to her that she may stop Ocean from destroying all life upon Earth. She sends me as her humble messenger that I may take the stone to her and return it safely to your keeping when all is done.' Not wishing to see the land covered by water, Mountain gave Triodon the stone and said: 'When Earth is safe from my sister Ocean, bring me this stone so that none may rule Earth alone.' And Triodon lied. 'I will.' And so Mountain was deceived."

Krik heaved a long sigh.

"With the four stones, Triodon now ruled the four corners of Earth. But the Fates, hearing of Triodon's treachery, were not to be deceived. Deep into Mountain they fled to a place called Erebus and there they guarded the three remaining stones for many years until, weary at last, they fell asleep. And as they lay sleeping, Triodon crept into Erebus, and from the hand of each Fate he took one black stone."

Rafi was spellbound. Never in her life had she heard such a story. It was simply too impossible to be true. And yet there sat upon her bed a talking mantis, three singing rats and three stones. One look around the room told her that these were no ordinary stones. Somehow, it all added up. But as to what 'up' was she had not a clue.

"Are you telling me that these are three of the seven stones?" she asked in a hushed voice.

"Three of the Seven Stones of Erebus," corrected Krik. He nodded so vigorously that it did not look like he needed Mrok for his head to fall off. "These are the stones of the three Fates: Wisdom, Beauty and Grace. Triodon has the other four in his keeping. But he now knows that the three have been found and his servants have been unleashed for one purpose alone – to find the stones and return them to him so that he may destroy Earth."

"I don't understand," said Rafi miserably, thinking about her family and friends and all of the miracles she had come to love upon the earth. "How can Triodon destroy Earth? I have three of the stones and nothing has changed."

"You have not thrown them, Rafi," said Krik. "For the hand that throws the stones will rule the fate of all according to such will as they possess. Even to throw one stone can cause great good or greater evil depending on the hand and heart that throws it. The runes on the stones are not for decoration. Each is an ancient rune and has meaning beyond understanding for they were written by day upon the night. What looks to you like a letter H is HAGAL, that which gives mere substance its reality. It is HAGAL that helps shape our intentions into what they are or will become. The X you see before you is NAUD. Time itself spins forever from NAUD's loom. From NAUD we determine what Time means to each and every one of us, however long or short it may be. The I is ISS, that which keeps our existence together. Without ISS we would simply fly into the dust from which we came. Whether we walk, crawl, fly or swim, it is ISS that gives us our strength to go on."

Instinctively, Rafi shrank from the stones. However beautiful they might have been, they now filled her with terror. For a horrible moment, she thought of nothing but throwing the stones out the window. But what if Krik's words were true? Were these three of the seven stones that once ruled Earth? It did not make any sense.

"I don't understand," she said slowly. "My father found these stones in the belly of a T-Rex."

"Along with Triodon's arm," said Krik calmly.

"Triodon's arm?" cried Rafi, not caring if she woke up half the neighborhood. "Krik, this is impossible! How can I believe such a tale? The dinosaurs became extinct millions of years ago. Yet earlier you spoke of Triodon as if he was alive. How could his arm ..."

"I'm sorry, Rafi," said Krik miserably, "but then, so are all living things. Sorry that they treated Triodon with contempt instead of friendship, sorry that the world has changed, and sorry to burden you with this history. But to answer your questions, the possession even of one stone gives long life and Triodon has four ..."

"But the T-Rex?"

"His name was Eidon," said Krik patiently, "and he was king of the dinosaurs. When the Fates awoke the next morning and discovered that Triodon now possessed the seven stones, they were helpless against him. They flew to Eidon to seek his help. And so it was that Eidon determined to fight Triodon in a last attempt to save Earth. But Triodon was waiting. He could not resist gloating so he taunted Eidon with the stones concealed in each of his closed hands. And although Eidon could not see how many stones were in each hand, he formulated a plan; a plan that his brave heart alone knew could destroy the dinosaurs but save Earth. He begged and pleaded with Triodon to return the stones, and if not, to spare his life so that he too could live in the new world. With this deception, he got closer and closer to Triodon until, suddenly, striking out with his great jaws he tore Triodon's right arm from his body, and in one gulp swallowed arm, hand, stones and all. But even in his agony Triodon realized his folly. Opening his left hand, he threw four stones. As each stone fell, so too fell the fate of Earth. The four stones thrown by Triodon exacted his revenge upon Eidon, his family and all of his kind. At the same time, the stones thrown by Eidon, even in his swallowing of Triodon's arm, saved Earth. And Earth shook to her very core to the cries of Mountain, Ocean, Fire, Wind and the three Fates."

Krik stopped for a moment to catch his breath. It was a lot to say for one so small. His tiny chest heaved with emotion, spelling Mrok with every breath. Bree came up from behind to pat him on the back, but the mantis waved him back.

"But Eidon didn't really throw the stones," Rafi pointed out. "He swallowed them."

"So he did," was Krik's ready reply. "But, even as Triodon's arm passed through Eidon, so too passed three of the seven Stones of Erebus. And so, Rafi," he went on, emotion still ringing in his voice, "now is the time for you to understand. We have traveled far to ask something of you that may be more than you can give. Let there be no doubt. You are the one we seek. You must help us return the seven stones to Erebus. You must join our quest."

"New friends," said Rafi, deeply moved. She looked at each of them with the greatest admiration. "With all due respect, you must be mistaken. I am not the one you seek. I can't be. While it is clear to me that these stones are a miracle and must be returned to their rightful owners, I cannot even begin to imagine what I can do that the Daughters of Earth were not able to do themselves. What makes you think that I could possibly help you?"

Krik looked at Rafi for the longest time. "Yes," he said to himself. "She is the one. It is written upon the stones and in the stars. Oh, but she is young. Strange that this child holds the fate of our world in her hands. Yet her heart is as pure as sunlight; her smile a drink of dawn." He sighed as he looked out the window. Soon darkness would give way to the gentle caresses of morning. He smiled at Rafi who was carefully looking for Dlop in her pajamas. That was enough to convince him. "The others have had their chance," he thought to himself. "Now it is in this Daughter of Earth we must place our trust."

He hopped onto Rafi's knee. Even from her knee, the intelligence in his eyes reached deep into her own. Together, their eyes sparkled as one.

"Rafi," he said, "there is no doubt that you are the one. There are many signs we can read even though you cannot. That crack above your bed is no ordinary crack. That is the rune PERTRA and it tells us that the future of the stones is in you as much as it is in Triodon. Then there is your hair. Have you not noticed how the letter in your hair resembles the runes on the stones? That is the rune BJARKA, and to us there can be no clearer sign that you are the rightful bearer of the stones. Of course, there is also the poem ..."

"What poem?" asked Rafi.

"We should leave soon," said Bree, still staring out the window. "Morning approaches."

"Your poem to be precise," said Krik. "More of a riddle, I suppose.

Dances with the daffodils,
Loves all living things,
Rain Walker,
River Talker,
Lives the song she sings."

"I don't know what to say," said Rafi, finally convinced that she was still dreaming. "Hard though it is to believe, let us suppose I am the one you seek. What is it you want of me?"

Krik took a deep breath. It seemed as though the moment he had been waiting for had finally come. Great tears rolled from his eyes onto the bed. Bree's and Pud's eyes were also wet. Holding paws, they looked up at Rafi.

"On behalf of Mountain, Ocean, Fire, Wind and the Fates ..."

"And the rats," added Pud.

"We respectfully request that you save Earth."

Unable to speak, Rafi picked up the stones. In her hands, they suddenly shone with a white light that filled the room. As if she had swallowed the sun, Rafi shone as brightly as the stones themselves. Beads of light breathed through her nostrils and lips as waves of chestnut hair fell around her autumn eyes like leaves in an enchanted forest. In a second that could only be measured in eternity she thought about her mother and father, her brother, the river, the trees and the flowers, and all of the sleepy citizens of Drumheller. As songbirds began to sing a new song outside her window, she promised:

"I will help you."

CHAPTER FOUR

FLIGHT FROM HOME

The sun was just beginning to blush across the eastern sky when Rafi lowered herself into the garden from her bedroom window. It was not the first time that she had left the Apple by her window, but with the strange events of last night still fresh in her mind, she wondered if this might be the last, and if she would ever see her home again.

"Are you sure about this, Krik?" she hissed at the mantis through the open window. Quite apart from fleeing from her home on the word of a mantis and an off-key chorus of rats, she could not believe what she was doing. What was she thinking? That she could save the world from a creature who walked and talked with dinosaurs, and then, as easily as dusting a table, wiped them off the face of the earth?

"This is madness!"

"Most definitely so," said Krik brightly. He hopped from the bed onto the windowsill. Reaching into his satchel, he pulled out six black riding gloves and began putting them on two at a time.

"Aphid leather," he explained, noticing the quizzical look on Rafi's face. His gaze strayed to a knapsack swinging heavily from her shoulder.

"Do we have enough food, Rafi?"

"How should I know?" Rafi asked miserably, even more convinced that she was out of her mind. In her mad haste to vacate the Apple she had thrown what little food she could think of into her knapsack along with a few useful items such as matches and a cooking pot. Somehow she doubted that three water bottles, four chocolate bars, a pound of cheese, a box of macaroni, raisins, peanuts, and a bag of carrot sticks would be enough to sustain five appetites (however small) in a quest to save Earth.

"You haven't even told me where we're going or how long we'll be gone."

"As to that," said Krik honestly, donning the last pair of gloves, "I don't rightly know myself. But I can tell you," he added hastily, seeing the stress soar in Rafi's face, "that we have until the new moon to save Earth. That is three moons – three nights – from now. After that, should our quest prove unsuccessful, you needn't worry about coming home."

"Meaning what, exactly?" said Rafi, although, judging from the tingling she felt down her spine, Krik's implication was clear enough.

"Meaning that there won't be anything to come back to," said Bree from where he sat on the bed cheerfully slapping Dlop's eyes open.

"Which all works out," said Pud cheerfully as he detached the mouse cord from Rafi's computer. He slung the mouse around his shoulders. "Because we'll all be dead."

"Did I hear something about food?" asked Dlop, waking up.

"Ignore them," said Krik crisply. All business that morning, he consulted his watch. "Nobody's dead – yet. And no one will die," he added, glaring at Pud, "if we all keep our minds on our jobs and not on ourselves."

"Can't you at least tell me where we're going?" asked Rafi irritably. Due to the lack of sleep, her excitement about saving Earth was evaporating as quickly as the dew. From the sound of Orly's cats across the street, it was garbage day. This was not a good sign. Orly was unusually punctual on garbage days and it was almost six o'clock in the morning. Once Orly was up and within reach of her telephone, The Mayor usually was not far behind.

"We must reach the Travelers' Nest by seven," said Krik smoothly. After making some final adjustments to his gloves, he hopped onto Rafi's shoulder. He looked every inch a boxing mantis. Commanding a view of the neighborhood, and fully aware of the light gathering in the sky, he called to Bree, Pud and Dlop who were engaged in a poor attempt at making Rafi's bed.

"We must hurry."

"The Travelers' Nest?" asked Rafi suspiciously. "That's a restaurant on the edge of town. What are we doing there?"

"There," said Krik patiently, the slight reddish tinge in his cheeks suggesting that he was not used to giving so many explanations, "we will turn east."

Rafi was shocked.

"East? But there's nothing out there but badlands!"

"Exactly," said Krik calmly. Military fashion, he boxed the air, evidently a signal for the rats to move out. "Our quest awaits us on the other side of the badlands ..."

"The other side of the bad..."

Krik raised a gloved claw. "I will explain everything in due time, Rafi," he said quickly. With another gloved claw he managed to push a tiny button on his watch, which ticked like a stopwatch except that the tick sounded like a cricket.

"We have a long road ahead of us," he said, putting away the watch. His eyes turned toward the street, surveying Orly's house and the roof-topped horizon. "The Travelers' Nest is just the beginning. But now is not the time for explanations, Rafi. Now is the time for act..."

On cue, Pud somersaulted through the window still wearing a sock on his head. He landed in a crowd of daisies. Pleased with his grand entrance into the garden, he stood up in the daisies like a court jester, scoring himself ten points. The computer mouse was still hanging around his neck. Dlop was not far behind. What he lacked in technique he more than made up for in distance, although it turned out that this was because Bree had thrown him through the window. He was lucky that Pud scored him a two.

Bree was less theatrical. Removing his glasses, he let them fall around his neck where they hung from a gold chain. After handing Rafi the green clothes peg, he jumped from the window into the garden where he joined Pud and Dlop.

Rafi reached up and closed the window. Then, with a sigh, she pegged the clothes peg on her shirt. She couldn't help thinking that it was a good thing she was fleeing Drumheller and not going to school. After all, a six-inch, green clothes peg and an equally noticeable mantis on her shoulder were bound to turn some heads.

But that was not the only thought on Rafi's mind. What would her parents say? Would they understand? She had never run away from home before although it occurred to her that saving Earth seemed to be a pretty good reason. She watched Bree and Pud try different flowers on Dlop's head as if they were hats. Tears wet her eyes as she imagined the worried faces an empty bed would give her mother and father when they discovered she was missing.

Slowly, she walked through the garden toward the street. At the edge of the garden she turned around and looked back at the bright green door of Newton's Apple. Anxious and confused, she prayed that someone – anyone – would open the door to stop her. She was so sad, almost desperate, that she would have even settled for The Mayor. Her heart tugged on the brass doorknocker, but, of course, the door did not open.

Affectionately, Krik boxed her ear. "You left a note, didn't you?"

Rafi sighed. A strange note was small consolation for a missing daughter. She reread the note in her mind, hoping that it would sound better now than when she wrote it.

Dearest Maman and Pupa;
Gone to save the world. This may take
awhile I expect. Won't be home for dinner.
Don't worry. My new friends will look after me.
(One of them can read!)
P.S. Pupa – it has to do with the T-Rex.
P.P.S. Sorry about the mess.

It didn't.

Unsure as to what would happen next, she gazed toward the east. As if it had been waiting for the right moment, a sunlit finger burst over the horizon, hurtled through the sky and touched her shirt. No longer hanging by the window, her latest creation, ablaze with light, seemed to leap from her shoulders into the morning, filling the world with color. On the front of her shirt, tied in knots of the finest Egyptian papyrus, hung three black stones.

"Wow," said Pud, looking up at her with wonder. "That's some shirt, Raffers. Too bad there won't be anyone to notice if Earth is destroyed."

"Thank you Pud," said Rafi sarcastically, her mood uplifting with a slight breeze. "If the world is going to end, at least I'm dressed for the occasion."

"Where's Dlop?" said Bree from where he was searching the flowers. "If he's walked off again for another snooze, I'll kill him."

Rafi watched Bree search the grounds along with Pud who was brandishing the cord of her computer mouse as if it was a whip, mercilessly thrashing the garden with the mouse end in an animated attempt to find Dlop. She did not blame Dlop in the least; life always seemed less complicated when you were asleep.

"Which way again?" she asked. She seemed to have lost all sense of direction. With nowhere else to go, she turned and faced the street.

The street looked lonely and strangely unfamiliar. From across the street, Rafi noticed that nine of Orly's cats had taken an unpleasant interest in Bree and Pud and were walking toward them. One of the cats, who appeared to be in charge, was as big and mean looking as a mountain lion. The others looked mangy and ugly. Bristling with confidence, the cats advanced in a column, an army of claws and fur. Fanning out into a row along the edge of the garden, they stopped, hissed and blocked the way.

"East," said Krik eyeing the cats darkly, and wishing that Mrok was nearby if only to prove that cats don't have nine lives.

Rafi tightened the straps on her knapsack. It felt as if it was filled with stones. East? Krik made it sound as if they were headed to the local mall. Without map or compass, what chance did they have in the wilderness? It suddenly occurred to her that a tent would have been useful while sleeping under the stars along with all the other things she had forgotten. Mentally, she reconstructed the food she had put in the knapsack along with a change of underwear, a toothbrush (she had forgotten to add toothpaste) and a bar of soap, none of which boosted her confidence.

But there was something else in the knapsack that attracted her attention. The knapsack breathed and snored, and seemed to have miraculously grown a tail. So that was where Dlop was hiding. She could not resist a chuckle.

Krik threw a punch at Orly's house. "Due east," he said. "Just put your back to the bright green door and walk."

"Run," suggested Bree who was studying the biggest cat. The cat was watching Bree, a triumphant grin playing below its whiskers.

"That will take us straight through Orly's garden," said Rafi, aghast. 'Garden' hardly described Orly's front yard. "Is there no other way? Orly will have a fit."

"Better fit than dead," said Bree, wondering if curiosity really did kill the cat.

Pud swung the computer mouse as if it was a mace and chain. "No," he said, an unfriendly gleam in his eye, "dead is definitely better."

Krik swelled until there was no doubt that he was a 'preying' mantis. "Now," he said.

"Run," Bree repeated, taking careful aim at the biggest cat.

"Kill," snarled Pud, picking up a rock in his spare paw as he gathered momentum.

"Cheese!" said Dlop from somewhere in the knapsack.

Rafi broke into a run alongside Bree and Pud. If Orly's cats had thought that breakfast was fast approaching, they were sadly mistaken. She rushed by two of them, launching the cats into orbit like flabby footballs. Bree grabbed the cat leader by the tail, and, swinging the shocked animal like a hammer, beat the others within an inch of their nine lives. Armed and deadly, and with many an 'ohoy!,' Pud introduced three of the cats to his mouse, 'rocking' the rest of them senseless for good measure. By any stretch of the imagination it was a 'cat'astrophe. Nine cats in a dryer could not have vented a more hideous display of yowls and flying cat fur.

Alerted by the noise and the smell of garbage, Orly opened her door. In a downpour of tails and cat fur she stared at Rafi, a look of complete bewilderment upon her face. She spotted Bree and Pud.

"Help! Thieves! Fire! Awake!"

Orly's screams could have awakened a dead rooster. She stumbled through her door and collapsed in her prized petunias where she lay screaming.

"Murderers! Assassins! Awake!"

There was no time to waste. In one jump Rafi cleared Orly's shrieking body. Without looking behind her, she vaulted the back fence and kept running as Krik held on for dear life. Bree and Pud were less polite. Following Rafi, they pawed a path over Orly's body and face, leaving a trail of muddy paw prints. In all the excitement, Pud bit Orly on the nose.

"Pestilence! Plague! Awake!"

Houses and fences flew by Rafi as she ran. She was by far the fastest runner in Drumheller, and her legs did not fail her now. It was only after she had run three miles at Olympic speed that her legs finally started to slow down. In need of a quick rest, she ducked into a back alley. She bent over to catch her breath.

The alley was deserted. Almost. Within seconds, Bree and Pud raced around the corner, collapsing at Rafi's feet where they lay panting and congratulating each other. Watching from the shadows, a platoon of garbage cans, bins and bags stood in sloppy salute.

"First time a cat was killed by a mouse," said Pud, unable to stop chuckling.

"And a rat," added Bree.

"First time I'll be chucked from Drumheller for sure," said Rafi. She was worried about Orly and her cats. "You didn't really kill it, did you Pud?"

"Nah," said Pud innocently, "just scared 'im, that's all." He winked at Bree. "Permanently."

Rafi sat on a garbage can and considered their predicament. Orly would have called The Mayor by now who would have contacted the police and the fire department. In another few minutes, the military would be combing the streets.

The knapsack groaned behind her back. Surrounded by danger as she was, Rafi let out a hearty laugh. Dlop might have been better off running. It was then that she realized her shoulder was aching. At first, she thought she might have adjusted the straps too tightly on her knapsack or had been the unintended victim of one of Pud's vicious mouse strokes, but the reason, unusually green and mopping his face with a red handkerchief, was kneeling on her shoulder. From all appearances, Krik had converted back to a praying mantis. His claws, even through the gloves, had dug deeply into Rafi's shoulder. For a moment, he looked as if he was going to be sick.

Standing on a garbage can, Rafi scanned the streets and buildings that stretched from the alley all the way to the edge of town. She groaned. The Travelers' Nest might just as well have been on the moon. Defeated, she looked at Krik.

"We'll never make it."

"Non…" said Krik, but he never finished. Without another word, he quickly disappeared into Rafi's hair.

"Rafi?"

"Mopsus!" Rafi could hardly believe her good luck.

"Is everything OK?" asked Mopsus, standing in front of his garbage truck, a confused grin upon his face. "The streets are a nightmare. The Mayor has declared Martial Law, and a tank almost hit my truck. But you look like you've seen a ghost."

Pud picked up a rock. "She was ugly too," he said.

"Ah." Mopsus stopped grinning as he noticed Bree and Pud for the first time. "If it wasn't so early I'd say that rat could talk. He has a most intelligent look about him too, and the other one looks like Thomas Jefferson." He shot a worried look at Rafi. "Don't tell me you've taught rats to speak. The Mayor will have a fit. He'll want them all driven out of town for fear of plague I shouldn't wonder."

"Plague indeed," snorted Bree, putting on his spectacles so he could get a better look at Mopsus. "As a matter of fact ..."

Mopsus dropped the bags he was carrying. He stared open mouthed at the two rats, and then at Rafi.

In an instant Rafi detected an ally. Mopsus had always been kind to her. Except for her father, Mopsus was the only person she knew who had a gift for making the impossible seem possible. In the distance she heard the sounds of police cars and fire trucks patrolling the streets as air raid sirens wailed over Drumheller. Mopsus was her only chance.

"Mopsus," she said breathlessly, her eyes wide with trepidation. "I have no time to explain. My friends and I must leave town to save Earth before The Mayor catches us. Will you help us?"

Mopsus braided a smile. No doubt Rafi was on another one of her adventures, he thought to himself. As to saving the world, he understood such childish fantasies, but last night he noticed that the moon had disappeared for half an hour. A wise man, Mopsus could put two and two together and not be frightened if the answer didn't add up to four. Disappearing moons and talking rats suggested to his mind that something was afoot in Drumheller. But in the end it was the picture he imagined of Orly's and The Mayor's contorted faces that caused him to point to the back of his truck.

"Get in," he said encouragingly.

"You can't be serious," said a testy voice from Rafi's hair.

"It's the only way," said Mopsus, keeping a sharp lookout, and unaware that Rafi had suddenly become a ventriloquist. "They'll search the front." He gently wrapped one of his giant hands around Rafi's elbow. "In with the garbage you go. Don't worry. I've only just begun. It shouldn't smell too bad."

"I am an ambassador to the League of ..." Krik protested, but Rafi drowned him out.

"East," she said, looking at Mopsus. None too eagerly, she mounted the back of the truck as two police cars and a jeep raced past the alley. Distracted by all the noise, including the 'wop, wop, wop' sound of an approaching helicopter, she fell between two bags of garbage.

"Due east," added Krik, still out of sight, and not sounding too pleased with this latest development.

"Lunch," sang Pud. With a magnificent jump he cleared the back of the truck, landing next to Rafi. Too dignified for such behavior, Bree let Mopsus lift him in.

For a wise man, Mopsus could not have been more wrong. The morning's garbage smelled as if it had been collected a month ago. Worse, in her haste to enter the truck, some of the bags had split open, spilling enough garbage all over Rafi, Bree and Pud so that even their own mothers would not be able to tell them apart.

The trip seemed to take forever. Slowly, the garbage truck clattered along busy streets sometimes followed by police cars and army vehicles, which pulled up closely, sirens wailing, before speeding off in search of Rafi.

Gazing out from the back of the truck, Rafi was sure that someone in a jeep had spotted her. She raised her hands to surrender but no one seemed to notice. Her disguise was impenetrable. Aside from garbage all over her clothing, both the ride and the smell had colored her as green as Krik.

Bree and Pud were in garbage heaven.

"Wow," said Pud. He held up a spare rib like a slice of watermelon, stripping the bone clean with his teeth. "A traveling restaurant!"

Bree was more practical. "There's good food here," he said. He started to separate garbage into disgusting piles. "Open your knapsack, Rafi. We can fill it along the way."

This was too much for Rafi and Krik. Simultaneously, they co-invented a new shade of green. Most unfortunately, this was followed by a fair imitation of two geysers. One of them was in Rafi's hair.

"Hot food!" Pud was delighted. So was Bree. Rafi was disgusted. So was Krik. And Dlop was still asleep.

The garbage truck lurched to a halt. A door slammed, and Mopsus's shaggy head towered above the garbage. He held out a callused hand.

"Rough ride?"

Aided by Mopsus, Rafi planted both feet on the pavement. She would have kissed the ground if only it would stop moving. Somewhere beyond her blurred vision, she could barely make out at least one Travelers' Nest.

"This is as far as I go," said Mopsus apologetically. He plucked a compass from a pouch on his belt. "But it's as east as east can be."

Rafi kissed the garbage man on the cheek. "Thank you Mopsus," she said, adding more garbage to his already stained overalls. "I hope we get the chance to repay you for your kindness once we have saved Earth."

"Think nothing of it, dear child," said Mopsus, picking banana and egg from her hair. "Due east, eh?" He spun on his boots and faced the restaurant. For several moments, his head nodded up and down as he studied the compass. A long, aristocratic finger with egg on it pointed to a haze of distant mountains rising above the badlands like a phantom ship with black sails.

"See that mountain in the middle with the top flattened like someone sat on it?" he said. "There's your heading, Rafi. Keep walking toward that mountain and you're headed due east. That is," he hesitated and looked at Rafi, his eyes full of concern, "if you're still prepared to go through with this."

Rafi brushed the garbage still littering her shoulders and hair into the back of the truck, careful not to include Krik who had remained hidden. It was not that the mantis did not trust Mopsus. Indeed, he had already made up his mind that, should Earth be spared, Mopsus would be named Earth Friend and receive the thanks of all creatures, great and small, for the rest of his life. Unfortunately however, for the time being, Mopsus would have to miss his opportunity to meet a Harvard educated mantis.

Aware of Krik's seclusion, and deeply touched by the garbage man's kindness, Rafi bowed before Mopsus.

"Again, our deepest thanks, Mopsus," she said. "If we are to meet again I will see to it that your kindness is not forgotten. Please tell my parents that I am well and protected, but tell no one else – especially not The Mayor."

She paused to watch the effect of her words. Mopsus seemed to have grown in stature as a mixture of love and pride spilled into his eyes.

"Look at you," he said wiping a tear from each eye, "covered with garbage from head to toe and looking every inch a queen." He let out a deep sigh as he turned, got back into his truck, put it into gear, and drove off.

Rafi watched Mopsus and the garbage truck rumble out of sight. They had made it. This far at least. Even Krik was elated with their progress after a brief consultation with his watch. Only a few more steps and they would be in the badlands beyond the clutches of The Mayor.

Krik stepped out from behind Rafi's ear, took off his riding gloves, and put them in his satchel.

"That was close," he said. "But I never lost faith for a minute."

Pud imitated a geyser. "You lost more than that," he said.

"None the less," said Krik, glaring at Pud like a 'preying' mantis about to run amok. "There is no time to lose. Once we're into the badlands we can follow the river for several miles so water should not be a problem. At least for now. I'm more worried about food."

"Then what didja go waste it for?" demanded Pud.

Krik tapped the knapsack.

"Remind me as to what is on the menu, Rafi."

"Well," she said, "as you well know, there was no time for shopping. However," she added, a little annoyed that Krik kept asking about food, "if you must know, we have four chocolate bars, a pound of cheese …"

"Half a pound," corrected Dlop, poking his head out of the knapsack.

"Cheese?" Pud snorted with disgust.

"I thought you would like cheese," said Rafi, crestfallen. "You are a rat aren't you?"

"Another myth," said Bree contemptuously.

"Garbage is starting to sound good already," said Pud.

"Macaroni, raisins, peanuts, carrot sticks …" Rafi mumbled.

"No Pud," said Bree, noticing the sad look in Rafi's eyes. "I meant that you're not a rat."

"Never mind," said Krik, none too cheerfully. "It will have to do. That is if a certain fat somebody doesn't eat it all before we leave town." He shot a reproachful eye at Dlop who sank back down into the knapsack.

"I'm sorry," said Rafi, wondering how she could save Earth when she had failed to pack dinner. "I guess I wasn't thinking."

"Don't mind us," said Pud, coming to her rescue. "We's used to adventure. Why, once Krik forgot to feed us for three days so we almost ate him while he was sleeping …"

"Perhaps," said Bree flatly, cutting off Pud, "we can tell Krik about how we almost ate him when we tell ghost stories around the next campfire. Honestly Pud, can't you keep your big mouth shut?"

"Just kiddin', Krik," said Pud sheepishly.

"Well," said Rafi, giving Krik, Pud and Bree the full measure of her eyes, "while I'm around, nobody will be eating anybody." She gave each of them another eyeful, including Dlop who poked his head out of the knapsack to see what all the commotion was about. "Are we clear?"

"More than ever," said Krik, who, judging by the injured look on his face, appeared to be nursing the wound inflicted upon him by Pud.

"I'm sure we will find some things to eat along the way. We always do, although we've never had to feed a Drog before. I've heard that rat fricassee is a delicacy in some countries."

"That's twice you've said 'Drog,'" said Rafi curiously. "What is a Drog?"

Krik hesitated a moment before answering. He gave Bree a sharp look.

"Well," he said finally, "you are."

"I'm a Drog?"

"It's what we call humans, Rafi," said Bree. "Those who came after the Nadi."

"The Nadi?"

Krik checked his watch. "The Firstborn," he said. "But this discussion will have to wait. It is not one that has ever been shared with a Dr ... er ... human before. Besides, we are not out of town – yet. I, for one, will feel better after we have put some miles behind us. We must hurry."

The Travelers' Nest loomed dead ahead, the last sign of civilization they would see before they stepped into the badlands. As Krik had carefully planned, both the parking lot and the restaurant were empty. The quest would be long gone before anyone knew where they were going.

"One small step for a rat," said Pud solemnly, "one giant leap for rat-kind."

"Miss Malawi."

They never saw him coming. Ablaze in his red sash and armed on either side by a large police officer, The Mayor stood behind them. A triumphant smile animated his moustache so that it looked like a hairy caterpillar someone had stepped on. The quest was finished before it had even started.

"Well, well, well," said The Mayor, stepping forward and looking rather pleased with himself. He had not yet noticed Bree or Pud as they had ducked behind Rafi's legs, or Krik, who had slid back into her hair. "What have we here?" With practiced flourish, he reached into his pockets, producing both pen and notebook, flipping it open like a cell phone.

"Your Lordship," said Rafi, bowing so low her head almost touched her shoes. "We ... I ask for your clemency." She knew that 'clemency' was a word The Mayor liked to hear even though he never granted it. "My friends and I ..."

"Silence!" The Mayor spat into his moustache. Bolstered by the presence of the police and energized by his growing anger, both pen and paper flew together in a grand gesture of authority.

"Rafiatu Malawi," he began as the pen scribbled in the notebook, "you are hereby cited for breaking the following laws and ordinances of the City of Drumheller. Ordinance RM21-08-77: No child under the age of eighteen years is either permitted or tolerated in the City of Drumheller between the hours of 8:00 p.m. and 8:00 a.m. (any time zone) without adult supervision. Ordinance RM26-09-39: All clothing worn in the City of Drumheller must not exceed three colors by design and must not be fastened or adorned by any non-commercial product or naturally occurring substance found within the vicinity of earth. Ordinance RM31-12-66: Imaginary friends of the accused are illegal aliens in the City of Drumheller and are subject to seizure and imprisonment."

The Mayor looked up from his notebook, pleased at his own scribbling. His moustache was about to have baby caterpillars when his face grew as dark as a rain cloud. He had not even gotten close to citing all the new ordinances he would write such as breeding rats within the city limits or biting Orly on the nose when, looking over his notebook, he noticed something long and green on Rafi's shirt and in her hair.

"What ... is ... that?" he bellowed like a wounded rhinoceros. Such was his fury when he saw the green clothes peg on Rafi's shirt and in her hair that veins popped out all over his head. Tufts of hair sprang from his moustache, littering the ground. The officers could do nothing to restrain him.

"How dare you!" he shrieked, gnashing his teeth until the points were ground flat, and shaking off the officers who, by this time, had produced handcuffs. By the confused looks on the officers' faces it was hard to tell whether the handcuffs were meant for Rafi or The Mayor. Followed by the officers he advanced toward Rafi, lowered his notebook and pen, and snatched the clothes peg from her shirt. He would have done the same to the one in her hair had it not been for Krik. The sight of The Mayor's finger rushing toward him, coupled with the fact that he had not eaten all day (minus what he lost in the garbage truck) combined to give Krik the strength and courage (and hunger) of ten 'preying' mantises.

It has long since been debated as to whether banshees or werewolves had moved into the City of Drumheller that day, but such was the indescribable noise made by The Mayor when Krik bit his finger that tourism went up two hundred and sixty-three percent. To this day, the written history in the town archives records the event as a 'close encounter of the green kind.' Orly even called the Vatican upon hearing about what had transpired that morning at the Travelers' Nest, reasoning that only a Pope could reckon with such events – however unnatural.

It was some time before The Mayor returned to earth. He dropped from the sky like an errant bowling ball, fell heavily upon the heads of the two police officers, who stood as still as rigid pins, knocking them both out cold and scoring a ten in the process. His black suit was covered in dirt, and his grand sash had blown away toward the east as if it was a kite. Worst of all, the end of his finger was missing. As he stared in disbelief, blood gushed out all over his suit.

"You … she … devil!" he cried, but his voice was smaller than Krik's. Defenseless and bleeding, without sash, pen or notebook, he just sat there sucking his injured finger, shaking and mumbling as if he had a fever. Still staring at his finger, he rolled over on his back.

"Rafiatu Malawi," he said weakly, looking up at the sky, "as Mayor and Chief Legislator, I hereby ban you from the City of Drumheller."

Pud suddenly appeared from behind Rafi's legs carrying a large rock. "Ban yourself," he said.

Rafi held up her hand. "No, Pud," she said. "The Mayor is only doing his duty. We are not in any danger." She looked at Krik who stood on her shoulder chewing what was left of The Mayor's finger. "Not any more, anyway." She looked back at The Mayor who was staring in disbelief at Pud. "We will have enough explaining to do when we get back without frightening His Lordship."

"I wasna going to frighten Lordy," said Pud, reluctant to let go of his rock. "I was going to ..."

"Pud," said Bree warningly. He lifted the eyelids of both police officers who were still out cold. "Rafi is right. The Mayor has done us no harm." He glanced up at Krik and Rafi. "Let's go before the whole town descends upon us."

Wondering how many laws she had just broken, Rafi picked up The Mayor's notebook and pen. After brushing them off on her pants, she held them out to The Mayor who simply stared at her in wordless horror.

She placed the notebook and pen into one of his torn pockets. "I am sorry, Your Excellency," she said with sincerity. "When there is more time I will explain." She looked at The Mayor as if for the first time. Sitting with his finger in his mouth and mumbling incoherently, he looked and sounded more like a distressed baby than the strong arm of the law.

"Rats," he whispered, unable to take his eyes off Bree and Pud. "Rats, breeding rats, talking rats, rats, rats, rats ..." This last word he kept repeating until it sounded like a singsong.

"Rats, rats, rats ..."

Rafi turned away. In spite of The Mayor's mean temper and the grief he had caused both her and her family, she was sorry to see him in such an awful state. One thing was certain. There was no returning to Drumheller, unless she came back with absolute proof that Earth was in danger.

"Well done, Rafi," said Krik after a loud burp. He reached into his satchel and produced a small bottle from which he squeezed a white liquid all over his body. Then he stuck his head into the satchel and reemerged wearing the world's tiniest pair of sunglasses. Every inch a movie mantis, he looked east.

"At this rate you'll be an ambassador to the United Nations in no time."

Rafi wasn't so sure. Facing east, she gazed at the distant mountains, hovering over the badlands like a broken crown. Suddenly she was struck by the enormity of her quest. A rush of fear and regret pulsed through her body. What lay at the other end of her travels? Would each footstep across the badlands bring her and her new friends closer to completing their quest?

Or were they walking toward certain death?

CHAPTER FIVE

THE OVERSEER OF
TAHW KNAR GNUD

Under the eternal gaze of the distant mountains, Rafi, Krik, Bree, Pud, and Dlop headed east. Soon, the Travelers' Nest was nothing more than a dirty speck behind them. For a mile or two they followed the river, but kept a safe distance from the bank just in case the navy had already set sail in an attempt to find them. From the east, the sun rose swiftly up the cloudless sky, warming their faces with a golden light that spread across the badlands.

Rafi wiped the sweat from her face with a tail from her shirt. Already badly soiled, it perfectly matched the rest of her clothes. Overhead, an F-16 fighter jet streaked through a clear blue sky. She watched its vapor trail slowly dissolve along with her hopes of ever returning to Drumheller. Regretful and worried, she glared at Krik, who was still sitting on her shoulder, looking rather pleased with himself.

"Really Krik," she said, venting some of her frustration onto the mantis, "I've never seen The Mayor so angry. What did you have to go bite his finger off for?"

"Not the whole finger," Krik protested innocently. "At the same time," he patted his stomach, "I won't deny that it wasn't a full course meal."

"Stinks too," said Bree, holding his nose. Using his tail like a whip he lashed out at the battalions of flies that had volunteered to join their quest. "Phew," he said, striking several of them dead with his tail, but the fallen flies were replaced by twice as many new recruits as quickly as they fell. "Give us a break. It's your world we're saving too!"

"Yeh," snapped Pud at a squadron of flies taunting him with their daring acrobatics. "Buzz this!" His lightning jaws snatched a foolish fly in mid air, ending what could have been a promising flying career.

"Now that you mention it," said Rafi, holding her own nose as she continued to glare at Krik. "When was the last time you had a bath?"

Krik produced a gas mask from his satchel. "I was just going to ask you the same question," he said.

"P-U" said Bree again, vying with Pud to be the furthest upwind. "It must be coming from you, P-U-D." After tripping Pud and tying him up with his own tail, he looked up at Rafi and Krik who were arguing about whether Krik had more gas masks in his satchel. He laughed.

"Garbage."

"No it isn't," Rafi argued fiercely, pointing at Krik. "He really stinks!"

"That's because he's covered in garbage," said Bree, an amused grin beneath his whiskers. "And so are you."

It was true. In their haste to escape The Mayor they had forgotten their new attire. Each of them was still covered from head to toe (and paws) with garbage. Rafi's shirt and pants were covered with spaghetti and a particularly nauseous crème sauce complete with maggots, while Krik was dressed in a disgusting puree of egg yolk and coffee grinds. Having licked most of their fur clean from garbage, Bree and Pud looked comparatively clean and respectable, although both needed a bath as well. Pud still had peanut butter on his shoulder.

Krik pulled a soiled tea bag from his satchel. "That settles it," he said. "Let's make for the river where we can wash and have a brief rest."

"Is the river safe?" asked Bree cautiously.

"Who cares?" said Rafi. She tried to wave away a cloud of flies buzzing cheerfully around her head. Maddened by the smell of rotting garbage, and eager to get their fair share, the flies attacked with even more determination. "Even if a thousand Mayors are after us, it won't stop me from taking a bath. What do you say to that, Dlop?"

She turned her head to look at Dlop. Furthest downwind, he rode in the knapsack as if he was a rich tourist on safari. He was fast asleep. Fastened on his nose was the green clothes peg.

"Thinkin' as usual," said Pud, trying to untie himself from his own tail.

"We'll have to chance it," said Krik. He studied the river with a tiny telescope. "Besides, after our narrow escape this morning I'm sure we could all use a drink. I haven't quite digested that raw finger."

The river never looked more inviting. In a twinkling they plunged into the cool water although Pud, in spite of Krik's harangue, would only consent to dangle his legs over the edge of the riverbank. Like most rats, he hated water, especially the bathing kind. In truth, he did not smell quite as bad as the others having acquainted himself with Rafi's perfume, but that did not matter because Bree, who was a good swimmer underwater, could not resist the temptation of swimming under Pud, grabbing his legs with both paws, and pulling him into the river. As for Dlop, he simply floated on his back (asleep) as if he was a fur-covered canoe. Worried that Dlop might float down river, Bree had strategically lashed his tail to a branch growing from the riverbank.

"Har, har," said Pud once his head had spluttered over the surface of the water, "very mature, you lug nut. I'll bet Thomas Jeffer's son never behaved like that."

"As if you would know," said Bree, laughing.

Krik watched with amusement from where he sunbathed on a floating leaf. He was an excellent swimmer himself owing to the fact that he had six arms and legs, but he had not forgotten about the fish in the river that darted curiously beneath the leaf in search of food.

Not far from Krik, Rafi bathed herself using the bar of soap she had gratefully retrieved from her knapsack. Under other circumstances, she would have never used soap in the river since she had studied the effects of pollution at school. But with half of Drumheller's garbage on and in her clothes, in her hair and in her ears, she made an exception. She hoped that the river would forgive her.

After a luxurious bath complete with its breathtaking view of the badlands, Rafi washed her clothes. Sadly, she counted the rips and tears in her pants and shirt, a result, no doubt, of her desperate flight across town in Mopsus's truck. Unworried, she dived into her knapsack, producing both needle and thread, and mended her clothes until they looked, so to speak, comparatively new. Beneath the hot sun, she laid them out on the riverbank to dry.

"What happens now?" She sat down beside Krik who was drying himself off with a red towel that looked more like a postage stamp.

"We must keep heading east," said Krik, his eyes on Bree and Pud who were guarding the stones on Rafi's shirt. Taking turns, the rats munched on a fish they had caught in the river. "If my calculations are correct, we should find the Overseer of Tahw Knar Gnud by mid afternoon."

"The Overseer of Tahw Knar Gnud?" asked Rafi, chewing thoughtfully on a carrot stick, "who or what is that?"

"He is," said Krik, standing perfectly still as he watched a ladybug creep along a blade of grass, "the Overseer or sentinel who watches over the gates that lead to the land of Tahw Knar Gnud. At least that is what the Nadi call it. Perhaps you have another name." One of his eyes looked at Rafi as the other eye remained glued to the ladybug. "You must understand, Rafi, it is here that our real quest begins. The Overseer is wise, and none too friendly toward strangers. You must be careful when you speak to him, and call him Great One as often as you can. He'll like that. However, if we do not offend him, and he offends easily, and if he does not eat us, he may tell us where we can find the Oracle."

"The Oracle?"

"*The* Oracle," said Krik. His legs quivered ever so slightly as he prepared to lunge. "The most powerful being on Earth. He has no name having forgotten it himself, living for so many long years alone, but it is from him that I hope to understand how we may find and defeat Triodon. It is great honor to meet the Oracle. No Drog has ever been awarded this privilege. Remember when you speak to him that you are speaking to the oldest and most powerful creature that ever walked Earth."

"I shall remember," said Rafi, awed by the thought of meeting such an august and powerful being. She plucked several long blades of grass from the riverbank and began to weave a hat. "I can only hope that one so powerful will understand that I am only a young girl, and not turn us away."

Krik leaned forward a little. "Fear not your youth, Rafi," he said. "It is the greatest gift that Earth has given you. Yet you are wise beyond your years, and the Oracle knows and sees all. But I will teach you in the ways of politics and protocol for I have much experience in such matters. Think of it as training for when you shall become a U.N. ambassador."

Rafi looked surprised. "How do you know that I want to become an ambassador?"

Krik smiled ever so slightly. "Do you remember the caterpillar you kept finding in your pocket? That was no coincidence. She's one of my agents, hired to gather information about you …"

Suddenly, Krik launched himself at the ladybug, who, under other circumstances, would have preferred a proper introduction. He turned away so that Rafi needn't watch what followed. Wings first, he devoured the ladybug limb by limb.

"Well," he said, a leg still kicking out of his mouth, "that will have to do for lunch. Besides, I ate a big breakfast." He looked over at Bree and Pud who were looking for Dlop as usual. "Time to address the troops."

By this time Rafi's clothes were dry. While Krik disappeared momentarily along with his satchel she put them on, checking to make sure that Bree and Pud had not failed in their duty to protect the stones. To her intense satisfaction the stones were still there, bound in knots that would have stumped the world's greatest magicians. She picked up the knapsack. Still heavy, she noticed that Dlop had taken up his usual residence, and was already snoring. She strapped it on, and was about to call Bree and Pud, who were having a heated argument about whether Pud should have dashed The Mayor's brains out with a rock, when she felt something move up her pant leg.

Her mouth almost hit the ground. For, marching up her leg, wearing a three star general's hat on his head, a swagger stick thrust under one arm, was Krik. With perfect military cadence, he marched up her pants and shirt and onto her shoulder where he stood with some authority before executing a sharp about-face.

"Brothers and sister," he began in an important voice. He stopped to give each of them an imperial stare as if judging their character and fitness for what lay ahead. With a snort of disgust he climbed over the knapsack and cracked Dlop smartly on the nose with his swagger stick. Dlop squeaked a little but slept all the same. After this painful exercise in discipline, he marched back over the knapsack onto Rafi's shoulder and resumed his address.

"Today we stand on the edge of destiny as Earth trembles beneath our feet. Your determination, your resolve, your friendship, your love for one another, and, not least, your strength in times of fear and darkness, shall rule the lives of many in the days to come. For now, great deeds must be done, not by those great in size or strength or riches alone, but by those with hearts full of greater valor. For it is in you that Earth has placed her trust. And so you shall be named Companions of Earth if you are willing to accept the quest for which you have been chosen."

A hand and two paws answered in crisp salute.

But apparently Krik had not finished. After giving Dlop another crack on the nose with his swagger stick, to which he added a violent dusting with his hat, he returned to Rafi's shoulder where he stood like an officer on parade. One of his stars was missing.

"It is well," he said looking at the Companions, his voice shaking with emotion. Removing his hat, he looked down at the earth and then up at the sky through the great tears that had filled his eyes.

"We, the Companions of Earth, do hereby accept our quest. We may fall, but we will not fail. For where one Companion falls, another shall stand in that very place until we are gone or Earth is safe once again. May our hearts guide our footsteps, our loyalty cement our resolve."

Krik placed his hat back on his head and saluted Rafi, Bree and Pud with his swagger stick. He even saluted Dlop who had managed to keep one eye open during these last words although it was unclear as to whether Dlop's eye was on Krik or on the swagger stick.

"Well spoken," Bree called up to Krik as the mantis packed away his props. "Might I suggest that before we leave the river, we all take a drink. It is unlikely that we will find any more water before nightfall."

"I have already filled the water bottles," said Rafi.

"Agreed," said Krik, who, after his speech, was rather thirsty indeed. "However, we must not linger. There are many miles between us and Tahw Knar Gnud. We mustn't be late."

"Speaking of late," said Bree, looking curiously at Krik, "what happened to you back at the Apple? I thought that we were supposed to meet in the hedge long before you showed up with your infernal clothes peg. We could have used your help."

"It was only because of the clothes peg," said Krik grimly, "that I was able to show up at all. You were not the only ones who had visitors last night. I'm sure it did not escape your notice that Megaera wasn't around to join your little party."

Bree gave Krik a sharp look. "I noticed something else too," he said. "If red eyes are to be believed, Alecto and Tisiphone weren't alone …"

"Megaera?" asked Rafi.

"Will have to wait, my child," said Krik, abruptly changing the subject. He shook his head at Bree. "Time presses and we have a hard road ahead of us. Take your drink quickly and let us go. Tahw Knar Gnud is at least a day's journey and the sun is already high."

"Don't forget your hats," said Rafi. She presented each of the Companions with a green hat made entirely of grass. Pud's wore a spider for decoration. Green headed, they might all have passed for distant relatives of Krik were it not that he now wore a tan sombrero. She plopped the last hat on her own head — a perfect imitation of a green beret. This done, her keen eyes surveyed the river and looked back toward Drumheller.

Krik added a poncho to his accoutrement. "What is it, Rafi?" he asked.

"Nothing, I suppose," said Rafi slowly. "Only I would have thought we'd have been captured by now. But I don't see any sign of activity anywhere. Surely The Mayor has not given up already?"

"The Nadi are not without resources," said Krik, a mischievous glint in his eyes. "Let's just say that, by now, I'm sure that your Mayor has other things on his mind."

It was with no great joy that they left the river. Even Pud was hesitant to say goodbye to the cool, life-giving water, and would have gladly traded the prospect of an endless trek across the bleak, sun-baked badlands for a long bath.

Mindful of Mopsus's directions, the Companions steered east. In a haze of heat and dust, the distant mountains rode majestically upon a bleak strand of horizon. But to the Companions, caught between the glare of the soaring sun and the hot earth that seared their feet and paws, the mountains, however majestic, might just as well have been anthills. Worst of all, once they had left the river, the flies had rejoined them in greater numbers and with even greater reverie than before.

"My word," said Bree, blowing on his sore paws. "This ground is as hard as cement and as hot as a skillet."

"Harder," said Pud miserably. He seemed to be attracting most of the flies, a result, no doubt, of his lingering perfume and the flies' revenge for a lost brother. He threw a rock at the sun and missed.

Bree shook his head and smiled at Krik. "Sun not a big enough target for you, Pud?"

"Well," said Pud. Simultaneously, he jumped as high as he could while throwing another rock at the sun. "If only I could get a little closer …"

Krik fanned Rafi's ear with his sombrero.

"You can't imagine what it means to me," he said looking down at Pud, a look of amusement on his face, "to know that one of the Companions of Earth is twice as dense as the sun."

"Got that right," said Pud. He rudely gestured at the sun with his paw.

"Or twice as hot," said Rafi. She sipped some water when she could have drunk a gallon. At Krik's insistence they had been careful with the water, sharing a half bottle every hour or so. But, after several hours of walking across the badlands, it seemed that as soon as the water had passed their lips, the sun sucked it right back out of them.

Bree had been right. Water, if there was any to be found, eluded them. Only rock Hoodoos – fantastic, multicolored mushrooms as tall as a house – and the occasional bone kept them company along the way. Sometimes, when she needed a rest, Rafi would stop and examine the bones, putting some of the smaller ones in her knapsack along with rare or beautiful shells and stones. Wondrously colored in the reds, yellows and oranges of the badlands, the stones shone like jewels upon the ground as if some traveling merchant had dropped them along the way. Other stones were jet black in color and extremely heavy for their size, suggesting, as Bree had said, that they were tiny meteorites that had fallen from the sky. Whether the bones were from dinosaurs or from some other long forgotten creature, Rafi was too tired to say.

"We must find shade," she said despairingly at a point when all of the Companions' legs had unanimously declared an unscheduled stop. "We won't last long in this heat. The water is almost gone. There is a Hoodoo up ahead. Let us stop there and rest awhile. It's not very big but it will give us some protection against the sun."

"How much further?" asked Pud wearily, who up until this time had not uttered one word of complaint. Dragging his tail, even Bree's unflagging devotion to duty was beginning to show signs of wear.

"Far enough," said Krik glumly. He fiddled with an abacus he had pulled from his satchel. "We are falling behind schedule. But I agree about having a rest," he said quickly, looking at the mutinous faces gathered around him. "Still we mustn't linger. If I am not mistaken, the Overseer should not be far off unless he is hunting, but he usually does that at night."

The rest of the Companions were too tired to care. Overseer or no Overseer, they stumbled toward the Hoodoo and collapsed in a patch of beckoning shade. Hungry and thirsty, they ate a little food and drank the last of the water.

Looking west, Rafi could not believe how far they had come. In spite of her burning thirst and the crippling heat she could not help but admire the view. She turned to the east and looked out upon a vista of yawning canyons and snakelike coulees that, in ancient times, must have been formed by water. Preferring to not think about anything to do with water, she turned her head away.

"We can't stay here forever," said Krik less than five minutes after they had sat down. "Besides, the more we move around, the better our chances of finding water or the Overseer. Better yet, he may find us."

"I think he already has," said Bree, looking up at the Hoodoo's mushroom cap.

Not sure as to what he was talking about, the rest of the Companions scrambled out of the shade and joined Bree.

On top of the Hoodoo, looking down upon them with a face that was both expressionless and yet imperial, sat a Great Grey Owl. Its large eyes were as gold and intense as the sun, and its wings, although folded upon his back, were as tall as Rafi. For the longest time, the Owl neither moved nor spoke, but continued to look at them with those great orbs of eyes as if it was trying to stare them all the way back to Drumheller. Rafi was reminded of someone she had once read about in a book, but who that was she couldn't remember.

"Hoodoo," said the Owl, staring at all of them at once.

"We are well, thank you," said Rafi although this statement couldn't have been further from the truth. Forgetting her thirst, she bowed as low as her aching back would allow. But the owl did not return the bow, frowned and stared at her instead.

"Great One," she said, remembering both Krik's words and her manners, "it is an honor to meet you. What royal presence could be more beautiful, what wings more powerful and what eyes wiser that those that look upon us? Truly, your fame is well deserved, most Omnipotent Owl. Only, if I am not mistaken I was ... well . . . under the impression that Great Grey Owls ... ah ... lived in the forest?"

"Hoodoo," said the owl in a louder tone almost matching the intensity of those golden eyes.

"Ah," said Rafi, catching on and bowing lower than before. "My apologies, Great One. It is a great Hoodoo and one worthy of your magnificence, if that is indeed possible."

"Hoodoo," said the owl. The tone had an ominous ring to it.

"Perhaps he is warning us," suggested Bree. "I've heard that Hoodoo's can bring bad luck."

"Perhaps he is just stup..." said Pud.

"Great and kind owl," said Rafi, confused by the conversation, if, indeed, you could call it that. "We are travelers not wise in the ways of your wisdom. By 'Hoodoo,' do you mean to welcome us, warn us, or tell us something about the Hoodoo?"

"All of them at once," said the owl, obviously pleased at its cleverness. The voice was clear, almost human, but layered with a hint of hoot. "You do have a name I suppose?"

"Indeed we do," said Rafi, awed in the wonder that she was having a conversation with an owl, and a clever one at that. "This is Krik, our most noble ambassador to the League of Mantis, mentor and friend, and this is Bree and Pud, two chivalrous and brave rats who defeated the Nine Cats of Orly. Dlop is their most resourceful brother who, alas, is sleeping at the moment."

"Thinking," said Drop drowsily from where he sat in the knapsack. Eyes closed, his head lolled heavily to one side.

"And I am Rafi."

"Hoodoo," said the owl decidedly after looking her up and down. "You do have some intelligence and manners about you. For a Drog, that is most rare." The owl nodded at Krik. "Krik I have met before and he is welcome here. As for your other companions," the owl glared particularly at Pud, "I am less sure."

"Here's back at ya, bird brain," said Pud. He picked up a large rock behind his back.

"Careful my fat little friend," said the owl, whose eyes now burned hotter than the sun. "It occurs to me that I have not dined today and a fat rat would be a welcome meal. I've been feeding none too well of late. Game is both scarce and skinny here, which is why, I suppose, they call it the badlands. So I would not move or speak too quickly if I were you, and leave the talking to those wiser than yourself."

Pud hung his head and said nothing. Edging over beside Pud, Bree knocked the rock from Pud's paws.

"Much better," said the owl in an amused tone. "I see that you have been rock collecting but I would guess that there is more to your story than that. As for myself, I am Ademar, and I am the Overseer of Tahw Knar Gnud, the eyes of the Oracle. As for my story, I was born in a great forest far away from this place, but I was chosen by the Oracle himself to watch over his realm. Nothing escapes my surveillance ..."

"That's nuttin," said Pud enthusiastically, "we was surfin' just the other ..."

Bree clapped a paw over Pud's mouth as Ademar sharpened his short, hooked beak on a rock atop the Hoodoo. "You're not the only one who knows how to use rocks, my furry friend," he said menacingly. Deliberately, he stretched one of his feathered legs and inspected a set of three-inch razor talons. "And now that I have seen you," he added, scowling at Pud, "what is your business here?"

"Ademar," said Krik, bowing as he removed his sombrero. "It is good to see you again, my old friend. Long have I wished to hear your great wisdom since last we parted. As for my companions and I, we have come here to beg your guidance and help in a matter of utmost and universal importance." Here Krik gave Ademar a look that matched the owl's in its intensity. "We must speak to the Oracle and time is short. Of our quest I can say little. But, to an old friend, I am permitted to say that our destiny lies within the great hall of Erebus."

"Erebus?" Ademar hooted softly. "Say no more, Krik. It may interest you to hear that I know something of your quest although I did not know that this task had fallen to you. It is a great honor. Should you prove successful you shall have the favor of all living things until the end of your days, which shall be exceedingly long. But it gives my heart no joy to think of you in that dreadful place." Ademar's eyes click-blinked to Rafi. "Then this must be the Drog of whom the legends speak."

"That is so," said Krik, his voice resonating with reverence. "This is Rafi, River's Daughter, Keeper of the Three Stones of Erebus, who wears the mark of the Fates upon her hair. It is a great honor to meet her, is it not?"

Ademar bowed low. "It is indeed," he said, looking at Rafi as if for the first time. His eyes were as bright and intense as ever, but kindness and pity were mixed in them now. "My wings and tail are at your service, Rafi of the Three Stones. How may I assist you?"

"Great Ademar," said Rafi as Krik whispered in her ear, "whose heart beats above both wind and wings. Your gracious offer is worth more to us than you know. May the Fates reward your kindness with good hunting and a full moon. First, if we are to have any hope in fulfilling our quest, we must find water. Second, as our noble ambassador has told you, we must find the Oracle. Will you help us?"

"The Oracle," said Ademar slowly, "is many of your miles from here. Walking as you are you shall surely perish for there is no water between this place and Tahw Knar Gnud where the Oracle is to be found."

"Miles?" Rafi's hope sank. Thoroughly exhausted, she plopped down on a flat stone. It was so hot she could have fried an egg on it. But since eggs were in as short supply as water she remained where she sat, gazing forlornly at the iron clad mountains which, maddeningly, seemed even farther away than before.

"Maybe the Orc could meet us half way," suggested Pud.

Bree rolled his eyes at Pud. "Unbelievable," he muttered.

Weary beyond words, Rafi secretly agreed with Pud. If the Oracle was so powerful, why couldn't he have the decency to save them a trip across the badlands? Why couldn't he save Earth? Groaning, she stretched her legs, which were as stiff as ironing boards. Thoroughly disillusioned with their quest, she looked up at Ademar.

"Many miles," repeated Ademar, clicking his beak as if he did not know whether to laugh or cry or eat Pud. "Yet, the miles between this place and Tahw Knar Gnud are the least of your worries. For in order to speak to the Oracle you must first pass the Guardian who guards his realm, and that, I can assure you, is no easy task. Zigh is his name. In battle, no creature has ever defeated him. He is as fearless as he is strong, and I would be remiss not to tell you that mercy is a quality unknown to him, as evidenced by the bones surrounding his home."

This was unwelcome news to say the least. Bree and Pud looked uneasy as Dlop squeaked in his sleep. While she tried to hide it, Rafi felt a wave of fatigue and despair wash over her. Only Krik appeared to receive Ademar's news without alarm, checking his watch so often he might have been mistaken for a watch repair mantis.

"That being so," he said, deliberately tapping the face of his watch so that everyone could see, especially Ademar, "what course do you advise?"

"You were always one for getting to the point, my dear mantis," Ademar hooted graciously. "Patience was never one of your virtues just as diplomacy was never one of mine." The owl stretched his great wings, glancing casually at a passing cloud. "It is simple. I will take you there …"

Rafi's eyes almost popped out of her head.

"Do you mean to say that you will fly us there?"

"Indeed," said Ademar, highly amused. "Why walk when one can fly, my father always used to say. Quite honestly, I don't know how you Drogs manage without it. One can never truly appreciate the fine art of flying locked up in one of those infernal sardine cans that you call an airplane. Is it not so?"

"Perhaps we can answer your question once we are in the air," said Krik, eager to push on. "However, there is still the matter of water …"

"There is a water hole near Zigh's house," Ademar said evenly. "With a good wind I shall have you there before the red eye sits upon its mountain throne. There you can refresh yourselves, get a good night's sleep and prepare for your meeting with Zigh. There too I shall take my leave of you for I do not wish for Zigh to think that I am an intruder and discover his mistake afterwards. As for your quest, if the stones are with you, and if Zigh is not in one of his bad moods, perhaps he will guide you to the Oracle."

Krik looked as if a great weight had suddenly slipped from his shoulders. With a grand sweep of his sombrero he bowed three times before Ademar.

"Most gracious and noble friend," he said, "please forgive me. As you well know, the words from my mouth seldom do justice to the words of my heart. Once again, I find myself in your debt, and for that I am eternally grateful."

Ademar hooted softly with pleasure. "Nonsense," he said. "If you are successful in your Quest, it is I who shall be eternally grateful. But enough of what was and what will be." Ademar spread his great wings and sailed to the ground. He winked at Rafi and Krik. "The largest and the smallest shall ride upon my back," he said. "As for you two," he added, looking at Bree and especially at Pud with a dangerous glint in his eyes, "I will introduce you to sky surfing – owl style."

"Just one second …" said Bree. Having recently been airborne, he preferred to leave flying to birds.

"All aboard," said Ademar. Before Bree and Pud could blink an objection he had wrapped each of them in his great talons as Rafi and Krik climbed onto his back. He winced over his shoulder. "No need to pull my feathers, Rafi," he said, "you will not fall."

"But I'm not …" Rafi began. Then she spotted Krik whose pallor had changed to that of a withered onion. In anticipation of the journey the mantis had already pulled out four of Ademar's feathers which he was now attempting to push back into place.

"I won't," she called up to Ademar. She scooped Krik up in her hands, and held him tight. To ensure his on-flight security, Krik added several bungee cords, a padlock and chain, and the entire contents of a bottle of glue, which he had produced from his satchel. "Don't worry, Krik," she whispered reassuringly. "Somehow I doubt that Earth's future will depend on whether or not its greatest ambassador falls from an owl."

"It's not the falling I'm worried about," confessed Krik. He pointed at the hard ground. "Hitting, on the other hand, is an entirely different matter …"

In seconds they were in the air. With Krik's sombrero blowing somewhere behind them, they pulled up sharply from the Hoodoo, soaring higher and higher as the ground fell away from their feet. Before long, they were even with the clouds, flying still higher until the vast badlands shrank into a quilted blanket.

High above the earth, tears of joy flooded Rafi's eyes. She had never seen anything more beautiful. She ran her fingers through wisps of cloud, breathed them in and out again, and reached up to touch the sun. It was a miracle.

Filled with feelings she could never describe, Rafi stood up on Ademar's back, stretched out her arms, and sang to the earth, clouds and sky.

"Here I am
In the sky,
So high,
I can fly.

I can see,
Oh to be,
So free,
Fly with me.

Touch my hand,
Touch the Sun,
All hearts
Forever one.

Spread your wings,
Fly as far
To know
Who you are.

Know yourself,
Not a face,
In love
A deeper grace.

Look at you,
Look at me,
It's all
In how we see.

I love you,
You love me,
What more
Can there be?

Here I am,
In the sky,
So high,
I can fly.

I can fly,
I can fly,
I can fly,
I can fly."

"I can fly, I can fly!" Pud shouted at the great canyons that were now not much larger than himself. "Sure beats surfin'."

"I can die, I can die," Bree muttered under his whiskers. He did not altogether approve of heights or Ademar's talons that seemed to be sharpening themselves on his ribs.

"I wish I could fly," said Dlop sadly. He peered over the edge of the knapsack, overcome with the wonders unfolding around him.

But it was Krik, upheld upon Ademar's wings and Rafi's song, who rose higher than the sky itself as great tears rolled from his eyes and fell upon the clouds. High above the earth he so cherished he soared in blissful spirit, calling each cloud and canyon by name as the precious earth looked up at him, child of her womb, so green and small, and yet more precious to her than all of the stars that shine at night.

The trip took less than an hour, and yet it lasted a lifetime. On outstretched wings, Ademar spiraled down through wind and cloud as the earth rushed up just in time for a perfect landing. Adding to the delight of his passengers, a small water hole beckoned from the shade of a nearby tree.

"Next stop, Albuquerque," said Ademar, and they all laughed.

"Greatest Ademar," said Rafi who would have liked nothing better than to fly with the owl to the ends of Earth, "how can we ever repay you?" With Krik firmly planted on her shoulder once again, she dismounted the owl, pecking him on the beak with a wet kiss.

"You already have, my child," said Ademar. Tears wet his eyes. "You already have."

Krik smiled up at Ademar. "As always, friend," he said, "you made the impossible possible. Water we see. But before you leave us, please tell us more about Zigh so that he may look upon us favorably as friends, and take us to the Oracle."

"Soon it shall be nightfall," said Ademar gravely, his golden eyes tinged with the reddish glow of the setting sun. "Tonight, you should camp by the water. Be wary, post a guard and be sure to get a good night's rest for you will need it when you come face to face with Zigh. At first light, make yourselves presentable and follow the bones over that rise to a grove of white poplar trees. In that grove is the House of Zigh. He will be waiting for you there. Remember, and this is very important, when you reach the bones do not move suddenly or speak loudly, and when you reach the poplar grove, sit down. If he does not kill you outright, he may be willing to take you to the Oracle."

"I can hardly wait," muttered Bree.

Ademar prepared to go. More than once the Companions asked if he would join their quest but each time he politely bowed his head and hooted his decline. With a benign smile, he gave each of them some parting words of advice.

"You have a brave heart, little one," he said to Pud who was examining some rocks near the water hole. "Have a care to measure your words as you would your friendship and loyalty. You have mine. But Zigh is not as patient and understanding as an old owl sitting on a Hoodoo. Out here, it is better to think twice and speak once if, indeed, one should speak at all."

"And you, my furry friend," he said to Dlop, "if I am not mistaken, one day, you too shall learn how to fly. Yet do not be too eager to spread your wings until you are ready, for many have perished in their quest to reach the stars."

After updating Bree that, statistically speaking, flying was still the safest way to travel, Ademar turned to Rafi. "Never have I flown as high as I did today. You have a wonderful gift and a gentle heart, and one day you shall be great among your people and ours. But wherever your path may take you I pray that you do not forget us in your songs. May your heart always be so gentle and your nest filled with the love you so freely give."

"Speaking of nests," Krik broke in, "Rafi's parents will be worried by her sudden disappearance, and it is safe to say that our departure from the Drog town could not have been more noticeable with a brass band. If it is not too much to ask, please send an envoy to her parents so that they will understand something of our quest and know that she is well. Also, send one to the Drog Mayor. It is time he learned that there is more to Earth than happy tourists and angry books. I will send word back to you as our quest allows, so that you may keep them and others informed."

"I will," said Ademar. And without another word his great wings filled the sky.

"Goodbye," they called after him, each waving with as many hands, paws or claws as they possessed. Soon Ademar's wings shrank into a dark wavy line fringed with the deepening reds of the setting sun. Then he was gone.

"I wish I could fly," said Dlop, waving an empty chocolate bar wrapper.

"Didja hear that everybody?" said Pud proudly. "He said I was brave. Brave. A brave sexy general."

"I don't like the sound of this Zigh," said Bree. He looked up at Rafi and Krik. "Perhaps the general and I should go alone. That way, if something happens, the three of you can run for it."

"To where?" asked Krik pointedly. He stowed his poncho back into his satchel, shaking his head regretfully at the loss of a good sombrero. "West? To flee that way will only serve to delay the inevitable as will fleeing in any direction save one. No, it is to the east we must go, whether we like it or not."

"Agreed," said Rafi although the prospect of returning to her family and a warm bed sounded infinitely more inviting than deliberately crossing the path of a known murderer. Looking west, she watched the dying embers of a glorious sunset flicker its affirmation.

"Companions we are and Companions we stay," she said, frowning at Bree and Pud as if daring them to disagree. Behind the rats she could see the unmistakable shimmer of water and, suddenly, the burning thirst she had felt back at the Hoodoo reasserted itself.

"Last one in cooks dinner!" she shouted. Her feet were already in motion.

Bree and Pud needed no more urging than that. With a bound and a shout they raced toward the water hole, heedless of Zigh, mindful only of the water which lay dark and deep beneath the quiet light of a jeweled evening. In spite of his distaste for bathing, Pud was the first one in. "I can fly, I can fly!" he sang, splashing up a fountain of water, which he drank in great gulps. Bree plunged in after him followed by Rafi and Krik with Dlop, still in the knapsack, bringing up the rear. Soon they were all neck deep in water, sucking up the precious nectar until each of them was ready to explode.

While no rules had been officially established, it was generally agreed that Dlop was last to reach the water hole. But as no one expected him to make dinner, and as he did not offer to make any, it all worked out. In the end, it was decided by vote that Pud would collect wood while Bree made a fire, and Rafi, who knew how to do such things, would cook dinner.

With the help of two sticks and his tail, Bree had soon made a roaring fire, aided by a plentiful supply of wood provided by Pud.

"That's enough wood for now, Pud," said Bree, moving closer to the fire. There was a definite chill in the air. "We're building a fire, not a house."

"But there's wood all around us," said Pud. He threw a log on the fire that was at least three times his own size and weight. A rain of sparks flew up into the night sky like a swarm of angry fireflies.

Krik watched the sparks fly from the comfort of his familiar chair that he had set up on a rock by the fire. "Curious," he said. "From the air I would have guessed that a great forest once grew here, but from what I could see it looked as if all of the trees had been knocked down. Yet I didn't see any sign of an earthquake."

"Zigh, no doubt," said Bree, his bright eyes staring at the fire. "I would hate to be on the receiving end of one of Zigh's battles." He sighed as he watched Pud throw another log on the fire. "This fire doesn't seem like such a good idea now. Zigh can spot us from ten miles away."

Pud threw two more logs on the fire. "Guardian, shmardian," he said. "At least we won't die of cold."

"Or hunger," said Rafi. She had been busily cooking macaroni and cheese in a pot held over the fire by a large bone she had found next to the water hole. Since most of the cheese was already inside Dlop it was really macaroni, but she did the best she could with what she had.

"What didja go eat all the cheese for, Dlop?" hollered Pud.

"I didn't eat all of it," snapped Dlop. "In fact, I only ate half."

"Exactly," corrected Bree. "You ate half, and then you ate another half, and so on until it was all gone."

"Like I said," Dlop persisted, "I only ate half."

As Bree, Pud and Dlop argued around the fire, Rafi dolled out large portions of macaroni and cheese. Even without cheese, it was a veritable feast compared to their meager rations throughout the day, which had consisted mostly of dried nuts and raisins.

"Tastes like chicken," said Krik as he preyed on a noodle of macaroni.

"When did you ever eat a chicken?" asked Bree, laughing. His face became serious. "No, wait a moment," he added dryly, "I don't think I want to know."

"I should have brought more food." Sadly, Rafi patted down the knapsack, which felt as limp as a punctured tire.

"Or less Dlop," suggested Bree.

Rafi scratched Dlop's ears. "You were right, Bree," she said. "By tomorrow night we'll wish we had filled the knapsack with garbage."

Krik almost up-chucked a noodle. "Never," he said. "Bite your tongue!"

Sitting by the fire, they talked far into the night. The sky was unusually clear, and Bree, who turned out to be something of an astronomer, pointed out the stars and constellations, calling them out by name as shooting stars smiled upon them. Caught in its starry web, the crescent moon swung like a silver spider above the haunting calls of lonely wolves.

"Nice doggies," Pud called out to the darkness, but the wolves gave no sign that they were nearby or even interested in approaching the water hole. Perhaps they were afraid of the fire or the possibility that Zigh was lurking somewhere nearby. Or, as Bree pointed out, perhaps the wolves simply wanted to avoid the two jagged rocks that seemed to accompany Pud wherever he went. In any event, the Companions did not appear to be in any immediate danger.

Yet they were not alone. Almost as bright as the blue and white stars across the heavens, countless eyes watched the Companions from the far side of the water hole. Transfixed by the fire, aglow with flame, they hung suspended like living lamps upon an altar of darkness.

"Red and yellow eyes," squeaked Dlop. Terrified, he closed his own, burying his head in one of Rafi's shoes.

"There is nothing to fear," said Krik lazily from where he contemplated the stars, a slender blade of grass notched between his teeth. "These animals are here for water. If they were here for anything else they would have Zigh to contend with. And while I cannot be sure, I would guess that anyone intent on doing us harm is an enemy of the Oracle."

Rafi stared at the eyes watching her from across the water. Krik was right. These were not the same eyes she had seen through the window at Newton's Apple. Absent of the angry reds and malicious yellows she had seen the night before, somehow they seemed more fair than foul. Not entirely sure of this, she stoked the fire with the bone she had used to cook dinner, sending a shower of sparks toward the moon.

"Krik," she said finally, her eyes staring fixedly upon the fire. "Last night you spoke of the servants of Triodon." She threw another log on the fire and settled next to the mantis, who had cranked one of his legs into a footstool. "Who are they?"

Krik plucked the blade of grass from his teeth and threw it into the fire.

"They are ..." he began.

"No, don't," squeaked Dlop, who was even less sure about the eyes than Rafi. Unnerved by the prospect of unwelcome visitors during the night, and not a little hopeful of dreams yet to come, he padded over to where Rafi lay beside Krik and curled up on her stomach.

"Dlop's right," said Pud, yawning. He nudged Dlop over with his nose until he had enough space to lay an equal claim to Rafi's stomach. "We don't need to know. Not now, anyway. How about next week sometime? I'm free on Tuesday."

"Next week?" snapped Bree. He gave Pud a shot in the ribs and then settled comfortably on Rafi's chest, taking great care to cover the stones. "At the rate things are going, what with Dlop eating everything and you not taking a single word seriously, it will be a miracle if there is a next week, never mind Tuesday!"

"I'm sorry, Dlop," said Krik firmly, but there was a warmth and understanding in his voice beyond the fire. "But it is time for Rafi to know something about the enemy." He collapsed his chair, stood up, stretched and then resettled in Rafi's hair. Bathed in firelight, his small body and limbs cast a huge shadow upon a rock where it towered over the Companions like some gruesome god from a bygone era.

"If you remember," he said at length, "when Eidon fought Triodon for the mastery of Earth, he tore off Triodon's arm right down to its socket, and for a moment, one impossible moment, it looked like Earth would be saved. But even as Eidon swallowed Triodon's arm and the three stones still grasped within his hand, Triodon's blood gushed from his wound, staining the Earth black. And from his blood sprang the three Erinnyes, Alecto, Tisiphone and Megaera, a darkness more cursed and cruel than Triodon himself, for though they were born of his blood, their true parents were none other than Hatred and Malice. Dlop is right to fear them. They are terrible. No creature or refuge is safe once the Erinnyes have declared their doom, not even the light of day."

"Bats!" Dlop cried in his sleep. "Bats!"

"More than bats," said Bree in an undertone as he licked his shoulder. "But that's not all. Is it, Krik?"

Krik continued.

"Legend also tells us that when Triodon lost his arm, there rose from the blackest drops of his blood the three Empusae: Lilam, Lamia and Neith, the daughters of Death. It is said that when the Empusae opened their eyes for the first time, even Death became afraid and fled to Erebus where all shadows must pass. It is also said that when they dare to walk upon Earth they take the form of black scorpions filled with a venom that delivers an agonizing and certain death."

"It's no legend," added Bree. His eyes smoldered like small fires. "I saw them. The Empusae ride upon the backs of the Erinnyes. They are worse than you describe. Back at the Apple, it was only by sheer luck and the Erinnyes' passion for eating living flesh that I am alive today. Death was wise to flee to the place where only shadows lie. Having looked into their eyes, I can safely say that a raging volcano could not be more merciless."

"Bats and scorpions!" wailed Dlop.

"I saw such eyes," said Rafi. She tried to warm Dlop with her hands but her hands were as cold as ice. "Last night in my window. Were those the Erinnyes and the Empu...?"

"Empusae," said Krik emphatically. "And it is with no small thanks to Bree here that we were able to save you that night. While I expected trouble I did not think that they would attack so soon, not with all the miles that lay between us and Erebus."

Rafi kissed Bree on the forehead. "Thank you, Bree," she said. "Is that why your shoulder was bleeding?"

"It was nothing, Rafi," said Bree, his cheeks more ruddy than the fire. "Only a scratch."

"We was guarding too," said Pud. He hung his whiskered head. "Only we fell asleep. Surfin' is hard work."

"I know it," said Rafi, kissing both Pud and Dlop. As quickly as it had departed, the warmth crept back into her hands. "What miracle could be greater than having such wonderful friends?"

"Here's back at ya, Raffers!" said Pud.

Bree listened carefully to the wind. "Remember what Ademar said," he advised the others. "We must get some sleep."

"Agreed," said Krik. Along with the receding flames, his shadow dwindled to that of a mere mantis. "I will take the first watch."

"Dlop and I will watch together when it is our turn," said Rafi. "Won't we, Dlop?"

Dlop snored in reply.

Soon the fire had burned down to a bed of coals. Still burning brightly, the stars twirled around the moon like sparkling starfish in a deep, dark sea. Down below, Rafi, Bree and Pud closed their eyes and in an instant they had followed Dlop to a land of curious thoughts and dreams. As for Krik, he pulled a crossword puzzle from his satchel to keep him company during his watch.

After midnight, Krik woke Bree and instantly fell asleep on Rafi's hair. As for Bree, he sat by the dying fire, gazing up at the stars, and wondering how many throws it would take Pud to reach them with a stone.

And so the Companions watched and slept beneath the jeweled twinkle in the sky. Tonight, wrapped in the sweet arms of sleep and companionship they would dream about Orly's cats, The Mayor, their flight across the badlands and meeting the Oracle.

Tomorrow, they would face the wrath of Zigh.

CHAPTER SIX

ZIGH

At Krik's orders, both Bree and Pud were up and patrolling the water hole well before daybreak. There might have been some initial grumbling about 'sleeping in,' but in the end the rats did not seem to mind as the early morning air was brisk and damp, and, as Pud had pointed out, anything was better than sitting around and waiting for Zigh.

Content with these arrangements, Krik went alone to reconnoiter the entrance to the Road of Death that, according to Ademar, led to Zigh's house. It was not that he would not have liked some company. Indeed, as he crawled and hopped over a mound of boulders and bones, the smallest of which could have crushed him to a grain of sand, he never felt more alone or insignificant. But Krik was not fearful for his life. He was fearful of his plan. And that meant keeping Rafi and the others safe.

Unconcerned with these activities, Rafi lay sleeping by the fire. Having almost burned itself out during the night it now lay in a smoldering heap of gray and black coals. As for Dlop, he lay where Bree had deposited him on Rafi's chest as a last defense to protect the stones. However, with one eye open and one closed, it was not entirely clear as to whether he was awake or asleep.

By all accounts, the night had passed without any disturbance. Other than the endless howling of wolves and the unnerving glare of red eyes, only the moon had looked in on them casually, more preoccupied with admiring its own reflection in the water hole. But as morning approached, the wolves had given up their calling, the eyes had vanished and even the moon had tired of looking at itself and wandered off to make room for the coming dawn.

"Hup, two, free, six." Dutifully, Pud marched around the water hole, a huge rock hoisted above his head.

Bree rounded a corner. "Pud," he said warningly, "drop that rock. If Zigh sees it, we're done for!"

"Zigh or no Zigh," said Pud unapologetically, "if anyone attacks Raffers, they'll have me to deal with."

"Ridiculous," said Krik, having finished his inspection of the road. There was an air of calm about him as if he had come to peace with whatever had been on his mind before he had set out to explore the road. "Zigh is not one of Orly's cats. Look around you. Don't you see the bones? Does their size not tell you anything? While Rafi could tell you better, I would say that many of these bones belonged to dinosaurs. Very large dinosaurs. And that's not all. Some of them don't seem to be that old if rotting flesh is any indication. But, believe me, in any event, Zigh will not be dispatched by a rock or even a boulder, regardless of the hand that wields it."

Pud dropped the rock on Bree's tail. "Paw," he said.

"Good morning," said Rafi, awakened by the sound of her name and Bree's screaming. "What's up?" Now that Pud had joined in on the screaming, she jackknifed to her feet, launching Dlop off her chest and into the cooking pot. Empty of macaroni and cheese, it was now full of Dlop.

"Nothing yet," said Bree, both his paws wrapped around Pud's throat. "Not Dlop. Not even the sun."

"I'm up now," said Dlop, groaning.

"It was an accident!" protested Pud. "Tell 'im, Krik!"

"Assuming Ademar is correct, and he usually is," said Krik, ignoring Pud and pointing east, "our path lies beyond those rocks."

"The Road of Death," said Bree softly. Noticing that Pud was turning blue, he released his brother's throat.

"The Road of Death," echoed Krik. As if to make his point all the more clear, he brandished a splinter of bone he had picked up on his way back to the water hole. For a six-inch mantis, it made a perfect staff. He pointed over the mound of boulders and bones which, as it turned out, was shaped like a hand with an extended finger pointing east. "It's not a long walk," he remarked casually, "although unpleasant enough I dare say. I expect that Zigh will be waiting for us at the other end. We must get ready."

Bree drew a target on Dlop's buttocks with the burnt end of a stick he had pulled from the fire. "Ademar said something about making ourselves presentable," he said. "How does one approach a mass murderer?"

"Shhh," said Krik sternly. "Do not speak so of Zigh even in jest. If he is listening, I doubt that he will enjoy the joke. And remember what Ademar said about manners." The mantis swung one eye so that it was looking directly at Pud. "Remember that when you speak, even a single word, you are no longer speaking for yourself – you are speaking for the Companions of Earth. You heard Ademar. Zigh is incapable of mercy. Any wrong word or movement by anyone will be the end of us all. Worse, it will be the end of our quest."

"I wasn't joking," said Bree flatly, "and you haven't answered my question."

"Enough!" snapped Krik. He signaled a double time out with his claws. "I haven't got all the answers. May I suggest that, instead of debating this pointless drivel, our time would be better spent eating breakfast and making ourselves as presentable as we can. What do you think, Rafi?"

Rafi rummaged through the knapsack. "As to breakfast," she said, "we have nuts and raisins, two chocolate bars ..."

"One chocolate bar," corrected Dlop, still lying in the cooking pot. Worried that breakfast might include something other than nuts and raisins he gingerly stepped out of the pot, looking hungrily at the knapsack.

"Nuts," said Pud despondently. "You'd think we was chipmunks or something!"

"A definite improvement in your case," snapped Krik.

While Krik and the rats argued over breakfast, Rafi pulled a hairbrush and a pair of scissors from the knapsack. Tapping the brush on her outstretched palm, she studied Bree, Pud and Dlop as if she was Mrs. Wheeze about to go where no hair stylist had gone before.

"I can brush you while you eat," she said finally, stuffing a large walnut into Pud's mouth. "And your whiskers need trimming."

Pud spat the walnut at Dlop. "Any perfoom in there?" he asked hopefully. With a nauseated look, he pointed at Bree's armpits where his nose had spent the better part of their discussion while Bree was choking him.

"As a matter of fact," said Rafi. Slyly, she reached into one of the pockets of the knapsack, extracting a small bottle of perfume. Without warning, a perfumed blast knocked each of the rats head over heels and onto their tails where they sat spluttering in objection except for Dlop who had fallen asleep again, not caring whether he was perfumed or not. She doubled over with laughter.

"Do you like it boys?" she asked, giving Pud a second blast. "I call it Badland Breeze. How about you, Krik?"

"Thank you, no," said Krik who had already moved a good distance away. "We're here to talk to Zigh, not poison him. As for myself, I prefer to rely on my natural pheromones."

"I thought Krik wasn't afraid of nuttin," Pud whispered to Bree.

Bree rolled his eyes.

"Your outfit would be a nice touch, Krik," said Rafi seriously. She held Dlop by his tail as she brushed him upside down. "I'm sure that Mrok would approve."

Pud coughed up a cloud of perfume. "With or without his head?" he asked.

A nasty, 'preying' look darkened Krik's eyes. For a moment, it looked like Pud was going to have an intimate conversation with Krik's staff, but, getting the better of himself, the mantis leaned on it instead. "If we could be serious for more than two seconds at a time," he snapped. "It occurs to me that Zigh might want a gift. Any suggestions?"

"It's a little late for shopping," said Bree.

"What do you give a mass murderer?" asked Pud. He held his chin up with one of his paws as if he was thinking. It was doubtful that any ideas would spring forth any time soon.

Krik covered his face with two of his claws. Apparently, this was not enough, for after several seconds of tense silence he dropped his staff, adding as many claws to his face as he could without falling over. Only a series of muffled groans mixed with numbers escaped the claws as he counted to ten. Upon reaching ten, which appeared to calm him down, he removed his claws, picked up his staff and smiled encouragingly at Rafi. It was obvious that he had not counted high enough to look at Bree or Pud.

"Rafi," he said evenly. "You packed the knapsack. What gifts do we have worthy of a Guardian?"

"You missed fifteen," interjected Pud.

"None really," said Rafi, wishing that she had packed a suitcase and not a knapsack. "Some shells, bones, stones, thimble, thread …"

Pud looked around. "He already has bones," he said.

"I have an idea," said Rafi, noticing that Krik was so angry at Pud, he had just counted to twenty-seven on his way to one hundred. "When we Drogs buy a gift for someone we usually like to know something about them. Or at least know something about their home so the gift fits in with the décor. I suggest that we first visit Zigh, see where he lives, and if he doesn't kill us, get him a gift he will value."

"Bone china?" wondered Pud.

Bree looked down at Krik who was now doubled over, getting his numbers mixed up. "You might have mentioned the gift earlier," he said.

"As usual," exploded Krik, who, while he had not managed to count to a hundred, was so red he did not need his outfit, "I can't think of everything at once!" He threw down his staff where it clattered upon the rocks, his arms and legs gesticulating so wildly they started to tie themselves into knots. "Do you think it's easy being an ambassador?" he roared in a loud voice. "I didn't ask for this! I was appointed this job and I accepted it without thought or personal consequence just so that someone might help save your miserable … flea … bitten … hides!"

"There go the fleas again," said Bree.

"Rafi doesn't have fleas," said Pud.

"Yeh, she does," said Dlop, "I noticed one just …"

Pud's face suddenly brightened. "I have it!" he said triumphantly, looking around at the others. "We could send Zigh a gift! We could include a self-at-rest, stamped envelope so he can tell us whether or not he wants to kill us! Only," he buried his chin in his paws in thoughtful repose, "who would deliver it?"

"Great idea, Pud," said Bree in mock support. "One way courier. Think of the money we'd save on benefits."

"Shut up!" Krik's voice carried across the water, echoing amongst the rocks and bones. Finding his staff, he picked it up and stormed behind a rock. Strange numbers, completely out of order, filled the air. "Twelve, two hundred, sixty four, twenty one, seventy nine …" Krik's head popped out from behind the rock as if it had been fired from a cannon. The look on his face would have made an elephant forget. In a staccato voice, he barked out a barrage of orders.

"We will adopt Rafi's plan at once! Do you hear? End of story. Wake up, shape up and shut up! Now get ready! The sun will be up any moment now!"

As if Krik had the sun on a string, the first ray of dawn stained the eastern sky a bloody red. Red light oozed up the sky.

"Red sky in the morning, rats take warning," said Bree prophetically.

Having brushed and trimmed the rat pack to her satisfaction, Rafi sat down to a hurried breakfast of nuts and raisins complemented by some dusty remnants of chocolate with the corners nibbled off.

Then, watching the rising sun paint the sky red, she washed her face and brushed her hair, periodically inspecting her reflection in the water hole. It was only after ten minutes of hard work, washing and combing what looked like months worth of grime and tangles, a young, not-so-unpresentable girl stared back at her. Her gaze fell upon the rune streaked across her hair. For the first time in her life, she began to understand. Once the object of so much gossip and ridicule, the rune now filled her with hope. She reached out to the water, touching it with her finger, but both the rune and her reflection rippled into the worried looks of her mother and father. She waved at them, but they only looked up into the sky as if they had lost something, conversing in silent ripples until Krik's voice broke through her reverie.

"All fed and ready?" he asked.

"If you want to call that feeding," complained Pud. "Personally, I'd prefer to go to my death on a full stomach!"

Having run out of numbers, Krik appeared to have calmed down considerably, and was just able to let Pud's remark go. He looked splendid in the full wardrobe of an Arab sheik to which he had added a tarboosh. Armed with his staff he might have passed for a prophet. With a well-aimed leap, he landed on Rafi's shoulder, his robes fluttering in a warm breeze.

"Let's go!"

"No one is going to die," said Rafi, although she was not entirely sure about this. "We have come this far together and that in itself is a miracle. I can't imagine that Ademar would be so willing to send us to our deaths."

Bree woke up Dlop. "Unless Ademar is in league with Triodon," he said. "That is, after all, possible, is it not, Krik?"

"Possible," said Krik, "but unlikely. Triodon has many servants gathered around him, but I doubt that his one arm stretches as far as Ademar. It is a good observation though. Do not trust anyone but ourselves. But do not worry. I'm sure that the Oracle will at least hear us out before allowing Zigh to add us to his furniture."

"Good point," said Bree. He picked up a small bone that lay by his feet and thrust the sharp end deep into a tree stump, pulling it out again as if the stump was made of butter. Gnarled bone spurs completed a handle, making it a perfect sword.

"Couldn't have said it better myself," said Pud, laying his paws on an even bigger bone that was shaped like a scimitar and honed with a serrated edge. With a yell, he swung the bone sword down upon a large rock, splitting it in two.

Krik watched from Rafi's shoulder. "You have a good blade, Pud," he said. "As your tongue is ever ready and sharp for your friends, make sure that your sword is equal to the task when we face the enemy. Just have a care as to which is which."

Bree selected yet another bone. "This sword will do well for Dlop," he said. He looked up at Dlop who had rejoined the knapsack now securely slung on Rafi's shoulders. "That is if he ever wakes up."

"It's hard work up here," said Dlop who might have looked more offended if his eyes were open. "I'm the lookout rat."

"Yes, we know all about that," said Bree thickly. "Well, Sir Lookout, I'll carry your sword for now. But if anything happens, you had better get down here pronto."

"Or you up here," Dlop pointed out.

Ademar had been true to his word. Not far from the water hole, a large road of bones stretched east toward a grove of white poplar trees. The Road of Death. Never had a name been more aptly given. The road, complete with sidewalks, handrails and a tollbooth, was made entirely of bones – small bones, large bones and bones as tall as a house – all painstakingly assembled into a grotesque avenue of demons and nightmares. If Ademar had not told them their destiny lay on the other side of that road, the Companions would have surely headed west by the quickest way. But there was no other road. There it lay, gleaming white under the gathering sunlight, pulling them forward as if by some unseen force, calling each of them by name.

"I have never known fear," said Bree grimly, looking up at a colossus of bone that threatened to come crashing down upon their heads, "until now."

"Look!" cried Rafi, astonished. She pointed to a flower bed that ran the length of the road, filled with a variety of exotic flowers assembled from bones. Not surprisingly, a bone watering can lay nearby.

"There's one on the other side too," said Bree, aghast. "Did one ever see such a thing before?"

"This is not the first time we have looked upon Death," said Krik bravely, although his voice sounded as if it was coming from inside his satchel. "These are only bones."

"We've never walked on no bones before," pointed out Pud.

Bree sniffed the air. "Everywhere, the smell of Death," he said.

"There is no other way," said Krik simply. "Don't look. Just walk." He tugged on Rafi's ear to redirect her gaze, which was glued to the watering can. "There is no turning back now. Bones or no bones, we must see the Oracle."

With one sharp intake of breath, the Companions stepped onto the road. Here and there along the road, they found their progress watched by silent skull sentinels as flaps of dried skin waved from the bones like forgotten flags from battles lost. More bones crunched beneath their feet, packed straight and true so that every step was a nightmare completed by a 'surround sound' of bone snapping pops.

"See here," said Rafi, pointing out a skeleton that could have swallowed them whole had they not already been standing between its ribs. "This was once an Albertosaurus, a huge and terrible dinosaur not unlike the T-Rex," she said. She pointed to the next skeleton. "And this," she gasped, "this is a Daspletosaurus. Its name means 'frightful reptile.' With a skull like that I can certainly see why." Suddenly, she fell upon her knees before a great skull with a complete set of serrated teeth the size of bananas. "I must be dreaming. Is this a Nanotyrannus?" She pointed to the eyes that watched her disinterestedly. "Look how the eyes face forward as if it is watching us." She brushed away years of sand from the skull that, in another age, could have swallowed her whole. "A complete specimen. Oh, I wish Pupa was here." She stared at the skull in disbelief.

"What's wrong Rafi?" asked Krik, for it had not escaped his notice that she was crying. "These are only the bones of our ancestors. They cannot hurt us now. They are but white shadows of what once was. Time has healed their pain as one day it shall heal our own."

"It's not that," said Rafi. Her hands caressed the skull of the Nanotyrannus as if she was mourning a lost loved one. Tears fell from her eyes, splashing white upon the skull. Were it not for those grinning teeth, one might have thought that the Nanotyrannus was crying.

"They were so ferocious and yet so magnificent. How could such life rule the world for millions of years and then disappear? And yet, had they not, where would we be today? Why could we not have lived together and learned through each other's lives instead of trying to see a world we shall never see through such empty eyes?"

"I do not know" said Krik, impressed yet saddened by the child's wise words. "Yet I cannot say that they are gone. There is some of them in you and in all living things. Perhaps it is only in our own demise that we may begin to understand theirs."

Rafi rose to her feet, brushing sand from her knees. "You speak wisely, Krik," she said. "Such matters are beyond a young girl." She looked up and down the road, which seemed no more inviting one way or the other. "One thing does bother me though. As far as I can tell, all of these skeletons are Tyrannosaurids, the largest, fiercest predators the world has ever known. Who could kill such monsters, and then lay their bones out as if paving a driveway? Besides," she went on, noting that some of the bones were dressed in rags of skin, "I thought that Triodon killed all the dinosaurs. Did some survive?"

Krik did not answer.

"Will you look at that?" said Bree.

"Now there's something you don't see everyday," said Pud.

Rafi looked up. Not far off down the road, perched among a

graveyard of white trees, was a house. As far as the Companions could see it was constructed entirely from skulls and bones held together by some unseen force. Through shuttered eyes and a rot-iron door, it stared and grinned upon the road.

While the road had filled them with terror, it was nothing compared to the house. A tower of white, it gleamed ominously above the white trees, twisting and popping in the breeze as if extending an invitation for the Companions to join into some macabre dance to which only Death might be a willing partner.

"Zigh must be powerful indeed," said Bree, his teeth chattering louder than the bones, "to live at the end of such a road and in such a house." Paws shaking, he put on his spectacles and looked up at Krik. "What hope do we have against such a formidable adversary?"

Krik removed his tarboosh. "That which is in our hearts," he said. With a white handkerchief he mopped a tide of sweat from his brow. As it was, his own heart was in his boots, shaking no less than some bones dancing from a grisly weather vane set upon the roof of the house. He put on his tarboosh. "The goodness that makes us who we are and keeps us together."

"I'd settle for a good rock," said Pud though, he too, was having trouble finding any heart as he looked upon the house of Death. "And some dinosaur rats to carry it. Rafi, rats ..."

Without warning, the road stopped before a clearing, which might have served as a front lawn had it not included yet another graveyard full of skulls and bones. Oddly enough, a small bone table, complete with seven bone chairs, sat uninvitingly in front of the house. But, where the house had stood only moments before, it had suddenly been replaced with a large, dark wall.

"So ..." said Pud.

"Big ..." said Bree.

"Who ..." said Rafi.

"Zigh!" said Krik.

The ground shook beneath their feet as the wall moved toward them, growing larger and darker with every step. It was then that the Companions came to the horrid realization that the wall was breathing and had suddenly grown a body, head and tail. Piercing the darkness, which had blotted out the sun, two ferocious eyes, sheathed in yellow and writhing like angry snakes, skewered them to the road.

Standing before them was an enormous Tyrannosaurus. It stood as tall as a two-story house and its head was large enough to swallow a small car. Still more terrible, an army of butcher blade teeth completed a cruel mouth stained with blood and gore. But most terrible of all were those serpentine eyes that seemed to leap from their sockets, riveting the Companions into wordless silence.

"Well, hello, my little friends," said the Tyrannosaurus in a deep voice that rattled the Road of Death into a frightful dance. "Three appetizers, an entrée and a mint toothpick out for a stroll I see." Impossible as it seemed, the Tyrannosaurus curled back its lips to reveal even more teeth. "And from out of the whole, wide world you chose to stroll … to me."

With that, the Tyrannosaurus let out a deafening roar that sent an avalanche of bones crashing down around the Companions. Rooted in terror, transfixed by the Tyrannosaurus's piercing eyes, they did not move or speak. Any proud words they had prepared to greet the Guardian were irretrievably lost with the bones strewn upon the road.

Rafi had never seen anything so terrible as the Tyrannosaurus. No longer did it stand proud but harmless as she had seen it in her father's museum. Now it stood less than ten feet away, earth's most efficient predator since the beginning of time, filled with both life and death, at the height of its raw power. She tried to scream or run but her screams were clotted in fear, and her legs locked in terror. Krik did not appear to be doing much better. Only his bulbous eyes could be seen above one of Rafi's ears as he stared at the Tyrannosaurus in equal terror, a clicking noise issuing from his lips as he tried to speak. As for Bree and Pud, they simply stood so frozen in fear they could not even look at each other or say good bye. But most curious of all was Dlop. Eyes open, as white as the bones around him, he sat like a frozen ratsicle in the knapsack.

"Zzzziiiggh!" said Krik finally, looking no less terrified as he emerged from behind Rafi's ear.

"Ahhh," said the Tyrannosaurus in a tone that froze the Companions' blood right down to the marrow of their bones. "The smallest but bravest speaks first. Krik, isn't it?" The Tyrannosaurus flexed nostrils the size of basketballs and spewed a green, sticky residue all over the Companions. "This is one time you'll wish that you minded your own business, little twig." The coiled eyes struck out with a knowing look. "Yes, I know of your quest. Do not be surprised. Your names, as you can see, have not escaped me. And neither will you."

"Great Zigh," Rafi began hopelessly, finding strength in Krik's voice, however small. She was certain that not even the United Nations could contend with this Tyrannosaurus. "Please hear our …"

"Now the youngest speaks," said the Tyrannosaurus in mock interest. The coiled eyes folded into daggers of gold. "And you would dare to speak to one such as I, who roamed the earth since before the dawn? Foolish Drog. Thinking all along that you and these silly creatures could save Earth? A miserable, pathetic, little pipsqueak like you?" The eyes were laughing at her now. "Rest assured that you still have a small part to play in your quest, but I call that dinner."

"See here, Zigh," said Bree, surprised at his own daring. "You have no right to speak to Rafi …"

"Right?" The Companions were blasted off their feet and onto their backs by the fury of the Tyrannosaurus's roar. Unblinking, they lay in a sea of spit, snot and bone. "You speak to me of rights? A rat? Enough of all of you!" With one powerful step the Tyrannosaurus's foot crushed the road before them as a row of spinal columns, along with the tollbooth, disintegrated under one powerful sweep of its tail. Thundering into position, its massive jaws hovered only feet from Rafi, a thick syrup of saliva dripping upon her face and in her hair. "Drog!" bellowed the Tyrannosaurus. "Give me the stones you bear! With the stones I shall challenge Triodon himself for the mastery of Earth. Give me the stones, Drog, and you may choose whom I shall eat last!"

"The stones?" Krik's eyes widened with comprehension. "You aren't ..."

"The stones," roared the Tyrannosaurus, possessed with a fury that was hideous to behold. "Give them to me!" A pair of arms which hitherto had gone unnoticed clawed the air in a futile effort to rip the stones from Rafi's shirt, but the arms were too short and the Tyrannosaurus too angry to make the connection.

"They are not mine to give!" cried Rafi from where she lay upon the road. She tried to cover the stones with her hands but Bree, Pud and Krik had already mounted a triangular defense upon her chest. Swords and staff drawn, they stood in steadfast silence. Trapped somewhere beneath her, she could feel Dlop struggling to free himself from the knapsack.

"Then enjoy your last meal," snapped the Tyrannosaurus. Adjusting its tactics, the monster's mouth flew open, revealing a railway tunnel filled with teeth. "Mine!"

Rafi closed her eyes and screamed. Even with her eyes closed, she could still see the gaping jaws of the Tyrannosaurus lunge toward her. A strange end, she thought. This can't be good for tourism.

The strike never came. With a roar of surprise and pain, the Tyrannosaurus reared itself onto its great legs, turned its head, and began snapping its jaws across its back and sides as if fighting some unseen assailant. The sound was deafening as it stomped and staggered and danced around the Companions, almost crushing them in its fury, its bus-sized tail scattering rocks and bones as if they were grains of sand. Inexplicably, a river of blood gushed from gaping wounds that formed along its body, raining down upon the Companions where they lay upon the road too frightened to move. Confused, unable to see anything but the agony of the Tyrannosaurus, they simply watched what they could not understand.

"You!" snarled the Tyrannosaurus, biting everywhere and

anywhere as fast as its jaws could move. "I thought it was you. Small matter. You, at least, shall die first!"

From under a veil of spit and blood, Rafi watched the Tyrannosaurus dance in a seemingly endless parade of agony as fresh wounds sprouted up all over its body. In spite of its bold words, the look on the Tyrannosaurus's face was one of mingled fear and wonder. At first, she could not determine the cause of such grievous wounds, but then she saw what looked like a small black bundle moving at dizzying speed all over the Tyrannosaurus's body. Without warning, but with ominous intention, the bundle stopped moving just below the monster's throat.

"Mercy," cried the Tyrannosaurus stamping the road into dust and shaking the very ground upon which it stood, but nothing could shake off the black bundle. "Mercy," it cried again in a voice that brought tears to Rafi's eyes. "I would not have hurt them. Forgive me … I …"

It was of no use. No matter how madly the Tyrannosaurus pleaded and begged and stamped for its life, the black bundle remained locked on its throat as fresh chunks of flesh and gore fell upon the Companions, entombed as they were upon the Road of Death. Then, with a sudden intake of breath, the Tyrannosaurus stopped moving. For a moment, it stood as still as stone except for the serpentine eyes that almost leapt from its head in a desperate search for something on the road.

Somehow, Rafi knew what the eyes were searching for. In a moment that turned her stomach more than blood and gore, she realized that the eyes were searching for the one thing more precious than any stone upon the earth, and yet the only thing the black bundle would clearly deny. Life. Unwilling to look up and yet unable to resist, her eyes intertwined with the serpent's stare in a shared look of infinite sadness. Slowly, slower than the melting of ice, the timeless light that once filled those eyes began to fade. Never had she been in a room so empty. Then, standing like the tallest tree, as magnificent in death as it was in life, the Tyrannosaurus crashed to the earth, scattering rocks and bones in every direction.

It was some time before the Companions could even think. Paralyzed with fear, they lay in their bed of flesh, blood and bone as if they were sleeping, unwilling to ever rise again. Under a cloud of confused dust, the Tyrannosaurus lay upon the ground, blood still running down its sides like an active volcano. Spears of sunlight vaulted across the sky.

On top of the red heap that was once a Tyrannosaurus, something black and red looked down upon the Companions with black, gimlety eyes. Of all the things they had just seen, this was the most remarkable.

It was a wolverine.

"Not the time I would have chosen for a nap," growled the wolverine. From under a veil of blood, patches of thick, black fur bristled in sunlight surrounded by a mane of gold.

"Well?" The gimlety eyes rolled furiously in their sockets. Full of anger, merciless in their roll, the black eyes terrorized the Companions into new levels of horror. Yet there was something else rolling in those eyes, suggesting a hint of humor.

"I haven't got all day! It's enough to have my breakfast disturbed by some blundering fool of a T-Rex than to find you lot taking a nap on my road. In case you haven't noticed, this isn't a hotel!"

"Zigh!" cried the Companions together. Slowly, painfully, they rose to their feet except for Dlop who lay slumped over the knapsack, feeling too crushed and sick to be afraid. Miraculously, Krik was still clinging to Rafi's ear. One look at each other told them there was no point in trying to look presentable.

"Who else were you expecting?" roared Zigh in a voice that would have shamed a lion. Lazily, he cleaned one of his paws with his tongue. "The Pope? Does this look like the Vatican to you? Even so, you might have combed your hair before you wrecked my road. Look at the mess you made! Who's going to pay for all this damage?"

"He's not much bigger than Bree," whispered Pud.

"Oh, I get it," growled Zigh, his gimlety eyes fixed on Pud. "Small is as small does, is it? Well, it serves that T-Rex right, lumbering in here as if he owned the place. Should have picked on someone his own size. But that's just like a dinosaur. Big and stupid."

Rafi bowed as low as she could without slipping on the blood-bespattered road. Try as she might, she could not pull her gaze away from the Tyrannosaurus's eyes, which still watched her like deep wells that had run out of water.

"You were magnificent, Zigh," she said breathlessly. "Thank you for saving us."

Zigh looked up from where he had just bitten the Tyrannosaurus. "Eh?" he growled. "What's that? Well, yes, I suppose it was magnificent, now that I think about it, although I should have given him a half nelson before I ripped his throat out." He licked a beautiful set of golden teeth. "As to saving your lives ..." He paused, stroking his chin thoughtfully.

"Great Zigh," said Krik, taking advantage of the silence. Miraculously, his tarboosh had stayed on during the battle, but it was as red as a poppy. "Please consider our quest before you pronounce our doom."

Zigh rubbed his paws together in anticipation. "Did you bring me a present?" he asked.

"Well ... no," said Krik guiltily, sure that the eyes of Bree and Pud were upon him. "Not yet anyway. We thought it best that we ..."

"... would first visit your magnificence to see what gift would be most appropriate for your ... er ... home," said Rafi, looking up at Zigh with the biggest, brownest eyes she could muster.

"No present?" asked Zigh disappointedly. A flash of anger swept the humor from his eyes. "And you want to be a U. N. ambassador?"

Rafi hung her head. "Forgive me, Zigh," she said. Her bloodied fingers twisted around the stones dangling loosely from her shirt. "My companions are blameless in this matter. The fault is mine alone." She looked up at Zigh. "Is there anything you need?"

"What I need is peace and quiet," snapped Zigh. Then, over the corpse of the Tyrannosaurus, he performed a victory dance followed by a four-pawed moon walk. For the first time, the Companions noticed that he had a short, stubby tail.

He glanced angrily at his tail. "Bitten off in a fight," he explained, "by an Albertosaurus." He nodded at an enormous skeleton lying further down the road. "That's her over there. So I bit hers off just to teach her a lesson. It seems like yesterday although I think it was more around the time when you Drogs first showed up. You know, before you started burning up the place."

"Remarkable," said Rafi. "What do you do when you're not fighting?"

"Oh," said Zigh nonchalantly, looking at the road and the grounds in front of his home. "I have my bone collection. Water my flowers. Eat, sleep ... mostly I play 'I Spy' with the Oracle. He cheats though."

"And is the Oracle in?" asked Krik hopefully and bowing low. "For, if it pleases your clemency, Most Wondrous Zigh, we greatly desire to speak to him."

"Certainly no one ever comes here to speak with me," growled Zigh. "As if I have nothing important to say next to that old crank." He scowled in the direction of the bone house. "You pick up a few things over millions of years you know." He gave the Companions a look that suggested he had not quite made up his mind as to whether or not he should kill them. "I must be getting soft letting you in without a present. Still, I suppose I should let you pass. Are you sure you didn't bring one?"

"Most Astonishing Zigh," said Rafi who was truly amazed by the wolverine. "I love playing 'I Spy'. I give you my word that if we live through our quest it will be my greatest honor to play the game with you and learn from your great wisdom gathered over the ages. And between games I can clean up the mess we made until your road is as good as new. That is, if my gift pleases Your Excellency."

"She doesn't cheat either," said Pud.

"Not now, Pud," said Bree through clenched teeth.

Evidently, Rafi's offer pleased Zigh immensely. His dark eyes grew bright and merry, and his stubby tail wagged ferociously.

"I accept your gracious gift, Rafi of the Three Stones," he said imperiously. "Tuesdays work best I think. That is if we're not all dead by then." He gave the Tyrannosaurus another bite. "Now, let's go see the Oracle."

Zigh jumped down from the Tyrannosaurus. As Pud had said, Zigh was not much bigger than Bree, but, having just seen his amazing victory over a T-Rex, the Companions were willing to accept him as the true Guardian. Only his small, gimlety eyes seemed larger than life, alternating between looks of inestimable fury and sweeping laughter. Pud was particularly impressed.

"Have you ever used rocks?" he asked.

"Rocks are for amateurs," scoffed Zigh. He picked up a large rock, crushing it into dust. "You must be the rock if you are to win. Only stronger. Much stronger. Stronger and faster than anything you know and don't know. Get it? It's all in the mind, you see."

"All in the mind," repeated Pud. He glared at a rock as if he could split it in two.

"I'd stick to rocks if I were you, Pud," said Bree, laughing.

They followed Zigh toward the bone house. After their horrific adventure with the Tyrannosaurus it seemed unlikely that a house of bone could cause them any further alarm but the mere sight of it filled them with terror. In every bone they sensed an unhappy and unending tragedy made all the worse by row upon row of white washed skulls, fused together into one astonished look of regret that stared impenetrably upon the Road of Death.

Bree looked uneasy.

"I can't help feeling that Zigh's house has a life and death of its own," he said darkly. "A life beyond living and a death beyond dying as it were. It fills me with a great foreboding I have never felt before."

"What Bree means," Pud called up to Dlop, "is that this place gives him the willies."

"Does the Oracle live in the bone house?" asked Rafi with a shudder. The thought of stepping inside the bone house almost paralyzed her with fear. She could only think that it would be like living in a skeleton.

"No," said Zigh. The Companions shared a sigh of relief. "That's *my* house. The Oracle lives behind. He wants the extra bedroom, and I suppose I could spare the room, but, quite frankly, he stinks."

"Stinks?" said Rafi. She crinkled her nose. This struck her as rather odd as Zigh, covered with filth and blood, did not exactly smell like a flower.

They passed the house as quickly as they could without offending Zigh. Wagging his tail, he looked each of them up and down for approval.

"Wait until you see the basement!"

In spite of her growing fear, Rafi could not resist the temptation to look inside. Judging by the spaces between the bones, it was almost as if the builder had intended to welcome prying eyes inside along with the sunlight that bleached the bones to a deathly white. At first, she thought the house was empty, but then she spotted a heap of skulls piled high in the middle of a large room. Unable to come to any other conclusion, it suddenly dawned upon her that this was Zigh's bed. Shivering with horror, she pulled her shirt collar tightly around her neck as if she was about to catch a cold. She sneezed.

"Lovely!" said Krik, who had turned just in time to appreciate the full impact of the sneeze. A palette of disgusting textures and color, his flowing robe and hat could have passed for a soiled tissue. "First, we have a hot bath complete with dinosaur sized booger bath pellets, and now you. I'm so stiff wearing all this crud I can hardly move."

"I'm sorry, Krik," Rafi whispered. She tried to clean him off using one of the tails of her shirt, but it only made things worse. Her eyes floated in a pool of tears. "It's the T-Rex, it's this house, it's … everything. I have never seen such hatred, anger, despair and laughter all in one day. It's as if my body can't take in any more and wants to let it out." She sneezed again.

"I know it, Rafi," said Krik who did not really seem to mind another coating. "It's an awful thing to stare into the eyes of Death, but worse still to see it forever close the eyes of another. Life is a gift that no one has the right to take away. Yet in death, there is life beyond the grave. In the world of the Nadi, the lion kills the antelope, the sheep graze upon the grass and I eat the ladybug, but we are all one and the same. One cannot live or die without the other. It has always been this way. It is much the same with Drogs, but you never think about the consequences of what you do. Every animal you kill, every rain forest you destroy, a little of you dies with it. You are only as alive as we are, and when we are gone you shall wander lost and witless until the days when you shall follow."

Rafi wiped the tears from her eyes. "I understand, dearest Krik," she said. "Knowing this hurts me more than you know. But if I live to become a U. N. ambassador, I will carry your message throughout the world until they will listen."

"Here we are," growled Zigh, stopping behind the house. They now stood upon a bone courtyard surrounded by a bone palisade. Here and there, bone trees stood in bone planters flanked by numerous flower beds of bone. In the middle of the courtyard lay a bone pool complete with a bone slide and diving board, which was not of much use since the pool was empty.

"Leaks," growled Zigh, watching their astonished faces.

Stunned, the Companions could only stare at the pool.

Zigh looked up at the sky, which was unusually bright. "I will take my leave of you now," he said. "It's laundry day and I have a road to mend." He sat on a skull, impaling each of the Companions with a swift look from his piercing eyes.

"You are standing on sacred ground," he said warningly. "For in this place dwells the Oracle, the oldest and most powerful being on Earth." The faintest trace of humor drained from his eyes as if they were bone pools. "Now listen carefully," he added, "all of you." His eyes lingered on Pud. "If His Eminence favors you with an audience, you must prostrate yourselves before him until you are lower than the dust. Do not move or speak or even think for the Oracle knows all. If you are granted the rare privilege of speaking, speak clearly, and in few words. Above all, and this is very important, never, never, ever turn your back on him." Zigh winced as if the consequences of this action were too painful to explain. "I have done much to let you come this far but I deem you to be worthy folk. Do not make me regret my decision."

With these words, Zigh left them, waving his stubby tail good bye. "Don't forget Tuesdays," he called back to Rafi. He disappeared into the bone house.

"Who could be more powerful than Zigh?" asked Pud.

"Pud," said Bree, his voice and temper rising, "if you value our lives, be silent."

They waited and waited. Other than the sun inching its way up the sky, no one moved or spoke. In an added show of respect even Dlop had been retrieved from the knapsack, propped up between Bree and Pud, his eyes held open by splinters of bone.

"Is it just me," whispered Bree, "or did the ground move?"

"I felt it too," Rafi whispered back. She pinched Dlop's fur just in time to prevent him from falling over. "What's happening?"

"Silence," hissed Krik. "You heard Zigh. No matter what happens, stay where you are. Don't speak or think unless I tell you to. The last of these shouldn't be a problem for you, Pud. Now be quiet."

Ten minutes passed. Just as the Companions thought that they had been imagining things, the ground swayed violently beneath their feet. Before they even knew what was happening it heaved back and forth, a pitching sea, rising into the air, falling around them into depths unknown until they stood upon a patch of ground barely seven feet wide. Below, the earth belched and rolled as if the end of time had already come, spitting fire and brimstone into the air.

"Can I think now?" asked Pud as Dlop deposited the remains of his breakfast all over him.

As if in answer, a wall of flame shot up in front of the Companions as tall and wide as a cloud but as hot as the sun, searing the air and filling their eyes and mouths with smoke and ash.

"I guess not," added Pud, choking.

Helpless, the Companions held on to one another in a seemingly futile attempt to prevent themselves from falling into the fiery abyss below. But it did not seem to matter. To their added horror, inch by inch, their small, desperate refuge disintegrated into the mouth of the encroaching fire as rocks and bones catapulted across the sky. Then, just when the end seemed certain and Krik was about to crown Pud with his staff, the fire burst into a new holocaust of flame, setting a dreadful dragon upon the sky. Enraged, a pair of wings as large as a forest fire beat a merciless cloud of heated dust toward the Companions as two volcanic eyes fixed them with a stare that would have melted steel.

"Behold," the dragon spoke in tongues of flame. "The Oracle approaches."

"Look!" cried Rafi, unable to contain herself any longer, and pointing to the ground in front of them.

Bathed in the heat and glow of the dragon, the ground cracked before their feet. Terrified, the Companions watched as the crack widened into a hole about the size of a melon from which emerged an equally sized ball of dark earth. This was followed by an assortment of black legs and horns. Their terror turning into fascination, they watched the ball complete its exit directed, as it seemed, by the legs and horns until both ball and pilot stood directly before them. It was only then that they realized the dragon and flame had vanished, but the air was filled with a suggestive odor that had them wishing the dragon would return. Bewildered, choking from smoke inhalation, and forgetting to prostrate themselves in front of the Oracle, they stared dumbfounded at this semi-miraculous sight.

Perched upon a dung ball as if it was a throne, wearing an acorn hat, sat a dung beetle.

CHAPTER SEVEN

THE ORACLE

The Companions stared at the Dung Beetle in awed silence. Dressed in thick plates of polished black armor it sat menacingly upon the dung ball. Below two lance-like antennae, a pair of grim looking horns clashed like swords in the sunlight. Ablaze in metallic sheen, fitted with a tread of dung, it looked more like a small tank than a large, smelly insect.

Mindful of Zigh's warning, they watched and waited for the Dung Beetle to speak. But for all they waited, it uttered neither word nor sound, only glaring at the Companions from where it sat imperiously upon the dung ball as if to challenge any one of them to break the awkward silence.

Well coached by Zigh, the Companions said nothing. They stared back. The same thought raced through each of their minds. What does one say to an Oracle? Not just any Oracle. *The* Oracle. Ageless, all knowing, the oldest, wisest and most powerful being on Earth. There it sat upon its throne of dung in pungent majesty. What words were courteous enough, what words brave enough to address this timeless vessel of power and knowledge?

Without warning, the Dung Beetle suddenly toppled off the dung ball, landing headfirst upon the ground. Helpless, it stood on horns and head, its crown still intact, waving its legs and antennae in the air. For a moment, the Companions wondered if this was a sign that they too should stand on their heads, but the contrived, almost comical nature of the Dung Beetle's fall made them warier than ever. And so, fighting every instinct and courtesy to help the Dung Beetle, they remained still and silent, knowing that any wrong word or movement meant certain death.

Rafi gave Krik a knowing look. Unbelievably, it appeared that the Dung Beetle was trying to trick them into conversation. And so it was. After a few moments, it righted itself with a grunt, climbed back up the dung ball and glared at them even more ferociously than before. After two more elaborate dives, the last of which, along with a theatrical groan, put the Dung Beetle flat on its back, it appeared to give up the game and began pedaling the dung ball for all it was worth back to the dung hole.

"Did you say something?" asked the Dung Beetle, suddenly stopping and turning around. The voice sounded old and shrill, resonating with a power that seemed to come from the earth itself. Without waiting for an answer, it furiously pedaled the dung ball back to the Companions. Expertly braking the dung ball as if it was a small car, the Dung Beetle screeched in a skid mark of dung. Majestically, it gazed upon the Companions, a triumphant smile rising up its face and antennae in insolent swagger.

"No, Glorious One," said Krik, knowing that he must break the Companions' silence or condemn them all to an awful death. "Since you asked first," he added hastily.

"Liar!" snapped the Dung Beetle angrily. Robed in black, it sat like a judge upon a bench that smelled worse than an outhouse.

"Truly, Most Illustrious, August and Unrivaled One," said Krik in measured tones, "we did not."

The Dung Beetle glared at each of the Companions. "Are you sure?" it asked suspiciously. "I know I heard something, and I know everything." The Dung Beetle waved an accusatory antenna at Bree. "You said something, didn't you?"

"Not I, Exalted One," said Bree with great obedience.

The Dung Beetle glared at Pud with grim satisfaction. "Then it was you," it said.

"Not I, Knobbly One," said Pud.

"Noble!" whispered Bree.

"Aha," said the Dung Beetle, looking up at Rafi. "It was you!"

"Not I, Puissant One," said Rafi.

"Puissant?" asked the Dung Beetle.

"It means powerful," said Rafi, unthinkingly.

The earth trembled beneath the sky. "I know what it means!" roared the Dung Beetle. "I'm The Oracle. I know everything!"

"You forgot about Dlop," said Pud.

Krik glared at Pud, readying his staff. "Who is asleep, Fabled One," he added.

"Then he talks in his sleep!" snapped the Dung Beetle, crowning itself in smug superiority. "I knew it! Or," the Dung Beetle's face lit up as if suddenly inspired, "there is another talking member of your party!"

"No, Imperial One," said Krik, who was fast running out of titles. "Who would dare to speak first before the Great Oracle whose wisdom is unsurpassed by even the stars? Surely not your humble servants that sit before you."

"You're sure it wasn't you?"

"No ... Most ... Elevated ... One," said Krik, racking his brain for a new title. "I only wish that it was me or one of my companions, so that the guilty might learn from your supreme justice, and so assuage your anger."

"Well," the Dung Beetle roared as bolts of fire and brimstone rained down from the sky. "Then who was it? I distinctly heard somebody say, 'Did you say something?', and somebody's going into the flames one by one until I get an answer!"

Bree scribbled on a piece of paper and handed it up to Rafi. After a quick glance, she held it up for Krik to read.

"O, Most Commanding and Olympic Oracle," he said with a sigh of relief, reading aloud the new titles Bree had written down. "Forgive us our minds of mud, but we thought you said that."

"I did?" asked the Dung Beetle, amazed. From the look on its face, Rafi could tell that the Dung Beetle was doing some fast thinking. "Moi?" In evident alarm, it pedaled back and forth on the dung ball. In a spray of dung, both ball and beetle hurtled back to the Companions.

"Well," said the Dung Beetle with a slightly beaten look, "maybe I did. But for my part I am prepared to give you the benefit of your doubt. And now that I know that all of you spoke first, who are you, and what do you want?"

"So much for knowing everything," muttered Pud, unfortunately in a voice loud enough for the Dung Beetle to hear. Rafi and Bree froze in terror. As for Krik, he threw his staff upon the ground and hung his head.

"A doubter!" snapped the Dung Beetle, steering the dung ball toward Pud. "As for your sorry self, I know all about you. You're a …"

"Pud," said Pud, suddenly aware of the danger glinting in the beetle-black eyes. In an effort to redeem himself, he bowed so low his nostrils filled with dung.

"Silence!" wailed the Dung Beetle as if it had suddenly fallen in a trance. "For what passes in your mind has already passed through mine. You are a … Pud!"

As if they had rehearsed it in a play, the Companions gasped in wonder at the Dung Beetle's revelation. Having finally come to his senses, even Pud was ready for the part he must play.

"Truly astonishing, O Magma Brain," he said, bowing again. "I apostrophe myself before your um … nipple … tents."

"Omnipotence," hissed Bree.

Pud lay upon his stomach. And, to the shock of everyone including the Dung Beetle, he heaped paws full of dust and dung upon his head.

Kirk watched Pud, a look of disbelief and admiration upon his face. "Incredible," he said, meaning Pud.

"Isn't it?" agreed the Dung Beetle proudly. In its excitement, the Dung Beetle took a great bite out of the dung ball, which it chewed exultantly before making an awful face.

Krik consulted his list. "Undeniably Transcendent One," he said. He bowed humbly, winking at Rafi and Bree.

"Is there nothing that escapes you?" he went on, looking up at the Dung Beetle from where he lay in a cloud of dust. "Lower than the dust beneath our feet we can only look upon you as blades of grass look at the sun. Otherwise, how is it that you know my name is Krik, and that I am the Ambassador to the League of Mantis?"

"How is it," said Rafi, taking up the game, "that you know my name is Rafi, and that bound upon my shirt are three of the Stones of Erebus?"

"How is it," said Bree, "that you know my name is Bree, and that I am Pud's older and wiser brother?"

"How is it," said a sleepy voice from inside the knapsack, "that you know my name is Dlop, and that where there were four chocolate bars, now there are none?"

"It is," shouted the Dung Beetle, waving its legs, horns and antennae as it danced madly upon the dung ball, "because I am the Oracle! Outstanding. Remarkable. Astounding. Clever. Learned. Enlightened. O-R-A-C-L-E. Wisest of All. Supreme Authoritarian. Keeper of the Sacred Knowledge. Been there. Done that. Seen it all a thousand times. The One and Only Oracle. Isn't that right, Klik?"

"Krik," corrected Krik, wincing at the not-so-modest Dung Beetle who, in its excitement, had fallen once again from the dung ball. "Which brings us to our quest of which you, undoubtedly, know so much."

"It is true, it is true!" cried the Dung Beetle, tears of joy streaming from its eyes.

Krik risked a glance at his watch. "That being so," he said, "we humbly beg your great wisdom and guidance in a matter that concerns us all …"

"Do you play 'I Spy'?" asked the Dung Beetle excitedly.

Krik picked up his staff. "Ah … yes," he said. "Or rather, we know how to play. However, as you already know, now is not the time to …"

"I spy with my little eye," said the Dung Beetle, looking intently at the sky, "something that is blue."

The Companions shifted uneasily. Other than the sky there was not a visible speck of blue for at least a hundred miles. Hemming and hawing, they stared awkwardly at one another, the ground, the Dung Beetle and everywhere but the clear, blue sky. For added precaution, Bree clapped a paw over Pud's mouth. As for Krik, his body deflated into a long sigh. Obviously discouraged by this delay, he appeared to be inwardly debating whether or not to count to ten or rush up and thrash the Dung Beetle within an inch of its oracular life before it had a chance to condemn them to the flames.

"Something that is blue," repeated the Dung Beetle, delighted by the silence and still staring at the sky. "Come now. Do not be afraid. It's not that hard."

"Thhh ssca?" said Pud from behind Bree's paw.

"Those red rocks?" guessed Bree, pointing to a rock formation.

"No, not the rocks," chortled the Dung Beetle.

"Thhh ssca?" said Pud.

"Zigh's house?" guessed Rafi doubtfully.

"No, not *my* house," said the Dung Beetle with great emphasis as to whose house it was.

"Thhh ssca?" said Pud.

"The clouds?" guessed the knapsack.

"No, not the clouds," said the Dung Beetle nervously. "You'll never get it."

"Well," said Krik, throwing caution to the wind, "we can't think of anything else that is blue. Unless ... of course ... it can't be ... the sky?"

"The sky?" asked the Dung Beetle evasively.

"Yes," said Krik as if he was still not sure, "and now that I look at it I see that it is a kind of blue. How clever of you to choose something as high and almighty as your beetling self."

"Is that your final answer?" asked the Dung Beetle as if to suggest that the answer was wrong. "The sky is not actually blue you know. It only appears blue due to the scattering of light by dust particles smaller than the wavelength of the visible spectrum."

"Yes," said Krik, not to be fooled by the Dung Beetle.

"Oh," said the Dung Beetle, dreadfully disappointed that the game was both over and lost. "Well, since time is short and I'm in a good mood I'll give you that one. Now tell me, how are you going to enter Erebus?"

This was unexpected. Just when the Companions had become convinced that the Dung Beetle had lost its mind, it had now posed a serious question. More importantly, it really did know something about their quest.

"I must confess, Omniscient One," said Krik. "It is to learn the answer to your question that we have journeyed here. For while the legend of Erebus is known to me, I know not where it is or how to enter the dark land from where no one has ever returned. But this I do know. Before the coming of the new moon, two moons from now, we must find and destroy Triodon, and return the Stones of Erebus to the Daughters of Earth."

"That's quite a plan, Ambassador," said the Dung Beetle, looking at Krik with new respect. "You know when but not where or how. Yet you five expect to find Triodon, the destroyer of all that once was, force him to relinquish the four, while you somehow protect the three from falling into his hand, and so save Earth?"

Krik held his staff high. "Such as we are," he said proudly. "That is, if it pleases Your Excellency."

"You certainly are the bravest and most polite cricket I have ever known," said the Dung Beetle.

"Mantis," corrected Krik.

"Rafi of the Three Stones," said the Dung Beetle, its shiny ball bearing eyes upon her, glinting with curiosity. "It is clear to me that you are the One, but tell me, how do you propose taking the stones from Triodon?"

"Rafi believes ..." Krik interjected hastily.

"Let the child speak," said the Dung Beetle. "Do not fear, mantis. You have done well. But the future of Earth lies heavily upon her and the time has come for her to speak."

"Great One …" Rafi began. Even as the words formed upon her lips, her mind went completely blank.

"Call me Uncle Oracle," said the Dung Beetle kindly.

"Uncle Oracle," said Rafi, wondering whether having a Dung Beetle for an uncle would be a welcome development in Drumheller. "Strange as it is to me, through a chance discovery by my father and the meeting of new and dear friends, I find myself in a world of miracles beyond my own. Yet I understand that the earth we cherish is threatened to change forever if we do not return the Stones of Erebus to the Daughters of Earth to whom they rightfully belong. How this is to be done I do not know, though others," she nodded at Krik, "believe that in this quest I have some small part to play. But I must tell you in all truthfulness that I may be a poor choice for your quest for I cannot bring it upon my heart to destroy Triodon, either for what he did or for what he might do. For, if the legends are true, he was good once as all things were meant to be, and so it is my hope that we may yet save him from his own destruction. No matter how we must win the stones, I wish him no harm."

"Yet you have not seen him," said the Dung Beetle. "As Rikk could tell you, countless creatures, entire species, have died at his hands."

"Krik."

"So it would seem," said Rafi. "But I wonder in a world of such miracles if he would have thrown the stones had not others laid seven times as many stones upon his heart. It seems to me that a stone that breaks a window is more easily thrown once the glass is already broken. And so evil may grow in a place now broken, even though it was once good and whole."

"Sometimes the cruelest stones are those we never see," murmured Krik.

The Dung Beetle smiled. "Truly, you are the One," it said. "But tell me, daughter of Drogs who, in their own destruction of Earth have surpassed even Triodon, should you find the power of Earth in your hands, what sort of a world would you wish for?"

"Wish?" asked Rafi. She fingered the three stones that now blazed openly upon her shirt. Once empty, her mind filled with the smiling faces of her mother, father and brother, Mopsus, Krik, Bree, Pud, Dlop, Ademar, Zigh and, should she have dared to say so, the Dung Beetle. A miracle of miracles indeed.

"I wish," she said, as each stone sang a clear and beautiful note, "for a world that is as large in a drop of water as it is hanging in the sky. A world that comforts hatred with love, embraces loneliness with friendship and colors prejudice with understanding. A world where all living things live for one another. Where no sacrifice is too great for the love of all. I wish …

I wish to hear a world of words,
In anger never spent,
Voices raised in love and praise,
In understanding meant.

I wish for those, all born to age,
Shall never grow so old,
That life has lost its mystery,
No miracles unfold.

I wish to see a songbird's nest,
In each and every tree,
Filled with songs of happiness,
Spirituality.

I wish to feel love in the air,
A smile, in hope sincere,
In truth, the only wishing well,
In prayer, an angel's tear.

I wish to live in dreams undreamed,
Where wonders never die,
A world of light and spirit loved,
More we instead of I.

I wish for all who look for Gold,
Shall find one letter less,
A world where trying always wins,
And leaves the loser blessed.

I wish no road be walked alone,
No grief without a grace,
Togetherness is all it takes,
One world, a better place.

I wish, I wish,
I wish to wish,
Wish I wish,
A wish."

The dung ball ran with the Dung Beetle's tears. "So let it be written," it said, "that in the light of the new moon, all shall sing your song."

"If that is going to happen," Krik put in anxiously, "we must find Erebus."

"A fact I had not forgotten, Kirk," said the Dung Beetle. "But the way is long and hard, and though you may not feel it, your companions are hungry and weary. Besides, any further travel today would be both foolish and dangerous for the Erinnyes are not as far away as you might think. Here is what I propose. Tonight, you shall rest by the water with little to disturb your sleep for no one, not even Triodon, would dare to attack you here. There you will find that a great feast awaits you, as well as food to keep you on your quest, for Ademar has been busy between the realms of Drumheller and Tahw Knar Gnud. Go now, wash and prepare yourselves, and I will join you in your feast. Then, when the moon and stars come out to play their game of ball and jacks in the sky, I will tell you how you may enter the dark paths of Erebus."

"No more chipmunk food," Pud declared happily. He dropped a stack of firewood next to Bree who was lighting a fire. "We's having lasagna!"

"Not just any lasagna," said Rafi, having just bathed and washed her clothes in the water hole. "In one hour you will be eating my mother's twice baked, three cheese lasagna – the best, the very best lasagna in the whole world." She hung her clothes on some hangers next to the fire, which looked remarkably like Tyrannosaurus teeth.

Bree nodded at a bone candelabra set in the center of a bone table. "Zigh thinks of everything," he said.

"As does Ademar," sang Rafi. She danced with Pud who, as it turned out, danced very well. She could not believe her eyes as she looked at all of the good food that Ademar had brought them from her parents and the good citizens of Drumheller. With the exception of the lasagna, everything had been carefully chosen for a long journey including two canteens donated by the local hardware store. There was dried beef (and more cheese) for Bree, Pud and Dlop, a box full of ladybugs for Krik, an assortment of dried fruits, nuts, raisins and protein bars for Rafi, and enough chocolate bars, chips, licorice and cookies to feed an army. Dlop was so excited he could not sleep.

"Is everything ready?" asked Krik. He was especially pleased with the gift of ladybugs from Mopsus. "Based on the smell of that lasagna I would guess that Zigh and the Oracle will be here soon."

"More than ready," said Bree surveying the fire, which burned brightly, now that the sun had dropped out of sight. He sniffed the delicious smells bubbling up from the lasagna. "But I'm guessing this won't be the only smell we'll smell tonight."

Krik took his seat on the table. "True," he said. "But be careful of what you say in their presence. Remember that you are speaking to the Guardian and Oracle of Tahw Knar Gnud. We mustn't offend them on any account."

"I'm more worried about you, Irkk," said Bree, laughing, and recalling the Oracle's fondness for getting Krik's name mixed up. "And from the smell of that east wind, I'd say they're already here."

"What's that sme… ow!" yelled Pud. Gingerly, he extracted Bree's elbow from his mouth.

From the east and into the firelight emerged the unmistakable shapes of Zigh and the Dung Beetle. Much to Zigh's disgust, which he wore openly upon his face, the Dung Beetle and a dung ball rode upon his back on a small bone dais. Slowly and regally, they proceeded toward the fire and the table, the Dung Beetle looking every inch a venerable king as Zigh growled as if he would have liked nothing better than to throw the Dung Beetle into the fire.

"Welcome," said the Dung Beetle to eliminate any doubt as to whose party it was. To everyone's distress, both the Dung Beetle and, more alarmingly, the dung ball chose to sit uncomfortably close to the lasagna.

"Smells delicious," said the Dung Beetle, flinging a lump of dung dead center into the lasagna.

Rafi did her best not to gag. "You'll have to give me the recipe," she said politely. She glanced at Krik, but the mantis appeared to have developed a sudden interest in his satchel.

"Dung," said the Dung Beetle. "First, you need to …"

Zigh did not seem to be in the mood for exchanging recipes. "Perhaps another time," he growled. "Assuming no one wants to barf on the feast, let's eat!"

Cutting carefully around the dung, Rafi doled out generous

portions of lasagna to all. The centerpiece she reserved for the Dung Beetle who, for all its power, did not seem to mind being served last.

"Delicious," said Bree.

"Awesome," said Pud.

Dlop held out his bone plate. "More," he said.

"Not bad." The Dung Beetle nodded encouragingly at Krik who had not yet begun to eat. With pinpoint accuracy, a lump of dung flew into Krik's lasagna.

"Don't even think about it!" snarled Zigh.

"Not hungry, Krik?" asked the Dung Beetle.

"No, Your 'Poop'entate," said Krik, although he looked hungry enough to eat the Dung Beetle. "It seems that too much excitement has spoiled my appetite."

The Dung Beetle topped Krik's dinner with yet another lump of dung. "Maybe it just needs more seasoning."

"Four … actually … five," said Krik, barely able to contain his anger, "I'm … seven … more … nine … hungry for information. Pray tell us, O Fecal Pharaoh, what must we do to find and defeat Triodon?"

"First," said the Dung Beetle, its mouth full of steaming lasagna, "you must cross the Anvil."

"The Anvil?" asked Rafi.

Krik contemplated the dung decorating his dinner. He looked at the Dung Beetle interrogatively. "Does that mean …"

The Dung Beetle nodded.

"Nod Dega Mra."

Everyone stopped eating. They did not need to understand the Oracle's words or its tone to know that something worse than dung was about to spoil their dinner.

Bree braved the silence filling their plates. "What is it, Krik?" he asked. "I've never heard of the Anvil before – is that a place? And what is Nod Dega Mra?"

Krik paced up and down the table. "A place," he said gravely, "and a time." He looked down at his feet only to realize that he was standing in his lasagna. "For the Anvil is the path that Triodon took east after he threw the stones and fled to Erebus. As for Nod Dega Mra," he winced uncomfortably, "legend tells us that, once the stones are found, Earth will move closer and closer to the sun until all seven stones are returned to the Daughters of Earth. As I am sure you can guess, this means …"

Bree whistled. "… Armageddon," he said. "The beginning of the end."

Rafi shuddered. The prospect of being burned alive by the sun on an anvil was not a promising career path for becoming a UN ambassador. Yet, having come this far, she could only put her trust in Krik.

"Nod Dega Mra," repeated Krik. "Once before such a thing has happened and only after Triodon stole the stones. Tomorrow marks the day, two days before the coming of the new moon." He looked searchingly at the Dung Beetle, his face an hourglass of hopelessness. "In that heat, every second will seem like hours. How shall we survive?"

"Not to worry," said the Dung Beetle. Apparently satisfied that the Companions, and especially Krik, had enough on their plates, it turned to Zigh. "I have prepared an ointment for you that should, at least, protect you from the sun. There is hope yet that you shall cross the Anvil."

"Ointment?" squeaked Rafi in a voice more like Dlop's. Of all the horrifying things she had just heard, the thought of rubbing herself with an ointment made by the Dung Beetle seemed by far the worst.

Zigh glared suspiciously at the Dung Beetle. "Don't worry, kiddo," he growled. "I prepared the ointment myself, mostly out of powdered bone. Dung Brains here never got near it unless it was while I was interviewing the T-Rex." He handed Rafi a bone box with an eyeball on the lid for decoration. "Rub this on your skin," he said, "and under your clothes. That includes you too, my furry friends," he added, glancing at Bree, Pud and Dlop. "And if you don't want your food to rot in less than a minute, it wouldn't hurt to give the knapsack a rub either." Growling at the Dung Beetle, he stalked off into the night.

"Well," said Pud encouragingly, "let's look at the bright side. A pleasant walk, sun tanning, hot food … should be a piece of cake!"

The Dung Beetle cleared its throat.

"There's more?"

The Dung Beetle's sigh was all the Companions needed to hear to know that 'more' did not include a game of beach volleyball.

"Once across the Anvil," said the Dung Beetle, "you must cross the Tears of Agony."

Krik looked shocked. "The Tears of Agony," he repeated slowly. It was not a question. The expression upon his face was enough to make the others creak uneasily in their bone chairs. "I thought the Tears were just legend. Yet, even if they exist, what have they got to do with our quest?"

The Dung Beetle pushed back its plate. "Everything." Then, to everyone's horror, it rolled and lit up a dung cigar.

"As you may recall, when Triodon fought Eidon for the mastery of Earth, he threw four of the seven stones, killing his enemies in the process and, indeed, most life upon Earth. But to his everlasting horror he discovered that the new world he had just created was even lonelier than the one he had destroyed. Just as he had hated the others for living, now he hated them for dying. And so, shaking his one fist defiantly at the unforgiving sun, he walked lonely footsteps, filled with his own tears."

"His footsteps filled with tears?" Rafi shook her head. "That is so sad."

The Dung Beetle blew exotic smoke rings that paraded around the fire like animals from some ancient zoo. "Sad indeed for those who died," it said. "I remember their countless faces as if it was yesterday."

"You remember?" said Rafi, too astonished to join Krik who, at the smell of the cigar, was making more room for his dinner. "But I thought that Triodon threw the stones ages ago."

The Dung Beetle stubbed out its cigar on Krik's plate. "So he did," it said. "But I was there even then. Yet, as Triodon's throw destroyed a world that you shall never know, Eidon's sacrifice saved the lives of many including my own." The Dung Beetle smiled. "Unlike the one who unexpectedly greeted you today, not all T-Rex's are evil."

"So," said Krik. Nervously, he watched the Dung Beetle raise its pitching arm as Rafi slid him a fresh plate of lasagna. "The Tears of Agony were Triodon's tears after he had tried to destroy Earth."

"Ironic, isn't it?" observed the Dung Beetle. "With his enemies destroyed, the sun and the moon almost completely to himself, he sought refuge in the oldest and darkest place on Earth."

"Erebus," joined in Krik.

"But you speak of the Tears of Agony as if they are a place," said Rafi.

"Many places," said the Dung Beetle. "Further east you shall find them once you have crossed the Anvil. There you must look for a canyon as black as Triodon's heart." As if to demonstrate, he squashed a heart shaped lump of dung right in the middle of Krik's lasagna. "But I must warn you. No longer bitter footsteps, the Tears are now deep, acidic wells of quicksand and fire, unseen by living eyes and yet filled with living death. They are perilous. To this day no one has ever survived them. But through the Tears you must go."

"Oh, goody," said Pud, "a barbecue!"

"Not that we don't like challenges," said Bree anxiously, "but couldn't we just go around the Tears?"

"That is not your destiny," said the Dung Beetle with alarming calm. "For it is only by crossing the Tears that you will find what you need to pass the three sentinels that guard Triodon's realm."

"Only three?" asked Pud.

"I remember," said Krik darkly. "Legend tells us of three levels leading to Erebus, each one guarded by an unknown terror of the ancient world."

"I get it," said Pud, clapping his paws together. "If we don't get melted, sucked in or blowed up, we can always count on three sentences to do us in!"

"What will we find in the Tears of Agony?" asked Rafi. Truth be told, she did not quite share Pud's humor. "First they filled me with sadness. Now they fill me with terror."

"That I cannot tell you," said the Dung Beetle, "for it is part of your quest. Yet your quest is not without hope. The Tears will tempt you with gifts as you make your way through them. Choose wisely, and you will live to choose again. Choose poorly, and you will be trapped forever in either the quicksand or the fire depending on your choice."

"I see," said Krik, who, nodding slowly along with the rest of the Companions, could see only too well. Clearly, their prospects were not good. In spite of his raging hunger, he had not touched his dinner.

"What can you tell us about the three levels of Erebus? Who are the sentinels?"

"Only that they lead to Triodon," said the Dung Beetle. "And that none are to be trusted. Know that they serve Triodon alone, although each secretly desires the stones so that they may escape his will."

"If the Tears of Agony are unseen," said Bree, "how will we know when we have found them?"

"You will know," said the Dung Beetle.

Without warning, Zigh reappeared, carrying what looked like an odd assortment of bones. He growled approvingly at Bree, Pud and Dlop. "I see that you have already found swords," he said. Then he presented each rat with a fine bone helmet and shield along with a pair of bone grieves. Thinking perhaps that Krik had everything he would ever need in his satchel he passed over the mantis, but to Rafi he presented a staff of bone and a magnificent bone helmet complete with a dinosaur-plated plume. "Use it as a staff or a javelin for all I care," he growled, "just be careful not to put it through your toe or one of your friends. It's that sharp."

Unable to find words, Rafi hugged Zigh even after the Dung Beetle had started pelting the wolverine with bits of dung. Almost hidden beneath their suits of bone, Bree, Pud and Dlop stuttered a round of thanks.

Krik bowed before the Guardian and Oracle of Tahw Knar Gnud.

"Let us hope," he said, "that through your gifts we shall meet again. Long may your home be full of dung."

That was enough for Zigh. Growling with disgust, he stalked over to the Dung Beetle.

The Dung Beetle mounted the dais on Zigh's back.

"Rely not on your strength," said the Dung Beetle, taking great care to wipe its feet on the dais, "but on your wits and courage. Even a warrior with the strength of Zigh could not hope to defeat Triodon in mortal combat armed with only three of the stones. Be wary, trust in one another and temper what may seem to be good council with the wisdom in your hearts. Help and danger may appear in the unlikeliest of places."

"We will," said the Companions not knowing which was worse, the Dung Beetle's help or the end of Earth.

The Dung Beetle waved goodbye. "You may keep the dung for breakfast," it said imperiously as Zigh took a last, longing look at the fire. "I'll send some to your parents, Rafi, with Ademar. It would be a shame coming so close to making the best lasagna without adding the secret ingredient."

"It was the best lasagna, Rafi," growled Zigh.

"Don't," said Rafi before she could stop herself. The thought of dung balls raining down over Drumheller was too much for her already shattered nerves. "I mean, Uncle Oracle, should we survive Nod Dega Mra, perhaps it would be better if we celebrate together."

"You are right, Rafi of the Three Stones," said the Dung Beetle gleefully. "That will be one party I won't miss. Tomorrow, I shall start baking in anticipation of your return. Will you help me, Zigh?"

"You know I won't, dung head," growled Zigh. "And quit putting them in my parlor!"

"I spy with my little eye," said Rafi, her face wet and shiny in the glow of the fire, "two wonderful new friends." She kissed her hand, touching each of them under the chin. She knew that Zigh would understand.

Bree bowed his helmeted head. "I shall never forget this day," he said.

"Mind over matter," said Pud, winking at Zigh.

"Did someone say something about baking?" asked Dlop. He started to bow but fell asleep half way down so that his head got caught between his knees.

"Remember your promise, Rafi," said Zigh.

"I will," she said. The lump in her throat was the size of a dung ball. "I only wish that we could play tomorrow instead of beginning a journey that may yet play to another end."

"And remember," added the Dung Beetle who could not resist having the final word, "some journeys cannot be measured in hours or days just as no creature can be measured by size or color alone. When all seems lost, look to find yourselves in one another."

In a procession of sniffs and growls, Zigh and the Dung Beetle disappeared into the night. From somewhere in the darkness, the Companions could hear them still arguing as to whether or not the Dung Beetle should start sleeping in Zigh's house. They listened, expecting at any moment to hear the crunch of beetle, but the sound never came.

Rafi gazed up at the stars. "What a day!" she said. "A T-Rex, Zigh, the Dung Beetle – I would never have thought such miracles were possible."

"The only miracle I need right now," said Krik, who looked like he was about to pass out from hunger, "is a slice of your mother's lasagna. Never have I been so appalled at the thought of eating a meal and yet considered eating it anyway."

Just to be sure that his dinner had not been soiled by the Dung Beetle, Krik helped himself to a fresh slice of lasagna.

"The Oracle was testing you," said Bree, laughing. "I think it's safe to say you passed the test, O Greatest of Ambassadors."

Krik shoveled down mouthfuls of lasagna before answering.

"I suppose that's true," he said, laughing in his turn. He was so full of lasagna he looked like a fat, green noodle. The mantis helped himself to another slice. "Sure beats ladybugs."

Rafi lay down next to the fire. "I wish this day would never end," she said dreamily. She looked at Bree and Pud who stood waiting for a warm place to sleep. Somehow Dlop had already beaten them to it and lay curled up on her stomach. Moments later, a chorus of squeaky sniffs and snores filled the air.

With the moon and stars for company, Rafi and Krik talked far into the night. Miraculously, they had survived the Guardian and the Oracle of Tahw Knar Gnud, but it seemed certain that greater challenges lay ahead. Would they survive the Anvil? How and where would they find the Tears of Agony? What secrets lay buried beneath the Tears? And who or what were the three sentinels of Erebus? And if by some impossible chance they made their way into Erebus, would they find Triodon in time to save the stones and fulfill their quest?

Krik was still awake when Rafi nodded off to sleep, her last words lingering softly upon her lips. He gazed at her face for the longest time. Two nights ago they had met under the same stars for the first time in her bedroom. Somehow, she seemed brighter than them all. He looked up at the moon blazing brightly in the night sky as if it already knew this might be for the last time. Suddenly, a weariness he had never known effused throughout his body. Exhausted, he climbed Rafi's ear and lay down upon a bed of fragrant hair. Closing his eyes, he whispered up to the starry sky.

"It was the best lasagna."

CHAPTER EIGHT

BADGERS IN BEDLAM

Drumheller was in an uproar. News that Rafi had fled town spread throughout the valley like wildfire. The army, the R.C.M.P., the F.B.I., the K.G.B. and Scotland Yard had already been summoned to Town Hall. Just to be sure that no one was forgotten Orly had called the Pope and Buckingham Palace. Mopsus had been arrested four times that day for his part in 'the conspiracy,' as The Mayor called it, but since there was nothing to charge him with other than collecting garbage, the charges were dropped.

The town furor did not stop there. Orly and her cats had taken over a wing at the hospital and The Mayor had insisted that every citizen of Drumheller be vaccinated against Plague, Rabies, Tetanus, Cholera, Yellow Fever and just about every disease known to mankind. Rat specialists were flown in from every corner of the globe as news agencies and movie makers descended upon the town, both by the hour and by the dozen, in hopes of getting an exclusive interview with a talking rat. The biting clothes peg was front-page news in the daily tabloids.

At the same time, there was a brief but unsuccessful attempt to hide certain facts from the public and the press. For Ademar had been true to his word and had sent special envoys to both Rafi's parents and The Mayor. In fact, none other than Ademar himself visited Mr. and Mrs. Malawi, explaining to them what was happening to the world and their daughter who, he assured them, was in good paws. Mrs. Malawi was hysterical at first and had to lie down, but when Ademar told her that any interference would only make things worse, and that Rafi had been chosen by all living things to save Earth, her face beamed with pride. As for Mr. Malawi, he was visibly shaken, and spoke little throughout the days that followed if, indeed, he spoke at all.

The Mayor's situation was grave by comparison. In his hospital bed, he was first visited by a badger and then a grebe and later at Town Hall by a barbershop quartet of singing crickets. Everywhere he went creatures of every size and color followed him, ignoring his screams as he wrote them up in his little black book. The jail was full of the oddest assortment of rats, ducks, snakes, dragonflies and other creatures seen anywhere on Earth, but, ignoring all by-laws, they kept wandering or flying through the bars and out of jail only to be arrested again. When the night cleaners discovered that only their mess remained behind, they went on strike. Dubbing The Mayor 'The Pied Mayor of Drumheller,' the press had a field day.

"Find her!" he roared at an emergency Town Hall meeting. The room was so packed with government agents, dignitaries and reporters from all over the world that it was hard to breathe as all of the available air had already been sucked up by The Mayor who ranted and raved against Rafi for over half an hour. A throne had been flown in and placed at the front of the hall in the event that anyone from the Royal Family made an appearance. As nobody did, The Mayor wasted no time using it himself.

"Can you imagine?" he spat at the assembly from his throne until they all looked like they had fallen in the river, "explaining to the President of the United States that the most powerful ruler in the world is a ... dung beetle? And," The Mayor grappled with a vein snaking across his forehead, "he's invited it to the White House!"

"Mr. Mayor," said the reporter from VNN, "what can you tell us about this dung beetle?"

"And where can we find the dung beetle?" asked the reporter from the Herald.

"And is the dung beetle married?" asked the reporter from the

National Post.

"And if so," said a reporter from the Star, "do they live in a dunghill?"

"And," said the reporter from the tabloids, "do they wear dungarees?"

"And who is Rafi?" asked a reporter from the Times.

"More importantly," said a ferret who had wandered into the proceedings along with a hoary marmot, "when's lunch?"

"No offense," said the marmot looking up at The Mayor, "but is that a dead muskrat holding up your snotty nose?"

"As far as I know," The Mayor screamed at the reporters as he recorded the ferret and especially the marmot in his little black book, "the dung beetle, who appears to live at no fixed address, doesn't even pay taxes!" He glared at the reporter from the Times. "Miss Malawi – Rafi – and her raffish behavior is why there is a ferret and a hairy marmot in Town Hall. She is why one of our oldest and most respected citizens no longer has a nose and why I am missing a finger." He held out his mutilated hand to the 'oohs' and 'aahs' of the crowd. Amidst a flurry of camera flashes, clicks and whirrs, he continued. "And I dare say," he bellowed as the ceiling dusted the assembly, "that if the world is indeed coming to an end – she is bound to have something to do with it!"

"That's hoary marmot to you, ferret face," said the marmot.

"Hey," the ferret said to the marmot, "there's no need for insults!"

"Arrest those fermots!" The Mayor screamed at sixty-two police officers scattered throughout the hall. But to his dismay, the reporter from the Times was already interviewing the ferret, and the marmot had signed an exclusive interview with the tabloids. The vein on his forehead grew so large he looked like he had grown another head. At a loss for words, he simply gnashed his teeth, foaming at the mouth until some paramedics arrived, who carried both him and his throne out of Town Hall and into a waiting ambulance. He was still spitting up a rainstorm when they closed the doors.

Amidst the squawks and squeals of sirens, he was raced to the hospital closely followed by two dozen police cars, three fire trucks and a tank.

CHAPTER NINE

THE ANVIL

T he next morning, Rafi awoke to discover a mailbox overlooking the water hole. Constructed entirely of bone, upon
which someone had painstakingly spelled Malawi in
knucklebones, it even featured 'in' and 'out' jaws for receiving and
posting mail. Inside the mailbox was – not one – but three letters.
She recognized the handwriting on two of the letters immediately.
Eagerly, she ripped open the first letter.

Rafi Dearest;

*We can only pray that Ademar and this letter find you safe.
Imagine our little girl off to save Earth! Naturally, we are both
worried sick, but Ademar and Erech (an eagle that is guarding the
house) have convinced us that you are safer with your new friends
than here with us.*

*As for your father, he's had a trying day. A Velociraptor applied
for a job today at the museum as an assistant curator. Naturally,
she got the job (she was highly qualified) but misunderstood the
cafeteria rules and ate three tourists. The Mayor had a fit.*

*Please write back soon! We need to know that you are safe. I
never thought when I told you that you could conquer the world
that you would take me so literally. But that's our daughter! Always
living her dreams!*

We could not be more proud.

Your loving Mother and Father
P.S. Be careful, mind your manners, and don't forget to brush your teeth.

Rafi laughed. Inside the envelope was a pen, some writing paper, and a tube of toothpaste.

The second letter was from her brother Motu.

Dear Rafi;

What are you playing at? Mother and father are beside themselves with worry and, more importantly, it's your turn to do the dishes tonight. As for The Mayor, he is doing everything he can to make our lives difficult. Yesterday, I was arrested for being your brother. Personally, I don't blame him. In my legal opinion, a world without laws (and lawyers) is hardly worth saving.

As to this alleged Dung Beetle being the most powerful ruler on earth, I find such nonsense highly questionable. He doesn't even have a law degree (I checked), and, as everyone knows, no one could possibly assume any position of power without one. I can only hope that your other friends are more credible (which is highly unlikely since only one of them can read).

In any event, as I am applying to law school next year, I trust that you will do your best to save Earth. Hoping you are well, I remain (legally)

Your Brother,
Motu
P.S. If, by any chance, the Dung Beetle went to Harvard, please have him put in a good word for me.

The third letter bore the official seal of The Mayor's office.

Rafiatu Malawi;

Upon receipt of this letter, you are hereby charged with (and have already been found guilty of) the following offences, contrary to all laws of Drumheller:

-**T**he attempted murder of Miss Orly Thumbottom

-**T**he attempted assassination of The Mayor

-**B**reeding rats within city limits

-**R**esisting arrest

-**F**leeing town without a license

-**B**eing a general public nuisance and threat to society

Report immediately to the nearest authorities, alone and unarmed, so that Earth may be saved — not from the fantastical fantasies of creatures unknown — but from **Y**ou.

Sincerely,

The **M**ayor

Bree used the last letter to light a fire.

After writing and posting a quick letter back to her family, Rafi sat down to an early morning breakfast with Krik, Bree, Pud and Dlop. Over a table laden with dried fruit, potato chips, raisins and granola bars, the conversation soon turned to the grim prospect of crossing the Anvil. Was it far? How many miles would they have to endure before they reached the Tears of Agony? And where were the Erinnyes? With nothing more to comfort them but the Dung Beetle's words and Zigh's ointment, they waited for the dawn. Soon it came, first appearing as a thin ribbon of light that stretched across the east, and then as a ring of fire creeping slowly up the azure-blue sky. Already warm, the morning was turning into a sauna.

"If this heat is any prelude," said Bree, finishing his breakfast, "I'd hate to think of what's coming."

"You won't have long to wait," said Krik, who, after breakfast, had assumed the shape of a dried apricot. With apologies to Mopsus, he had decided to let the ladybugs go, feeling that, with only two days remaining before Earth might come to an end, they should spend more time with their families. He gazed at the dawn, and then looked up at Rafi, Bree and Pud who had gathered nervously around the ointment box, a look of pure disgust upon their faces.

"Is there a problem with Zigh's ointment?" he asked.

"The Dung Beetle's you mean," said Rafi. She pinched her nose as she gathered up a handful of ointment. "This stuff stinks!"

"Well," said Krik sympathetically. "It can't be worse than a garbage truck. Considering the alternative, I don't think we have much choice. As for myself ..."

"I'm glad you feel that way," said Rafi. Before Krik could hop for cover, she had covered the mantis with a generous supply of ointment. She smiled sweetly. "After all, we are Companions, are we not? All for one, and one for all?"

"I am an ambassador ..." protested Krik.

"It's not that bad," said Pud. White with ointment, he looked like a whiskered ghost.

"No, you don't, Dlop," said Bree. Before Dlop could escape into the knapsack, Bree and Pud had grabbed him by the tail, giving him a rather violent ointment massage. "No Companion of Earth ever walked to Erebus in a knapsack. It's paws for you now, Dlop."

"That's what I had in mind," said Dlop miserably. "Pause."

"Speaking of paws," said Krik, who looked like one of Zigh's bones, "be sure to cover the bottoms of your paws and feet. Don't forget Achilles' heel."

"Do chilies have heels?" asked Pud.

At that moment, the sun vaulted over the horizon, bathing the badlands with bright, colorless light. Even beneath Zigh's ointment, the Companions felt the heat.

Bree shaded his eyes with a paw. "Wow," he said. "It's going to be a scorcher."

"Helmets," barked Krik. Staff in claw, he marched up Rafi's ghostly figure, settling upon her shoulder like an alabaster figurine. "Unless I'm mistaken, Zigh's gifts will protect us as much from the sun as they will from any weapons possessed by the enemy."

Rafi donned her helmet, which was conveniently equipped with a sun visor made from teeth. It fitted her perfectly.

"What about you, Krik?"

Krik removed his satchel. "Not to worry," he said. Within seconds, the mantis had transformed into a musketeer right out of the French revolution. Resplendent in matching boots and gloves, a white cape and a French cocked hat, the sun seemed dull in comparison.

"You see," he said innocently, "A mantis must always appear to be a gentle-mantis, whatever the occasion."

Laughing, Rafi put on her knapsack. Laden with food and water, it was heavier than ever (even without Dlop), but somehow the weight comforted her. At any rate, they would not starve as they crossed the Anvil.

Krik gazed down a tiny checklist.

"Water?"

"Three bottles full," said Rafi dutifully. "I've also filled the canteens."

"We'll take the bottles, Rafi," said Bree, much to Dlop's dismay. "You can't carry everything."

"I can carry enough for two," said Pud defiantly.

Rafi handed the water bottles down to Bree. "Then I'll fill the pot with water. It will be heavy, but it should give us a head start before we touch any of our other supplies."

Krik folded up his list. "Good thinking, Rafi," he said. "We'll need every drop we can carry."

They faced east. Still miles away, wrought in mantles of silver and gray, three grave mountains brooded under the glittering glare of the morning sun.

"Behold the Three Sisters," said Krik solemnly.

"Magnificent," said Rafi. She gazed up the mountains, which, together, rose like an iron crown into the steel blue sky. Just as Mopsus had said, the middle mountain was flat as if a giant had sat on it. In its center, much to everyone's surprise loomed a giant eye.

Bree contemplated the eye. "Will wonders never cease," he muttered.

Krik pointed from left to right. "Urd, Verdandi, and Skuld," he said. "It is in Verdandi, the middle sister that I expect to find Triodon. For in her, our fate awaits."

Bree raised his sword.

"To Erebus," he said.

"Erebus." The Companions' voices echoed from a forest of staffs and swords.

Erebus. In spite of the growing heat, the word sent a shiver down their spines. Sizzling like an egg yolk in a heated blue pan, the sun watched them say good-bye to the water hole and Zigh's house. Without another word, they set out upon the Anvil.

On and on they walked. Watching their every step, the sun rushed up the sky, larger and hotter than ever. It was not long before the Anvil took its toll. Caught upon its face of steel, pounded from above by the hammer-hot rays of the sun, they trudged in silence. The sky steeped into a hot blue tea. Within an hour, the pot and one of the water bottles were empty.

Much to everyone's surprise, Dlop kept up although he asked about meals every half hour or so and needed to be constantly reminded that drinking water did not necessarily decrease its weight. Just to be sure that he did not fall asleep and get left behind, Bree and Pud took turns tying his tail to their own.

Perhaps another hour passed – they had lost all count of time – but using the eye as a guide they crossed the Anvil as straight as the crooked canyons and peculiar rock formations would allow. Sharp stones cut their feet and paws, and, more than once, they staggered and fell into unexpected holes that seemed to have minds of their own.

Before long, all of the water bottles were empty. Only the two canteens of water remained.

They stopped for a brief rest every mile or so, drinking as little water as they dared knowing that, in this heat, running out of water meant certain death. Only Krik refused to drink any, claiming that mantises were distant relatives of camels. As for food, they only ate enough to fill their stomachs without feeling nauseous, a strategy suggested by Krik to which even Dlop assented.

If there was one thing that did not worry them, it was getting lost. The Three Sisters were rarely out of sight, and the eye, which had inexplicably moved to the sister on the left, pulled them almost hypnotically across the Anvil. Walking ahead of the others, Bree jokingly observed that, unlike the explorers of old, the real danger was not so much in not finding their destination as it was in finding it. At least, he ventured, when one generally gets lost there is a good chance of being found, unless, of course, you happen to be sucked into the center of Earth by quicksand or consumed by fire. Nobody laughed.

Without warning, Bree suddenly stopped dead in his paw prints. If it was not for Rafi's lightning reflexes, he might have been crushed into a hairy pancake right then and there, but as it was, she did a somersault right over him, landing gracefully on her feet. Amazingly, Krik had managed to stay on her shoulder. Unfortunately, Pud was not so lucky (or graceful), and did a complete header over Bree.

"Problem?" asked Krik testily. In all of the commotion, he had fallen from the chaise lounge he had made with his legs, dropping a letter he was writing to Mrok.

Bree pointed to the sister on the right, which now wore the eye. "I swear that eye just winked at me," he said.

"That makes two of us," said Rafi, laughing. She dusted off Pud who sat glaring and chattering at Bree.

"Three," said Dlop. He gave a yawn that covered so much of his face it was hard to imagine he could notice anything much less a winking eye. He leaned heavily on Pud.

"That settles it," said Bree. "A winking mountain." No sooner had Pud turned his back to look upon the eye, Bree whacked his behind with the broadside of his sword. "Whoever heard of such a thing?" He turned to Krik who, having found his letter was busily reconstructing his chair. "What do you make of it, Krik?"

"The eye is ever watchful," said Krik, scrutinizing the others from over his letter. "Fear not. I, for one, know this eye. Be glad that it looks upon you. I can think of more unfriendly eyes in the world watching us from both above and below."

Pud rubbed his behind. "There's a comforting thought," he said.

"I think it is a beautiful eye," said Rafi. She winked back at the middle sister that had somehow reacquired the eye. "It reminds me of," she looked wistfully to the west, which had turned the color of sour milk, "my mother and father." It was not the last time she thought about her family, and how strange it was to be walking across the badlands with three rats, a mantis, and a winking mountain. For all the well-meaning townsfolk of Drumheller had told her that miracles were just pleasant fantasies of the mind, she seemed to have walked right into one. Yet, there were no answers to this miracle – just more questions that made it all the more miraculous.

As if the mountain had heard her thoughts, the eye winked again.

"Let us rest here awhile," said Bree, looking around. "This place seems as good as any, and I'm not embarrassed to say that Dlop isn't the only one who is tired. Even with Zigh's ointment, this heat is unbearable."

Before Krik could object, they had claimed a patch of shade. While Bree, Pud and Dlop watched eagerly, Rafi measured out three small but equal shares of water. The three rats drank as if they had not touched a drop of water for days. She offered a capful of water to Krik. The mantis refused.

"Save it for the others," he said, his face screwed into his telescope. "You have all walked far, and you'll need to gather your strength before we start again, and that will be soon enough." He collapsed his telescope, glanced up at the sun, and then at Rafi. "By my reckoning, we are only half way across the Anvil. Much as I hate to say it, the worst is yet to come. We will need every drop if we are to have any hope in reaching the Three Sisters by nightfall."

"But surely even ambassadors must eat and drink," said Rafi. She pressed the cap toward him a second time along with a slice of apple, but still he refused.

"Don't worry, Rafi," said Krik. "I caught a fly or two a while back so I am not completely without sustenance." He smiled dryly. "As for water, we mantises are known to go for weeks without it."

"If only we were all descendants of camels," said Rafi, taking a drink. Somehow, she knew that Krik was not being entirely truthful about his heritage.

"Tell me, Krik," she added, certain that ambassadors are made and not born, "have you always been an ambassador?"

"I was wondering when you would get to that," said Krik sheepishly. From the tone in his voice, this was clearly a subject he did not care to discuss. "Why do you ask?"

"Well," said Rafi, "it's not everyday one meets an ambassador to the League of Mantis."

"No, I don't suppose it is," said Krik, who had taken a sudden interest in his hat. He clawed a tiny feather, staring awkwardly into the bowl. "I suppose I do owe you an explanation …"

Bree smiled at Rafi. "Nooo," he said. "A bedroom break-in, a Drog-napping, an escape from town that even Houdini would have been proud of, a forced march across the badlands, an attempt to cross the Anvil where none survive, and you owe her an explanation?"

"An expaltation?" said Pud, trying to wake Dlop. "Say it ain't so."

"If you are going to tell a story," said Dlop, his eyes still closed, "perhaps we should stop and eat."

"This is stop and eat, nitwit," said Pud.

"Ahem," said Krik. Having finished clawing and twisting his beautiful hat into a dishrag he put it back on his head where it flapped like a discombobulated butterfly. He glared at Bree, Pud and Dlop.

"If the rat trap have finished," he said hotly, "perhaps I can begin. But it is a long story and the sun is already high. You will forgive me, Rafi, if I leave certain parts out, for now is not the time for stories, not when the worst half of the Anvil and the Tears of Agony still lie before us. Perhaps, when our quest is done and Time is in safer hands, you shall hear the story in full. Even so, I should like to answer your question."

"If you'd rather not discuss it," said Rafi, "I understand."

"Not at all," said Krik. He hopped onto her knee, folding his legs into a barstool. "It is precisely because you do not understand – could not begin to understand – that I must tell you." After a deep sigh, his penetrating gaze settled on Rafi's face.

"I know, Rafi," he said prophetically, "that the last two days have not been 'every-days' for you. But there comes a time when one day is greater than all the days that shape what was and is to come. Such are the days of our lives. Yet in living, we must think of others, for it is only through others that we live. I live through you; you live through me. And so we shall live forever, however long or short our lives may be."

Even without water, Krik's eyes filled with tears.

"For as long as I shall live," he said, "I shall never forget the moment you decided to join our quest. It was a moment when all life's forces, and all living things, came together as one. And it was only through you, Rafi, my dear, that such a thing was possible. Who would have expected such purity of love and spirit in a Drog? In joining a quest that at the time was doomed to failure, you gave us our one chance to succeed. Yet, unlike our whiskered friends here, on this subject I fear to say too much, for even the strongest and most noble spirit may break upon the longest road."

Rafi watched the ever-fickle mountains change the eye once again. "The road is long," she said. "And dark. Yet, honored am I above all Drogs to share this road with you, Krik. But I would be lying to say that I do not fear for my family and friends." She lowered her eyes. "And for myself."

Krik nodded with understanding. "Fear is not what fear is made of," he said. "It is what we do that gives fear a name."

"I think I understand, mantis," said Rafi. "At least I hope to understand when the time comes. You have great faith in me, which I trust you have not misplaced. It is a shame you don't have children, Krik – you would have made a great father. Though we have only just met, you are more precious to me than all the stones on Earth and those that shine up in the sky. Great as the stones may be, and though they may light our way into Erebus, you light the way to my heart, Krik. Triodon may not know it yet, but such love cannot be lost, such a road cannot be broken."

"I know it, gentle Drog," said Krik, weeping openly beneath his hat. "Such love is why I am an ambassador." He paused to catch his breath, which spilled from his tiny chest like blasts of wind. "But I … I was not always an ambassador. Once I was the prophet of my people. Once I was a Praying Mantis."

He paused, apparently lost in thought.

"In our world, my word was law. And, like generations of my kind before me, I dispensed wisdom and justice throughout the land. We were happy. As my fame spread throughout the world, others sought my council and resourcefulness. With fame came responsibility. With responsibility came decisions. And then, not so long ago, about the time when you came to this place, I was asked by a powerful lord to serve as both guide and minister to three of his servants to whom he said he had given the smallest of tasks."

Rafi smiled at Bree, Pud and Dlop.

"Protecting me?"

Krik's kind face turned to granite. "Quite the opposite," he said. "For the three were none other than the Erinnyes, the dark servants of Triodon who were commanded to kill you the moment you set foot in this land. For Triodon knew of a prophecy foretelling that one day a young girl would challenge him for the mastery of Earth. For this service, he promised both me and the League of Mantis eternal life in the new world he would create. Yet I refused, bringing his wrath down upon my people. 'Fool,' they cried, 'what is the life of a useless Drog when measured against immortality?' Still I refused, and so I was cast out from among my people. 'Go,' they said as they threw sharp stones at my head, 'if you love Drogs so much over your own kind, you can be their ambassador to the League of Mantis. Only you will never be welcome here in this world or the next.' And so, here I am, a lonely ambassador, with neither past nor future, shunned by my own kind."

"And that," said Rafi quietly, "is why you are a 'preying' mantis." It was now so hot her tears evaporated before they hit the ground. "Oh Krik, this story is too horrible to imagine."

"Too horrible to imagine," Krik agreed, "yet the same story repeats itself in your world every day. So now, I must defend myself and that which we cherish against the harsh realities of our time. Whereas Triodon would have you destroyed, now I must destroy Triodon. And that a 'preying' mantis could never do. In the beginning, it almost destroyed me. Like you, I could wish no harm or destruction upon another. But, as you will discover yourself, Rafi, on your way to becoming a young woman – and an ambassador – life is about choices. The difficulty is always in making the right one. What is easiest is seldom wisest. So, I gathered to myself three worthy companions who could stand up to the Erinnyes as I myself plan to stand up against Triodon. Yet, as you can see, our strength is not in size or nobility, but in the friendship and love that bind us together. The most difficult choice of all. Three knights in shining armor could not be more worthy."

Rafi looked shocked. Never in her life could she have imagined such a horrible fate – to be stoned and shunned by one's own people. As if in prayer, she held out her hands to Krik.

"Krik," she cried, her heart almost breaking. "Oh, most kind and compassionate of ambassadors. To you I owe my very life. Only what have you lost in return? Surely not a future for the future has yet to be written. Yet my life is not worth such cruelty and sadness."

Krik gazed deeply into her eyes. "You are wrong, Rafi," he said. "The sparkle in your eyes alone is worth more to me than many lifetimes of happiness. In your heart beats the spirit of Earth. That which gave life, gives life, and never takes it away. For in you is life itself, not life for merely living, but life by which only life can live."

"I love you, Krik," said Rafi. Gently, she picked him up, holding him against her cheek. "All of you," she added tearfully, looking round at Bree, Pud and Dlop who sat watching in silence. "Who in this world or the next could have such wonderful friends, Companions to the very end?" Her eyes flashed beneath the visor on her helmet. "But know this – all of you. While there is life in me, there shall always be life in you. We share a present that is worth more than any future. Together we shall seek this Triodon who has done you so much wrong. Yet I fear that he shall pay for what he has done. If not in life, it shall be in the shadows of his own doing."

"In the shadows of his own doing," Krik repeated sadly. "Shadows are as much of who we are as that which we project to the world. For it is only in the dark, and when we are alone, that we truly know who we are. Shadows are one of Earth's greatest gifts. Thrown as they are by the light of the sun and the false brightness of our own self worth, they serve as a lifelong reminder as to whom we really are. Only in Erebus are we without shadow, where all is flat and gray."

"I shall never look at shadows the same way again," said Rafi, curiously watching the shadows gathered around her. "And yet," she confided, "I know what you mean. In the world of Drogs, as you say, sometimes I feel like I'm a shadow looking in, as if I don't really belong. If The Mayor had his way, I would be locked up in a zoo where people could gawk at me all day and be glad that those who are born or dare to be different are safely behind bars. It hurts me to no end to know how much embarrassment and pain I have caused my family."

"Those who see only fleeting curiosities behind bars are the ones that don't belong," said Krik. "Until Drogs learn to see beyond that which is merely seen, they will never truly belong to Earth. While they know it not, they are but a passing fancy in a history and future that reaches far beyond their science and technology. Yet, while there are Drogs like you, Rafi, there is still hope. Never let fear or prejudice change who you are. Instead, change those who fear and judge others by helping them become who they were always meant to be. Then you will no longer need your shadow."

It was almost noon. After another drink of water, they crawled out of the shade and stepped into the glaring sun. Around them, the Anvil bleached with hostility.

Since morning, they had traveled some nine or ten miles, although, as Bree had said, it felt more like a hundred. High above, the sun fixed its fierce eye upon them even as the mountains' eye winked to the east. Slowly, painfully, they crept across the Anvil, mile after painful mile, hammered beneath the sun's relentless blows and their own doggedness to fulfill their quest. Walking above their own shadows, shaped and reshaped upon the Anvil like living pieces of iron, the Companions forged on toward the east.

"Ohhh," groaned Rafi, utterly exhausted. Her legs felt like red-hot pokers thrust into a fire. "If only I had two more legs instead of arms."

"Wish it was that easy," gasped Bree, who was scouting ahead with Pud. He held his shield over his head in an attempt to deflect the sun's hammer. "Two, four, six, eight – this Anvil would run the legs off a centipede."

"Are we there yet?" asked Dlop.

"Thank goodness for Zigh's ointment," said Krik, who was studying every inch of ground with his telescope. Owing to the fact that he had not walked across the Anvil he was in less distress than the others were, but his mind, always active, burned with new thoughts. He lowered his telescope.

"Dung," he muttered to himself as if the sun had already taken its toll. "Dung." His arms flailed about as if he was a European mantis. "Don't you see? It's all so simple. A lump of dung in steaming hot lasagna."

"Krik's gone sun happy," said Bree. "We'd better stop and get some rest."

"And water," croaked Dlop.

"He's not the only one," said Rafi. For the last mile she had become quite light-headed, and was afraid to tell the others that a salmon, broiling on a barbecue, had mysteriously joined their quest. Knowing what she would find, she reached for the last canteen. It was almost empty. Followed by Bree, Pud and Dlop, she staggered to a patch of shade barely large enough to cover a mouse.

She flung herself upon the ground. "One drink now," she observed dryly, "and we're out of water."

While the others drank and shared a little food, Krik was madly reemployed with his telescope. Only after he had pointed it in every direction, and had played several tunes upon his abacus, did he speak again.

"Not sun happy," he said finally, "dung happy. Why didn't I see it before?"

"See what before?"

Krik helped himself to an unsalted raisin. "The Dung Beetle was sending me a message," he said excitedly. "It's all coming back to me now. When Triodon crossed the Anvil, he descended into a black canyon where he hoped to find refuge from the sun. Finding none, it was there he cried the Tears of Agony, and so resolved to enter Erebus."

"And that is going to help us, how?" asked Bree.

Krik pointed east with his telescope. "Because," he said, "there is a black canyon just a mile or two ahead."

Rafi shuddered, hot as it was. "A mile or two?" she said. "Even with the Erinnyes at my heels I couldn't walk another step." She waved the canteen in front of Krik. Only a capful of water remained.

"You haven't seen the Erinnyes," said Bree.

"If we stop here," said Krik desperately, "we'll die." Standing on Rafi's shoulder, he reached down and tried to pull her to her feet, an impossible task even for the mantis. "And when we die, everyone dies. Do you understand?"

"Everyone?" said Rafi. Through bleary eyes, she looked at Bree, Pud and Dlop, but found herself looking at her mother, father and Motu. As if helped by unseen hands, she staggered to her feet.

And so, with the fate of Earth upon their backs, the Companions walked, crawled and dragged themselves east. They did not dare to eat any more food for they knew it would only increase their thirst, and except for the remaining capful of water, there was no hope of finding any in that dreadful void. Silently, steadily, the Anvil did its work. Finally, exhausted beyond measure, cooked from within, and hammered into powdered pulp, they collapsed only a few feet away from the canyon. Defeated, they curled up to die.

"Too bad we couldn't find the Tears of Agony," whispered Rafi. Too weak for anything else she shook paws with Bree, Pud and Dlop. "If we had, we could have drunk them."

"Don't even think such a thing," said Krik who, miraculously, still had his wits about him. Alarmed, he hopped back and forth from each Companion, pinching their cheeks as he tried to open their eyes. "We'll find water soon enough. I promise. But we won't find it here."

Rafi did not hear him. Not content with sucking every drop of water from her body, the sun had begun to boil her brain. She was almost pleased to see that the salmon had returned and lay grilling on its barbecue surrounded by seven hazelnuts.

"Nuts?" asked the salmon.

"Almost," she said.

"It's cooler in here," said the salmon. Striped from the grill, it looked more like a zebra than a fish. "Pull up a grill and make yourself at home."

Rafi took her place alongside the salmon. "Don't mind if I do," she said.

The salmon flipped on its other side. "Help much?"

"Not much," said Rafi, unsure as to whether she was ready for flipping. "However do you manage it?"

"Ahhh," said the salmon. "Now that's a burning question." The salmon disappeared.

"Rafi?" A voice like Krik's sounded frightened and far away.

"Rafi!"

"Rafi, are you all right?"

The familiar voice jerked Rafi back to her senses. Suddenly, she felt as if something had gripped her by the stomach and flung her to the ends of Earth. The sound of rushing water greeted her ears, and she wondered if she had landed in the river. She tried to sing but no words came. Then, just as she was sure the end had come, a giant cucumber swam up to her and looked deep into her eyes. Slowly, the cucumber changed into a green head wearing the ugliest water lily she had ever seen. Beneath his outrageous hat, Krik's face popped into focus.

"Where did the salmon go?" she asked hoarsely. She was not sure which was worse – the disappearance of the salmon or Krik's face pressed against one of her eyeballs as if he was an optometrist (which, as a matter of fact, he was).

"Water," cried Dlop in his sleep. "Mummy, get me some water."

Hearing Dlop's cries, Bree and Pud awoke from their stupor. They looked at each other through hollow eyes. For the first time in their lives, their strength had left them, and they could no longer be strong for their brother. "Water, water," they cried.

"Water," whispered Rafi.

Desperate, Krik scrambled to the edge of the canyon. If he had hoped to find water there, he was sorely disappointed. Black even under the mid afternoon sun, the canyon yawned like a giant grave. The sight filled the mantis with dismay. If only they could find water.

"Water," he said. The one thing that kept them from their quest. Even for a mantis, he felt the heat for, like all living things, he needed water to survive. Yet, he refused to give in or cry out, knowing that a cool head was all that lay between survival and certain death. With only seconds to think, he formulated a plan.

"Water," he cried. He jumped on Rafi's chin, hammering her eyelids with fists of fury. "Give me some water!"

Rafi opened her eyes. "There's not enough," she gasped, almost pleased to see that the mantis had his breaking point. With trembling fingers, she unscrewed the cap from the canteen.

"There's enough for me," bellowed Krik.

"Water!" Bree, Pud and Dlop croaked like a chorus of dried out frogs.

"Not a chance," Krik snapped angrily. His face grew dark under the brim of his hat. "This water is mine. Not a drop of water has touched my lips since we left the water hole."

"You don't have any lips," wailed Pud.

"Ha," Krik scoffed as he tugged on the canteen. "Always making fun of me. Did it never occur to you as you drank all the water that I might want my fair share? Did you think I was content to watch you drink what I might have drunk myself?" Krik held out his barbed claws. "Rafi, give me the water!"

"Krik's right," said Rafi regrettably. "It's only fair. There's not enough water here to save anyone but Krik." Three times she tried to fill the cap with water, but her hands shook uncontrollably, and, where there had been one cap, now there were three. Finally, after much effort, she counted the last drops of precious water fall into the cap. For a moment, she considered hurling both cap and water down her parched throat. But in the end, she handed the cap to Krik. It was the hardest thing she had ever done.

"That's right," said Krik, taking the cap. Greedily, he stared at the others from over the cap, rays of sunlit water shimmering upon his face. "I'm just as thirsty as you. Thirstier, in fact, if you consider that I'm green (it was all that he could think of at the time). Deliberately, he raised the cap to his mouth.

For a moment, the world stood still. All eyes were riveted on Krik as the cap touched his lips. Unable to move or even smack their own lips, the others watched in open-mouthed torment.

"Water!"

Then Krik did a curious thing. Without drinking the water, he turned the cap upside down, pouring the water on the parched earth where it was sucked greedily into the soil. Not a trace of water remained. Amazed, the Companions looked at the soil, Krik, and then at each other. The same thought rushed through their minds like a raging river. Krik had not wasted the water on the soil. It was as if each of them had had a long drink. If Krik could survive without water, so could they.

Krik's cape set sail upon the wind. "Up, up, Companions of Earth!" he cried. He pointed a claw at both Earth and sky, and seemed to have grown three times in stature. "Destiny awaits. Let no foe or element keep us from our appointed path for ours is the darkest road. Yet, dark though it may be, it is the light in our hearts that shall bring us a new day. Drink, drink, drink from the soil and the well of your own inspiration. Drink. Let their strength be your strength, and none, not even the Anvil, shall defeat us."

Rafi rose to her feet. "You are our leader," she said. Bree, Pud and Dlop cheered, clapping their paws and giving their tails the high five.

"Arise, my Companions, and my friends," said Krik who could hardly believe his own miracle. "Into the canyon we must go for it is time to give the Anvil a taste of its own medicine. There, even if we do not find water, at least we shall find ourselves."

Incredibly, the ground darkened about their feet, and a roar and a rush thundered above their heads. Suddenly, it became difficult to see, but it was the most wonderful sight they had ever seen. It was raining. Above them, black storm clouds chased the sun further west. Below the clouds and still wearing the eye, the middle sister seemed to smile approvingly as the rain soaked both skin and fur, filling open mouths. Frustrated and angry, the sun stormed behind a cloud.

They had defeated the Anvil. Impossible as it seemed, through grim determination, sheer courage, and selfless leadership, the quest, like an iron pulled from a fire, was ready for its next challenge.

Waiting somewhere at the bottom of the canyon, unseen and yet deadlier than a thousand Anvils, lay the Tears of Agony.

CHAPTER TEN

ᚠᛖᚱᛗᛁ

I t was a hot afternoon under a shiny blue sky when Fermi reached the stately road that led to Town Hall. He had never stepped foot in Drumheller before, although he remembered with great fondness the tales his father had told him when he was a young lad filled with a desire to see the world.

"It's a strange place, Fermi," said his father Tycho. Up until last year, Tycho had been the chief potentate (ruler) of their village just outside of Drumheller, the same year Fermi was elected for the job. Tycho was so proud of his youngest son who was the fifth generation of his family to serve the village with such distinction.

"Dearest father," said Fermi, "is not everything strange until it becomes familiar? A first winter or spring flood may seem strange, and yet, which is stranger, that which is or that which we believe?"

"Winters are constant," said Tycho, admiring the wisdom of his son, "and even floods are constant in their own way. But Drogs are different, Fermi. There is nothing constant about them unless it is their indifference to what is constant in the world. They care for no one but themselves, and even then very little. Never go where you are not welcome, my son. That's all I can say."

Fermi wondered why he had not visited the town sooner. The lilacs were in full bloom, and the scent of tulips and daffodils sweetened his nostrils as he walked along the tidy sidewalks that brought him closer to Town Hall. Contrary to his father's advice, the people he met were exceedingly friendly. Bowing and removing their hats with flourish, they even introduced him to their friends.

Still, the town was not without mystery. By some strange coincidence, everyone he met was going to Town Hall. This was no easy task since three tanks, four jeeps, an ambulance and a helicopter blocked the road and sidewalk. Everyone ran and pushed to get ahead of him (obviously to get a better seat at Town Hall), but he did not mind for they were frightfully polite about it, and even a tank moved so he could pick his way deliberately across the green lawn and white steps that would usher him into the hall.

The hall was filled with chairs and people. A few chairs were empty, but most people preferred to stand so they could better see The Mayor. He sat on the throne like a puffed toad, arguing volubly with a general who wore a green uniform. Wearing more creases on his face than in his pants, the general did not appear to be enjoying the conversation.

As this was Fermi's first visit to Town Hall, he sat in the shadows at the back of the room where the acoustics were more pleasant to his sensitive ears. Rather than deliver his message outright, he thought he would first study his new surroundings before approaching the front of the hall. It was just as well for an owl had swooped down on the proceedings, interrupting both The Mayor and the general with a shower of owl droppings.

"Order!" snapped The Mayor. "We must have order." He banged a book of by-laws against one of the arms of the throne, and then threw it at Scart Loitersack, the Malawi's next door neighbor, who had blown him a raspberry. The heavy volume rebounded off Scart's nose, landing in Ira Gammerstand's tea, which flew up all over the general. British to the core, Ira asked the general if he would like some sugar with his tea. Above the din, The Mayor could be heard begging the police chief to shoot the owl. However, the chief, whose name was Ezel Gleed, simply shook his head, nodding toward Gardyloo Blowmaunger who now wore the owl as a hat. As for Gardyloo, who worked at the Post Office and blew trumpet in the local band, she took no notice of the owl since she had fallen asleep just in time for The Mayor to begin his speech.

But for all The Mayor called for order, he received none. A delighted group of onlookers watched as Erasmus Rince Pytcher, who worked with Mr. Malawi at the museum, reenacted The Mayor's last trip to the hospital. He was just at the point where The Mayor had discovered that the marmot had accompanied him into the ambulance, giving him mouth to mouth resuscitation, when Mrs. Grogblossom sneezed all over Pucksy Tootle, ruining the punch line. A frantic search for towels ensued in which two squirrels and a rabbit tried to help (but were eventually used as towels). When Mrs. Grogblossum (Groggy to her 'distant' friends) sneezed, it was best to be at least as far away as the nearest town. Poor Pucksy. She had hardly needed the full blast of Groggy's sneeze to remember that Groggy's nose had received three honorable mentions in the annual cabbage competition at the agricultural fair.

Things might have continued this way for some time had it not been for the general. Losing patience, he fired three shots from his pistol into the ceiling, narrowly missing a bandicoot that had taken refuge in a chandelier. At the sound of the shots, all snores, sneezes, chatter and breezes came to a complete stop.

"Silence!" The Mayor shouted needlessly. Almost. At the back of the room, frightened by the gunshots, Flotch Piggesnye could be heard burping up her lunch with the precision of a jackhammer. Standing on the throne so he was at least as tall as the tallest person in the room, The Mayor addressed the citizens of Drumheller.

"The general has just informed me that our efforts to apprehend the delinquent desperado Rafiatu Malawi and her murderous accomplices have been in vain. He has only just returned from the battlefield to give his report. General?"

Mr. and Mrs. Malawi looked shocked. "Battlefield?"

Before the general could respond, many of the townsfolk, Mopsus not least, attempted to reason with The Mayor before things got out of hand (a little late admittedly). Already that morning, Matilda Bagslops had injured her leg after being chased by a tank, a paratrooper had landed on Stiles Whatish, and Snooks and

Gammon's billiard hall had been blown up by the army (an added bonus according to The Mayor) after a rooster and a hen had been seen entering the premises.

But no amount of reason could convince The Mayor to stand down. Finally, the bandicoot had to take matters into its own paws, sending a shower of odoriferous spray into The Mayor's upturned hat, which he had removed in a gesture of parley.

Practiced in diplomacy, the general waited until the room and the bandicoot had settled down. He was a tall, sharp looking man with piercing blue eyes, a jaw that opened and closed like a vice, and a shock of grizzled hair.

"We can't find her," he said. He brushed owl droppings from his uniform. Unfortunately, this made his uniform whiter, and his temper blacker, than ever. He glared at The Mayor. Since the army had arrived in Drumheller, they had been dive bombed by just about every bird known to ornithology, including a Dodo.

He rubbed a chin that was set into his face like a brick. "Fact is," he said, "we can't even follow her. Everywhere we go, the ground opens up like an earthquake. It's as if we're expected. Worse, our troops are blocked and harried by every plague and toil imaginable. Locusts, wasps, bees, ants in our pants, things I can't even describe crawling around in our underwear, dung balls in our socks and our soup – I haven't seen this much action since Normandy."

"The planes?" asked The Mayor anxiously.

"Grounded." The general swallowed his temper just in time to sidestep a special delivery from the bandicoot. The bandicoot waved cheerfully from the chandelier. "All the steering mechanisms have been chewed through, and the fuel has been contaminated with … well … ask the bandicoot. Yesterday, we caught two raccoons befouling the jet engines with … whatever. Today, there are three bears sleeping in my tent." The general looked at The Mayor and the townspeople gathered around him in dismay. "What kind of town is this?"

"This is an orderly town," snapped The Mayor, "where criminals are punished to the full extent of the law. Have you nothing to report on the illegal movements or whereabouts of the felonious miscreant Malawi?"

"Nothing," confirmed the general. Eying the bandicoot, he removed his hat and scratched his head. "Only that, if in some way, these creatures and even the earth are protecting this girl, entire countries would be well advised to steer clear of Rafiatu Malawi."

"Utter nonsense," The Mayor spat from the throne. He wrote up the general in his little black book. "Obviously, when I asked you to lead the assault on Miss Malawi, I should have entrusted this simple request to someone more worthy of the task. An entire army reduced to a gaggle of whitewashed tourists by a small but, admittedly, resourceful girl? So much for our armed forces. Beaten by worms and crickets. Or," his eyes surged with suspicion, "you are, perhaps, in league with her?" He nodded at Chief Gleed. For a moment, it looked like the general was to be arrested.

The general tapped his holster significantly. "Don't tempt me," he said.

Disgusted, The Mayor turned his back on the general, facing the crowd. Deliberately, he avoided looking at Mr. and Mrs. Malawi who, as usual during his briefings, sat bravely in the front row.

"Does anyone have any information pertaining to Ms. Malawi?"

"She's a witch!" screeched Orly. Her nose, green from infection, could have given Mrs. Grogblossum's a run for her money. "Burn her!"

"Undoubtedly," replied The Mayor over Mr. and Mrs. Malawi's objections, "but I prefer to leave such conclusions to the story tellers and ballad makers that populate the school library. What I mean is, does anyone have any useful information that will help us locate and arrest this misdemeanant?"

"Burn her!" Orly screamed until Mopsus not so accidentally introduced her nose to his elbow. Her head fell next to Gardyloo's where, along with Mrs. Grogblossum, their upturned noses would have shamed a cabbage patch.

"Ahem." In one cough, Fermi cleared his throat and the back of the hall. His way now clear, he waddled up the hall and toward The Mayor, nodding pleasantly to the astonished townspeople. Upon reaching Mr. and Mrs. Malawi, he bowed three times reverently. Then, after exchanging a few kind words with Mopsus, he greeted The Mayor and the general. As they both appeared to be at a loss for words, he turned and spoke to the assembly instead.

"Good citizens of Drumheller," he said in a clear voice. He had read somewhere that this was a wise way to address a congregation of Drogs. "If it pleases the court, I have a message."

Orly woke up in the cabbage patch. "Is that a cat?" she asked.

"It's a skunk!" Primula Pullikins and Isabelline Pruttock screamed simultaneously just before they fainted. It was the first and last time they agreed on anything.

"No kidding," said the bandicoot. "These Drogs aren't as stupid as they look."

With all eyes focused upon him, Fermi lifted his tail to eliminate any doubt. Any hunter would have given a month's hunting to bag Fermi's tail. It was the blackest and bushiest tail north of Texas, perfectly combed, with two white stripes painted down the middle.

"His Excellency, the Dung Beetle," he said, "bids I inform you that the Companions of Earth have crossed the Anvil."

The two squirrels, the rabbit, and the bandicoot cheered.

"An anvil?" The Mayor looked up at the ceiling as if expecting one to fall upon him at any moment. Frightened, he looked at the general. "Have we got an anvil?"

"The Anvil," said Fermi patiently. "It is but one of many tasks the Companions must pass in their quest to save Earth. Even as we speak, they stand, tired and weak, before the Tears of Agony where none of this age has stood before. That this young Drog, who is called Rafi, has made it this far, and is determined to go on against great hardship for your sake and mine, is something for which we should all be grateful."

"Agony," spluttered The Mayor. He clutched his sides, swaying back and forth as if he was going to split in two. On cue, four paramedics ran up, strategically positioning themselves around the throne as Peers Fustilugs and Josiah Windy-Wallets, who owned the local drugstore, took bets as to which way The Mayor would fall.

"Your Drogship," Fermi said to The Mayor, "surely even you must know that all we hold dear is close to passing. No, you will not find the signs in your little black book. Look instead into the eyes of these good people who stand before you. Know that, through them, there is hope even for a Drog – a human I should say – like you."

A hall full of heads nodded in assent. Somewhere in their hearts, most of the townspeople knew that the world was different, was changing right before their eyes, and it was only when they joined hands that they felt safer in the unfamiliar warmth of one another. To The Mayor's horror, the general had joined hands with Mopsus and the bandicoot.

"Remove this vermin from my sight," The Mayor spat at the assembly. Other than the bandicoot, nobody moved. "Out, out, you filthy beasts," he roared at Fermi and the bandicoot. "We are not gathered here to listen to the grunts and snorts of dumb animals. Remove your disgusting quadruped selves to a place where such filth is welcome. I have no doubt that Rafi and her kind are waiting to applaud your arrival."

"Such words sadden my heart," said Fermi. He turned his back on The Mayor, stamping his feet. "If only we could be friends in this, our hour of need."

The Mayor was still trying to work out if he had been called a Drog. "What," he bellowed at Fermi in a gathering wind, "would a skunk, and a slovenly one at that, know about friends? Pest, I say, and an uncivilized pest at that. A pest and a plague. And I say to you sir, a plague upon your house of pests, of which I have no doubt you have already exceeded a decent amount."

Fermi smiled at Mr. and Mrs. Malawi. "She is well guarded," he said, spreading his magnificent tail toward The Mayor. "Know that many would gladly give their lives to protect her. She will only be in danger when the rest of us have fallen."

"Out!" roared The Mayor. "Out! Save your rabid dementia for those living in the wretched hole from which you crawled. Drog indeed!"

"Drog, I say," said Fermi. As if he was a rear gunner on a battleship, he made a final adjustment to his tail. His nose crinkled at the crowd standing breathlessly before him. "No offense."

It is a fact that, after Fermi's visit, no one gathered in Town Hall again (without a clothes peg) until the following spring. Fermi, like generations of his family before him, was not the chief 'potent'ate of his village for nothing. The pungent blast that escaped his tail at that town meeting would have staggered a herd of wild elephants. As for The Mayor, lift off was achieved when the blast blew him off his feet and the throne and through a stained glass window. According to the army seismologist, the fallout was enormous, covering three square miles, and sending over half of city council to the hospital along with The Mayor in one fell (foul according to some) swoop.

CHAPTER ELEVEN

THE TEARS OF AGONY

A mazed by their good fortune Rafi, Krik, Bree, Pud and Dlop soaked up gallons of precious rain. Down it fell in a liquid volley of spears and arrows, penetrating willing throats and skin, overflowing, until they could drink no more. Having almost perished from thirst in the Anvil, they had never tasted anything nicer. Then, as abruptly as it came, the rain stopped.

Krik returned a shower cap and a bar of soap to his satchel. "I don't know what we would have done without that rain," he said gratefully. "For a moment there, I thought we were finished."

"I don't know what we would have done without you," said Rafi, even more gratefully. She refilled the canteens and water bottles from the pot, which she had wisely placed on the ground when it had started to rain. "I'm beginning to see there is much more to being an ambassador than exotic trips and parties."

Krik acknowledged the compliment with a diplomatic bow of his head. "That is why a good ambassador must first learn to observe," he said. "No one is born knowing all the answers. It is only by studying others that we learn. Those we admire," here he gave a long sigh, "as well as those we pity and revile. What I did, I learned from an old friend of mine many years ago. His name was Alexander. For a Drog, he had a short life and yet, by observing and learning from others, he built a kingdom more powerful than any king. And so, he has lived for thousands of years."

"If only we could observe lunch," observed Dlop hungrily.

"We've had lunch," said Bree, laughing. "But I wouldn't say no to something to eat either." He looked at Krik. "After our ordeal in the Anvil, I'm sure our ambassador would have learned it's time for some food and rest."

"He has," said Krik, smiling. "And I want all of you to know how proud I am of how you handled yourselves in the Anvil. One day, even if Earth survives and we do not, someone will sing songs in memory of what you accomplished today. You are stronger now for your experience, as strong as folded steel, and though you know it not, there is new strength in you, forged between the hammer and the fire. And it is with such folded hearts and minds we shall prevail."

In spite of the rain, it was still dreadfully hot. However, whether it was because of Zigh's ointment or the Companions' jubilation at crossing the Anvil, no one complained. At Dlop's urging, they found shade behind some rocks overlooking the canyon, and sat down to a badly needed meal.

"What are these?" asked Pud. He helped himself for the third time to a large bag of chocolate covered nuts and raisins. "When we get back home I'm going to pig out on these for a week."

Rafi sorted the candies with her finger. "These little ones are raisins and the larger ones are peanuts," she said. "My mother bakes them when we have been especially good." She crinkled her nose. "But these larger, darker ones – I've never seen them before."

"Maybe they're chocolate covered walnuts," suggested Bree.

"Or pecans," said Dlop. Having tried one, he had decided he liked them at least as much as Pud.

"Or dung," said Krik.

"Dung?" Pud nearly fainted.

Unsure as to whether she had eaten several dung balls herself, Rafi changed the subject. She looked down the canyon. "Krik," she said, "why is the canyon black?"

"You mean as black as Pud's tongue?" quipped Bree.

With a look of immense satisfaction, Krik rolled one dung ball after another into the canyon.

"It was here, alone and broken-hearted, that Triodon looked down into the canyon even as we do now. Bleeding, and in agony he fell, blinded by his own folly. Yet he survived, for no injury could cause him greater harm than his already injured pride. Slowly, he made his way to the three sisters where he knew he would find sanctuary, even as the rest of the world was destroyed. It is because of his fall, the fall of the dinosaurs, and, not least, our failure to have loved him when the world was young that we call this place the black canyon. Now, it is only remembered in the tears he shed – not just for himself but for all the Nadi – that await us below."

"I still don't get it," said Bree. "If the Tears are Triodon's footprints, and we know the Tears are invisible, that would mean his footprints are also invisible. Right?"

"The answer to your question, Bree," said Krik, "lies at the bottom of this canyon. There is only one way to find out."

Rafi strapped on her knapsack.

"Shall we?"

Bree looked up from where he had been studying the canyon wall. "It's not that deep," he said. He rolled a large stone into the canyon. Gathering momentum, it sent what might have been a promising pathway crashing onto the rocks below. As if this was nothing to worry about, he started down the wall. "I had better go first," he called back to the others. "From what I've heard, there are enough tears down here already without adding our own."

Pud raced after him. "And me!" he shouted. "Rocks are my specialty."

"Wait," cried Dlop, following his brothers. "You'll need a supervisor."

With Bree leading, the Companions descended into the canyon. As if they were an advance team of engineers, the three rats debated each proposed route, comparing it to others, as Pud applied his own version of 'rock'et science. Once each route was thoroughly discussed and 'rat'ified (as Bree called it), Dlop would deliver their report back to Rafi and Krik. For the most part this plan worked, but even the rats could not test every inch of ground. More than once, Rafi and Krik found themselves scrambling for safety just as the ground beneath their feet collapsed into a cloud of gravel and dust. Yet, with Bree, Pud and Dlop to guide her along, and with Krik's endless stream of advice at every stop, step, and turn, Rafi soon found herself standing on the canyon bottom.

"There," said Krik with an intense sigh of relief. "That wasn't so bad."

"Easy for you to say," Rafi said testily. She counted the new rips and tears in her pants she would have to repair that evening. "I hope my almost getting killed three times didn't disturb you too much?"

Krik ignored the remark. Now that they were in the canyon, his eyes and mind were focused on nothing else. "The Tears," he said almost frantically to himself, "we must find the Tears."

Bree glanced casually at the ground, swinging his arms. "So …" There was more than a hint of sarcasm in his voice. "Does anyone see what can't be seen?"

"Maybe if we look for nothing, we'll find it," suggested Pud.

"The Oracle said we will know when we find them," said Rafi.

"Well," said Bree indifferently, "that's no mystery, is it? Believe me, when we're lit up like torches or neck deep in quicksand, we'll know all right."

"Not if I can help it," said Krik thoughtfully. He was studying a round boulder not more than fifty yards off. Almost identical, another boulder lay just beyond the first. In the distance, yet more boulders lay strewn about the canyon as if some giant had dropped its marbles.

Krik grinned. "Dung."

Pud twirled a paw around his ear. "Krik's gone batty again," he said.

"Quiet, Pud," said Bree. "Krik's next thought could decide the fate of Earth."

Krik let out a chuckle. "I should have known," he said. He

pointed to the closest boulder which, with a little imagination, looked just like a giant dung ball. "Dung marks the spot. If I am right, that boulder marks the beginning of the Tears. It would certainly explain why the Oracle kept pitching dung balls in my dinner. Which means," he added, looking at Rafi, "Triodon must have walked this way."

"What proof is there of that?" demanded Bree.

"You're standing in it," said Rafi. She pointed to a large indentation pressed into the ground beneath Bree. It was very old. Had her father been a dentist or an accountant she might have thought nothing of it, but as her father was none other than Amos Malawi, paleontologist, her keen eyes saw what no one else would have dared to believe.

It was a footprint.

Rafi examined the footprint using a brush from her knapsack. "Unbelievable," she said. "See how it has four claws and …" She gasped, pointing to five unmistakable toes.

"Here's another one!" yelled Pud.

"Well done, Rafi," said Krik, knee deep in one of the toes. "There can no longer be any doubt. We are following the footsteps of Triodon."

Bree measured the footprint with his tail. "Literally," he said.

"But we can see these footprints," pointed out Dlop.

"Naturally," said Krik. "Triodon wasn't crying when he made these footprints. Remember, it was only when Triodon's footprints filled with tears that they became invisible."

"Or," said Bree, unwilling to risk the fate of Earth on a footprint with four claws and five toes, "these are somebody else's footprints."

"I see no reason to doubt that these footprints were made by Triodon," said Krik. He used his staff as a pointer. "For starters, look at the size and shape. As Rafi can tell you this footprint was never made by any run of the mill dinosaur. And, with claws like these, we can safely assume a giant Drog didn't make it either. No, I for one am convinced that we stand where Triodon once stood many long years ago."

Bree remained unconvinced. "Let's assume you are right," he said. "What does it mean?"

"It means," said Krik, eyeing the boulders once more, "that where these footsteps end, the Tears of Agony begin. We must be very careful. Any wrong move will be the end of our quest."

"A real tearjerker," said Pud.

"A tearful farewell," added Dlop.

"This is no laughing matter," said Krik warningly. "We knew what we were getting into when we crossed the Anvil. Sun, heat and thirst, however deadly, are familiar adversaries. Yet there is nothing deadlier than the unknown, for it preys upon the heart and mind as much as any limb. Here, our foe is unseen."

"Speak for yourself," muttered Dlop.

"I will go first," said Bree.

Pud picked up a rock. "Not a chance, big B," he said. "I am the strongest so I will go first."

"This is no time for male bravado," said Rafi. The light in her eyes flashed amusement and concern. All the same, she did not doubt for one second that both rats would have gladly sacrificed their lives if it meant the others would be safe. "Let's get practical here. I am the tallest, and can see the farthest, so I will go first."

"Not true," said Bree, who had an analytical mind for such things. "Once we reach the Tears, which are unseen, you will have to crawl, making you no taller than the rest of us ..."

"Except Krik," put in Pud.

Bree stared down Pud's rock. "Therefore," he continued, "it is only right that we go first because we are expendable, whereas you are not."

"Expendable?" Rafi could barely choke out the word. "Expendable? Bree, I am appalled! Let's get one thing straight here. You and Pud are no more expendable than I am, or anyone else, for that matter. We are Companions, are we not? And as Companions we shall go together, or not at all."

Krik had been dreading this moment. "Rafi," he said gently. "Listen. Bree is right ..."

"No, mantis," she snapped. Her eyes swirled into an approaching storm. "For once in your life, you listen. We shall go through the Tears together."

"Brave, Rafi, my dear," said Krik, his face brewing as if the decision had already been made, "but impractical ..."

"My dear mantis," retorted Rafi. She stood up, towering over Krik. "If we do not go through the Tears together, I shall return the stones to you now and go home. Alone if I must."

"Oh," said Krik, not knowing what else to say. He looked at Bree and Pud, but the two rats only shrugged their shoulders and grinned. Unable to think of anything else, he decided to appeal to Rafi as one ambassador to another.

"That leaves little room for negotiation," he said craftily. "Rafi, a good UN ambassador ..."

"... would not let others take all the risk," said Rafi, knowing that Krik would have a tough time getting out of that one. Through tearful eyes, she looked at each of the Companions. "You all say you care about me, but where would I be without you? Don't be so eager to leave me when I need you most. Dearest mentor and gallant knights in whose hearts ride the greater glory, without you there is no quest."

"Very well," said Krik. In spite of the compliment, he could not have looked gloomier. "As there appears to be no other way, we shall go together. What do you propose?"

Rafi leaned on her staff. "I agree with Bree," she said. "Once we reach the Tears it will be safer if I crawl on my hands and knees. Krik, you shall ride on my head and be our guide along the way. No quest could have a finer navigator." She smiled at Bree, Pud and Dlop who were sword fighting for the honor to be first into the Tears. Even Dlop had managed to get in one or two good blows before he fell asleep. "As for our noble knights, they shall ride upon my back as in the days of old, always ready to lend a paw." She studied her staff closely. For the first time since she had left Tahw Knar Gnud, she noticed that one end intertwined like two snakes. "With this staff of bone we shall feel our way through the Tears," she said, "unless," she knelt down and touched the footprint, "the Tears of Agony are as deadly to the bones of the dead as they are to the living."

Krik hopped on her shoulder. "A fair plan, Rafi," he said. "Are we agreed?"

"Agreed!" shouted the rats.

And so, with much trepidation in their hearts, the Companions walked in the footsteps of Triodon. It was a strangely exhilarating experience, especially for Rafi who, for the first time, walked in footprints made when the earth was young, knowing that the maker was waiting for her, alive and well, at the other end. It was all too hard to believe.

Sure enough, Krik was right. Upon reaching the first boulder, they discovered that the footprints had mysteriously disappeared.

"Dung marks the spot," muttered Pud.

Rafi held up her hand. Not leaving anything to chance, her keen eyes searched the ground. But wherever she looked, the ground was flat and bare as if the footprints had suddenly sprouted wings and flown away. She reminded herself that Triodon had wings, but, she reasoned, if the stories were true, it was unlikely that even his great wings could have lifted such a broken heart.

"This is it," she said breathlessly. "I know it." She laid her staff upon the ground, dropping beside it on her hands and knees. Then, as if she was a knight about to enter the joust, she picked up the staff and made ready to advance into the Tears.

"The Tears of Agony," muttered Krik. His own staff was precariously close to impaling Rafi's nose. "Who would have thought it would come to this?"

"Indeed," said Bree. He piled onto Rafi's back along with with Pud and Dlop. "That the Tears bring death we already know. Yet, as I understand it, our job is not to avoid them, but to find the Tears so we that can get what we need to enter Erebus. If that isn't insane, I'd like to know what is."

Rafi groaned. "I thought you guys had lost weight in the Anvil," she complained. "What have you been eating – rocks?"

Pud was unapologetic. He patted a pile of rocks on Rafi's back. "Just some friends I brought along," he said, "in case we need to perform a rock concert."

Groaning under her load of rats and rocks, Rafi swept the ground with her staff.

Nothing happened.

Pud brightened. "Maybe there are no Tears," he said.

"Wishful thinking, my good rat," said Krik. He was studying the situation through his telescope, a sextant, and a transit. "But I see no reason to doubt the Oracle."

"Yeh," scoffed Pud, "he knows everything. Except maybe his own name."

Krik examined Pud through his sextant. "Then by all means," he said encouragingly, "lead the way. I've never witnessed a 'rodenticide' before."

"Rodenticide?" snapped Rafi. Already stressed to tears (literally), she could have sworn she was walking on her nerves instead of hands and knees. "Krik, if that is what I think it is, we don't need any rat suicide missions right about now." Not content with admonishing Krik, who was now prodding Pud with his staff, she glared at Pud. "Pud, if you move one inch, I'll throw you into the Tears myself." She clenched her teeth, not at all pleased to discover several new nerves she had never felt before.

The staff swept the ground.

"What did I tell you?" said Pud exultingly. "That batty beetle is out of his mind."

"That would make two of us," snapped Rafi.

"What is it Rafi?" asked Krik.

Rafi prodded a patch of earth with her staff. "I would have bet a million dung balls that a footprint should have been right here."

She buried the staff three inches deep into the ground. "I don't know about you, but back there when we could see Triodon's footprints I measured them for distance using my own footsteps. On average, they were nine of my feet apart and almost as wide give or take a few toes. Now, my hands are about the same size as my feet. According to my calculations, we should have already discovered at least one footprint."

Krik wielded a theodolite and a slide ruler. "I agree with Rafi," he said. "From up here I estimate one hundred and thirty seven feet."

"My count was twenty three, one hund'erd and five," said Pud.

"Six," said Dlop.

"So much for that," said Bree. He shook his head at Pud and Dlop. "What's next?"

"Perhaps our rock musician could help us there …" suggested Krik.

"Krik …" said Rafi warningly.

"You misunderstand me, Rafi," said Krik. "I am merely pointing out that we are forgetting a critical element of our story. Injured as he was by his fall into the canyon, shunned by moon and sun, it was only when the full weight of Triodon's heart pressed his feet deep into the earth that he cried the bitter tears that would become the Tears of Agony. Such agony, as one might expect, would make his footsteps most …"

"… unpredictable," said Bree. "Meaning," he groaned, "his footsteps could be anywhere."

Krik packed away his instruments. He pointed to a patch of ground. "Pud," he said, "let's see if you can throw better than you count. Throw one of your rocks just ahead of that dead cactus."

A large rock thudded next to the cactus.

"I feel lighter already," said Rafi.

"A little more to the left." said Krik.

Another rock thudded pointlessly to the ground.

"A little more …"

Without warning, a pillar of fire burst from the earth. Swiftly it rose up the sky, a seemingly endless torrent of blue flame, burning a hole through a passing cloud. At the base of the fire, caught up in a swirling curse of agony and flame, lay a silver shaft.

"Look!" cried Pud, pointing. "That old dungbat was right! A sword!"

Unbelievably, behind a veil of flame, a magnificent sword now lay upon the ground where Pud's rock had fallen, glittering with a star-like twinkle as if it had fallen from the sky. Deeply set in its silver handle, between two wings of solid gold, shone a blood-red stone.

"What do we do now?" asked Bree, breaking the awed silence. "Run through the flame or skewer ourselves on the sword?"

"I wish I knew," said Rafi, glad that somebody else had asked this excellent question.

"Call the fire department?" asked Pud.

Abandoning all formalities, Krik ran down Rafi's arm. "The staff, Rafi!" he cried. "Use the staff!"

"Careful, Rafi," advised Bree. "If that bone acts like a conductor we'll all be fried to a crisp."

"Crisps with salt and butter," said Dlop wishfully.

"Trying!" Rafi cried frantically. After several failed attempts to hook the sword out of the flames with her staff, she changed tactics, leveling a barrage of well-aimed and powerful blows to the sword hilt. However, other than an eerie gong that cried 'doom' each time the staff struck the hilt, the sword did not move.

"Harder!" cried Krik, adding his own plentiful arms and legs to the staff.

"Melting!" yelled Pud. "The sword is melting!"

Much to their horror, Pud was right. The sword was melting right before their eyes. Before they could even think about what to do next, both sword and flame had disappeared.

"That was fun," said Pud.

"So much for crisps," said Dlop.

"Save your sarcasm," snapped Krik. Almost blue with worry, he stomped back up Rafi's arm. His eyes met Rafi's in a look of shared defeat. "It was a good try, Rafi," he said. "But somehow I think we are better off leaving that sword in the ground. Perhaps we shall have better luck at the next Tear."

"That shouldn't be hard," Pud whispered to Dlop.

Fuming at Pud, Krik vaulted into Rafi's hair. After several deep breathing exercises, he scooped up two reins of Rafi's hair. He pulled to the right. "Try over there," he said.

Rafi winced. "I'm not a stagecoach," she complained.

"That reminds me," said Krik. He whipped open his satchel. Within seconds, he had transformed into a cowboy from the old west, complete with a black vest, a red neckerchief, chaps, spurs, and a cowboy hat. He drawled out his instructions as he pulled on the reins. "Pull left – left, pull right – right. Equal pull – forward. Hard pull – stop. Got it?"

"Ouch!" cried Rafi.

"Right," corrected Krik.

"Do I smell beans?" asked Dlop.

"Danged if I know," drawled Krik.

Painfully guided by Krik, Rafi crawled right, sweeping the ground with her staff. It was not long before two tugs brought her to a screaming halt.

"Krik," she howled, "must you pull so hard?" She watched several strands of her hair flutter to the ground. "Isn't crossing the Tears enough agony without you ripping my hair out?"

"Much obliged, Missy," drawled Krik. Not to be dissuaded by a little hair loss, he restocked his claws with hair. "Just getting used to the steering. I think I have it now." He pulled left. "Unless I'm mistaken, the next Tear should be right …"

"Back!" yelled Bree. "Back!" The ground swelled beneath Rafi's feet. Instinctively, she threw herself backwards, spilling Companions everywhere. Right where they had stood only seconds before, the ground yawned into a sucking mouth of bubbling …

"Quicksand!"

Bruised and frightened, they watched in horror as the mouth bubbled and shrieked, sucking in everything above its wake including a cloud and a flock of passing birds. Wondering what or who would be next, they hung desperately onto the ground and each other with every ounce of strength they possessed.

The ground burped.

"Jumping sand fleas!" said Pud. "Talk about sucking up!"

Amazed, Rafi watched the mouth splutter a tongue of sand. Then, in an atrocious display of manners, it swallowed itself back into the ground. "There's nothing there," she said disappointedly. "Where's the gift?"

Bree brushed his fur free of sand. "At least we're still here," he said.

"Maybe we were supposed to get the bubbles," said Pud.

"Would you mind?" snapped Krik. He glared ominously at Pud. "We could have another try, you know …"

Bree gave Dlop a paw up Rafi's back. "It is clear to me that not all Tears bear gifts," he said. "I suppose that is part of the agony."

"And our quest," added Krik. "Thank you, Bree, for correcting my slight miscalculation. I must have been thinking in meters and not in yards. As usual, your intuition could not have been better timed. If you don't mind, I could use a little more of your intuition up here."

With Bree's assistance, Krik steered the Companions east. As if she was a human minesweeper, Rafi swept the ground relentlessly with her staff. Before long, more than a dozen Tears lay behind them. Impossible as it seemed, each Tear was more terrifying than the last, setting passing clouds on fire, or sucking them down a horrific vortex of swirling sand. Yet, for all their efforts, the only gift offered up by the Tears was a single acorn.

"Probably one of the Dung Beetle's bad jokes," said Bree.

"I'm not so sure," said Krik. "A golden acorn might prove very useful once we descend into Erebus."

"That is if Dlop doesn't eat it," said Pud.

"Maybe that sword was our only chance," said Bree.

Krik wiped his brow on the reins. "We'll never know," he said. "We have come this far. Let us not give up hope when hope may be as close as the nearest Tear."

"I hope my hair grows back!" snapped Rafi.

Even as she spoke a comet of flame shot skyward from the earth, almost wrenching the staff from her hand. In the middle of the flame, looking like a small replica of the sword, lay a golden shaft with silver wings. Between the wings sparkled a blood-red stone.

"A scepter!" Krik whispered hoarsely.

With no time to waste, Rafi swung the staff into the flame. Taking careful aim, she speared the scepter beneath one of its silver wings.

"I've … got … you!"

"Slowly, slowly," urged Krik. Almost blinded by fear and excitement, he took a firm grip on Bree's fur.

"That's it, Rafi," said Bree. "A few more inches. A little more …"

"Come on, Raffers!" Pud yelled encouragingly. "That skeptic's as good as ours."

Empowered by these words and an added shriek from Bree, Rafi lifted both staff and scepter out of the flame. Exhausted, she laid both staff and scepter upon the ground to cool.

Krik was jubilant. "Well done, Rafi!" he cried. Still clutching Bree's fur, he looked like he was wearing a muff.

Bree wrestled back his fur. "Not that I don't need a haircut," he snapped, "but I'd prefer to wait 'till this is over."

They had barely rested five minutes when Rafi felt a familiar pull on the reins.

She groaned. "Here we go again."

It was madness. As if by some grand design, each newly discovered Tear seemed even more determined to end their quest. Even from a distance, the swirling fire was almost more than they could bear and, more than once, Rafi came perilously close to being sucked into quicksand. Worse, other than the acorn and the scepter, the Tears had relinquished but a single crystal about the size of a lemon. In the center of the crystal, which was cut like a diamond and as clear as ice, shone a blood-red stone.

They went on. After several more Tears, and the onset of a nagging backache, Rafi did not need a pull on the reins to know that she must stop and rest. Every bone in her body screamed bruised or broken, and her hands and knees were covered with blood and sores. So thirsty that she could barely talk, she swallowed some water between a handful of nuts and raisins.

"Much further?" she croaked.

"See for yourself," said Krik.

She gazed east. Much to her overwhelming joy, she found herself looking into the shadow of Verdandi's eye. Distant no longer, its flat head wreathed in cloud, the mountain gazed down a skirt of green and gray.

"We're here!"

"Almost," said Krik cautiously. "Don't get too comfortable – yet. Too often, it is when one believes that the task is done the true measure of the task is revealed – usually with disastrous results. I know you have already given us more than we deserve, however, I must ask if you can bear us just a little further."

"Comfortable?" demanded Rafi. Having had enough of the Tears, not to mention Krik's driving, she struggled to her feet. "You call being driven like a mule through fire and quicksand comfortable?" The Tears boasted nothing next to the flame in her eyes. "That is if you want to call whatever you were doing in my hair driving. Aside from needing a wig from the way you pull on the reins, I think that last Tear singed off my eyebrows. Well, I've had it. I'm walking from here."

"I hate to say it, Rafi," said Bree sympathetically, "but Krik's right. My brain tells me we are through the Tears, but my tail doesn't quite agree. If tails are to be believed, there's still something out there."

"And if knees are to be believed, I need a new pair of legs," sulked Rafi. She slung the staff across her shoulders. "Do whatever you want. As for me, I'm walking …"

"Rafi!"

She never saw it coming. Before she had barely started, Rafi found herself neck deep in bubbling quicksand. Only the staff, to which she hung on for dear life, saved her from being sucked into earthy bowels unknown. Having lost their ride, Bree, Pud and Dlop watched in terror. As for Krik, who had remained in Rafi's hair, soliloquizing on the foolishness of youth, he grabbed as much hair as his claws could hold to prevent being swept away in a tornado of sand.

"Hold on! Hold on!" he cried unnecessarily.

Rafi choked on mouthfuls of sand. "Can't …"

"The stones, Rafi!" hollered Krik, "use the stones!"

Not knowing how she possessed the strength to do so, Rafi released her right hand. Somehow, even as the quicksand sucked her free arm into the swirling void, she managed to grip one of the stones bound upon her shirt. Then, in an effort not to be believed, her hand reemerged from the quicksand.

A black stone flew through the air.

As if by magic, the deadly quicksand suddenly relaxed into a stairwell of sand. Only feet away, white and smoking hot, ISS lay where it had fallen upon the ground.

Literally in agony, Rafi crept up the stairs and out of the quicksand. She did not need any further lectures from Krik or Bree to know that her decision to walk through the Tears had been foolish, almost to the point of disaster.

Aching all over, she picked up ISS, reattaching the stone to her shirt. "I …" she began.

"No worries," Krik lied. Like Rafi, he seemed to have grown several inches and looked inclined to be sick. "Often the burned hand teaches best. Next time, you'll know."

"Well, at least we know the stones are real," Bree said supportively to Rafi. She did not hear him. Bent almost double, she was introducing the ground to her lunch.

"As does anyone who is watching," added Krik cautiously. He glanced at Rafi who, without asking, had already laid down in a heap of misery. "All the same, I think a break is in order. Bree, perhaps now is the time to show us what you learned from that Swedish masseuse …"

After a brief rest, which included a vigorous neck and back massage from Bree, Rafi began the arduous and painful task of finding any last Tears. Her joints now stiff from rest, the journey was even more painful than before. Three times, they came upon a Tear, barely escaping with their lives, but each time the Tear yielded only fire or quicksand. She was in so much pain she wondered if she would ever walk again. Hoping that Zigh would loan her another staff, if only so she could use them for crutches, she swept the ground.

As if someone had turned on a searchlight, a pillar of fire blasted up the sky, illuminating the deepening mountain shade. Had a cloud not moved as the sun threw a glorious sunset over Mount Verdandi, Rafi was sure that the fire would have burnt a hole right through it.

More glorious than the sunset, their eyes marveled at a wreath of silver and gold lying majestically in the flames. Set into its center was yet another blood-red stone.

"A crown!"

Not wasting one second, Rafi thrust the staff into the fire and through the center of the crown. Amidst regales of applause and laughter from Krik, Bree, Pud and Dlop, she carefully withdrew the crown and set it upon the ground.

She collapsed next to the crown. In spite of her pain, she could not help but marvel at the crown, which, in addition to its magnificent red stone was ringed by nine black diamonds. "A scepter, an acorn, a crystal and a crown," she said wearily. Ignored for much of the afternoon, the sky gushed with gold. "That's got to be of some use getting into Erebus."

"And that's not all," said Krik, smiling. He pointed at the ground. Instead of a fiery Tear, there sat an enormous dung ball.

"We have done it," he said proudly, his eyes aflame in tears of amber and gold. "You have done it." He bowed his head to each of the Companions, not forgetting Mount Verdandi whose eye looked down from beneath an eyebrow of crimson cloud. "I cannot tell you what an honor it has been to have come with you so far."

Bree helped Rafi put the crown in the knapsack. "You know," he said, "I'm beginning to think that there is hope for our quest after all."

"Hope?" asked Rafi. She gave the rat a sidelong glance. Having only just survived her ordeal in the quicksand, she was terrified of what challenges may yet be lurking both on and in the mountain. She had never felt so low. "Does hope really ever make a difference?"

Bree gave her a sympathetic look. "I'd like to think so," he said thoughtfully. "I don't suppose we'll ever know."

Helped by Bree, Pud and Dlop, Rafi rose to her feet. It was a strange feeling to walk again after crawling through the Tears. The pain in her hands and knees stabbed like knives, but she was almost grateful to exercise the pain from her legs as Krik debated where they should camp for the night. Not surprisingly, he chose a sheltered spot next to some trees and a delightful mountain stream.

While Bree made a fire, Rafi lost no time introducing herself to the stream. In minutes, she was washed and combed, emerging from the stream in considerably better spirits than when she had entered it. On a rock, under which she had hidden her clothes, were two letters.

With trembling hands, she opened the first letter.

Rafi Dearest,

How are you? Fermi (a skunk, if you please) tells us that you are fine, but, even so, we cannot help but worry. The thought of you crossing the Anvil (as Fermi called it), and in such heat (Madame Mool's Wax Museum melted), is more than we can bear.

As you can well imagine, Drumheller (and you) are front-page news. Most (if not all) of the world's leaders are here (including a penguin from the North Pole) and tents are pitched everywhere, including our garden (the Gorgonzalias will never be the same I fear).

As far as other news, the Velociraptor (now a vice president at the museum, having eaten her last three bosses) has invited itself over to dinner tomorrow night. Amos told her that we are rather busy right now what with you missing but she insisted, saying that she is looking forward to meeting our family.

As for Motu — well — I'll let him explain in his letter. In spite of the prospect that the world may soon end, I've never seen him so excited ...

Please write back soon. I know you're busy what with saving Earth, but a nice long letter would do much to ease our concern. Everyone (except The Mayor) has been wonderfully kind, but we need to know that our not-so-little girl is safe.

Your Loving Mother and Father

P.S. While you're out looking after the world, be sure to look after yourself! If something were to happen to you, our world would already be at an end.

Wiping tears from her eyes, Rafi opened the second letter.

Dear Rafi,

I miss you Sis! In all the years we've been together I've never realized up until now how very special you are — not because of what you are doing, but because of the emptiness I feel in my heart when you're not around. Coming from me, I'm sure this comes as quite a shock but there it is – I love you, Rafi. I always have and I always will. I only hope that, soon, I will get the chance to tell you in person.

On another note, I don't know how you did it, but I have received a full scholarship from every major law school in the world! Even Harvard is begging me to come but has requested that I leave my dung balls at home (whatever that means). I can't put into words what this means to me. However, as I am currently in jail (I was arrested for helping a mongoose cross the street), it doesn't seem to matter. But don't worry about me – this gives me some time to write my defense ...

Praying that you are safe,

Motu

Almost as wet from tears as she had been while bathing in the stream, Rafi joined the others. Then, having read her letters to Krik and Bree, she melted some chocolate in the pot and, with the help of her knapsack, introduced everyone to a chocolate fondue.

"Do Drogs always eat this way?" asked Dlop. After sharing the better half of a bag of marshmallows with Pud, he dipped his fourth banana chunk into the vat of bubbling chocolate.

Bree helped himself to a chocolate covered macaroon. "Not if they want to live," he said.

"These mallowmarshes are delicious," said Pud.

Full of chocolate fondue, and having written a letter to her family, Rafi quietly mended her clothing by the fire. She was dreadfully tired but could not sleep. Already nodding by the fire, Bree, Pud and Dlop lay in chocolate content. Even Krik was unusually quiet having worn himself out driving.

He fluffed a marshmallow pillow from where he lay upon Rafi's hair. "Now," he said, "let's have that letter once again."

Unable to think about anything but her family, Rafi was only too pleased to oblige the mantis.

Dearest Maman, Pupa and Motu;

Thank you for your letters. It seems like ages since I left home, but of all the miracles I have seen while on our quest, knowing that I have such a wonderful family is, by far, the greatest miracle of all.

Unbelievably – to me, at least – we made it through the Anvil and the Tears (try to imagine crawling through tornadoes of fire and quicksand). If it wasn't for Krik, I'm sure that we would have died. I don't mean to frighten you, but I can't pretend that we are not constantly in danger. The Erinnyes and the Empusae (bats and scorpions) are still on our tail and tomorrow morning we must climb Mount Verdandi on our way to Erebus. I must confess that I don't like the sound of Erebus. Aside from Triodon, I keep imagining that The Mayor is waiting for me down there. Wouldn't that be something! But Krik is with me, and so is Bree, Pud and Dlop – four dear friends who will stop at nothing to protect me. I know that I shall always feel safe as long as I am with them.

Motu – congratulations on your scholarships. I'm sorry you're in jail but, right now, it's probably the safest place to be on Earth. Good luck on your defense.

Speaking of safe, Krik wants you to tell both Ademar and Erech about the Velociraptor – says that one can never be too careful (he sounds like you, Pupa!).

Maman, if you were here right now you would be telling me to go to bed. And so I must, knowing that, tomorrow, we have a date in Erebus. Somehow, I don't think it will be anything like going to a prom (at least from what Motu has told me). Yet, as Pupa has always said, miracles often hide in the unlikeliest of places.

Please know that I love you all

Dearly,

Rafi

Krik yawned. "Good letter, Rafi," he said.

As if it did not know how to behave, a patch of moon struggled up the sky. After disappearing for half an hour, it returned, looking even less enthusiastic than before.

"The new moon," said Krik sleepily. He fluffed a marshmallow. "By this time tomorrow night it will all be over – one way or another."

"One way or another," repeated Rafi. She looked suspiciously at Krik. "You mean life or death, don't you? How is it, mantis, that you accept death as if it was as easy as putting on a pair of socks?"

Krik looked up at the stars before replying. "I wasn't afraid to be born," he said simply. "Why should I be afraid to die?"

"I see," Rafi lied. "Are you saying that all ways ultimately lead to the same eventuality? Then, doesn't Triodon know that, without good in the world, what he is doing has no meaning?"

Krik was too tired to even think about posting a guard. "Well," he said, closing his eyes, "you can ask him that yourself tomorrow."

CHAPTER TWELVE

QUEENS AND QUILLS

O rly could not believe her eyes when the Queen of England
stopped to ask directions to Town Hall. Flushed with excitement and cat hair, she personally escorted the Queen to
the Buzz and Blow so she could have her hair done before meeting
The Mayor. But if Orly was surprised at meeting the Queen, Her
Majesty was equally surprised when she was almost run down by
the Popemobile, driven by the Pope himself with no less than three
cardinals in tow, and followed by a brigade of police vehicles and
a black limousine. In the back seat of the limousine, waving to the
startled onlookers packing the streets, sat the President of the United
States.

The Mayor was no less pleased to greet his visitors on the steps
of Town Hall where he awaited them in a black tuxedo and top
hat ablaze with a magnificent new sash. Having almost recovered
from his encounter with Fermi, and having just received the Prime
Minister of Canada, he was in a jolly good mood, and nothing, not
even Mrs. Grogblossum smelling like she had inherited a liquor
store, could remove the unnatural smile upon his face. It was only
after the Queen tipped him, thinking he was an usher, and after the
Pope, Presidents and Prime Ministers asked him to wash their cars,
that his mouth showed even the slightest signs of irritation. After
all, he thought, what city or town or borough or Mayor anywhere in
the world could boast having such dignified guests all in one day?

After receiving the Dalai Lama and the Grand Duke of
Luxemburg, he hustled into Town Hall to give his daily report. He
was not a little disappointed to see the Queen sitting on his throne.

However, having some skill when it came to rising above such situations, he chose to give his report from the balcony where all, including the press, could see him. That the balcony also provided a safe haven, should any of Fermi's associates or relatives show up, was an added bonus.

"Most honored guests," he said with a grand flourish of his hat, "most noble Queens, Popes, Presidents, Prime Ministers, Llamas and ..." he glared at Mopsus and the press, "... riffraff. It is my distinct pleasure to speak to you today from the center of the world, indeed, the center of the universe, our fine town of Drumheller."

"I'll drink to that," sang Mrs. Grogblossum. And she did. Frequently.

"What's he going on about?" snapped the Queen who, along with all the other dignitaries, had received a personalized gift from the Dung Beetle, as well as a note advising them that Earth was in danger, and that answers to any questions would be provided at Town Hall.

"Something about being self-centered," said the Russian President.

"Perhaps he should read one of my books," suggested the Dalai Lama.

"Perhaps he should read any book," said the Pope.

Adrift in the rafters of Town Hall, hearing nothing but the sweet sound of his own voice, The Mayor continued his lofty address. "I can only hope the fair citizens of Drumheller take note of this magnificent and austere gathering that has come to pay their respects to none other than your Mayor." Removing his hat, he bowed graciously to the assembly.

"Where's my general?" demanded the Prime Minister of Canada.

"Where's this Dung Beeble?" snapped the President of the United States.

The Queen signed an autograph for Mrs. Scandalmonger. "Where is Rafi?" she asked.

"Ahhh," said The Mayor, looking at the Prime Minister. His smile shrank so violently it almost sucked his ears through his face. "Generals are no longer allowed in Town Hall since they have proved ineffective against the wiles of a misguided girl. As for the alleged Dung Beetle, we believe this estranged personage to be pure taradiddle – a fanciful creation of a warped ..."

"We know what it means," snapped the Queen. Leaning forward, she slapped Stiles Whatish on the hand for trying to touch her crown.

"... mind," ended The Mayor flatly. He found it difficult to enjoy the sound of his own voice with so many people talking in the room. He was about to write the Queen up in his little black book when he remembered his speech was being telecast to telemissions throughout the world. Sensing danger, and seeing the Queen holding Mrs. Malawi's hand, he decided to try a different tact.

"As for Rafi," he said thickly, "this creative and precocious sorcer... girl ... our efforts to locate her have been in vain. How she hoodwinked the generals ... I mean ..."

"Oh, shut up," snapped the Queen. "We didn't come all this way to listen to some striped blow fly with an ego the size of a circus tent. We are here to find Rafi, and understand what is happening to our world. In England, we can no longer see the moon. And according to others gathered here, worse may be yet to come."

"It's snowing grasshoppers in Berlin!" cried the Chancellor of Germany.

"The Great Wall of China is sinking!" cried the President of China.

"The Grand Canyon is full of water!" cried the President of the United States.

"Zee cheeze won't curd!" cried the President of France.

"There, there, my cheesy friend," said the Queen. She patted the French President on the hand. "I'm sure someone will sort out your Roquefort while the rest of us attempt to save the world." She looked majestically around the room, purposely ignoring The Mayor, who was so shocked at being told to shut up, by a Queen no less, he spluttered all over his sash until it looked like a baby's bib.

"Therefore, I say again," she said, "where is Rafi?"

"Rafi of the Three Stones stands before the walls of Erebus," said a scratchy voice. Mr. and Mrs. Malawi started visibly. "If Your Majesty will permit me," continued the voice, "I will answer your question and shed some light on the evil events that plague our world."

"Finally," said the Queen. "Someone who knows what's going on. Forward, good sir, and tell us this tale."

Cries of 'ouch' and 'make way' parted the crowd. Then, to everyone's horror, an enormous golden porcupine covered from head to toe with long, sharp quills, the size of knitting needles, approached the Queen. Staring out from amongst the quills, a kind and intelligent face looked upon the assembly. On its right eye hung a monocle.

"Look," cried someone, "a hedgehog!"

"Do you see any hedges around here?" the porcupine asked kindly. It pawed its way toward the Queen like a heavily armored caboose. Several of the Queen's guards stood up menacingly, but she waved them off impatiently. As for the porcupine, it let out a great sneeze, rattling its quills along with every nerve in the hall. Judging by the way it bumped into legs and chairs, it could have used another monocle. Nevertheless, it rattled, bumped, and sneezed its way across the floor until settling in a hedge of gold before the Queen.

"Your Majesty," the porcupine said most respectfully, "and to all of you gathered here today. My name is Aye, and I bring you greetings from the Nadi. Long has it been since our ancestors spoke together in the common tongue of the Druidae. But then it was a simpler world after all."

"Then it's true," said the Queen, her voice full of awe. "In my country we know something of this history when the ancients were one with the world. Yet I have always thought it was more myth than fact ..."

Aye bowed his head. "Your Majesty, too often history becomes legend even as legend becomes the mirror of our past. May we look forward to renewing our ties in the days to come."

To everyone's astonishment, the Queen bowed her head to Aye.

"You have asked about Rafi of the Three Stones, Your Majesty," Aye went on. "This much I am permitted to say. Though none of my world – the world of the Nadi – would have believed it, a Drog – that is a human, Your Majesty – has crossed the Anvil and the Tears of Agony. Even now, she prepares to scale the long face of Mount Verdandi and find her way into the dark halls of Erebus. Who could have imagined that a Drog – a child no less – would give us hope as we stand upon the edge of the destruction of our world?"

Tinkling like the sound of rain upon a tin roof, Aye bowed his prickly head three times before Mr. and Mrs. Malawi.

"Tell us, Aye, if you will," said the Queen, "what is it that is destroying our world? And why, given the vast resources gathered here, can we not help Rafi in her time of need?"

"Alas, Your Majesty," said Aye, "I cannot answer your first question for only the bearer of the stones may know the secrets of our past. This much I can tell you. If Rafi is successful in her quest we shall meet again, and I should like nothing better than to hear your voice which speaks the wisdom of the Druidae. However, should her quest fail, should our champions not succeed, your world, our world – all that we know and cherish – will be destroyed at the coming of the new moon."

Gasps rang through the assembly and throughout the world as Aye pronounced earth's doom. Orly fainted. In a cloud of cat hair, she fell into the open arms of the Pope who blessed her on the way down.

"We're getting a new moon?" the President of the United States snapped at one of his aides. "Why wasn't I informed about that?"

The Queen touched her forehead with regal grace. "I would not have thought this possible, most gracious Aye," she said, "had I not seen the moon disappear over the Thames with my own eyes. Yet you say our efforts to help Rafi will bear no reward?"

"It is true, Your Majesty," said Aye, "you would only hasten your own destruction. For it has been foretold that only Rafi can save us, and for that we should all be grateful …"

"Enough!" The Mayor's voice exploded from the balcony, blasting dust off the rafters as several people fell to their knees. "Enough!" All cameras zoomed in on his face and sash as he raced down the stairs. Pushing and swatting his way through the crowd with his hat, he stormed angrily toward the Queen.

"Your Majesty," he cried as real tears ran down his face, "only now do I see the true purpose and evil design of this devil child raised by …" he pointed to Mr. and Mrs. Malawi, "these demons. Who, not content with the destruction of our town, have now determined to pollute the world with their mischief. And you may ask, what proof is there of that? Let me tell you." The Mayor turned and spoke directly to the cameras, which could hardly keep up as he spit washed the lenses. "Talking rats, biting clothes pegs, shameless creatures that should be locked up in zoos or worn as hats befouling our streets and halls with filth, skunks launching weapons of mass destruction, and now, this vermin, this foul-mouthed, putrid pin cushion with the scruples and brain of a knitting needle has the audacity to speak of this … this enchantress as if she is some kind of … hero." Pausing for breath, he whipped out his little black book.

"Did he say biting clothes peg?" asked the Pope.

"Did he say weapons of mass destruction?" asked the President of the United States.

"You scum," The Mayor spat at Aye. As for Aye, he sat patiently between the Queen and the Pope, not looking the least bit out of place. A factory of abuse, The Mayor continued spitting out as many insults as he could think of at Aye until he finally collapsed in a chair. "Now comes the doom of which you speak," he said, "only the doom is not ours – it is yours." With a sanctimonious nod, he flipped open his little black book, searching for his pen. "As Mayor of Drumheller I hereby sentence you to …"

"Knighthood," said the Queen. One of her aids handed her a sword.

"Sainthood," said the Pope.

"Okay," snapped the President of the United States, glaring at the crowd, "fess up. Who's got the weapons of mass destruction?"

"Knighthood?" The Mayor squeaked like a mouse with its head caught in a mousetrap.

"Draw your lance," said Aye. Deeply offended by The Mayor's remarks about Rafi, his body had already launched into motion. Gathering speed, he tinkled toward The Mayor like an open drawer of sharp knives.

"Onward, fair knight," cried the Queen.

"Heaven belt him," whispered the Pope, excommunicating The Mayor in the same breath.

"Don't you dare …" The Mayor began, getting up from his chair.

"Charge!" cried the citizens of Drumheller.

It is a fact that the film footage of Aye's charge on The Mayor as photographed by the press won an Academy Award for best documentary horror picture. Never in the history of the Academy had anyone captured on film such raw horror and pain etched in a human face without special effects, and on such a low budget. The contortions of The Mayor were so remarkable and varied, based on two hundred and fifty six entry points, that the Society of Acupuncturists bought the rights for a training film.

With the help of the fire department, two engineers, and an anesthetist, The Mayor was raced to the hospital. As for Aye, he was knighted by the Queen to the delight and applause of the crowd, as the Pope and Cardinals heard confession from anyone who felt guilty about cheering Aye on to victory.

As for the rest of the world, people nervously watched the sky to see what was and was not there. And in voices speaking every language, and heard in every corner of the globe, the citizens of Earth said a heartfelt prayer for Rafi.

CHAPTER THIRTEEN
MOUNT VERDANDI

While Drumheller sent good thoughts to Rafi, Rafi dreamed that she was back in Drumheller. "If you would only listen," she pleaded to The Mayor who was writing her up for stealing the moon, "you would understand. I'm not stealing it, I'm borrowing it." The Mayor ballooned with indignation. "Stealing the moon, Miss Malawi," he thundered venomously, "is against the laws of Drumheller." His pen bled red ink across every page of his little black book. Much to her horror, his sash, no longer red but covered with green and black scales, turned into a giant snake with nine heads. Terrified, she gripped one head in her hands and pulled as hard as she could, spinning him like a top. Round and round and round he went, spinning a thousand different shapes and faces, all staring at her with the same vengeful eyes. Then, one by one, the faces joined until, finally, only one face remained. She gasped. A cruel laugh, as cold and sharp as an icicle, stabbed through her heart. In pain, she fell to her knees. Before her shone a bright light. "That's right, Drog," said the light. "Worship me now as all others have done before you. Worship me now as you would a ..."

Rafi opened her eyes to a sea of blue. Where was the light? For a moment, she lay disoriented until something green on her nose pointed a telescope north. She breathed easier. Against a gathering light in the sky, Krik towered as tall as Mount Verdandi.

If Krik knew she was awake, he did not show it. He was too busy arguing with himself in at least six different languages. But in any language, it was clear as to what he had decided to wear up the mountain. From the cap on his head right down to his shirt and shorts and a rope coiled around his shoulders, he was a swirl of Spandex™. On one end of the rope was an open safety pin.

"Fortuitous," he said to his telescope.

"Sorry," said Rafi. She slipped her hands behind her head as she marveled at this most remarkable mantis. "What's fortuitous?"

Krik collapsed the telescope. "A Drog."

"A Drog?"

Rafi sat up. Already in training, Krik's safety pin made a perfect landing in her hair as he swung from his rope. Not so perfectly, Bree, Pud, and Dlop tumbled into her lap from where they had been sleeping on her chest. She peered through a ragged bush. Sure enough, a young boy was picking his way through the rocks to their very position. Behind the boy was a motorcycle.

"A Drog?" said Pud. He grabbed the nearest rock. "You want us to kill it?"

"Not yet," said Krik. He hauled himself up the rope and hid in Rafi's hair. "It's a young Drog, not much older than Rafi. He must have seen the smoke from our fire."

"What are you orders?" asked Bree quickly. "I doubt even you foresaw this turn of events."

"Or opportunity," said Krik unexpectedly.

Bree shook his paw at Pud, now suited in bone armor, and still holding his rock. "In either case," he said, "I doubt that cold blooded murder is the solution."

"What should we do?" asked Rafi nervously. She could not begin to imagine how she must look having worn and slept in the same clothes for three days. "Maybe he was sent to spy on us by The Mayor."

"Maybe," said Krik. He motioned for Bree, Pud and Dlop to take cover behind a rock. "But judging by his clothing and the rope around his shoulder, I would say he came to climb this mountain. Now, it occurs to me that, other than myself, none of you have any mountain climbing experience."

"Bree can fly …" began Pud.

Krik smudged his face with shoe polish, which did little to camouflage his cap. "Shhh," he said. "He approaches."

Rafi stood up.

"Hey there," said the boy in a friendly drawl. Sharp blue eyes looked out from a mop of blonde hair. Beneath a smile a canyon wide, he extended a hand to Rafi. "Hot enough for ya? Where did you come from? My name's Peter."

"Hi, Peter," said Rafi, returning his handshake and smile. He stood a head taller than she did but she guessed his boyish grin to be no more than two or three years older than herself, which would make him about thirteen or fourteen years old. She tried to think of something else to say, but she could not tear her eyes away from Peter's outfit, which perfectly matched Krik's right down to the rope on his shoulder.

"My name is Rafi. I live in Drum…"

"Rafi?" said Peter incredulously, "you're …"

"Is that your motorcycle?" she asked. "I can't believe I didn't hear it."

Peter swept a wave of blond hair from his eyes. "Nah," he said carelessly, "it's my dad's. I'm just borrowing it for the day to do some rock climbing." He gazed almost unbelievingly at Rafi. "I've heard of you. Is it true that you once …"

"You mean you drove it here by yourself?" asked Rafi. She wondered what The Mayor would have to say about thirteen year olds driving motorcycles in and out of Drumheller.

"Sure," drawled Peter. "Dad lets me drive by myself all the time." He gave Rafi a wink of blue. "As long as he doesn't know about it." He glanced casually over his shoulder at his motorcycle. "Didn't think I'd make it though – engine kept overheating." His sharp eyes narrowed as he looked back at Rafi. "Besides, from what I've heard about you, I can't imagine anything would surprise you. Is it true …"

"Reckless Drog," said a voice in Rafi's hair.

"What?" asked Peter.

"No... nothing," said Rafi awkwardly. "Are you here to climb the mountain?"

"Yes!" said Peter. His blue eyes sparked excitement as he looked defiantly at the mountain. "I've wanted to climb this ol' rock ever since we moved here from Texas – my dad's in the oil business see – and now, what with all that's going on – he says we're going home tomorrow. Says if the world is going to end, he would just as soon it end in Texas. So, you alone?"

Krik's voice buzzed in Rafi's left ear. "Ask him if he'll help us climb the mountain."

"Stop crawling around in my hair," whispered Rafi.

"And ask him if he's certified," buzzed a voice in her right ear. "I'm a level six myself."

Filthy, alone, seemingly talking to herself, and with voices coming out of her hair, Rafi could imagine that she must have seemed strange to Peter. In the end, however, she decided to make a full confession. There was something in Peter's eyes and his smile that made her think he was not a threat to their quest, and while she would have never told Krik, the rope on Peter's shoulder boosted her confidence in a way that Krik's never did. But before she could speak, however, Peter held up his hand.

"Let me guess," he said, looking up the rock face of Mount Verdandi. "You want to climb this mountain and you need my help to do it. Don't ask me how I know. Something made me come here today. I can't explain it, but it is clear to me that I was meant to be here. And from what I have heard, not to mention the acrobatics in your hair, I'm guessing you are not alone. Am I right?"

Rafi was elated. What might have taken years to explain to someone else, Peter had guessed in less than a minute.

Krik's green and smudged head popped out of Rafi's hair. "Greetings, wise Drog," he said, "I can only hope your mountain climbing is better than your driving."

"The biting clothes peg!" cried Peter, both shocked and delighted.

"Krik, if you please," said Krik.

"And the Knights of Rattus," said Pud, emerging from behind a rock with Bree and Dlop. Equally resplendent in bone armor, the three rats formed an impenetrable wall in front of Rafi.

"This is Pud," said Rafi, laughing. She picked him up, kissing him on both cheeks. "And these are Bree and Dlop."

Peter was beside himself with wonder. For several minutes, he said nothing, staring at the Companions as if he was in a dream. At first, he could not take his eyes off Krik who, aside from his outfit, was already asking him if he had climbed Mount Everest. Even so, he marveled at Bree, Pud and Dlop, standing in front of Rafi, looking both grim and deadly, as if they would have liked nothing better than to do battle with anyone intent on doing her harm. Finally, his gaze fell upon Rafi. Of all these wondrous sights, she seemed to him the most remarkable of all. Never in his life had he seen such a girl, aflame in the innocence of a morning's light, as sturdy as a young oak, her bright eyes filled with leaves of wisdom beyond her years. In torn pants and a dirty shirt, she stood before him, holding her staff of bone as if she was a fairy princess who had just stepped from the mountain.

"Pleased to meet you," he said dreamily to Krik although his eyes never left Rafi.

"Down to business," announced Krik. He performed some dizzying calculations on his abacus. "Assuming this is not your first climbing expedition, and that your papers are in order, we would like to secure your assistance in climbing this mountain." He pulled a tiny roll of parchment from his satchel. "Our terms are as follows: first, we will pay you in gold – fifty percent now and fifty percent to be paid upon reaching the summit safely before nightfall; second, upon any failure or breech of duty on your part – payment is forfeit; and third – food, water, and insurance are, of course, at your own expense." He held out one claw in which lay three gold nuggets, each the size of a tooth filling. In another claw, he held a tiny pen. "Sign here."

"You drive a hard bargain, Krik," said Peter, giving Rafi another wink. He took the pen and signed the parchment although it was hard to say whether his signature landed on the parchment or Krik. "Keep your gold for now. What I would do with such a fortune is beyond me, and I could never accept payment until I had satisfied your terms to the letter. Besides, once we are up the mountain I may be of more use to you yet."

Rafi smiled approvingly.

"That," said Krik, carefully stowing the gold along with the parchment back into his satchel, "we shall see. First, we need to get up the mountain."

"I'll get my gear," said Peter amicably. "As to getting up the mountain, have no worry." After giving Rafi another long look, he set off for his motorcycle.

"Be back in fifteen minutes," Krik called after him. "Now," he said turning to the Companions, "that gives us fifteen minutes to eat and get ready." None too happily, he glanced up the mountainside. "In sixteen minutes we climb."

Bree nodded at the sun, rising menacingly in the east. "I hate to be the bearer of bad news," he said, "but that sun isn't finished with us yet." In his paws, he held out a box, which smelled frighteningly familiar.

Pud mimicked Krik as Bree rubbed ointment on his face and in his fur. "In fifteen minutes, we eat," he said, "in sixteen minutes, we climb. In twenty minutes we …"

"Had better be ten minutes further up the mountain than from where we started," said Krik irritably. "Are you ready, Rafi?"

Rafi thrust the scepter into her belt. "As ready as I'll ever be," she said. She put on her helmet and shouldered her staff, which she had strung like a bow with some of Peter's rope. She looked up the mountain and her hopes waned. It seemed to have grown to twice its size since Peter had left for his motorcycle. She sighed at Bree. "I suppose it's like climbing trees – only I don't see any branches."

"You know, Rafi," said Bree with complete honesty, "if we ever get through this I just might take up surfing."

After a hurried breakfast and another ghastly encounter with Zigh's ointment, they waited for Peter. He arrived with a minute to spare, heavily laden with more ropes and pulleys.

"What happened?" he said, noticing (and smelling) Zigh's ointment for the first time. "You all look like you've seen a ghost."

"You could say that," said Bree. He threw the box of ointment to Peter.

"You're not serious," said Peter. He held the box an arm's length away. "This stuff smells like ..."

"It's in our agreement," said Krik testily. "Paragraph twenty seven, clause six. Believe me, in another hour you'll be grateful for it."

"Don't get your rope in a knot," said Peter disgustedly. He rubbed ointment all over his skin. "I'll do it just as long as there's not another clause in there saying I'll have to eat it too."

"As a matter of fact ..." began Pud.

"Never mind," said Peter. He threw the empty box back to Bree. "I don't want to know. Now," he said in a business like tone that even drew Krik's attention, "other than Krik, who else has any rock or mountain climbing experience?"

Pud sniggered. "Did you say rock throwing or climbing?"

"I'll take that as a no," said Peter. "Anyone else? No? Well, then ..." He measured out several lengths of rope with his arms, "there are only two rules for first timers: never leave the rope, and don't look down."

"That's not what Sir Edmund Hillary said ..." began Krik.

Peter looked at Krik in amazement. "You know Sir Edmund Hillary – the world's most famous mountain climber?"

"Percival," said Krik.

"You'll get used to it," said Rafi, smiling.

"Right," said Peter, unsure as to whether he should continue or ask Krik for his autograph. "There is a third rule: pay attention to what you are doing. Sometimes even the smallest detail can make the difference between life and death."

"Now we're getting there ..." said Krik approvingly.

Having stated all that was necessary under the circumstances, Peter looked hungrily at the mountain. Then, after a final check of his equipment, he began to climb. Even Krik stirred in admiration. Climbing like a human fly, he stopped every few feet or so, inspecting rocks and crevices, hammering in metal pegs with a hammer he had produced from a bag hanging around his waist, until he soared fifty feet above their heads. After securing another peg, to which he attached an end of rope, he let the other end fall to the Companions waiting below.

"There," he said, standing on the peg like a flightless bird. "Let's see what you make of that. Don't worry if you can't make it up by yourself, Rafi," he called down hopefully, "I can always come down and help you."

"Ready boys?" asked Rafi. She glanced at Bree, Pud and Dlop. Swords sheathed and shields behind their backs, each rat grabbed a tail of her shirt.

Looking every inch a mountain mantis, Krik threw his safety pin.

She launched herself into the air. Together, what with Krik's safety pin swirling around her head and the rats swinging dangerously by the tails of her shirt, they looked like an exotic ride that should have been banned from an exhibition. Her strong hands and feet gripped both rock and peg, pushing and pulling the Companions up the mountain. Within minutes, she looked down at Peter who stood on his peg open mouthed in disbelief.

"Strong girl," he muttered to himself. Even so, he hauled up his rope and began the arduous task of securing pegs and rope all over again. In another few minutes, they had climbed the same distance and looked out toward the west.

From the east, rising in anger, the sun burned the blue out of the sky. Still fuming from yesterday's defeat upon the Anvil, it lashed the mountainside with wave upon wave of blistering heat.

Completely exposed to its fury, rocks and pegs burning their hands and feet, it was all Rafi and Peter could do to stay on the ropes and climb the mountain. Within minutes, even Peter was wishing for more ointment.

"That stuff really works," he said, watching a plant shrivel up right before his eyes. "Where did you get it?"

"You don't want to know," said Rafi. She handed him a bottle of water. He drank gratefully under Krik's watchful eye as the mantis made a deduction on his parchment.

Possessed with a fury that out rivaled the sun's, they climbed and climbed. Up, up, up they went, climbing, walking, and crawling their way up the mountain. They stopped for breaks only as Krik would allow, getting what little rest and water they could while the sun soared past them, well on its way to winning the race to the top.

They were glad Peter was with them. Aside from his good-natured smile, he had a quiet efficiency about him, and he was always careful to ensure that everyone was safe, checking his pegs and lines twice before calling them up.

It was midday when Krik announced an unexpected lunch. The sun had long arrived at the mountaintop where it now hung brazenly like a maddened eye. Exhausted, they collapsed on a ledge of rock barely providing enough room for Krik.

"Look at that view," said Peter. He helped himself to some chocolate covered peanuts as Krik made more deductions. "Isn't that something?"

"Some things are best left to the imagination," said Bree, who, facing the mountain, clearly did not approve of mountain climbing any more than he did of flying.

"Have another du... chocolate, Peter," said Pud encouragingly. "Here's a nice big one for you ..."

"It's a miracle," said Rafi, admiring the view. "From up here it looks like a quilt of gold. And yet," she said thoughtfully, "I cannot help but think that we are the hand in a quilt of gold that wove the quilt in the first place. When we are gone, who will thread the needle when such miracles unfold? That, to me, is Triodon's greatest sadness. He seeks the quilt of gold alone – not the hand that made it."

"Who's Triodon?" asked Peter.

Krik ignored the question. "A quilt and a crown," he said bitterly. "Never think for a minute, Rafi, that Triodon will share an ounce of his gold, a scrap of cloth, or even a snip of thread. It is his own hand that would thread the needle, and it is the thread in you he covets most."

Rafi touched the stones bound upon her shirt. As if they shared Krik's bitterness, they hung heavily upon her without the faintest trace of a single rune.

"You don't fool me for a minute, mantis," Bree snapped at the wall. "Something else has been bothering you ever since we got up this morning. That something wouldn't happen to have wings, would it?"

"The Erinnyes?" asked Rafi.

"The Ee-rihn-ih-eez?" asked Peter. "What's that?"

"Who," said Krik gravely. "And yes, Bree, you are quite right." He paused thoughtfully. "I am having trouble understanding why they did not attack last night. It was a perfect opportunity. There we were, tired, weak, without shelter or guard, completely vulnerable, and yet they did not attack – even in the blackness of a moonless night. Why?"

"Maybe they're just scaredy-bats," said Pud. "Here's some more, Peter. Help yourself ..."

"No," said Krik flatly. "Fear is an emotion unknown to them and known even less to their riders." He sighed deeply. "They are planning something, you can be sure of that."

"Maybe you answered your own question," said Bree. "It was natural and expected that they would attack at night so they didn't."

Krik's eyes widened with comprehension. "Is it possible?" He looked up the mountain. "Could they be planning an attack in daylight?"

"This place is as good as any," said Bree flatly. "Day or night."

Krik jumped to his feet. It was a sure sign that lunch was over. "You speak wisely, Bree," he said. "I was foolish down below. Keep sword and shield ready. They will have the advantage should any attack come from the air." He drew from his satchel a silver belt fitted with four magnificent swords clad in jeweled scabbards. "Besides," he said with a gleam in his eyes, "there may be other servants enslaved by Triodon who wait for us in the shadows above."

"Who's Triodon?" asked Peter louder than before.

"We have no time to explain, Peter," said Krik. "At the same time, I was not wholly honest with you down below. For now, it should be enough for you to know that the three Erinnyes are our mortal enemies, and when it comes to fighting, you must stand aside. Against the Erinnyes and the Empusae, you have no defense. As for Triodon, just be thankful you shall never meet him, and let us leave it at that."

"Empu, empu…" Peter spat the last dung ball Pud had given him over the ledge where it fell to a noiseless world below. He creaked to his feet. "Erinnyes or no Erinnyes, we need to get a move on if I am to earn your gold."

Krik brightened. "A Drog after my own heart," he said. He scrambled up his rope and onto Rafi's head where he made ready with his safety pin. "Remember," he called down to the Bree, Pud and Dlop, "you are our eyes and ears while we are on the mountain. Let no suspicious movement go unchallenged. Watch every shadow."

"No worries," said Pud. He poked Dlop in the ribs.

"We'll show dem bats, won't we, Dlop?"

Dlop looked up at the sky with fearful eyes.

With the added weight of the Erinnyes on their minds, they progressed even more slowly up the mountain. The ascent was tiring work in such heat, especially for Peter and Rafi although Rafi could hear the rats' groans and squeaks as they hung dutifully onto the tails of her shirt. Pud seemed to be enjoying himself. Dlop kept his eyes closed most of the time but now he was much too scared to fall asleep.

Peter hammered in another peg. "This is harder than I thought," he gasped.

"Try doing it with four fifths of the quest on your back," said Rafi wearily.

Bree groaned. "Try doing it without moving your arms for two hours," he said. "My arms are at least two inches longer than when we started."

"Better for sword fighting," said Pud. He waved at Bree, hanging on to Rafi's shirt with one arm.

They climbed higher and higher. Almost a mile below, the ground yawned with increasing disinterest as the sun, having grown weary of waiting for them at the top of the mountain, stalked disgustedly to the west.

During a brief rest, Peter went ahead to reconnoiter a vertical expanse of rock, soaring above their heads. After several minutes, he returned with a whitish face.

"This next part is going to be ugly," he said. "More than a hundred feet and as flat as a pancake. I can peg it for you," he went on with his usual efficiency, "but if you lose your footing, only the ropes and a prayer will save you." He looked at the startled faces of the Companions. "Call out if you get into trouble."

After what seemed like an eternity, interrupted only by the tap, tap, tap of Peter's hammer, a rope magically appeared next to Rafi.

"Eyes open, little brother," Bree called over to Dlop. "We're counting on you. Keep your eyes on that sky. If anything moves, even a speck of dust, I want to know about it. Pud, you watch for anything coming up from below."

Pud saluted. "Aye, aye, captain," he said.

"Take your time, Rafi," said Krik. He could almost feel her hair curl around his legs with apprehension. "We're almost at the top. If anything happens, I've got you." He threw his safety pin.

Rafi pulled herself up the rope. "Who's got you?"

"Easy does it," Peter cried down the mountain.

"This is anything but easy," muttered Rafi. Strong as she was, her arms were exhausted from hauling herself up the ropes, and the pegs, which had seemed so comforting once they had started up the mountain, stood out from the rock face like pins. Delighted to have found some added support in a small crevice, she had just reached the next peg when ...

Without warning, a bird shot from the crevice, almost striking Rafi in the face. Shocked, she recoiled in terror, losing her grip on the crevice, and – worse – her feet slipped off the peg. Had it not been for a rope clasped around her waist and firmly held by Peter, the quest would have ended in one inglorious flight onto the rocks below. As it was, she swung precariously back and forth, polishing the rock wall with her shirt and pants.

"Rafi, you okay?" A strong arm reached down, pressing her against the mountain.

"I'm ... alright," she lied, pausing for breath. "Much further?"

Peter flashed an encouraging smile. "About thirty feet," he said. "You're doing great. A born natural. I know some experienced rock climbers who wouldn't have climbed this rock on their best ..."

"Draw your swords!" shouted Bree. "Eyes to the west. The enemy is upon us!" His own sword flew from his side like a bolt of lightning as he scrambled up Rafi's back. "Dlop, stay where you are and protect Rafi's legs with your life. Pud, get up here pronto. We must protect her at all cost. Make every stroke count."

Unsure as to what was happening, Rafi and Peter watched the sky. At first, they could see nothing. Then, out of a sickly swirl of white, three black discs hurtled toward them at frightening speed.

Even in all of the confusion, Rafi heard the sharp ring of steel. Something long and wispy fell between her eyes. It was Krik's rope. Swords drawn, swinging on the rope like a pirate gone mad, he waited for the Erinnyes.

"Move away, Drog!" he shouted at Peter who hung dumbfounded

above their heads. "Your position puts us in danger for the Erinnyes miss nothing, and stabbing you, only to have you fall on our heads, is as good a way of ending the quest as killing us outright. Stand aside, and be ready to haul us up should we prevail!"

The Erinnyes wasted no time in their attack. In tight formation, they swarmed around Rafi like overgrown bees. Their wings, which were as black as the stones upon her breast were drenched with blood; their eyes possessed of a diseased yellow; and on their heads coiled snakes of hair. More hideous, a giant black scorpion rode upon each of their backs like an armored horseman, swinging two sword like claws and a spiked tail. Instead of eyes, blood-red nightmares glared at Rafi.

"It is death for you, my pretty," snarled Megaera.

"Yes," hissed Tisiphone, "give us the stones now, and we'll let you die with the rest of the Drogs."

"What? And spoil our sport?" spat Alecto. She flew closer to Rafi. "Let me draw blood first."

"Evil witch!" cried Bree. His sword blocked a tail thrust from Lilith aimed at Rafi's heart. As he parried the blow, Rafi could see drops of venom ooze from the scorpion's sting even as its claws snapped at her face and neck. Furious that Rafi was still alive, Alecto bit and spat at Bree, but the noble rat never flinched an inch as he drove her back with his sword, inflicting an ugly wound on her forehead.

"Pud, Dlop!" he cried. He drove his sword through one of Lilith's eyes. "Talk to me!"

"Fine time for a chat," yelled Pud. He slammed Tisiphone's head into the mountainside. "You okay, Dlop?"

"I'm fighting a giant bat with a scorpion on its back," wailed Dlop. "Do you think I'm okay?" Surprisingly, through either a unique fighting style or sheer ineptitude with a sword, his strokes baffled Megaera and Neith. Even so, fighting in his worst nightmare, the rat fought bravely, his confidence growing with every stroke.

"That's it, my hearties!" cried Krik, his swords flashing, a knife between his teeth and a patch over one eye. Swinging from his rope, he attempted to board Alecto, but she was too quick for him, slapping the mantis back into Rafi's face with one of her wings.

Helpless, Rafi watched the battle unfold. She knew even the slightest movement could mean the difference between a missed sword stroke, or worse, give victory to those who would kill her and her friends. How she stood still in that awful onslaught of bats' wings, claws, teeth, and scorpions' tails could only be imagined. Once or twice, she looked at Peter. Shocked and angry, he faithfully obeyed Krik's instructions, hanging on his rope, ready to grab anyone who might fall. At one point he leveled his hammer at Tisiphone and would have joined the fray had Krik not shook his head.

"Begone, foul demon!" cried Krik. He swept aside Lilith's tail as the scorpion attempted to put out Rafi's eye in exchange for the loss of one of her own. "We are the Companions of Earth! It shall take more than you to keep us from our quest."

"To me, to me," Megaera cried to her sisters. "Hear the old fool rant as if he had a choice in the matter. Never since the beginning of time have the Erinnyes failed once we have named our prey."

"Less talking," snapped Neith. She jabbed Megaera in the neck with her tail. "Or worse is yet to come."

Maddened with pain, Megaera withdrew, followed by her sisters. With a hideous cry, the Erinnyes regrouped, and in concentrated fury drove straight for Krik and Bree.

"Pud, Dlop!" Bree gasped as blow after blow of scorpions' tails rained down upon him. "My brothers, help me!"

"You were saying?" said Pud. His sword blocked Lamia's sting within an inch of Bree's face.

"I'm coming!" cried Dlop, scrambling up Rafi's legs.

"Now," cried Megaera, her eyes full of hatred and venom. She pulled back even as her sisters howled against Krik, Pud and Bree.

With all the cunning and wickedness she possessed, Megaera struck hard and fast. Between the raging battle, and Dlop who was fast approaching from below, Rafi hung unprotected on her rope.

There was nothing anyone could do.

Pud had guessed Megaera's plan even as she moved in for the kill. Poised above her head, the inch long sting in Neith's tail glistened in the fading rays of sunlight.

In another second, it would all be over.

"No!" he cried.

"Pud!" Rafi screamed as she hung helplessly against the wall.

But Pud could not hear her. He had already thrown his body between Rafi and Neith's deadly sting.

"Pud!" cried Bree who knew what must happen. Suddenly possessed with the strength of a mountain lion he slammed Lamia off Tisiphone with one stroke of his sword and then drove his fist into Tisiphone's face. With another vicious stroke, he hacked off one of Alecto's ears even as Krik hooked Lilith off Alecto with his safety pin. Howling with fury, Lamia and Lilith fell to earth with Alecto and Tisiphone in hot pursuit.

It was too late. With a look of sinister joy, Megaera pulled away even as Pud's blood dripped from Neith's sting. Enraged, Bree colored Megaera's brow with a vicious stroke of his sword. For the first time in her life, she felt pain. Hearing her sisters call, she spiraled down to earth.

"Oh," gasped Pud. Indescribable pain shot throughout his body. Without another word, the light in his eyes collapsed as the strength in his once powerful grip relaxed. With nothing to hold onto, not even the comfort that he had saved Rafi's life, he fell.

"No, you don't!" roared Peter, catching Pud. "I've got you!" He thrust Pud into his bag. Around him he could hear the others weeping and then realized he was weeping himself. "Up, up," he cried. "There is no time to lose!"

Krik was the first to understand the sense in Peter's words. "Companions of Earth," he cried, taking up Peter's call, "let no tears stand between us and our quest. Up, up the mountain we must go!"

Rafi could not believe it had come to this. Blinded by tears, her heart breaking, she flew up the mountainside as if she had wings. Hanging by the tails of her shirt, Bree did his best to console Dlop.

Within minutes, they had reached the summit. Where there might have been joy, there was now only a sense of profound sadness as Peter gently removed Pud from his bag, and laid him upon the ground.

"We showed 'em, didn't we Raffers?" gasped Pud. His brown fur was turning white before their eyes and his face had turned an ashen grey. A mixture of blood and venom oozed from the wound in his chest as more blood trickled out of the corners of his mouth.

"You showed us all," cried Rafi. She buried her face into Pud's fur. "Surely life cannot be so cruel." She turned to Krik who was searching frantically through his satchel. "Is there nothing we can do?" Reluctantly, she placed Pud in the open arms of his brothers.

Krik pulled something small and jagged from his satchel. It looked like a broken fragment of gold leaf, tarnished and very old. Standing over Pud, he inserted it deep into the wound. For several minutes, nothing happened. Then, to everyone's astonishment, Pud's breathing became less erratic, and a slight tinge of color crept back into his face and fur.

"Rafi," he said, "come with me."

Reluctantly, Rafi followed Krik. Once they were out of earshot from the others, he stood perfectly still, his face, still wet, adrift in the glow of the setting sun.

"I understand things better now," he said with some difficulty as he watched the others try to rub some life back into Pud. "The Erinnyes attack in daylight, though not completely unforeseen, tells me that Triodon is getting stronger. By now, he will know that we are at the very doors of Erebus. Great peril awaits us on the other side."

"What you put into Pud," said Rafi, not caring if Triodon had to wait until the end of time, which was only one day away, "will it save him?"

Krik let the sunset dry his tears before replying. "I will not lie to you, Rafi," he said. "I have given Pud all that remains of an ancient and powerful magic. At best it will ease his pain and perhaps extend his life another day. Who can say? He is very strong. But just as Pud did not fail in his duty, we must not fail in ours, for to fail now means the end of everything we cherish. Pud knows this, and has given his life for it – and his love for you."

"It should have been me!" Rafi sobbed bitterly. "What joy is there in a world without Pud or Bree or Dlop or you?" She looked desperately at the mantis for answers but she knew he had none hidden in his satchel.

"No one," said Krik, "shall lament Pud's death more than his brothers and I. We have traveled together for many of your years and death has been our constant companion. But there is more you must prepare yourself for, Rafi. No true ambassador has looked death in the face and not become the better for it. All of us must die at one time or another. It is how we are survived that gives life meaning."

"I don't understand," cried Rafi, getting angry. Her pain echoed across the mountaintop. "Why must others die so we can understand life?"

"That I do not know," said Krik. "But this I do know, for it was foretold to me before we left Tahw Knar Gnud, and there is nothing you, I, or anyone can do about it." He paused.

"What is it?" Rafi demanded, not caring about Tahw Knar Gnud, not caring about duty or Triodon or the Erinnyes and, least of all, not caring about their quest.

"If we are to be successful in our quest, two of the Companions must die."

CHAPTER FOURTEEN
BEAVERS AND BEES

"End of the world!" screamed Canada's National Post. "Queen of England rules Drumheller!" roared the London Times. "Weapons of Mass Destruction!" howled USA Today. "Human Porcupine Terrorizes Small Town!" tattled the tabloids.

It was true. In a unanimous decision at Town Hall, the Queen had been elected to rule Drumheller. So remarkable was her extended visit (permanent according to the tabloids), British soil was flown in from London and placed beneath her throne, under her bed, and in her shoes. As for her bed, partly out of a growing affection for Mr. and Mrs. Malawi, and partly to annoy The Mayor, she chose to stay at Newton's Apple. "A most magical place," she informed the press after she awoke the next morning in Rafi's bed to a choir of crickets singing God Save the Queen.

With The Mayor still in the hospital compliments of Aye, the Queen, the Pope and the Dalai Lama presided over Town Hall while the Presidents and Prime Ministers played golf. Radiant with sculptures, tapestries and artifacts from around the world, Town Hall was a sight to behold. Even more magnificent were the personal escorts sent by the Dung Beetle: to the Queen he gave a lion and a monarch butterfly; to the Pope, a stag and a flamingo; and to the Dalai Lama, a dove and an elephant. Each monarch also received a generous gift of dung balls.

At two o'clock, The Mayor's customary time for addressing Town Hall, there was much to discuss. In Russia, a herd of Woolly Mammoths had taken over the Kremlin. In space, an international moon mission had to turn back because the astronauts could not find the moon. Worst of all, in France, all the wine had gone sour.

"Mon Dieu!" cried the French President. "First, zee cheese, now zee wine. What are we supposed to do?"

"There, there, my whiny friend," said the Queen, patting the French President on the hand. "At least the bonbons are safe."

"The wine has gone sour?" asked Mrs. Grogblossum frantically.

"What news, Your Majesty?" cried a reporter from the Herald.

"Where is Rafi?" cried a reporter from the Tribune.

"Where is the human porcupine?" cried the reporter from the tabloids, referring to The Mayor.

"All in due time," said the Queen. She frowned majestically at the reporter from the tabloids. To everyone's delight, he was bounced out of the hall by the elephant. "Before we begin, is there anyone who wishes to address this assembly?"

"Surely," slurred Mrs. Grogblossum indignantly, "the assembly can dress itself." Having drank and heard enough for one day, her head made a perfect landing on Ira Gammerstand's lap.

"Quite," said the Queen. She stroked the butterfly where it sat upon her shoulder, gently flapping its wings. "Is there anyone who wishes to speak before we begin our address?"

"Indeed," a weak voice croaked from the back of the hall. The crowd parted quickly to avoid any new catastrophe only to discover The Mayor standing on crutches. His nose was so badly bandaged he looked like an anteater, and his face, which was white and puffy, looked like a pincushion without the pins. "If it pleases Your Majesty, and those who are gathered here, I would like to say something." Without waiting for an answer, he made his way painfully to the front of the assembly. On either side of his crutches marched a beaver dressed in the full serge uniform of the Royal Canadian Mounted Police.

"I am pleased to see you have come to your senses," said the Queen. The Pope and the Dalai Lama nodded in approval. "Perhaps you are not such a gimcrack (a showy, useless thing) after all."

"As I lay in my hospital bed," began The Mayor, who seemed to have misplaced his sash, "it occurred to me that I might have been unjust in my comments toward Ms. Malawi …"

"There's a revelation," growled the lion, scowling.

"Unjust," continued The Mayor, "in thinking this mere child of circumstance, this imaginative and inspired adolescent, could be expected to shoulder the burden of an entire world …"

"That's better," growled the lion.

"A world," The Mayor looked at the press with big blue eyes, "to which I most deeply and humbly apologize."

"There goes dinner," lamented the lion.

"Excellent," said the Queen. "There is hope for you yet …"

"Yet I am not finished, Your Majesty," said The Mayor. "I …" His cheeks reddened as he spotted Mr. and Mrs. Malawi holding hands. Mr. Malawi had a Koala bear sitting on his lap while a nest of gerbils played hopscotch on Mrs. Malawi's hair. Behind the Malawis, Mopsus sat talking to a raccoon. Unnoticed by both the Queen and the press, Mopsus and the raccoon tried to outdo each other by making rude gestures at The Mayor.

"Pity," said the Queen.

"Pity?" said The Mayor. The red in his cheeks soured until his face looked like a bowl of seedy grape punch. "Pity?" His knuckles popped as he squeezed all the maple syrup out of his wooden crutches. "Pity was my undoing." His once unctuous tone rapidly decayed into one of growing resentment as he glared at those gathered around him. "Pity for an ungrateful town," his voice grew louder, "pity for garbage men who think beyond their station, pity for parents of hooligans and lawbreakers that challenge the sinews of just government …"

"Pity you don't shut up," said the Queen.

"Come to momma," growled the lion, licking its lips.

"Pity," The Mayor screamed, his voice rising in hostility as he swung on his crutches like an orangutan, "for demented fools who degrade themselves by talking to filthy beasts and …" He spied the gift of dung balls on a table in front of the Queen. Convinced the gift belonged to him and to no one else, he stuffed every dung ball within reach into his mouth as he continued screaming, giving a whole new meaning to eating and talking at the same time. "Pity for some useless, poetic tramp with no common decency, without shame or morality, demons in her heart, bugs in her hair …"

"Your Majesty," said the butterfly. "Her Majesty approaches."

A buzzing sound streaked through the hall, cutting off The Mayor. After zooming three times around the hall the buzzing stopped as something alighted on the Queen's knee. It was a Queen Bee.

"Your Majesty," said the Queen and the Queen Bee. Everyone in Town Hall bowed except The Mayor who, cut off in mid sentence and choking on a dung ball, was wondering where he had left off.

"The Companions stand upon the crown of Mount Verdandi," the Queen Bee buzzed sweetly. "However, in a noble act that saved Rafi's life, our valiant Pud has fallen to the Erinnyes. They mourn him now before the gates of Erebus."

Mr. and Mrs. Malawi's eyes filled with tears. Watching from across the hall and from across the world, every mother, father, sister and brother shared their pain. Even the reporter from the tabloids could be heard bawling outside.

"This is ill news, Your Majesty," said the Queen sadly. "That Pud should have fallen in such a heroic attempt to save Rafi, and a world others choose to not understand," she glared at The Mayor who was still spitting up dung balls, "is a grief beyond the borders of any kingdom. Could not a knight be sent from my own kingdom to replace the valiant Pud?"

"With all due respect, Your Majesty," said the Queen Bee, "no knight of your vast kingdom except perhaps the knights of old could replace the virtuous Pud. Even now, the Companions carry him with great honor into the depths of Erebus where his shadow shall pass no more."

"Pray tell us of Erebus, Your Majesty," said the Queen.

"That I cannot, Your Highness," said the Queen Bee, "for such knowledge is better left in dark places where none of your kind can see."

"Then tell us," said the Queen, "if there is any hope for those of us who pray for Rafi and mourn for Pud? Or have we done such wrong in this world that even the good earth has turned against us?"

"Yes, tell us, Queen!" Bellowing like a foghorn, The Mayor's voice pierced through a gathering mist of spit and bad breath. "Tell us of the moon and the stars, the future for a thousand years, why some live as others die, the meaning of life, why we are here …" He laughed derisively as flies, overcome by his breath, fell in battalions from the walls and ceiling. "That we should need to ask such things of a bee, and a sap sucking pantywaist at that …"

The Queen bowed her head in embarrassment. "How I wish I had my army," she said.

"No need, Your Majesty," said the Queen Bee. "I have mine."

What The Mayor was about to say next no one found out. Sounding like an errant hydro pole badly in need of service, a black storm of angry bees burst into the hall, saluted both Queens, and made a beeline for The Mayor. He would have made a run for it had it not been for the beavers. In three seconds, they had gnawed through his crutches, causing his bandaged face to connect painfully with the hard floor. What happened next is beyond description. A convention of horror novelists could not have imagined a more ghastly scene. Even the press shielded their lenses and looked away in horror as the two Queens bowed their heads in silent and majestic approval.

As for The Mayor, he lay upon the floor like a fallen hive clotted in blood and honey. Eventually some paramedics arrived with a stretcher, and with the help of some smoke and shovels, he was lifted onto the stretcher, slid into an ambulance and raced to the hospital yet again.

CHAPTER FIFTEEN
INTO THE MOUNTAIN

Rafi couldn't believe what she was hearing. "Two of us must die?"
"Not so loud," Krik whispered urgently. Pools of amber swirled franticly in his eyes. "None of the others must know."

"They have a right to know ..." Rafi began.

"You don't understand ..." said Krik.

"Oh, I think I understand perfectly, you mischievous mantis," she hissed. "By not telling the others that they or someone they love may die, you think your miserable quest is safe, that everyone will tag along since any option is better than waiting for the end." Deliberately, she turned to rejoin the others. "Well," she said, her face a portrait of defiance, "I'm going to fix that part of your little quest right now."

"Rafi," said Krik desperately. "Listen. You don't know Bree, Pud and Dlop as I do. It is precisely because two of us must die that they will want to go on. This knowledge will seriously affect their judgement, and their willingness to sacrifice themselves at the first opportune moment so that someone else may live. Don't you see? We must put our faith in the unknown rather than choose to play a part we may have never been meant to play. As Pud has proven, we shall defend you to the death, but death, when it comes, must arrive on the wings of chance and circumstance – not on some foolish notion of heroics that was never meant to be."

Rafi was unmoved. "And what about me?" she demanded. "I know two of us must die. Why don't I just throw myself off the mountain and save everybody the trouble of wondering who is next? With Pud and I gone, no one else needs to die."

Krik buried his face in his claws. "Because," he said miserably, "if you die, everybody dies, and not just the members of our quest. You must remember, Rafi, without you we may as well hand the stones over to Triodon right now. And another thing," he looked up from his claws with eyes neither happy nor sad, "I have seen many miracles in my long life. Do not be too quick to rule out Pud. He is wonderfully strong, and there is time yet for new miracles to happen."

"And Peter?"

"Peter's role in our quest is finished," said Krik. "If we survive, he will be more than adequately compensated for his efforts. Whatever future awaits him, it shall not be in Erebus. But this I know, Rafi – even if Peter was to share in the knowledge you bear – his choice would be the same as the others. He has a brave heart, and a lot of the recklessness that clouds a youthful mind."

"What am I to do?" asked Rafi. Beyond tears, she gazed upon the sunset, which did little to lighten her weary eyes. "If I don't tell the others, two of us must die. And if I tell them, everyone dies."

"You are an ambassador," said Krik patiently, "although you don't know it yet. And ambassadors know that sometimes, while they visit strange, new countries and talk to grand assemblies, others die. And sometimes, they die themselves. It is the badge of every ambassador to know that the difference between life and death often hangs, not on the edge of weapons or war, but on the edge of words. For no sword ever forged cuts as deep as a sharpened word; no war ever conceived was launched on words truly spoken."

"It is only now," said Rafi in a hushed voice, "behind the singing of anthems and the waving of flags I begin to understand the true meaning of being an ambassador. Now that I have seen Pud, I am no longer sure I want to be one. To have such power over life and death, and yet be so powerless in the face of it."

"So it is with all ambassadors," said Krik, "until they realize that power rests not in an anthem or flag, but in the choices we make. That is, after all, what miracles are, is it not? The difference between a burden and a blessing, intolerance and enlightenment, a house and a home …"

Bree's haggard face loomed in front of Rafi and Krik. "We need to get moving," he said. From the droop of his whiskers and shoulders, he looked as if he had aged ten years in as many minutes. "Aside from another attack by the Erinnyes, we need to get Pud underground where he will be safe from birds, and any other predators looking for an easy meal. You okay, Rafi?"

"How's Pud?" she asked, still gazing far beyond what her eyes could see. She could not bring herself to look at Bree, knowing what she knew, and that he too would gladly give his life so she might live.

"We've done all we can for him," he said. He looked at Krik who, having cleaned out the better part of a box of tissue, was blowing his nose. "What do we do now?"

"Find the doors of Erebus," said Krik, sniffing.

Peter and Dlop joined them.

Bree watched Pud out of the corner of his eye. "And how do we do that?" he asked.

Krik pulled out his telescope. "Look for a grove of black poplar trees," he said. "Five to be precise. Legend tells us each tree is stunted, more twisted than a tortured thought, and blacker than the depths of Erebus itself." He sighed. "It is also said that, beneath its roots, there lives a monstrous serpent. Once that serpent is destroyed, the trees shall grow again."

"There," said Peter. He pointed east. Twisting ominously, five black trees haunted a descending halo of light. "And you're right – spookier trees I've never seen in my life."

Krik nodded grimly. "Very well," he said. There was no emotion in his voice. "To Erebus we shall go. Let us get Pud, and be on our way …"

"Pud!" cried Bree.

Pud was missing.

"He can't be far," yelled Bree. He ran wildly to where they had left

Pud, kicking himself as he ran. "Make for the edge of the mountain! If I know Pud, he's crawling away to die."

In desperate and frightened voices, they called Pud's name.

"Pud!"

"Pud!"

"Pud!"

"Here he is!" cried Peter. He knelt down only inches from the mountain's edge.

"Let me die!" Pud gasped as he crawled another inch. "I am nothing but a burden now. I will only slow the others down. I beg you Peter, pick me up, and throw me off the mountain!"

"Not a chance, little brother," said Peter, wiping his eyes. Gently, he picked up Pud, and laid him next to the giant lump in his throat.

"Thank goodness, Peter!" cried Rafi, running up. "You found him. Pud, whatever were you doing so close to the edge of the mountain?"

"He was disoriented," said Peter. He stroked Pud's fur, which, alarmingly, fell off in his fingers. "That's all. Let me carry him."

"Impossible," said Krik, although the mantis had already guessed that Peter had said less than he knew. "For to carry Pud would mean you are going to Erebus, and that I cannot allow."

"Why not?" said Peter angrily. "You have nothing to fear from me. I helped you up the mountain and I want to help more. You know it as well as I do, Krik. You can't be fighting Erinnyes, Triodon, and heaven knows what else with Pud on your backs. Can you?"

"Peter has shown himself to be a good Companion, and there is no question we could use his help," Bree joined in. "Upon Pud's life, I cannot imagine that crawling down the mountain's throat will be any better than climbing its face. Besides, I have a good feeling about him."

Krik spun on his heels and looked at Rafi. She knew what he would say even before he said it. "It's your choice, Rafi."

She groaned inwardly as Krik's words drove into her heart. She must choose whether Peter should join them, knowing that yet another Companion must die. She wished Krik had never told her. Yet somehow, she knew this had been his plan all along. As an ambassador, it was not enough to save the world by offering her own life; she must do it by offering the lives of others. In cruel condemnation, the last rays of sunlight daubed each of the Companions a bloody red.

"Peter," said Rafi, "you cannot imagine the danger that awaits us once we cross into Erebus."

"Neither can you," said Peter. "Besides, you can't stop me. I'll follow you anyway, all the way to Erebus if I have to. But I would be of more use to you by your side than skulking around in the dark. Let me come. If the world is going to end, I'd just as soon see it end with you."

Unconvinced, Rafi's watery gaze rested upon Pud. "But I don't even know you."

"What's to know?" asked Peter, trying to make light of the remarkable events that had, so far, bound them together. "Born in Texas, moved to Drumheller, mountain climber extraordinaire, handsome …"

Grateful for a moment's reprieve from her pain, Rafi pretended to consider very deeply. "Well," she said finally, "three out of four isn't bad …"

"Which three?"

Rafi smiled.

"Besides," Peter pressed on, pleased to see that he was giving Rafi something to think about other than Pud. "From what I've heard on the news, I feel like we've already met." He counted off his fingers. "Let's see. Your name is Rafi. You live in an apple. Your hair can spell better than most kids at my school. You're on a first name basis with rats and skunks. And, for the past week you've occupied numbers one through ten on The Mayor's Most Wanted List. Shall I go on?"

Rafi gave in. "If that is your answer," she said, giving Peter a hug, "let the Companions, old and new, set forth." Her face grew hard as she looked at Pud. "We have a score to settle with Triodon. Quite apart from destroying the world, I cannot allow him to destroy my friends."

Bree drew his sword. "To Erebus!" he cried. "To Erebus we go, and when we get there, if nothing else, I shall show Megaera the true meaning of hell."

"If we are going to Erebus," gasped Pud, "somebody give me a rock."

Pud's humor was a good sign, which did much to lighten their hearts. With Pud on Peter's shoulder, and Krik in Rafi's hair, they made their way to the poplar grove. In growing darkness, they counted five black trees, twisting up from the earth like splintered swords. Behind the trees, open-eyed and open-mouthed, lay a skull of rock.

They had found the Mouth of Erebus.

Dlop shivered. "Are we sure we want to do this?" he asked. He could only imagine how many bats were waiting for him on the other side of that mouth.

"Want," said Krik darkly, "has nothing to do with it. Once we pass through the mouth there is no turning back unless it is in eons of time. We've no time to waste. Into the Mouth of Erebus we must go."

"Shan't," croaked a voice above their heads.

Bree and Dlop whipped out their swords, scanning the trees. A strong wind had found its way up the mountain, making the trees sway as black leaves dropped on their heads. Hanging upside down in the boughs of the nearest tree, visible only by one bright and wary eye, sat a black raven.

Krik motioned for Bree and Dlop to lower their swords. "Good Raven," he said, "what news have you of Erebus? No doubt you know of our quest. Have you words from the Oracle? Nonetheless, we must enter Erebus."

"Won't," croaked the raven.

"Will somebody give me a rock?" gasped Pud from Peter's shoulder.

"Until you hear what I have to say," continued the raven.

They stepped closer. It was then they noticed the raven had only one eye, cut and colored like an amethyst. Where there should have been another eye, only an empty socket glowered in descending gloom.

"Pecked it out myself," boasted the raven proudly, "so I could see better."

Odd as this was, Rafi did not doubt the raven for a second. From the moment she looked into the raven's missing eye, she felt as if she had been suddenly transported into the mountain. At first, she found herself surrounded by complete darkness. Then, she stood in a great cave stuffed with treasure, which turned into a golden tree. Beyond the tree, three old crones sat in filthy rags cooking something in a pot. Much to her horror, two of the crones looked at her with the faces of her mother and brother. But the third crone did not look up from where she sat staring into the pot. Instead, she held out a twisted claw, in the palm of which lay seven stones.

"O stately Raven," she said, trying to remember everything she had learned about ravens in school, "of the saintly days of yore. Tell me, why do you hang upside down?"

The raven hesitated as if it did not understand the question. "It is a difficult question to answer," it said finally, "because I am not upside down. How do you know you are right side up?"

Before Rafi could answer, a curious thing happened. The raven's head suddenly changed into the head of a lion even as its body changed into a goat. Instead of legs, there sprouted a serpent's tail.

Amazingly, this strange creature then changed into a platypus.

"A shape shifter!" said Krik.

"Haven't … quite …" said the platypus, changing into a mongoose, "got the hang of it yet." This became even more evident when the mongoose turned into an armadillo and fell from the tree.

"illo," said the armadillo, lying on its back. After an exclamation, it turned back into a raven.

"Why are you all upside down?" asked the raven, looking up with one eye.

"We're not," said Bree testily. All this changing was making him dizzy. "And we are in a hurry. What can you tell us about Erebus?"

"Many dark things," said the raven unhappily. "Put me back up in my tree and I'll tell you."

"Shan't," croaked Dlop in a fair imitation of the raven.

As soon as Rafi had placed the raven back in its tree, it began a little dance, which was an odd thing to see because the raven was still upside down.

"Triodon awaits you at the fourth level of Erebus," croaked the raven. "As to how you will get there, you must trust to your own wits and strength. But this I can tell you. Each level is guarded by one of Triodon's most powerful servants, great beings from another age that none have passed or conquered since Time was young. It does not give me confidence to see you standing, upside down, without arms other than sticks and bones. You will need more than that if you are to descend into the abyss where no shadow grows. But before you can reach the three guardians of Erebus, you must first cross the River of Death. And that you will not do unless you each have a penny."

"I don't have a penny," said Rafi.

Peter searched his pockets. "Neither do I."

"Then you will not cross the River of Death," croaked the raven. "No one crosses without a penny. And if you don't cross the river ..."

"We will not find Triodon," said Krik. He bowed to the raven. "Good raven, if that is all you can tell us, we thank you. Yet, nothing shall stop us from reaching Erebus, be it a penniless pocket or a legion of Erinnyes."

"Good luck to you all," croaked the raven as it tried to peck out its remaining eye. Then it disappeared.

"What an odd fellow," said Bree.

"Speaking of odd …" the raven reappeared looking more like a kangaroo with the face of a puffin. It looked at Rafi or rather tried to look because both of its eyes had been pecked out. "That scepter you bear is no ordinary scepter," it said. "In Erebus it will give you the power of invisibility. Use it well." The raven disappeared for a second time.

"Rafi, how's our …" began Krik.

"If you need water," croaked the raven's voice from somewhere up the tree, "there is a patch of snow on the north side of each tree. Drink long and deep, for there is no drinkable water in Erebus. Only death …"

Peter sighed. "If I hear that word one more time," he said, "I'm going to start wondering what I've gotten into."

"And I'm going to need a therapist," squeaked Dlop.

Rafi quickly packed the canteens and water bottles with snow. "How's Pud?"

"Barely breathing," said Peter, helping himself to some snow.

She pressed a handful of snow to Pud's lips. "Oh, Pud," she said, stroking his cheeks, which looked sunken and hollow, "how can I ever repay you? No ambassador could ever lose such a faithful friend. Yet somehow, I do not believe you shall ever leave us for ours is a friendship that will never die."

With great difficulty, Pud opened one eye. "Don't worry about me, Raffers," he said weakly. "You just look out for yourself." His eye closed.

"You should eat something, Rafi," said Krik kindly. "The next leg of our journey will be more challenging than anything you have ever faced before, and you will need your strength. Do not worry about Pud or what the future may bring, for many a future has been wrongly guessed only to discover that the future is just that – a time and a place whose ultimate end we may never know."

Fighting back her tears, Rafi opened the knapsack. "Anyone hungry?" she asked. But before any of the Companions could answer, a bright light sprang from the knapsack, illuminating her astonished

face along with the equally astonished faces of Krik, Peter, Bree and
Dlop. For a moment, she thought a star had fallen from the sky.
Hands trembling, she reached into the knapsack and withdrew,
not a star, but a flame that filled the grove with light. She held it
high above her head as if to place it back into the heavens where it
scintillated beyond the mere twinkling of stars.

"The crystal!"

"Not a moment too soon," said Krik, admiring the crystal. "We
will need it where we are going. As my father always said, 'fear of
the unknown is best confronted in a well lit room ...'"

"And from as far away as possible," added Dlop.

"As for food," Krik continued, "we can eat along the way. I
don't know about the rest of you, but I'd feel better once we put a
few miles between us and the mountaintop before we sit down to a
proper dinner."

Not sure if they entirely agreed with this, the Companions helped
themselves to some food, and made ready to enter the Mouth of
Erebus. If given a choice, there was nothing they would have liked
less than step inside such a dark and dreary hole, not even being burnt
alive. Only feet away, the Mouth of Erebus lay etched in rock and
agony, twisting in torment like a scream that would never end.

Frightened and hungry, Dlop did his best to bury his fear in a
chocolate bar. "What's that clacking noise?" he squeaked.

"Our knees," said Peter. He was not kidding.

They stepped into the mouth. Rafi was too excited to eat. With
the crystal in one hand and her staff in the other, she led the way
until they were all inside. Turning around, they looked back through
the mouth, gazing upon a star strewn darkness and a faint sliver of
sickly moon.

"Let us hope," said Bree, "this is not the last time we shall see
the moon."

Reluctantly, they turned and stared down the mouth's throat. It
was really a tunnel, which went deep and down and dark into the
mountain like the twisted belly of an angry snake. Had it not been

for the crystal, they would have gladly fled back into the night, which was infinitely less frightening than the black shades of Erebus. But as it was, they could only go forward.

"Bugs!" cried Peter. He noticed with a shudder that the roof, floor, and walls of the tunnel were covered with insects. Attracted by the light of the crystal, bugs of every description rained down onto their clothing, hair and fur.

"Not bad," said Krik, munching on a cockroach. "Needs salt though …"

"Bats and scorpions and bugs!" wailed Dlop, who had just lost his chocolate bar to a gang of termites.

Down, down, down they went. It was a horrible journey, a never-ending nightmare that grew more foul and gruesome with every step. Even with the crystal, the tunnel was dark and cold, and so infested with bugs and other strange creatures it seemed to be alive.

"I have the distinct feeling I'm being swallowed," said Bree. "If this is the entrance to Erebus I hate to think of what lies ahead." His whiskers stiffened. "Say – does anyone smell smoke?"

"I do," said Peter, sniffing. "And a moment ago I thought I saw a flash of light further down the tunnel. Only lasted a second. Now it's gone."

In spite of their fear, they pressed on. Soon, the unmistakable smell of smoke filled their nostrils as a faint sound like a falling rock echoed through the tunnel. In the distance, they heard the sound of footsteps. Then silence.

"Something is not right," said Krik. He peered down the tunnel. "While I have never been in here before, I would bet my life we are nowhere near the first level of Erebus. Yet, danger is nearby, it seems. If I did not know better, I might have thought it was the Erinnyes, but they never use fire. Still, there may be other creatures that choose to welcome us for unwholesome reasons of their own."

"Maybe the mountain is still active," suggested Peter.

"Unlikely," said Krik. He extracted a giant beetle from Rafi's hair, which he threw to the ground as if exacting his revenge on some relative of the Dung Beetle. "Or rather I should say it's possible, but mountain fire smells nothing like this. Can't you smell the wood? Besides, no footsteps were ever made by a mountain." He dropkicked a stick bug and three cockroaches out of Rafi's hair. "Curious," he added. "If we were above ground I would say it was a Drog's fire, but no Drog would choose to live in Erebus, not unless …"

"I will go first," said Rafi, not wanting to hear why anyone would choose to live in such an awful place. Anticipating an argument, she blocked the way with her staff and a frown. "It's time I did something other than watch the rest of you kill yourselves," she said. She handed her staff to Peter and then reached for the scepter still hooked on her belt by one of its golden wings. Without another word, she disappeared.

"Wha…!" cried Peter.

As if held by unseen string, the crystal dangled in the air. "Shhh," Rafi whispered. "It's the scepter, remember? It makes me invisible. Bree, follow me."

Bree drew his sword. "Gladly," he said, although there was not a shred of gladness in his eyes. "Dlop, stay here and look after Pud."

"Us," corrected Krik's voice, for he, too, had disappeared along with Rafi the moment she had touched the scepter. "Follow us."

With her friends on, beside, and behind her, and danger possibly ahead, Rafi was in no mood for lessons. "Not now, mantis," she hissed.

"Accuracy is an important virtue of diplomacy," Krik's voice persisted as the crystal bobbed its way down the tunnel. "Imagine if two nations …"

"Are about to meet," whispered Bree. Anyone watching would have thought the rat walked alone. "Honestly, Krik," he said, doing his best to keep up, "this is no time for lessons. Words did not save us on the mountainside, and I doubt they are of any better use here." As if to illustrate this point, he donned his helmet and shield.

Without warning, the tunnel suddenly opened into a large room. Giant sized stalactites shaped like rusted knives dripped a gooey, reddish liquid onto a rock-strewn floor. In the center of the room, surrounded by rocks, the remains of a small fire lay smoking. Next to the fire, a torn, shabby blanket lay upon a flat rock that might have served as a pillow.

Rafi stood quietly at the edge of the room. Alert and wary, cloaked in the power of the scepter, she listened intently for any sound that might betray someone hiding in the room. But for all she listened, the only sound she heard was the plop, plop, plop of the stalactites, taking their time to paint the floor a bloody red.

She stepped inside, followed closely by Bree.

"It's just a rat," a voice whispered from somewhere above her head. The voice, which was deep and flavored with a heavy accent, sounded almost relieved.

"What izzat on its 'ead and in its 'ands?" said another voice, softer and no less accented than the first. "Throw a rock on its 'ead and squish it dead. Then we can 'ave it for dinn'air."

"What about the light?" the first voice added cautiously. "Surely lights don't travel on their own?"

"It is true," said the second voice with an air of unsettling calm, "throw a bigg'air rock on its 'ead, and let us see wheth'air lights 'ave wings or legs."

Rafi had heard enough to know they were in danger. "Show yourself," she called out to the voices. She brandished the scepter but then realized no one could see her. "Show yourself," she said again, although her heart was in her shoes. "And you have nothing to fear."

Bree's sword split the air so fine it would have made a sword master jealous. "Drop a rock on my head," he said, "and I'll give you that, and more besides."

Peter rushed into the room along with Dlop. "As will we!"

"'ear them," said the second voice softly. "'ear the liars and fools who demand we show ourselves. Show yourselves, I say. Then we shall see wheth'air we 'ave nothing to fear."

Not wishing to reveal the scepter's secret, Rafi stood deliberately over the smoking ashes of the fire. Before Krik could say two words, she thrust the scepter back into her belt.

"Don't ..." Krik began.

"Here I am!" she cried, releasing the scepter. Wreathed in light and smoke, she rose like a wingless phoenix from the ashes.

"Here we are," Krik announced with a sigh.

Above their heads, the air filled with the sound of hurried voices.

"It's a girl!" cried the deep voice in disbelief. "Come right out of the fire. You never said anything about a girl."

"Ridicule," said the other voice, "I 'ave known such tricks in my time. Marie could do the same trick even aft'air she 'ad lost 'er 'ead."

"That would be some trick," said Dlop.

"Please come down," said Rafi. She stepped away from the fire as Peter placed the staff in her hand. "We wish you no harm."

"What about that one, yes, the Drog with two 'eads, one with the face of a dead rat but no less ugly than the oth'air. Does 'e wish us no 'arm?"

Peter held out his hands. "I am unarmed," he said. "And Pud is injured. He cannot hurt you."

"Don't be too sure about that," gasped Pud.

"Liar," retorted the voice. "The Drog 'as two arms as certainement as 'e 'as two 'eads. And the oth'air two that greet us with swords and fill our 'ome with stink, they are also unarmed?"

"We are armed to fight our enemies," said Bree proudly. Deftly, he sheathed his sword, nodding at Dlop to do the same. "Since you have yet to declare yourselves our enemy, you have nothing to fear."

"Per'aps we are friends, non?" The voice prickled with the sweetness of a bitter lemon. "Then allow me to introduce myself." Clickity-click, clickity-clack, clackity-click, two reddish claws appeared over a ridge of rock followed by two beady, brown eyes.

"A crab!" shouted Peter.

"Not a crab, you fool!" the crab shrieked back at him. "I am none oth'air than Turgot de Bois-Guilbert, chief adjutant and advisor to Louis XVI of France."

"You're a little out of your way," said Bree.

"And your time," said Dlop.

"Silence, les deux comiques," snapped Turgot. "Out of your way you mean, my bubonic rattlebrains."

"We meet again, Turgot," said Krik, who up until that time had remained hidden in Rafi's hair. He now sat in his familiar chair, watching Turgot with bright eyes. "I would have thought after that business in France you might have tried another occupation."

Turgot looked shocked. "Can it be?" His eyes waved madly on their stalks. "I 'ave 'eard that voice before, and I curse the day when it first filled my ears with pain." The eyes leaned forward. "Is that you, Krik? Ahhh, mon ami, it is you. Aft'air all these years, we meet again."

"Indeed," said Krik, who looked every bit as surprised as Turgot. "I never thought I would ever see you again. I would have thought you would have returned to the sea by now where you could find bigger fish and homes to destroy than the ones you have destroyed already. Was the sea not large enough for you, Turgot? What are you doing here, O Hermit of Hermit Crabs?"

"Such was the tongue I rememb'air," spat Turgot, turning bright red in anger. "Always the one to give advice, but nev'air accepting a shred of it yourself." Such bitterness was in his gaze that his eyes almost popped off their stalks. "It was you who killed my Marie!"

"No doubt that is what you remember," said Krik. "But I repeat my question. What are you doing here? And who is your companion? Not Louis, to be sure."

"Not that it is any of your – how you say – business," snapped Turgot, "but I live 'ere." He waved one of his claws. "As for my comrade, my friend, 'e shall speak for himself." With one eye fixed on Krik his other eye swung around, looking behind the rock. "Come, Talat. Do not be shy. We are among friends, yes?"

A tumbled mass of black hair rose slowly from behind the rock, revealing a rectangular face that looked neither kind nor evil, set with two jet-black eyes, a hawk's nose, and a mouth curled by the weight of too many sad memories. Beneath the head was a neck that might have belonged to a bull, and below that, rose a muscular body fitted with even more powerful limbs. By all appearances, the young man standing beside Turgot was not much older than Peter.

For a moment Rafi stood rooted in the same wonder that silenced her friends. She gazed up at Talat and Turgot. Suddenly, it occurred to her that she was not the only one possessed of strange and exotic friends. Yet, whereas she felt only warmth and love from the Companions, she felt and saw none in those black and brown eyes.

"Greetings Talat and Turgot," she said cordially. "I am Rafi. Krik, it seems, you already know." She extended her staff and a smile to Peter, Bree and Dlop. "This is Peter, who climbed Mount Verdandi as if it was a hill, and on his shoulder is Pud, a brave knight who rests from his labors. Here also are his brothers, Bree and Dlop, great knights of valor and renown. That we should meet like this in such a time and place, gives me hope we can be friends."

"Bonjour, Mademoiselle," said Turgot. He bowed graciously for a crab. "You 'ave a courteous tongue for a Drog. It should serve you well in this wicked world. In fact, you remind me of my Marie, so bold and yet so beautiful."

"Hi," said Talat. His deep voice rumbled like a shower of stones. "I am Talat. It has been a long time since I have seen another Drog. If all Drogs, people I mean, were so courteous, I wouldn't be living in a cave."

Peter gazed at Talat with growing dislike.

"Where are you from, Talat?" he asked.

Talat's neck cracked like a whip as his black eyes bore down on Peter.

"Afghanistan."

"I knew it!" whispered Peter. "A terrorist!"

"Yes," hissed Talat coldly. "I come from a family of terrorists. My mother was terrorizing the kitchen with my younger brother when the bombs fell on their heads, and my father was terrorizing a mosque with his prayers when they shot him dead. Obviously, you are an American. Was it your father or brother who my family terrorized as I terrorize you now?"

Peter opened a jackknife. "As to that," he said, "you are not the only one who has lost a brother. One September day, not so long ago, my own brother watched a roof crash down upon his head. Yet, I do not fear you, Talat, and I wonder why, coming from such a noble family, you choose to live in a cave."

Turgot's beady eyes watched Peter's knife. "Armed and yet armed again," he muttered.

Talat stepped from behind the rock. In one of his massive hands there curved a scimitar at least three feet long. "As to my living in a cave," he said mockingly, "in my country, nobility is not measured by three car garages or gilded halls. No home will I call my own while my family's blood goes unavenged. For no home could ever hope to be warmed by such love, no room embraced in such joy, and no frame ever picture such sorrow."

"Please, Talat," said Rafi. She felt his pain from across the room. "Come down and tell us your story. Tell us of your family. And you, Turgot. Lay aside your differences with Krik, and tell us how you came to be part of a history, which others can only read."

Moved by Rafi's words or perhaps for reasons of his own, Talat descended from his hiding place with Turgot on his shoulder. And even as Krik whispered in Rafi's ear, Turgot whispered to Talat. Yet for all Talat and Turgot towered over Rafi and Krik, it was Rafi and Krik who radiated with power. Talat must have sensed it too, for he measured his steps as if approaching a queen. Standing no less proud, he bowed his shaggy head.

"You are kind," he said. His black eyes reached deep into Rafi's, where they seemed less harsh and cold. "Perhaps, when I know you better, I will tell you something of my family. For now," he added, "I will only say that, after they were murdered by his kind," his sword pointed at Peter, "I was adopted by a family in Drumheller. In their own way, they opened their hearts and home to me, but it was too late; the door to my heart and home had closed even as I closed the eyes of my family. Filled with such emptiness, I fled east until I reached these mountains. These I climbed, if only to look out upon this cruel world before throwing myself into a better one. But, just as I was about to see my family once again, a voice brought me to this place. Here I met Turgot who, at least, understands something of my grief."

Turgot nodded approvingly. "It is true," he said. "Both of us 'ave suffered much by the 'ands of oth'airs." His eyes bulged at Krik. "But, as they say in my country, misery loves company. And, may I ask, what misery brings you 'ere?"

"That, Turgot," said Krik quickly, "we cannot say. Moreover, as our meeting was unexpected, it must be short. We will leave you now for our destiny lies, not with acquaintances old and new, but with another whose home is no less empty than your own."

"So you say," said Turgot smoothly, "but I wond'air — when you find yourself deep in the mountain's eye and stand before nine passages, eight of which lead nowhere, and one, only one, which leads to the great hall of Erebus — which passage will you choose? And, if you are lucky enough to choose the right passage, who will guide you when left is no longer left and right is wrong? Tell me that, O Insufferable Mantis."

"You know the way to Erebus?" asked Krik doubtfully.

Talat ran his thumb across his blade where it dripped as red as the stalactites over his head. "He knows," he said. "I have journeyed far with him, as far as the river, and in places darker than the souls of men."

"No way!" cried Peter, sensing what was to happen. His eyes filled with horror. "This is one terrorist who is not going to lead us into a trap! Who would choose to live in a cave if he wasn't up to any good? They are devious beyond anything you can imagine.

Believe me, we Americans know something of the breed." His voice faltered as he brushed aside an unintended tear. "No more than I," he added proudly, "for I count my own brother among the dead. Krik, Rafi, don't do this!"

Rafi was appalled. "Peter!" she snapped angrily. "How can you judge someone you have only just met? However deep your anger and grief, surely it does not run so deep as to include everyone?"

"Who would choose to drive people from their homes and into caves unless they were up to no good?" shouted Talat.

Krik looked long and hard at Turgot.

"We have no choice, Peter," he said resignedly. "Turgot knows this. I do not know how much he knows, but it is clear to me that, without him, we risk getting lost in Erebus. I have journeyed with him before; he was always one for knowing the deepest and darkest paths. More importantly, he is the best tracker I have ever known. As for Talat, he is somehow bound in our quest, for good or for evil I cannot say."

Talat sheathed his sword. "And whether your quest is bound for evil or good, I cannot say."

"It's settled then," said Rafi. She threw her arms around Talat even as she encouraged Krik and Turgot to shake claws. "Alone, we stand alone. Together, we shall save the world."

"From whom I wonder?" muttered Bree. He turned to Dlop. "I don't trust these two. Especially Turgot. Keep your eyes on that one, brother."

"You speak for me also, Bree," said Peter quietly. "Keep your eyes and swords on both of them!"

Krik and Turgot released claws. It was only after Rafi stepped back that she noticed Krik had also released the hilts of his swords. "Lead on, Turgot," he said warily. "I only hope our trust is not misplaced in you, as much for your sake as our own."

"But, of course." Turgot's words slid from his mouth like butter. "Nev'air fear, my distrustful mantis. I will guide you to Erebus. You 'ave my word. I do not wish for a world where choice is measured by death or servitude. No, mon ami, even I, Turgot de Bois-Guilbert, would choose death ov'air the empty promises of Triodon. 'e is our common enemy, yes?"

No one replied.

"I see," Turgot went on as if interpreting their silence. "In your arrogance, you thought that you alone knew about Triodon. 'ow typical. Per'aps before you meet him, you will find that there is much already known that you do not know."

With these words, he led the Companions to the far side of the room. Behind some rocks, hung like shades upon the walls, three grave tunnels beckoned to places dark and unknown.

"Aha!" cried Turgot. "Three passages. One for yesterday, one for today and one for tomorrow. Only which do you choose? The left? The right? Today? Tomorrow? Myself, I do not choose. For to choose is death for all."

Without explaining these strange words, Turgot whispered to Talat. Much to everyone's surprise, Talat swept by not one, but all three passages, stopping only when he stood before a large slab of stone. He spit in his hands, squared his great shoulders and threw himself at the rock, pushing with all his might. For a moment, nothing happened. Then, to the sound of grinding stone, a black door slowly opened on the wall.

"Come, come!" cried Turgot. His eyes and claws beckoned madly. "So begins your quest. Where would you be now without your Turgot?" His words broke like glass diamonds upon the stone floor. "Who else but Turgot could 'elp? Who else but Turgot could lead you to your 'eart's desire?"

Without waiting for the others, Talat and Turgot descended into the passage. The Companions followed, Peter's warning still heavy in their hearts, each wondering what lay ahead even as they remembered the loved ones they had left behind. More than ever, they were glad of the crystal, which lifted some of the gloom in the passage as well as in their hearts.

"Will this take us to Erebus?" Rafi asked Talat.

"I don't know," he said, looking startled as if waking from a deep dream. "I have only been as far as the river."

"The river?"

"The River of Erebus," said Krik darkly. "The most loathsome of all rivers on and under Earth. I had forgotten about the river. Could it be?" His face suddenly grew darker than the tunnel, which seemed to close in around him. "Without a penny, what hope do we have?" He fell silent.

"Pennies I don't have," said Talat, "but if you are so minded to cross the river, gold and silver are everywhere down here." He scraped his sword against the rock, holding the blade high for Rafi to see. It glinted with flakes of gold. "Not that I think it will do you any good," he added. He glanced at Rafi, his eyes distant and impenetrable. "Once I saw him. A man on the river, if indeed it was a man and not a ghost. He pulled up to the riverbank in that crazy boat of his and waited as if he was expecting someone. But no one got on and no one got off. The stench of death was about him. I watched as long as I could and then fled back up the passage."

"Gold will not help us," said Krik, "for Styx – that is his name – will ferry only those who pay the toll."

"And if we don't pay the toll?" squeaked Dlop.

Krik did not answer.

They crept further down the passage. Even with the crystal, it was impossible not to bump heads on the many mischievous rocks that suddenly appeared out of nowhere, or fall down any one of the dark and seemingly endless holes that sprang up from the floor.

"I don't know which will get us into more trouble," said Bree. "Falling into one of these holes or following Turgot."

"Not much further," grunted Talat.

"And yet it is only the beginning," said Turgot. The cold flame in his eyes stalked Rafi and Krik. "It is not too late to turn back for those who do not wish to die."

"Think well of your words, Turgot," said Krik sharply. "Our feet are bound to one path that even you cannot lead astray. With or without you, we shall prevail."

"But, of course," Turgot said cheerfully. His voice did little to still the anger spilling from his eyes. "Those who live shall see."

Before anyone could digest the meaning of his words, the passage opened into a vast cavern, a thousand times the size of Talat's dreary cave. Even so, the crystal filled the cavern with a soft light. They gasped in wonder. Before them, a fleet of stalagmites rose from the floor, as large and tall as ships, sailing under masts of stone, which pointed to a ceiling swirled with gold, and studded with precious stones.

Peter was awestruck. "Sure beats Texas," he crowed.

Rafi pointed to a ribbon of darkness just beyond the stone ships. "The river!" she shouted.

Other than Talat and Turgot, no one had ever seen such a river before.

Bree spoke for all of them. "This is no river," he said. All the emotion had drained from his voice. "This is a nightmare from which one never wakes." He shuddered. "Death I have seen before, but now I feel the eyes of Death upon me."

"Styx knows we are here," said Krik. "He will be along any minute now. We can only hope he has heard of our quest, and will ferry us, penniless as we are, across the river."

As Krik spoke, a sudden chill settled in the air. Colder than the death of night, and more haunting than a last farewell, it gripped their already frozen senses right down to the marrow of their bones. Even Pud stirred in his sleep at the river's edge.

"Who died?" he asked, and then his head fell on Peter's shoulder.

"Look!" cried Rafi. Something blacker than the river was fast approaching the riverbank.

"Death is coming for us on a boat!" screeched Dlop.

"Death," said Talat grimly. "If only it was that simple."

The boat, if it could be called a boat, was unlike anything they had ever seen. Upon black tipped waves it came, a torrent of dread and shadow, changing size and shape as often as the waves upon which it sailed. In the back of the boat, hooded and cloaked, a tall figure skillfully punted across the river with a long white pole. More ghastly than the figure, ten bony white fingers gripped the pole.

"Be'old the 'ands of Death," said Turgot.

Krik bowed his head. "Styx."

Styx beached his boat. Eyes and spines locked in fear, the others could only gape at the ferryman, except Talat who saluted Styx with his sword. Then, in a motion as fluid and hair-raising as the river, Styx pointed a single finger at each of the Companions, as all light collapsed back into the crystal.

Death had indeed crossed the river.

CHAPTER SIXTEEN

THE BATTLE OF ZIGH

"**D**RUMHELLER AT WAR!" Headlines literally screamed across newspapers throughout the world. For once, even the tabloids agreed, adding, however, that Drumheller had declared war on no less than sixty-seven nations including the United States, Britain, France, Australia – and the Vatican.

Of course, none of this was true. In fact, while the outside world trembled between headlines, in Drumheller, the world's leaders were busily engaged in a bingo game at Town Hall.

"B – twenty-nine," pronounced the Pope.

"Bingo!" cried a hall full of hopeful heads.

The French President dropped pâté all over his bingo card. "Impossible!" he complained loudly to anyone who would listen. "'e 'as only called one numb'air!"

"What are they doing?" a bewildered bobcat asked an orangutan.

The orangutan daubed the number twenty-nine under each B on his bingo cards with red ink. "It's a Drog game," he said. His red pen singled out the Pope. "When the Drog with the funny hat calls out a number, you mark it on your bingo cards …"

"I – forty-seven," proclaimed the Pope.

"… and when you have five numbers in a row," continued the orangutan, "you call out 'Bingo!' and you win a prize."

"Bingo!"

At the same time, newspaper headlines were not completely untrue. Under the pretence of protecting Drumheller and the world's leaders gathered at Town Hall, The Mayor had mustered the army on the eastern front of town, where it had been rumored by a barn owl that an attack was imminent. While exact details were scarce as to who or what was attacking, and why, the armies of seven different nations including Canada and the United States were surprisingly supportive, thinking that a joint military exercise might ease the growing tension amongst the troops.

Under tents, and fitted with portable air conditioners, both equipment and troops dug in under the blistering heat as anyone over the rank of sergeant lunched on sushi at the Travelers' Nest. Having been promoted to temporary field commander, Sergeant Strigil reviewed the battlefield through a pair of binoculars. By his side, smartly dressed in army fatigues, The Mayor read out a list of armaments from his little black book.

"Artillery?"

"Fifty-four."

"Tanks?"

"Sixty-two."

"Bombers?"

"Nine."

"Gun ships?"

"Fifteen."

"Missiles?"

"Forty-one."

"Troops?"

The sergeant smiled grimly. "More than we'll ever need."

"Excellent!" The Mayor slapped shut his little black book. Even without his sash and top hat, he looked more imposing than ever, having swelled to almost twice his normal size being, as it turned out, allergic to bees. "Drog, is it?" His beady eyes surveyed a mass of tanks and artillery. "Let's see what stings, knitting needles and perfumed behinds make of that ..."

"Sergeant!" Unflappable in salute and air conditioner, Corporal Flitch handed the sergeant a coded message.

"Problem?" asked The Mayor.

Sergeant Strigil focused his binoculars. "Sector Alpha 9 has reported contact with the enemy."

"Fire!" screamed The Mayor.

"Hold your fire," the sergeant barked into a walkie-talkie. "I see it now." He handed the binoculars to Corporal Flitch. "Probably a badger ..."

"Fire!" screamed The Mayor.

"All positions hold your fire," the sergeant blasted into the walkie-talkie. He glared at The Mayor. "Corporal, remove this civilian from the War Theater ..."

Corporal Flitch handed the sergeant a second message.

The sergeant scooped up his walkie-talkie. "Alpha 9, this is Base Command. State your situation. Over."

The walkie-talkie squawked its reply. "Base Command." Squawk. "This is Alpha 9." Squawk. "Enemy has demanded safe conduct into Drumheller."

"Denied!" barked Sergeant Strigil.

"Uh ... sir" squawked the walkie-talkie, "perhaps we should reconsider ..."

"Fire!" screamed The Mayor.

"Denied!" barked the sergeant. "Alpha 9, what is enemy position?"

The walkie-talkie hesitated before replying.

"Alpha 9?"

"Sir," squawked Alpha 9. "Enemy position is sitting on my tank." Squawk. "He's demanding our complete," squawk "and unconditional surrender, sir."

"He?"

Squawk (gasp). "Base Command, we are under fire. Do you copy?" Squawk. "Repeat. We are under fire (gasp). Gas attack ..."

The walkie-talkie went dead.

"Alpha 9?"

"Fire!" screamed The Mayor.

"Fire!" screamed Sergeant Strigil.

"Fire!" screamed every tank, artillery, bomber, gunship and missile commander.

To anyone lunching at the Travelers' Nest, it seemed as if Fireworks Day had come early. For ten minutes, every bomb, bazooka, barrel and bullet pummeled the badlands outside of Drumheller. 'Bad' could not even begin to describe it. The crater caused by the shelling was enormous, and has since revealed so many new dinosaur remains that only public outcry prevented the provincial government from turning it into a lake.

Sergeant Strigil raised his binoculars.

"What the?"

"Incoming!" roared Corporal Flitch.

The Mayor staggered against a table. "Is that ..."

Before the Sergeant or Corporal could respond, they had already passed it.

"Gas!"

The foul wind blowing in from the east was nothing compared to what happened next. Suddenly, the sky went black as an endless barrage of dung balls pelted every tent, tank and soldier until the War Theater was a struggling mass of dung. Generously filled with dung, gas masks only made it worse. In the Travelers' Nest, even the sushi had turned to dung.

However, dung was not the only bombardment raining down on Drumheller. Tanks, artillery, gun ships and jeeps flew through the air like leaves, crashing down upon one another like pieces of an unknown puzzle dropped from the sky.

Based on experience, The Mayor lost no time deserting his post. He was almost half way up to the Travelers' Nest when an airborne tank fell on his toe. As you can well imagine, his screams only added to the dungy carnage unfolding below.

Under a soiled flag, and only half finished with their lunches, the generals had no choice but to surrender.

Infuriated over losing a tooth to a gunship, Zigh was in no mood for friendly terms. "Next time pick on someone your own size," he growled.

"There, there," said the Dung Beetle, consoling each General with a conciliatory gift of dung balls. Not content with polluting the War Theater, the Dung Beetle lit up one of its dung cigars. "No harm done. Perhaps, Zigh, now that the landscape has been redecorated more to my liking, we should visit more often."

"Wouldn't that be a treat," growled Zigh.

The American general pointed enviously at the Dung Beetle's cigar.

"Cuban …?"

So ended The Battle of Zigh (as chronicled by the press). Such was the complete and utter devastation of the army that, to this day, foreign powers bent on destroying Earth can lease the badlands for military exercises, complete with soiled artillery and tanks, in exchange for helping to bury the world's largest latrine. For nowhere else on Earth can fighting men and women relive the realities of war with such personal conveniences followed by such a superb lunch.

Flush(ed) with victory (in more ways than one), Zigh and the Dung Beetle left the generals to clean up the mess and headed into town where they had a dinner date with the Malawis and a not-so-unexpected guest.

CHAPTER SEVENTEEN

DRAIG

Styx pointed to a clay pot in the bow of the boat. Inside, black with age, lay a single penny. Out of the growing darkness, which seemed to pour from the ferryman himself, a bony arm pointed to the far side of the river.

"'e wants 'is monnaie," said Turgot. He threw two pennies in the penny pot. "Once again, mantis," he crowed triumphantly, "I 'ave what you want. Per'aps, if you scrabble in the dirt one thousand years, you might find a penny for yourself." Bitter waves of laughter broke upon the shore. "Then we shall meet again on the oth'air side." His smile twisted ominously. "Although, I 'ave a feeling that, aft'air tonight, you won't be meeting anyone again. Come, Talat."

Talat did not move. Instead, his hawk like gaze pounced on Rafi's face, wrestling its way through the darkness and into her eyes as if to look upon and within her deepest thoughts. In turn, he gazed no less intrusively, eye to eye, heart to heart, into each Companion. A full minute had passed before he finally released Peter from his gaze.

"I'm not going without them," he said.

Turgot looked furious. "Not going?" he cried, his shell almost exploding with rage. "Not going, you fool?" One of his claws fell dangerously close to Talat's throat. "I, Turgot de Bois-Guilbert, command it! Get into the boat before I lose my monnaie!"

"No," said Talat stiffly. With lightning speed, he gripped Turgot's claw in his powerful hand, cracking it like a shell at a dinner table. "You are not my father. Orders I take only from him." His piercing gaze fell once again on the Companions. "And my father says that death waits on the far side of the river. Nevertheless, I shall cross it, for death at the hands of an enemy is nobler than treachery at the claws of a friend." He looked back at Turgot. "But, I will only go when the pot is full of pennies."

"But I 'aven't got any more monnaie!" screamed Turgot. Spit and bits of shell flew into the penny pot. "What are these Drogs and traitors and rats to you? Where were they when you cried yourself to sleep at night?"

"I do not know," said Talat darkly, "but if we all scrabble in the dirt, perhaps it will take only a hundred years to buy our passage across the river."

"Once again, Turgot," said Krik quietly, "you have what I never want."

"Bah!" Turgot sprang from Talat's shoulder, landing in the bow of the boat next to the penny pot. "So ends your quest, mantis. Too bad the fools who chose you to save the world will not live to regret their decision. Ha, ha." He glanced up at Styx who was still pointing across the river. With a magician's skill, he reclaimed a penny, hiding it in his shell.

Having had enough of Turgot, Krik appealed directly to Styx.

"Styx," he said, "Master of the River, Ferryman of the Dead, we, the Companions of Earth, beseech you to grant us safe passage into Erebus. Pennies we do not have, but if you know anything of our quest, you know it cannot be bought or sold, neither for a penny nor for all the riches on Earth. Yet, should we fail, I fear your boat, however enduring, will sink forever beneath the ponderous waves of so many souls. Nay, I foresee even a pot full of pennies will not bring you comfort in the world ahead. And so I ask, indeed I beg, on behalf of all souls, living and dead, that you grant us this request."

Styx did not reply, but the darkness around him grew. For a moment, the shrouded face seemed to gaze upon Krik, not with eyes, but with the dread judgment of death. Yet in death there loomed a thousand unseen eyes as the finger pointed once more to the penny pot.

"He won't let us cross," said Bree bitterly. "All this way for nothing. Poor Pud."

"Ha!" Turgot fairly danced in his triumph, his claws snapping like castanets. "So much for Krik the prophet; so much for Krik the ambassador; so much for Krik the fool! 'e who would bargain with the living, but cannot sway the dead. Imbecile, why not throw yourself into the river and save this bag of bones the trouble of ferrying you across!"

Before Krik could answer, Styx turned his black face toward Turgot. Though the specter never moved nor spoke, Turgot leapt backwards as if he had been struck an awful blow. White with fear, the crab's head, eyes, legs, and claws retreated into his shell even as a penny flew out from the shell, landing in the penny pot.

"That should shut him up for awhile," said Bree.

"So much for Turdo duh blah full of hot air," said Dlop.

"Insults are of no use here," said Krik. "What we need right now is clear thinking. I was foolish to think that Styx could be swayed from his due. Any suggestions?"

"Could we swim across?" asked Peter doubtfully.

"I said clear thinking," said Krik irritably. "To even touch the water is death, a death more agonizing and everlasting than you can possibly imagine. Do not speak of such things – especially in front of Styx. Even now, he reads our thoughts. No, there is no other way."

"Then why," demanded Peter, irritated in his turn, "did you bring us to this accursed place?" He picked up a stone. He was about to throw it in the river when a chill sprang up his spine, electrifying his limbs. Sheer panic drained the color from his cheeks. Styx's bony finger was pointed at his face.

"Eh?" Peter cried. He had never felt more alone. "What does he want now? I haven't got any pennies." Frantic, he showed his empty pockets to Styx.

"Styx is pointing at Pud," said Krik. He looked down at Bree and Dlop with sympathetic eyes. "Things are worse than I feared.

He is claiming him, for all dead souls must cross the river. While Turgot never intended it, his penny has bought passage for Pud at least."

"But Pud's not dead!" Dlop's wails were enough to wake the dead. Great tears fell from his eyes, each a thousand times more moving than the river. "He can't be dead! Are you, Pud?" He looked up at Pud who lay, eyes closed, like a sack of corn on Peter's shoulder.

"Don't leave us, Pud!"

Rafi hugged Dlop.

"Don't cry, Dlop," she said through her own tears. "Somehow my heart tells me that Pud is not ready to cross the river. Not with the dead at least. And, until he is ready, no power – not even Styx himself – can claim him. In a world so full of miracles, together we shall pray for one more."

She turned to face Styx, but the ferryman had already departed, accompanied by Turgot. With a heavy heart, she watched the ferryman's fingers and pole swirl against the black light until they too were consumed by the river's gloom. Her only comfort was the crystal, which began to shine only seconds after Styx's boat had left the shore.

"Turgot was right," said Krik miserably. "I was a fool to think I could reason with the dead. Here I am trying to teach you how to become an ambassador and all I have done is fail my people, Earth, and now you."

"Nonsense, Krik," said Rafi. "There is no such thing as failure and you know it. At worst, we can only try. That in itself is a miracle. After that, we must leave miracles to other hands. And may I say, mantis, where I come from, your worst is better than best. No one else could have got us to the river. And I, for one, am going to cross it shoulder to shoulder with Earth's greatest ambassador – you."

And with that, Rafi turned to the river and began to sing.

"If I had a penny for each flower 'neath the sun,
For each warm smile they smile at me when all good deeds are done,
I'd have a pot of pennies, crimson towers in the sky,
Forever set, to pay my debts, while never knowing why.

If I had a penny for every song and story told,
Of timeless myths and legends, of ancient heroes bold,
I'd have a pot of pennies deeper than the restless sea,
To meet all ends, look after friends, yet never to be free.

If I had a penny for each thought, in silence bound,
Clipped of wings in ridicule, conversations never found,
I'd have a pot of pennies, weary faces worn of words,
Never spent, not saved nor lent, no interest incurred.

If I had a penny for every star that shines at night,
Distant worlds of wonder, wondering what makes them bright,
I'd have a pot of pennies, poppies red, in fields unknown,
Light lost, unspent, in what we meant, without, to each we own.

If I had a penny for each frown and flag unfurled,
Launched in words of anger, aimless insults hurled,
I'd have a pot of pennies, petaled soldiers, armies tall,
To grace all trees with penny leaves yet not prevent their fall.

If I had a penny for every sign, embrace or tongue,
Unending spokes of language, dialect or sum,
I'd have a pot of pennies, in meaning all the same,
A copper 'could' instead of should, but who is there to blame?

If I had a penny for each call from God above,
Put on hold or waiting, lost in disconnected love,
I'd have a pot of pennies, dearly paid, yet always free,
A guided call to one and all, words dialed in destiny.

But if I had one penny, I would give it all to you,
For any smile is worth ten miles in anybody's shoes,
And then I'd have no penny, nor a pot to put it in,
But I would be the richest me without one cent of sin."

And so, Rafi's song floated on and in the river. Lifted by her song and indomitable spirit, the crystal joined her, singing in growing brightness as both light and words floated into their hearts and into the river. Stirred to depths beyond even Styx's pole, moved beyond pain and sorrow, the river rocked and rolled on Rafi's song.

"Do I hear drumming?" asked Dlop.

Peter pointed over their heads. "Look!"

"I don't believe it," said Bree.

"Leave miracles to other hands," said Krik. His face shone as bright as the crystal. "Rafi, you did it! You are our miracle."

From the mist sprang Styx and his boat. Across the river he sailed, faster than before, and they wondered at his strokes for they would have seemed almost happy had the hands of Death not made them. Expertly, he landed the boat next to their feet by the shore. Then, in a majestic sweep of cloak and bone, Styx invited them in.

"Thank you, Styx," said Rafi. Awed by her own miracle, and the unprecedented privilege of taking Styx's hand, she stepped into the boat.

Krik pointed astern. In the back of the boat was a set of drums. "There's your miracle, Rafi," he said. "Death is a drummer. You gave Styx the one thing he valued more than a penny – music."

Bree bowed before Styx. "Charmed, I'm sure," he said. Deliberately, he sat upon Turgot who still lay hiding in his shell. "Looks like no one's home," he said innocently.

Dlop's sword rang the crab's shell like a doorbell. "Although," he said, imitating Turgot, "I 'ave a feeling that, aft'air tonight, 'e won't be meeting anyone again."

Escorted by Styx, Rafi sat down between Peter and Talat. She sighed. Taut as bowstrings, both boys sat like bookends pushed apart by too many dark covered books no one cared to read.

She looked awkwardly at the deck rolling like waves beneath her feet. "Strange," she said, "I feel as if I am sitting in water, as if the boat is part of the river."

"And not just the boat," said Krik. He looked up from his telescope through which he had been studying Styx. "Styx isn't master of the river. He is the river."

Krik was right. What had looked like cloth and bone only moments before now swished with the rush and ripple of the river as Styx and his pole pushed the boat away from shore.

Peter peered over the side of the boat. "I can't see my reflection in the water," he said.

"That is because we have crossed into Erebus," said Krik. "Here, there are no reflections. No shadows. Only that which is truly you walks in Erebus, for what you have seen of yourself in the light, in front of mirrors and crowded rooms, remains above. Here, you exist only as you see yourself, as if in a darkened room."

Styx landed his boat on the opposite shore. Terrified at the prospect of what might lay ahead, it was some time before anyone stepped out of the boat. However, in the end, it was Rafi, accompanied by Krik, who first set foot on the black shores of Erebus.

As the others slowly disembarked, Rafi pulled a ring from her finger and laid it in the penny pot. Alerted by the clink of metal on clay, Turgot's head and legs shot out of his shell. He wasted no time in using them. Clicking like a keyboard gone mad he ran past the others, and did not stop until he was a good fifty yards from Styx.

Rafi bowed before Styx. "Master of the River," she said. "Please accept this ring. One day I will bring you two pennies, but until then, let this ring be a token of our friendship and our trip together on the river. And with this ring I also give you my love, for without love, I fear that even Death will eventually lose its meaning."

Styx picked up the ring and slid it on his finger. For a moment, the river seemed less dark and foreboding. Then, with a sweep of his robes and a push of his pole, the boat shot from the riverbank and into the river. The boat was barely on its way when, amidst a strange, bone chilling sound, it slowly slipped beneath the black waves along with Styx.

Styx was singing.

"Goodbye, Styx," Rafi called after the ferryman, "I hope we meet again …"

Appalled, everyone glanced at Rafi.

"Oops," she said sheepishly. "I only meant …"

Turgot popped out of his shell. "Au revoir, bone'ead," he said. Delighted to be rid of Styx, he clicked back to the Companions.

"Such bravery in the face of Death," muttered Bree.

"And why not?" spat Turgot. He seemed to have no memory of what had transpired on the riverbank. His eyes swelled into a grin as his claws opened in friendship. "Mes amis," he crowed in friendly falsetto, "'ere we are, togeth'air again. How you say? Peas in a pod. And what bett'air pea than Turgot, your friend and ev'air faithful guide?"

"What bett'air flea you mean," said Bree. A cloud of disgust passed over his face. "Only a river ago you sold us out." He looked incredulously at Krik. "Surely we're not going to listen to this crustaceous cheat?" He eyed the fleshy part of Turgot's throat even as his sword rang by his side.

Krik looked down at Turgot. "Trust?" he asked. "No, Bree. Yet there is more use in Turgot than you know. Like a flea, he is more comfortable in darkness than light, and no one knows the foul places of Earth and Sea better than he. No, trust him we shall not, but even so, he shall be our guide."

"Certainement," said Turgot. His voice waxed smoother than his shell, which, now that Styx was gone, piqued a rosy red. "These places I know like the inside of my shell. Yet to me they do not seem so foul, mantis. But then, that was always our difference, non?"

Krik's gaze almost bore a hole through Turgot. "Swear to us," he said, "that you shall guide us faithfully to Triodon without deceit. And do not swear on your mother's grave as you did back in

Germania. I happen to know she is still alive and well in Bali."

"A misunderstanding, distrustful mantis," said Turgot. His rosy red simmered a bright orange. "On my Marie I swear I shall lead you faithfully to Triodon."

Bree rolled his eyes. "That's good enough for me."

"We are wasting time," said Krik. "On the subject of trust, that is as much as we will get from Turgot." He peered into the darkness looming beyond the shore. "Lead on, Turgot," he said. "And, for your own sake, do not play us false or we will be having crab's legs for dinner."

"Crab's legs with salt and butter," said Dlop, moaning.

"Talat," said Turgot airily, "give an old friend a warm shoulder so the way is not so lonely. My short legs are many, but no match for the ones of these Drogs."

"My shoulder and friendship you had," said Tatat grimly, "right up to the river. But they are not so easily bought as was your passage across the river. Think well before you betray us again." He picked up Dlop who now lay asleep beside Bree, perching him on his shoulder. Knight that he was, Dlop awoke, driving his sword straight through Talat's cheek before realizing his error. Chuckling, Talat pulled the bloodied blade from his cheek, and handed it back to Dlop.

"Us?" hissed Peter. He glared at Talat. "Where did you get us? Terrorist. You're no more trustworthy than Turgot."

Before Talat could answer, Rafi stepped between them, both staff and crystal upraised in her hands. Joined in light yet divided by the staff, the two boys' faces raged into one mask of blood, hate, and fury.

"Us," she said firmly. As if by magic, the mask melted back into two handsome faces that, in other times and places might have been friends. "Companions all. Gathered together with one purpose – to save the world. But in order to save the world we must first save ourselves. As for me, I can only pledge by this staff, given to me by the Oracle, that I will not fail you. All I ask is that you do not fail each other."

Despite his short legs, Turgot led them at a furious pace deeper into the gloom. Gone now were the stalactites and stalagmites that watched from above and below, gone were the swirls of sparkling dust and stones that had hung above their heads like a jeweled heaven cast up into the sky. Now, only darkness remained, a shapeless void of unseen walls and distance, more terrifying than a cemetery of open graves.

Talat had better eyes for the dark. "Something's up ahead," he grunted.

"I see it," said Krik.

"See what?" said Peter, squinting.

"I see it too," said Rafi. She held the crystal high above her head. Not far away, nine dark holes, each a phantom within a greater abyss looked out from an appalling face cut deep into the rock.

"Nine passages," scoffed Turgot, "and only seven of you. Even with your trusted Turgot, you could not 'ope to discov'air the mountain's secret as I 'ave done through a lifetime of misery in dark places." Ahead of the others, but still within range of the crystal, his eyes twirled lighthouses of approaching doom.

"Get on with it, Turgot," said Krik.

"Unless, of course, you don't know," scoffed Dlop.

"Know?" Turgot howled like a wounded dog. "Careful, mon ami, or it will be Turgot who will be 'aving rat's legs for dinn'air. Maybe with a pinch of salt and butt'air." He clicked with unnerving precision until he stood beneath the dark face, his eyes oddly luminous in the light of the crystal.

"Let me see," he muttered as if talking to himself. "Left is left and right is right and nev'air the twain shall meet ..."

"That's plagiarism," hissed Bree indignantly. "He stole that from a poem."

"Only," continued Turgot, "when right is right and each is long, what is left when right is wrong? Tell me, mantis, do you know?"

Krik did not answer.

Turgot swelled with pride. "Of course, you don't know," he

said. "But Turgot knows, and that is why you 'ate 'im. For knowing that which you shall nev'air know." His shell deflated a little. "Poor Turgot. Always 'ated, nev'air understood." He glared at Krik as some of the hardness cracked back into his shell. "But understand this, mantis. Follow me now, and I shall lead you to Triodon, and more besides."

"It's the more that worries me," squeaked Dlop.

With a wicked laugh, Turgot plunged into the third passage from the left.

"Left, left, left!" he screamed, almost insane in his excitement, the click of his legs echoing tenfold as he made his way further down the passage. "Left is our friend in the darkness, when right is left to chance."

"Tell me, Krik," whispered Rafi, peering after Turgot. "What is it between you and Turgot?"

"Yes," added Bree who, along with the others, was having serious doubts about Turgot. "What's all this business about Louis and Marie?"

Krik shook his head warningly. "This is neither the time nor place for such discussion," he said quietly. "Aside from reopening old wounds with Turgot, I too carry the scars that wounded so many during such dark and turbulent times." His eyes grew darker than the tunnel. "It was in France during the French Revolution when I found myself opposed to Turgot as to the fate of their king, Louis XVI, his wife Marie Antoinette and their son the Dauphin. Working secretly with the king, I tried to negotiate a compromise with the revolutionaries but Turgot, once the King's most trusted advisor, but having been slighted by the Queen, further diseased already ambitious minds, which ultimately resulted in the deaths of the royal family. It is my belief that Turgot, in his own way, was in love with Marie, but like Triodon, discovered only too late that vengeance is a bitter substitute for love."

As Krik would say nothing more, they scrambled into the passage after Turgot. Not as far down the passage as they might have suspected, Turgot was more than a little annoyed at the delay.

"Keep your secrets," he hissed disapprovingly at Krik. "As you should know by now mantis, secrets can nev'air be truly kept until all but one is dead." He laughed. "Per'aps Turgot 'as a secret or two 'imself."

Whatever Turgot's secrets, the passage revealed some of its own. Every few feet competing passages crossed and tangled with their own so that, before long, the Companions had no idea as to where they were or where they were going. During a brief rest even Bree had to admit that Turgot made a fair guide, 'providing,' as he had said, 'he isn't leading us to an awful death.' In the end, however, it was always Turgot who sorted out the tangle, leading them by secret ways deeper and deeper into the mountain. Here and there, he would stop and 'listen to the air' as he said, while his eyes spun on knotted cords, looking deeper into dark places no one but he had ever dared to look before.

"Dieu merci," he muttered each time he pried his eyes away from the darkness. "Clos'air we are, mes amis. Clos'air we are." Closer to what he would not say.

"Is it just me," asked Rafi, "or is the crystal getting darker?"

"I was just wondering that myself ..." Krik began.

Suddenly, all light left the tunnel.

"The crystal!"

"Silence," Turgot whispered through the dark. His clicks were now fewer and far between. Holding their breath and onto each other, the Companions followed, trusting only to a soft hissing further down the tunnel, which they knew to be Turgot.

"Yes, yes," he hissed. "This way, mes amis. That is, if you are not afraid."

They breathed a sigh of relief when Turgot's voice hissed only inches away. Suddenly, they became aware of a heavy breathing sound synchronous to an unsettling pulse of blue flame. Drawing closer, they looked through a doorway cut into the rock, and into a chamber of pulsing gloom.

"Be'old the Third Level of Erebus," Turgot said quietly. "For it is 'ere the first Guardian awaits." Between pulses of blue light, Rafi saw Turgot give her a withering look. "Drog," he said, "I 'ope you 'ave more magic than my Marie. For, against the 'ydra, there is no escape."

"What did he say?" squeaked Dlop.

"The Hydra," Krik repeated slowly. No one needed the pulsing light to sense the look of anxiety upon his face. He looked pensively at the flame. "Now I understand something of the tales of old," he said. "Of all the foul creatures ever to walk Earth, few are as foul as what we are about to meet in that room."

"Perhaps we should come back later," squeaked Dlop. He climbed up Talat's head to get as far away from the chamber as he could. "Maybe in a hundred years ..."

"You are forgetting," said Rafi, too afraid to ask what could be more foul than a T-Rex, "if we don't pass the Hydra, there is no later."

"Which brings me to a question," said Peter. He grabbed Pud just in time to prevent him from sliding off his shoulder. "What is a Hydra?"

"Me!" Wreathed in flame, a voice as horrible as anything they could have ever imagined echoed down the tunnel.

"Me. Me. Me. Me. Me. Me. Me. Me."

The dreadful chorus rose and fell between spurts of flame.

"Come," the voice continued mockingly. "Neither fear nor bravery can save you now. Do not be afraid." Each word wreathed the doorway in flame. "I would, at least, like to know your names before I strike. Come." No longer welcoming, the last word sounded like a command. "Though you may not know it, I have already honored your presence as you should honor mine for I have never bothered with names before." A cruel laugh shook the chamber. "But in your case, I shall make an exception." Suddenly, the voice grew harsher than stone. "Do not try my patience. Come out from your hole for I wish to see those who would dare face the Hydra."

Rafi leaned her staff against the wall. "Join hands," she said quickly.

"Join 'ands?" Turgot spat incredulously. "What madness is this? Marie, I must protest."

"Magic," said Bree, catching on to Rafi's plan even as she picked him up and placed him on her shoulder next to Krik.

She nodded at Peter to do the same with Turgot.

None too kindly, Peter slapped the still protesting Turgot on his shoulder opposite Pud. Then, with a look of utter contempt on his face, he held out his hand to Talat. As for Talat, he appeared to be considering whether to take Peter's hand or cut if off with his sword. It was only after Rafi gave both boys a sharp look that they buried their fury into a handshake instead of each other.

Then, to the howls of Turgot, the Companions disappeared from sight.

"Mon Dieu," said Turgot, who had not lost his wits along with his nerve. His eyes fixed greedily on the scepter in Rafi's hands. "Magic and yet not magic," he muttered to himself. "Marie and yet not Marie."

"Careful, Rafi," Krik whispered in her ear. "Do not stray too far inside the chamber. The Hydra has powers beyond anything in our world. Above all, beware of its tongue. Trust nothing it says."

Krik's warning did little to boost her confidence.

Terrified, she stepped into the chamber.

The chamber was unlike anything they had expected. Hewn out of solid rock, it was as large and magnificent as any temple. Great stone columns joined the floor and ceiling, which, along with the walls, were as smooth as polished glass. A little further on lay a great hill, which could only be described, as Dlop had said, as 'a sparkling darkness' until a burst of flame shot over their heads, revealing the hill for what it was – a king's ransom in gold and jewels. Behind this priceless hoard lay yet another hill, larger and darker than the first, and without the sparkling. Upon this hill sat, what appeared to be nine thrones.

"Help yourselves," said the voice encouragingly. "For tonight, at least, you shall be the richest creatures on Earth." Suddenly, as if alive, the thrones rose mysteriously into the air, and began to weave a strangely hypnotic dance.

"If I wasn't dreaming," said Bree, "I'd say those thrones were …"

"The 'eads of the 'ydra," said Turgot.

"Nine of them to be exact," said Krik.

"Don't be exact," squeaked Dlop.

Nine bursts of flame singed their heads, melting rocks and pillars into lumps of molten glass.

"OK, nine," squeaked Dlop.

"Whatever happens," Rafi whispered to the others, "don't let go. As long as we stay invisible, we may have a chance."

"I can't let go," Dlop added unnecessarily.

In all of the years Rafi had studied dinosaurs with her father, nothing could have prepared her for the Hydra. It was massive, beyond any scale or imagination of dinosaurs, or indeed, of any creature that swam, flew, or walked upon the earth. In terror, she watched the nine heads weave their deadly dance upon necks as long as a tree, and thicker than any forest. Then, just as she was debating whether to throw down the scepter and plead for mercy, or run for her life, the hill moved, revealing a body in shape like a dog's, but so large the chamber suddenly seemed smaller than a broom closet. Six legs, each the size of an elephant thundered across the floor, scattering treasure in every direction. Above such calamity, two jewel-encrusted wings filled what was left of the chamber as a barbed tail, shaking like a giant fist, pounded walls of solid granite into dust.

But it was not the Hydra's body that filled Rafi with terror. Unable to help herself, she gazed horrified at each head as if she was the tiniest fly caught in the greatest of spiders' webs. One head alone would have set entire worlds into panic, and there she stood facing nine of them, each armed with a pair of curved horns that could have skewered a herd of buffalo. Below the horns, nostrils flared, filling the air with a noxious fume made worse by a mouth so cruel it was hard to notice the escaping bursts of scorching flame. But such terrors were nothing compared to the Hydra's eyes, each its own chamber of horror, as large as a crescent moon, and as hard and red as the giant rubies strewn upon the floor.

"Snakes!" Rafi gasped as smoke and fumes filled her lungs. "It had to be snakes."

"Bats!" squeaked Dlop, "it had to be bats."

"Goodness me," said the middle head. Being in the middle it appeared to speak for the others. "Three Drogs, three … er … two rats, and a cricket. Yes, yes," the head went on carelessly, "I can see all of you as clear as noonday, although I must confess I haven't seen one of those since I came from the egg. However, in spite of the fact that I am going to eat you, I am pleased to meet your acquaintance. I am Draig, daughter of Druella, the First Guardian of Erebus."

"Perhaps you could make an exception," said Bree.

"We won't tell anyone," said Dlop hopefully. "Honest."

"Now, now, my brave little rats," continued the middle head as the other heads fumed in anger, "exceptions become rules and you know it. No, eat you I must, but surely this is not the way to greet your host. Are there none but rats who would speak for your party?"

"Some party," said Dlop.

"Draig …" began Rafi and Krik.

"Let the Drog speak," said Draig superciliously, "I do not speak with rats and crickets."

"Mantis," corrected Krik.

"Draig," said Rafi, wondering if she had left her heart back in the passage along with her staff, "Daughter of Druella, First Guardian of Erebus, greetings! Honored are we, the Companions of Earth, to meet your esteemed calamity."

"Good, good, Rafi," Krik whispered in her ear. "I have heard Hydras like that kind of talk. They're like dragons so you might want to try a riddle …"

A blast of flame shot over Rafi's head almost taking Krik and Bree along for the ride.

"They do not," said the middle head emphatically, whose ears were evidently as good as its eyes. "Although I do like a good riddle from time to time …"

"Which reminds me," said the head on the far left, "did you hear the one about the …"

"Shut up," snapped the middle head, "or I'll riddle your head with more than foolish words!"

"Hey, you can't talk to me,

        me,

            me,

                me,

                    me,

                        me,

                            me,

                                me

like that," fumed the other heads.

One look from the middle head appeared to be enough to put the other heads in order. "As for dragons," Draig continued loftily, "they are nothing like us. For starters, we are three times stronger …"

"Fourteen times braver …" said the head on the right.

"Fifteen times smarter …" said the head on the left.

"Nine times deadlier …" said a head whose neck was so entangled with the other heads it was hard to tell which head it was. "Why, our venom is so deadly it flows through lance, sword, or shield as easily as skin and bone, killing the bearer instantly. Nothing can survive one touch of our venom …"

"Shut up," fumed the middle head. "I think they get the picture." Quite deliberately, Draig's eyes singled out Talat. "And in case you get any other ideas with that sword, you should know that, even if you succeeded in cutting off one of our heads, two will grow in its place …"

"… making us twenty-six times …"

"Give it a rest," hissed the middle head.

Draig sat smugly on her haunches. "And if that isn't enough to make your last thoughts unpleasant, you should also know that one of my heads is immortal. Had you a thousand swords and as many warriors at your disposal, you would never dispose of me. Indeed, there is no power on Earth that can harm me, neither sword nor scepter, weapons of mass destruction …"

"Did she say …" began Peter.

"Except our own venom," put in the tangled head.

"It all seems so right and fitting," said Rafi, not knowing how the words formed upon her lips, "that Draig, Daughter of Druella, is as immortal as the sun that lights the sky. Truly, O Draig, of all the miracles I have seen, you are the most miraculous. Who else but an immortal could be blinded by such wealth, and yet see through the power of the scepter as if it was a toy?"

"Er … yes," said Draig, trying to work out the compliment. "And no doubt you thought to catch me napping and relieve me of some of it."

"Nothing, O Draig," said Rafi, formulating a plan, "could be further from the truth. In fact, we come, not to steal, but to contribute."

"Really?" scoffed Draig, her ruby eyes wide with greed. "Not that I wouldn't welcome some salt for my meal, but I doubt you have anything worthy of my treasury."

"Not even this?" said Rafi. Without explaining a word to the others, she handed the scepter to Peter. Before anyone could protest, she stepped forward, instantly becoming visible along with Krik and Bree. In a movement faster than the serpent's greed, she opened her knapsack, pulled out the gold and silver crown, and held it high above her head for all of Draig's greedy eyes to see.

"Surely," she said, turning the crown to reveal every aspect of its magnificence, "not even your treasury would refuse a magnificent crown set with nine black diamonds, and a ruby, the like of which could only be matched by your eyes."

All heads drooled greedily. "Mine!"

"Yours," affirmed Rafi, "if you let us live."

Draig laughed loud and long. "Well, well," she said. "If this isn't the nicest conversation I've had in a millennium of Sundays. And gifts too. Only, I would have thought you had better manners than that. A gift is only a gift if the giver seeks nothing in return." Draig's eyes narrowed into blades of flame. "What is your name, little one? When I look upon your bones from time to time I should like to remember them with a name."

Rafi lifted her head proudly. "I am Rafi, Daughter of Amos and Myra Malawi, Companion of Earth. These are my friends …"

"Those were your friends," said Draig, pleased at the conversation, but knowing that all good things must soon come to an end. "Yet, I should like to return your gift, for though bravery is a foolish and pointless act, it must be honored with a gift. Give me the crown, and I promise to eat you last. Amusement for me, a longer life for you."

"Where have we heard that before?" muttered Bree.

Rafi stepped forward as if she liked the idea. "That seems only fair," she said.

"Really, my dear," said Draig, visibly impressed, "you are a brave little Drog. And I see you have a letter in your hair. B for brave, I shouldn't doubt." Draig's voice dripped with sarcasm. "But know this, little B. One letter does not make an alphabet. Many have stood where you stand now and could not find a single word until I showed them the only way out of my realm." Draig opened all nine of her mouths, flashing an army of fangs that made Talat's sword look like a pin. "Others tried to run back up the passageway only to wish they had saved themselves the trouble." One of Draig's heads belched a jet of flame into the tunnel where it glowed red-hot.

Rafi lifted the crown higher. "Certainly, O Draig," she said, "I know escape is impossible. Only," she paused as if in doubt, "on whose head shall I place the crown? While it is clear to me that all nine of your heads are equally deserving of such tribute, the fact remains that there is only one crown."

"Easy, easy," hissed Draig's middle head. "Since I do most of the talking around here, I shall wear the crown."

"Not so fast, Miss Center-of-Attention," hissed the head on the far right. "By all accounts the crown is rightfully mine!"

"Not a chance, Ms. Self-Righteous," hissed the head furthest to the left, "by all rights, the crown should be left to me!"

"And what are we?" snarled the second, third and fourth heads to the left. "Leftovers?"

"Yes," hissed the other heads. "What about us?"

"You?" The middle head fumed with indignant flame. "Why would you wear the crown? You're just ... extras!"

"Extras?" hissed the heads on the right.

The others howled. "Leftovers!"

"Look," said the middle head in a voice suddenly filled with more fright than fury as the other heads nodded dangerously, "we'll share the crown. But, as I'm center, I'll wear it first."

Without warning, the head on the right sank its fangs deep into Draig's middle head. With an awful scream, a thick palette of blood and venom oozed from the stricken head even as it crashed to the floor.

"Who's center now, chief?" snapped the head on the right.

"Not you," snarled the head on the left, sinking its fangs into the other head. The Hydra's venom quickly did its work as one more head crashed to the floor.

"Or you,

      you,

           you,

                you,

                    you,

                        you," screamed the Hydra. And with each scream another head fell lifeless to the floor.

Only one head remained.

"I have won!" the last head proclaimed after a dizzying melee of fangs, fire, and venom. Dazed and bloodied, Draig looked down upon her fallen sisters, suddenly aware of her folly.

"You!" The two remaining eyes searched mercilessly for Rafi who had taken refuge behind some rocks with the rest of the Companions. But the eyes, no longer red, were as gray as lumps of burned out coal, and the voice, once so commanding, seemed to have lost its power. Unable to comprehend what had just happened, Draig lashed out with fire and tongue, but no fire issued from her mouth, as her tongue cracked and fell to the floor. Then, in a scream as horrid as it was pitiful, Draig's once immortal head and body crashed upon her sisters and the floor.

"It's dead!" cried Bree in disbelief.

As if to confirm Bree's words the crystal sprang into light.

"Killed by its own venom," said Krik jubilantly, and still smarting over being called a cricket. "Rafi, that was brilliant!"

"No, Krik," said Rafi sadly. There was no flush of victory in her face. Even the light glowing from the crystal brought her no comfort in the otherwise dark room. "There is no brilliance in death." Her adrenaline all but gone, she staggered up to Draig, and placed the crown upon one of her horns. Tears fell from her eyes.

"Draig, Daughter of Druella, First Guardian of Erebus," she said. "How I wish I had crowned you in life rather than death – you, who were safe from everyone – except yourself. May you wear your crown better in the years to come."

Peter thrust the scepter back into Rafi's belt. His face instantly reappeared along with Pud, Turgot, Talat, and Dlop. For once, he and Talat had something in common. Beyond words, they looked upon Rafi as if she was something more than human.

"You should rest," he said gently. He looked round at other faces too tired to speak. "We should rest. It's been hours since we've had a break, and after seeing that," he nodded at Draig, "I'm positively exhausted. Besides, if this was the first guardian of Erebus, I'd hate to think of what's waiting for us at the second level. We will need our strength. Why not rest here? Thanks to you, I cannot think of a safer place."

Rafi turned a weary eye on Krik. "It is for Krik to decide," she said although, at any second, she felt as if she was going to drop next to one of the Hydra's heads.

Krik searched for his watch. "Must have lost it back in the tunnel," he said. "However, we mantises have something of an internal clock. It's something we seldom use, having invented watches and clocks, but seeing that neither is available, not to mention the moon, it will have to do. Either way, I'm afraid we can only spare an hour or two." After a brief consultation with Bree, he set off with his satchel and a stethoscope to tend to Pud.

Peter threw himself on a makeshift bed of precious stones. "Two hours of sleep," he grumbled. His head jerked toward Talat. "That should give you just enough time to slit our throats while we're sleeping."

"Two hours," mumbled Talat. From where he sat, his muscular back could have easily been mistaken for a column. "What I would give for two hours of sleep." Unnoticed by the others, massive fingers wrung tears from his eyes. "Father," he moaned in a low voice so that only the rocks could hear. "Father, look what you have done."

Weary as she was, Rafi still had enough strength to kick Peter's bed, burying him in an avalanche of precious stones. "More than enough time then," she snapped irritably, "to sleep some sense into you. Honestly, Peter, after seeing Draig, how can you be worried about Talat? If only Talat and his sword stand between you and the next guardian, you may regret your treatment of him."

Peter shifted uncomfortably under his jeweled blanket. "That I'd like to see," he said.

"He worries," snapped Talat, his anger rising as he searched for just the right diamond with which to sharpen his sword, "because worrying is America's national pastime. Worrying about its next car, a new house, everyone else's business but its own ..."

Rafi rolled her eyes. "Perhaps you two might be more comfortable sleeping together. You certainly have made the same bed. As for me, I'm more worried about the Second Guardian of Erebus."

"The second guardian," said Peter, reminded that worse things than Talat might be waiting for them further down the passage. "What do you suppose it is?"

Rafi shook her head. After meeting Draig, she could not possibly imagine what other horrors lurked in the deepest, darkest levels of Erebus.

"Whatever it is," said Talat, studying Rafi closely, "I am bound to say that it will find an even match in you. Shortly after I had moved to Drumheller I heard about a young girl who, it was said, lived in a dream and yet brought dreams to life. In the little time I have known you, I can see that you are that girl. In my country, you would be a Queen."

Peter nodded his assent. "A queen in any country ..."

Rafi blushed. Caught between the admiring gaze of two older boys, she awkwardly inspected her staff. "Thank you," she said without looking at either Peter or Talat. "But I would prefer to be just me."

"Just me, then," said Peter, yawning.

"And then some," muttered Talat.

Upon Krik's return, their conversation shifted to Pud.

"How's Pud?" asked Rafi.

"Still alive," said Krik slowly, "at least as near as I can tell. I can do nothing more for him. Only time will tell now but I fear that Pud's time is growing shorter by the minute."

Peter held up a heart shaped ruby. He looked at Rafi and Krik. "Are you thinking what I'm thinking?"

Having guessed Peter's mind, Rafi tore a thin strip of cloth from her shirt. Together, under the watchful eyes of Krik and Talat, they fashioned a crude Purple Heart necklace, which Rafi lovingly placed around Pud's neck.

Aware of Pud's heroics on the mountainside through Dlop, even Talat rounded off the Companions' heartfelt salute.

Rafi kissed Pud. "No heart could ever replace yours, Pud," she said.

With less than two hours before Krik would undoubtedly end their break, Peter, Bree and Dlop wisely used the time to sleep. Against a backdrop of Peter's snores and the monotonous diamond scrape of Talat's sword, Rafi recounted the day's events with Krik.

"You have done well, Rafi," said Krik admiringly. "Today you were the teacher, and I was the pupil. Never in all my years have I seen anyone overcome such odds. You have given us all much more than we should have ever dared to ask or expect. Thank you, Rafi, for being you."

Rafi lay her head upon the knapsack. "Mantis," she said sleepily, "if I have done well, it is only because I had the best of teachers. I want you to know that, even if we fail in our quest, I would not trade the last three days for all the days of my life. Now that I know Earth has a heart, I am sure it is no bigger than yours. Sleep, my gentle mantis so that for the next two hours at least, the world does not rest upon your shoulders. And if you will not do it for yourself then, as a friend, do it for me." She closed her eyes.

"As a friend," said Krik, "how can I refuse?" Wearily, he climbed up her hair, and without another word, he fell fast asleep.

Talat looked over from where he was sharpening his sword. There was not a trace of sleep in his eyes. "Go to sleep," he said. "I will keep watch."

Peter rolled over on his treasure bed. "Oh, there's a comfort," he muttered to himself. Even so, it was not long before his worry, whether real of imagined, dissolved once again into a deep and dreamless sleep.

Rafi listened to the chilling scrape of diamond upon steel. Unlike Peter, she was glad to know Talat's sword watched over them as they lay in the gloom of the Hydra's lair, the smell of death still lingering in the air. With this comfort in mind, she picked up Pud from where he lay and placed him lovingly upon her chest where she knew he would still protect her, if only in his dreams.

Dlop woke up if only to tell Pud about their most recent adventure for the tenth time.

"You should have seen it, Pud," he said, unable to contain his excitement. "There she was, the biggest bat of them all, with a hundred heads and a thousand eyes, and Rafi clipped its wings as if it was a fly. She crowned it all right. Almost made me feel that I'm not so small after all. Did you see it Bree?"

"Believe me, Dlop," said Bree, opening his eyes. He reached over and gave Dlop a reassuring squeeze. "I couldn't have been any closer. Almost singed the hair off my head."

"How silly of me," said Dlop. "You're always looking out after us. I wish I was as brave as you and Pud. But I only seem to get in the way."

Bree sat up. "That you do not," he said. "Don't misunderstand me, Dlop. Ever since we were attacked on the mountain, you have become a warrior, one that even Pud would have been proud to be. But I should also tell you that Pud always wanted to be more like you. And for that matter," Bree smiled warmly, "so do I. Don't change too much, little brother. If we were all the same there wouldn't be any difference. And then Earth wouldn't be worth saving after all."

"Amen," said Rafi, yawning.

As Rafi, Krik, Bree and Dlop slid from words into dreams, Turgot watched silently from the shadows. He had not said a word since the Hydra's fall, nor offered even the slightest objection after Peter had cracked his shell on a broken column next to Talat 'to keep all traitors and terrorists together.' Certainly, the Hydra's fall had not been part of his plan; his beautiful plan where he would be spared in exchange for a good dinner. Such was the plan he had discussed with Draig one dark night when the Companions lay innocently beneath the stars. But there were parts to his plan even Draig had not known, for the Hydra knew nothing of the stones. That was the best part of his plan. If Draig had consumed the stones along with Rafi it was of small consequence, for Turgot knew, like all solid waste, the stones must soon pass. He was used to the dark and foul places of the earth. Crawling through the waste of an inexpensive dinner was nothing compared to the value of the stones. But now, along with Draig, his beautiful plan lay in ruins.

"Marie," his mind babbled insanely so that only he could hear. "'ow could you? 'ow could you fail your faithful Turgot? For that you must be punished, non?" His eyes burned through the darkness as he watched Rafi sleep surrounded by her guard. Alive or dead, the Drog made no difference to him. The stones were what he was after. But in order for his plan to work he had to steal the stones before they reached the great hall of Erebus. And for that he needed another plan.

Not far below, in a place where even the Hydra dared not go, waited the Second Guardian of Erebus.

CHAPTER EIGHTEEN
SHEPHERD'S PIE

Delighted, Mr. and Mrs. Malawi ushered their new guests into the Apple. As advised by Ademar, Amos and Myra both wore clothes pegs on their noses, as did the Queen (who was still staying at the Apple).

"Welcome, welcome," cried the Dung Beetle to clear up any misunderstanding as to whose house it was. "You'll be staying the night of course?"

"Of course," echoed Mr. and Mrs. Malawi. "May we come in?"

The Dung Beetle settled comfortably into Mr. Malawi's favorite armchair. "Certainly, certainly," the Oracle gushed in more than words. "My home is your home. Zigh, make mine a martini and don't forget the du…"

Impressed with Mr. Malawi's bone collection, Zigh's gimlety eyes spotted a conspicuously small but ferocious looking skeleton. "Hey," he growled, "that's my cousin, Bert!"

Mr. Malawi hastened to cover Bert with a tablecloth. "S… s… sorry!"

"Not to worry," growled Zigh amicably. "It's nice to see him doing something useful for a change. Never had much sense …"

The Dung Beetle gazed imperiously around the room. "It occurs to me that two things are missing – Motu – and my martini."

"Motu is still in jail, Your Dungness," said Amos, properly schooled by Ademar as to how to speak to the Oracle, "and sends his regrets."

"And as far as your martini, Dung Brains," growled Zigh, "get it yourself."

Not wishing to see her home become a dung hole, Myra fixed everyone drinks.

The Dung Beetle stirred in the most important ingredient. "Zigh apologizes for arriving so early, but we thought it best to have a quiet chat before my other dinner guest arrives. Isn't that right, Zigh?"

"Whatever you say, Feces Face," growled Zigh. He turned to Mr. Malawi. "A Velociraptor, is it?"

"Sue," said Mr. Malawi, wondering which was more odd – calling a Velociraptor by its first name – or talking to a wolverine. "Says she wants to meet our family …"

"… which is precisely why we are here," said the Dung Beetle, suddenly looking serious.

The Queen, who had been silent up until that time, patted Mrs. Malawi's hand. "I must confess," she said, "I do not altogether like the sound of this Sue, and I am bound to say that I question her intentions." She sniffed majestically. "If there is any meaning to the word, I think that 'meating' the Malawis is more as to what Sue has on her mind. Which is why," she lowered her voice, "my guards are waiting upstairs." She nodded fondly at a lion sleeping next to her chair, one of the Dung Beetle's magnanimous gifts presented to her at Town Hall. "Not to mention Leo."

"Or us." Ademar, the owl, and Erech, the eagle, looked down from where they had perched on Bert.

"You are wise beyond Drogs, Your Majesty," said the Dung Beetle, impressed. "But guards won't be necessary. Zigh will entertain our guest while we make dinner, won't you Zigh?"

"You know it, Grand Pooh-Bah," growled Zigh.

Mr. Malawi put his arms around his wife. "Then it is as I feared. Sue is coming to kill us."

"Yes," confirmed the Dung Beetle. "Triodon was never one for leaving loose ends. It would serve him well if both of you were dead, not to mention Motu, before he meets Rafi in the great hall of Erebus. It is his belief that, with all of you gone and nothing left to live for, Rafi will abandon her quest or better – give him the stones."

"The rogue!" snapped the Queen.

"Rafi is safe?" asked Mrs. Malawi, almost hysterical.

The Dung Beetle refilled the martini from its own vast resources. "For the moment."

Mr. Malawi put down his drink. With Sue, the assassin, on her way to the Apple, his son in jail and his daughter in grave danger, he asked the one question nearest to his heart.

"Why Rafi?"

"Ahhh," replied the Dung Beetle, slopping a little martini on Zigh. "Now you are asking too much. Yet, as you are the parents of the One, I am compelled to answer your question." The Dung Beetle sipped its martini.

"Rafi is not your daughter ..."

"What?" Mr. and Mrs. Malawi looked shocked (not to mention the Queen).

"... in a manner of speaking," added the Dung Beetle. "Perhaps the simplest explanation is that Rafi comes from a bigger womb."

Mr. Malawi smiled. Fond memories flooded his mind: Rafi singing in the river, kissing rainbows, mailing letters to a cloud, showing her report card to a tree ... "Let me guess," he said. "Earth."

"Earth," confirmed the Dung Beetle. "Rare indeed, especially for a Drog, but there it is. Rafi is a Daughter of Earth. So, when Earth was in trouble, she did what any mother would have done. She called her daughter – your daughter – and no mother or father could be more proud."

"Did you hear that, Amos?" Mrs. Malawi smiled through her tears. "Our daughter comes from a big family."

Mr. Malawi helped himself to the Dung Beetle's martini. "But aren't we all, each in our own way, children of Earth?" he asked.

"True," said the Dung Beetle, fixing itself another drink, "but Earth only names those children destined to inherit a world beyond their own."

Mr. Malawi slapped his forehead. "The letter in Rafi's hair ..."

"Rune," corrected the Dung Beetle. "Rafi's Earth-name is Bjarka, meaning 'she who belongs.'"

"Rafiatu Bjarka Malawi," said Mrs. Malawi proudly.

"Incidentally," the Dung Beetle went on, "it was no coincidence that Rafi was born into your home for you too have the favor of Earth. That rain in Mogadishu when you first met under an umbrella was no random event. That meeting had already been decreed by Earth long before you were even born." The Dung Beetle passed around a plate of chocolate hors d'oeuvres. "As a child of Earth myself, that would make us family." The Dung Beetle gave both Mr. and Mrs. Malawi a squishy hug. "I am your brother – your much older brother – Horace."

"Horace," said Mr. and Mrs. Malawi together, too stunned to say anything else.

"What delightful ordure's," said the Queen, not wishing to offend the Dung Beetle.

There was a knock on the door.

"Ah," said the Dung Beetle, having finished its sixth martini, "I see that our guest has arrived. Amos, Myra, Your Majesty, you will join me in the kitchen where I will show you how to create the perfect Shepherd's Pie. Meanwhile Zigh will show Sue your lovely garden ..."

As Amos, Myra and the Queen unwillingly joined the Dung Beetle in the kitchen, Zigh opened the bright green door of Newton's Apple. On the doormat stood an enormous Velociraptor. Cradled in its arms was a bottle of red wine.

"Good afternoon," said Sue, somewhat surprised at finding someone other than Mr. and Mrs. Malawi or the Queen at the door. "You must be the family dog ..."

Zigh looked Sue up and down with his gimlety eyes. "Woof," he growled.

Sue's voice sank to a whisper. "After dinner, if you're a good doggie, you can have your pick of the bones."

Zigh wagged his stubby tail.

The door closed.

There is no need to describe the horrible events that followed. In fact, at the request of the International Association of Psychiatrists, the author has agreed not to be too specific as there are already enough people in therapy without frightening any more of them, children no less, by telling the world what happened next in Mrs. Malawi's garden. Let it only be said that the bottle of red wine, while a cheap and questionable Shiraz, was a perfect match for raw Velociraptor and, to this day, Sue's skeleton, as modified by Zigh, makes a perfect sprinkler for the garden.

As for Zigh, replete from dinner and exhausted from battle, he curled up in Mr. Malawi's arm chair as Amos, Myra, Leo, Ademar, Erech, the Queen and her guards and the Dung Beetle sat down to Earth's dungiest Shepherd's Pie.

CHAPTER NINETEEN
MASTER OF HALLS

Two hours had passed before Talat woke the others. It's time," he said. He showered each of their heads with a fistful of diamonds. A hint of amusement almost betrayed the grim smile upon his face.

"Time for what?" snapped Peter irritably. Having just slept on a bed that would have shamed the treasuries of Europe, he had no further use for diamonds, or indeed, of any riches upon the earth that did not include breakfast, a blanket, or a pillow.

"Two hours," grunted Talat. He pointed to a pool of water cleverly hidden behind some rocks. "There's water over there if you need it. Clean too."

"Well done, Talat," said Krik, stretching. Instinctively, his glance strayed to the column where he had last seen Turgot. Much to his relief, Turgot was still there, his bulging eyes fixed upon the mantis.

Peter sat up. He rubbed his eyes as several of the heavier diamonds bounced off his head. "Yes," he said, looking up at Talat. "Well done, Talat. It must have taken some effort to keep your sword at your side instead of in ours. Yet I've heard about your kind. Plotting something more sinister I shouldn't wonder ..."

A fistful of diamonds hit him squarely in the back of his head.

"Speaking of effort," said Rafi, yawning, and sitting up in her turn, "I had hoped by now that you two would have become friends."

Peter rubbed the back of his head. "Funny how a single letter separates a fiend from a friend," he said. Seeing Rafi's face, he hastily changed the subject. "What a dream I had," he went on. "First, a giant hammer beat me to a pulp, and then an eye as big as a house swallowed me whole …"

"Too bad the hammer didn't beat some sense into you," Rafi retorted. She looked supportively at Talat but the young man was once again sharpening his sword. She glared at Peter. "I, too, had a dream," she said. "We were attacked by a nine headed dragon and …" She turned to Krik only to be confronted with Draig's middle head. Stripped of light and fire, the once ruby eyes glared back at her accusingly. She shook her own head in disbelief. "It wasn't a dream!"

Krik pulled a miniature chalkboard out of his satchel. He looked appraisingly at what was left of Draig, and then wrote the number 1 across it in green chalk.

"One," he said methodically. He looked up from his chalkboard at Bree who was taking sword-sharpening lessons from Talat. "How's Pud?"

"Still alive," said Bree coldly. He nodded at Pud who lay in a contorted heap beside Dlop. "If anyone could call that life."

"Where there is life, there is hope," said Rafi soothingly.

In answer, Bree inspected his sword. Honed to a razor's edge, it glittered with diamond dust. In focused fury, both rat and sword hurtled down upon a large ruby, neatly spitting it in two. Diamond hard, the blade was no match for the piercing look in his eyes. "Which is more than I can say for Megaera," he said darkly, "when we meet again."

Something rumbled in the chamber.

"What was that?"

"My stomach," Peter confessed. "What's for breakfast? Hopefully not smoked Hydra."

Rafi threw him a chocolate bar. "Not much," she said. "From now until the end of Earth it's nothing but chocolate for you." She counted out six nuts each for Bree and Dlop. "And nuts for you."

"I could live with that," said Peter, grinning.

"Only," she added, with the merest twinkle in her eye, "you'll have to share it with Talat."

"No, thank you," said Talat coldly. He looked up from his sword. It was difficult to tell which was harder – the diamond, his sword, or the look in his eyes. "I'm not hungry."

Peter threw half of his chocolate bar at Talat. "C'mon, Talat," he said. "Even terrorists have to eat."

"Peter," Rafi looked angrier than he had ever seen her. "Give Talat a break, OK?" She picked up Pud. "Don't you understand? If you and Talat can't reconcile your differences, what is the point of going on? Do you want to live in the Hydra's world? In Triodon's? If you choose to find old enemies only hours before the end of Earth, how can you possibly expect to find new friends should we survive?"

"I'm sorry, Rafi," said Peter, his mouth full of chocolate.

"Don't apologize to me." She nodded at Talat. Having had enough of bickering boys, she dribbled some water down Pud's throat. His tongue was black.

Peter walked over to Talat. "Sorry, Talat," he said, extending both a smile and his hand. The smile was genuine. "I have been rather crude, haven't I? Rafi's right. Let's start over, shall we?"

Talat stopped sharpening his sword. For the first time since they had met him, some of the grimness haunting his face upturned a smile. Lowering his sword, he took Peter's hand.

"That was our problem, Peter," he said. "We never started."

Peter admired the giant bear paw swallowing his own hand. "You remind me of my brother," he said.

Something clicked on the column.

"Ahhh," said Turgot, whose mood had thawed along with the air, "friends we are again, non?"

Peter and Talat glared at Turgot.

"Non!"

At Krik's urging, everyone ate and drank, and prepared to go. Turgot, however, was in no mood for going on.

"Why should I 'elp?" he demanded. He waved an imperial claw.

"Friendship and chocola' you 'ave for yourselves, but insults you give to me. Even aft'air I 'elped defeat the 'ydra."

"'elped?" said Bree incredulously.

"Defeat the 'ydra?" said Peter even more incredulously.

Turgot's claw lost nothing in translation. "'ad it not been for me," he crowed triumphantly, "there would 'ave been nothing to defeat, non?"

"He does have a point," said Krik. Other than Turgot, everyone knew the mantis was joking. He hopped onto Rafi's shoulder.

"Look, Turgot," he said, "there's no denying you've helped us get this far, but nobody forced you to come either. I have no doubt your eagerness to be our guide is no charitable act; it did not escape my attention that the Hydra did not include you on its menu."

Rafi looked up from where she had been administering to Pud. "I must confess, Turgot," she said, "I was wondering about that myself."

"Clearly, I am misunderstood," Turgot shot back, deeply wounded. "Marie, 'ow could you?" For a brief moment, their eyes shared a sea of sparkling and yet indifferent stones. But even in that moment, Rafi sensed that a deeper and more indifferent sea rolled somewhere beneath the waves of discontent flooding Turgot's eyes – eyes that counted only three stones, even in a room full of treasure.

"Clearly – misunderstood," observed Bree. "There's an oxymoron for you, Dlop."

"No," said Dlop, "that's just a moron."

"A plague on you!" Turgot's shouts echoed throughout the chamber. But his eyes, now pale and luminescent, never strayed far from Rafi.

"Save it for the next level." Krik's voice bellowed above the din. "Or we will never get there." He clasped his sword belt around his waist. "Bree, Dlop, I am surprised at you. You are Companions of Earth; keep your minds on your duty. As for you, Turgot, I'm in no mood for playing games. Time is not only short – it's getting shorter. If we have offended you, then, for my part, I apologize. Are you with us or not?"

"But of course," said Turgot after some effort. He pulled his gaze away from Rafi long enough to tell the mantis that insults were not the only thing on his mind. "Insulted I am, but I 'ave a 'ard shell. If oth'airs kicked it less often, per'aps they would find me more – how you say – sociable. 'elp me down and I will show you the way."

"How far?" asked Krik.

Dlop surveyed the column. "About three and a half feet, I'd say," he said.

Krik rolled his eyes. "To the second level of Erebus I mean."

"An 'our and an 'alf an 'our," said Turgot.

Peter swept Turgot from the column. It was by no accident that Turgot fell most of the way. "Where are you taking us?"

Peter's gesture was not lost on the crab who, being without a nose, thrust his shell high in the air and began a deliberate march around the Hydra.

"That the Drog shall see."

Burdened as she was with stones, knapsack, staff, scepter, and the crystal, Rafi knelt down to pick up her most precious charge of all – Pud.

"No," said Peter gently, "I'll take him." He laid Pud on his shoulder. "You worry about Earth; I'll worry about Pud." He smiled appreciatively. "Believe me, I've got the better deal, no matter which way you slice it. Besides, ever since the mountaintop, Pud and I have a special understanding. A bond you might say."

Rafi looked sharply into Peter's eyes. There was nothing in his eyes to suggest that his words were nothing more than a casual remark.

"It is all of these special understandings that you wear so well," she confided as she looked at Peter, Krik and Bree, "that concern me most. Promise me you won't do anything that will have us carrying you as well."

Peter flashed his most innocent smile. "Don't worry about me, Rafi," he said. "I can take care of myself."

"That's exactly what worries me," she said.

They followed Turgot around the Hydra. Even in death, Draig was magnificent to behold, her heads lying like toppled thrones upon a treasury too magnificent to be believed. Still haunted by Draig's boasts of immortality, they bowed before each head, that is, except for Turgot who spat upon the Hydra as if the monster was no better than a flea.

"Bah," he snapped his claws most disrespectfully, "nine 'eads, and not one as smart as Turgot." He cast a sly look at Krik. "But then, that could also be said of oth'airs, non?" He laughed wickedly.

All this time the crystal lit their way through the chamber until, at last, they stood before a vast passageway descending further into the mountain. In front of the passageway lay a mountain of unwrought gold.

"Wow," said Peter. His eyes welled into cauldrons of gold. "There's enough gold here for each of us to buy our own planet."

"Let's save the one we all share first," quipped Rafi. Raising the crystal high above her head, she stepped over Turgot and into the passageway. She gasped. Neither dark nor dreary, the walls, floor and ceiling were made of solid gold.

Even Talat whistled in wonder. "A golden passage," he said. He ran his fingers along the wall, which was as smooth as glass. "If I didn't know better I'd say the Hydra pays tribute to someone down below. She must melt the gold from up here so that it flows down the passageway, for what purpose I cannot say. Why else would all this gold be here?"

Peter seemed lost between comprehending the Hydra's inestimable wealth and the meaning of Talat's words. "T... t... tribute?" he stammered. "The Hydra? To whom in this world would something like that," he pointed to one of Draig's heads, "pay tribute?"

"Who indeed," said Krik. He looked sharply at Turgot. "What is it that awaits us below?"

Turgot almost rolled over in his delight. "What does it matt'air?" he said. Echoes of laughter, magnified within the chamber, assailed the Companions from every direction. "You must find Triodon and this is the only way. Can it be? Is the mantis afraid …?"

"Only a fool would not be afraid," muttered Krik. He looked at the others, none of whom looked any more eager to explore the passageway, however rich its gilded walls. "He's right, of course. Our quest stops for no one. Those who stand between us and destiny are merely fleeting means to an unyielding end."

"Or an end to all means," squeaked Dlop.

Turgot was in no hurry to end his sport. "Means end, end means," he scoffed, "or per'aps a mean end." He laughed uproariously. "Who can tell?"

Unable to answer this question, they plunged down the passageway. Decked in gold, bathed in the warm light of the crystal, and without a single rock or hole to impede their progress, the trip would have seemed almost heavenly were it not for the tap, tap, tap of Turgot's feet. A prickly heat gradually spilled into the passageway from down below. Here and there, they stopped for a brief rest and some water, but never for long as Krik was anxious to reach the second level, being more afraid, it seemed, of being late for an appointment than meeting an awful death. Soon the heat was almost unbearable.

Rafi leaned heavily on her staff. "Now I know what it feels like to be a baked lasagna," she said. She sipped some water, taking her time to sweat on Krik. "And I thought we had finished with the Anvil."

Bree winked wearily at Dlop. "Maybe the second level of Erebus is an oven," he said.

"And the guardian is an haute chef," said Dlop.

"Not funny," said Krik. Across his forehead, he wore a black sweatband with the word PYSCHE written across it in red letters. "Just imagine you are freezing in an igloo at the North Pole. Think about how nice it would be to put on a warm coat or light a roaring fire." He tapped his headband significantly. "Don't give in to what you feel – fight heat with heat and fire with fire. Fight with your minds."

"Fighting." Dlop slumped wearily against Bree. "Only the igloo has a hammer and I'm getting a headache."

Bree fanned Dlop with his sword. "Don't give in, Dlop," he said. "You heard Krik. Fight with your mind."

"He's fighting better than the rest of you," said Peter suddenly. "Have you no ears? It's the same hammering I heard in my dreams!"

They listened. From somewhere down below they heard the unmistakable tapping of a hammer.

"We must be getting close," said Rafi.

"Close we are, Marie," said Turgot. "But clos'air we shall be."

A few turns and several minutes later, Turgot's prediction appeared to be coming true. With every step, the passageway grew hotter and hotter until the hammer clanged like an avalanche of iron pounding a freight train. With each blow, the Companions sailed into the air as if they had jumped on a trampoline.

"Hammer and tongs!" cried Krik. "Turgot, is that what I think it is?"

"What diff'airence does it make?" snapped Turgot, unafraid. He moved closer to Rafi. "It is what it is."

"Builder of walls; Master of Halls,
From gold are trinkets spun,
One-eyed sire; worships fire,
Beats gold upon the Sun."

Krik looked shocked. At first, he stood rigid with horror until, in terrible distress, he paced back and forth on Rafi's shoulder. More than once, he almost walked off her shoulder into thin air. It would have been a long fall but nowhere near as long as the look upon his face. Farther down the passageway, the hammer rang in thunderous blows.

"C'mon, Krik," said Bree bravely. "We can take it. What could be worse than a Hydra?"

Krik groaned. "A Cyclops," he said. Far too late, he tried to hide the wave of worry that washed his face. "You can't imagine what is waiting for us on the other side of that hammer." He stopped pacing. "I had not counted on such a foe. Even a Hydra would think twice before challenging a Cyclops."

Krik's words fell upon the Companions like boulders dropped from above. Even Talat gazed longingly back up the passageway.

"Surely we're not turning back," said Rafi, surprised at her own courage.

Krik looked knowingly at each Companion. His words came as no surprise. "There is no turning back," he said. "Even if we did it would only give us a few more hours."

"That seems fair," squeaked Dlop. Propelled by his tail, he started back up the passageway.

"Is it?" asked Rafi. She shielded her eyes from the crystal. Apparently unaware of any danger, it burned brighter than ever. "I don't know about you, but if we and our families are going to die, I'd hate to think several hours from now that we could have prevented it. I couldn't live with myself."

"Not for long anyway," quipped Bree, holding on to Dlop's tail.

"You are right, Rafi," said Krik. "To give up now is to give up forever. We have faced many perils together, the Hydra not least, and now is not the time for turning back or second thoughts." He stared down the passageway for the longest time. Boom, boom, boom, went the hammer. When, at last, his face turned upon them, it was as blank as stone without even the slightest hint of blame or suggestion.

"Who is with us?" he asked.

"I am," was Bree's ready reply.

"I think I am," squeaked Dlop.

"I am," said Peter and Talat together. Grinning awkwardly, they shook hands.

"I am," croaked a weak voice. "Only where are we going?"

"Pud!"

Such was the Companions' jubilation that, for a moment, everything else was forgotten. Before Peter could even lower Pud into their arms, Bree and Dlop were already kissing and licking his face as the others smiled enviously. But just as quickly, their smiles faded. Only the faintest gleam looked out of Pud's eyes.

"Thought you'd hog all the action, didn't you," he whispered.

Bree lovingly caressed his brow. "Pud, there is no action without you. It's only because of you that we're here, brother!"

Dlop's eyes almost spun out of his head with excitement. "You should have seen it, Pud," he said. "Rafi saved us from a giant bat with nine heads. Nine heads! And bad breath, too. But she crowned 'em all. Just like them cats …"

Pud closed his eyes and smiled. Orly's cats still drifted as pleasant memories through his mind. He held out his paw. "Give me my sword," he said. He said no more.

"Give him his sword," said Krik with the greatest respect, "for he is a Companion of Earth, and a sword in Pud's paw is enough to make any of our enemies think twice before they step between us and our quest. Who else could survive the sting of the Empusae for so long, and even now, gives us hope before the storm?" His face grew as hard as the gold glistening above his head. "Companions of Earth, prepare to enter the second level of Erebus."

Rafi set aside both staff and crystal. "Give him to me," she said to Bree gently. Under the ever-watchful eye of Turgot, she placed Pud inside her shirt. Then, after knotting each stone securely back into place, she picked up the staff and the crystal.

"If the stones were made to protect Earth," she said simply, "perhaps they will also protect Pud".

Bree's sword pointed to the crystal. "If that thing burns any brighter," he said, "we could light our way to China."

Rafi nodded. "Only what does it mean?" she asked. "I'm sure it went dark before to protect us from the Hydra, but now it burns as if for the whole world to see. Do we take it with us? If we do, the Cyclops will only need one eye to know something is amiss – even if we use the scepter. If we don't, there's no guarantee the scepter will protect us from the Cyclops; it may turn out that the crystal is exactly what we need. Who can solve this riddle for us?"

"What about the acorn?" asked Dlop. "Maybe we could throw it at the Cyclops. If he eats it, it might grow into a tree and he'll choke on it."

Turgot rolled his eyes. "Listen to me, you fools," he said, "for whatev'air this 'umbug 'as told you," he glared at Krik, "I 'ave advised the great of your world and mine for ov'air two thousand years. And although 'e will nev'air admit it, even this … this narcissistic mantis has sought my advice when 'e had less faith in 'is own." Turgot's eyes swelled with pride. "And I tell you now that your magic tricks are nothing compared to the Cyclops. 'e is a master of deception and chicane. Per'aps it was 'e who made the scepter …"

Krik tapped his feet impatiently. "Where are you going with this, Turgot?" he asked.

"Let me finish," snapped Turgot. The mere sound of Krik's voice spun his eyeballs into orbit. "As the mantis knows, the Cyclops worships both fire and sun. This is 'is strength but," Turgot chuckled, "behind every strength there is weakness, non?" His eyes twisted deviously on their stalks. "Yes, yes," he muttered as he stared at the crystal still burning brightly in Rafi's hand, "I see it now. An eye for an eye. A sun for a son. That is a magic 'e might understand."

"Meaning?" asked Krik impatiently.

"Meaning that you are a fool," snapped Turgot. Clearly, his hatred for Krik went much deeper than his eyes. "Don't you see, idiot?" His voice softened as Bree's paw crept to his sword. "It is simple, mon ami. The Cyclops worships the sun, and the sun I see in your 'and. Give him the sun in return for safe passage through his realm. As for the scept'air, keep it secret until all else fails. Then, when 'e least expects it we may yet steal away with more than our lives."

"That settles it," said Bree. He seemed to despise Turgot as much as Turgot hated Krik. "Let's leave the crystal here and use the scepter."

"You 'ave a bett'air idea, I suppose?" Turgot laughed as if he already knew the answer.

All eyes turned to Krik.

"I don't know, Bree," he said slowly. "It is clear to me Turgot is not telling us everything, but I agree with him about the crystal. Cyclopses have always been fascinated with fire and bright lights, and the crystal is sure to catch his attention. As for the scepter, it makes sense to use it as a second defense should the need arise. Yet, I cannot imagine, even for a second, why a Cyclops would spare us in exchange for the crystal. Such gestures are not in its nature." He looked questioningly at Turgot.

"Because, fool," Turgot crowed triumphantly, "I know this Cyclops."

"This is getting better by the minute," said Bree incredulously.

Turgot ignored Bree. "For once, the mantis is correct," he said scornfully. "To know one's enemy, one must know its nature, yes?" He raised an authoritative claw. "By trade, the Cyclops is a goldsmith. 'owev'air cruel its nature, it lives but for one purpose and one purpose alone – to make beautiful things. But for that they need gold and jewels." His eyes widened into golden passageways of their own. "Lots of gold and jewels. And for that ... it needs the 'ydra."

There was silence in the passageway. Even the Cyclops's hammer ceased to ring as Turgot approached his next point with calculated relish.

"Many years ago while exploring this mountain I stumbled across the Cyclops's cave. Nev'air had I seen such riches – priceless treasures beyond even the imagination of Drogs. In I went – to steal something I admit – but the Cyclops caught me even as 'e slept for, fool that I was, I 'ad forgotten that 'is gold is charmed, and can speak to 'im in ways we will nev'air understand." His eyes swelled with fear. "What was I to do against such an adversary? I did the only thing I could ..."

"Lie," snapped Bree.

Turgot shot Bree a venomous look. "There I was, trapped like a rat, but little did I know the Cyclops 'ad a use for me. 'Gold', 'e said, 'tell the Hydra I need more gold, seven tons of it, and two hundred and fifty six of her finest diamonds. Alas, my last messenger recently met with an untimely end, and so you shall go until I have no further use for you.'" Turgot shivered appreciatively. "And so I became the – 'ow you say – messeng'air between the Cyclops and the Hydra. The Cyclops would tell me 'ow much gold it wanted and the 'ydra would send it down this passage. That is why it is paved with gold. With one breath, she would melt the gold where it flowed like a riv'air all the way to the Cyclops. As for me, I 'ad to carry all those 'eavy stones myself. Poor Turgot."

"Fascinating as this story is," said Bree with a sidelong glance at Krik, "and 'story' being the key word here, what use is that to us? The Hydra, as you may have noticed, is dead."

Turgot's eyes glinted malevolently. "Dead, yes," he said, "but not forgotten." His voice sank to a whisper. "To those who know – she is dead – but to the Cyclops she is still very much alive, non? 'e knows nothing about Triodon. Tell 'im you stole the sun from the 'ydra and that there is anoth'air, even bett'air sun, deep in the mountain on the oth'air side of 'is cave. Make 'im a – 'ow you say – deal. If 'e lets you go on, you will give it to 'im upon your return." Turgot shrugged within his shell. "Aft'air all, 'e 'as nothing to lose. 'e knows there is no oth'air way out of the mountain. In 'is cruel mind, it will give 'im great pleasure to kill you when you return, wheth'air or not you bring back the sun."

"You've obviously given this a lot of thought, Turgot," said Krik. "And a very clever idea it is. It's so crazy it might just work." He looked at the others. "I'm open to suggestions."

There were none. After whispering something in Rafi's ear, Krik looked back at Turgot. "Assuming we can trust you, Turgot," he said, "there remains a problem ..."

"That's two problems," countered Bree.

Krik went on. "However clever, that is a lot to explain to a Cyclops. As a rule, they are known to kill first and ask questions later, indeed if they can talk at all. Other than you, we are unknown to him. What's to stop him from greeting his guests with a hammer?"

"Ahhh," smiled Turgot. "That is why you 'ave your Turgot." His eyes never looked more hopeful. "Let me be your ambassador to the Cyclops. Upon your command, I will speak with 'im and 'elp you save Earth. Only," Turgot looked up helplessly from where he sat upon the floor, "it is 'ard to be noticed and 'eard from down 'ere. Let me sit on Marie's shoulder – opposite yourself of course – so that togeth'air, when all magic fails, we can win the day with words. It will be like old times, non? Aft'air all, three 'eads are bett'air than one."

"Let's make that four heads," said Bree suspiciously. "Krik, if you are intent with going on with this madness then I suggest you sit up top. I'll watch Rafi – and Turgot."

"Certainement," said Turgot innocently. His eyes orbited wildly around their stalks. "Of course, I could always sit with anoth'air Drog should you pref'air."

Krik looked at Bree and then at Rafi. "What do you think, Rafi?"

Rafi gazed deep into Turgot's eyes. In his eyes swirled a darkened room. On the far side of the room, bathed in a faint, flickering light was a half-open door. Wonderingly, she headed for the door, but before she could reach it, the door closed. Somewhere in the darkness, she heard the snick of a lock.

Turgot looked away. His shell blushed like a ruby. "Marie," he protested in embarrassment. "Do not look too deep inside your poor Turgot. Louis will be jealous, non?"

Rafi nodded at Krik. She had seen enough in Turgot's eyes to know he could not be trusted, yet in the darkness, she had seen many other things both painful and sad.

"I accept your offer, Turgot," she said. "It is my hope there is some good in you yet. Perhaps, before we are done, you shall learn that small friends, who care for one another are priceless when measured against larger friends, who care for no one but themselves."

"Amen," said Krik. He scrambled up Rafi's hair where his green head poked through her curls like an unripe chestnut in a chestnut tree. Somewhere along the way, he had traded in his sweatband for a tee shirt that read 'NOBODY.' "This way," he said, looking at the confused faces around him, "whatever happens, it will be NOBODY'S fault. Get it?" He barked out his orders.

"Rafi below. Bree on my right. Turgot on my left. Dlop, you're with Peter. Talat, if ever we needed your sword, it is now. I do not doubt for a moment you know how to use it. Rafi, had I known it would come to this, I would have better prepared you for meeting the Cyclops. Remember that Cyclopses are bigger than most countries, have no government, and kill, not out of need, but for amusement. Your instincts are likely a better guide than anything I can tell you." He called each of them by name except Turgot. "But whatever happens, know it happened to the Companions of Earth."

"What was that part about kills?" squeaked Dlop.

Rafi looked at her staff. "I wish Zigh was here," she said longingly. "He'd know what to do. What good is a staff of bone in the hands of a girl against … a monster?"

No one answered.

Their hearts beating even louder than the Cyclops's hammer, they inched further down the passageway. Suddenly, with an earsplitting crash and a flash of light, the passageway opened into a vast cave, many times larger than the temple of the Hydra, but roughly hewn out of rock.

The Cyclops was enormous. Bathed in the light of a great fire, every one of its gruesome features was plain to see. On two cloven hooves and goat's legs it stood as high as a stacked fleet of double-decker buses, moving about on its great legs as if it was a man that had never ceased to grow. The two arms were equally grotesque, muscular beyond comparison, covered with hair, and each ending with horned, three fingered hands. One hand gripped a set of tongs over an anvil as large as a factory, holding a red-hot lump of gold. In the other hand, the Cyclops wielded a hammer that could have easily crushed a house had it not already been employed in the beating of the metal. All of these frightful aspects the Companions saw as they watched the Cyclops, but it was only when they looked upon his face they knew the true meaning of fear. One glance was enough to know there was no mercy in that face. Thin and cruel, the lips hung in a lopsided grin that pulled on a nose the size of a battleship. Most hideous of all was the single eye that looked beyond the anvil and the fire, as large as a full moon, but burning darker than the meanest lump of coal.

"Oho," boomed the Cyclops in a voice that shook the mountain. He placed his tools on the anvil, stretched his great limbs, and cracked his knuckles so loudly they sounded like a six-gun salute. "I do not get guests very often. Guests usually have an … ah … unexpected stay with the Hydra." He laughed but there was no humor in his voice. "Who are you and what do you want? My name is Brontes."

"Brontosaurus, more like," whispered Bree.

Rafi's first impulse was to grab the scepter, a thought shared by the others, but something held her back. Instead, as waves of horror choked her throat and mind, she looked around the cave. In heaped delight, mountains of gold and precious stones lay on either side of the Cyclops, some made from the unwrought metal waiting for the fire and anvil, while others sparkled in riches that, in ancient times, must surely had been meant for the Gods. There were golden shields, weapons, and suits of gold, golden chairs, thrones set with sparkling jewels beyond the riches of kings, golden tables as large as halls, statues of solid gold so real they seemed to speak from beyond the ages, golden chests, beds, shrines, ornaments and jewelry, and even a golden chariot pulled by twelve horses made of solid gold.

"Brontes," she said breathlessly, looking at the golden miracles wrought by the Cyclops's hammer, "great smith of the golden hall, you are indeed the master of all. Never have we, the Companions of

Earth, ever looked upon such power and yet such stunning beauty. Our tragic world pales in comparison to the magnificence of your cave. Surely there is not another."

"Companions of Earth," Brontes snorted, for there was a bird's nest in his left nostril, "I care not a jot for the puny earth and the weak insects that call it home." His eye flared with cruelty. "But tell me what your name is, and what it is you hold in your hand."

"Tell him NOBODY," whispered Krik.

Drowned out by the noise of two great bellows, which blew upon the fire, Rafi did not hear the mantis. "My name is Rafi," she said bravely, although it seemed to her that her heart had stopped beating along with the Cyclops's hammer. She held the crystal before her shining face. "And this is the Sun of Agony that has guided us along our way. As for my friends ..."

"Your friends are of little interest to me," Brontes cut in. He picked up his hammer and strode over to the Companions. The ground shook with every step. "But give me the sun and I shall spare your lives. It is but a trifle to you, and shall find a welcome place in my home. Surely, it is mine already, for it could only have belonged to Fire, who, as you must know, is my mother."

"Gladly," said Rafi as Krik whispered in her ear, "but surely such a treasure is worth more than our lives. Even so, we give it willingly for there is yet another, even greater sun beyond your cave in Erebus. Let us live and we shall get it for you. It is a fair offer, is it not? For even the world above has but one sun, and you shall have two."

Brontes looked suspicious. "And why should you wish to go there?" he asked gruffly. "For years uncounted I have allowed naught but the Erinnyes to pass through my realm." The cruel monster's eye softened to the hardness of jagged quartz. "Yet, even this I grant you if you give me the sun – now." He held out his hand. "Ah, and here they are," he said as three black shadows flitted into the cave. He smiled lopsidedly. "I do not doubt you already have some business to settle with the Erinnyes," the smile stretched in meaning, "and others perhaps."

Bree bristled with fury. "Megaera," he said.

"Ignore them," said Krik firmly. "One Cyclops is enough to handle for the moment. Remember your duty to Earth."

"I remember," said Bree through gritted teeth, "and so shall the Erinnyes."

"The sun," Brontes reminded them. Even bent double, he was so enormous he had to use his tongs so that Rafi could hand him the crystal. Horrified, she placed the crystal between the tongs where it scintillated like a newborn star. She stepped back.

Joyfully, Brontes raised the crystal to his eye where, much to his surprise, it burned brighter than ever. Immersed in light, he gazed upon the crystal like a child rapt upon a toy.

Rafi's hand slid toward the scepter. "With your leave, Brontes," she said. "We shall go."

"I think not," said Brontes, still entranced by the crystal. "I am not as dull as you think me. It occurs to me that one who carries such treasure, and is so eager to give it away, may yet have other treasures to reveal. And I am not unacquainted with the legends that idle minds spin upon the earth. You would not be here were it not for some greater purpose. You forget that I have lived in the mountain even longer than Triodon, and that my mother is Fire." Brontes reared himself to his full height as his fist closed around the crystal. The cave suddenly grew darker along with his tone. "Give me the stones and only then will I spare you. But the bearer of the stones shall be spared alone to be my slave. The others I shall add to my evening meal."

"Alas, Brontes," said Rafi, her fingers closing in on the scepter, "the thing you ask, is the one thing I cannot do."

Brontes raised his hammer. "Then," he said evilly, "the one thing you have, I cannot grant. Life."

"Now's your time, Turgot," said Krik.

With an awful shriek, Turgot leapt into the air. "Kill them!" he shouted at Brontes. "Kill them all!"

Bree drew his sword. "I knew it!"

Then, everything that could have happened, happened all at once.

Most alarming of all, Brontes's hammer prepared to squash the Companions into jelly. Metal gray and fringed upon jagged shores, it hovered in the air like a vast island about to crash upon their heads.

Their end would have come soon enough had it not been for the Erinnyes. Worried perhaps that the stones might be lost forever beneath the awful might of the Cyclops's hammer, they flew up into his face as if to distract him, calling him by name in their fell voices.

It was all the time Turgot needed. Before anyone even knew what was happening, he had landed on the scepter still hanging from Rafi's belt. In a flurry of cries and claws, he cut through the cords binding each stone upon her shirt. One by one, they fell into his claws, each stone a ponderous weight, and yet as light as a feather when compared to the greed that bore them.

"The stones!" cried Krik.

"The hammer!" warned Peter.

Turgot's plan would have been perfect had it not been for Pud. Upon hearing Krik's cries, the noble rat thrust his sword through Rafi's shirt, stabbing Turgot through both eyes. Shocked and angry, maddened with pain, Turgot somehow managed to keep his footing on the scepter, his claw cutting through Rafi's belt as he hastened to complete his plan. Invisible to those who watched in horror, blind to himself, Turgot, stones and scepter clattered to the ground and disappeared.

Krik stared helplessly at the frayed cords on Rafi's shirt.

"We are lost!" he cried. "Turgot has the stones!"

"Lost!" Turgot's cries mocked him from the shadows. Bittersweet, they sang a song of triumph hushed by sobs over his lost eyes. "Lost you are," he cried in an insane mixture of merriment and misery, "nev'air to be found!" His voice rose loud and shrill. "Once again, I 'ave defeated you, mantis. And you, Marie," he added between sobs of pain, "parting is such sweet sorrow. It is a shame that one so bold and beautiful should die, but die you must, and die you shall, but not by my 'and. The Cyclops will see to that."

"Not that you'll ever see it, Turgot!" roared Bree.

Unforgotten, hovering like a tombstone over a moving grave, Brontes's hammer was about to make Turgot's prediction come true. Yet even Brontes was not without surprise. Even as the monster raised his hammer, and would have made an end to the Companions in one blow, the crystal, still in his hand, burst into flame. Amidst howls of pain, the stroke fell wide. As if struck by a missile, the ground exploded, blowing both rocks and Companions skyward in every direction until they fell, bruised and scattered, upon the hard ground.

"Stay together!" shouted Krik.

Peter leapt to his feet. Blood poured from his nostrils. "No!" he cried. "That way one blow will finish us all. We must confuse him!"

The same thought had occurred to Talat. Racing toward Brontes, his great sword flashing like the crescent moon, he slashed the Cyclops's legs. Rivers of red sprang from ugly wounds, drenching him with blood.

"Run!" he cried with another furious stroke of his sword.

With one sweep of his hand, Brontes brushed Talat off his feet as if he was a fly. Airborne, Talat flew across the cave, slapping hard against a wall of rock. For a moment, he hung suspended upon the wall as if he was hanging on a peg. Then, with a groan and a crash, he fell upon a mountain of gold and rolled out of sight.

Shocked that he was not already picking bits of each Companion off his hammer, Brontes rubbed his bleeding legs. Burning hotter than the crystal, his enraged eye searched the cave until it frosted over with the unnerving placidity of chilled steel.

"There you are!" he bellowed, spotting the Companions as they painfully crept across the cave. The voice fell upon them like a thunderclap as avalanches of rock slid down the walls from every direction, hemming them in. "Death is too sweet an end for you. I will tear you limb by limb and eat you alive. Such is your reward for spilling but one drop of my blood." He dropped his hammer and fell to his knees, turning the air into an asteroid belt of flying rock.

"The way is blocked!" cried Bree.

Peter spun on his heels. "We're surrounded!" he cried.

"Where's Talat?" cried Rafi.

"Make for the Cyclops!" yelled Krik. "It's the only way!"

"You've got to be kid..." said Dlop.

They never made it. Having guessed their escape route, Brontes blocked the way with one of his horned hands. "So ends your merry dance, my brave little frogs." His ugly face closed in, one bright and shining eye. Through a graveyard of broken, yellow teeth, hot breath steamed the air as his eye swelled to the size of a hot air balloon and bore down upon Rafi.

"Give me the stones!"

Rafi pointed to the dangling cords on her shirt. "Can't you see?" she cried. "Turgot has stolen them. And while you are playing with us, he is getting away!"

Brontes smiled more lopsidedly than ever. "You lie," he said.

"She lies," cackled Megaera. Flanked by Alecto and Tisiphone, she hovered above Brontes's head, lustful for slaughter. "Remember, Brontes, the stones are not for you."

Rafi drew herself up proudly. She smiled grimly at Krik, Bree, Dlop and Peter. If she was going to die, at least she would die with her friends.

"What are the stones to you?" she asked, hopeful of a few more precious seconds of life. "Your world will be no better than Triodon's."

Brontes laughed a deep, hearty laugh. "My world," he said. He opened his hand. Upon a blackened welt of skin the crystal burned faintly. "What would you know about my world? See how I have already tamed your magic lamp. Do you not know? Not all things must be destroyed; only those that are weak and infirm. Even slaves have their purpose in an ordered world." His eye darkened. "However, that is one luxury you shall not have."

"Cruel monster," said Rafi. "What is a world without love?" She scooped up Bree, Dlop and Krik, assembling them on her shoulders and in her hair. Krik's head was covered with blood.

"You're bleeding!" she cried.

"Seemed ... to ... have ... bumped my head," he said painfully.

"What does it matter?" bellowed Brontes. "Better he die now than face the peril that awaits the rest of you. Starting with you, my fine Drog." And with these words, he snatched up Peter in one of his powerful hands.

"Allah!" With a great shout, Talat hurtled across the cave, his broad chest gleaming in a breastplate of gold. Such was his speed and fury, Brontes could only watch dumbfounded as Talat's sword connected with his thumb. In a fountain of blood, the thumb sprang from Brontes's hand. As for Peter, he had not been idle, driving his knife all the way down to its handle into Brontes's thick skin.

Brontes dropped Peter. "Father Zeus!" he cried. "Is there no end to these troublesome guests?" He picked up his hammer.

"Goodbye, Companions of Earth," he said.

The hammer zeroed in for the kill. Beneath the hammer's shadow, surrounded by a wall of rock, Rafi, Krik, Bree, Dlop, Peter and Talat looked helplessly at each other. Above, the island seemed to mist before their eyes.

"Hey, hammerhead!" At the sound of Peter's voice, the hammer shunted abruptly back into sharp focus. "If it's the stones you want, let's see if you can catch me!" In seconds, he was away, leaping over rocks as if they were grains of sand, running as hard as he could zigzag fashion away from the Cyclops.

"Peter, no!" cried Rafi.

Down flew the Cyclops's hammer. With a deafening roar, walls of stone seemed to disintegrate before their eyes even as the floor collapsed beneath their feet. Deadlier still, fragments of rock blew like shrapnel in every direction.

Rafi looked up from where she lay in a painful heap beside Bree, Dlop, Pud and Talat. Miraculously, Krik had somehow managed to stay in her hair. Even more surprising to Rafi, her staff still lay in her hand.

"Ha, ha! Missed me!" Laced with pain, Peter's voice roared above the din as he continued his deadly game of hide and seek. Springing to her feet, Rafi looked over to where she had last seen him just before the world had turned upside down.

Not far away, Peter stood in front of the Cyclops like a young tree about to be crushed by an avalanche of iron. One of his arms hung awkwardly by his side, obviously broken. In spite of his pain, he managed a smile, pointing with his good arm straight through the Cyclops's legs.

"Run! Now!" The words fell, slowly, painfully, like the haunting notes of a funeral march. Worst of all, their meaning could not be more clear. Peter was going to sacrifice himself so the others might have a chance.

"Peter!" cried Rafi, knowing there was nowhere to hide. "Come back!"

But Brontes was in no mood for games. "A fast little fly you are!" he bellowed, as Peter collapsed to his knees under the sheer weight of the giant's breath. His hammer ratcheted over Peter's head like some gruesome machine. Defeated at last, smiling only to himself, Peter shielded his eyes for the end.

"Cyclops!" A voice thundered that no one had heard before. "Stop! I say this shall not be! You shall not harm my friends!"

Too injured to do anything else, Peter looked over in amazement. Standing upon a rock, shining more brightly than any golden statue cast by Brontes's able hands, Rafi raised her staff above her head. Inexplicably, for Turgot had taken the stones, or so the others had thought, HAGAL, NAUD and ISS – the three stones of Erebus – burned brightly around Rafi's neck.

"Look, Dlop," said Bree, pointing. "The constellation Rafi."

Equally amazed, Brontes almost dropped his hammer. "Shall not be?" he cried. "Worthless Drog, you may have escaped the Hydra, but you will need more than a stick to worry me. As for your friend, he is already dead ..."

"Cyclops," Rafi repeated. Poised and ready, she threatened Brontes with her staff as if it was a javelin. "I say this shall not be so."

Brontes ignored her. With an eerie whoosh, his hammer fell toward Peter even as Rafi's staff flew from her hand. Straight and true, it streaked like an arrow through the air, bursting into flame.

"By the Gods ..." began Brontes.

He never finished. Before the Cyclops could react the sharp end of the staff found its mark, cutting through his eye like a hot nail through butter. Driven by the power of the stones, thrown by an arm spirited by friendship and not by gold, the staff drove deeper and deeper into the soft tissue. How the eye sizzled, bubbled, and boiled! From the wound gushed a putrid waterfall of blood and jelly.

With a dreadful shriek, Brontes dropped his hammer. Falling like a meteorite out of the sky, it crashed upon a golden ship complete with diamond-studded sails and golden oars, crushing it as if it was an egg.

"Alas," he cried but no tears fell. His eye, once so bright, was no more than a fire extinguished by a raging sea. He stumbled backwards until his back rested against a wall. Then slowly, almost gently, he slid down the wall where he sat upon cloven hooves. "So the prophecies come true," he said weakly. He looked around the cave, now dark and empty. "Little did I know that such a puny runt could use my own words against me. Once before, a long time ago, a Drog robbed my brother of his eye but that was when the Gods protected us." He sighed deeply. "Who will protect us now? For I am the last of my people. And with my passing, much shall be lost to the world."

"Brontes!" cried Rafi. Blinded with tears, her eyes dimmed as if she too had fallen before the flight of her staff. "You were going to kill Peter," she added miserably. Hands upon her head, she fell to her knees, rocking back and forth in agony. "You were going to kill us all."

Floating upon a stream of blood, a low moan rumbled from Brontes's lips.

"A gift for a gift," he said in a voice not much louder than Krik's, "for you have conquered in fair battle." His massive head rolled to one side. "If you would still seek Triodon, there is a passage to his realm beyond the fire. There the third guardian awaits. Beyond the Guardian you shall find Triodon soon enough. May his fate be better than mine. But if you live, to you and you alone, I relinquish all of my treasure, aye, and that of the Hydra too, for it is protected by enchantments of my kind so that none can remove it without suffering a life of misery and despair. This I willingly give to you along with my life, Rafi of the Three Stones."

Rafi choked back her tears. "Thank you, Brontes," she said. "I only wish that such enchantments could save you now. Please forgive me for what I have done."

Brontes smiled. "To forgive is to forget, little one." With some effort, he raised the crystal to his eye. For the first and last time, his fierce eye glowed with a soft light. "And I shall never forget you, Drog. Perhaps in the next world we shall meet again." Without another word, the crystal fell from his hand, striking the earth where it suddenly disappeared.

"Earth to Earth," pronounced Krik. Somehow, in all the commotion he had managed to bandage his head.

"And the Erinnyes to their master," said Bree. He pointed up at Megaera, Alecto and Tisiphone who, after seeing Brontes fall, were almost colliding with one another in their haste to leave the cave. He turned to Rafi. "And you, Rafi," he added, his eyes shining with pride, "however, did you manage it? I thought for sure Turgot had stolen the stones. Just another one of your miracles, eh?"

"No, not a miracle," said Rafi, who had never felt so low. "I switched the stones just before we climbed the mountain. I had hoped it would make a convincing decoy while the real stones remained hidden. Only Krik seemed to notice, but we agreed to keep the secret to ourselves."

"A secret wise is a secret kept," said Krik. "Who knows who is listening to us even now?" He clawed Rafi's hair affectionately. "Do not grieve overmuch, Rafi. Believe me, it was the only thing you could have done. In times of life and death, even the humblest of ambassadors must rise above humility, even if it means becoming someone who, under other circumstances, we might have never expected to be."

Rafi nodded. "I feel like a 'preying' mantis," she said dolefully.

"One and the same," said Krik sadly, "and yet ever apart. Unfortunately, when the going gets tough, words and good intentions are not always enough." He brightened visibly. "But look at the bright side – we are all still alive – and that is as good as any intention I can think of." He retrieved his chalkboard and chalk from his satchel. "Two," he added.

"An eye for an eye," said Bree, thinking of Brontes and Turgot.

Peter hobbled up to the others, helped by Talat. "Which reminds me," he said, grimacing with pain, "where is that little devil?" His face was as white as snow except for the bloody beard that daubed his chin. Below his elbow, splinters of bone protruded from his arm.

"Knowing Turgot, he can't be far," said Krik. "He would have wanted to watch us die, if only to be sure of his odds before he reaches the next level. Rest assured, he is somewhere nearby, watching, fearful, but dangerous just the same."

Dlop was indignant. "Yeah?" he snapped. "Well hear this you wormy crab apple! When we meet again, we'll do more than put out your eyes! Good one, Pud!"

"He's fainted again," said Rafi. Now that her secret was out she reattached the stones to her shirt. After stowing Pud inside, she then made a sling for Peter's arm.

"It's a little dirty," she said guiltily.

Peter sniffed the rag, making an awful face. "A little?" he said, jokingly. "It smells of garlic."

Glad to be alive, they looked gratefully at each other. Not one of them had escaped the Cyclops without a wound: Krik's head was bleeding through his bandages, Peter's arm had been almost snapped in two, and Talat was finding it difficult to breathe, a result, no doubt, of his collision with the wall. And although she didn't know it at the time, Rafi had thrown her staff with such force, she had badly dislocated her shoulder. To complete their list of injuries, Bree had a nasty hole right through one of his ears, and in all the excitement, Dlop had managed to stab his own tail.

"Shrapnel," said Bree as Rafi tended his ear.

"Things could have been worse," said Krik. He looked repulsively at the Cyclops. "Give us a lift, Rafi my dear. I don't think I'm up to walking."

"I wonder," said Rafi, still grieving over the death of Brontes and worried about Krik who was spitting up blood and seemed to have forgotten that he was already in her hair.

Bree looked concernedly at Krik. "Brontes said there is a passage beyond the fire. Should we stop here and rest awhile or go on?"

"We … must … go … on," Krik coughed in reply. "We haven't a second to lose, and by now Triodon is sure to know about Brontes. A drink and a bite standing will have to do. Collect your things and let's go."

Bree loosened his sword as he looked at Dlop. "Watch out for the Erinnyes," he said.

"And Turgot," added Dlop.

Led by Rafi, they made their way around the fire. Here and there, they paused to admire the magnificent handiwork of the Cyclops, which, in terms of art and craftsmanship, surpassed anything they had ever seen before.

"Rafi," said Peter. Painfully, he picked up a golden buckler adorned with an eagle that looked so real it could have flown away.

"What does it feel like to be the richest person in the world?"

"Worried," said Rafi in perfect truth. "Worried about my family, worried about you, worried about the world that is to come, and worried that, in the end, I may be the poorest wretch alive."

"Not if we can help it," said Bree.

Before long, they found themselves standing in front of a giant crack cut deep in the mountain wall. Hundreds of feet high and at least as wide, it looked to be an entrance of an underground canyon. As if waiting for visitors, dozens of wooden torches, both large and small, lay neatly stacked against the wall. Beyond the entrance, on either side of a rock-strewn floor, walls of rock rose dizzily to heights unknown. Nowhere could they see any sign of a guardian.

"Maybe the guardian is hiding in the rocks," squeaked Dlop.

"Maybe the guardian is the rocks," suggested Krik.

"Anoth'air riddle, my resilient mantis," said a voice.

"Tall as Mountain, Oceans deep,
Distant shores, in death will meet,
Ever moving, never walks,
Symplegades, the Clashing Rocks."

"Turgot!"

"The same," sneered Turgot. Even cloaked in invisibility, his voice rang of envy and hatred.

Bree offered up his spectacles. "How are your eyes, Turgot?" he said.

"Bett'air than your broth'air's," snapped Turgot angrily, "and just as good as yours. Without the scept'air you are as blind to me as I am to you. But what does that matt'air? Invisible, I alone may pass the third guardian un'armed, but you," Turgot spat, "will remain here forev'air." He laughed insanely. "Or at least until the coming of the new moon."

Krik peered into the canyon. "You may be right, Turgot," he said in a clear voice, "but I warn you now as someone who was once your friend. Join us before it is too late. Triodon has nothing to offer you and something tells me that even the scepter cannot protect you here. You may not know it, but I believe you are in great danger."

"Bah!" cried Turgot. "Danger I was in when that filthy rat put out my eyes! And you, Marie," his voice seethed with anger, "you tricked your faithful Turgot even as you did once before. Ahhh, but then I 'ad the last laugh did I not?" His voice calmed suddenly. "But enough of old memories. It is time to leave the dying with the dead. Goodbye, mes amis."

Clickety-clack, clackity-click.

"Turgot ..." cried Krik.

It was too late. Suddenly, the canyon shook as walls of rock hurtled down from above as if the entire mountain was about to collapse, crushing everything in its path. Somewhere beneath it all, Turgot let out one piercing, heart wrenching scream, which was followed by a sickening crunch. Within seconds, the entire canyon had filled with rocks as a great cloud of dust rose like a white specter above a graveyard of death.

Symplegades, the third guardian of Erebus, had spoken.

CHAPTER TWENTY
BOOTS AND BARROWS

Troubled clouds gathered over Drumheller. In the aftermath of Zigh's battle, the army had resigned, Greenland was missing, the bonbons had melted in France and someone had stolen the American President's boots. If that was not enough to worry about, there was still the fact that, in a few hours, there would be no (living) humans left on Earth.

With nothing else to do other than look for the President's boots, the people of Drumheller voted at Town Hall as to how they should spend their remaining hours together. In the end, at the recommendation of Canada's Prime Minister, it was decided to start a World Wildlife Scholarship Fund for those less fortunate animals who could not afford to get a proper education. That could mean only one thing …

"A garage sale?" spluttered The Mayor. Having just been released from the hospital, he stood in a wheelbarrow where, for some unknown reason, his injured foot had been set in cement. Oddly enough, his aides did not seem to mind, citing that it was the first time they could push him around.

Tents, balloons and 'GARAGE SALE' signs adorned the city. Everyone came out, some to sell – others to buy – to ensure that the sale was a complete success. The Queen sold tours of her palaces, the Dalai Lama sold books, the Pope sold the Popemobile, Australia sold New Zealand, the American President auctioned off Senators and Members of Congress and the Canadian Prime Minister held a contest to see if anyone could remember his name. But that was not all. Touched by the town's generosity, the Nadi were equally creative:

Ademar and Erech sold rides, Zigh sold dinosaur bones, Fermi sold perfume, Aye sold chop sticks and knitting needles – the list went on and on. Easily the most successful venue was the Dung Beetle's where, for one dollar, you could buy a bag of chocolate not-so-sweets or a cigar.

"Ships in a bottle!" cried Mrs. Grogblossum. Sober now that the world had run out of wine, she held up a variety of wine bottles – each containing its own ship made entirely of cork.

Orly Thumbottom's voice rose from a cloud of cat hair. "Kittens!"

"Ride with Rafi!" cried Mopsus and the town garbage men. Starting at five dollars, interested parties could reenact Rafi's daring escape from Drumheller in a garbage truck – complete with rats and garbage.

"Poutine?" guessed the President of the United States.

"No, not Poutine," said the Prime Minister of Canada.

"Gretzky?"

The Prime Minister shook his head.

"I know! I know!" The President held out another dollar. "Prince Edward Island?"

None too happily, the Prime Minister took the dollar. "Sorry …"

"Suzuki?"

Not missing a thing from his wheelbarrow, The Mayor had never been angrier. Aside from the fact that garage sales were illegal in Drumheller, his aides had deserted him in an effort to do some last minute shopping (literally).

"Citizens of Drumheller," he pleaded as shoppers, mistaking his wheelbarrow for a trash can, threw dirty cups and plates around his feet. "Listen to me." He scowled at Mopsus who had added a spare rat to his wheelbarrow. "See for yourselves how, when laws are broken, a troubled girl, encouraged by unfit parents and an untutored public, has reduced our fine town to a rubbish heap. Yet even now I hold you blameless in this matter, for the guilt lies with one and one alone. If only I had acted sooner, before these," The Mayor sniffed at a Prince, President and Prime Minister fighting over the last bag of dung balls, "these truffles and hangers-on, bored with their own kingdoms, saw fit to destroy ..."

"Excuse me," said Scart Loitersack, finding a half-eaten sandwich in the wheelbarrow, "will you be eating that?"

"... mine."

"Too late," confessed Scart, his mouth full of sandwich.

"I see that you have found a more fitting vocation," said the Queen, stopping by after giving the American President a few hints as to the Canadian Prime Minister's name. "Is the light red or green?" Not waiting to find out, she hurried off to see Zigh to purchase some new dinosaur exhibits for the British Museum.

Stunned that his own world had seemingly come to an end while Senators were still selling for a dime a dozen, The Mayor hung his head. Confused and angry, he did not even notice the Popemobile park beside his wheelbarrow.

"Do you like it?" asked the Dung Beetle, having traded in his dung ball for a new set of wheels. "Smells of leather but we'll fix that." The Oracle's gaze fell upon the wheelbarrow. "Shift or automatic?"

The Mayor cried openly in his wheelbarrow. "Why," he asked, turning his tearful face to the sky, "do you torture me? Is it not enough that you have set, not a girl, but a ghoul against me, filled my home with beasts and bogtrotters, and destroyed my town only to have me waylaid by a Dung Beetle?"

"Still you remain removed from your fellow creatures," said the Dung Beetle. "Have you learned nothing from a child's innocence, the heart of a people, a town, a world or, indeed, Mother Earth herself? Is your world so indifferent to ours that you cannot bring yourself to look upon us with love instead of laws?"

Getting no response from the sky, and finding himself the object of a lecture by a Dung Beetle, The Mayor almost flew from his wheelbarrow. Clearly, his mood and mind were set no less hard than the cement around his foot.

"Mother Earth!" The Mayor scoffed in disgust. "What is Earth if nothing but a place upon which to hang a business or a home or, for that matter, a realty sign? What is Earth without laws as to how to dispense its use, control its citizens unable to contribute to a greater cause or mete justice upon those who, under the pretense of love, cannot follow a few simple rules?" Loathing spilled from his eyes, overflowing his wheelbarrow. "And you, an animated bit of dung, have the audacity to ask me if I have learned anything from Mother Earth or a reckless child that, as I understand it, was fouled from the same womb?" In a rage, he threw his little black book at the Dung Beetle. "There," he said, laughing, "if dung is all you know, eat that, and perhaps one day you shall fill the world with something better than yourself. As for me, I resign as Mayor of Drumheller. And if I have uttered one word of a lie, let your precious Earth strike me d ... de ... where I stand. Yet surely even Earth cannot be so cruel ..."

He was wrong.

As if to announce the garage sale was over, a bolt of lightning zigzagged across the sky, striking The Mayor on his other foot. What happened next could only be described as a fitting ceremony for The Mayor's resignation. Against all laws of physics, The Ex-Mayor and his wheelbarrow set off into space for a full minute before landing on a passing hot air balloon. Even from the balloon, his screams could still be heard raining down upon exhausted but contented shoppers.

The President of the United States was impressed. "NASA should see this," he said.

With all eyes upon The Mayor, Stiles Whatish idled up to the President.

"Interested in a fine pair of boots?"

CHAPTER TWENTY-ONE

THE FATES

Horrified, the Companions watched as tons of rock crashed down upon Turgot. Down it came in a never-ending rush of rock until the canyon was completely blocked. From out of the canyon, a cloud of dust settled upon them, filling their eyes, ears, and mouths with the bitterness of chalk made even bitterer by the realization that, had they taken another step, they would have shared the same fate as Turgot. Then, as if the rocks had never fallen, they sank beneath the canyon floor.

Rafi covered her eyes, thinking of Turgot. Visible or invisible, it was a horrible way to die. "I can't bear to look," she said.

Bree peered into the canyon. "It's not that bad, Rafi," he said cheerfully.

She gazed into the canyon. In a pool of blood, almost crushed beyond recognition, fragments of broken scepter and Krik's shattered watch lay beneath the mangled remains of Turgot.

Bree winked at Dlop. "See?" he said. "It's not that bad."

"Well, whaddaya know," said Dlop. "He was a 'rock' lobster after all."

Krik lowered his head. "Do not rejoice too quickly, my rock hearted friends," he said solemnly. "Turgot was many things both dark and unpleasant, but once he was also my friend. He was not always possessed of an evil mind. Much knowledge has died with him today, and I, for one, grieve at his passing." He lifted a claw in salute. "Salut, Turgot."

"Sorry, Krik," said Bree. "Sometimes it's easier to forget than remember. Certainly we would never have made it this far without him."

"Nev'air," said Dlop.

Then, as if to mourn Turgot's passing, bits of scepter, watch, claw and shell sank beneath the ground.

"So the Scepter of Agony returns to Earth," said Krik.

"What now?" Peter asked anxiously. Rivets of pain had sprouted up all over his face. Helped by Talat, he slumped on a rock as Rafi removed bone splinters from his arm. He closed his eyes. Beneath a mantle of gray dust, he suddenly looked much older. "I don't know about the rest of you," he gasped, "but my arm and shoulder feel like they're in there with Turgot. If we are going to do something, we had better do it quick."

Talat ran a finger down the length of his sword. "Flesh and blood I understand," he said grimly. He bent down, picked up a golden mask, and threw it into the canyon. Instantly, the mountain roared as a fresh avalanche of rock hurtled down from heights above, filling the canyon. Just as mysteriously, the rocks and mask disappeared. He shrugged his shoulders.

"How does one reason with rocks?" he asked.

"How indeed?" said Bree, having just exhausted all of the possibilities in a game of rocks and scissors with Dlop.

"If anybody understands rocks," said Dlop, "it's Pud."

Rafi checked Pud who lay seemingly comatose in her shirt. "I'm afraid even Pud can't save us this time," she said.

"Maybe there's another passageway," suggested Bree.

"That there is not," said Krik firmly. "We can be sure of that. Turgot would never have risked entering the canyon if he knew there was another way. Foolishly, he thought that Symplegades would fail to penetrate the scepter's invisibility. How wrong he was."

"Then we must trust our own strength," said Bree wearily, "only I'm not sure I have any left."

"I'm sure you speak for all of us, Bree," said Krik. "Yet one never knows what strength or reason one possesses until confronted with the ultimate choice. It is only when the root of our greatest fear pulls us toward difficult choices that we discover who we really are. Pud made that choice back at the cliff as did Talat and Peter in the cave. And so have you all, each in your own way."

"Except me," Dlop whispered dejectedly. Only Talat heard him.

"Roots and rocks!" Rafi cried suddenly. Her face wore the expression of someone who had just solved a problem. "Krik, that's it! It's so simple!" Reaching into her knapsack, she withdrew a flash of gold.

"The acorn!"

Krik applied several new bandages to his head. "Well done, Rafi," he said approvingly. "I can't imagine why I didn't think of it myself. That fall in the Cyclops's cave must have scrambled my brains."

"I don't understand," said Peter. "How is an acorn going to save us from being pulverized into dust?"

Rafi looked jubilant. "It won't," she announced excitedly to the confused faces around her, "but a tree will. Don't you see? The Oracle knew we could never defeat the guardians on our own. That's why we had to cross the Tears of Agony – to get what we needed, remember? But the gifts weren't meant for us; each gift was destined to be given to a certain guardian. Without the crown, we would have never escaped the Hydra, and I don't want to think where we would be right now had it not been for the crystal. That leaves the acorn …"

"I get it, Rafi," said Bree, catching on. He gazed wonderingly at the acorn. "Rock is stronger than acorn, but tree is stronger than rock – if only given enough time. And this …"

"… is no ordinary acorn," finished Krik. He nodded encouragingly at Rafi. "Well, Rafi," he said, "I can't think of anything else. Throw it as far as you can into the canyon and let's see what happens."

She kissed the acorn. "Acorn," she said, "please forgive me if, by my hand, you are never to be reborn. Yet, even as I release you back into Earth's miracle, I pray that you will grow into a miracle of your own." Then, with an added prayer for her family and friends, and for all creatures upon the earth, she threw the acorn. On golden wings, it sailed into the middle of the canyon where it fell in a splash of gold upon the ground. From the earth rose a deep, resonant sound as loud and beautiful as a church bell.

Breathless they watched hopeful of a miracle. They did not have to watch for long. In seconds, to the tune of clashing rocks and drum, walls of rock crashed down into the canyon. The mountain held nothing back – dropping the Empire State Building upon the acorn could have done no less damage than the world of rock that buried it now. Drained and defeated, the Companions watched their one and only hope crushed out of sight by the merciless rocks. Then, just as mysteriously, both rocks and acorn disappeared beneath the earth.

"It's gone!" cried Peter.

"So much for strength," said Bree sadly.

"Waste of a good dinner," said Dlop.

Then, just when their spirits fell, a golden shaft sprang up from the earth where the acorn had fallen. Up, up, up it grew, growing taller and wider by the second as new shafts of gold sprouted outwards and upwards into the canyon like the never-ending branches of a tree. Within seconds, golden branches had sprouted golden leaves, filling the canyon with gold. But it did not stop there. The tree grew and grew, pushing back the clashing rocks with all of its golden might, punching through the mountainside as if it was a paper bag. Only then did the tree cease to grow, its magnificent golden boughs crested by a crown of seven stars pinned above the crescent moon.

Bree shook his head in disbelief. "Good thing you didn't eat it, Dlop," he said.

"Unbe-leaf-able," said Dlop.

Rafi could not believe her eyes. "A golden tree!" she exclaimed. Shimmering in appreciation, golden leaves danced on moonlit boughs. "Who am I to see such wonders upon the earth?"

"One who sees," said Krik, who had eyes only for the moon.

Bravely, the last sliver of sickly moon tried to resist the dark penumbra slowly creeping across its face. Soon its face would be completely black.

"The coming of the New Moon!" cried Bree.

"The New Moon!" Krik pointed to the moon, moving irresistibly toward two bright lights that refused to twinkle in the black sky. "Jupiter and Saturn," he said. "Three hours from now they will align with the horns of the crescent moon. For seven minutes, the entire world will be plunged into complete darkness. This will be the Moment of Truth when the stones must fall, either to save Earth or change it forever for those few who survive. By then, if we are to succeed in our quest, we must have the Seven Stones of Erebus. Nothing less will do."

Bree's face set with determination. "Then nothing less will happen," he said.

Krik raised his staff. What little light left shining in the sky fell delicately upon his face. "Companions of Earth," he cried in a trembling voice, "now the final road begins. Yet travel not this road with your feet, but with your hearts for it shall take you to deep places within Earth and, indeed, within yourselves. Let none hold back while the fair moon still lives in the sky, for he that would rob us of life and home awaits. We shall not disappoint him. And should we fall along the way, better we fall, not into the closed abyss of hatred and greed, but into the open arms of a friend."

Impassioned by Krik's words, they sprang into the canyon, Rafi leading, Pud in her shirt, Bree on her shoulder and Krik in her hair. High above their heads they heard the ominous clashing of rocks but, miraculously, the golden tree held firm. On winged feet, they flew through the canyon under a canopy of silver and gold. Such was Rafi's speed that Krik's bandages almost blew off his head. But the mantis never faltered for a moment, shouting encouragement to failing legs and quaking hearts as, at every second, a mountain of rock threatened to fall upon their heads. Fearless and proud, he stood taller than any tree, his staff pointing to a distant door. Behind

Rafi, heavy boots stumped upon the earth as Talat tried to keep up, his great sword swinging by his side. On his shoulder, squeaking at every step was Dlop. Last of all, finding strength in the deepest recesses of his pain, staggered Peter.

One by one, they screeched to a halt before the door.

"That run would have tired a racehorse," said Bree, deeply impressed.

Rafi wondered if her lungs were about to explode. "Too ... bad ... we don't ... have one," she gasped.

Reminded of his contract with the mantis, which had not included dragons, a Cyclops or living rocks, Peter forced a smile. "How much gold am I getting?"

Krik missed the joke. "I am prepared to renegotiate your contract in due time," he said. Preoccupied with his chalkboard, he wrote the number three upon it in green chalk.

"Three," he said.

Rafi stared intently at the door. Inscribed with beautiful objects and pictures, massive beyond any human that ever walked the earth, and seemingly made of solid gold, it stood like an ancient portal to some long forgotten past. On either side of the door burned a flaming torch, its flickering light falling upon the inscriptions, almost animating them to life. Rafi knew at once that they were hieroglyphics, even though she could not read them.

"Egyptian, are they not?"

"Gypsum," Dlop said importantly to Bree.

Krik studied the inscriptions. To those watching him, there was no question about it – Krik could read hieroglyphics. He nodded in his usual way.

"It's Egyptian all right," he said admiringly. "And very good Egyptian at that. The inscriptions are flawless."

"What does it say?" asked Bree.

Krik hesitated. "Many dark things," he said, "but only one of them concerns us now." He pointed to an oval. Inside were most beautiful inscriptions of all.

"The cartouche of Triodon," he said.

Slowly, deliberately, the doors opened.

Beyond the door, more torches conducted them into a great hall where new hieroglyphics, looking as fresh as if they had been painted the day before, guided them throughout the hall and its adjacent rooms – all stuffed with treasure. However, unlike the many wonders in the Cyclops's cave, each crafted object appeared to have been made for a single owner. There were chairs, thrones, and beds made of gold, footstools of ebony and ivory, headrests of lapis-lazuli, alabaster vases and lamps, exotically carved canes and sandals, golden chests, chests, and yet more chests, all overflowing with jewelry and precious stones. Every few feet, grim statues of exotic animals with human hands and feet, life size and terribly life like, stood over the treasure as if guarding it from those who would dare to intrude. The mere sight of it was overwhelming.

"That chair," said Peter, pointing, and momentarily forgetting his pain, "is worth more than Drumheller and everything in it."

"More like ten Drumhellers," corrected Bree.

Krik appeared completely oblivious to the marvelous objects around him. "Worth," he said disgustedly, "has nothing to do with it. There is many a smile and kind word in Drumheller that is worth more than that chair and, indeed, everything in here."

Rafi thought about her family and friends back in Drumheller. "How true," she said. Stale air filled her nostrils. "Is this a tomb?"

"Hopefully not our own," said Peter.

Talat laughed for the first time since he had left Afghanistan. "Oh, I don't know," he said. He picked up a beautiful two-handled vase of alabaster, gazed at the decorative inlays, and put it down again. "I can think of worse places to die."

"Hurry," Krik implored. "Every second counts. Tomorrow, should we live, there will be plenty of treasure for everyone. Until then, our one and only treasure lies beneath our feet."

"Earth!"

Reluctantly, they proceeded down the hall. At the end of the hall stood yet another door, smaller, and made of wood. In front of the door was a table. Upon the table was a gourd of water and a bowl of fruit.

Krik surveyed the fruit. "A long overdue snack, and then a powwow I think," he said, and in a moment, his face was buried in a grape that smelled of hyacinth and honey.

Rafi was appalled. "Krik!" she cried. "What if the fruit is poisoned?"

"How little you understand Triodon, Rafi," he said, his mouth full of grape, "if you think he allowed us to come this far only to poison us. This is just his way of letting us know that he is here and still in charge. Believe me, he is torn between disappointment and admiration that we have managed to come this far. Besides, Triodon never did anything without an audience. It would give him his greatest pleasure to look upon our faces as it dawns upon us that our time has finally come. More likely, this is his idea of a reward."

"Or our last supper," said Peter.

Bree wrestled with a large banana. "In either case," he said, famished. "Eat!"

Without another word, they fell upon the food and water provided by their unseen host, wondering if this was, indeed, the last meal that would ever pass their lips. Certainly, it was the most delicious.

Suddenly, the mountain shook, making the gourd and remnants of fruit dance upon the table.

Krik shook along with the table. He pointed a grape-stained claw at the wooden door. "Listen to me – all of you. There is precious little time to explain, and there are some things you should know before we walk through that door." He paused to catch both his balance and his breath. "There is much that I would say to each of you now," he added, his eyes misting, "if only we had more time." He bowed to Bree and Dlop. "To old friends, whose friendship and loyalty have never wavered in the face of loss or danger. To new friends," his bow extended to Peter and Talat, "whose single deeds speak louder and truer than most nations and ..." His voice faltered as he gazed lovingly into Rafi's eyes. "To a friend as deep and timeless as love itself in whose voice and song live the dreams and flowers that, once planted, will grow into gardens that shall never end."

He dried his eyes on his satchel. "But beyond this door," he went on, his voice now strong and steady, "wait those who care nothing for gardens, love, loyalty, or friendship. Death is their garden, and in that garden we shall find the Erinnyes, the Empusae, and, if we are lucky, Triodon himself. But, more importantly, beyond this door, you shall find your past, present and future. Whether it beckons bright and joyous, or to places dark and unknown, I cannot say."

"Is that all?" said Bree carelessly. "Are you sure you don't want to put us under any real pressure before we go in?"

"Danger," Krik continued, "will be around us at every step and turn. And yet all of you have proven yourselves equal to those who would end our quest. Do not imagine for a moment that our victories over the Hydra and the Cyclops have gone unnoticed. Fear gnaws at our foes even as your own fear gives you the strength to go on. But know this: Triodon's power is not in his strength, though he is strong enough; nor in his courage, though he is brave enough. His power lies in his words and guile. Remember that his tongue alone softened the hearts of no less than Wind, Ocean, Fire, and Mountain. Remember too, that he already possesses four of the seven stones. That in itself gives him the mastery, and, should he throw them in a sudden rage, our quest will have been for naught."

"We are tired and weak," said Rafi suddenly sensing the futility of their quest. "And some of us are injured. Against such odds, where shall we find hope?"

"Hope remains our most fickle Companion," said Krik. "It comes and goes like a never-ending tide, and yet it shall never leave us as long as we are true to ourselves and each other. Do not fear. There is still every hope that we may yet defeat Triodon and rescue the stones."

Rafi touched the stones bound once more upon her shirt.

Suddenly she was fearful that she might lose them. It was only then that she realized the stones had become a part of her as precious as life itself. A part that, either way, would soon be over.

"Perhaps," she said wistfully, "there is still hope that Triodon will see reason and not throw the stones. You said yourself that he was not always evil. Perhaps these long years of torment have given him reason to forgive those who have wronged him. Could he not have changed," she looked round at Peter, Talat, Bree, and Dlop, "just as we have changed?" She stroked Pud. "As I have changed?"

"Dearest Rafi," said Krik, his eyes no less revealing than her own, "the question you ask can only be answered by the Fates, the three sisters whose stones you bear upon your breast if only for a little while. Fortune telling is of no use here. Only one charge do I put upon you and you alone. Under no circumstances are you to let Triodon have the stones."

"I understand," she said miserably. "But why must new beginnings begin with so much death? First, the Tyrannosaurus, then Draig, Brontes and Turgot. And what about Pud? Must he die too? Who else must die to save a world that seems less worth saving with every step we take? Surely the Fates did not intend it to be so."

"That I cannot say," answered Krik. "But save the world we must, or at least try. And if not for us, for those who cannot save themselves."

At these words, the door creaked open. Behind the door lay a passageway, dark and forbidding.

"So it begins," said Bree.

"So it begins," echoed Rafi. She gazed at each of the Companions, and her friends. There was Peter, bent awkwardly as if he was a broken stick, the forced smile upon his face belying the pain that everyone knew was tearing him apart. Next to Peter stood Talat, a grim smile fixed upon his face, his strong fingers drumming on his sword as if he was about to begin a recital. Sitting on the table, Bree held Dlop's paw, whispering something in his ear. Still in her shirt, gripped in an internal battle somewhere between life and death, lay

Pud. And there was Krik, gazing lovingly at his satchel, which he placed upon the table. Looking at Krik, Bree, Dlop, Pud, Peter, and Talat as if for the first time, she knew what an honor it was to be a Companion of Earth.

Krik held out a claw. "For Earth," he said.

Over the table soared a pyramid of hands and paws.

"For love," said Rafi.

"For those who live," said Talat calmly.

"For those who shall never die," said Bree.

"Let's do it!" said Peter.

Rafi slid off her knapsack. Now empty, she placed it next to Krik's satchel. "Let us hope," she said, "that we shall wear these again in better times."

"Make way for Rafi of the Three Stones!" cried Bree. He nodded to Krik, knelt down before the mantis, letting him mount his back as if he was a horse. After a brief argument about the use of spurs, he ran up Rafi's arm where he stationed himself upon her shoulder. Drawing his sword, he signaled for Dlop to join Talat.

Through the doorway they went. It seemed as if they had stepped into a darkness that would never end. For several minutes they stumbled on, speaking only in whispers, wondering whether Triodon or the Erinnyes would suddenly spring out from the darkness, catching them unawares. Almost imperceptibly, a faint light penetrated the darkness – from where they knew not – revealing a stone path that led up a hill. Grateful for the light, they headed up the path until they stood at the top of the hill. Then they gasped.

Below the hill stretched a vast plain. A stone Sphinx shaped like a lion with a man's head and beard cast its majestic gaze over a wide black chasm that snaked like a river across the plain. Beyond the Sphinx, each dressed in white polished limestone and under an apex of black granite, three colossal pyramids brooded timelessly over the plain.

Peter rubbed his eyes in disbelief. "Is it just me," he gasped, "or did we just walk into Egypt?"

"I see it too," said Rafi, equally amazed. She thought back to her eighth birthday when her parents had taken her see the pyramids of Egypt. "I've seen the real ones in Egypt, or at least I thought I had up until now. Somehow, these seem larger – grander – as if time itself had never touched them. How is this possible?"

"She cheated," crackled a voice.

Beyond further astonishment, Rafi turned toward the voice. "Pardon me?" she asked.

"Not you," the voice crackled impatiently. "Her!"

Without any explanation, Krik quickly dismounted Bree. He lowered his head, indicating for the others to do the same.

"Wise Ones," he said reverently, his head still bowed, "please forgive our intrusion. Little did we expect to find you here where old endings and new beginnings meet. But then, where else would one expect to find Wisdom, Beauty and Grace? Daughters of Earth and Erebus, I bid you greeting."

"The Fates," whispered Bree.

Rafi bowed as low as she could without catapulting Krik and Bree onto the plain below. She had already forgotten about the pyramids. For under the branches of a white cypress tree sat what appeared to be three old women. It was hard to tell as, between the three of them, they shared only one eye, two mouths, three noses and four ears. Their hair, if it could be called hair, sprawled from their heads like old tree roots. Almost as tree-ish, their arms and legs, which happily appeared to be of the right number, hung from shapeless, potato sack garments in varying degrees of filth and shabbiness. In their hands and fingers, which were severely bent and knobby, they each held five cards.

"The Three Sisters," Rafi muttered in awe. It was then that she noticed each sister sat upon a large tortoise, each wearing a different colored shell. In a crude circle, they sat around a small, black pot.

"Four," snapped the sister who happened to be wearing both mouths. Seemingly better off than the other two, this sister also wore the eye, a nose and two ears except that one ear grew from her chin while the other sat on top of her head. She was old, very old, and yet she looked younger than the sister on her left who sat like an ancient ruin, cracked and mossy, apparently having a bout of the sniffles. Youngest of all, the third sister perched upon her tortoise like an old tower, a ruin in the making, looking at her cards through two ears, which she wore as eyes.

Apparently, this remark was meant for the eldest sister. After scratching her nose with twiggy fingers, she carefully withdrew four cards from a card deck she held in her right hand. Not so deftly, a fifth card slipped under her tortoise's aquamarine shell.

"Cheat, I say again," said the sister with the eye. She took the four cards, showing them to her tortoise who sat glumly under a shell of bronze. While looking at her cards, her voice crackled once more.

"Welcome, Companions of Earth," she said. "It is no small feat that you have passed through Earth and Fire, and now stand at the very gates of Erebus. Our greatest respect and admiration you have, but nothing more I fear. For Triodon has four of the stones that, in ages past, ruled this world along with the three that you bear. He awaits you down below."

"Am I to u… understand …," stuttered Krik, a stunned look upon his face, "that you are playing cards?"

"Not cards," snapped the middle sister, offended. She ripped an ear off her head and threw it into the pot. "Poker!"

"P… p… poker?" said Krik incredulously. "The fate of Earth is governed by a poker game?"

"Five card stud to be precise," the sister snapped, an exasperated look upon her face. "Ante up!" she roared, boxing her older sister around the ears except that she did not have any. Without waiting for an answer, she leaned over, ripped off her sister's nose, and threw it into the poker pot.

Suddenly, Rafi understood the mystery of the mountain's eye.

"They're playing for the eye," she whispered.

"Not just the eye," said the middle sister. "Ears, eyes, mouths

— we tried playing for noses but it's too hard to concentrate holding one's breath for so long." She eyed her older sister who, while having been spared the sniffles, was turning blue. "We play for pennies when we have them, although we haven't seen that lay about Styx for ages. You haven't got any, do you?"

"No, Your Graces," said Rafi, highly amused. It was a strange sight to watch the Daughters of Earth curse and shriek at one another, ripping off each other's faces, throwing all and sundry into the poker pot.

By virtue of wearing both mouths, the middle sister went on. "Since you want to know," she said, "my name is Verdandi. I am the Fate of all that is present." She pointed a knobby finger at her sister desperately in need of air and the ace of hearts.

"That's Urd, " she said, scowling. She threw a penny in the pot, giving Urd her nose back. "Urd is the Fate of all that is past."

Urd breathed gratefully.

The youngest sister shuffled the cards.

Verdandi jerked her head. "Skuld," she said, "the Fate of that which is to come."

"Speaking of the future," said Krik, who seemed to have found his wits but forgotten his manners, "it is our understanding that we are perilously close to not having one. Is there anything you wish to tell us before you bargain our lives within an ace of Triodon's?"

Verdandi concentrated on her cards. "Patience, mantis," she said. "This game is not for your lives. That game is between you and Triodon. Should he win, we too shall suffer. Even so, we cannot help you in your quest."

The mountain shook ominously as the Fates anted up for a new game.

"You must hurry," said Verdandi. "Unlike us, Time is not your friend." Having managed to retain one mouth, she smiled at the Companions. "Take the stone path down to the plain and make for the Sphinx. There you shall see a bridge that leads across the Chasm of Hope and Despair. Across the bridge you must go. On the other side, you shall find Triodon."

"Thank you," said Krik, mollified to learn that the fate of Earth as well as his own life did not lie hidden in the hearts and clubs of a five-card spread. "Not just for now, but always. For it is only through your gift that we may learn to understand the miracle of those around us – and ultimately – of ourselves." He bowed low. "What more could be said of Past, Present and Future – the fairest Daughters of Earth."

Desperate for answers, Rafi could not help but ask the question that, more than even Krik, Bree, Pud, and Dlop, had been her constant companion ever since she had left the Apple.

"Daughters of Earth," she said, fighting back her tears, "is there nothing you can tell me about my family? Are they alive and well? Or are their hearts filled with sadness over a foolish daughter and sister, as empty of hope as mine is now?" As beautiful in despair as in hope, her tear stained eyes looked upon Skuld.

Verdandi studied Rafi now that she had won back the eye. "Daughter of Earth," she said, "for you too have earned this honor though you know it not. Even if Skuld had a mouth, she could not tell you that which your heart most desires to hear. But this I can tell you if only for the present. Together, your hearts beat as one, as all hearts were meant to be, and the fate of Earth could rest in no better place." She held out a single letter. "Perhaps this shall ease your pain." Then, to everyone's astonishment, she threw an ear into the poker pot, only the ear was not her own – it was Rafi's. "Now go, ere the heart of Earth bleeds before the light of the new moon."

Pleased that Verdandi had not ripped out her eyes, Rafi read her letter.

Rafi Dearest,

Wherever you are, know that we are safe. Thanks to Zigh and the Dung Beetle, Sue the Velociraptor is now a sprinkler in our garden. If you can believe it, she was sent by Triodon to kill us.

*Oddly enough, with the help of your friends, our survival (Motu
is safe too!) gives us new hope that you are alive and well. In fact,
after our visit with the Dung Beetle, not a moment goes by that
we don't see your face in a cloud, feel your touch in the rain or
hear your voice upon the wind. Earth's Daughter, only now do we
begin to understand that, whatever happens, you never left us.*

*Know too that we shall never leave you. Ours is a love that will
remain long after we are gone. Should Triodon prevail, so shall
you — as will we all — for the Miracle of Love lives by one hand
alone.*

*Even so, we pray for your safe return. There is much to discuss
— Motu's upcoming trial, your father's promotion at the museum,
our new Mayor! — not to mention your quest and the fact that we
have a new relative (your Uncle Horace) in the family!*

*May Earth's and our love shine upon you when you face
Triodon. As one mother to another, I know that Earth loves you
no less or more than we.*

Love
Mother, Father and Motu

With tears both happy and sad, the Companions proceeded
down the stone path that led to the plain. Once level with the plain,
they made their way toward the Sphinx.

"There's the bridge," said Rafi. She pointed to four black obelisks,
as tall as trees, anchoring a great slab of black stone that spanned
the chasm. Behind the bridge stood a wall of painted stone, at least
twelve feet high, and painted with colorful hieroglyphics.

"And there are the Erinnyes," said Bree darkly. They counted
three black shadows perched upon the nearest obelisk. "If I could
only fly, I would send them packing to their master soon enough.
Wing by wing, and claw by claw."

"You may yet have your chance," said Krik. As if they had heard

Bree's threat, the Erinnyes deserted their perch, flying low across the chasm where they settled upon the wall.

At Krik's command, the Companions stopped at the bridge.

Talat shaved a razor thin layer of skin from his thumb with his sword. "I don't like the feeling of this," he said grimly. "It's a trap if ever I saw one. Once we cross the bridge, we will be caught between the wall and the chasm. This Triodon is powerful, is he not? Once across, what is to prevent him from swatting us like flies and sending us into the chasm? It's a trap, I say again. Even without the stones which he bears – behind the wall, on his own ground – he has every advantage."

"Triodon has chosen his defenses well," Krik agreed, surveying the wall. "I do not doubt for a moment that you are right in this, Talat. We could have used your cunning during the Mantis Rebellion of 6771. Yet we have no choice. We can only go on. Are you ready, Rafi?"

"I'm ready," Rafi lied. Even as she spoke, she knew that this statement could not have been further from the truth. Her skin tingled in fear and excitement. With a deep sigh, she laid Pud at the foot of an obelisk with a rock for a pillow. "He will be safer here," she said sadly. Looking down at Pud she suddenly felt unsafe for the first time in her life. "That is, if 'safe' has any meaning down here."

Bree saluted Pud with his sword. "Rest, my brother," he said. "If you don't mind, I'll be needing that." Pud's sword grinned in Bree's paw. "It is time for a debt to be repaid. Never fear. One way or another, we shall return."

"Goodbye Pud," Dlop cried miserably in Talat's ear. "Somehow I don't think we shall ever see each other again."

"Nonsense," said Krik, overhearing Dlop. "Friends are forever."

Rafi stepped onto the bridge. Against her better judgement and Krik's advice, she gazed into the chasm. One look was enough to make her regret her decision. Far below, endless black miles yawned up at her with unnerving incredulity. She turned to Peter. Staggering in pain, he looked back at her with misty eyes, as if only sheer nerve and adrenaline kept him on his feet. Behind Peter, Talat and Dlop followed as rear guard, neither of them happy at the prospect of crossing the bridge.

Oddly enough, Talat appeared to be afraid of heights. "I would sooner fight an army," he grumbled, "than cross a bridge."

"And I would sooner cross that bridge with an army," squeaked Dlop.

Once across, Talat was not alone in his joy to have reached the other side. Somehow, for different reasons, each of the Companions found that they had not only left Pud at the foot of the bridge – they had also left their fear. It was not that they felt any braver; perhaps it was because, like the frayed strings of a violin, their fragile nerves had been plucked so hard and so often they had no more notes to play.

Cautiously, they approached the wall. Of all of their ordeals together, these last steps seemed the worst by far. Step by step, their every thought chilled by the cold brush of impending doom, they inched closer to the wall, their quest and – ultimately – themselves.

"Give me a rope," Peter gasped, almost doubled over with pain, "and I could climb that wall as if it had stairs."

"No need," said Bree. He pointed to the wall. "Look!"

Trembling, they watched unseen hands draw long straight lines upon the wall. Then, to the horrific high-pitched shriek of levers and stone, the lines widened into cracks, opening toward them as a dark doorway grew upon the wall. Beyond the doorway loomed a courtyard, no less dark and foreboding, in the center of which stood seven pylons, encircling a massive throne of black stone. Upon the throne, wreathed in a shadow of irrepressible gloom, two glittering eyes bore down upon the Companions much as distant stars, however bright, might envy the lesser moon.

"Companions of Earth," said the shadow. The voice was neither threatening nor unkind. "Welcome to Erebus. Many are the years since I have welcomed such brave and noble visitors to my home." Strong and clear, the words lingered above the plain, deep as a ruddy wine, and yet as light as air.

Krik bowed his bandaged head. "Triodon," he said.

Rafi, Bree and Peter bowed their heads as well. Upon hearing the voice, which was a delight to hear, some of the gloom seemed to lift from the figure seated upon the throne. Yet, deep in their hearts, the darkness grew.

A large shadow, somewhere in size between that of a man and a monster, rose from the throne. On clawed toes, it stepped forward with the majesty of kings, dragging a long and powerful tail as regal as any robe, yet more deadly than a host of armed men. Behind its back stretched a magnificent pair of golden wings as if some ancient deity had suddenly stepped into a world unready to gaze upon such impossible things. Bright now was the handsome face, lit with a profound grace and wisdom beyond the ages, transcending a body both primitive and strong. Upon its brow was bound a blood-red stone. Deliberately, almost playfully, a single arm, made even more conspicuous by the absence of the other, shook a closed fist as a child might shake a rattle, filling the air with a clacking sound more deadly than any dice.

For the second time since the beginning, Triodon stood ready to destroy Earth.

CHAPTER TWENTY-TWO

TRIODON

Triodon turned and faced the east. Above the plain, framed in a window cut straight through the mountain, the tattered horns of the crescent moon inched its way across the sky. Beaming brightly, the planets Jupiter and Saturn waited for the moon like errant dance partners, ever hopeful for the last dance of the ball. Soon, it would all be over – one way or another.

He laughed. Loud and clear, it rang across the plain, above the pyramids and the Sphinx, into the deepest reaches of the chasm, and as high as the distant moon. Only after the laughter had ended with an audible sigh, did Triodon lower his fist. Deliberately, it came to rest upon his heart. Turning, he retraced powerful steps back to the throne, collapsing his great wings like an exotic umbrella. Turning once more, he stood before the throne, King of Kings, eying each Companion with a look as inviting as it was unnerving, a portrait of tranquil majesty wrought upon a troubled heart.

He sat down. Instantly, the pylons around the throne burst into flame, filling the courtyard with light. Black as pitch, for no light could touch them, the Erinnyes and the Empusae settled upon the back of the throne, glaring at the Companions through eviscerated eyes.

Triodon bowed his head. "Welcome, I say again," he said. Starlight eyes filled with the red glow of a coming dawn. Above his head, under a crown of shooting stars, Jupiter and Saturn bowed before the crescent moon. Beneath his feet, growls of hot magma stirred the chasm. Enthroned in Heaven and in Hell, Triodon gazed upon Rafi, Krik, Bree and Peter.

Rafi could not believe her eyes. It was as if millions of years of evolution of every creature ever born had suddenly come together into one distinct and yet impossible form. Yet, not twenty feet away, Triodon sat in strange but unquestionable glory. The face was a kaleidoscope of creatures both great and small – many that she had seen before – and others she could not have possibly imagined. At first, she thought the face was that of a reptile or mammal, or that of a bird, insect, or a frog – and yet each face was distinctly human in some beautiful but bizarre way. Suddenly, it occurred to her that, for all Krik's obsession that Triodon would destroy Earth, such a thing was not possible until he had destroyed himself.

Triodon smiled a thousand faces. "You must be tired," he said. "For you have traveled far, farther than I would have ever thought possible, and for that, you have my undying respect and admiration. Undying, I say, for I have never died. Yet, never in my long life have I seen such persistence and devotion applied to a duty. A duty no one, however powerful, should have asked of another. And yet a duty, I should have said, that could not have been better given."

Bolts of lightning flashed across his eyes. Gone now was the dawn as dark clouds stormed across his face. And though he never touched nor even looked upon the Erinnyes, they howled in pain from where they sat upon the throne, bolting for the wall where, along with the Empusae, they quailed as if some unseen force had plunged them into depthless agony.

"If only I had had such devoted followers," Triodon said softly. As quickly as they had appeared, the storm clouds vanished, revealing a sea of blue. "What a world it would have been. For, when all is said and done, stones are poor comfort, and even poorer company, as years turn into ages and ages into years."

"Amen," said Krik, his tiny face set adrift in waves of Rafi's hair.

"But you, Krik," said Triodon, his eyes suddenly as green as the mantis, "you never cease to amaze me." His voice rose and fell in admiration. "If only I had been more successful in my attempt to recruit you for an enterprise that, I assure you, would have made you every inch the king you are. The League of Mantis would not have been alone in worshipping your crown. Even Eidon was not worthy to lick your feet."

"Most worshipful Triodon," said Krik cautiously. "Your very gift was why I had to refuse. As you should know by now, no crown should outweigh the lives of its subjects, and kingdoms alone measure no true king. Eidon knew this, and his choice was the same as mine – there cannot be another – to live and let live until living draws its very life from the love and sacrifice of others. If need be – dying for that which is closest to one's heart."

"Love." Triodon's green eyes rolled from gray to white, freezing into sheets of ice, but not before a single tear fell and sizzled upon his throne. "Do not speak to me of love. Where was love when my eyes first looked upon the world? Where was love when, with my first words, I greeted those who only looked upon me with hatred and disgust? Where was your precious love when I begged them to let me into their world?"

"Truly, Triodon," said Krik, his own eyes wet with memories suddenly reopened like old wounds, "I cannot say. Yet, as always, you confuse love with fear. And you forget that, unlike fear, love that is freely given is more powerful than any unrequited love received. You, who had the power of the stones and could have reshaped our world into a better place, choose instead to rid Earth of all that you perceived to be against you, rather than understand one simple truth – that it was love that opened your eyes, formed your first words, and made you into who you are. Then, as now, though you know it not, it was love that made you different, love which placed you upon the greatest of all thrones. You, above all living things, were the scepter chosen by Earth to welcome in a new age. Yet the throne you chose was as hard and black as the one you sit upon now."

Triodon wept bitter tears, which sizzled upon his throne. "Don't I know it, mantis," he said. "I sit upon this throne of black salt to remind me of the bitterness of my youth. Not a day goes by that I do not regret my folly and shortsightedness that you have so admirably recounted to me." The ice in his eyes melted into pools of shining light. "But such talk is wearisome for those who hang upon our words, especially the young Drog of whom the legends speak, and who wears the stones I lost so long ago. It is a heavy burden for one so young. Perhaps she will tell me of herself and her family, and how it is that she wears three of the stones that shaped the earth when even the Fates were young. And then, when she is ready, she can explain to me why she has come to rob me of all that I have left, my life and misery not least, after I have given her and her kind everything I had ever wished for myself, but was denied."

Rafi brushed away the tears she shared with Triodon. His sad story was not lost upon her for she knew something of the words some people said, often without meaning but always mean. The sight of Triodon sitting upon his bitter throne, recounting long years of misery in words both wise and fair, overwhelmed her like a rushing tide. This was no monster sitting before her; she was reminded of a just and venerable king, wounded not with arrows, but by the lifelong sting thrust upon the pointed thoughtlessness of others. No less magnificent in his wisdom as he was beautiful, in any age, Triodon stood beyond presidents, popes, and kings.

"Am I to understand, Triodon" she asked, feeling unworthy to say his name, "that you once ruled mankind?"

"Once?" Spears of anger flew from Triodon's eyes. So frightening was his gaze that, for a moment, the Companions felt as if they had already died. Hardly expecting to live another second, they each breathed a sigh of relief as Triodon released them from his gaze, looking down upon the pyramids and the Sphinx as only he could do.

"I forget that you are so young," he said, smiling once again, "and that history, so dim and distant to your mind, is but to me the days of the week. And for one of those days – many lifetimes to you – I did indeed rule your kind. For though I had long dwelt in this land, I confess that I grew weary of loneliness. From Wind I had heard of a Drog nation emerging upon the Nile, and so I flew across the sea to see for myself what manner of creature these Drogs were, and whether, indeed, my time had come to rule more than mud and stones. There, in a place I was to call Egypt, I built my home. There too I built my pyramids, set my face upon the Sphinx, built my temples, obelisks and pylons – all so that those who served would know me as their rightful king. Pharaoh, they called me, and worshipped my feet until, preferring my own company to their small and sniveling ways, I returned to this place to await the day when the stones should be found. Yet, even so," Triodon sniffed at the pyramids and the Sphinx, "I keep such trinkets as I desire to remind me that Drogs still walk upon the earth."

Rafi suddenly understood. Before her stood the faces, not of Triodon, but of history itself. Was not the face written upon the Sphinx the same face that gazed upon her now? Were not the treasures she had seen both in Egypt and in Erebus – those depicting a pantheon of Gods and guardians – wrought upon Triodon's throne in living flesh and blood?

Triodon's gaze flew like arrows, penetrating her deepest thoughts. "Think of it, Rafi," he continued in a voice not unlike her father's, "today you stand before me because of who I was. It was I who placed mankind's cradle upon Earth, I who named their destiny and fathered the golden age that set their feet upon the path that brings you to my throne." More arrows flew from exalted skies as each Companion fell captive to a gaze of gold. "And with your help I shall rule Earth once again – together, I should say – for a new Earth needs its share of Kings and Queens. Clearly, there are none whose nobility measures up to your own. Join me now and your every wish is already granted."

"Now more than ever," snapped Bree, alarmed by the silence that seemed to paralyze the plain, "are we reminded of our noble ambassador's warning." He aimed an accusing paw at Triodon. "Hear the liar. Such honeyed words are not without their sting." The Erinnyes' scorching glare was no match for the fire in his eyes. He shook his sword at Triodon. "If I was only half as big as you, and as brave as Eidon, I would tear your heart out, and I do not doubt for a moment that it is as black and ugly as your throne."

"Peace, my fearless friend," Triodon said graciously. His fist tightened in an audible crack of bone. "Krik chose you well, the wisest of three brave brothers, who have given much of themselves so that others might live to see another day and cast their wishes upon the stars."

Bree opened his mouth to speak, but remained silent. All the same, his fur bristled with fury, and he did not sheath his sword.

"Bree's right," Peter cried angrily. Somehow, his anger helped defeat the pain sweeping mercilessly throughout his body. Even so, the color in his face was as pale as the failing moon. He gripped Rafi's shoulder with a bloodied hand.

"Don't listen to him, Rafi," he gasped. "His words are fair, but if ever I smelled a cheat and a liar, it's him. Remember Draig, Brontes, and even Turgot, all friends I'm sure of this monster who would now have us believe he is our friend. And remember Pud who gave his life so that freedom could reign instead of this miserable trickster who would throw us into the chasm as easily as he would throw the stones."

Triodon's eyes crystallized into shards of steel. "How little you know me, Peter," he said smoothly. "Draig, Brontes, and even Turgot had their uses, but am I responsible for the choices made by others of their own free will? Their motivation was their own: Draig's obsession with riches, Brontes's love of power, and even Turgot in his unending hatred of Krik – quite remarkable for one so small. But there are other kinds of motivation no less powerful and equally convincing. Yours, for instance. How is it that you can withstand the pain that almost wrenches your arm from your shoulder? I know that pain well as you can plainly see." He pointed at an armless lump of flesh that had once been a shoulder. "And I marvel that you still have the strength to go on, along with, I might add, a good measure of audacity to upbraid a king in his own palace. But let us not bandy words over trifles. Your motivation is clearer than the pain that fills your eyes: your quest for freedom, your passion for justice, and, not least, your love for Rafi."

Peter hung his head. Having lost so much blood, he could not have blushed if he tried. At that moment, not for all the riches on earth would he have dared to look at Rafi. Instead, he turned to speak to Talat – only Talat was not there. Neither was Dlop.

"Now where are they?" he cried, echoing the thoughts of the others who, up until then, had no idea that either Talat or Dlop were missing.

Triodon smiled a thousand smiles. "Last I saw of them," he said, "they were running as fast as their legs could carry them away from my realm. It would appear that not all of you are united in your quest."

The Erinnyes croaked and chuckled.

"The big one has wits sharper than his sword," hissed Alecto. Her eyes smoked at Rafi. "Who's going to save you now, Drog? Not that filthy little Pudder, to be sure!"

"What does it matter?" snapped Tisiphone. "Once these vermin are dead, they shall all die."

Megaera had eyes only for Bree. "Leave the ugly one for me," she spat. A battered wing rubbed an ugly wound upon her brow. "There is a debt to be settled here."

Krik hopped onto Rafi's shoulder where, small as he was, he could be plainly seen. "Ridiculous," he said. "For, unlike you, Triodon, I do not judge others before the facts are in. We, the Companions of Earth, are as united now as we were when Brontes gave us an offer no less offensive than your own. The bridge has not been made that could divide us now."

Triodon shook his head. "That is your greatest weakness, mantis," he said. "Dreaming is for poets – not for kings. Brave you are, as I was brave once, but in this harsh world bravery is not enough. Ask your friends who are now hiding in the rocks. They know your quest is futile; that doom is close at hand." He looked at Rafi. "But what is doom?" he asked her in a voice that would have sounded reasonable had it not hinted at the end of Earth. "With each new age comes new life. And with each new life comes death. For as it is truly said, only through death does life begin to have meaning. And so we begin the cycle once again. Life, death, life, death – it is all the same. Such is our doom."

"Such is your doom," said Rafi, not knowing how she found the strength to challenge Triodon, if only in empty words. On legs as heavy as pyramids, she stepped toward Triodon whose bright eyes, infused with surprise and amusement, watched her every move.

"There is much I do not know," she admitted truthfully. "Why Earth was born, where Wind sleeps at night, when Mountains cease to grow, what makes Fire dance, Ocean sing, and how it is that I am blessed to look upon the stars. And you, Triodon," she continued passionately as she looked deep into his eyes, "never have I looked upon a star so bright. You shine with a light beyond the stars, and in your eyes I see so many miracles I could not count them upon blades of grass." Standing taller than the Sphinx that gazed admiringly upon her, she smiled at Krik, Bree and Peter. "But this I do know. Life is what we choose to make of it. Not just for ourselves, but for all who live. Its meaning is not hidden in death but revealed in life, every minute, every hour, every day – not in who we wish to be, but in who we are. And if we choose to see only that which others see in us, then a little of us dies with every minute, every season and every year. So the river told me. Who do you see, Triodon, when you look upon yourself in the water? Which face do you see when you are alone and in the dark? And why, when there are so many stars above, do you wish to look upon the stars by yourself?"

Then Rafi began to sing.

"Do my eyes deceive me,
Are you that single flame
Who lit the lamp of destiny,
And gave the earth its name?

Tell me of your story,
Were you the first to grieve,
Sing a song, right a wrong,
Say a prayer, or disbelieve?

I see in you the splendor,
Of Egypt, Greece, and Rome,
Shining through the ages,
Yet one house without a home.

In every race, I see your face,
The dawn of living time;
Fathers, mothers, sons and daughters,
Stars of the most divine.

Yet your eyes are filled with sadness,
Your heart weighed in seven stones,
One life, never loved nor lived,
In worship, just a throne.

So why can't we be friends today,
Tomorrow, and beyond?
Together, let us make a world
Where everyone gets along.

For Hope was never meant to be
A future shared alone;
As life cannot be won or lost
It was never ours to own."

NEVER OURS TO OWN.

The last notes of Rafi's song echoed sweetly above the plain. Higher than the greatest pyramid they fell, filled with joy and sorrow, touching the hearts of all who listened, penetrating even to the ears of a Sphinx of stone. And as they fell, so too fell the three stones of Erebus – HAGAL, NAUD, and ISS – into her outstretched hand. Yet, for all the power they wielded on Earth, the stones felt strangely small and insignificant.

"Krik," she confided to the mantis, "I have never felt so afraid."

Krik said nothing, but his grip tightened on her shoulder, his every breath, eye, and limb movement focused upon Triodon. On her other shoulder, Bree waited in equal anticipation, his bristling whiskers, ears and eyes alert for any movement or sound. Ever defiant, still gripping his buckler Peter stood beside her, his once bright blue eyes now dim and far away. She had seen the same light in Talat's eyes at their first meeting. She glanced up at the moon, hopeful even in its passing, and then down to the Erinnyes who swayed mockingly upon the throne. Where were Talat and Dlop?

As for Triodon, he neither moved nor spoke. Throughout Rafi's song, he had sat in salted misery, hiding his face with his fist as he wept great tears that fell and sizzled upon his throne. An acid mist rose about him.

"Rafi," he said finally, wiping great tears from his eyes, "sweet child of Earth. I have heard of your songs that stir both the living and the dead, but never could I have imagined such memories as your song stirs within me now. Your words cut deeper than you know. Well I remember the days that brought me here. They were no less kind or less in number than those who hated and reviled me – not for who I was, but for who I was born to be." Fresh tears swept through Triodon's eyes. "Shunned for my superiority, they judged me," he said haltingly, casting an accusing eye at Krik, "as others would have me judged. It is a long story."

"And one that I would gladly hear," said Rafi. She glanced again at the ailing moon, flickering ominously in the sky. If only she had more time, perhaps both Earth and Triodon could be saved.

"You are kind," said Triodon, reading her thoughts. "But not if you had lived for a thousand of your lifetimes could such a story, so full of sadness, betrayal, and death, be told in full. And even then you would not understand." He frowned majestically. "How could you understand? You are a Drog. Understanding is not in your nature. And if my words do not ring true, look at what your kind has done to the world. Our world. My world. But then, such has always been your fate."

"Surely," said Rafi, wondering at her own words, "fate is what we make of it?"

"Surely," Triodon agreed. "And is it not fate that we find ourselves here, in this place, where tired endings and new beginnings meet? Where Earth shall be reborn?" He shook his fist significantly. "Why do you fear change? It is only through change that you are here." A long sigh broke upon his lips. "Change is the one constant through the ages. So the river should have told you. Your eyes, which are so young and innocent, have yet to see what my eyes have seen." His eyes, no longer palpable, shone as beacons of clear light. "I envy you your youth, Rafi. Treasure it now for, once lost, you shall never reclaim it. That is what sets Drogs apart from all other life. They only believe in miracles of their own making." He leaned forward on his throne. "Listen to me, Rafi. The world you live in is what is left of my creation. It is I who gave you your parents, your life, and the river to whom you sing. Does that count for so little when measured against the short and fickle bond of love? Am I not the father of your fathers? And does a father not know what is best for his children? Would you kill your own father?"

As he spoke, his face changed. At first, the faces were large, brutish, and hairy. Then the eyes became less deep-set, the nose less flat, the jaws less massive as patches of skin grew over a mat of hair. Endless, each face was distinct from the others and yet different, and then – Rafi found herself looking into the eyes of her own father.

"Pupa," she said, as if awakening from a dream. "What are you doing here? Where are mother and Motu? Is it the end of time then? Was I too late to save Earth?" As if to remind her that Earth could yet be saved, HAGAL, NAUD and ISS burned brightly in her right hand. No longer real, Mr. Malawi's face sank beneath two bright and piercing eyes.

"Patricide!" the Erinnyes howled from behind the throne. "She that would kill her own father!"

Reminded of her parents' last letter, Rafi glared at Triodon. "You tried to kill my family," she said coldly. "Only now do I begin to see through you, Triodon. If death is the best fate you can think of for your own children as well as Earth, perhaps it is your bond upon us all that is so short and fickle."

Triodon glanced up at the moon, now dangling feebly in the center of the window. Unwavering in their courses, Jupiter and Saturn hung only minutes away from its oncoming horns, bracing themselves for that inevitable kiss, never to be the same.

"I see that you prefer to die with your friends than accept my offer," he said. His voice rose impatiently. "Yet even now, I will spare them if you but willingly give me the stones. It is a fair trade, is it not? One soul for each stone."

Rafi almost dropped the stones. "And all other souls?"

Triodon's silence spoke in words too terrible to hear.

"Surely," Rafi gasped, unable to comprehend the countless lives she held in her hand including those of her own family, "you cannot believe that we survived the Anvil, The Tears, Draig, Brontes and the Clashing Rocks only to give you the stones so that you can destroy Earth?"

Impatience chilled into anger. "Drog," snapped Triodon, "you are perilously close to greeting those who would follow you on Styx's boat. As for your survival, I can tell you now that you are here only by my design. It was I who placed the sword, scepter, crystal and crown in my own tears." He touched the blood-red stone bound upon his brow. "If you were as old as I am you would learn to never trust a servant any more than you would trust a friend. In the event that the Erinnyes and the Empusae failed in their duty, I needed a way to ensure that you would pass the guardians and find me here.

That I have provided along with your lives. Now that you are here, it is only fitting that you return the favor."

Sure that she was in a dream, Rafi looked at Krik, Bree and Peter.

"Never!"

Black as a thundercloud, Triodon rose from his throne. Through the window above the plain, no longer stepping on Heaven's toes, the moon disappeared even as Saturn and Jupiter braced for a final kiss. He opened his fist. In the palm of his hand lay four black stones.

For the first time, Rafi gazed upon the stones of Erebus once wielded by the four corners of Earth. In lines of fiery red, four runes revealed their secrets to an anxious world: UR – Ocean – that which is to become; THURS – Wind – Herald of Law and Order; KEN – Fire – the Light and Power from within; and GIFU – Mountain – the Gift of Time. Together, they whispered in cosmic sound.

"Give me the stones, Rafi," Triodon commanded. "You know yourself that you cannot say whether the world I shall create will be any worse or better than the one you stand in now. Give me the stones and I promise you, your family and your friends a place in the new world."

Rafi opened her fist. It was a small fist compared to Triodon's, and yet, she sensed an unseen power in her hand beyond the will and words of kings. Then, to her utter joy, in a language she could not read, but completely understood, HAGAL, NAUD, and ISS revealed themselves in a breathless burst of light.

"That, Triodon," she said stubbornly, "I cannot do."

"I had hoped you would see reason, Drog," said Triodon. The smoothness in his voice fractured like frozen steel. "My words, too late, have fallen upon deaf ears." His gaze blazed a path toward Krik. "You have done your job well, mantis. Ever the youth are corrupted by those who refuse to see."

"There is still time, Triodon," said Krik anxiously, "if only a little. Give us the stones so that we may return them to Earth. They are a matter too great for us who are made of flesh and blood. Such things are best left to those who made them for the better of all who walk upon Earth."

"Fool!" Triodon shouted. Enraged, he shook his fist at Krik. "Idiot!" I should have known you would not see reason!" His voice blew like a thunderstorm. "You were not there. You did not see. They despised me. They hated me. *They laughed at me!* All of your precious friends who filled the earth with their small and sniveling ways. Can you hear them? They're not laughing now, are they? I wiped their grins from the face of Earth as easily as the rain clears away the mud!"

Krik nodded at Bree. "And so the world has changed," he said quickly, "for better, and for worse. I would have thought Drogs were more to your liking, Triodon. What makes you think this time will be any different?"

"Drogs!" snapped Triodon, clearly disgusted. "They follow no one but their own destructive path. Once I gave them hope and they worshipped me, but even then, as with all inferior creatures, they did not fail to disappoint. But armed with the seven stones, I shall show them the true meaning of disappointment. Along with their bones, so shall their memory pass forever into mud."

"And so you would repeat the history that has caused you so much despair?" Krik asked sadly. "Is there no end to your madness? Like many Drogs, you cannot imagine an Earth for everyone; you can only imagine an Earth for yourself. But Earth does not belong to you, Triodon. You belong to Earth."

Triodon rubbed his injured shoulder instinctively.

"Kill them," he said to the Erinnyes. "And bring me the stones!"

Krik lost no time rallying the Companions. "To the bridge!" he roared. Spinning like a whirling dervish, his four swords leapt from their scabbards. "To the bridge! Bree, remember Pud. Strike hard and fast. Peter, be ready to help Rafi should we fall. Rafi, if all else fails, throw the stones into the chasm. Even Triodon cannot reach them there."

"Let nothing happen to the stones," Triodon barked at the Erinnyes, "or you will curse your very lives!"

"Dlop!" Bree cried, drawing both Pud's and his own sword in a glitter of diamond dust. "Where are you? We need you, Bro!"

At Triodon's urging, the Erinnyes attacked. Led by Megaera, they howled against the Companions, beating their wings as the sound of their voices split the air. Upon their backs rode the Empusae, black-hearted and infernal-eyed, their pincers and stingers dancing to a macabre tune of death.

Triodon inspected his claws. "Kill them," he reminded the Erinnyes. He gazed happily through the window. Far away, Jupiter and Saturn looked back from where they hung transfixed upon the moon. In a world now measured without time, seven minutes remained: one minute each for Mountain, Ocean, Fire, and Wind; and one minute for each of the three Fates who bowed their heads in silent wonder above the plain. Seven minutes, all told, for the Daughters of Earth. An eternity for all.

Triodon hummed a little tune.

His gaze never left the window. "Spare the Drog!" he said. "Leave enough life in her so that she can see that not all songs end in happiness."

Fighting desperately, the Companions fell back. Inch by inch, they fought their way out of the courtyard and past the wall until they stood next to the bridge. Rafi watched helplessly, guarding the stones with her very life, as Bree and Krik swung their swords effortlessly from her shoulders and hair, repelling attack after attack as Peter, almost possessed in his fury, hammered at the Erinnyes with his buckler. Behind them, a wall of flame shot up from the chasm, ringing the plain with fire.

Krik saluted the unseen moon with one of his swords. "One minute for Mountain!" he cried.

Krik was not the only one watching the window. For the first time in his long life, fear clouded Triodon's face. "Time presses," he roared at the Erinnyes. "Are you not the Erinnyes and the Empusae?

Where is your nerve and daring? There are six of you against four of them and only two of them are armed. Are the tales of old merely bedtime stories meant to frighten young children? If so, be sure that death will be but the beginning of your agonies should you fail."

Spurred on by Triodon's threats, the Erinnyes and the Empusae attacked with even more fury only to be thrown back by the rat and the mantis who seemed to have become almost supernatural in strength. Aided by Peter, who wielded his buckler like a champion of old, they held the bridge.

The chasm roared.

"One minute for Ocean!" cried Krik.

"There might only be two," gasped Tisiphone, almost dizzy from dodging Bree's and Krik's sword strokes, "but they fight like an army!"

"Thank you," said Bree. He punched out three of Tisiphone's teeth with the pommel of one of his swords. "Up close, you're not so ugly after all."

"Really?" Tisiphone spat through her broken teeth.

"Nah," said Bree. He caught Lilum's tail in a cross of swords. "'Tis, I'd say you're uglier. Far uglier." In a scissors like motion, he snapped his wrists, thrusting the diamond-coated blades upwards and outwards. In a spurt of blood and venom, Lilam's stinger sprang from her tail. Howling in pain, she watched her stinger tumble into the chasm.

Lilam rammed her pincers into Tisiphone's head. "Fall back!" she screamed.

"Not so fast, Scorpio," shouted Bree. Pretending to give way, he suddenly leapt forward, striking Lilum between the eyes with a thunderous blow. In a river of blood and gore, her head split in two. Even Tisiphone felt the diamond blade cut through shell, hair, bone, and tissue, stopping only at her brain. Disengaging his sword, Bree watched with satisfaction as Tisiphone crashed into the bridge, catapulting what was left of Lilum to follow her stinger into the chasm.

As if to greet the fallen, the chasm roared again.

"One minute for Fire!" cried Krik who, fighting both Alecto and Megaera at the same time, was too busy to applaud. "And one for Bree! Don't ever let it be said that diamonds aren't a girl's best friend." Faster than any eye could follow, his sinewy arms flickered tirelessly, frustrating both the Erinnyes and the Empusae as they tried to bring him down.

"What took you so long?" he added as the rat joined him.

Bree was unapologetic. "I took Tis on a date," he said. He nodded at Tisiphone who lay next to the bridge. Her wings were wrapped around her head in a bloody ball. "Only I think she got bored and fell asleep."

"Perhaps," said Krik, neatly slicing off one of Megaera's ears, "you might prefer one of her sisters."

"Perhaps," repeated Bree, slicing off Megaera's other ear, "I would."

"No you don't!" Peter roared at Alecto. In an evil attempt to strike Rafi from behind, the Erinnye had tried to circumnavigate Bree's impenetrable swordplay. His buckler rang against Alecto's skull, propelling both Alecto and Neith in a head on collision with the wall.

It was all the time Bree needed. Enraged by the injuries inflicted upon her sisters, Megaera charged straight at him as Lamia stabbed the air in an impossible rhythm of pincers, stinger, and tail. Clearly, their plan was to kill the meddlesome rat before Peter's buckler could reenter the fray. But Bree had other things in mind. At the last moment, he stepped aside and the attackers, expecting to find Rafi alone and defenseless, found Krik instead. Well armed and rested, the mantis did not disappoint. Suddenly, Megaera and Lamia found themselves in a forest of swords, and that was precisely when Bree made his move. With a terrible yell, he pounced on Megaera from the side, his sword ringing down on Lamia's back. The diamond-encrusted blade did its work, cutting through Lamia's armor like butter, neatly dividing the scorpion in two.

But Lamia was not so easily dispatched. For a moment, she danced in two pieces across Megaera's back, her stinger and back legs advancing like some fearless robot as her head and pincers lunged at Rafi's face. Once again, Krik came to her rescue. As two of his swords engaged Lamia's pincers, the other two hacked them off, leaving only waving stumps. Not taking any chances, Bree slashed the stinger from its tail, sweeping what was left of Lamia into the chasm.

Surging up from the chasm, the fire roared its approval.

Krik's voice rose above the flame. "One minute for Wind!" There was no emotion in his voice; neither troubled nor triumphant, he counted off the minutes that would soon end along with Earth.

"One minute for Future,
One minute for Past,
One minute for Present,
Thus first shall be last."

Discouraged by Lamia's fall and the wall of flame, Megaera initiated a quick retreat.

"Going somewhere, Megaera, my dear?" sang Bree. He stabbed the Erinnye clean through her wing. Then, dropping one of his swords, his paw flew up, snatching Megaera's throat in a grip of iron. "You're next, Megaera," he added coldly. From the sky, his sword fell in a glittering diamond-toothed smile.

"No!" cried Rafi, knowing already that she was too late.

Miraculously, the blade stopped a hair width away from Megaera's skull. Like a Roman gladiator of old, Bree looked to Rafi for further orders.

"Bree, spare her," she appealed to the rat, appalled that she had served as a theater for such a grisly battle. Her gaze fell upon Megaera who, either through injury or fatigue, hung helplessly from Bree's paw.

Bree tightened his grip on Megaera's throat. "Rafi, are you sure?"

he asked. "Even without Lamia, I fear that Megaera has not lost her sting."

"Tisiphone and Alecto too," she pleaded, having noticed that the two Erinnyes were in no condition for any more fighting. Tisiphone could be heard groaning beneath her wings. Alecto lay slumped against the wall, her head swollen to almost twice its normal size. Jabbing Alecto with her stinger, Neith berated the almost unconscious Erinnye in a maelstrom of spit and venom.

"Swear," said Bree, looking deep into Megaera's eyes, "that you will not harm Rafi."

"I swear," said Megaera. No longer filled with hatred, her eyes shone with a light Bree had never seen before. "I swear," she said again, this time looking at Rafi, "and I speak for my sisters as well. The time has come for the Erinnyes to choose again. Only this time we choose to die with those that would spare us in death rather than live with one who would destroy us with life. Have we not chosen, my sisters?"

Tisiphone poked her bleeding head from between her wings. "I swear," she answered.

Alecto opened her eyes. "I swear," she said. It was then she noticed Neith, who had not quite finished drumming her pincers on Alecto's head. With one furious blow of her wing, she sent Neith howling into the chasm.

"One minute for Urd!" counted Krik.

"So," Triodon snarled. Countless faces contorted in disbelief as he gazed at the Companions now joined by Alecto, Tisiphone and Megaera. "The dreaded Errinyes fall to the swords of a mantis and a rat, and, worst of all, to the childish dreams of a little girl." Nonetheless, he stepped toward the Companions with the pride of a wounded lion, stopping between them and the wall. In his palm, UR, THURS, KEN, and GIFU glittered red.

"That's Drog to you, Triodon," said Rafi. From her outstretched hand, HAGAL, NAUD, and ISS glittered white in answer.

Triodon shook his head as a dark shadow crept along the wall.

"Drog," he said, "your foolish dreams cannot stop me. Your efforts, however valiant, have been in vain. With the four stones, I alone control Earth. Armed with the three as you are, the best you can pray for is a kindly death. Yet even now, if you give them to me, I will spare your lives, except for the Erinnyes who have betrayed me and that miserable mantis who has thwarted me up until this very hour."

Rafi glanced up the wall. Right above Triodon's head the shadow grew, severed by a crescent smile at least a yard long. She wondered what new terror this might be.

Her hand stretched over the chasm. "No, Triodon," she said. "The stones are not mine to give. And if you only had eyes as bright as the stones in your hand you would see that it was not the Erinnyes who betrayed you – you betrayed yourself."

Flames rocketed over the chasm.

"One minute for Skuld!" cried Krik, his voice breaking with emotion. "Stand ready, Companions of Earth, for this is the minute of Doom!"

"Your doom," said Triodon, unconcernedly. Deliberately, he stepped back toward the wall.

But even as he stepped, the shadow sprang from the wall. In a blur of hot muscle and cold steel, it hurtled down upon him with the speed and fury of a striking snake. Then, to Triodon's shock and the others delight, Talat had gripped Triodon's arm in mortal combat. Driving his sword repeatedly in Triodon's head was Dlop.

But that was not all. With a cry that would have thrown Viking villages into panic, Pud boarded Triodon's shoulder, a rock in each paw.

"Ahoy, Triodon!" he called, bloodying Triodon's many faces beneath an onslaught of rocks. His voice was but a shiver of pain upon the wind. "Take that, you royal pain in the ..."

"No!" cried Triodon. With more pressing matters upon his mind, he bit savagely at Talat whose bright sword rang almost musically as curved steel bit against angry teeth. Back and forth they struggled before the wall, locked in a desperate dance of doom, as each fought to control the stones. As for Dlop, the rat's sword rammed into Triodon's head like a piston, his high-pitched voice squeaking at every stroke.

"Now, Rafi," said Krik.

With a prayer for Talat, a prayer for them all, Rafi threw the stones into the chasm. As they fell, three jets of white light blasted through the window where, touching the moon, Jupiter and Saturn, they connected in a triangular shaft of light.

Outsized and out muscled, Talat relaxed his grip. Using his legs, he swung upside down from Triodon's arm as if he was about to fall, and then, when all seemed lost, his sword flew up, wounding Triodon deeply across his face. From Triodon's brow fell a blood-red stone. Enraged, Triodon struck out at him with flailing teeth, once, twice, wounding his legs and arm, but as he rushed in for a third time, Talat blocked the blow with the broadside of his sword, and then, with an economical twist, the sword, as if wielded by the heavens above, rained down upon Triodon's wrist.

"The stones!" cried Triodon, but it was too late. In a waterfall of blood, his wrist sprang from his arm as Talat held on to both Triodon's arm and severed hand for dear life. Maddened with pain, yet driven by a madder hope, Triodon rushed toward the chasm.

Unable to hold on any longer, Pud thudded to the ground.

"Talat!" cried Rafi. She saw only too clearly what was passing in Talat's mind. His legs still wrapped around Triodon's arm, his mind wrapped upon nothing but the stones, he managed to pry open Triodon's severed fist even as Dlop rushed to his side. In a tumbled mass of bodies and stones, Triodon, Talat and Dlop approached the edge of the chasm. For several seconds they struggled upon its edge, a would be God, a man, and a rat trapped between Hope and Despair. During the struggle, the stone GIFU slipped through Triodon's fingers, falling into the chasm. Yet even as it fell, so too fell the three combatants as the stars, moon, planets, and the Companions watched in rigid horror.

Talat released his legs, letting Triodon fall beneath him. As for Triodon, he never said a word, his every face a look of pure astonishment. Powerless, with neither hand nor stones, the fire rushing up to consume him, he disappeared into the chasm.

Victorious, riding upon a flying carpet of wind and fire, Talat held aloft three stones. He placed one stone in Dlop's astonished mouth. With his last breath, he threw UR and KEN into the chasm. Then, his grim smile fixed forever upon his face, he waved goodbye.

"For you, Father!" he cried.

"For my brothers!" cried Dlop, who, to his utter delight, had finally learned how to fly. Without even the smallest squeak, he spat THURS into the chasm.

"Dlop!" cried Bree.

A cry of dismay rose from the Companions even as the Erinnyes launched into the air like a squadron of jet fighters, arching over the bridge and into the chasm. Seconds passed like years. Then, just when it appeared that they too had perished, there was a shout as three black shadows shot from the chasm. Three times they circled around Rafi, Krik, Bree, Pud and Peter. In Megaera's claws, hung Dlop – asleep.

"There was nothing else we could do," said Alecto sadly as Megaera deposited Dlop in Bree's waiting arms. "He's gone."

"Gone?" Rafi tried to comprehend Alecto's words. For the longest time she stared wordlessly where she had last seen Talat. Then, taking one of Krik's swords, she cut a lock of her hair, letting it fall into the chasm.

"Talat," she said. "We will never forget you. You were our Hope at the edge of Despair. I only wish that all who were saved today by your smile and your sword will one day look up and remember you."

Peter threw his buckler into the chasm along with his pride. "Talat," he said, "before I met you I knew what it felt like to lose a brother. Now I know what it feels like to lose a brother and a friend. I, for one, will remember you when I look upon the stars."

"Brother!" Bree cried, almost squeezing the life out of Dlop. "You were magnificent! I could not be more grateful or proud. Wait 'till Pud hears that you can fly!"

For all Dlop was happy to be alive, his whiskers drooped into the chasm. "Goodbye, Talat," he cried, "thank you for teaching me how to fly."

They had not forgotten about Pud. They found him resting peacefully against the wall, still wearing his Purple Heart, Triodon's dusty, blood-red stone bound upon his brow. His body was black and broken, but his eyes were as bright as the light that poured down from the beckoning moon.

"Pud!"

"I hope we have a good benefits package," he said, looking at Krik.

Krik smiled through his tears. "The best," he said. "Just like yourself."

"Moon sure is bright," said Pud feebly. "Where's Bree and Dlop?"

"Beside you, bro," said Bree, his grief an endless sea. "Where we always were and always will be."

"Did you see, Pud?" cried Dlop. "Did you see me fly?"

Pud smiled. "That I did, Dlop," he said. "Always knew you had it in you." He looked up with unseeing eyes. "Peter?"

Peter choked down the lump he had felt up on the mountaintop. "I'm here," he said.

"Thanks …"

Seeing beyond a world of light and shadow, Pud smiled at Rafi.

Rafi lifted Pud's paws and heart into her own. Even in a world filled with new hope, she knew he was dying. "Pud," she said. "In you, I found the greatest miracle of all. For what is a miracle but a heart that is given to others, in a word, a smile, a deed that will live on forever as long as hearts still beat upon the earth. As for mine, it beats for you, now and always. Farewell, gentle Knight. May your armor always shine as warm and bright as your everlasting eyes."

Pud kissed Rafi's hand. "Rock on, Raffers," he said. He looked up at the moon. "Oh, there you are Talat. I was wondering when you would show up …"

He never spoke again.

And so the prophecies had come true. Two of the Companions had died in their quest to save Earth. Beyond grief, they knelt beside Pud, remembering Orly's cats, his innocence and his strength, and his final battle before the wall.

Krik turned to the Erinnyes who had gathered around Bree and Dlop. "Thank you," he said. "I had hoped to teach Rafi something about becoming an ambassador but, instead, she taught me. Perhaps you will find a new master in the new world – yourselves."

"It is us who should be grateful," said Megaera. "For, in the end, understanding and kind words proved far more powerful than the scorpion's sting." She bowed to Rafi. "You released us, and for that, we thank you."

Rafi nodded graciously. There was no need for further words. Together, as friends and enemies, they had saved Earth. She picked up Pud. Stroking his chin, she turned to face the pyramids and the Sphinx where they towered above the plain, not in size, but in new meaning. However magnificent, like Triodon's throne, they were only stone after all. Through the window, bright of face and full of song, the moon danced upon its black-lit stage of imperishable stars. She smiled at Krik, Bree, Dlop and Peter, for in their eyes hung the brightest stars she could ever hope to see.

"I only wish that we had been able to save Triodon," she admitted. "In spite of our saving Earth, I cannot help but think that I have failed. Is there any hope for me as an ambassador?"

Krik was shocked. "Great Heavens, Rafi," he said. "How can you ask? Earth has been saved, but in the end, not least for Talat and the Erinnyes, it was only worth saving because of you. Only time will tell whether or not the stone that fell from Triodon's hand fell blessed with your words and song. Perhaps, as you have said, there was hope for him after all." He gazed happily at the moon. "We must be getting back. No doubt the Fates will want to speak to us, and I'm sure that at least one of you is thinking about going home."

"Home," said Rafi and Peter together. After all their wondrous adventures together it sounded a strangely exhilarating word.

"Home."

And with this word beating in their hearts, they retraced steps up paths both old and new to see the Fates.

CHAPTER TWENTY-THREE

A NEW DAY

"The quest has ended!" Verdandi's strong voice echoed above the plain. "Triodon is dead!" Still in possession of the eye, she ripped it from her face, holding it in front of her as she adjusted her hair. Satisfied, she anted the eye into the poker pot. "The Companions have fulfilled their quest!"

"Earth is safe!" barked Urd. In filthy rags, she rocked back and forth upon her tortoise as inch long talons ripped an ear from behind her head, throwing it into the poker pot. "Ha, ha," she cackled. "Earth is safe once more!"

Skuld shot a quizzical look at both her sisters as if she did not quite agree. However, being without a mouth, she said nothing, crinkling her nose as if it was a moldy prune Danish. Apparently unwilling to part with either her nose or ear, she tossed a penny into the pot.

Verdandi turned her eyeless face toward the Companions. "Companions of Earth," she said most respectfully, "you have done well." She shuffled the cards. "Step forward that we may pronounce your fate."

Urd not so accidentally dropped the five of clubs beneath her tortoise only to pick up the king of diamonds. "Killed him," she cackled, adding the king to her hand, "killed him dead!"

Rafi gave Skuld a questioning look. Something about the way Skuld had looked at her sisters made her feel uneasy, as if Earth's fate – and possibly that of Triodon's too – had yet more to reveal. As for Skuld, she tapped her tortoise once, grabbing a card from Verdandi's hand before she could pass it over the poker pot. From where it still lay in the pot, the eye blinked disappointedly.

"Earth is safe," said Krik contentedly. He untied the bloodied bandages around his head, letting them fall to the earth like a wounded sail.

Rafi gasped. Nowhere on his head could she see any sign of a wound. She looked at Verdandi, but the Fate only smiled and shook her head. Then she knew. Krik had never been wounded in the Cyclops's cave after all. Krik's injuries had all been an act.

"You see, Rafi," he admitted sheepishly, "in the end, when those around you are in need or danger, most often the answers are found not in others, but within yourself. What did you find?"

Rafi thought for a moment. It was only then she realized how much she had grown since leaving the Apple.

"I found," she said, "that life's greatest miracles come not from what we learn about ourselves, but from what we learn about others. From this miracle blooms love – and from love – responsibility. And it was in this responsibility that I found you, my mother, my father, Motu, Mopsus, and even ... The Mayor. In his own way, I now believe that he loves Drumheller as much as I do except that he chose to express his love in the only way he could – rules."

"Hear her!" Urd wailed, having just lost both her ears to Skuld.

Krik nipped Rafi's ear affectionately. "You found well," he said. "Yet, as you grow up and become an adult, and Earth's greatest ambassador, remember that adults are merely children with greater responsibilities – often without the experience to know how to deal with them. That is what makes Drogs so tragic. You grow up, forgetting the child that is within you, and within us all. Too often, this child becomes buried in a world of responsibility, diminishing the wonder, when, in the end, our lives extend only as far as our sense of wonder. For there, hidden somewhere in the unknown, we shall find the miracles of today and tomorrow."

Peter pointed to the window in the mountain, which seemed to follow the moon. "Look!" he cried. "The full moon!"

"The full moon," Verdandi echoed triumphantly, having just won back the eye. "Never have I looked upon anything brighter." Against a black sky, the moon danced brightly in her new white dress complete with its necklace of diamonds and pearls. "A new age has begun. Let great joy and happiness return to Earth." She turned to Rafi. "Yet you are not happy, Rafi of the Three Stones."

Rafi nodded. Deep inside, beyond the light of the joyous moon, her heart felt troubled. "Your Grace," she said mournfully, "my heart aches for Pud and Talat."

Skuld reshuffled the cards.

"It is true," said Verdandi, "that the noble Talat has joined his family in a place no further away than your own hearts. Long will his name be remembered, for to give one's life to protect others is the greatest gift of all." She sighed as Skuld revealed the seven of diamonds. "His life, he gave to the chasm, but, in the throwing of the stones, his love, he gave to all. And for that, his image shall forever be placed among the imperishable stars."

Peter wept openly. "Forgive me, Talat," he said. "I promise you that, one day, in better times, I shall visit your country where such hearts are born. For it occurs to me now that there, as well as in my own land, I have more than one brother."

"And Pud?" asked Bree indignantly. "Surely, he too has earned his rightful place among the stars ..."

Skuld revealed the rest of her cards. Beside the seven of diamonds, dressed in mold, three kings stared up at the Companions along with the three of hearts.

Verdandi studied the cards. "Alas," she said finally. "It has been decreed that Pud shall not reign with Talat among the stars. I'm afraid the best we can do is to return him – to you."

Bree was speechless.

"For this very night," Verdandi continued, "Pud shall be reborn."

"Reborn!" wailed Urd.

Bree looked shocked. "I don't understand," he said incredulously.

"How is that possible?"

Verdandi smiled at Urd and Skuld. "Because," she said simply, "the three of us – the Fates – say it shall be so."

"Pud reborn?"

The Companions looked at each other in disbelief. Verdandi's words, so clear and simple, were impossible to comprehend. Pud reborn? Exhausted beyond measure, wounded in heart, body, and mind, they each waited for someone else to speak, to comprehend, to know that, once again, they would soon hear Pud's voice or look into his deep blue eyes. As for Pud, he lay still upon his shield, rigid in death, the smile upon his face more alive than most mortal men.

"Are you saying ..." Rafi began.

"So it is written," Verdandi decreed softly. "By your own hand Pud shall be reborn." She threw a penny into the poker pot. "For it was your hand that planted Gried – for that is the tree's name – beneath the Clashing Rocks. And as Gried has been restored to us from the Tears of Agony, so too shall Pud be restored to you, for Gried has power beyond life and death and, indeed, beyond the leaves of all living things." She bowed her twiggy head. "And so," she added, smiling, "the time has come for friends – old and new – to say goodbye. I do not doubt that your leaving us will be less adventurous than your quest – except perhaps when you speak with Gried."

"Your Graces are kind and wise," said Rafi, bowing in her turn. No matter how hard she tried, she could not wipe the grin from her face as Bree and Dlop danced a not so Irish jig. "Yet, while I long to see my family, it is hard to go."

"Go you must," said Verdandi kindly, "but know that you five are always welcome here."

"Five?"

Verdandi drew the ace of hearts. "Krik shall not be going with you."

The Companions looked sharply at Krik. At first, Rafi wondered if the mantis was still holding out on her, but the stunned look upon his face made it clear that he was no less surprised than the others, who looked on in disbelief.

"If I have offended ..." he began.

"Never fear, mantis," said Verdandi sympathetically, "but for you, your quest remains unfinished. You still have much work to do only ... you shall do it here."

"Don't ... understand ..." said Krik awkwardly.

Verdandi lovingly stroked Urd's hair with her hand.

"Urd is dying," she said sadly. "For seven ages my sisters and I have ruled Earth. As Urd is the Fate of all that is Past, she is the eldest, and as each age does turn but another page, so too must another sit in her place. You."

"Poker?" said Krik weakly. The prospect of wearing one of Verdandi's ears or Skuld's nose did not sound like a promising future for an ambassador.

"The stakes are high," Verdandi went on, "for not only will you sit in Urd's place – you shall help us rule Earth." The three Fates bowed their heads so low their hair swept the ground like old brooms. "Krik," she went on, her one and only eye shining upon him, "because of your unwavering love and selfless devotion to all living things, you have been appointed as one of the three Fates, and an honorary Daughter of Earth. Do you play five card stud?"

Krik looked stunned. "It is a great honor, your Graces," he said, his eyes wet with tears, "however, my wife Mrok ..."

"... is on her way here," replied Verdandi. "Yet, other than the fearless Mrok and three old crones, you shall not go wanting for companions, for you have also been appointed as Grand Ambassador of Earth. You may visit your friends at any time, that is," she added hastily after Skuld made a face, "unless we are playing in a poker tournament against Mountain, Fire, Ocean and Wind."

Krik clawed his throat. "There is, perhaps, something you should know ..." he began.

"Mrok will not be relieving you of your head," said Verdandi, reading his mind as easily as the cards before her. She laughed. "Although I can't guarantee the same once you join in our game. Your head is needed now – more than ever – and, of course, your children will not appreciate a headless father."

Krik's face colored a rainbow above the plain. "Ch... ch... children?" he stuttered.

"Children and grandchildren beyond your wildest dreams," said Verdandi after studying Skuld's cards. "Though your life shall now be counted in ages rather than years, one day, even you must die. By then both Skuld and myself will have joined Urd, and the most able of your sons and daughters shall reign in our place, as one shall eventually reign in yours. So shall the League of Mantis rule Earth."

"Most ... kind ..." stammered Krik, overwhelmed by his good fortune as Rafi, Peter, Bree, and Dlop lined up to congratulate him.

Verdandi reshuffled the cards. "So much for our noble ambassador," she said. She would have looked over her nose at Bree and Dlop except that it had slid off her face into the poker pot.

Bree and Dlop shifted uneasily on their feet. Happy as they were for Krik, they were anxious to move on if only to see Gried.

"You three," she went on, "have been appointed Knights of Earth. No knight, of any age, could stand in greater honor as you stand before us now. As for companions, you shall have the Erinnyes who, having refused Triodon and saved Dlop, shall henceforth be known as the Virtues. Together, you shall be known far and wide as the Powers." She dealt two cards to Skuld. "Your first task, not surprisingly, is to protect Rafi and Peter on their way home."

Bree and Dlop shuddered. It was hard to imagine serpent-haired bats accompanying them to parties. But, as it was only courteous to do so, they turned to face the Erinnyes only to discover that their former enemies had changed into the most beautiful rats they had ever seen. Born upon golden wings and starlit eyes, Megaera, Alecto and Tisiphone looked back at them as if for the first time, and no gem or jewel from the Hydra's lair ever shone so sweetly as the tears that flowed between them now.

It was Megaera's tears that fell on Pud. "Pud," she said, "forgive me for my part in giving you this grievous wound. But I swear, as Triodon's hatred and the scorpion's sting drove my heart to do evil things, so let the love and happiness that fill it now protect you until the end of my days."

His face an ashen gray, Pud lay silent in a growing pool of tears.

"Dead!" wailed Urd.

"Soon to be reborn," Verdandi reminded her sister. She nodded at Rafi, Krik, Bree, Peter, Alecto and Megaera. Together, they looked at Dlop and Tisiphone. Arm in arm, eyes closed, and whiskers intertwined, the two rats lay – fast asleep.

Reborn. All past forgotten, Bree and Alecto gazed lovingly into each other's eyes.

Verdandi turned to Peter. So much had happened that day, the others had forgotten his injuries, which he had borne with a humble and sainted grace. As for Peter, he stood in silent wonder, convinced that the last two days were nothing more than a dream – the most wonderful dream of his entire life.

Verdandi's cards totaled twenty-one. "Son of the Eagle," she said, "your part in saving Earth is in no way less diminished than Talat's, for today a part of you has also died in Erebus. Yet we have nothing to give you, for in your heart already dwells the most precious gift of all. Tell us, Peter, what gift did you bestow upon yourself?"

Peter touched his injured arm. Miraculously, the arm had completely healed, leaving no trace of any wound. His face bloomed with color.

"That understanding," he said in a voice that grew stronger with every word, "is more powerful than knowledge. That neither nations, politics, symbols nor words are as strong as a heart that is true. It is only when we seek to understand the hearts of others that great nations shall be born."

"Long life to you, Peter, Companion of Earth," said Verdandi. "Great riches shall be yours, but these you shall win yourself, and one day your words shall spread beyond where even the bravest Eagle flies."

Peter bowed low. If this was a dream, he wished it would never end. Something tugged on his pants even as a hand slid into his own. Through his tears, he smiled at Rafi and Bree.

Verdandi laid another card on her tortoise. Two heart shaped eyes, as rich and deep as autumn leaves in a forest, looked up from the card into her own.

"Rafi," she said, "Companion and Daughter of Earth. There is much that we would say and give to you today, and always. We three have seen much joy and sorrow upon Earth, and yet, old and wise as we are, you have renewed in us a hope we have not felt for many ages past." Her mouth continued speaking even after she had ripped it from her face. "Without hope, there can be no future. And so," the mouth added as she handed it to Skuld, "the time has come for Skuld to speak."

Skuld took the mouth. Evidently, she was not used to having one for she placed it upon her head like a bow.

"River's Daughter," she sang in a voice as gentle and cool as green grass blowing in the wind, "how does one reward the earth for dancing 'round the sun? How does Earth reward the One when all great deeds are done?

How does one reward the Sun
For shining in the sky?
How do friends remember friends
When one and all must die?
Is it not enough to shine,
And know that friends are true?
That love is born of friendship,
And who you are is you?

How can friendship light a heart
That fills the darkest sky?
How can hearts be broken
When hearts can never die?
For is not love a song with wings
That never says goodbye?
Sings the dreams that make us shine
Within each other's eyes."

"Eyes," sang Urd, although she did not have any, and her voice sounded like a dentist drilling on a blackboard.

Skuld smiled at Rafi. "Tell us, Daughter of Earth," she said. "What song does a mother give her daughter? You have only to name your gift and it shall be yours."

"Nothing," said Rafi truthfully for Skuld's song went on singing in her heart. "It is enough to have helped my friends and to have heard your song. And since you have already decreed that Pud shall live again, no other song could better sing my heart's desire."

"Then go with our blessing, Rafi of the Three Stones," said Skuld, "who shall now be known far and wide as …" she consulted her cards, "er … Rafi. But to you we give the gift of speaking to all living things so that you may sing your songs to those who have not yet learned to sing. May this help you on your way to becoming Earth's greatest ambassador."

Reluctantly, Skuld handed the mouth back to Verdandi. Afraid perhaps that her sister might change her mind, Verdandi had snatched it back almost before Skuld had a chance to remove it from her head.

Her smile set back in place, Verdandi and her sisters bowed their heads as one.

"Until we meet again, Rafi," said Verdandi. Unblinkingly, she raised her head, her voice ringing above the plain, over the mountain, and, indeed, throughout Earth. "But know this," she decreed. "Until Drogs understand the meaning of your songs, you alone shall always be welcome here."

Urd reshuffled the cards except three aces, which fell beneath her tortoise.

Verdandi gave Krik an encouraging look. "Krik," she said, "come and take your place beside Urd so that we may begin."

Rafi felt her heart drop into the poker pot. Suddenly, after all she had been through – the T-Rex, the Anvil, the Tears of Agony, Draig, Brontes, the Clashing Rocks, the Erinnyes, the Empusae, and, finally, Triodon himself – she realized that she had only just reached the most difficult part of her quest – to say goodbye to Krik.

The lump in her throat did not make it any easier. In the three days they had spent together, Krik had been her mentor, guide, and protector, but more than that – he had become her best friend. Beneath the grateful moon, they turned to one another. In tender moonbeams of quiet light they reached for the stars in each other's eyes, talking, laughing, living – without saying a single word.

"Goodbye, Krik" Rafi said finally, showering the mantis with her tears, "at least until we meet again." She pulled the green clothes peg from her pocket and handed it to Krik. "In case you run out of eyes."

Mantis that he was, Krik could not resist giving Rafi a final bit of advice. "Between friends," he said softly, "there are no good-byes. Besides, we shall meet again, sooner than you think." He lowered his voice. "And don't worry. I won the Mantis World Poker Tournament six hundred and fourteen times in a row ..."

Her heart beating merrily once more, she kissed Krik on the forehead, placing him beside Urd on her tortoise. If snapping was any indication, neither Urd nor her tortoise were happy with the new arrangement. Judging from the indignant look on Krik's face, the feeling was mutual.

She turned to go. With the Virtues to help them, Bree and Dlop had already hoisted Pud above their heads who, laying upon his shield, his sword and smile set peacefully in place, never looked more glorious. Together, they headed back up the stone path, singing sad songs about a brave knight soon to be reborn.

Unable to help herself, Rafi cast one last look at the Fates. She laughed. Krik was right. She need not have worried. Already dressed in Verdandi's eye and two of Skuld's ears, which flapped like wings, he looked like a mad bat.

And so, with the exception of Krik who, along with the Fates, would now rule Earth, and Talat, who, it is said, watches over them from the stars, the Companions began their journey out of Erebus. In minutes, they stood before the Clashing Rocks where Turgot had betrayed them only to betray himself. In the center of the canyon stood a golden tree.

"I cannot imagine," said Rafi, marveling at the tree, which stretched a sunrise of leaves and gold above their heads, "of a more beautiful place to be reborn."

Bree and Dlop placed Pud on the ground next to Gried's massive trunk. "I hope this works," said Bree doubtfully. "But what are we supposed to do? The Fates never said anything about that."

"Just wait, I suppose," said Rafi, suddenly feeling embarrassed that she had never bothered to ask the Fates how Pud should be reborn. She looked anxiously at Pud.

A deep voice thrummed upon the wind.

"Rafi of the Three Stones."

Rafi looked at the others in amazement. But no one – not even Bree – gave any indication that they had heard the voice. Then she remembered Verdandi's last words. It was the tree!

"Daughter of Earth," hummed the tree, "I am Gried, son of Gur. Long ago, my people were the shepherds of Earth when our forests filled the land from sea to almighty sea. Now, thanks to your hand and those gathered here, our forests shall grow once more."

"Gried, son of Gur," cried Rafi with shining eyes, "it is I who must thank you. Never have I looked upon a more beautiful tree. Trees have always been a miracle to me, giving me hope and shelter, and the very air I breathe. It is a great honor to be the hand that has returned you to Earth."

"Your words are fair, River's Daughter," said Gried. "Child of the sweet Earth that gives life to us all – the honor is mine. And it is through this path that life shall be given once more." Gried lowered a golden branch studded with golden leaves. "Take three of my leaves and place them upon the valiant Pud. From these leaves, he shall be given that of which he most freely gave. Take too this acorn – my first-born. Ginn is her name. All I ask is that when you return to your home you give Ginn back to Earth as you have given me."

Rafi plucked the acorn and three leaves from Gried. In her hands they shone like a temple of gold, even as a leaf seemed to catch in her throat. "I promise," she croaked.

Then, as the others looked on in astonishment for they had not heard a single word of her conversation with Gried, she explained what they must do. She was about to place the leaves upon Pud when suddenly she had an idea.

She placed the first leaf in Bree's paws. "Come, Bree," she said. "Take this leaf and lay it upon Pud. It is only fitting that his older brother, who protected him in life, should be the first to give it back to him."

With tears of gratitude streaming from his eyes, Bree laid the leaf lovingly upon Pud.

Next, she woke up Dlop. "Dlop," she said, "take this leaf and lay it upon Pud. It is only fitting that his younger brother, who followed him in life, shall now return the gift so that he shall follow you."

Dlop squeaked in sleepy revelry as he laid his leaf upon Pud.

Finally, Rafi knelt down beside Megaera where she lay next to Pud. Burdened by tears and a guilty heart, Megaera lovingly stroked his head with her wing. "Megaera," she said, "take this leaf and lay it upon Pud so that he shall be restored to life by the wings that guided the scorpion's sting."

Megaera kissed Rafi's hand. Then, for there were no words that could speak to her loving eyes, she kissed the leaf and laid it upon Pud.

Beneath his mantle of gold, Pud lay like a great king that had fallen from the pages of a storybook, for no king of flesh and blood had ever looked so beautiful. Only how would the story end? With shining eyes, they called him by his name and titles, fearful that no one could ever return from where he had gone, and yet hopeful of a miracle.

"I wish Krik was here," said Rafi.

Peter squeezed her shoulder. "I think he is," he said gently. "He'll always be with you, Rafi." He nodded at Bree, Pud and Megaera. "It was a wonderful thing you did – giving the leaves to his brothers and Megaera."

They watched. Beneath Gried, Pud lay in his bed of gold, rocked upon Earth's gentle bosom while, worlds away, stars swirled curiously around the moon, leaning in closer and closer to see if, indeed, miracles do happen.

In a wink of wonder, a pulse of light blew across the heavens in alternating rings of red and blue. In the center of the rings, there suddenly appeared a giant star, brighter and more beautiful than any star they had ever seen. From distant shores, it lit upon their faces, striking its rightful claim to both heaven and their hearts. It was a miracle.

"Good thing we didn't eat Krik," said Pud lazily. No longer covered in leaves, he sat up in an armored suit of gold. "Now I know why you sleep so much, Dlop. I've never felt better." He picked up a large stone in his paw, crushing it into dust. In disbelief, he looked at Bree and Dlop, who were covered in golden armor no less magnificent than his own.

"Wow!" squeaked Dlop. "You're as strong as Zigh!"

Bree gave Pud a great rat hug. Their armor clanged with perfect pitch as star after star rang greetings to hearts both above and below. "Welcome back, bro," sang Bree. "I can't tell you how happy we are."

Rafi kneeled before Pud, pressing her wet face into his warm fur. "Thank you, Pud," she said, listening to his heart, which once again beat the song she had so longed to hear. "Thank you for saving me.

Thank you for everything."

Pud licked her face. "It was nuttin', Rafi," he said. "Just a pin-prick, and then a bee-you-tiful sleep. Jumping Erinnyes!" he cried, noticing Megaera for the first time. "Is that Megaera?"

Megaera put her paws into Pud's. "I am Megaera," she sighed, blessing their paws with her tears. "As I was once your enemy, let me now be your wife, companion, and friend so that I may love and protect you until the end of my days."

Pud added his own tearful blessing. "I know it, Megaera," he said. "And I shall be your husband, to have, and to hold, and protect you with all that Earth has given me until the end of my days."

Rafi smiled contentedly at the Powers. Paw in paw, Bree, Alecto, Pud, Megaera, Dlop, and Tisiphone smiled back, united in the tears and joy that had brought them together. "Of all the miracles I have seen," she said happily, "this is the most wonderful. Truly, love is our miracle."

She looked up at Gried, who stood in a silent altar of gold. "Thank you, Gried."

Forever grateful, they said goodbye to Gried. Pud bowed many times. "Don't you worry about Ginn," he said after a final bow, as Gried's golden boughs waved goodbye, "if anyone comes to hurt her, they'll have me to deal with." Picking up a chair-sized rock, he threw it clear across the canyon where it exploded into grains of sand.

"And then some ..." Bree added admiringly.

Bree, Pud, and Dlop picked up their shields. No longer made of bone, each shield was shaped like an oak leaf set in solid gold.

Bree slung his shield over his back. "You did it, Rafi," he said, looking up at her, the wonder still alight in his eyes. "You saved Earth."

"We saved Earth," corrected Rafi. She picked up Dlop and Tisiphone who, now that their quest was over, seemed determined to get some sleep.

Not long after leaving Gried, they entered the Cyclops's cave. In a pool of blood and dust, Rafi's staff still protruding from his eye, Brontes sat where he had fallen. Perched on the end of the staff, unperturbed by their intrusion, five crows pecked at each other and Brontes's eye.

Rafi lowered her head. For a moment, she considered running back to Gried, but somehow she knew in her heart that not all of Gried's leaves together could return to Brontes a life that he had treated with such contempt. She looked at her shoulder, expecting to find Krik, but then she remembered that the mantis was already eyes, ears, mouths, and noses deep in his latest quest. If only there had been another way.

Peter squeezed her hand. "It couldn't be helped, Rafi," he said, sharing the sadness in her heart. "You had to make a choice, and I, for one, am glad that you made the choice you did."

After admiring Brontes's magnificent handiwork one last time, they lit some torches in the fire, and began the arduous journey back up the passageway. At the end of the passageway, dreaded but not unexpected, lay what was left of Draig, a charred crown still dangling from one of her horns.

"Queens are only made in the eyes of others," said Bree solemnly as they looked upon the beast, felled not by a sword, but by her own evil vanity.

Rafi nodded prophetically. "Then we are all Kings and Queens," she said, "whose royalty can only be measured by our love for one another. If only Draig had known that her own crown was much more beautiful than one made of gold and jewels."

Styx was waiting for them at the riverbank. The penny pot was empty. If the ferryman was disappointed that business had been slow since the Companions had saved Earth, he did not show it, and with one push of his pole they shot across the river. After everyone had disembarked as quickly as their legs could carry them, he presented Rafi with his pole, which seemed to have shrunk by just the right amount to replace her staff.

She gave Styx a hug. Being only cloth and bones there was not much to hug, but it is said that on that day, Death better understood those who cling to life for, within his bones, Styx felt a force that, to this day, lives beyond the grave.

Love.

Cheered on by the Virtues' songs, they had soon left the dark recesses of the mountain. They reemerged, changed but not forgotten, into the black poplar grove that marked the door to Erebus. Only now, the poplars' leaves fluttered green under a sky of delicious blue. To the east, bathing the earth with growing delight, the sun nodded approvingly over the horizon.

"So begins a new day," said Peter.

"So begins every day," said Rafi, rejoicing in the morning's reds, blues, greens, and yellows. She held out her hands. "For every day is what we first choose for ourselves and then give to others."

Forever blessed, blissful hearts joined hands and paws. Together, each as different as the moon is to the stars, they stood above an imperfect world in perfect Truth, Harmony, and Love.

EPILOGUE

E scorted by Peter and the Powers, Rafi spent an informative if not uncomfortable night in the House of Zigh where the Dung Beetle had moved in with all the pomp and pungency afforded to his high estate. Under an enchanted sky, they talked well into the night, waving appreciatively at the ever-watchful Talat, forever guarding the heavens with his smile and his sword. The next morning found them rested and well fed (luckily, the owl Ademar had provided some alternatives to dung balls). After a heartfelt parting from Zigh and the Dung Beetle, Ademar flew both Rafi and Peter back to Drumheller with the Powers in hot pursuit.

Never before had such a crowd gathered at the Travelers' Nest. From the air, it looked as if the whole town had come out to greet them. But that was not all. You can imagine Rafi's surprise when she was greeted by none other than the Secretary General of the United Nations who, with a wombat and a wallaby on his shoulders, thanked her publicly for saving Earth under the proud and loving gaze of Amos, Myra, and Motu.

Reunited at last, Rafi, her parents and her brother hugged and kissed to the sound of tumultuous applause.

Motu was already sporting his new Harvard jacket. On his shoulder sat a Colobus Monkey. "You did it, Sis," he cried. "You saved Earth!" He pointed at the monkey. "This is Xanthus, my new roommate at law school …"

Mr. and Mrs. Malawi's hugs and kisses were all the words Rafi needed to hear.

Much to her surprise, even the Mayor had joined the long line of well-wishers that seemed to never end. However, to her utter delight, he bore a striking resemblance to Mopsus who, as it turned out, had turned in his garbage man's overalls to become the new Mayor. Naturally, the Ex-Mayor blamed all of his troubles on Rafi, but he soon found a promising career as a child psychologist and writer. His Pulitzer Prize winning books, <u>Stop and No – First Words to Teach Your Children</u> and <u>Hobbies for Parents to Prevent the Spread of Children</u> are best sellers to this day. Some things never change.

As for Orly Thumbottom who still lives across the street from Newton's Apple, she became a nun and started a convent after a visit by the Pope. To this day, her home remains one of Drumheller's favorite tourist attractions largely thanks to Orly's cats who collect donations and sing in the choir.

Rafi did not forget her promise to Gried. Before she would even consider walking through the bright green door of Newton's Apple, she planted Ginn in the middle of the garden next to the fountain. Unable to contain her excitement, she camped in the garden with Peter and the Powers. The next morning, she could hardly believe her eyes.

In a pillar of gold no less magnificent than Gried himself, Ginn towered over the fountain and the Apple, and from that day on Drumheller became (and remains) the number one tourist attraction in the world. Proudly, she stands over Myra's latest creation – a breathtaking sculpture of a beautiful young woman in whose outstretched hands dance seven stars and seven stones. At her feet, three rats in golden armor look up at her with shining eyes, as a Praying Mantis, clutching a staff upon which is set a tiny Earth, whispers in her ear.

But the real Rafi could never stand so still. On weekends, often accompanied by her father, she played I Spy with Zigh and the Dung Beetle, and, after fixing Zigh's road, the grateful wolverine helped Amos assemble the greatest dinosaur collection in the world, which can still be seen in the local museum. On special holidays, she visited Krik, Verdandi, and Skuld (Urd died later that year), often accompanied by the Powers who were now married and planning to have children. (They neglected to read The Mayor's book). Summers, she worked as a Junior Ambassador to the United Nations.

And so, with the help of some friends, a young girl saved Earth for you and me. I hope that one day you will meet Rafi walking the streets of Drumheller, dancing in a tree, or singing to the river. But if you cannot make it to one of Earth's gentler places, look no further than the light that shines in the eyes of all living things or, if you are alone, in your own heart, for there is something of Rafi in all of us.

About the Author

F. M. Perrin was born in Toronto, Canada where he developed an early passion for writing fiction and poetry, graduating high school with a scholarship in English Literature before acquiring his degree at the University of Toronto.

Mr. Perrin was last seen in Winnipeg, Canada where it is rumored he married a fairy princess and befriended a miniature dragon.

This is his first novel.

Lost Legends

Three girls from a land. They shall fight untill the end. Something will stop each girl. They will concer there fears. In the end.

—SCHB

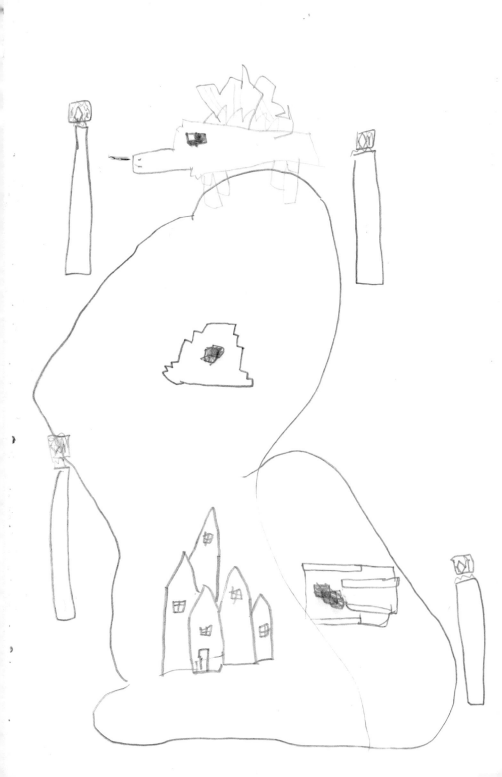